SOLDIERS OF THE TSAR

SOLDIERS OF THE TSAR

ARMY AND SOCIETY IN RUSSIA
1462–1874

JOHN L. H. KEEP

CLARENDON PRESS · OXFORD
1985

947.04 (handwritten, top left)

Oxford University Press, Walton Street, Oxford OX2 6DP

Oxford New York Toronto
Delhi Bombay Calcutta Madras Karachi
Kuala Lumpur Singapore Hong Kong Tokyo
Nairobi Dar es Salaam Cape Town
Melbourne Auckland
and associated companies in
Beirut Berlin Ibadan Mexico City Nicosia

Oxford is a trade mark of Oxford University Press

Published in the United States
by Oxford University Press, New York

© *John L. H. Keep 1985*

British Library Cataloguing in Publication Data
Keep, John L.H.
Soldiers of the tsar: army and society in
Russia, 1462–1874.
1. Soviet Union—Armed Forces—History
I. Title
306'.27'0947 UA772
ISBN 0-19-822575-X

Set by DMB (Typesetting), Oxford
Printed in Great Britain
at the Alden Press, Oxford

CONTENTS

Contents

ILLUSTRATIONS

MAPS

FIGURES

INTRODUCTION

THIS is a study of the armed forces' role in sustaining autocratic government and shaping social life in Russia. For about four hundred years the realm of the tsars was a 'service state': that is to say, the most important element in the experience of most of its inhabitants was the performance of duties designed to bolster the country's external and internal security. Nowhere else in medieval or early modern Europe was the principle of service to the Crown pressed so far as it was in Russia, where there were no autonomous social estates (*états*, *Stände*) or other public bodies that could act as a countervailing force to the claims of the monarchy. The Tatar conquest in the thirteenth century arbitrarily truncated and distorted Russia's legal and institutional development. When the principalities of the Volga–Oka basin came together two hundred years later under the hegemony of the Grand Princes of Moscow, power rapidly became concentrated in the autocratic ruler and his household or *dvor*. This simple early system of administration soon gave way to a more bureaucratic one, and by the seventeenth century we may legitimately say that Russia had a state order. It was organized on principles that owed much to the credo that Muscovy had inherited from the Byzantine empire the task of preserving and extending the lands where the true religion, Orthodox Christianity, was practised. In the accomplishment of this mission a major role fell to the land forces, as was only natural since until the early eighteenth century Russia was all but cut off from the sea. Even after Peter the Great (1689–1725) had forced an opening to the West, built a navy, reformed the army, and established his new empire as one of the great powers of Europe, the political and social pattern still owed much to the Muscovite legacy.

In that formative era laymen had by and large been classified as members of one of two social categories: servitors (*sluzhiliye*) and taxpayers (*tyaglye*). The duties and rewards of men in each group, and in the various sub-categories which each of them comprised, were closely regulated, at least in intent, by the central power—by the *vlast'*, to use the expressive Russian term. Officials in the capital and in the major provincial centres laboured hard to ensure that each adult male performed his allotted obligations. Servitors were expected above all to bear arms in the field against the tsar's foreign foes or rebellious subjects; and even when they acted as civil administrators or landlords their functions often had a martial flavour. The taxpayers' job was to provide the wherewithal in cash and goods that made this service possible.

It was a system that in practice had many lacunae. Most notably, it did not prevent the more favoured groups from turning it to their own advantage and converting about half the peasants into their personal dependants (serfs), with the authorities' tacit connivance. The actual relationship between the state power and the *dvoryanstvo*—the Russian equivalent of the European nobility[1]—was from the start one of interdependence, not just one of vertical subordination. Nevertheless these servitors were unable to institutionalize their gains in the ways that European noblemen did; indeed, in the early eighteenth century, under Peter I's draconian rule, their state obligations were increased. Not until 1762 did a monarch permit them to decide (in peacetime) whether they wished to serve or not; and even so for the next hundred years most members of the gentry found it necessary or expedient to spend at least part of their lives in military uniform. Commoners, too, had their burdens greatly increased during the Imperial era.

In this way the traditional service state survived the turmoil of the French revolution and its aftermath, when Russian arms helped to liberate the continent from Napoleonic rule, until the middle of the nineteenth century. It was only in the wake of the Crimean War (1854–6) that it was dismantled. This did not come about by revolution from below, but was carried through in a more or less controlled fashion by officials anxious to modernize the empire's institutional and socio-economic structure. The reforms were incomplete and elements of the old order lived on into the twentieth century, leaving a deep imprint on the minds of people in all classes.

One of the reformers' objectives was to enhance Russia's military efficiency in order to meet the challenge posed by other European states whose way of life and thinking had been drastically transformed by the industrial revolution.[2] This goal was difficult to achieve without shaking the existing social order, which the late-nineteenth-century tsars and their advisers, as deeply conservative individuals, were loath to do. In consequence the Russian army suffered a number of defeats in the field and eventually collapsed during the First World War, bringing the monarchy and empire down with it. Yet this failure should not be allowed to obscure the fact that in earlier centuries the Russians were remarkably successful in keeping up with the international arms race. It is this earlier age that is the concern of this book, which ends precisely at the moment when the advent of modern technologies was radically altering the nature of warfare. Specifically, the closing date is 1874, when Russia went over to a modern system of selective conscription. There is no lack of literature on the events and dilemmas of the last hundred years, whereas for the pre-industrial era, as one might call it, the English-speaking reader at least has hitherto been very much in the dark.

Thematically this volume is only indirectly concerned with state 'defence' policies, armaments, or warfare, the stuff of conventional military history until recent years. Our focus, as the title indicates, is on the soldiers who bore

---

[1] In conformity with accepted practice, the terms 'nobility' and 'gentry' are used here in reference to the *dvoryanstvo*, but they are inexact translations; a clumsier but more precise appellation is 'privileged servitors'.

[2] See W. H. McNeill, *The Pursuit of Power: Technology, Armed Force and Society since* A.D. *1000*, Chicago and London, 1982, pp. 232–41.

the brunt of the sacrifices that the service state demanded. By 'soldiers' we mean primarily the men in the ranks, but the officers have not been neglected. The armed forces were both the instrument and the victim of coercive state policies, and so an investigation of the internal life of the troops can tell us a lot about the entire political and social system of which they formed an integral part.

The tsarist state may in our view quite properly be characterized, over most of its long history, as manifesting both *despotic* and *militaristic* features. These are contentious terms, frowned on by some contemporary social scientists, and therefore their employment here calls for a word or two of explanation. Neither term is used in an emotive or value-laden sense. The extensive use of force by those in authority (as officials and landlords as well as members of the armed forces and 'specialists in violence') was after all a fact of life in Russia for centuries, and no good purpose is served by ignoring it. This use of force 'from above' had its counterpart in acts of rebellion—notably the four great Cossack–peasant uprisings of the seventeenth and eighteenth centuries, but also countless smaller disturbances—in which the disadvantaged or oppressed sought to wreak vengeance on their overlords. The agents of authority also encountered a good deal of passive resistance from the simple folk with whom they had to deal. Violence was never far from the surface of Russian social life, particularly in the countryside, and members of the armed forces were often to be found on either side of the firing-line.

The reasons for the pervasiveness of conflict are fairly evident. They may be sought first of all in the inhospitable natural environment, which made the struggle for physical survival a desperate matter for most people; and then in the country's cultural isolation and backwardness, allied to the lack of a developed legal and institutional order that has already been mentioned. These factors and others besides helped to shape a political culture that, at least prior to the reforms of the 1860s, was characterized by a great deal of official arbitrariness (*proizvol*) and corruption. The evils of absolute government loomed larger in Russia than they did elsewhere in Europe at the time. They were the target of criticism by a growing number of enlightened individuals from the 1790s onward, among them a fair proportion of military men, but their efforts to change things were not particularly successful. One sympathizes with the aggrieved subaltern who during Nicholas I's reign lamented that 'in Russia everything is secret and false'.[3]

To categorize either Muscovite or Imperial Russia as 'despotic' *tout court* would be unjust, but to deny that despotic elements existed in public life is to err also. The problem is to ascertain their importance—and to weigh the part which the armed forces played in sustaining the system.[4] Undoubtedly some

---

[3] Mombelli, in *Delo petrashevtsev*, i. 308.

[4] In its time C.-A. Wittfogel's *Oriental Despotism: a Comparative Study of Total Power* (New Haven and London, 1963) evoked lively controversy among Russian specialists, as has A. Yanov's *The Origins of Autocracy: Ivan the Terrible in Russian History* (Berkeley, Los Angeles, and London, 1981); see the author's reply to his critics in *SR* 42 (1983), pp. 247–52, and E. L. Keenan

features of this form of government (for example, paternalism, informality) were beneficent; and it is likewise true that it commanded a high degree of acceptance (paradoxically, in view of the popular rebelliousness), since few were able to envisage any practical alternative. Not until the twentieth century was the regime's legitimacy widely called in question. Russia produced a fair crop of rulers with a tyrannical disposition—Ivan IV, Peter I, Peter III, Paul I, Nicholas I—but much more is involved here than the personality of the autocrat. In their efforts to conceptualize this problem institutionally and sociologically, sophisticated modern scholars should not overlook the insights of contemporary observers such as the nineteenth-century Polish officer who maintained, with reference to what he called unambiguously 'le despotisme d'un seul', that:

Since Peter I all the emperors have taken particular care of the army, which is the object of their continual solicitude . . . The army is in fact the preponderant element in the state, for upon it rests the Sovereign's power; and it is through it that civilization spreads within the empire.[5]

Was pre-reform Russia also militaristic? Of the eight features which students of the phenomenon have identified as characteristic, Russia manifested all but one. It cannot be shown that the military, as a distinct interest group, intervened overtly or covertly in the process of political decision-making, in the manner of the Prussian general staff—although a sceptic might say that it had no need to since it received very generous resource allocations. The other features, listed in ascending order of importance, are:

   (i)   a heavy emphasis on military ceremonial;
   (ii)   an ideology supportive of military ideals;
   (iii)   the regular inculcation of these values through the educational system;
   (iv)   heavy state expenditure on military projects;
   (v)   a willingness to incur high casualty tolls in warfare;
   (vi)   a readiness to commit the armed forces in foreign and domestic conflicts;
   (vii)   extensive controls over the life of society for military ends.[6]

in *Problems of Communism* 33 (1984), 1, pp. 68–72. An interesting discussion on the nature of Russian absolutism was staged by Soviet scholars in 1968–71. From the ample semi-popular literature T. Szamuely, *The Russian Tradition* (London, 1974) deserves to be singled out. In our view none of these works appreciates sufficiently the military component in the tsarist power structure.

   [5] Tański, *Tableau*, p. 3.
   [6] This list is based on L. I. Radway, 'Militarism', in D. L. Sills (ed.), *Encyclopedia of the Social Sciences*, New York, 1968, pp. 300–4; H. F. Reading, *A Dictionary of the Social Sciences*, London and Boston, 1977, p. 131. Both these definitions rest upon the pioneering work of S. Andreski, M. Janowitz, S. P. Huntington, J. van Doorn, F. Vagts, and others. For the whole controversy see now V. R. Berghahn, *Militarism: the History of an International Debate, 1861–1979*, Leamington Spa, 1981, and for the Russian case my 'Origins of Russian Militarism' (forthcoming in *CMRS*).

Certainly, one might question whether Russia had a state ideology before the 1830s, and if it did whether this was not as much religious–patriarchal as militarist. It is also largely a matter of subjective judgement how far any of these characteristics were present in excess of what was necessary for the country's defence, in view of its long exposed borders and the magnitude of the threats to its security. Perhaps the significance of the militaristic features in Russian society may be easier to assess in the light of the evidence adduced in these pages. Two general points may be made in this connection. First, the Russian military ethos differed in quality from the Prussian variety, which has generally been taken as normative. Russia lacked a tradition of feudal chivalry, a *Standesgeist*, which officers could invoke to justify their special interests and views[7]—although in the later nineteenth century some efforts were made to provide an artificial substitute for it. Second, militaristic traits were not just a German import, a product of 'the decadent West', as some chauvinistic writers have implied, but seem to have been of autochthonous origin, a homespun response to the problem of maintaining 'order' in the face of 'subversion'. To some extent, too, attitudes characteristic of serf-owners carried over into the military domain—although this argument can be overworked. The pre-1861 Russian army was not simply an extension of the serf-based rural economy; likewise its officers' mentality was more powerfully shaped by professional experiences in the service than by childhood reminiscences of some 'nobleman's nest'. Indeed, from the 1760s onward the military ethos was often transmitted to the rural milieu by officers who retired to take up farming, or their ex-NCO bailiffs, who embarked on ill-considered attempts to systematize the management of their estates.

Since the reader will find little discussion in what follows of the warfare in which the troops engaged, it may be as well to outline here the major occasions when military power was used in support of the tsars' foreign policy objectives. It was the principal ingredient, along with diplomacy, in bringing about the remarkable territorial expansion which turned the insignificant principality of Moscow into an empire covering one-sixth of the globe's land surface. Warfare was almost continuous along this empire's remoter borders, although these campaigns were generally small-scale and involved irregular (especially Cossack) forces rather than regular troops. The amount of coercion applied varied a great deal. As a rule the brutalities associated with the initial conquest were succeeded by more statesmanlike policies—unless the natives rebelled, as they frequently did. At the start of our period most of the people brought under the tsar's 'high hand' were ethnically and culturally akin to their new masters, and so assimilated fairly easily. But the so-called 'gathering of the Russian lands' also involved absorption of fellow Slavs who were already

---

[7] Cf., for Prussia, G. Ritter, *Staatskunst und Kriegshandwerk: das Problem des 'Militarismus' in Deutschland*, i. *Die altpreussische Tradition, 1740–1890*, Munich, 1954, pp. 149–52; Ritter offers some interesting observations on pre-1914 Russian militarism, ibid., ii. (1960), 98–114; cf. also Stein, 'Offizier'.

nationally distinct (ancestors of the Ukrainians and Belorussians) as well as of various non-Slavic peoples in the Volga valley, some of whom were Muslims; thereupon Muscovy expanded across the Urals into Siberia, subduing the scattered indigenous groups (Turco-Tatars, Yakuts, Buryats, etc.).

In the early eighteenth century it was the turn of the peoples of the eastern Baltic littoral. The partitions of Poland then brought within the empire many Jews and Lithuanians as well as Belorussians and Poles. In the south Catherine II (1762–96) implanted the cross of St. George firmly on the shores of the Black Sea, absorbing the Crimean khanate, and initiated action to win control of the Caucasus. In the course of this epic eighty-year struggle Russia acquired sovereignty first over the peoples of the Transcaucasian valleys (Georgians, Armenians) and then over the hardy mountaineers (Daghestanis, Chechens, Ossetians, and others), who were subdued only after repeated military forays into their territories. By the end of our period Russia was enlarging her Asiatic dominions at both ends, so to speak: in the Far East (Maritime province) at the expense of China, and in Turkestan at the expense of the independent Muslim khanates. Meanwhile, Finland was won in 1809 and in south-eastern Europe Russia obtained Bessarabia (1812), of which she had to cede part in 1856, and a sphere of influence in the Balkans.

This imperial expansion played a major part in instigating the wars which Russia fought with other European powers. This was the case with the many armed conflicts with the Polish–Lithuanian Commonwealth, Sweden, and the Livonian Order. In the 1670s the Ottoman sultan entered the list openly in support of his vassals, the Crimean Tatars, as Moscow's power extended southward across the Ukrainian steppe; and thereafter the two empires found themselves at war roughly once in each generation until 1914–18. War with Persia occurred twice (1804–13, 1826–8) after Peter I's reign, and was similar in character. On the other hand, Russia's participation in the European coalitions formed against Prussia (1756–62) and post-revolutionary France (1799–1800, 1805, 1806–7) was motivated primarily by a desire to maintain an advantageous balance of power. In 1812 the empire was itself the victim of aggression by Napoleon's Grande Armée, which contained a large international contingent; but the invaders' defeat led the Russian armies in hot pursuit across the continent, from Moscow to Paris, in 1813–14. The hegemonic position which Russia enjoyed in European affairs for the next forty years owed a good deal to fear of her armed might, demonstrated *inter alia* by the action taken against Polish and Hungarian insurgents in 1830–1 and 1849 respectively. That 'the giant had feet of clay' was not apparent until the Allies invaded the Crimea. Even so, the Russian troops fought back well, as they had done on earlier occasions; it was not so much Nicholas's army that failed but its supply system and the underlying political and economic structure.

While there are several good studies of Russia's imperial wars,[8] the historical significance of which is undeniable, there has been no work in any language

---

[8] Two excellent recent Western studies are Duffy, *Russia's Military Way* and Curtiss, *Russia's*

specifically devoted to the men who were expected to do the fighting. This is surprising: after all, countless monographs have appeared on the intelligentsia (numerically a smaller group), and a respectable literature exists on peasants, nobles, and even townsmen; in recent years, officials and clergymen have begun to attract the attention that is their due. The neglect of the soldiers may in part be attributed to a feeling among historians that the subject ought properly to be left to their military confrères. This sentiment is no doubt justified with regard to the more technical aspect of the topic, such as weaponry or tactics, but surely not with regard to matters that are of wider interest. Unless adequate attention is paid to the armed forces' prominent place in Russian public life, historians will labour under serious misconceptions and draw one-sided conclusions. Indeed, much of the existing literature suffers from this distortion of vision. Writers on the so-called 'Decembrist movement' have almost without exception viewed it as a civilian phenomenon—a chapter in the history of the intelligentsia or of Russian political thought—although most of those involved were army officers, and it needs to be seen as an instance of 'Praetorianism' (see below, ch. 12). Similarly, the military settlements (chs. 13–14) are often regarded as an epiphenomenon of serfdom, or as an aberration on the part of Alexander I and his minister A. A. Arakcheyev, instead of as an early attempt at social engineering designed to produce a military caste that would be under firm control and particularly reliable. By placing military service in the centre of attention, where it belongs, we can gain a truer understanding of the way Russian society operated and of its leaders' code of values.

Another reason for neglect of this subject is more political in nature. In tsarist Russia matters affecting state security or the good reputation of the armed services were considered very sensitive. The same attitude, *mutatis mutandis*, has been perpetuated in the USSR, at least since the 1930s. Before the revolution professional military historians concentrated on 'safe' subjects such as administration or strategy; they regarded what was then called *voyennyy byt*, or 'the military way of life', as of trivial importance. In so far as they dealt with it at all, they concerned themselves with the officers, whose experiences were thought to possess entertainment value. This attitude carried over to the many Russian serving or veteran officers who wrote their memoirs. The practice was encouraged rather than frowned on, as in Prussia, and in the last decades of the nineteenth century produced a great crop of autobiographical and similar material.[9] Writers had to take care not to give offence to the

---

Crimean War. Ye. V. Tarle has given classic accounts of three of these conflicts: *Severnaya voyna i shvedskoye nashestviye na Rossiyu*, Moscow, 1958, *Nashestviye Napoleona na Rossiyu*, Moscow, 1938, reproduced in id. *1812 g.*, Moscow, 1959, and *Krymskaya voyna*, 2nd rev. edn., Moscow and Leningrad, 1950.

[9] An invaluable bibliographical guide to memoir literature has recently been provided by Zayonchkovsky, *Istoriya dorevol. Rossii*. For an evaluation of military memoirs on the pre-reform era, see our 'From the Pistol to the Pen'.

censors. Most of them accepted these limitations[10] and their works often echo the caste spirit and chauvinism characteristic of that age; nevertheless they constitute a valuable body of source material. Still more important are the various collections of laws and parts of the War Ministry's official history (1902–11), while numerous foreign visitors to, or residents in Russia (some of whom served in the forces), also left observations of interest, particularly if they published their accounts abroad.

Soviet scholars have added considerably to knowledge of the subject, even though 'the armed forces and society' (as it is termed in the West) is not yet an acknowledged sub-discipline and historians' interpretation of the material has sometimes been stridently nationalistic, not to say militaristic. This bias can be allowed for, as can the ideologically motivated temptation to acclaim any dissent or mutinous activity as evidence of 'class struggle'. No one can afford to overlook the studies by V. I. Buganov, M. D. Rabinovich, or the late lamented P. A. Zayonchkovsky and the dean of Soviet military historians, L. G. Beskrovnyy. Specialists in other areas such as demography or agrarian relations also have a great deal to add. Whatever mental reservations may be harboured about Soviet historians' methodology, they have the inestimable advantage of ready access to the rich archival holdings.

In 1978 I was kindly allowed to see some material from the Central Military-Historical Archive (TsGVIA) in Moscow which relates to life in the ranks during the late eighteenth century. An extensive sojourn in the USSR would be necessary in order to write an authoritative, comprehensive account of this subject. The present volume does not claim to be more than an introduction which may perhaps encourage others to study some of the themes touched on only episodically here: for example, the organization of the supply services, the militia (*opolcheniye*), or the rewards system, which included the bestowal of remarkably lavish gifts on individual servitors by the tsar, a practice that must have done much to foster loyalist sentiments. Ideally, the social history of the Russian army should be dealt with in a comparative all-European context, but this can scarcely be done until more preliminary studies have been written. We have to walk before we can run. Happily work in this field is under way.[11]

Little has been said here about the autonomous Cossack warrior communities of southern Russia, partly for reasons of space and partly because this topic is best handled by specialists on the Ukraine. *Aficionados* of quantitative history

---

[10] G. G. Kartsov, one of the best known of these writers, admitted that, in describing a mutiny, he had 'toned down' what seemed to him to be extreme or out of line with the views of those who regarded the matter 'calmly': 'Semenovskiy polk', p. 332.

[11] I owe a particular debt to the pioneering work of R. Hellie and J. S. Curtiss. Studies in progress include those by E. Kimerling-Wirtschafter on soldiers in the early nineteenth century, B. W. Menning on the Cossacks, C. B. Stevens on the Razryad, and W. McK. Pintner on the defence budget. Among authorities on the period 1874–1917 are J. Bushnell, P. Kenez and A. Wildman. I had not seen D. Beyrau, *Militär und Gesellschaft im vorrevolutionären Russland*, Cologne, 1984, when this manuscript was sent to press.

may wonder why this volume does not contain more statistical exercises tabulating military expenditure per man, casualty ratios, and the like. An effort to reconstruct expenditure on the armed forces between 1789 and 1825[12] convinced me that many of the essential data are highly unreliable. Even for a period as late as the Crimean War estimates of the Russia army's actual size (as distinct from the official establishment figure, or *shtat*) vary tremendously, and casualty figures are even less trustworthy. This, too, is a task for the future.

The ranking system in the post-Petrine army was of the standard European type, with ensign (*praporshchik*) as the lowest commissioned rank; officers from ensign to captain inclusive were classed as subalterns (*ober-ofitsery*), and majors to colonels as staff officers (*shtab-ofitsery*); general ranks extended from brigadier to full general (*general-anshef*). Minor differences of designation between various arms of service have been disregarded. The term 'soldier' as used here usually refers to the *nizhnye chiny*, who included warrant officers, non-commissioned officers (NCOs), and privates (in American, enlisted men). A verst is equivalent to 1.067 km. (1166.4 yards), a *desyatina* to 1.09 hectares (2.70 acres), a *pud* to 16.38 kg. (36.11 lb.), and a *funt* to 409.4 gr. (0.90 lb.).

A number of friends and colleagues kindly read parts of the manuscript and made helpful suggestions; none are responsible for such errors as remain. I should like to thank them and also the John S. Guggenheim Foundation for its generous financial support.

---

12 'Russian Army's Response', pp. 521–3.

I

MUSCOVITE ROOTS, 1462–1689

1

MOSCOW'S MEN ON HORSEBACK

In the fourteenth and early fifteenth centuries the Grand Princes of Moscow acquired a position of pre-eminence over the other lands of north-eastern Rus´. Historians have traditionally emphasized the political, economic, or ideological aspects of this feat. The Danilovichi, as political tutees as well as lineal descendants of Alexander Nevsky, exhibited a remarkable pliancy towards the Tatar overlord; they managed to siphon off much of the tribute that was channelled through their hands; they used some of it to attract peasant immigrants, who appreciated the relative security of this forested area; and they won valuable support from the metropolitans of the Orthodox Church, who legitimated their rule in the eyes of the faithful.

These factors were certainly important; but perhaps the main ingredient in Moscow's success was its skilful manipulation of the warrior élite. All Ryurikid rulers had noble servitors, but those who took employment with the Grand Prince of Moscow enjoyed higher status and richer rewards. In return for these favours they put their swords at his disposal with a will and consistency not apparent elsewhere. This was the foundation on which arose the formidable liturgical and service state of sixteenth- and seventeenth-century Muscovy: a realm with a strong sense of its individuality, of its sacred mission, a realm in which the well-born found fulfilment in loyally furthering the interests of the autocrat. Sigismund von Herberstein, the Habsburg diplomat who first visited Moscow in 1517, heard notables mock the grandees of Lithuania who failed to carry out their sovereign's orders. ' "That does not happen with us here," they say with a smile; "if you want to keep your head on firmly, ride off at each command." '[1] Later Western travellers also noted, with no little astonishment, the submissiveness and martial character of the Russian *dvoryanstvo*. 'The soldiers of Russia', wrote the Englishman Giles Fletcher in 1591, 'are called [*deti*] *boyarskiye*, or sons of gentlemen, because they are all of that degree by virtue of their military profession . . . The son of a gentleman (which is born a soldier) is ever a gentleman and a soldier withal and professeth nothing else but military matters.'[2] Forty years or so later Adam Olearius remarked on the fact that leading noblemen 'are obliged to live in Moscow and, even though they may have no business there, must appear daily at court and beat their heads to the tsar.'[3]

In the 1550s compulsory service was imposed by decree on all (secular)

[1] Von Herberstein, *Moscovia*, p. 101.
[2] Fletcher, *Russe Commonwealth*, in Berry and Crummey, *Rude and Barbarous Kingdom*, p. 177 (Schmidt edn., p. 75).
[3] Olearius, *Travels*, p. 220; cf. Margeret, *L'Estat*, pp. 13–15; Van Klenk, *Posol'stvo*, p. 486.

nobles, most of whom performed it as cavalrymen, accompanied by their dependants. Later the obligation was extended from the well-born to a sizeable segment of the non-privileged or 'taxpaying' population, in conditions that were generally much more onerous. There gradually developed a complex military structure that comprised several distinct groups, each with its specific duties and (theoretically at least) rights. These corps could almost be called castes, since they recruited new members primarily from the children of those already enrolled. They were not hermetically sealed, but service was hereditary; thus transfer from one group to another became increasingly difficult and usually occurred only when the central authorities required it for reasons of their own. Administratively, the Muscovite troops were something of a hodge-podge, and co-ordination of their efforts in the field left much to be desired. Nevertheless these defects were exaggerated by historians writing in the Imperial era, when it was taken for granted that the Russian army was a creation of the 'tsar–reformer' Peter the Great. It is now possible to take a more balanced view, and to recognize that in many respects the pre-Petrine armed forces were reasonably well adapted to the relatively limited tasks they faced. The system of military administration, though cumbersome and often chaotic, had a flex-ibility and immediacy that were sacrificed under the rigorous bureaucratic centralism of St. Petersburg. In Muscovy, at least until the mid-seventeenth century, service was usually rendered on an annual basis, for a single campaign, and so involved less dislocation for those concerned or for their dependants.

The origins of the Russian service state are not easy to pin down. There are precedents in the Byzantine empire, which in the *pronoia* developed a fore-runner of the Muscovite *pomest´ye*, i.e. an estate held on conditional tenure in return for the performance of military duties (see below, p. 44).[4] However, there is no evidence of conscious emulation. Nearer geographically, if not culturally, were the Tatar khanates. Yet two and a half centuries of domination by the Kipchak ('Golden') Horde left remarkably few direct traces on Russian social life or institutions, important as its indirect consequences were. Some knowledge in the fields of military equipment, communications, nomenclature, and perhaps tactics was transmitted.[5] Jaroslaw Pelenski has recently pointed to 'the striking similarities' between the *pomest´ye* and the *soyūrghāl* of the Kazan´ Tatars; but his claim that there was a 'reception of Kazanian institu-tional models and societal arrangements in Muscovite Russia' must remain, in default of supporting evidence, only a provocative hypothesis.[6] Parallel developments are not in themselves proof of cross-cultural influences. It seems more reasonable to infer that these two neighbouring but antagonistic societies, which faced similar problems in mobilizing their scarce resources for

[4] G. Ostrogorsky, 'Agricultural Conditions in the Byzantine Empire in the Middle Ages', *Cambridge Economic History of Europe*, 2nd edn., i. ed. M. M. Postan, Cambridge, 1971, pp. 221–6; Uspensky, 'Znacheniye', pp. 21–7.

[5] G. V. Vernadsky, *The Mongols and Russia* (A History of Russia, 3) New Haven and London, 1953, pp. 362–6.

[6] Pelenski, 'State and Society', p. 163.

defence, adopted similar solutions independently. After all, the concept of universal service was common to a number of ancient and oriental polities, which developed monarchies, nobilities, and armed forces in broadly comparable ways; and most religions have accommodated themselves fairly readily to the notion that it is virtuous to bear arms and risk death for the 'common good' as defined by the political power. More specifically, Muscovites could read in their chronicles that Kievan Rus´, too, had been a war-like society, and that its fall had been due to bitter feuding among its princes; memories of this tragedy, kept alive by the Church, helped to make the demands of the new *vlast´* seem more acceptable.[7]

In its concrete particulars, at any rate, the Russian service state was the fruit of harsh experience, above all in trying to protect the long steppe frontier against Tatar attack. It is important to see this problem in the context of the authorities' overall 'defence posture'. In effect Muscovy had *two* foreign and military policies, one eastern and one western, which were not adequately coordinated until the mid-seventeenth century. Whether this was the product of circumstance or of a failure to decide priorities realistically is open to debate. It is certainly a curious paradox that, although the steppe 'front' was the most vulnerable, and fighting went on along it almost without interruption, it rarely held first place among the leaders' preoccupations. As a rule their eyes were fixed on relations with the West. The tsardom's main objective, they thought, should be to recover from Lithuania and Poland (united in a Commonwealth from 1569) those lands inhabited by Orthodox eastern Slavs that had once formed part of the Kievan realm. Yet this was a matter of prestige rather than a strategic necessity, whereas in the east Muscovy faced a life-and-death struggle against the other 'successor states' to the Kipchak Horde.

This confrontation with the Crimean and Nogay khanates was forced upon her by the fact that these hordes were not reconciled to Muscovy's hard-won independence and considered her their legitimate prey. To further their claims to sovereignty, and also to obtain the slaves vital to the maintenance of their mainly nomadic, parasitic, and war-like polities, they launched continual raids on Muscovite territory. The first recorded attack took place in 1468;[8] thereafter they occurred almost annually. The skilful diplomacy of Ivan III (1462–1505) secured something of a respite until 1504, but then the political constellation changed, partly because of Muscovite encroachment on the Kazan´ khanate. During the first half of the sixteenth century a total of forty-three raids were recorded, the most serious of them in 1507, 1512, 1521, 1531, and 1541.[9] Von Herberstein, who witnessed the attack of 1521, relates that

[7] Rüss, *Adel*, p. 7, goes so far as to speak of 'the *druzhina* [Kievan princely armed retinue] character of the Muscovite polity'.

[8] Fisher, *Crimean Tatars*, pp. 26–7, who comments: 'Viewed from a less emotional or nationalistic perspective, these slave raids can be seen as a very successful economic activity that produced means by which the Tatars developed a lively urban and cultural society.' This is to take revisionism too far.

[9] Kargalov, 'Oborona', p. 141; id., *Na stepnoy granitse*, pp. 39, 43, 56–67, 80, 100.

Mahmet-girey crossed the river Oka (which formed the boundary), 'laid waste the country terribly' and came within reach of Moscow; the Grand Prince fled and allegedly hid under a haystack; 'gifts' (that is, tribute) were handed over, whereupon the khan withdrew with 'an incredible number of prisoners', some of whom were massacred shortly afterwards. 'For the elderly and sick, who do not fetch much [on the slave market] and are unfit for work, are given by the Tatars to their young men, much as one gives a hare to a hound to make it snappish: they are stoned to death or thrown into the sea . . .'.[10] Several tens of thousands of warriors might take part in a major raid. The Tatars were aided by their robust physique and superb horsemanship, strong clan affinities, knowledge of the local terrain, and skilful use of *ruses de guerre*. They often managed to take their slow-moving foes by surprise. They were inferior, however, in 'modern' equipment (firearms, artillery), a factor that explains why they seldom persisted with sieges of towns or fortified places.[11] All in all, they posed a formidable threat. The history of this epic conflict can scarcely be written, given the scantiness of the sources. The vulnerability of Russia's borders in this era scarred men's minds and left lasting traces.

The Russians responded by developing an alert system based on fixed defence lines and a mobile reserve, which will be considered further below. Manning it was the *raison d'être* of the gentry cavalry, although the bulk of the troops involved were of humbler origin. Particularly important was the role of Cossacks and other border peoples (for example, *sevryuki*) with a similar life-style, who acted as scouts and harassed the invaders from the flank as they withdrew. They showed more initiative and combativeness than the privileged servitors, not least because they had a direct interest in protecting their homes and families.[12] The defence system seems to have originated spontaneously as a local enterprise, to which the central authorities soon supplied direction. The first fortified line, of simple palisades and earthworks which took advantage of the natural obstacles, ran along the rivers Oka and Ugra. In the 1530s it was pushed forward as far as Tula, and after Ivan IV's conquest of the Kazan' khanate in 1552 another line was built along the Volga against the Nogays (see map 1).[13] The reserve forces were concentrated at Kaluga or Serpukhov, whence they could be sent to the most vulnerable sector. How far did these measures, and the control from the centre they implied, help or hinder the people on the spot? Most of them probably welcomed the additional protection but resented the obligation to build, maintain, and garrison the forts, especially where high-ranking superiors seemed to be concerned less with providing effective leadership than with furthering their own careers.

[10] Von Herberstein, *Moscovia*, pp. 163–8.

[11] On Tatar tactics see Kargalov, *Na stepnoy granitse*, pp. 12–18; there is a lively account in Fletcher, *Russe Commonwealth*, pp. 191–202 (Schmidt edn., pp. 90–103).

[12] Kargalov, *Na stepnoy granitse*, p. 74; id., 'Oborona', p. 146.

[13] Kargalov, 'Oborona', p. 147; id., *Na stepnoy granitse*, pp. 80, 101; Belyayev, *O storozhevoy . . . sluzhbe*, p. 5.

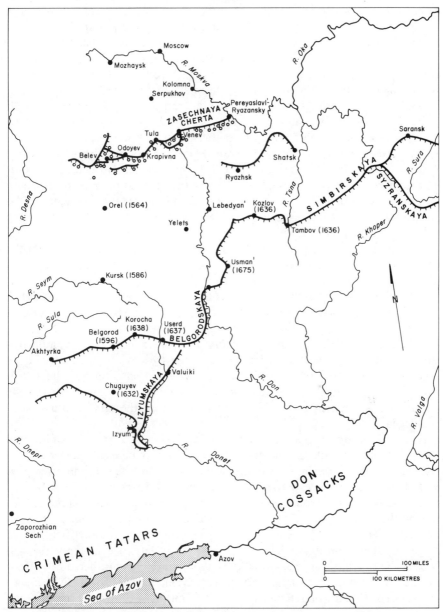

Map 1. Steppe Frontier Defence Lines, 16th–17th Centuries

The extension of Moscow's power down the Volga waterway in the 1550s promised to revolutionize the strategic situation in the steppe region. Yet the opportunity to undertake a major offensive against the Crimeans and Nogays was not taken. Since no records of the policy-making process in Moscow have survived, one can only speculate as to the reasons for this. It has been argued that an overland campaign across the waterless steppe was technically unfeasible (the river routes being too insecure), and that it would have embroiled Russia in an unequal duel with the mighty Ottoman empire, the Crimean Tatars' suzerain power. Perhaps 'structural' military constraints were also involved: to be successful, such a campaign had to be waged in Cossack style, or at least with active co-operation from frontier-dwellers whose loyalties, in Moscow's view, were uncertain. In any event Ivan IV took the fateful decision to move west, not south. In 1558 he launched an ill-prepared offensive against the lands of the enfeebled Livonian knights. The war that ensued dragged on for over two decades, until 1581, and brought Russia no ultimate advantage. On the contrary it strained her resources to breaking-point and directly or indirectly led to a major political and social crisis. Her European neighbours, more advanced culturally and technologically, rallied against the menace from the east and deprived her of the precarious toe-hold she acquired on the Baltic shore. By the 1560s there was growing disaffection among the élite servitors, which aroused exaggerated suspicions of treachery in Ivan's unbalanced mind. The defection of a leading general, Andrey Kurbsky, in April 1564 was a particularly shattering blow. The tsar set out to eliminate all opposition, real or imagined, by establishing the *oprichnina*: a separate 'emergency administration' for part of his realm, staffed in the main by servitors picked for their readiness to obey the ruler's whims. The *oprichniki* had complete licence to investigate and punish alleged traitors. Their violent misdeeds terrorized the population, since their blows fell indiscriminately on the privileged and non-privileged.

Although the *oprichnina* was formally abolished in 1572, the level of internal tension remained high for the rest of Ivan's reign. One consequence was to weaken the border defence system, which in the 1550s the tsar had attempted with some success to regularize. On the other hand, the terror also resulted in a massive spontaneous migration by peasants and other commoners to the border region, where they constituted a potential reservoir of soldiers and labourers. In 1566 the ruler spent a month visiting the fortifications at Kozel'sk, Belev, and elsewhere;[14] but five years later Devlet-girey reached Moscow with a large army, burned the city's suburbs, and inflicted heavy loss of life. According to Fletcher, 'Ivan Vasilevich, leading forth his army to encounter with him, marched a wrong way, but, it was thought, of very purpose, as . . . he doubted his nobility and chief captains of a meaning to betray him to the Tatar.'[15] However this may be, the raid occurred only a few months

[14] Nikitin, 'Oboronitel'nye sooruzheniya', p. 122; Yakovlev, *Zasechnaya cherta*, p. 19.
[15] Fletcher, *Russe Commonwealth*, pp. 191–2 (Schmidt edn., p. 91).

after M. I. Vorotynsky, a leading commander who twice fell into the tsar's disfavour, had undertaken, in consultation with experienced representatives from the area, a thorough-going review of the border defence arrangements.[16]

The statute issued after this conference listed in detail the various sectors of the front, from the Polish-Lithuanian border to the Don, with their respective forts and guard towers, and laid down how the watchmen and patrols were to carry out their tasks. Each station (*stanitsa*) was to be under a chief (*golova*), who in turn was responsible to the field commander (*voyevoda*, voivode). The latter reported to the principal military chancellery in Moscow, the Razryad (see below, p. 35). This body, not the local commander, was to issue assignments to the servitors in each town—a characteristic example of creeping bureaucratic centralism that could not but stifle the initiative of men in the field. During the last quarter of the sixteenth century the arrival of settlers pushed the border further southwards into the steppe and several new fortified towns were established (for example, Voronezh 1585, Yelets 1592, Belgorod 1595).[17] An order of 1577 setting up an additional agency of supervisors (*dozorshchiki*) to combat absenteeism[18] suggests that morale was not all it might have been. In fact Moscow's hold on the region at this time was still tenuous. In 1598 the Ryurikid dynasty expired and shortly thereafter public order collapsed. It was the restless southern borderlands that furnished most of the thousands of malcontents who joined the various popular militias that were formed. Comprising Cossacks and other lower-grade servitors, non-Slavic tribesmen, fugitive peasants, and slaves, these makeshift armies waged one campaign after another, under the banner of false pretenders to the throne or simple bandit chieftains, with the object of avenging themselves on their former masters and refashioning the social hierarchy to suit their sectional interests. Foreign powers joined in the fray and Russia plunged into chaos. The conventional term for this period (1598–1613), 'the Time of Troubles', scarcely does justice to the horrors that befell ordinary folk. Millions fell victim to famine and disease.

When the country began to recover after the accession of Tsar Michael Romanov (1613–45) the political and military establishment was reconstituted much as it had been before. The weakness of the new dynasty and the general misery forced Russia's leaders to adopt a cautious foreign policy. However, Patriarch Filaret, who managed affairs from 1619 to 1633, was eager for war with Poland–Lithuania. His immediate aim was to recover the key fortress of Smolensk, lost in 1612. The Smolensk War of 1632–4, limited in scope, demonstrated once again the Moscow government's difficulties in co-ordinating policies on two exposed flanks; for while Russian troops were investing the city

---

[16] *AMG* i. 1–2 (also in Beskrovnyy, *Khrestomatiya*, pp. 64–8); Zagorodsky, *Belgorodskaya cherta*, p. 56; Belyayev, *O storozhevoy . . . sluzhbe*, pp. 11–17. On Vorotynsky see also Kleimola, 'Mil. Service', p. 53, and 'Changing Face', p. 488.

[17] Belyayev, *O storozhevoy . . . sluzhbe*, pp. 22, 31, 33.

[18] Ibid., p. 24.

the Tatars attacked from the south. Servitors with land in the region hurried home to repair the damage.

Over the previous twenty years the border defences had been neglected and undermanned.[19] In 1638 a major new effort was undertaken with the rebuilding of the disaffected fortified line (*zasechnaya cherta*) which ran for some 600 versts from Shatsk to Belev by way of Tula. In sections it was doubled or even tripled; ditches were dug and earthen ramparts erected; the twenty-one most vulnerable points ('gates', as they were called) received particularly thorough protection.[20] Some 10,000 men were engaged as artisans (*delovtsy*) while another 20,000 labourers were mobilized to perform the most onerous physical tasks: taken by force from their communities, they had to toil in mud and water for a modest remuneration, of which some were subsequently cheated.[21] At the same time a beginning was made on the Belgorod line further south; a second phase of construction followed in 1646–51 and a third in 1654–8. This impressive building programme and the continued expansion of settlement in the border region considerably reduced the threat of Tatar raiding. The main danger in this quarter now came from the tsar's own potentially insubordinate subjects, notably the Cossacks of the Dnieper and Don.

In the historic region around Kiev, in south-eastern Poland, the population had grown rapidly. It consisted mainly of Ukrainians ('Cherkassians', as the Muscovites called them), who were becoming more aware of their religious, social, and national identity. By 1653 Tsar Alexis Mikhaylovich (1645–76) felt strong enough to risk a major new confrontation with the Commonwealth in order to bring the area under his sovereignty. The Thirteen Years War (1654–67) that followed was as costly in blood and treasure as the Livonian War had been a hundred years earlier; but the results were less disappointing— the Ukraine was partitioned between the belligerents—and security in the south was vastly improved. Moscow contained a major Cossack–peasant rebellion on the Don, led by the colourful chieftain Sten´ka Razin (1670–1), and skilfully exploited to its own advantage the continuous feuding among the Cossacks on either bank of the Dnieper. By the late 1670s Russian forces had at last come to grips with the Turks, and although 3,000 captives were still taken in 1680[22] the Tatar menace could be said to be under control. In the eighteenth and nineteenth centuries several other defence lines were built on the empire's Caucasian and Asiatic borders, but they were of less significance than their forerunners in the Muscovite era, both strategically and in terms of social mobilization for military ends.

The heart and brain of the Muscovite political and military order was the tsar's court (*dvor*). During the late fifteenth and early sixteenth centuries it under-

---

[19] Ibid., pp. 36, 41–2; Yakovlev, *Zasechnaya cherta*, p. 14; A. A. Novosel´sky, *Bor´ba mosk. gosudarstva s tatarami v I-oy pol. XVII v.*, Moscow, 1948, p. 205.

[20] Yakovlev, *Zasechnaya cherta*, pp. 38–9.

[21] Ibid., p. 280.

[22] Vazhinsky, *Zemlevladeniye*, p. 46.

went a remarkable expansion which kept pace with the realm's territorial growth. Around 1550 it was about 3,000 strong.[23] Thereafter the pace slackened: reduced to a mere one thousand or so by the Troubles, it rose again to 3,500 by the 1690s.[24] The courtiers did not see themselves as specialized functionaries but as servants of their sovereign prepared to carry out assignments of any kind. In the nature of things most of these had a war-like flavour, since there was no clear distinction between military and civil administration.

In Ivan III's reign, so long as the apanage (*udel'nye*) princes still retained a vestige of their former autonomy and had their own military forces, members of the Grand Prince's court would be attached to these contingents as overseers.[25] Subsequently their duties were confined to the forces under the nominal (and sometimes actual) control of the autocrat. When the tsar went on a major campaign, practically his entire court would accompany him. It made a splendid sight: Richard Chancellor (1553) reported that the ruler was 'richly attyred above all measure' and that his pavilion, 'covered eyther with cloth of gold or silver', was fairer than those of either the English or the French king.[26] Under the young Ivan IV the court led an especially peripatetic existence, as is clear from the official military registers (*razryadnye knigi*). Thus in 1547/8 (7056 by contemporary reckoning) it marched on Kazan' and the following year twice moved to Kolomna on the Oka, on watch for Tatar raiders; thereafter it was stationed from time to time at Ryazan', Murom, and Tula.[27] When there was a pause in operations it returned to the Moscow Kremlin. Here life assumed a more somnolent and torpid character, if the French officer Jacques Margeret, who served in Moscow in the 1590s, is to be believed: in summer nobles attended court from dawn to 'the sixth hour', went home to dine and rest, and then returned from 'the fourteenth hour' until the evening; in consequence, he noted, they were obese from lack of exercise.[28] The senior men, especially holders of the top two ranks (*boyare, okol'nichiye*), might help to frame policy in the tsar's council, rather misleadingly termed by historians the Boyar Duma; some courtiers had administrative functions in the palace, while others supervised the central chancelleries (*prikazy*), served as provincial governors, or ran various errands. The complex ranking (*chin*) system, which developed under Ivan III and was modelled in part on Byzantine precedents, divided courtiers and senior servitors ('metropolitan nobles', in our terminology) into two main groups, 'Duma' (*dumnye*) and 'Moscow' (*moskovskiye*), each of which had subordinate gradations (see figure 1). This 'civilian' aspect of upper-class life need not concern us further here.

The military registers recorded pedantically major appointments and assignments, but gave tantalizingly few other details. All notables with command

23 Alef, 'Aristocratic Politics', p. 98.
24 Bobrovsky, 'Mestnichestvo', p. 257.
25 Alef, 'Crisis', p. 51.
26 Vernadsky *et al.* (eds.), *Source Book*, i. 168.
27 *RK*, pp. 117, 127, 132, 143, 147, 151.
28 Margeret, *L'Estat*, p. 15.

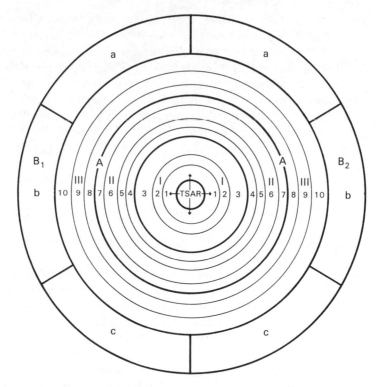

Fig. 1. Structure of the Ranking System in Muscovite Russia.

This diagram represents schematically the various ranks (*chiny*) of servitors in order of proximity to the source of power and favour. A circular form is preferable to the vertical one of modern organization charts, since to the Muscovite the objective of the 'service state' was to safeguard the security of the Sovereign Autocrat, seen as the embodiment of true piety (*pravda*), against threats from without. The terminology of the ranks varied slightly.

Key:

A. Men in hereditary service (*sluzhiliye lyudi po otechestvu*)
  I. Members of the tsar's council (*dumnye chiny*)
    1. Boyars (*boyare*)
    2. *Okol′nichiye*
    3. Duma nobles (*dumnye dvoryane*) and secretaries (*d′yaki*)
  II. Men serving from the Moscow register (*chiny moskovskiye, sluzhiliye lyudi po moskovskomu spisku*)
    4. *Stol′niki*
    5. *Stryapchiye*
    6. Moscow nobles (*dvoryane moskovskiye*)
    7. *Zhil′tsy*
  III. Men serving from provincial towns (*sluzhiliye lyudi po gorodovomu spisku*)
    8. *Vybornye* ('the select')
    9. *Deti boyarskiye dvorovye*
    10. *Deti boyarskiye gorodovye*

functions were enumerated according to rank, from members of the dynasty down to junior gentrymen (*deti boyarskiye*) who looked after the tsar's horses or battle standard. Senior commanders (voivodes) were usually titled aristocrats.[29] A recent study of the registers for 1520–50 shows that, of 1,018 regimental command positions, 771 went to members of princely clans; the rate rose from 61.5 per cent under Vasiliy III (1505–33) to 79.4 per cent in the ensuing period of 'boyar rule'.[30] A distinction was drawn between 'palace' and 'regimental' commanders. The former, who included the treasurer (*dvoretskiy*), mounted guard over the notables and supervised the ordinary gentrymen; the latter were assigned to the various regiments (*polki*) or to the artillery (*naryad*), supply train, etc.[31] The term regiment is a little misleading: in pre-Petrine Russia this was a large unit, usually combining different arms, as is clear from the record (which is unusually full) of Ivan's march on Polotsk in 1563: the 'tsar's regiment' had 6,731 men—15 per cent of the total (32,000)—of whom 5,566 were privileged servitors; the others varied in size from 5,789 for the main regiment down to 1,877 for the scouting force (*ertoul*).[32] From 1550 regiments were ranked in order of seniority or precedence: right wing, vanguard (*peredovoy*), left wing, and rearguard (*storozhevoy*); the artillery stood somewhat apart.[33]

The reason for this was the curious practice of 'place-seeking' (*mestnichestvo*) which grew up among courtiers in the late fifteenth century and later spread downwards through much of the élite. Recent research has done much to clarify the character, origins, and significance of this important institution.[34] R. O. Crummey defines 'the rules of the game' as follows: 'no one could be made to serve in a subordinate position to someone to whom he was superior according to the ranking system, which was based on a combination of one's genealogical distinction and the service record of oneself and one's

[29] Alef, 'Crisis', pp. 27, 55.   [30] Kleimola, 'Mil. Service', p. 51.
[31] Buganov, 'K izucheniyu', p. 57 (1549); cf. *DRV* xiv. 350–2 (1578).
[32] Yepifanov, 'Voysko', p. 368; 30,000 horsemen were also fielded in the 1578 campaign: ibid., p. 343.
[33] *PRP* iv. 582–3.
[34] See particularly the works of A. Kleimola (with full bibliography); Crummey, 'Reflections'; and Shmidt, 'Mestnichestvo i absolyutizm'. Markevich, *Ist. mestnichestva*, remains the classic study.

B. Men recruited for service (*sluzhiliye lyudi po priboru*)
   1. Old formation (*russkiy stroy*)
      a) Musketeers (*strel'tsy*)
      b) [Serving] cossacks (*gorodovye kazaki*)
      c) Artillerymen and fortress guards (*pushkari, zantinshchiki, vorotniki*)
   2. New formation (*novyy* [*inozemskiy*] *stroy*)
      a) Infantrymen (*soldaty*)
      b) Cavalrymen (*reytary*)
      c) Dragoons (*draguny*)

Based on Filippov, *Uchebnik*, p. 438.

kinsmen.'[35] If a man were appointed to a position that he and other members of his clan considered dishonourable, he would submit a petition to the tsar for redress of grievances, citing the precedents: that he or, more frequently, a close kinsman (within the last two generations) had served at an equivalent or superior level to an ancestor of the individual now nominated as his superior. The plea would be adjudicated, usually with dispatch, either by a commission of boyars or, if the matter were thought important enough, by the ruler in person. A successful plaintiff might be given a different assignment which would keep him away from the man whom he had challenged; alternatively—and this was more common—he would be granted a document called a *nevmestnaya gramota* certifying that his service in the position assigned was not to be accounted a precedent. If his plea was rejected, he might be reprimanded, committed briefly to prison, or even handed over to the defendant for ritual public shaming, which might well involve a sound beating administered by one of the defendant's slaves.[36] Such an apparently humiliating outcome was not in itself thought dishonourable: what counted was that one had stood up for one's correct placing. On the other hand, those who litigated unsuccessfully to excess could expect to do poorly in the matter of official preferment.

It was this competition among nobles for relatively scarce offices, with the prestige and material benefits they conferred, that lay at the origin of place-seeking. During Ivan III's reign nearly all the surviving apanage principalities were absorbed into the Muscovite domain; their rulers had no practical alternative but to take service with the Grand Prince, and their kinsmen, nobles, and other retainers followed them to the capital. This put pressure on the untitled Moscow boyars, who considered that the service their ancestors had rendered to earlier Muscovite rulers qualified them for favourable consideration *vis-à-vis* the titled newcomers. *Mestnichestvo* began with seating arrangements on ceremonial court occasions, which for all their apparent triviality had symbolic implications, and from such matters spread to public appointments as these gradually became distinguished from court assignments. It was a method of keeping tensions within the burgeoning élite at an acceptable level; it enabled clans and individuals to ascertain their proper place on the service ladder and in the eyes of the sovereign. It is important to recognize that it was not the contestants' *rank* that was at issue, at least directly: for this was conferred by the ruler and belonged to the autocratic prerogative. Nor could one have claimed the right to hold (still less to purchase!) a particular office. *Mestnichestvo* contests were fought over the *relative* standing of the servitors in question, usually when offices or commands were assigned. At the same time, though, appointment to such posts, and meritorious performance of the duties involved, would normally qualify a man for promotion in rank.

[35] Crummey, 'Reconstitution', p. 206. [36] Bobrovsky, 'Mestnichestvo', p. 253.

Both in making such promotions and in settling precedence disputes the criterion adopted was *otechestvo*, which can be roughly translated as seniority. Yet this was a vague term, open to various interpretations. Etymologically, it derived from *otets* (father), and at first probably meant genealogical descent. But with time greater weight seems to have been accorded to one's ancestor's service record. This was certainly the case by the sixteenth and seventeenth centuries, when the system became more routinized and chancellery officials played a greater role in deciding such matters. A family of ancient lineage whose members failed to perform a service, or performed it badly, would lose status—would 'grow thin' (*zakhudet'*), as the terminology of the day put it expressively. When filing precedence pleas, men would lay less emphasis on their family origins than on their forbears' achievements in the tsar's service.[37] Crummey cites the extreme case of a contest fought in 1623 between members of two branches of the Buturlin clan: the *okol'nichiy* F. L. Buturlin successfully withstood his challengers by arguing that, although their branch could indeed claim genealogical seniority, its members had served as provincial nobles in Novgorod rather than in the capital, and so had lost status.[38] Plaintiffs also came to make a further distinction between purely administrative assignments and those in the military domain. The latter, termed 'Razryad service' (*razryadnaya sluzhba*), was accounted more meritorious. To complicate matters even more, military service in one region might be considered more honourable than that in another, even though its actual character had been much the same.[39]

Noble servitors were under constant pressure from other members of their clan to avoid loss of status by inadvertently carrying out some dishonourable task. The more ambitious engaged in a kind of informal surveillance over the conduct of their kinsmen and, so far as they could, over people in other clans as well. To this end families would compile unofficial genealogical records (*rodoslovtsy*) in which details of all service rendered would be noted down; these records would be conserved carefully, like buried treasure. They often contained errors, some of them deliberate, even though they might be based in large part on official documents. It was of course these latter sources alone that counted when a dispute came up for adjudication. This gave a great deal of power to the officials who controlled the information in the various registers. They had a professional interest in restricting the number of contestations and so tended to pass judgements that went against the plaintiff. They were not, however, necessarily opposed to *mestnichestvo* on principle, partly because such cases gave them power (and sometimes profit) and partly because it was an element of the 'ancient tradition' (*starina*) that Muscovites valued so highly. Although officials took much trouble to verify the precedents, there was a great deal of arbitrariness in the settling of disputes, especially when the

---

[37] Ostrogorsky, 'Projekt', pp. 89–90.
[38] Crummey, *Aristocrats and Servitors*, p. 35.
[39] Bobrovsky, 'Mestnichestvo', p. 249.

monarchical power was weakened.[40] Thus in 1578/9 I. F. Mstislavsky and I. P. Shuysky, two prominent boyars, instituted proceedings against members of the Golitsyn clan. Ivan IV ordered their plea to be duly registered and sent for adjudication. But in the following year, when A. P. Kurakin refused to serve under M. P. Katyrev, and several other men raised similar objections, the tsar made them all serve 'according to the list', while in other such cases an adjudication was promised at the conclusion of the campaign.[41]

Mestnichestvo was clearly an obstacle to military efficiency: it limited the choices open to those who took decisions on senior appointments and increased the likelihood that these would go to men of ancient lineage but indifferent talent. Why then did not so autocratic a ruler as Ivan IV simply abolish it? The reason is not, as used to be thought, that the tsar's power was limited by reactionary aristocrats, for whom precedence ranking was a weapon to bolster their selfish interests against the Crown.[42] In fact Russia's autocratic monarchs appreciated the usefulness of this custom in keeping the élite divided and subservient. Their attitude was ambiguous and their reform efforts half-hearted. There were many complaints about the harm done by *mestnichestvo* to the country's defence effort, but even those provisions made to limit its impact were not always observed in practice. According to the chronicle account in 1550 Ivan IV, after consulting with the metropolitan and 'all the boyars', issued a ruling to the effect that 'princes and nobles [shall serve] in the regiments with their commanders without [contesting] places, shall go on all assignments [and] shall replace [other] people with all their commanders, and in this there shall be no diminution in their seniority . . .'.[43] The terminology is confusing; nor is it much clearer in the text contained in the official register. It was issued after precedence disputes had obstructed earlier offensives against the Kazan´ khanate, and may have been intended to apply only to the current campaign. In any event, the tsar later sat in judgement on pleas submitted while fighting was under way, which suggests that he did not consider it universally binding.[44] Ivan seems to have appreciated that *mestnichestvo* could be manipulated in such a way to further the monarchy's interests. It was particularly handy in ensuring the loyalty of descendants of the formerly independent princes, so integrating them into the service. Partly for this reason he consistently favoured those progeny of Gedimin, Grand Prince of Lithuania, who had come to Moscow over nobles of Ryurikid stock.[45] Kleimola observes that 'preoccupation with *mestnichestvo* concerns served to atomize the élite by keeping its members in a constant state of watchfulness and rivalry'; the fact

[40] For example, in the era of boyar rule (1533–47): Kleimola, 'Status, Place and Politics', pp. 205–9.   [41] *RK*, pp. 153, 295, 307.

[42] This was the view of pre-revolutionary and earlier Soviet historians such as Smirnov (*Ocherki*, pp. 399–406), whose arguments are ably countered by Zimin, *Reformy*, pp. 343–4 and Shmidt, 'Mestnichestvo i absolyutizm', p. 284.

[43] *PRP* iv. 583.

[44] Kleimola, 'Status, Place and Politics', p. 213.

[45] Shmidt, 'Mestnichestvo i absolyutizm', pp. 291, 294.

that 'no litigant, however firm he believed his precedence claims to be, could ever be certain of the outcome of his complaint . . . from the sovereign's point of view led to a desirable lack of security among the élite.'[46] The endemic quarrels and mutual suspicions among Muscovy's leading families help to explain why they offered no sustained opposition to Ivan IV's reign of terror. Those tempted to seek safety by fleeing abroad knew that they would be treated as traitors, and that the reprisals would affect not only their immediate kin but generations yet unborn, since their entire clan would fall several degrees in precedence ranking and might even be excluded from it altogether.[47]

When *mestnichestvo* was officially abolished in 1682, as many records as possible were solemnly destroyed. We shall therefore never know for certain how many pleas were filed in different periods or how they were settled. There must have been a diminution during the Troubles, when normal government business was interrupted and even well-born nobles had a hard struggle to survive. Under the first Romanovs the practice resumed. A study of the tsar's council between 1613 and 1689 shows that its total of 427 members engaged in no less than 294 known precedence disputes; the frequency of such cases declined after mid-century and very few are recorded after 1667.[48]

The practice will have been less prevalent among provincial cavalrymen, but the very fact that it spread to lower echelons of the élite made it less attractive to their social superiors. Its abolition was but a question of time. The government was no longer so beholden to its privileged servitors and had a rudimentary bureaucratic apparatus to do its bidding; and so the damage could be contained more easily than before. The 1550 decree was explicitly reaffirmed in 1620. Many official assignments, particularly military ones, were declared 'without places' (*bez mest*), that is, exempt from considerations of precedence. A blanket order of this kind was issued at the outset of the Thirteen Years War in 1654. Again it was not universally adhered to, but the disputes as a rule did not affect commanders in the field.[49] There was an important exception in 1659, when two generals failed to reinforce another, so allowing an enemy army to escape; but indiscipline of this kind was a problem that extended beyond that of precedence ranking. Nineteenth-century historians, writing in an age of 'rational' military organization, tended to exaggerate the negative impact of *mestnichestvo*, which, it is now clear, 'should take only a small share of the blame for the inconsistent performance of the Russian army in the seventeenth century'.[50] Far more serious was the fact that few senior Russian officers were professionals, and that the armed forces were dependent on foreigners for so much of their technical expertise.

---

[46] Kleimola, 'Up Through Servitude', p. 215; cf. id., 'Changing Face', p. 486.

[47] Shmidt, 'Mestnichestvo i absolyutizm', p. 280.

[48] Crummey, 'Reflections', pp. 270–1.

[49] Markevich, *Ist. mestnichestva*, p. 527; Crummey, 'Reflections', pp. 275–6; cf. Kleimola, 'Up Through Servitude', pp. 226–7.

[50] Crummey, 'Reflections', p. 279.

Precedence ranking, as we shall see, could be abolished in 1682 without provoking any noticeable opposition within the élite. The more broad-minded senior nobles had long since recognized that it has lost its *raison d'être*; they could hope to do well under a more modern system of preferment which downplayed genealogical origin or ancestral feats in favour of individual merit (*razum*, or intelligence) as well as one's service record (*zaslugi*).[51] In the new ranking order which Peter I would introduce (see ch. 6) there was much that was familiar; indeed, traditional habits of thought survived among Russian *dvoryane* long into the Imperial era—just as the service state did.

The metropolitan nobility comprised only a small fraction of the service élite, whose total size at the end of the sixteenth century was probably around 80,000—exclusive of families and retainers—and over 200,000 a hundred years later. Administratively, the provincial servitors were distinguished from those we have been discussing by the fact that they were enrolled on the register of their locality (*gorod*, 'town') rather than that of Moscow. As a rule they were referred to officially as *dvoryane i deti boyarskiye*.[52] Socially, economically, and psychologically the difference between the two groups was considerable, even if there was no legal or customary barrier between them and in many cases the divide might be bridged by kinship links. These differences widened as time went on.

The *deti boyarskiye* are first mentioned in 1433, when Moscow was wracked by dynastic strife; it was this conflict that called them into being and enabled some of the more enterprising to rise up in the Grand Prince's service.[53] All the autonomous or quasi-autonomous apanage princes had cavalry servitors; and as these forces were gradually absorbed into the Muscovite army in the late fifteenth century the elements of a nation-wide gentry militia (*opolcheniye*) came into being. However, it lacked cohesion. Neither the local lieutenants (*namestniki*) nor the officials of the central military chancellery, when this took shape in the 1530s, exercised much real authority. Herberstein speaks of provincial *deti boyarskiye* being mustered and registered every second or third year,[54] but this statement cannot be confirmed from native sources. He puts

[51] Medvedev, *Sozertsaniye*, p. 19; Volkov, 'Ob otmene', p. 57.

[52] The two elements in this designation were not clearly differentiated. The term *dvoryane*, which in Imperial Russia came to mean nobility *tout court*, is first met with in 1175. Originally it meant courtier, one who served in a prince's household: it was an office or function rather than a rank or title. In the Muscovite era it was applied both to certain rank-holders in the metropolitan nobility (*dumnye, moskovskiye dvoryane*) and to the provincial élite; the rest of the provincial gentry were *deti boyarskiye*. This term literally meant 'boyars' children' (that is, dependants), and reflected the patriarchal relationships in noble households of the apanage era; but by our period it had nothing to do with kinship and was purely a social category. On early nomenclature see Sh., 'Dvoryanstvo', pp. 557–61. Richard Hellie calls the provincial servitors the 'middle service class', indicating that they stood between the metropolitan nobility and the lower-grade musketeers, Cossacks, etc.

[53] Alef, 'Crisis', pp. 45–6. One of these, Fedor Basenok, fell into disfavour early in the reign of Ivan III, who had him blinded: ibid., p. 52.

[54] Von Herberstein, *Moscovia*, p. 101.

the size of the levy on the southern border at 20,000 men. The combat unit was the 'hundred' (*sotnya*) or company, whose chiefs initially had a fairly free hand in recruiting and remunerating personnel or in deciding on operations. The scope of their undertakings was limited by the cavalrymen's inability or reluctance to venture far from their lands, whence they obtained food, clothing, and mounts. Weapons were not standardized but were simple to manufacture; some were bought—or looted.

These easy-going ways changed in the early part of Ivan IV's reign. The drive to conquer the Kazan´ khanate was a major military enterprise which required a greater degree of organization than any previous campaign. The new tsar (he took the title in 1547) was eager to consolidate his authority and, according to the conventional view at least, already distrusted some of his boyars. It made excellent sense to expand the monarchy's power base by currying favour with other elements in the élite. The rivalry between noble clans was in part a matter of 'ins' versus 'outs', seniors versus juniors—a state of affairs which some historians have confused by trying to fit it into the anachronistic mould of a 'class struggle'.[55] During Ivan's minority the country's administration had run down and the self-confident young ruler and his close advisers sought to eliminate what they saw, not unreasonably, as grave abuses that could not be permitted in a truly autocratic and Orthodox realm. It was not a matter of undermining the boyars as a group, still less the entire metropolitan nobility, but rather of strengthening it by infusing new blood, mostly from the provinces, and so rendering the monarchy more secure.

To this end in 1550 Ivan ordered one thousand (actually 1,078) servitors, all but 28 of whom were *deti boyarskiye*, to be given estates on conditional tenure in an area within 60 to 70 versts of the capital.[56] Such compulsory transfers (*vyvody*) were a hallmark of despotic rule. They were unusual in Muscovy, although there was a notable precedent: in 1487-9 Ivan III had undertaken a reshuffle of noble servitors in the newly conquered lands of Great Novgorod that had involved some two thousand land-holders.[57] A new judicial code (*sudebnik*) issued in the same year removed the provincial gentry from the jurisdiction of the princely lieutenants, who had made themselves unpopular with their exactions. Shortly afterwards these governors were phased out and replaced by locally elected authorities. This measure benefited the gentry in those regions—and they were fast becoming the majority—where they owned or held land. Since these districts had to pay for the privilege of self-government and were soon subjected to tighter control by agents of the centre, the reform should not be seen as a step towards 'democratization' but rather as

[55] Alef, 'Aristocratic Politics', p. 97; Rüss, *Adel*, p. 20.

[56] *PRP* iv. 581-2, 596-7; A. A. Zimin (comp.), *Tysyachnaya kniga 1550 g.* . . ., Moscow and Leningrad, 1950. Zimin doubted whether this measure was actually implemented (*Reformy*, pp. 366-75); the evidence is inconclusive. Cf. also Smirnov, *Ocherki*, pp. 407-22; Veselovsky, *Feod. zemlevladeniye*, i. 314-26 (where the military security aspect is, however, played down).

[57] Alef, 'Aristocratic Politics', pp. 83-4; id., 'Musc. Mil. Reforms', p. 98; Veselovsky, *Feod. zemlevladeniye*, i. 290-2; id., *Issledovaniya*, pp. 77-8; Shapiro, *Agr. istoriya*, p. 333.

an effort to associate the local élite more actively with Moscow's policies. As such it was certainly a step in the right direction, and it was a pity that, largely owing to the Livonian War and the *oprichnina*, this deconcentration of authority was not sustained.

The high point for the gentry came in the summer of 1556 with the so-called Service Code (*Ulozheniye o sluzhbe*). Its historic significance lay in the fact that it formally extended the obligation to serve the tsar to all land-owners or -holders. Over and above that it prescribed a fixed relationship between the quality of their service and their entitlement to compensation. 'From each hundred quarters of good arable land [c. 400 acres] one man [shall be provided] with a horse and full armour, and with two horses for a distant campaign.'[58] The original order has not survived and the texts available are characteristically laconic. It was laid down that if a servitor brought more men (and horses?) than his norm, he was to receive a bounty—and the men 2½ times more than the standard monetary grant. Substitutes could be provided by those who—presumably on account of age or sickness—did not serve themselves. The code did not state explicitly that the servitor was to report for duty himself, evidently because this was taken for granted. Nor did it make clear that he had to bring enough supplies to maintain himself and his men for the duration of the campaign. He also of course had to bring his own weapons, the nature of which was left to his judgement. Like their Tatar adversaries, sixteenth-century Russian gentry cavalrymen preferred cold steel to the new-fangled firearms, which they evidently considered too clumsy and inaccurate, and so of limited use when fighting on horseback; they were also expensive.[59] One can sympathize with them up to a point, but on a long-term view this choice marked them out for technological obsolescence.[60] The compensation scales were not mentioned in the Service Code, but these matters were settled by subsequent legislation and practice.

From the 1550s onward the gentry militia assumed a more regular shape. In each district—particularly those situated in a great semicircle south of Moscow, where gentry estates were concentrated—there developed a skeleton organization responsible to the centre for the mustering and compensation of all cavalrymen who lived there.[61] It enjoyed a measure of autonomy but, as with the local government reform, the essential decisions were soon being taken in the capital or by military commanders appointed by the centre. They were supposed to supervise the proper functioning of the *gorod* (literally, 'town', as this service organization was simply called), and not to interfere in

---

[58] Vernadsky *et al.* (eds.), *Source Book*, i. 141–2; Russ. texts: *PRP* iv. 586, 600–1; Beskrovnyy, *Khrestomatiya*, pp. 62–4.

[59] A battleaxe or a good spear cost 10 roubles, as much as a musket: Brix, *Geschichte*, p. 118 (for weapon types, ibid., pp. 108–10). This was more than a provincial servitor's annual salary.

[60] Nasonov *et al.* (eds.), *Ocherki*, p. 330; this point is stressed by Hellie, *Enserfment*, passim, who perhaps makes too much of the 'gunpowder revolution' in the Russian context. Gentry who served in the new-model forces (see ch. 4), and no doubt some others, did have firearms.

[61] The best studies are by Novosel'sky: 'Prav. gruppy', 'Raspad'.

its inner workings, such as the electoral act; but this rule, as one might expect, was difficult to define and even harder to observe in practice. All too often local initiative was closely circumscribed. More concretely, what usually seems to have transpired was that the voivode, as the representative of the central authority, reached an informal arrangement with the 'better'—that is, senior in rank, wealthier, and more privileged—elements of the local gentry community. Such collusion could be vindicated as essential for the smooth operation of the system; yet it was likely to offend the poorer and disadvantaged *deti boyarskiye* and to make them feel that they were being exploited by their fellows. All servitors were bound by a network of sureties (*poruki*)[62] whereby the signatories—kinsmen, neighbours, or comrades—pledged themselves to answer for those who misbehaved or stepped out of line. This was a powerful instrument of social control which reinforced outward conformity of thought and action. In practice, however, the cohesion of each organization was under constant strain.

In Muscovy the election of any official (for example, for revenue collection or as judicial assessors) had the character of a duty rather than a right. So it was also with the compensation entitlement officials (*okladchiki*), whose job it was to evaluate the service which each of their fellows had rendered, or were expected to render, and on that basis to place them in a particular category in regard to rewards. (These rewards, in cash and land, will be discussed in ch. 2.) It was only natural that the individuals chosen for such a responsible and delicate task should themselves be men in the most senior category—not least because, in principle at any rate, they had to be able to reimburse the state for any losses incurred by their error or malfeasance. In practice, as data for the late sixteenth century show, they had more personal servants (slaves)—and probably also more land—than any other category of provincial servitor.[63] This marked them out as local leaders, and as logical allies of the voivode, both in fulfilling the authorities' legitimate behests and in sharing the pickings: for instance, at Yelets in the 1630s the voivode colluded with one Dmitriy Snetin who used a false-bottomed bucket when issuing grain allocations to his comrades.[64]

Those who objected to such practices could complain—that is, submit a petition-cum-denunciation—but the central authorities were notoriously tardy in investigating such complaints, especially if they stemmed from the relatively junior ranks. True, the central military chancellery, the Razryad, sent out officials to the provinces to assist in mustering, inspecting, and awarding compensation. In the seventeenth century they operated in permanence from the voivode's office. These senior functionaries' opinions normally carried a good deal of weight. However, they could not easily verify the information submitted

[62] Shakhmatov, *Kompetentsiya*, pp. 176–8; Kleimola, 'Up Through Servitude', pp. 217–18, 221–2; for the beginnings of this system in the 1520s: Rüss, *Adel*, pp. 78–84.

[63] Hellie, 'Musc. Prov. Elite', p. 8A.

[64] Chistyakova, 'Volneniya', pp. 258–9.

to them; the record-keeping system was cumbersome, and the data in local service registers (*desyatni*), land cadasters, and so on rapidly became obsolete. The same difficulties, it should be noted in fairness, confronted the *oklad-chiki*. Although they took an oath 'not to favour their friends' or take bribes,[65] it seems that they were frequently tempted to ease conditions or increase rewards for their kinsmen and fellow-servitors in the senior grade. The corollary was that men in junior categories faced heavier or more disagreeable tasks, or might receive less compensation than their due.

Men in the three provincial grades were termed respectively *vybornye* (literally, 'the select'), *dvorovye*, and *gorodovye*. The assignment to a particular class, and with this the specification of the entitlement (*oklad*), was called *verstan´ye*.[66] It normally took place in circumstances that one might term an 'inspection parade' if this did not convey an impression of formal ceremony that was usually lacking.[67] No rules existed as to the frequency of assignments, which depended on the whim of the government and its officials; they would take some account of the current military situation and of representations from below. In an emergency, or perhaps just for administrative convenience, the two principal events in the gentry cavalryman's service life, mustering (*razbor, sbor*) and *verstan´ye*, might be telescoped. They would be announced by the town crier or by messenger (*pristav*). At first many poorer noblemen in the vulnerable southern border region resided in their local town, with its protective citadel, and had to be ordered to live on the lands they had been allotted.[68] Those who had moved out would be summoned back to attend these official functions, which offered them an opportunity to meet socially as well as to obtain some material benefit.

Promotion from one grade to another depended in theory on one's merit (either already demonstrated on active service or *in spe*), and was granted in response to a petition in which the servitor detailed his accomplishments and needs. He began his career as a novice (*novik*) at the age of 15 and then served in the lowest grade as a *gorodovoy*, later advancing to *dvorovoy* and, if he were particularly fortunate, to *vybornyy*. Needless to say, in real life matters were more complicated. At Kolomna in 1577 some novices went directly into the second category, perhaps because of the manpower shortage induced by the war.[69] Besides individual merit, genealogical seniority played a part in the

---

[65] *DRV* xvi. 334.

[66] For a typical order: *DRV* xvi. 331–9 (1652).

[67] The term *smotr* (inspection) occurs in the documents, for example *AMG* i. 374 (1632). The first ones were apparently held in 1556, after regularization of the levy: Likhachev, *Razryadnye d´yaki*, app. iv. Troitsky, *Russkiy absolyutizm*, p. 108, dates them from 1622. They would not have satisfied the disciplinarian drill-masters of a later age: wealthy high-ranking servitors appeared on fine war-horses (*argamaki*) in full armour with a large suite, while 'the poor man turned up on a miserable nag, an ancient sabre at his side and a bag of hard tack, borne by an emaciated slave' ('Petr Velikiy i yego armiya', pp. 229–30).

[68] *AMG* i. 229, 245 (1629); Chistyakova, 'Volneniya', p. 255.

[69] Storozhev, 'Desyatni', p. 45.

assessor's decision; so too did wealth, measured by the amount of land owned or held and the number of dependants (slaves, serfs). It was a basic assumption of Muscovite political life that, the higher one stood on the social scale, the more responsibility one should bear; and conversely, that extra duties brought opportunities for additional gain.

How far the provincial gentrymen were socially mobile is not easily ascertained. Most of our data come from the seventeenth century, when the barriers were going down. I. K. Rudakov of Tver', who entered service in 1616, was listed as a *gorodovoy* in 1621 and 1631 and as a *dvorovoy* in 1634, 1649, and 1658—when he must have been nearly 60; his poor showing was probably due to misconduct in 1634, when he left the front, as so many did, without being properly discharged.[70] The objective of every provincial servitor, one assumes, was to rise to the top category (significantly, the *vybor* was the only one to have a name!), since this offered the prospect of ascent into the upper nobility. The term apparently originated with the great transfer of men to the capital in 1550.[71] Later other provincials were 'chosen', on a more restricted scale and on a routine basis. Once in Moscow they received the lowest metropolitan rank, *zhilets* (literally, 'resident'). There were generally about 200 of these men, who performed ceremonial duties and served in the sovereign's personal bodyguard.[72] Margeret states that 'the principal gentlemen are chosen from each town where they have their land, who are called the *vybornye dvoryane* of each town, according to its size—16, 18, up to 20 or even 30 [men], who reside in the city of Moscow for three years.'[73] In principle, then, the assignment was temporary: those who did well would join the 'Moscow ranks' and the rest would return home. The proportion who were siphoned off in this way is not known. One man served nineteen years as a *zhilets* without leaping the hurdle.[74] During the seventeenth century there was a considerable growth in the number of places to be filled at court and in the central administration, but this expansion could not accommodate all *vybornye* with ambition and talent. Men might also be down-graded from the metropolitan nobility to serve in the provinces: this was the fate of eleven men who in 1646 rashly petitioned for exemption from service on grounds of poverty; it was held that their conduct showed lack of zeal.[75] As the competition at the top became fiercer, more *vybornye* were obliged to remain in the 'town' to which they were ascribed, where they formed the local élite. The growing porportion of *vybornye* among provincial servitors may be taken as an indicator of greater prosperity and social stability. The authorities did not prescribe any arithmetical relationship between men in the three grades, leaving it to local officials to assess each indi-

---

[70] Hellie, 'Musc. Prov. Elite', p. 7A, based on V. N. Storozhev, *Tverskoye dvoryanstvo*, Tver', 1891–5, ii. 137–8.

[71] But cf. Kargalov, *Na stepnoy granitse*, p. 99 for a mention from 1541. The main study of the *vybornye* is Novitsky, *Vybornoye i bol'shoye dvoryanstvo*.

[72] Brix, *Geschichte*, p. 172.   [73] Margeret, *L'Estat*, p. 22.

[74] *AMG* ii. 76 (1637).   [75] *AMG* ii. 268.

vidual's worth. This flexibility was beneficial in so far as it gave servitors an incentive to do their duty and better themselves.

As to the nature of these duties our sources are largely silent. Service on the frontier had a seasonal character. The 1571 statute laid down that cavalrymen should serve in rotation for three-month terms, from 1 April to 1 July and from 1 July to 1 October or 'the great snows', whichever came first.[76] In 1578 I. A. Tyutchev left Ryl'sk on Easter Day, 8 April, for a ten-day patrol to the Donets with 93 men; on 13 June he was replaced by I. Semichev of Bryansk with 78 men, who in turn gave way on 21 August to A. Panyukin with a party of similar size; what they actually did we are not told.[77] A routine order of 1624 lists the men from various 'towns' who were to make up each of two shifts; those who lived far from the border were to serve in the spring, those from the vicinity in the autumn; however, the final stand-down order was not issued until 7 December.[78] They were ordered to keep good watch 'lest [Tatar] warriors approach our borders and do damage without [intelligence] information [being provided]'. If the enemy did appear, the second-shift men were told simply to call back the men from the first shift—although it would clearly take weeks for them to reassemble, by which time the Tatar raiders would have long since returned home and disposed of their loot. At other times a more activist strategy was indicated, but one gets little sense from the documents of provincial gentrymen carrying out their tasks with zeal. They were obsessive petitioners: for leave, discharge, transfer, promotion, or extra compensation; and they seem to have tried whenever possible to pass on their obligations to their dependants or substitutes.

The authorities prescribed severe penalties for dereliction of duty: fines, beatings, imprisonment, confiscation of property, and even death.[79] But these threats lacked credibility. Gentry cavalrymen were under oath 'to serve the Sovereign loyally and wish him well in everything, without any deceit'[80]—a promise that many failed to live up to. There were at least two good reasons for this. One was sheer poverty, at least among *deti boyarskiye* on the border; another was the pettifogging (and inefficient)[81] regimentation they had to endure from functionaries of the Razryad.

---

[76] *AMG* i. 1–2, 19, 22.   [77] Belyayev, *O storozhevoy . . . sluzhbe*, p. 28.
[78] *AMG* i. 175, 177; cf. i. 194 (1627), ii. 328 (1648). In 1632 a four-month term was specified: ibid., i. 322.
[79] *AMG* i. 99, 102 (1615), 117, 119 (1618), 148 (1622), 179 (1625), 233, 264 (1629).
[80] *AMG* i. 198 (1627).
[81] Plavsić, 'Seventeenth-Century Chanceries', seeks to revise the common assessment of the *prikaz* officials' skills. Their problems were compounded by vast distances, excessive centralization of decision-making, lack of proper record-keeping procedures, inadequate knowledge of arithmetic (Arabic numerals were introduced to Russia by Peter I), and the complexities of contemporary orthography and grammar. In the circumstances it is indeed commendable that the administration was not even more chaotic. Nor can one agree with the assertion by a recent student of the ranking system that 'before Peter's day . . . what supervisory institutions there were exercised minimal control' over noblemen's service (Bennett, 'Evolution', p. 13). Precisely the reverse is the case—although whether the controls were effective is another matter.

'The dominant bureaucratic organization in early modern Russia',[82] the Razryad still awaits its historian. Its archive has yet to be thoroughly surveyed, and it is only in recent years that some of its most important records, the service books (*razryadnye knigi*), have been published in scholarly editions.[83] The bland title of this powerful institution is in itself indicative: *razryad* means no more than 'category', and the office's chief function was indeed to categorize the privileged servitors in regard to their duties and rewards. These lists, called *razryady*, which are known to have existed from the 1470s, subsequently gave their name to the office which compiled them. It was not called the Military Service chancellery, as one might have expected, since most of the tsar's subjects, not just the nobles, were engaged in military or military-related service of some kind. The convenient English translation 'Military chancellery' obscures the fact that besides the Razryad there were other central offices concerned with military affairs (musketeers, new-model forces, foreigners etc.). Until the late seventeenth century these were independent bodies—evidently because it was thought politically unwise to concentrate too much armed force in the hands of a single individual; although it is also true that the Razryad acquired a general supervisory role, notably in war-time.[84]

Its institutional life began at least three decades before 1566, when it is known to have had separate premises (*izba*). The conflict with Lithuania in 1512–22 enhanced the role of the *razryadnye d'yaki* (secretaries), who were already well-known figures in Moscow public life.[85] As a rule there were three (later four) of them—an unusual feature, since most chancelleries were headed by a member of one of the top two ranks. The reason for this exception was that precedence-conscious senior servitors would not readily have accepted orders issued by a social equal, whereas secretaries were seen as executants of the monarchical will. They were indeed guardians of the interests of the central *vlast'*, despite the fact that they owned land and led lives much like those of other metropolitan noblemen (*d'yak* was a rank as well as an office). The Razryad chiefs also had a voice in the Duma.[86] They tended to serve for a lengthy time-span, which made for continuity and may have given them a more professional approach to their duties. In Russia, as in most other European countries, it was the military administration which led the way in the 'rationalization' of government. The Razryad had eight—later ten—departments, called 'desks' (*stoly*), which were arranged systematically according to functional and territorial criteria;[87] it was also the first chancellery to order its

---

[82] Brown, 'Musc. Bureaux', p. 89; cf. Brix, *Geschichte*, p. 78: 'the whole realm was subordinate to it so far as service was concerned'.

[83] *RK*; see also Buganov's articles, esp. 'K izucheniyu', '"Gos. razryad"', 'Obzor spiskov', 'Sokr. redasktsiya', etc.

[84] Brix, *Geschichte*, pp. 323–4; Brown, 'Musc. Bureaux', pp. 21, 89.

[85] Leont'yev, *Obrazovaniye*, pp. 78–85; Zimin (*Reformy*, p. 105) holds to the view generally shared earlier that the Razryad was not formed until the 1550s.

[86] Crummey, 'Reconstitution', p. 204; Demidova, 'Gos. apparat', p. 125.

[87] Kalinychev, *Prav. voprosy*, pp. 95–7.

archive.[88] In these departments and their provincial extensions there toiled a vast army of clerks (*pod'yachiye*): by the 1690s more than two thousand of them.[89] The Razryad and the Service Land chancellery (*Pomestnyy prikaz*) were among the largest employers of labour in the country.

The growth of a provincial apparatus is particularly significant, not only because (at least potentially) it intensified the degree of bureaucratic control over noble and other servitors, but also because it led to the creation of what one may term militarized zones. The most important of these, centred on Belgorod in the south-west, took shape in the 1640s and by 1663 had no less than 33,000 men in its charge, of whom 12,000 were gentry servitors.[90] Most of these troops manned the new defence line. They comprised the so-called Belgorod 'regiment' (the word *polk* was used here in a more comprehensive sense; to add to the confusion, the administrative division itself was called a *razryad*). Another force, based on the nearby town of Sevsk, in that year had 76,000 soldiers, of whom just over 10 per cent were gentry servitors.[91] *Razryady* were later set up to cover other regions, but few were so heavily militarized as those in the south-west. The large concentrations of troops here were built up partly by taking men from the central regions, which in turn affected the character of its administration.

It was in the seventeenth century that Russian local government first acquired a pronounced military character. Previously field commanders (voivodes) had been sent out only to areas where action was expected or under way; but the experience of the Troubles so frightened the government that commanders were appointed throughout the country, one to each of 150 or so districts (*uyezdy*). They were a reincarnation of the prince's lieutenants (*namestniki*) in the sense that they could abuse the local inhabitants with little fear of being called to account; the difference was that the voivode was formally invested with full military and civil power. Appointment to this office came to be regarded as a suitable reward for a middle-aged or incapacitated nobleman with ample military experience.[92] It was understood that the holder, who generally served a two-year term (to prevent him striking root too deeply in the area) was entitled to receive, in lieu of salary, 'gifts' and other income—

[88] Gozdavo-Golombiyevsky, 'Istoriya', p. 9; cf. pp. 5–6 for details of the various departments' responsibilities, also Ivanov, *Opisaniye*, p. 9.

[89] In 1669 the Razryad had the third largest staff of all Moscow chancelleries, which one early historian (Ivanov, *Opisaniye*, pp. 53–69) put at 64—perhaps an under-estimate, since by 1686/7 it had almost doubled to 125 (Demidova, 'Byurokratizatsiya', p. 216), and by 1698 had reached 242 (including 28 secretaries); those in provincial bureaux numbered 1,873 (id., 'Gos. apparat', pp. 130, 133–4, 144).

[90] Including relatives. Stashevsky, 'Smeta', pp. 64–7, 70–1 (our computation). In 1678 they numbered about 20,000: see *DAI* ix. 106, pp. 257 ff. For a map: Zagorodsky, *Belgorodskaya cherta*, p. 157.

[91] Stashevsky, 'Smeta', pp. 82–3; Vazhinsky, *Zemlevladeniye*, p. 69, dates the formation of this force to 1666.

[92] In 1632 S. Lykov, after 30 years' service during which he was wounded several times, was appointed voivode of Uglich: *AMG* i. 322.

more plainly, tribute—from the population, within the limits established by local custom.

The voivode was invested by the centre with enormous responsibilities but given next to no financial resources with which to carry them out. His job was to collect revenue, not to disburse it. This in itself forced him to cultivate members of the local élite—an alliance from which the interests of the state and the taxpaying population both suffered. In this partnership the dominant role fell to the voivode for three reasons: he belonged to the metropolitan nobility (with the rank of *stol'nik* at least); he had the aura that surrounded a personal representative of the sacrosanct autocrat; last but not least, he had at his disposal a body of troops which, especially in the border regions, might be of considerable size.

No instance is known of a voivode using these troops in a sense contrary to the wishes of the central power: this was not the direction in which these men's ambitions lay. Nor did the privileged elements in the local service organization urge them to do so. For the Muscovite provincial cavalrymen had little in common with the nobilities of central, still less western, Europe. They constituted something of a warrior caste[93]—yet paradoxically one that was not very belligerent. Senior Russian servitors told a Swedish diplomat in 1647 that peace was better than war and strongly condemned the Western practice of hiring mercenaries.[94] Unlike the Polish or Hungarian élites, to look no further afield, they did not conspicuously cherish the memory of deeds of valour performed by honoured fellow-soldiers of noble ancestry: for this they lacked the individualistic and chivalric spirit of the Latin West. Rather their attention was directed to the routine execution of their allotted tasks, especially in border defence. The Muscovite servitor was a bondsman of his sovereign: indeed, in petitions he would commonly refer to himself as his *kholop*, which literally meant slave—a practice that amazed status-conscious Western visitors. His loyalty was buttressed by the surety system, even though in practice such sureties might be rarely called in. In the next chapter we shall explore a little further the mentality of the privileged servitors in the light of the socio-economic milieu in which they lived.

---

[93] This term (also used by Crummey, 'Noble Officials', p. 62) is a little strong, since the *dvoryanstvo* did not form a closed corporation but was open at the base to new entrants from the under-privileged groups—a major weakness in its relationship with the Crown.

[94] K. Pommerening to Queen Christina, 15 Sept. 1647, in Yakubov, *Rossiya i Shvetsiya*, p. 410.

2

THE NOBLE SERVITOR AND HIS WORLD

'THE Muscovite army', states the invaluable Herberstein, 'always pitches camp in open field. The notables put up tents, while the common soldiers build huts of reeds, cover them with their cloaks, bring in their weapons, especially their bows and arrows, and seek shelter there from inclement weather.' The frugality with which men existed on campaign he found remarkable. When leaving home the cavalryman would take two or three little bags of ground millet and some salt pork; a spoonful of this with salt—only the wealthy added pepper—comprised his meal, unless he happened to camp in an area where game, fish, onions, or fruit were to be found. 'Master and servant are equally content with this economical meal. But it may occur that the master is very hungry, in which case he eats everything himself and his servants may fast splendidly for two or three days.' Metropolitan nobles would sometimes enter-tain their humbler fellow-servitors to a proper meal, after which they would not eat again for several days.[1]

An English traveller added: '[the soldiers'] lying in the field is not so strange as is their hardnesse: for every man must carrie and make provision for him-selfe and his Horse for a moneth or two, which is very wonderfull . . . I pray you, amongst all our boasting Warriors how many should we find to endure the field with them but one moneth?'[2] It was a refrain that Western observers would echo for centuries.

That masters should have lived and eaten better than their men is not sur-prising; the degree of inequality is not excessive. What foreign visitors did not report—and it probably began only as Chancellor wrote—was that, although self-maintenance was the norm, a rudimentary official 'supply service' also existed. Grain was sent to the forces marching on Kazan' in 1552, and a few years later we hear of it being collected from Novgorodian peasants for the campaign into Livonia.[3] In the seventeenth century the Razryad arranged mat-ters in more systematic fashion, with a rudimentary network of magazines.[4]

When supplies gave out, troops took what they could find from the local populace, despite official prohibitions and exhortations, much as they did everywhere else in Europe. 'Prisoners taken as slaves, movable wealth and cattle were prized. Both the rank of a servitor and the size of his following of

---

[1] Von Herberstein, *Moscovia*, pp. 106–7.
[2] Vernadsky *et al.* (eds.), *Source Book*, i. 168; cf. Fletcher, *Russe Commonwealth*, p. 184 (Schmidt edn., p. 82).
[3] Yepifanov, 'Voysko', pp. 375–6, citing *DAI* i. 70.
[4] *AMG* iii. 77, 159 (1660).

personal retainers governed his share of the spoils.'[5] The lure of booty was a powerful incentive for those fighting on the western front; but the Tatars did not lightly surrender the few goods they carried,[6] which leaves one wondering how far this factor accounts for the indifferent morale of servitors in the southern border region.

Certainly they could expect little help from the authorities if they were wounded or fell sick. In 1566 Grisha Nashchokin 'was wounded in the leg by a musket and has a bullet in his foot'. He submitted a petition to the Razryad, which ordered officials in Novgorod to send him a 'skilled doctor' (*master lekar'*, that is, a native healer).[7] Whether he removed the bullet is not stated; the oddest aspect of the case is the degree of bureaucratic centralization it reveals. It was long believed that no care at all was given until the seventeenth century, when a few Western doctors were hired to treat casualties. Several are known to have been active during the Smolensk War. Apparently they then returned home, for in 1638, when several men in Belgorod died from scurvy, the authorities simply recommended that the sick should be discharged—in secret, lest morale be adversely affected![8] Gentry servitors were sometimes granted compensation in land or money, but after the Troubles the treasury was empty. The unfortunate B. S. Gubarev, with 43 years' duty behind him, 'has his left arm cut through below the elbow by a sabre so that he cannot use his hand' and had also lost an ear; he was nevertheless ordered to soldier on until his sons could succeed him.[9] However, by mid-century conditions had improved. The Apothecaries' chancellery recruited more foreign medical men, who were paid generous salaries; they were posted to the front and sent supplies; training courses were also set up for about 30 native youths.[10] In the Crimean campaign of 1689 65 carts were assigned for the evacuation of casualties (reportedly 20,000 men were killed): a mere gesture, but one which anticipated methods still employed during the Crimean War.

Lucky invalids, if they were men of rank, would be granted leave or, if their wounds were serious, discharged.[11] However, veterans were still not regarded as free men—another trait that would endure. They might well find themselves sent to hunt down bandits or to do guard duty in a fortress—as happened to P. F. Lubyatinsky of Arzamas, who in 1636, having retired after 50 years in the ranks, petitioned that the local voivode be told to stop harassing him.[12]

---

[5] Alef, 'Crisis', p. 22; id., 'Musc. Mil. Reforms', pp. 81–2; Rüss, *Adel*, pp. 8–9. On looting during the Thirteen Years War: Bobrovsky, 'K kharakteristike', pp. 182–3. Bobrovsky was one of the few historians to break the nationalist taboo on discussing this matter.

[6] Russian enslavement of Tatar prisoners is noted by Paul of Aleppo, *Travels of Macarius, Patriarch of Antioch . . .*, tr. F. C. Belfour, London, 1829–36, ii. 286.

[7] Yepifanov, 'Voysko', p. 378, citing *DAI* i. 110.

[8] Lakhtin, 'Pomoshch'', p. 264.

[9] *AMG* i. 88 (1614); cf. i. 73.

[10] Lakhtin, 'Pomoshch'', pp. 266–9; id., 'Voznagrazhdeniye', pp. 610–11; A. S. Mulyukin, 'Inostrantsy svobodnykh professiy v moskovskom gosudarstve', *ZhMNP*, N.S., 17 (1908), 10, p. 328; Alexander, 'Medical Developments', p. 207.

[11] *AMG* i. 106 (1616); iii. 21, 35 (1660).

[12] Brix, *Geschichte*, p. 91; *AMG* ii. 45.

Discharge was considered a privilege, to be granted only for serious reasons; if they were medical in nature, applicants had to undergo physical inspection—by a bureaucrat, not a doctor.[13] Discharge was also granted, again as a special favour, to men who had fled, or been ransomed, from Tatar captivity. Similarly, home leave was granted 'very rarely, only in the event of some domestic catastrophe, and provided that no battle was imminent'.[14] One man was allowed it so that he could search for fugitive peasants, and several others because their homes had burned down; there were also a few—doubtless influential individuals—who merely wanted to get married or to help a kinsman gather in the harvest.[15]

The overwhelming majority of servitors, high and low, were thus in harness from the age of 15 until they dropped. Yet in principle the Muscovite noble cavalryman was but a seasonal or part-time soldier, and it is as 'feudal landowners' (and serf-owners) that they have entered the history-books. How much truth is there in the conventional image?

Before turning to the compensation system, two general points deserve to be made. First, the basic unit in early Russian society at all levels was the family, which at this time still generally meant an extensive kinship group or clan (*rod*);[16] this bond was much stronger than any that may have existed between men with common economic or professional interests. Second, the degree of pressure on 'society' exerted by the central *vlast'* (which from the seventeenth century we may call 'the state') varied greatly over time. Although the ruler's power was absolute in theory, in practice the noose was drawn most tightly whenever the country was involved in a major war or the throne occupied by a dynamic, determined ruler; it was slackened whenever the autocrat was incapacitated by age or sickness and the court became an arena of open factional conflict. On the other hand, if these struggles led to a breakdown of civil order, as they did in the second quarter of the fifteenth century and the first quarter of the seventeenth (and nearly did between 1533 and 1547), privileged servitors, along with everyone else, were gravely affected by the socio-economic dislocation: even they had few reserves on which to draw. There was, then, no 'golden age'. Certainly, conditions eased in the late seventeenth century, especially after the treaty of Andrusovo (1667) and the death of Tsar Alexis (1676), which was followed by confusion and even a certain political degeneration at the top; but such benefits as flowed from this were offset by

[13] Ivanov, *Opisaniye*, pp. 39–41; Stashevsky, 'Sluzh. sosloviye', p. 18; Torke, 'Adel und Staat', p. 285.

[14] Torke, loc. cit.

[15] *AMG* i. 57, 91, 92 (1614), 125, 127 (1619), 226 (1629); ii. 232–4 (1645).

[16] This view is not, however, accepted by all modern demographers. Data from the 1678 census suggest that among the taxpaying population there were on average 5–6 males per household (*dvor*): Vodarsky, 'K voprosu', p. 122. Among the privileged groups household size may have been lower; but family linkages of course extended far beyond the immediate household—as the rich Russian vocabulary for kinsmen (well over 100 terms!) suggests.

the fact that gentry servitors might well be forced into forms of military service far more onerous than the traditional levy (see below, p. 85).[17]

'Official' compensation (that is, disregarding booty) took three forms: jobs, cash, and land. The first benefited the metropolitan nobility in the main. During the sixteenth century no case is known of promotion to boyar rank of any individual who had not previously demonstrated prowess in the field.[18] This pattern continued under the Romanovs: one third of those who became Duma members between 1613 and 1645 (15 out of 48) had military experience (including terms as provincial voivodes), although this was not the main avenue to career advancement.[19] In a later study of a larger group, the 'boyar élite', Crummey found that over half 'functioned exclusively as officers or military administrators', while 'another one-fifth combined army duties with service in the civil bureaucracy during their apprenticeship'.[20] Once in the Duma, however, only one man in five concentrated wholly on military duties[21]—partly, it seems, because this involved prolonged absence from the capital, with all the political risks that this entailed. In the provinces, as we know, the commanders were men with active service backgrounds; so too were the elected *guba* elders, whose principal job was to track down and punish bandits. One of the few certainties about the holders of this office was that they were members of the provincial gentry.[22]

As the Muscovite sovereigns accumulated greater wealth, they could afford to recompense servitors in ways that did less obvious damage to their subjects' well-being. The treasury maintained a sizeable stock of valuables (furs, cloth, precious vessels, arms, etc.) which could be distributed as largesse to the favoured. After the Kazan' campaign Ivan IV held a three-day victory celebration at which 48,000 precious objects were given out.[23] During the Thirteen Years War one leading commander got three new fur coats with velvet trimmings within the space of a few months, and his colleagues fared almost as well.[24] Such practices were destined to have a long life, as we shall see. Medals were also awarded. Fletcher describes them as 'a piece of gold stamped with the image of St. George on horseback, which they hang on their sleeves and set in their caps'.[25]

---

[17] On the periodization of Muscovite history see Vernadsky, *Tsardom of Moscow*, ii. 752; cf. also our scheme in 'Musc. Elite', pp. 207–8, where, however, use of the Marx–Wittfogel concept of 'oriental despotism' requires modification.

[18] Rüss, *Adel*, p. 9.

[19] Crummey, 'Reconstitution', p. 207.

[20] Id., *Aristocrats and Servitors*, p. 37. The proportion was as high as 85 per cent in the first years of Tsar Michael's reign, and 87 per cent in the first years of his successor's; it fell to 66 per cent in 1634–44 and to 62 per cent in 1676–89: id., 'Noble Official', p. 64.

[21] Crummey, *Aristocrats and Servitors*, p. 44.

[22] Keep, 'Bandits', p. 208.

[23] Rüss, *Adel*, p. 8.

[24] *AMG* iii. 100, 151 (1660); cf. *DRV* xvii. 354–6 (1679).

[25] Fletcher, *Russe Commonwealth*, p. 186 (Schmidt edn., p. 85). For the beginnings of this practice see Alef, 'Musc. Mil. Reforms', p. 82.

Herberstein wrote that the Grand Prince fixed annual payments for all servitors when they were mustered, unless they were well endowed with land; but
later sixteenth-century observers were under the impression that no grants
were made in cash.[26] Neither view was quite correct. Such grants were exceptional, and in the main were made to individuals who had performed exploits
of unusual merit. Moreover, payment depended on the current state of the
treasury and the official estimate of the momentary usefulness of each particular group of servitors. Prior to 1576 the gentry of Putivl′ and Ryazan′—key
sectors of the troubled southern front—were said to have been paid only every
other year, except for the poorest who got nothing; they were accordingly
divided into five classes (*stat′i*) and awarded sums ranging from 7 (5 for
novices) to 12 roubles.[27] At Kolomna the following year *dvorovye* got between
10 and 14 roubles and *gorodovye* 6 to 14; and one year later at Pereyaslavl′-
Zalessky (north-east of Moscow and so further from the front) the rate was
only 5 to 7 roubles, with nothing at all for novices.[28] Boris Godunov, in an
obvious bid for gentry favour, ordered a general increase in the rates (and also
reduced the amount of duties specified in the 1556 code); but by 1606, as a
result of the crisis, the cash rate had fallen to 6–8 roubles.[29] Later virtually
each district had its own varying compensation scales, which were established
at each *verstan′ye* by the central officials in agreement with the local assessors.
The rates tended to vary over the years,[30] but in interpreting this fact one has
first to appreciate that they were *fictions* (frequent in Russian political and
administrative history) and that, although everyone recognized this to be so,
they continued to be taken seriously. Allocation to a specific class carried an
equally specific, but temporary, entitlement (*oklad*), measured in cash, land,
or both; and both the classes and the compensation scales were fixed afresh at
each *verstan′ye*. Entitlements were seen as desirable norms or 'targets', as we
would say today, or else as limits that should not be exceeded, rather than as
definite commitments by the authorities that these figures would be met. Their
object was to provide an incentive, or (take a more cynical view) to conceal the
government's miserliness behind a false mask of boundless monarchical
generosity.

The land entitlements for the men of Putivl′ and Ryazan′ just mentioned
ranged from 100 to 300 quarters (*cheti, chetverti*); high-ranking courtiers
might be awarded as much as 1,500 quarters. These were not precise measures
of land—which in the absense of a proper land survey would have been impossible to allocate—but vaguely determined areas of 'good' soil, which were supposed to be complemented by equal portions of average-quality and poor soil:
this was the normal way land was divided up among householders in a peasant

26 Von Herberstein, *Moscovia*, p. 101; Kappeler, *Ivan Groznyj*, p. 206.
27 *AMG* i. 16.
28 Storozhev, 'Desyatni', pp. 2–42; *AMG* i. 33.
29 Brix, *Geschichte*, pp. 144–5; Hellie, *Enserfment*, p. 48.
30 Hellie, *Enserfment*, p. 57; id., 'Musc. Prov. Elite', p. 5B.

community. Historians have assumed that servitors' allocations were rounded up similarly, and that a *chetvert´* was equivalent to 1⅓ acres in one field and about 4 acres in all.[31] It is not certain, though, that servitors, especially the poorer ones, were able to make good such a claim in practice. Even those who did had to be content with *actual* holdings that were only a portion of their entitlement, estimated at 25–60 per cent in the sixteenth century and 5–40 per cent in the seventeenth.[32] The 1649 law code (*Ulozheniye*) laid down a sliding scale, whereby those with allotments of 400 quarters were to get 70 'in one field', and those with 70 quarters 25.[33]

Men would try to bring their holdings up to the level of their entitlement. One way of doing so was to petition for an additional grant (*pridacha*), on grounds of merit or need. Thus in 1637 A. Kostev asked for extra land and cash because of his martial exploits nearly 20 years earlier and because 27 of his kinsmen had been killed in the tsar's service; he had also been a deputy to the Land Assembly (*zemskiy sobor*) 'and had done no harm to Thy, the Sovereign's, affairs'. He declared his entitlement to be 600 quarters and 65 roubles; an investigation showed that it was only 300 quarters and 30 roubles; yet 'for his relatives' blood' his norm was raised to 700 quarters and 70 roubles (presumably with an equivalent increase in the actual holding).[34] In 1648 the whole service organization of Belgorod, led by two *vybornye*, petitioned for additional compensation on account of their work in building the defence line, and were awarded 50 quarters each.[35] Sometimes the authorities took the initiative themselves: for instance, all those whose serfs had been killed in the Smolensk War were given an additional 50 quarters plus 1 rouble for each man (up to a certain limit).[36] In 1679, to celebrate an armistice with the Turks, the government granted land entitlements ranging from 500 quarters for a boyar to 100 for ordinary provincial servitors[37]—largesse on a scale that could not possibly be implemented and by now must have lost its propagandist effect.

One could also purchase extra land, especially in the frontier zone, where potentially rich but as yet thinly settled territory was relatively plentiful up to the mid-seventeenth century; or simply take possession of it by force. Servitors were under obligation to report their total holdings to the assessor and Razryad officials when the time came for a new *verstan´ye*, as well as to the census-takers (*pistsy*). In practice it was usually not too difficult to conceal at least part of one's holdings, although there was always a danger of denunciation by jealous fellow-servitors, who under the surety system were required to pass on precisely information of this kind. Officials were heavily dependent on

[31] Cf. Eaton, 'Censuses', p. 21. For purposes of the land tax, the unit of assessment (*sokha*) for gentry servitors comprised 800 quarters of good, 1,000 of average, and 1,200 of poor land; churchmen and 'black' peasants were assessed at a higher rate.
[32] Hellie, *Enserfment*, pp. 37, 290 n. 106; cf. Stashevsky, 'Sluzh. sosloviye', p. 21.
[33] Ulozheniye, xvi. 40.
[34] *AMG* ii. 74; cf. 34, 60; Vazhinsky, *Zemlevladeniye*, p. 80.
[35] *AMG* ii. 371.   [36] *AMG* ii. 1 (1635).
[37] *DRV* xvii. 312-13; cf. A. Vostokov, in Kalachov, *Materialy*, iii. 40.

such sources, since their own laborious procedures made it hard for them to keep up with the changes continually taking place on the ground. Servitors died, retired, or transferred; and since land was the only form of investment in a natural economy, their holdings changed hands with a frequency altogether surprising given the formal restrictions on ownership rights to so much of their land.

In early modern Russia, as is generally known, land tenure was of two types: the *votchina* was a hereditary 'patrimony' and the *pomest'ye* a 'fief' granted conditionally on service. But the Western terminology is misleading unless used with caution. Earlier historians sometimes wrote as if the owners or holders of these lands, respectively called *votchinniki* and *pomeshchiki*, constituted two distinct and rival classes, the former superior to the latter. This view is much too simplistic. Three points are particularly relevant here. First, in practice many individuals held land of both types: owners of patrimonies would often be compensated for their service with portions of land on conditional tenure, while land-holders who did well would try to acquire some territory they could call their own, since this gave them greater security and prestige. Second, the distinction between the two types of property was less absolute than might appear, since from 1556 onwards patrimonial owners were also compelled to render service, and their liability was assessed by the same criterion as that of *pomeschchiki*. Thus service was universally binding on male members of the élite: no one could escape the watchful eye of the tsar's officials. This did not, however, prevent noblemen, especially those with high rank and hereditary tenure, from easing their obligations and eventually turning the system to their own advantage.

A third factor, applicable to land of both types (though in different degrees), is that Russian servitors of this era seldom had estates in the Western sense of clearly delimited, perhaps even enclosed, territories that could readily be worked as independent agricultural units. The Muscovite land-owner or -holder was generally faced with a patchwork arrangement of small plots scattered about the area from which he served, and perhaps other districts as well. His plight resembled that of the late nineteenth-century peasant, which is more familiar. In such circumstances it was difficult to establish a homestead ('manor' in Western terminology) with demesne land tilled for the lord's profit by dependants. True, some such estates had come into being by the seventeenth century, such as those owned by great boyars like B. I. Morozov, which have been thoroughly studied,[38] yet they were not the norm. Even magnates might own parts of a hamlet, or even of a single peasant hut. It was easiest for a servitor to establish a farm on unsettled or waste land, which was available in the central region when this became depopulated during the late sixteenth-century crisis, and more especially along the expanding southern and eastern frontier.

Muscovite agrarian history is essentially one of a mass of smallholders thrusting forward into the steppe, pursued by a handful of big entrepreneurs.

[38] D. I. Petrikeyev, *Krupnoye krepostnoye khozyaystvo XVII v.*, Leningrad, 1967.

Most servitors were desperately short of capital and knowhow, and thus unable to contribute much to the agricultural economy (although their wives might do so).[39] Military duty forced them to neglect their lands precisely during the season when the major agricultural operations were under way. This hindered them not only from farming effectively on their own account but also from enforcing their rights to payment of dues by their dependants. The servitor was seen by 'his' peasants as an outsider, perhaps even as a parasite; such patriarchal bonds as had once existed were severed by the sixteenth-century crisis, which led to the enserfment of the rural population. Although lords still shared a common cultural background with their serfs, and had many of the same day-to-day concerns, they were not integrated into the life of the local community. The reason for this was not serfdom (*krepostnichestvo*), as many writers have too easily assumed—still less 'feudalism', which Russia conspicuously lacked—but the incessant demands of the service state.

One other important point deserves to be noted in this connection. The prevalence of the extended family meant that many land-owners and -holders exercised their rights jointly rather than individually.[40] The original *pomest'ye* grant would indeed be in favour of a certain individual, the servitor who did duty from that land; but his kinsmen, who might help him work it or look after it in his absence, considered themselves entitled to a share of its revenue. The clan spirit also helped to maintain the traditional practice of partible inheritance, whereby a family's property would be divided up among male heirs on the death of the paterfamilias. The ensuing fragmentation of property rights made management extremely complicated, and explains why officials found it so difficult to discover who held what, and why no general survey was taken before the late eighteenth century, although demands for one had been voiced for hundreds of years. The same problem confronted the compensation entitlement officials and Razryad clerks who endeavoured to reapportion service tenures in such a way as to preserve some rough conformity between the amount and quality of the land and the service due from it.

In theory a *pomest'ye*, being a holding, reverted to its ultimate owner, the tsar, if for some reason it passed 'out of service'. However, confiscations were rare. Even during the *oprichnina* dispossession was brought about by crude direct action rather than by invoking the sovereign's legal rights. Normally the authorities acquiesced in whatever testamentary provisions the *pomeshchik* made, provided that his son (or some other relative) performed service from the land in question, or else passed on the land to a surviving son on his death.[41] A complicated body of law grew up to regulate the transmission of

---

[39] The worthy *pomeshchitsa* Yulianiya Lazarevskaya (Osor´ina), whose biography was written by her son as a saint's life, spent most of her day in household toil; her husband, who had 400 quarters in Nizhniy Novgorod, was frequently away on service. T. A. Greenan, 'Iulianiya Lazarevskaya', *Oxford Slavonic Papers* xv (1982), 29.

[40] Got´ye, *Ocherk*, p. 53; Stashevsky, 'Sluzh. sosloviye', p. 26.

[41] For example, *AMG* ii. 17 (1635), 63 (1636).

such rights and duties. A holder's younger brothers, sons, and nephews would normally be 'ascribed' (*pripuskat´sya*) to his land until they had been mustered and received an allocation of their own. This intensified the pressure on the holder's resources, even if he received an additional grant in compensation; only the more influential dependant kinsmen managed to secure a separate property while the holder was still alive.[42] In the seventeenth century the laws were liberalized somewhat to protect the interests of widows of deceased servitors with young children to bring up: they would receive a small portion for their subsistence until death or remarriage.[43] Orphaned children were similarly provided for, the boys being enlisted as soon as they reached the age of maturity (15, later raised to 18) and the girls married off—to other servitors, needless to say!

Seventeenth-century *pomeshchiki* were also permitted to exchange their lands provided that they registered the deed. Their main purpose in concluding such deals was to consolidate their holdings and so make them more manageable.[44] From 1649 onwards they could also exchange their holdings for patrimonial land. This undermined the old principle that the territories exchanged should be of equal value.[45] Another concession was to allow service tenures to be leased under certain conditions. They were not supposed to be mortgaged or sold—but by the 1670s both these kinds of transaction are documented.[46]

In the early seventeenth century, according to a modern demographer, privileged secular owners or holders had 66 per cent of the theoretical maximum of arable and pasture;[47] the clergy held 16 per cent and the rest was split between the crown and 'black' (taxpaying) peasant communities. The breakdown between *votchiny* and *pomest´ya* is not known. The latter's share had been swollen by the population transfers and military reforms effected by Ivan III and Ivan IV. Throughout this period there was a massive expropriation of 'black' land to satisfy the appetite of the service class, particularly its more privileged elements. On the other hand, the effects of the *oprichnina* were felt by medium and low-ranking servitors as well as by those men who were the tyrant's ostensible targets. Between 1573/4 and 1584/5 the number of holdings

---

[42] This was called *verstan´ye v otvod*: for an example see *AMG* ii. 271 (1646); cf. *DRV* xvi. 335 (1632); Brix, *Geschichte*, pp. 133–4; Stashevsky, 'Sluzh. sosloviye', p. 24. The main legislative source, apart from the 1649 *Ulozheniye*, is the *Ukaznaya kniga Pom. prikaza*, reprinted in *PRP* v. 431–82.

[43] *Uk. kniga, PRP*, §§ 6, 52; Ulozheniye, xvi. 8, 10–11, 18–22, 56; Got´ye, *Ocherk*, pp. 50–3; Pavlov-Silvansky, *Gos. sluzh. lyudi*, pp. 198–9 (a mine of information on these and related issues).

[44] Hellie, *Enserfment*, p. 46.

[45] Got´ye, *Ocherk*, p. 63; Pavlov-Silvansky, *Gos. sluzh. lyudi*, pp. 200–1; Novosel´sky, 'Raspad', p. 251; Vazhinsky, *Zemlevladeniye*, p. 86. For legislation: *Uk. kniga, PRP*, § 36; Ulozheniye, xvi. 2–7; *PSZ* ii. 633, 644, 700.

[46] Got´ye, *Ocherk*, p. 64; Stashevsky, 'Sluzh. sosloviye', p. 26.

[47] 6.6 m. desyatines out of a total of 10.0 m. (including waste but excluding undeveloped land, also that held by towns or Cossacks). In the later Voronezh *guberniya* the proportion in secular hands was as high as 87 per cent: Vodarsky, 'Chislennost´´', pp. 220–1.

in Moscow district classified as 'waste' doubled, from 54 to 108.[48] During and after the Troubles the pendulum began to swing the other way. Lavish grants were made of land on patrimonial right,[49] from which the metropolitan nobles apparently did best. Much Crown land was distributed, and *pomeshchiki* were permitted to convert part of their land to patrimonial tenure.[50] The ratio of service to patrimonial land was highest in the southern border region; overall the latter are thought to have had the greater share—a reversal of the situation that had obtained one hundred years earlier.[51]

The process whereby servitors were turned into landlords, still in an initial phase, was economically beneficial in so far as it gave these men a stake in their lands, which they had first treated much as conquered territory. However, from the standpoint of the peasants it was a catastrophe, since they were debased to the condition of serfs. The gentry took the crude view that their land was of no use to them without a plentiful supply of labour, and that this could be assured only by degrading their dependants into human chattel. This tragic development is so familiar that we may restrict our discussion of it to three points which show that the military context exerted a decisive influence on events.

First, it was the misconceived Livonian War that lay at the origin of the sixteenth-century crisis. This fact would seem banal were it not for the disposition of so many historians to overlook it. The war touched off the wave of terror and destabilized the precarious agrarian economy; this in turn led many landlords to increase the rent demanded from their peasants (which they were permitted to collect in person). Since neither the secular nor the ecclesiastical authorities acted to limit this pressure, the peasants responded with passive resistance and mass flight; this in turn prompted measures to tie those who remained to their owners; and finally these measures did much to provoke peasant rebelliousness in the Troubles—in short, a vicious circle of monstrous proportions. While 'gentry greed' was certainly a factor in the imposition of

[48] Smirnov, *Ocherki*, p. 411. The gaps in the census data make it hard to evaluate the turnover rate among landowners during the *oprichnina*. Using the *pistsovye knigi*, Got´ye stated (*Zamosk. kray*, p. 284) that, out of 152 patrimonial properties in Moscow district in 1565, 45 were still in the same hands 20 years later; of the rest 33 passed to kinsmen and 74 to non-kinsmen. This suggests considerable disruption. Figures for Kolomna and Tver´ districts show greater stability, as one might expect. A more recent student of the problem concludes that between 1564 and 1584 no less than 456 patrimonies ceased to exist, most of their land being pledged to monasteries: Veselovsky, *Feod. zemlevladeniye*, p. 96.

[49] For example, [Khilkov] *Sbornik*, p. 50: grant to boyar Ye. A. Svechin (1614), who was allowed to convert 110 of his 550 quarters into a patrimony. In 1626 A. M. L´vov got 600 quarters: *AMG* i. 187. In 1632 622 *moskovskiye dvoryane* (⅔ of the total) owned 94,100 quarters of patrimonial land of which the source is known; of this 41,200 quarters (44 per cent) had been 'granted' or 'earned', 11,700 (12 per cent) inherited, and 18,400 (20 per cent) bought; 121 men had no patrimonial land at all, and for another 97 this accounted for 20 per cent or less of their property. Stashevsky, *Zemlevladeniye*, p. 17.

[50] *AMG* i. 176, 178, 188, 200; Maslovsky, 'Pom. voyska', p. 8.

[51] Hellie, *Enserfment*, pp. 40, 57; however, Eaton, 'Censuses', p. 81, puts the *pomest'ya*'s share in the late sixteenth century at only ⅓; cf. Rüss, *Adel*, pp. 30, 59.

serfdom, their self-interested behaviour was itself the product of Russia's cultural isolation and, more immediately, of the military burden which the government imposed—only part of which could be justified as necessary for the defence of the country's essential interests.

The second point relates to the 1630s and 1640s, when the privileged servitors became obsessed with halting the drain of peasant labour. In several collective petitions they urged the tsar first to extend the prescriptive term within which runaways, once discovered, could legally be returned to their former masters, and then to extend this period indefinitely—a step that was taken, under their pressure, in 1649.[52] This was a striking political innovation: the first time that the 'middle-class' elements of Russian society articulated demands in an organized way. The opportunity to do so was afforded them by annual mobilizations of the levy to ward off Tatar attacks. Such occasions did not occur at other junctures before this period, when the southern border was quieter, or after it, when the levy mattered less militarily.

Repeal of the statute of limitations did not solve the gentry's problems, for peasants continued to flee and their masters were soon appealing to the authorities for help in tracking them down. The government's response was ambiguous, since it had to balance sympathy for the landed interest against the country's security needs.[53] Not until the mid-1660s, under the threat of a general uprising in the border region, were so-called 'investigators' (*syshchiki*) sent out, armed with special powers and posses of troops, to bolster the proprietors' claims. But thereafter on at least three occasions a period of statutory limitation for the return of runaways was reintroduced, and on another four occasions between 1684 and 1698 punishment of fugitives was temporarily suspended. The authorities silently tolerated their recruitment as lower-class servitors (for example, Cossacks), whereupon they became ineligible for return. On the other hand, when major campaigns loomed in the south and the frontier servitors' co-operation was essential, concessions were made to their demands—sometimes at the expense of the metropolitan nobility.

Undeniably servitors as a whole succeeded in consolidating their social position during the seventeenth century at the expense of the peasants and the state. It is also clear that the high-ranking groups did best, and that this went hand in hand with growing social stratification within the élite. In the sixteenth century even metropolitan nobles had often fallen into debt on account of their military obligations;[54] political harassment, added to the fluctuations of

---

[52] The classic study of these petitions is P. P. Smirnov, 'Chelobitnye dvoryan i detey boyar-skikh vsekh gorodov v I-oy polovine XVII v.', *Chteniya* 254 (1915), 1, pp. 1–73. On the Land Assembly see our 'Decline of the Zemsky Sobor', *SEER* 36 (1957/8), pp. 100–22. R. Hellie is preparing a critical edition of the *Ulozheniye*. For the enserfment process see chs. 4–7 of Hellie's *Enserfment* and, for documents, R. E. F. Smith, *The Enserfment of the Russian Peasantry*, Cambridge, 1968. Torke, *Staatsbedingte Gesellschaft*, analyses thoroughly the gentry's limitations as an autonomous social force.

[53] The interpretation offered by Novosel'sky, 'Pobegi', is preferable to that offered in the more recent study of Man'kov, *Razvitiye*. Cf. now also Torke, 'Adel und Staat', p. 284.

[54] One boyar who possessed several patrimonial estates had to pawn his wife's clothes in order

the natural economy, made it hard to secure a regular income from their lands. Under the Romanovs their assets increased. In 1637/8 Duma members were said to have an average of 520 peasant households on their estates (*excluding* those in Moscow district), as against a mere 5 or 6 each for provincial *deti boyarskiye*.[55] This wealth was, however, unequally distributed within the group. Some metropolitan nobles pleaded that poverty prevented them from serving without a cash grant.[56] Their claim need not have been entirely groundless, for a survey taken that year of 303 *moskovskiye dvoryane* showed that their (nominal?) holdings ranged from 1,464 quarters to 142.[57] Figures for 1647/8 show that 10 boyars each owned an average of 1,827 peasant households; the wealthiest land-owner after the tsar, his kinsman N. I. Romanov, had 7,012.[58] The Soviet demographer Vodarsky offers a table[59] purporting to show that average holdings of *dumnye chiny* peaked in 1653 (1,045 households), as against 584 in 1638, 469 in 1678 and 572 in 1700; however, the number of individuals covered varies in each year; the polls were taken for different purposes and in different circumstances, and so are not readily comparable.

For the provincial servitors, fortunately, we have rather more trustworthy calculations. One recent investigator has concluded that in the sixteenth century fulfilment of the obligations imposed by the 1556 code would have cost 20 per cent of the rent a *pomeshchik* could extract from an area equivalent to a 100-quarter entitlement. Even for high-ranking servitors, he notes, 'the real cost of service from their land was considerably greater than the norm laid down by the service code'.[60] In the Starorussky district of Novgorod, where joint ownership of property was the rule (195 land-holders shared title to 104 *pomest'ya*), 90 per cent of the servitors had too little land to meet their obligations.[61]

Nor did the situation of provincial servitors change radically for the better after the Troubles. Landless gentry at Odoyev, on the southern border, affirmed in 1638 that they had to buy all their equipment on credit at high rates of interest and were 'dragging ourselves from one household to another [that is, begging for alms] and dying a hungry death, for we have neither food nor drink'.[62] Some allowance must be made for rhetorical exaggeration—such phrases were *de rigueur* in petitions—but the records abound with similar

to equip himself for service: Rozhdestvensky, *Sluzh. zemlevladeniye*, pp. 78–83; cf. Rüss, *Adel*, p. 19.

[55] Eaton, 'Censuses', p. 76; Crummey, *Aristocrats and Servitors*, pp. 114–15.

[56] *DRV* xvi. 328–31 (1632).

[57] Stashevsky, *Zemlevladeniye*, pp. 40ff., nos. 19 (T. Bezobrazov), 40 (D. V. Baryatinsky). The fact that much of their land will have been waste or thinly settled accounts for these differences and impedes their analysis. The average of 24 households per man (ibid., p. 31) seems far too low and must surely reflect concealment of their properties' true state.

[58] Rozhdestvensky, 'Rospis'; cf. Got'ye, *Ocherk*, p. 58 and *Zamosk. kray*, pp. 283–4; more recently Rexhauser, *Besitzverhältnisse*, p. 5.

[59] Vodarsky, 'Prav. gruppa', p. 74.

[60] Alekseyev, '15-rub. maksimum', p. 115.

[61] Degtyarev, 'Dokhody', pp. 88–9.

[62] *AMG* ii. 158.

pleas, and there is supporting evidence: at Bryansk in 1621 starvation among the local gentry reached such a pitch that several families had to be transferred elsewhere at state expense.[63] Cases occurred of provincial servitors falling into slavery, despite a formal ban (1641) on the practice.[64] Some cavalrymen sent to Tambov to work on the defences there found themselves worse off than the local musketeers, and besought aid to escape their humiliating predicament.[65] Land allocations in the region were then about 65–110 hectares per holding—more than ample, had they the wherewithal to develop this economic potential. As the century wore on, despite the constant warfare, a modest improvement evidently took place. A study of the Meshchersk region (in the forest zone south-east of Moscow) shows that in 1616 49 per cent of gentry 'estates' had no peasant households at all; by 1658 the figure had fallen to 35 per cent, and by 1678 to 8 per cent; those with from 1 to 3 dependent households accounted respectively for 18 per cent, 18 per cent, and 37 per cent, while those with over 25 households rose from 4 per cent to 6 per cent and 9 per cent.[66] There was, therefore, no massive concentration of property here. Only at the end of this period did a modest 3.6 per cent reach the 50-household norm which servitors generally believed to be necessary for them to go to war without receiving a cash payment from the state authorities (which in theory observed a 10-household limit).[67]

We do not have comparable data for the region further south, but Vazhinsky is correct in pointing out that from an economic point of view the *deti boyarskiye* of Voronezh could scarcely be distinguished from peasants.[68] A survey carried out in the 1670s, covering 1,078 gentry servitors in a number of southern border towns, revealed that they had a mere 849 taxpaying households between them.[69] A modern study of 1,966 such individuals in the Belgorod and Sevsk *razryady* in the late 1690s shows that only 45 (3.5 per cent) had 10 or more peasant households, and so were deemed fit to serve without supplementary payment; 96.5 per cent fell into the category of 'single-householders' (*odnodvortsy*), which would last into the Imperial era.[70] It is clear from these figures alone that by the late seventeenth century the gentry militia had lapsed into a critical state.

There were three principal reasons for its decline. One was technological: the new-model forces, to be discussed in chapter 4, were better armed, trained, and led; they comprised infantry as well as cavalry, and so were more suited to fight major wars against Turks, Poles, or Swedes.[71] The second was the

[63] *AMG* i. 142.
[64] *AMG* ii. 231 (1645); Hellie, *Enserfment*, pp. 65–6.
[65] Yakovlev, *Zasechnaya cherta*, p. 12.
[66] Dubinskaya, 'Pom. i vot. zemlevladeniye', pp. 129–30.
[67] Hellie, *Enserfment*, p. 50; Presnyakov, *Mosk. tsarstvo*, p. 65.
[68] Vazhinsky, *Zemlevladeniye*, p. 3.
[69] Chernov, *Voor. sily*, p. 157.
[70] Vazhinsky, *Zemlevladeniye*, p. 67.
[71] This aspect is fully covered by Hellie, *Enserfment*, and will not be discussed here.

improved security situation on the southern border after the construction of the Belgorod and other fortified lines (notably the Izyumskaya, built in 1679–81) and the acquisition of the left-bank Ukraine by the treaty of Andrusovo. The gentry helped to curb the Tatar threat, and in so doing deprived themselves of much of their *raison d'être*. The Thirteen Years War engaged them fully and inflicted heavy casualties, notably at the battles of Konotop and Chudnovo (June 1659, October 1660).[72] The bloodletting sapped their vitality and, apart from its effect on morale, reduced their military usefulness. Increasingly the government preferred to use gentry cavalrymen as part of a mixed force containing musketeers and other low-grade servitors.[73] Moreover, during the emergency many privileged servitors were simply assigned to these units, despite the loss of status which this entailed (see ch. 4). By the late 1680s, when two offensives were launched against the Crimea, the gentry militia supplied only 8,000 to 11,000 men, less than 10 per cent of total effectives.[74]

The third reason for the levy's decline was administrative. The Razryad officials found it ever harder to cope with their tasks now that many senior nobles, and some provincials too, were accumulating wealth and changing their life-style. A characteristic problem, which demonstrated that the unsophisticated *gorod* service organization was breaking down as social differentiation increased, was that servitors acquired property in districts other than the one where they were enrolled and then claimed that they were, or should be, registered there instead. The Razryad bureaucrats were not encouraged to develop the horizontal communication that would have been required to check how much service was being rendered and to reward it fittingly.[75]

The process of 'civilianization' was uneven—chronologically, regionally, and socially. Chronologically, it gathered pace during those years when the country enjoyed relative peace and stability, notably after 1667. Regionally, it was furthest advanced in the central districts, where so much land passed into the hands of the metropolitan nobility. And socially, it was this group which, with its wealth and influence, could secure non-military appointments or choose to live for part of the year on their estates, while hard-pressed provincials had no choice but to soldier on. It must be stressed that the decline of the levy did *not* mean a diminution of the ordinary gentryman's military role, since he was called on to fight in other capacities. One nineteenth-century military historian wrote that 'the *pomest'ye* system weakened the servitors' military character; an easy idle life [on their lands] undoubtedly attracted them more than onerous service, full of deprivation and hardship.'[76] This is to retroject an eighteenth-century situation into an earlier era, when it was true only of a relatively small privileged section of the noble élite.

---

[72] Hellie, *Enserfment*, p. 217.   [73] Stashevsky, 'Smeta', pp. 64–87.
[74] Chernov, *Voor. sily*, p. 195; Hellie, *Enserfment*, p. 272; the figures are in some doubt, however.
[75] Novosel'sky, 'Raspad', p. 223; cf. *AMG* ii. 164 (1639).
[76] 'Petr Vel. i yego armiya', p. 232.

What then of the widespread absenteeism among *deti boyarskiye*: is this not evidence of alienation and a desire to lead a civilian life as landlords? Tempting as this conclusion is, it must be rejected.[77] That is to say, there is no sign that they resisted or opposed the service state as such; they wanted an easement of their lot, but hoped that this could be achieved 'within the system', as we would say. In this their attitude did not differ radically from that of peasants or other commoners, who likewise sought to secure sectional advantages—although they used more violent means, which gentry servitors abandoned after participating in the Moscow riots of 1648. Absenteeism was characteristic of the lower servitors, too—as it was of armed forces throughout Europe at the time. Nevertheless its incidence among the gentry was certainly high. For example, in 1671 Yu. A. Dolgorukiy reported that of senior nobles on the Moscow roll 188 were present but 304 absent; for junior ones the figures were respectively 399 and 1,787, while only 'very few' provincial gentry appeared. No doubt most of them were busy defending their estates from Razin's rebel bands.[78] When the summons was issued for the 1687 campaign, 6,112 metropolitan nobles responded, whereas 711 excused themselves and another 719 were absent without explanation.[79]

The authorities at first dealt with offenders (and their sureties) by 'cruel punishment, beating in public without mercy', and sometimes even death; but later, as the rigour of the system slackened, by fines or confiscation of property, which was to be distributed among those of their comrades who did their duty.[80] But such menaces had lost much of their deterrent effect, and probably helped to make the problem worse. By fleeing from the colours gentry servitors expressed their discontent at the unfair and inefficient way in which the levy was run. They did not reach the point of openly questioning its necessity. Although they continued to submit collective petitions over specific grievances (for example, for a land survey),[81] their capacity for co-ordinated action was feeble. A century or so would pass before they realized that their corporate interests could be advanced by winning from the Crown guarantees of certain rights, notably exemption from corporal punishment[82] and other demeaning treatment.

To appreciate this deferential attitude we must remember that the provincial gentry servitor had no formal education and as likely as not could scarcely sign his name. A recent study of the Belgorod *polk* in 1669–71 shows that 22 per cent of its officers signed in Russian.[83] These were, however, mostly men in the

[77] This point has now been clarified in magisterial fashion by Torke, 'Adel und Staat'.

[78] Ibid., p. 287. In 1679 the proportion of absentees in various formations mobilized for active service was 17 per cent (14,156 out of 83,477): Brix, *Geschichte*, p. 377.

[79] Hellie, Enserfment, p. 369 n. 173; cf. *DRV* xvi. 405–6 for their regional distribution; *PSZ* i. 489.

[80] *DRV* xvi. 363 (1676); Rozengeym, *Ocherki*, pp. 17–22; Shakhmatov, *Kompetentsiya*, pp. 184–5; Torke, 'Adel und Staat', pp. 285–9.

[81] Keep, 'Musc. Elite', pp. 223–6.

[82] Even a voivode might be beaten in public: *AMG* ii. 1013 (1658).

[83] Stevens, 'Belgorod', p. 123; on p. 119 the author makes the figure 23 per cent.

new-model forces which contained a high proportion of foreign officers; some of these had assimilated and signed in Russian, while others used their native language. Stevens points out that the overall literacy rate (55 per cent) was high by international standards, but it would be rash to draw conclusions from this about the cultural level of Russian privileged servitors. These men left no memoirs, letters, or other personal documents, and so any conclusions as to their state of mind must be tentative. The impression one gains from official records is that their outlook was grossly materialistic and job-centred,[84] but this may be a little unfair.

Among metropolitan nobles we do find, by the last quarter of the seventeenth century, individuals who were beginning to reflect on the nature of their world. The boyar élite by and large upheld traditional attitudes and tried to live up to the Orthodox ideal, spending money on pious or charitable purposes; one man in ten donned a monk's cowl before death. Courtiers and officials rather than soldiers, they valued ceremonial and were obsessed with questions of family honour and standing, ever fearful lest some accident should cause them to fall from their lofty station.[85] If there were a few individuals among them who took a critical or reformist stance, this owed less to influences from the Protestant countries of northern and western Europe, as commonly supposed, than to the model offered by neighbouring Poland–Lithuania.

Those foreign soldiers of fortune who came to Muscovy, especially in the wake of the Thirty Years War, certainly made a contribution to Russian life, but this lay chiefly in the technical military domain. Culturally they had little to offer, and some of them converted to Orthodoxy, married Russians, and settled down comfortably on the estates they were granted. A few Commonwealth subjects (mainly eastern Slavs) took the same course, but the influence from this quarter was of a different order. Its aristocratic culture was attractive to men in leading Moscow families, including the ruling Romanovs, who sought to emulate the courtly refinements of their counterparts across the border; a few learned Polish or Latin.[86] The religious divide was of course a formidable barrier to genuine intimacy—but was this what leading Russians sought? Rather they looked on Muscovy's ancient rival as a land differing from their own mainly in its more secularized culture and in the superior status of its nobility. By emulating the Commonwealth's attainments in those fields alone, might not Russia surpass it in excellence?

The implication was that the metropolitan nobles at least should be emancipated from the constraints of the liturgical service state. This was the motive

---

[84] Hellie, 'Musc. Prov. Elite', p. 10A.

[85] Crummey, *Aristocrats and Servitors*, pp. 135–63.

[86] Rogov, *Russko-pol'skiye svyazi*; on the mediating role of the Ukraine: K. V. Kharlampovich, *Malorossiyskoye vliyanie na velikorusskuyu tserkovnuyu zhizn'*, Kazan', 1914. Klyuchevsky's well-known account (*Soch*. iii (1959). 282–98; *Rise of the Romanovs*, tr. L. Archibald, London, 1970, pp. 292–320) plays down the Polish element.

behind a fairly far-reaching 'reform programme' put forward during the reign of the adolescent Theodore II (1676–82) by several high-ranking officials, among them V. V. Golitsyn.[87] It covered military administration, central and local government, and ecclesiastical affairs. The scheme provided for a new ranking system based on the offices held by leading members of the Duma. There were to be 12 provincial lieutenants (*namestniki*: the old term for governor, as distinct from military voivodes) and another 10 commanders of military districts (*razryady*); the former, as civil functionaries, were to be superior to the latter. The chief position should go to a kind of prime minister, who would preside over a supreme tribunal (*raspravnaya palata*), while the leading military official would be the palace commandant.[88]

The attention given by the reformers to the civilianization of Russian public life is remarkable. Yet there was an aristocratic element in the plan as well: the provincial chiefs were to hold their appointments for life. This encountered strong opposition which doomed the entire project. Among its critics were the patriarch and leading boyars who did not relish the prospect of honourable relegation to the provinces; they were suspicious of the scheme's foreign (that is, Polish) flavour, even though this was carefully camouflaged by the use of Byzantine terminology; and above all they were jealous of the initiators for devising it behind their backs.

Largely as a result of this opposition the plan was dropped and Golitsyn's powers curbed. Appointed chief of a chancellery for military affairs (November 1681), he arranged for a commission to be set up to which representatives from various groups of servitors were summoned. It was this body that suggested the abolition of *mestnichestvo*. The deputies approached the matter indirectly, as an obstacle to a general reform of army organization. Their recommendations were approved with unusual promptitude, and early in 1682 the records of this practice—'hateful to God [and] created by the Foe', as Patriarch Ioakhim put it—were ceremonially burned.[89]

The metropolitan nobles who witnessed this historic scene must have felt confident that their family honour now stood on a firmer foundation than before. For they were expressly instructed to compile, with the aid of Razryad officials, genealogies that were to be entered into a special register. But this 'Velvet Book', when it was eventually put together, turned out to possess purely symbolic value and played no role in determining assignments. The reform seriously weakened their position.[90] Nothing had been said about limiting, still

---

[87] For a useful recent biography in English see L. A. J. Hughes, *Russia and the West: the Life of a Seventeenth-Century Westernizer . . .* , Newtonville, Mass., 1984; also Danilov, 'Golicyn'.

[88] Ostrogorsky, 'Projekt'.

[89] *PSZ* ii. 904–5; Shmidt, 'Mestnichestvo i absolyutizm', p. 301; Volkov, 'Ob otmene', offers a valuable fresh interpretation of the political background.

[90] Torke, 'Adel und Staat', p. 296. Some modern students of the Russian nobility (for example, P. Brown, 'Early Modern Russian Bureaucracy', Ph.D. thesis, Chicago, 1978, p. 532) take a contrary view, pointing to the major role that aristocrats played in public life under Peter and later; however, the crucial point is surely that they placed no limitations on the autocratic power. I am grateful to Ann Kleimola for this reference.

less abolishing, the nobles' obligation to serve the state, and their position in the official hierarchy now depended more completely than ever on the will of the monarch and bureaucrats subservient to him. Under a weak ruler such as the regent Sofia (1682–9) they did not need to worry unduly and could expect their background to be taken into account when appointments were made. But where would they turn for protection when the throne was occupied by a ruthless radical like Peter I?

The tsar-reformer would carry out a 'second service-class revolution',[91] greater in its impact than that of Ivan IV—one which, although it certainly brought the privileged elements in society many benefits, temporarily halted such progress towards civilianization as they had made in previous decades. In the early eighteenth century a new military emergency would lead the central *vlast'* to impose on the country's élite a more modern form of its traditional bondage.

[91] Hellie, 'Petrine Army'.

3

MUSKETEERS AND OTHER
TRADITIONAL FORCES

THE principal task of the underprivileged segments of the population was to provide the financial means with which the state met its heavy military commitments. In addition to this fiscal effort more and more ordinary Muscovites were called on to bear arms. It is with this service that we shall be concerned here, returning later to the question of human and financial costs.

Although Russia did not have an integrated standing army until the reign of Peter the Great, major steps were taken under earlier rulers towards creating such a force. In this they kept pace with other European monarchs, who from the late fifteenth century onwards were busily setting up 'royal militias' of various kinds.[1] This process was closely bound up with advances in military technology, especially the growing role of firearms. Militias differed from feudal levies in that they consisted of infantry (and artillery) rather than cavalry, depended on the Crown for most of their equipment, received regular remuneration, and were less impermanent. In some ways Russia was ahead of western European states in this development, a matter which has given satisfaction to historians of a nationalist persuasion, both pre-revolutionary and Soviet. Whether this advance deserves to be labelled 'progressive' must remain a matter of opinion: for whatever may be thought of the achievements of Russia's absolute monarchy ('the centralized multi-national Russian state', in Marxist–Leninist parlance), there is no doubt that the burdens of empire fell very heavily on those least able to bear them. The implication in much of the historical literature is that the sacrifices borne by the masses were ultimately justified by *raison d'état*—a claim of questionable validity where defensive action (especially on the steppe frontier) gave way to unalloyed expansionism.

Leaving aside such questions of interpretation, Soviet scholars deserve credit for clarifying the contribution which the lower classes made to the country's military efforts. Pre-revolutionary historians often gave the misleading impression that the privileged servitors alone mattered—partly from class bias, perhaps, but also because source material on the common soldiers is much scarcer.

At the base of the military establishment stood some all but forgotten men whose history bridges the centuries. In the autonomous principalities of Rus' in the Tatar era, as in Kievan times, it was taken for granted that ordinary folk

---

[1] Corvisier, *Armées et sociétés*, p. 60; cf. K. J. V. Jespersen, 'Social Change and Military Revolution in Early Modern Europe . . .', *Historical Journal* 26 (1983), pp. 1–13.

should defend their hearths in an emergency, whether or not they were called on to do so by the ruler. In some towns there were popular militias with a rudimentary form of organization—'thousandmen', centurions, and decurions—based in part on the Tatar model. These units survived into the Muscovite period, when the central power began to take an interest in them. Such soldiers were officially termed *pososhnye*, or '*sokha* men': the *sokha*, as we know, was the flexible unit of assessment for direct taxation, and it was on this basis that they too were levied. *Pososhnye* were provided as and when required, without any regular norm being set. Since they had no training, they were of less use in combat than as auxiliaries. They would help to construct defence works, cart supplies, haul the heavy field-guns of the era, and perform any similar task requiring physical labour. Their draught animals, carts, digging tools, and other items of equipment were provided by their community, rural or urban, at its own expense. Sometimes the obligation could be commuted by a cash payment, and certain privileged persons were exempted from it.[2] Chancellor (1553) estimated at 30,000 the number of 'such as goe with the Ordnance and Labourers'.[3] A German present at Polotsk in 1563 reckoned the number of 'peasants' in the army at 40,000, with another 6,000 'trench-diggers'. They formed a separate detachment (*polk*) under a relatively junior commander, who had 50 servitors to help him manage this force.[4] Twelve thousand *sokha* men are known to have taken part in the campaign of 1577.[5]

As the 'black' taxpaying territories fell under the jurisdiction of ecclesiastical and secular landlords, the function of choosing and despatching parties of such men for military service fell to their new masters. Accordingly they came to be known by other terms as well: 'boyars' men' (*boyarskiye lyudi*) or 'donated men' (*datochnye, peredatochnye*). The former seem to have been those who accompanied their lords (who were of course by no means all of boyar rank) on their martial duties, whereas the latter were individuals sent by their masters, eventually often as substitutes for themselves. Donated men lacked even that minimal protection which a lord could afford by his personal presence and were entirely at the disposal of the authorities, whose estimate of their human worth was likely to be even lower than that of their masters. For simplicity's sake we may call both categories 'recruits'. Some of them performed the tasks mentioned above, which although auxiliary were essential to the army's functioning, while others acted as bodyguards and servants to gentry cavalrymen, looking after their mounts, equipment, supplies, and so forth.[6] Occasionally they would assume a combat role. This will have depended on whether or not they actually had the horses and equipment with which their

2 *AI* ii. 145; *DAI* i. 94; Yepifanov, 'Voysko', p. 359; Nasonov *et al.* (eds.), *Ocherki*, pp. 334–5.
3 Vernadsky *et al.* (eds.), *Source Book*, i. 168.
4 Yepifanov, 'Voysko', p. 368; the independent-minded Pskov chronicler put the figure at 80,900, which is probably too high; it is, however, repeated by Maslovsky, 'Pom. voyska', p. 8 and Chernov, *Voor. sily*, p. 93.
5 Brix, *Geschichte*, p. 60.
6 Ibid., pp. 43, 94, citing *AAE* i. 205; ii. 78.

masters were supposed to provide them according to the 1556 service code. Non-privileged elements comprised a large but unknown share of the cavalry levy's total complement.[7] The Kolomna service register of 1577 shows that 268 servitors fielded 345 men, of whom 153 were well armed.[8] The servitors were listed roughly in order of seniority and wealth, and as one would expect the better-off brought more men and horses.[9] The general impression of indigence reflected the crisis of the 1570s. In Novgorod at this time only one master in five could appear with a mounted servant, whereas three-quarters had been able to do so in 1500.[10] The dependants' names, physical characteristics, or exact social status were of no interest to the officials who registered them, and *desyatni* compiled later provide even less information about them. Hellie assumes that all these men were slaves. Most probably were, since lords will have preferred to take household servants rather than agriculturalists who in theory at least could pay them rent; but some may have been fellow-servitors, or even kinsmen, who had fallen into personal dependence without signing a slavery deed (*kabala*). Expectation of loot would have given such individuals an incentive to accompany their masters on campaign.

In principle a lord was not allowed to loan a would-be debtor slave more than 5 roubles,[11] and the debtor had to find 15 roubles in order to buy his freedom. In the 1620s the loan limit, which had fallen to a mere 2 roubles or even less during the Troubles, was fixed at 3 roubles.[12] This illustrates the diminishing value of human life as Muscovite society settled into its rigidly stratified state. In 1621 a servant (*chelovek*) belonging to L. Davydov, a ser-

[7] Zimin's estimate of two-thirds (*Reformy*, p. 448) is probably too high: Hellie, *Slavery*, p. 467.

[8] Storozhev, 'Desyatni', pp. 1–58. There is some doubt as to the numbers since certain sheets of the original document are missing. Hellie ('Musc. Mil. Slavery', p. 1B) reckons that there were 280 servitors with 323 dependants, of whom 139 were 'combat slaves' and 184 'baggage-train slaves'.

[9] The distribution (excluding novices) was as follows:

	Compensation scale (quarters, roubles)	Dependants mounted on war-horse (*kon´*)*	Dependants mounted on ordinary horse (*merin*)	Dependants mounted on ordinary horse designated for carrying baggage (*s yukom*)
Top 10 *dvorovye*	350–400, 14	23	6	12
Bottom 10 *dvorovye*	200–250, 10–12	0	11	3
Top 10 *gorodvye*	200–300, 13–14	16	2	8
Bottom 10 *gorodovye*	100–150, 6–7	0	0	2

* including those in full armour but under-equipped, with a *prostoy kon´*.

[10] Degtyarev, 'Dokhody', p. 89.

[11] *Sudebnik, 1550 g.* § 78 (in *Sudebniki*); Alekseyev, '15-rublevyy maksimum', p. 111.

[12] Hellie, *Slavery*, pp. 319–24.

[13] *AMG* i. 144; cf. Hellie, *Slavery*, p. 122.

vitor of Bryansk, tried to flee to Poland–Lithuania; he was caught, tortured, and hanged.[13] Such an individual was a mere chattel, whose accidental death, if caused by the slave of another, entitled his owner to compensation in the form of one of the culprit's owner's slaves. The 1632 register of *moskovskiye dvoryane* shows that they were often diffident about bringing their men to service when summoned. The zealous I. V. Birkin promised 9 men, 6 of them for combat duty, although he admitted to possessing only 12 peasant households on his vast domain of 1,436 quarters; but T. Bezobrazov, who was similarly endowed (and said he had over twice as many peasants) would bring only 3 men, 2 of them for the baggage train.[14] Hellie offers some elaborate statistical computations based on this list,[15] but their value is limited by the fact that we do not know whether the statements were verified or whether these individuals were actually sent. But he is undoubtedly correct in assuming that the numerical decline compared with sixteenth-century data reflects a fear among owners, shared by the authorities, that an abundance of armed slaves might prove dangerous: they had shown in the Troubles their potential for rebellious conduct.[16] Yet those who were sent into combat fought well, or so at least we are told by Olearius.[17] Servitors' fears of mutiny were allayed by the new disciplinary methods that could be enforced, especially in the new-model forces, and so the decline in the number of hangers-on was not dramatic. In 1681 the metropolitan nobles listed as assigned to the various *razryady*, who were 14,625 strong, had in their retinue 21,830 *lyudi* (men), an average of 1.67 per head—proportionately more than the Kolomna servitors a century earlier.[18]

Recruits now increasingly went to war as substitutes for their masters. Sixteenth-century practice had been more exigent: they were permitted only in exceptional circumstances, when servitors were too old or ill to do duty in person and had no sons to send in their stead.[19] Substitution became more common during the Troubles, when the levy system all but broke down. In 1608–9 the northern town of Ustyug raised five detachments of *sokha* men to support Tsar Vasiliy Shuysky against the Second Pretender; nearby Soligalich collected 50 to 100 men per *sokha* and, when these were defeated, instituted another levy of 20 men which had better success.[20] Under the early Romanovs the provision of substitutes was closely controlled by the Razryad. In 1648 A. Baskakin, a privileged servitor for 50 years, was allowed to retire on condition that he supplied three *datochnye lyudi* in lieu.[21] Only one such recruit was demanded from

[14] Stashevsky, *Zemlevladeniye*, pp. 40 ff., nos. 19, 27.

[15] Hellie, 'Musc. Mil. Slavery', p. 3A.

[16] Hellie, *Slavery*, pp. 467–74.

[17] Olearius, *Travels*, p. 152.

[18] Ivanov, *Opisaniye*, pp. 71–92 (our calculation); there is some doubt about this figure, since servants are mentioned only for those metropolitan nobles in the Moscow *razryad*; if they alone owned such men, the ratio is four to one—and there were another 10,000 *datochnye*!

[19] Beskrovnyy, *Khrestomatiya*, p. 64 (late 1550s?); the order was repeated in 1604: Chernov, *Voor. sily*, p. 125; Hellie, *Enserfment*, p. 48.

[20] *AI* ii. 177; Platonov, *Ocherki*, p. 302. [21] *AMG* ii. 304.

B. A. Kalitin of Vladimir, who stated that in the course of no less than 68 years' service he had 'become feeble and deaf, and crippled by many wounds'.[22] The harsh fate that awaited these substitutes was somewhat mitigated by the fact that a fortunate few could rise up through service into the ranks of the privileged—whose estate (*soslovie*), though acquiring some traits of a caste, was not in fact hermetically sealed off to entrants from below.

Of greater military significance, and better documented, are the lower-grade servitors, or *sluzhiliye lyudi po priboru*. The main formal distinction between them and the privileged *sluzhiliye lyudi po otechestvu* was that they owed service, and were remunerated, collectively rather than individually. They formed a category, or more precisely a set of categories, that were as much professional groups as ranks (*chiny*). The principal groups were the musketeers (*strel'tsy*), artillerymen (*pushkari*), and serving Cossacks (*kazaki*). Service was obligatory for all males born into a particular category, and it was next to impossible to leave it of one's own volition—although in the seventeenth century men were frequently transferred from one body to another as state needs dictated. In principle service was for life, but it was not full-time, for as well as bearing arms lower-grade servitors would engage in economic activities in order to maintain themselves, since here as elsewhere self-sufficiency was the goal. What is of particular interest in our context is that the caste spirit which developed in this milieu generated organized opposition. Admittedly there is a risk of over-emphasizing this aspect and forgetting that most of these men, however discontented, remained loyal soldiers; nevertheless it is certainly significant that what the metropolitan and provincial nobility either could not or would not do was achieved in the late seventeenth century by the under-privileged musketeers. Unhappily for them, their dissident movement was ruthlessly suppressed by the absolutist state, aided and abetted by elements of the élite cavalrymen.

A certain rivalry between these two elements of the armed forces was present almost from the start. One early historian suggests that Ivan IV may have set up the *strel'tsy*, who were drawn from the free (non-servile) population, 'to obtain a counterweight to the powerful classes of nobility and gentry'.[23] There is, however, no firm evidence that this was so, and certainly Ivan's principal motive will have been of a technical military nature: experience in the first Kazan' campaign demonstrated the need for a professional infantry force trained in the use of firearms.

Elements of such a force already existed in the so-called *pishchal'niki*, men equipped with hand-guns (*pishchali*); their existence is attested in the sources from 1510.[24] Like the *pososhnye*, they were levied from the under-privileged

---

[22] *AMG* ii. 365 (1648); cf. ii. 430 (1650), 658 (1655), on grounds of poverty and sickness respectively.

[23] Brix, *Geschichte*, p. 93.

[24] Yepifanov, 'Voysko', p. 344.

classes and served for as long as they were needed. Some, the 'state *pishchal'niki*', were supplied with weapons by the authorities; they presumably enjoyed higher status and better conditions than those whose armament was provided by their communities. In 1546 some Novgorod *pishchal'niki* mutinied and clashed with a force of gentry servitors at Kolomna, where the young Ivan was then residing. The incident may have fortified his resolve to replace them by men who performed similar duties on a permanent basis and could be kept under tighter control.

The musketeers were set up in 1550, when 3,000 *pishchal'niki* were chosen to form an élite force, divided into six units.[25] They were settled in a body on the Sparrow Hills outside Moscow, where they were well placed to fulfil their task of guarding the monarch's security. In 1552 they accompanied him on the successful campaign against Kazan´ and first saw action. The number of musketeers grew rapidly: their children and other male relatives were encouraged (indeed, expected) to join, and volunteers were also accepted from outside the corps's ranks. In each case kinsmen or neighbours were required to stand surety for their good behaviour. The social distinction between the men who served in Moscow and those consigned to the provinces, already present among the *pishchal'niki*, continued and was accentuated. In 1563 13,000 musketeers went on the campaign to Polotsk, and by the end of the century they numbered some 18,000 to 20,000, of whom 7,000 served in Moscow.[26] The latter figure was given correctly by Fletcher, who put the total at 12,000; he also noted that 200 of the élite section were mounted, and that these '*stremyannye strel'tsy*, or gunners at the stirrup, are about [the tsar's] own person at the very court or house where [he] himself lodgeth'.[27] The existence of these cavalrymen raised the status of the whole corps, despite the growing social differentiation within it. Already at this time it was probably difficult for an ordinary musketeer to rise high in the force, or to transfer from the provinces to the centre. He could reach the junior ranks of decurion and quinquagenarian (*desyatskiy, pyatidesyatskiy*), but the centurion (*sotskiy*) and unit chief (*golova*) were drawn from the privileged servitors. The names and ranks (but not the social origin) of over two hundred such officers are known.[28] This 'promotion block' was a potential source of grievance to the rank and file. Materially, however, the musketeers were relatively well provided for. The annual pay of the first 3,000 men was fixed at 4 roubles, and by 1589, according to Fletcher, even provincials were receiving 7 roubles 'as well as 12 measures apiece of rye and oats'.[29]

[25] The initial term *stat'i* (categories or grades) soon yielded to hundreds (*sotni*) and detachments (*pribory, prikazy*). Chernov argues that some *strel'tsy* units came into being as early as 1545–7 ('Obrazovaniye', pp. 282–4; *Voor. sily*, pp. 46–7), but as Zimin has shown (*Reformy*, p. 346), this claim rests on dubious evidence.

[26] Yepifanov, 'Voysko', pp. 346, 368; Hellie, *Enserfment*, p. 162: 20–25,000; Fletcher, *Russe Commonwealth*, p. 180; Margeret estimated that in the 1590s the Moscow group was 10,000 strong (*L'Estat*, p. 22). [27] Fletcher, loc. cit.

[28] Bogoyavlensky, 'Strel. golovy', pp. 13–15; Yepifanov, 'Voysko', p. 346; Shpakovsky, 'Strel'tsy', p. 140.

[29] Fletcher, loc. cit. This may refer to the Moscow group.

By contrast in 1612, at the height of the Troubles, a rank-and-file musketeer could expect only 2 roubles and 6 measures of rye.[30]

The social crisis of the late sixteenth century accelerated the trend towards civilianization. Already the first units, as we have seen, were granted land—in principle for their use rather than as the property of the community concerned; the officers would then assign individual lots on which the men were expected to build homes, a small subsidy being allotted for the purpose. Residing in a particular quarter of the town, originally in a separate settlement (*sloboda*), they soon acquired not only vegetable-gardens but also arable land and pasture. The central authorities looked benignly on this development since it reduced demands on the Treasury, although it was bound to detract from the men's military value. Grants of cereals or of cloth for uniforms, and indeed payment of the annual salary, were often irregular or subject to delay. Sometimes cash grants would be made only until such time as the musketeer had established himself in a gainful occupation.[31] Thus in order to survive and support his family he was obliged to take up some kind of artisanal or commercial activity as well as to till the soil. One supposes that in general the chance to engage in such potentially profitable occupations was welcome; many men will have had previous experience of such work in civilian life. Some of them rented state-owned land or facilities (for example, mills) and ran barns, shops, stalls, etc., on which a modest fee was payable.

The musketeers' life-style differed from that of other town-dwellers only in regard to their military obligations. In an interior garrison in time of peace these were not too onerous. Guard duty lasted 24 hours at a stretch, but *strel′tsy* were seldom called on to perform drill or exercises. Generally they rendered service within the city precincts or in the immediate environs, for their earnings were too low to permit extended periods of absence from their settlements; nor did the central authorities have the means to maintain them when far from base. Many sixteenth-century Russian towns bore a wholly military aspect—not only along the southern border, where this was to be expected, but also in the north-west, which suffered so heavily from the Livonian War and Ivan IV's depredations. According to census data for 1585–8 the little town of Ostrov, near Pskov, had lost nearly all the 204 civilian households previously registered there, whose place had been taken by 120 lower-grade servitors, most of them musketeers.[32] Data for 1625 show that at Tula military personnel of this kind ran 111 of 356 trading establishments (31 per cent), including nearly half the forges, a skill that came naturally to them. They also specialized in meat and other foodstuffs, clothing, and footwear. Most of these men were close to the poverty line, possessing only 'shelves' or 'corners' of a shop or stall, but one, M. Pavlov, became a successful entrepreneur. The closer a town

---

[30] Brix, *Geschichte*, p. 147, citing *AAE* iii. 148.

[31] Chechulin, *Goroda*, p. 327.

[32] Ibid., p. 91; at Opochka almost half the cultivated land in the town was tilled by service personnel: ibid., p. 105.

was situated to the expanding southern border, the greater the role played by soldiers in its economic life: at Putivl´ in the same year they held 70 per cent of all shops and stalls. As conditions became more normal, a civilian urban community (*posad*) could grow up.[33]

The men in uniform seem to have identified quite readily with the town where they resided and whence most new recruits were drawn, even though they did not legally belong to the community. From time to time friction might develop with civilians over the fact that they were taxed separately, but the evidence suggests that they usually paid an equitable share of the common burden. Such disputes did not prevent the musketeers from becoming integrated into their milieu in a way that privileged servitors were not. From the state's viewpoint this created a certain security risk. If social tensions in a town became acute, the *strel´tsy* could provide leadership for other elements of the populace; they were armed, albeit mainly with antiquated weapons, and could bring to bear a measure of organization and discipline. The targets of their wrath were all those who, occupying an intermediate position between tsar and people, were so prone to abuse their authority: the voivode, such privileged servitors as resided within the city walls, and last but not least their own chiefs.

By the time of the first Romanovs the *strel´tsy* had become something of a doubtful asset. In terms of military efficiency they could not stand comparison with the new-model forces (see ch. 4), and although they continued to perform a valuable function in the southern frontier zone many were assigned to ceremonial and police duties. Musketeer detachments escorted foreign envoys to and from the border and guarded them while in the capital. Adam Olearius, who visited Moscow in 1634 in the suite of the Holstein ambassador, recorded that on reaching Nöteborg on Lake Ladoga his party 'entered a small overheated room, black as coal from smoke; the *strel´tsy* gave a salute with their flintlocks (which along with swords are part of their general equipment) without the slightest semblance of order, as if each wanted to be first to finish'. On another such occasion the salute 'was executed so carelessly that the secretary to the Swedish resident, who was standing by us watching the ceremony, had a large hole torn in his jacket'. In the evenings their musketeer escort entertained the travelling diplomats by playing the lute and disporting themselves with a chained bear—a popular pastime in seventeenth-century Muscovy.[34] For a foreign ambassador one company (*sotnya*) was the usual escort, but once a Muscovite envoy to Poland–Lithuania was accompanied by an entire 500-man unit (*prikaz*) in full panoply of war, whose presence was designed to lend emphasis to his arguments.[35] More routine duties included running errands for voivodes and other officials, convoying prisoners or army supplies, and tracking down bandits or absentee gentry servitors. (The latter task graphically underlines the narrow distinction between privileged and non-

---

[33] Aleksandrov, 'Strel. naseleniye', pp. 242–3, 245; cf. Eaton, 'Censuses', p. 211.
[34] Olearius, *Travels*, pp. 46–7, 52.
[35] Brix, *Geschichte*, p. 266.

privileged status in Muscovy.) Some *strel'tsy* were employed fighting fires in the capital—an important function, in view of the prevalence of wooden buildings, but scarcely a military one; after a fire, so Kotoshikhin tells us, they were paraded and beaten if they were found to have stolen anything.[36] When the army went on campaign, some musketeers were detailed to internal security duties: as many as six *prikazy* might guard a senior field commander.[37]

Even among these picked troops discipline was often a problem. In 1622 the authorities at Bryansk reported that Moscow *strel'tsy* sent to protect the town were behaving licentiously; an investigation showed that they had been liberally plied with alcohol by the local gentry, who were thereupon officially ordered to desist.[38] When civil disorders occurred after a major fire in Moscow in 1636, the musketeers joined the trouble-makers instead of combating them.[39] Twelve years later a peaceful request for redress of grievances by various elements of the population in the capital turned into a bloody riot after some units, which initially helped to maintain order, mutinied and refused to obey their commander B. I. Morozov, the young Tsar Alexis's unpopular favourite.[40] Their example was later followed by some of the service gentry: it was the last time that the two groups would act in concert. In the ensuing chaos three of the tsar's closest associates were killed by the mob. The troubles died down only after the government consented to convoke a Land Assembly (*zemskiy sobor*) to approve a new code of laws, the *Ulozheniye*, which came into force the following year. Olearius noted that after the riots 'His Tsarist Majesty feasted the strel'tsy who made up his bodyguard with vodka and mead' as part of his endeavour to ensure the corps's continued loyalty.[41] Several hundred men were exiled to Siberia for their part in the rising.

One reason for the musketeers' disaffection was that the Morozov regime, in its eagerness to improve the state's financial posture, had cut their pay, which in 1647/8 amounted to only 2 to 3 roubles (and 6 quarters of grain) for men in the ranks.[42] This reduction, coupled with burdensome new taxes and a Crown monopoly on salt, threatened their livelihood as it did that of other traders and artisans. The pay cuts seem to have been made good later,[43] but the

---

[36] Kotoshikhin, *O Rossii*, p. 91.

[37] Brix, *Geschichte*, loc. cit.; Shpakovsky, 'Strel'tsy', p. 145; Hellie, *Enserfment*, pp. 203, 214.

[38] *AMG* i. 146.

[39] Chistyakova, 'Moskva', pp. 307–8.

[40] S. V. Bakhrushin, 'Mosk. vosstaniye 1648 g.', *Nauchnye trudy*, Moscow, 1952–9, ii. 72–4; Hellie, *Enserfment*, p. 136.

[41] Olearius, *Travels*, p. 213.

[42] *DAI* iii. 36; cf. K. Pommerening to Queen Christina, 15 Sept. 1647, in Yakubov, *Rossiya i Shvetsiya*, p. 406: 5 roubles for *stremyanniye*, 4 roubles for other musketeers.

[43] Sakharov, *Obrazovaniye*, p. 161. Pommerening reported on 30 Dec. 1648 a grant (presumably once and for all) of 25 roubles—more than the 14 roubles initially promised: Yakubov, *Rossiya i Shvetsiya*, pp. 427–8, 433. However, Stashevsky shows ('Smeta', p. 72) that some musketeers on the south-eastern border received 8–10 roubles (cavalrymen) and 5 roubles (infantrymen). There was a tendency to remunerate men stationed in the provinces with land rather than cash (ibid., pp. 60–1). Such allotments might be reasonably generous: 8 quarters for an ordinary soldier and 30 for a centurion: Zagorodsky, *Belgorodskaya cherta*, p. 103.

musketeers' behaviour in 1648 evidently made the government more efficiency-conscious in their regard. More and more of them were obliged to earn their own living by trade or handicrafts, and as a rule only the privileged Moscow *strel'tsy* actually received the annual grain allocation. At the same time the authors of the new law code, anxious to appease the civilian townspeople, removed certain fiscal concessions which lower-grade servitors had previously enjoyed.

It is probably going too far to say, as Hellie implies, that the authorities made a conscious decision to down-grade the corps on account of its doubtful political reliability and military effectiveness, for if so they would scarcely have enlarged its size. In 1663 there were about 29,000 and in 1681 some 55,000 musketeers, over two and a half times as many as there had been a century earlier.[44] Admittedly the increase was largely due to natural reproduction within this closed caste, and so not wholly attributable to official policy, but on at least three occasions after 1649 peasants and townsmen were drafted into the corps; had the government wished to reduce it, it could have abstained from such a practice and acted more frequently than it did in transferring musketeers to the new-model forces. It is worth noting that the increase took place among the élite Moscow contingents rather than the provincial men, whose numbers remained more or less constant.[45] The former were no longer necessarily stationed in the capital but were posted to the provinces, where one of their tasks was presumably to exercise surveillance over the local men.[46]

During the long war with Poland–Lithuania, in which *strel'tsy* units played a relatively modest part, these troops' morale appears to have declined. In July 1662 elements of the Moscow populace rose up in protest at the government's deliberate devaluation of the coinage. Thirty-three *strel'tsy* were implicated, half of them from a single detachment (I. Monastyrev's *prikaz*). This was only a fraction of the number of men from the new-model forces (366 *soldaty* and 98 *reytary*) who were involved, but one of the leading activists, Kuz'ma Nagayev, was a musketeer.[47] After his arrest Nagayev was given fourteen lashes of the knout and 'burned with fire, but under this torture repeated his earlier evidence', as the investigation record states; nevertheless he was found guilty and sentenced, along with a civilian, L. Zhitkiy, to have his left hand and both feet cut off and his tongue torn out. Remarkably, Zhitkiy survived this fearsome punishment, from which his musketeer comrade died.[48] Gentrymen and soldiers from the new-model forces who were involved in the rising were spared torture and were sent into exile instead.

[44] Veselovsky, 'Smeta', pp. 26 ff. (our calculation; the Razryad clerks made it 29,244: Stashevsky, 'Smeta', p. 61); Chernov, *Voor. sily*, p. 162.

[45] In 1663 there were 15,900 and in 1681 22,500 Moscow *strel'tsy*. Chernov, loc. cit.; Hellie, *Enserfment*, p. 202.

[46] For a survey of their geographical distribution: Brix, *Geschichte*, pp. 259–65.

[47] Buganov, 'O sots. sostave', p. 314; id., *Mosk. vosstaniye 1662 g.*, pp. 40–3, 183–4; id. (comp.), *Vosstaniye 1662 g. . . . : sb. dok.*, pp. 43, 48–50, 76; Hellie, *Enserfment*, p. 364.

[48] Buganov, *Mosk. vosstaniye 1662 g.*, pp. 185, 209, 266.

In June 1670, during the revolt of Sten'ka Razin (1667–71), some *strel'tsy* at Astrakhan' went over to the insurgents, who characteristically formed their *own* musketeer units, and there was some disaffection in contingents stationed elsewhere along the Volga; but other detachments, particularly of Moscow *strel'tsy*, helped to suppress the rebellion, suffering 165 casualties in doing so.[49] By this time the musketeers may be said to have developed a sense of corporate identity and the rudiments of an ideology through which to express it. Hellie suggests that an awareness of their own obsolescence 'explains their fervent adherence to the eschatological Old Believer movement, for indeed their world was coming to an end'.[50] This must remain a suggestive hypothesis, since there is no hard evidence about their motivations or the extent of sympathy among them for these radical critics of the official Nikonian Church. Religious dissidents appear to have had more success in some units than others, which can be explained partly by the fact that their movement drew its support from certain regions,[51] and it was the detachments stationed there which came under its influence.

Opposition to the established order developed naturally out of dissatisfaction at material and legal disabilities. The musketeers were doubtless jealous of the new-model forces, which received much of the revenue from the tax known as 'musketeers' money' (*streletskiye den'gi*). This was usually in arrears, partly because it was collected by various central organs;[52] in 1679 the task was entrusted solely to the Streletskiy chancellery, but this measure does not seem to have improved the flow of funds. Officers in charge of musketeer units had ample opportunity to engage in corrupt practices. Frequently they would appropriate the men's pay or force them to work on their own lands. Not uncharacteristic was the conduct of one K. Yevlev, chief of a unit stationed at Belgorod, who was accused by his subordinates of causing the death of eight *strel'tsy* and the flight of seven others; those who dared to petition against his abuses 'he beats with cudgels and with his own hands, pulling them by the beard, and detains overnight in his own house'.[53]

Corporal punishment was the normal method of enforcing discipline. An instruction to the chief of a unit stationed near Pskov in 1677 prescribed beating for even a single day's absence without leave, 'according to [the gravity of] their offence'; in such cases the decurion was to be beaten too for neglecting his supervisory duties and kept in jail for as many days as the absentee remained at large. The rod was likewise to be applied to the backs of those who committed robberies, visited a prostitute, played dice, or sheltered fugitives in their homes.[54] There are touches of paranoia and sadism about this document, with

---

[49] Avrich, *Russ. Rebels*, pp. 75, 80, 82–6; A. A. Novosel'sky and V. I. Lebedev (eds.), *Krest. voyna pod predvoditel'stvom S. Razina: sb. dok.*, Moscow, 1954–62, ii. 136; iii. 187, 209, 224, 237, 248, 274–6.

[50] Hellie, *Enserfment*, p. 207.

[51] Mel'gunov, *Relig.–obshch. dvizheniya*, p. 65.

[52] *AI* v. 48.　　　　　　　　[53] *AMG* iii. 185 (1660).

[54] 'Strel. sluzhba', pp. 17–22; cf. *DAI* viii. 42 (1678).

its detailed catalogue of prohibitions and threats; officers are given no positive inducement to behave properly or to earn their men's respect.

The indifferent performance of the traditional forces in the campaigns of 1677–8 against the Turks and Tatars led the reformers in high places to revive the idea of turning the musketeers into Western-style soldiers, and perhaps of abolishing the corps altogether. In March 1680 the Moscow *strel'tsy* chiefs were given foreign titles of colonel (*polkovnik*) and the like to bring them into line with their equivalents in the new-model forces.[55] The move must have been unpopular, if not with the officers concerned at least with the rank and file, who were suspicious of alien influences. The following year, when Golitsyn set up the commission on military reforms, the *strel'tsy* do not appear to have been represented (or at any rate, if their leaders did attend, they were not elected).[56]

It is therefore not surprising that, when a dynastic crisis broke out a few months later, the *strel'tsy* should have become involved and helped to decide its outcome. During the troubled year 1682 they spearheaded a movement of social protest which generated a wide range of objectives—professional, political, and religious—that were not easily reconciled. The rebels also brought into being a rudimentary organization through which to press their claims, and these elected leaders tried to control the random destructiveness that marked the initial stages of the revolt. However, there is no denying that the men's political views were primitive; strong believers in the sacral monarchy and in traditional Orthodox values, they could not evolve a credible programme of political reform. This doomed the movement to failure. After a few months of uncertainty the government was able to restore order and to punish the trouble-makers. The uprising of 1682 was the first of a number of military revolts which broke out during the next century and a half; it is therefore worth examining closely, with the aid of sources that have recently been made available.[57]

The first sign of serious disaffection came in February, when men in B. Pyzhov's contingent charged their commander with arbitrarily docking their pay. An investigation was launched by I. M. Yazykov, a favourite of the tsar who shared responsibility for the Streletskiy chancellery with the aged and ineffectual boyar Yu. A. Dolgorukiy. The complaints were held to be unfounded and the petitioners severely punished. The *strel'tsy* in the capital appreciated that the political situation was becoming highly unstable. During

[55] *PSZ* ii. 812.

[56] *PSZ* ii. 905. The official record mentions *polkovniki . . . pekhotnye*, which might include the *strel'tsy* chiefs.

[57] Cf. Buganov, *Mosk. vosstaniya*; id., *Vosstaniye v Moskve 1682 g.: sb. dok.* The former offers a thorough critique of the sources, among which the most important are S. Medvedev, *Sozertsaniye kratkoye . . .* (preferable to the account by A. A. Matveyev on which most historians have relied) and Heinrich Butenant, *Eigentlicher Bericht . . .* , Hamburg, 1682, which we have tr. and ed. as 'Mutiny in Moscow, 1682'.

Theodore's reign power lay with the Miloslavsky clan, related to the dynasty by Tsar Alexis's first marriage. As the nominal ruler's health declined—he died on 27 April—this group lost influence to the Naryshkins, the kin of Alexis's second wife. On 23 April the *strel'tsy* submitted another petition, directed against the most unpopular of their colonels, S. Griboyedov. This time Yazykov had the accused man arrested, but freed him the next day. Such token punishment suggested that the authorities recognized the justice of the men's complaints but were unwilling to act on them. The petitioner was ordered to be publicly whipped, but his comrades freed him from arrest and assaulted several officials. Within days most of the nineteen musketeer regiments stationed in the capital were in uproar.[58]

On Theodore's death the Naryshkin family acceded to prominence with the aid of the patriarch, who tried to settle the succession in their favour by installing the ten-year-old Peter (born of Alexis's second marriage) as tsar. Many *strel'tsy*, notably those in A. Karandeyev's detachment, feared that this move heralded tough repressive measures; they were particularly nervous at the impending return to Moscow of A. S. Matveyev, a Naryshkin supporter who had been exiled under the previous regime. Thus what had begun as a simple protest over service conditions was now becoming politicized. The conventional view of the musketeers as mere tools of the ambitious Miloslavskys is no longer adequate. These embittered servicemen sought to exploit the power struggle in the Kremlin to advance their cause. Men in twelve units now jointly submitted a petition demanding redress of grievances. The panic-stricken officials arrested several senior officers against whom complaints of extortion were lodged and subjected them to the *pravezh*, that is, to a public beating, the normal judicial method of forcing a defaulter to pay his debts. This spectacle naturally whetted the men's appetites for vengeance, and they began to take the law into their own hands. At least fourteen colonels were beaten, two of them with the knout (an indignity from which officials tried in vain to save them), and forced to hand over large sums of money.[59] New officers were hastily appointed to take their place, but they exercised little authority.

By mid-May the mutinous troops were questioning the rights of all those who had held high office under the last administration. Their political ideal was a 'good' tsar, such as the feeble-witted Ivan, brother of the late Theodore, who they hoped would rule through officials sympathetic to popular aspirations. They did not challenge the existing system of government; they wanted a change of heart, a moral renewal, manifest in immediate changes of policy towards them and in the appointment of 'righteous' men to positions of authority. When Matveyev returned to Moscow (on or about 12 May) he committed the error of conferring secretly with Dolgorukiy. The musketeers felt

[58] Keep, 'Mutiny', pp. 414–15; Medvedev, *Sozertsaniye*, pp. 41–2; Buganov, *Mosk. vosstaniya*, p. 90; *Vosstaniye 1682 g.*, pp. 20–1.

[59] Keep, 'Mutiny', pp. 416–17; Medvedev, *Sozertsaniye*, pp. 47–8; Buganov, *Mosk. vosstaniya*, p. 117.

that the court factions were uniting against them. On 15 May they launched a three-day-long *pogrom*.[60]

More violent than the riots of 1648 or 1662, it cost the lives of 18 notables, including six boyars, and several dozen commoners; Matveyev, Dolgorukiy, and his son were among the victims, and several foreigners were assaulted or threatened. The property of those killed was seized and distributed. Notables whose lives had been spared were presented with further demands for money, and for the next few months the capital was to all intents and purposes under the musketeers' control. However, they did little or nothing to consolidate their power. This is understandable, since they saw themselves not as insurgents or revolutionaries but as loyal partisans of the established order who had been forced to act against 'traitors' in high places. This at least was the justification advanced by the men's elected leaders, who on 6 June successfully petitioned that their corps be granted the honorific title of 'court infantry' and that a column be erected in Red Square to immortalize its achievements.[61] Needless to say, the average musketeer, concerned above all with material enrichment, will not have bothered much about these transparent political fictions.

The riots strengthened the Miloslavskys' conviction that they alone could restore order. The ambitious Tsarevna Sofia was one architect of a curious compromise, announced on 26 May, whereby her brother Ivan was to rule jointly with Peter; shortly afterwards she was nominated regent. This solution to the dynastic problem was tacitly endorsed by the *strel'tsy*, whose leaders' compliance doubtless owed something to the hospitality they received at the court's expense; two regiments were entertained each day.[62] Many musketeers were also gratified by the appointment to the Streletskiy chancellery of A. I. Khovansky, a flamboyant demagogue sympathetic to the Old Belief. Among the 19 units in Moscow at this time nine were affected by religious dissent; it was strongest in that previously headed by Colonel G. S. Titov. However, this division of opinion among the troops was a major source of weakness which the government could turn to its own account.

The Old Believers, clerical and lay, petitioned for the convocation of a Church council which, they hoped, whould annul the Nikonian reforms and sanction a return to traditional rites. In the circumstances such a demand was provocative and utopian. Khovansky seems to have realized this, for he sought to mediate between the sectarians and members of the religious and political establishment. After some delay a public discussion was arranged (5 July) between partisans of the two viewpoints.[63] Such a confrontation could not possibly produce a compromise; indeed, neither side wanted one. Sofia in

[60] Keep, 'Mutiny', pp. 422–36; Medvedev, *Sozertsaniye*, pp. 52–7; Buganov, *Mosk. vosstaniya*, pp. 144–61.

[61] Medvedev, *Sozertsaniye*, p. 75; Buganov, *Mosk. vosstaniya*, pp. 236–44; *Vosstaniye 1682 g.*, pp. 36–46.

[62] Medvedev, *Sozertsaniye*, p. 65; Buganov, *Mosk. vosstaniya*, p. 173.

[63] Medvedev, *Sozertsaniye*, pp. 76–91; Buganov, *Mosk. vosstaniya*, pp. 210–35.

particular sought to embarrass and discredit the Old Believer delegation, and the meeting broke up in confusion. Those *strel´tsy* who did not support the dissidents, among them men in the Stremyannoy regiment (the ruler's body-guard), were again plied with alcohol, given money, and promised preferment. In this way the corps was effectively neutralized, allowing the authorities to arrest and punish the sectarian leaders (11 July).

After this move it was only a question of time before the musketeers in turn were suppressed. In government circles Khovansky, the *strel´tsy* commander, was rapidly becoming ostracized. On 13 July the court left Moscow for the first of two visits to summer retreats in the environs of the city. Since this was normal practice, the *strel´tsy* could not and did not try to prevent it. They remained in the capital and with Khovansky's tacit consent continued to press their claims. But opinion was now turning against them: townsmen and peasants begrudged paying extra taxes to meet their demands, which seemed to be motivated primarily by self-interest. Meanwhile Sofia acted with tactical skill. On 29 August she called the Stremyanniy regiment to attend on the court at the suburban palace of Kolomenskoye. Then, early in September, having moved on to the fortified monastery of Zvenigorod, she summoned the gentry militia and other forces under noble command to assemble in order to 'cleanse' the capital of the 'treacherous' musketeers. The latter were told to prepare for military duty in the south. Khovansky disobeyed the command, so giving Sofia the pretext she needed. He was summoned to her headquarters, arrested, and at once executed without trial in the presence of the court (17 September). His son and, it appears, as many as 37 of the musketeers' elected delegates were put to death with him.[64]

After this *coup de main* the government could proceed against the men themselves. Moscow was ringed with loyal troops, including some 5,500 metropolitan nobles, who were lavishly rewarded for their pains with grants of land (their men had to be content with the by now traditional dispensation of vodka). Early in October the patriarch helped to mediate a settlement whereby the rebels were pardoned on condition that they obeyed orders in future and informed on any of their comrades who acted disloyally.[65] The musketeers apologized for the violence they had done and asked for the commemorative column to be demolished, a symbolic gesture which the authorities hastened to carry out. The blame for the troubles was conveniently laid upon Khovansky and other scapegoats, and in November the court returned to Moscow. There was a mild disturbance in P. Bokhin's regiment the following month, but it was easily contained, half a dozen ringleaders being put to death.

Although some foreign accounts refer to hundreds of executions, there was no bloodbath—nor even a general investigation into the revolt. The repressive

---

[64] Medvedev, *Sozertsaniye*, pp. 106–11; Buganov, *Mosk. vosstaniya*, pp. 261–79; *Vosstaniye 1682 g.*, pp. 79–82.

[65] Medvedev, *Sozertsaniye*, pp. 124–51; Buganov, *Mosk. vosstaniya*, pp. 301–12; *Vosstaniye 1682 g.*, pp. 168–70, 175–9, 186–8.

measures taken were mild in comparison with those of Alexis—or of Peter I. Sofia wished to be thought an enlightened ruler and knew that her authority was weak. She was content to reduce by one-third the size of the musketeer forces in Moscow, which by December 1683 numbered 9,542 men in twelve regiments.[66] The others were sent to the provinces, where a screening operation was carried out. Men whose conduct was considered suspect were reassigned to other units, but it seems that none of them were discharged. Some were posted to a new composite (*sborniy*) regiment at Sevsk, where their families were allowed to join them. The hope of a return to the capital, and thus to favour, kept the exiles loyal. Despite or because of this lenient treatment there was continuing nervousness among metropolitan nobles at the security threat which the *strel'tsy* supposedly represented. 'They are most insolent whenever an occasion presents itself and inspire the greatest fear in Moscow', reported a Czech Jesuit who lived in the city from 1686 to 1689, here doubtless conveying the views of the noblemen he mixed with.[67] In 1687 there were signs that the government was easing its attitude to the musketeers, partly because they were needed to fight foreign foes and partly because they now seemed less menacing than the élite 'play regiments' (*poteshnye*: see below, p. 98) which the young Tsar Peter had been allowed to set up, ostensibly for his own amusement, and was industriously exercising under the tutelage of foreign officers.

It was from this direction that the fatal challenge to Sofia's shaky authority came in the summer of 1689. The government's prestige had been undermined by two fruitless and costly campaigns against the Crimean Tatars. To make matters worse, the returning army was publicly acclaimed as if it had been victorious and its commanders, including the regent's favourite V. V. Golitsyn, received unusually lavish rewards.[68] Peter found a pretext to provoke an open breach with Sofia, and for some weeks the two armed camps eyed one another with mounting suspicion, each fearing a *coup* by the other. Sofia's guard included several *strel'tsy* detachments, but their morale was uncertain. The regent, not wishing to antagonize her opponents, took no steps to win them over to her side. The dénouement came about almost accidentally on the night of 7 August. An alarming report prompted Peter to flee from Preobrazhenskoye, just outside Moscow, to the Trinity monastery. Here the Naryshkins proceeded to copy faithfully the tactics employed by the Miloslavskys seven years earlier, summoning various units in succession to attend. Two *strel'tsy* regiments, those of L. P. Sukharev and I. E. Tsykler, were committed to Peter from the start; indeed, it was several men from the latter unit who triggered the affair by reporting—mistakenly, as it appears—that Sofia was about to act. The other musketeers offered no resistance on Sofia's behalf.

---

[66] Medvedev, *Sozertsaniye*, p. 180; Buganov, *Mosk. vosstaniya*, p. 353; *Vosstaniye 1682 g.*, pp. 267–75.

[67] G. David SJ, *Status modernus Magnae Russiae . . .* (1690), ed. A. V. Florovskij, The Hague and Paris, 1965, pp. 86–7.

[68] *DRV* xvii. 284–355.

Nevertheless Peter suspected the entire corps of disloyalty. Their chief, F. L. Shaklovitiy, like Khovansky in 1682, was put to death after a secret investigation. (Unlike Khovansky, he was tortured.) There is no reliable evidence that he was responsible for any offensive move against the Naryshkin faction, but his fate was inescapably bound up with that of the regent, who was deposed and confined in a nunnery. A number of musketeer units were sent to the provinces, and in 1695–6 the bulk of the corps was sent to fight the Turks at Azov.[69]

While these actions were doubtless resented, it would be wrong to see the *strel´tsy* as harbouring a grudge against Peter personally or favouring his opponents: they had no such political commitments.[70] Their mutinous outbursts in 1682 and again in 1698 (see ch. 5) were motivated primarily by dissatisfaction at their service conditions, which were onerous. There is no truth to the view, assiduously spread by historians sympathetic to Peter, that they were 'spoiled' or 'cosseted'. Although there was a chiliastic strain in their thinking that was peculiarly Russian, in general their actions are comparable to those of military mutineers elsewhere in Europe at this time, who were often able to mount well-organized protest movements and to defy authority for a considerable length of time.[71] Some contemporary writers drew an analogy between the *strel´tsy* in Muscovy and the janissaries in the Ottoman empire.[72] Peter's official chronicler was one of those who made this allusion, in an attempt to justify the tsar's brutal actions against them.[73] Eventually this became something of a cliché. The parallels have yet to be examined, but it is clear that the *strel´tsy* never acquired or sought the political influence of their Ottoman counterparts. If they were feared and hated by partisans of Petrine absolutism this was because, of all the emergent interest groups within the armed forces, they were the most civilized and rooted in the populace. They had close ties with other urban groups who had good reason to resent the government's policies, particularly in the fiscal domain; as an armed and disciplined body, the musketeers could turn their passive opposition into active protest. These urban revolts, although easily suppressed, were damaging to the monarchy's self-image and prestige. Apart from the internal security considerations, the musketeers exemplified a flexible, permissive type of relationship between the state and elements of the service class—one for which there could be no place in the homogenized, rationally ordered society that Peter the Great would seek to introduce.

[69] On the crisis of 1689 see R. Wittram, *Peter I: Czar und Kaiser*, Göttingen, 1964, i. 96–9; Bogoslovsky, *Materialy*, i. 37–47; Kurakin, 'Gistoriya', pp. 58–60; Belov, 'Mosk. smuty', pp. 328–33.

[70] According to the well-informed J. G. Vockerodt, the charges levelled against Sofia were widely believed by the musketeers, of whom many declared for Peter in the hope of rewards: Herrmann, *Russland*, pp. 25–6.   [71] Corvisier, *Armées et sociétés*, pp. 191–2.

[72] Foy de la Neuville, who visited Russia during Sofia's regency, calls them 'un espèce de milice comme les janissaires de la Porte': *Relation*, p. 39; cf. Korb, *Dnevnik*, p. 245. Hellie, *Enserfment*, p. 348, offers some other references.

[73] Golikova, *Astr. vosstaniye*, p. 12; cf. Buganov, in Shunkov *et al.* (eds.), *Voprosy*, p. 46.

The *strel'tsy* rising lived on in the popular imagination. A folk song portrays a Cossack ataman riding to Moscow and asking the tsar why he was angry with his troops, whose loyalty and bravery were beyond all doubt; dissatisfied with the explanation he is given, he hurries back to 'the *strel'tsy* army' to warn it that a massacre is impending—or, in another version, that they have been pardoned and rewarded.[74] The motifs of such songs were traditional, and the ataman here represents a popular hero in the most general sense. Nevertheless this legend may reflect awareness of an important historical fact: that in their rebellions the musketeers were *not* actively supported by the Cossacks of the southern river systems, who had manifested violent antipathy to the Muscovite social order on so many other occasions.

One of the early Romanov tsars' most signal successes was to win over elements from the autonomous Cossack communities and to integrate them into their own forces. They were called 'town Cossacks' (*kazaki gorodovye*), a term which indicates, not that they were urbanized, but that they performed service 'from the [provincial] towns' in much the same way as most privileged servitors did. During the sixteenth century the practice developed of engaging bodies of Cossack troops from the Don and Volga, and less frequently from the Dnieper (who were known to the Muscovites as 'Cherkassians'), to fight various foreign enemies. These auxiliaries were led by their own elected chiefs (*atamany*) and were apparently free to return home when their services were no longer required. Some of them chose not to do so; others entered Muscovy as individuals (or in small bands) and enrolled in the tsar's forces. Although these men were in most cases former serfs or slaves, they were not returned to servitude, for it was considered that claims against them by their former owners had lost validity once the runaway had spent two years beyond the southern border: 'Don air makes one free', ran the popular saying.[75] (No doubt there were breaches of this principle in practice, especially after the legal establishment of serfdom.) On entering the tsar's service these Cossacks were normally exempted from taxes and given land allotments which they, like the *strel'tsy*, held collectively. A document of 1594 instructed the commander of Voronezh to ensure that their huts were built in a row so that their unit chief (*sotnik*) had them under surveillance and control.[76]

Apart from the Cossacks in Siberia, who cannot be considered here, such settlements were most frequently located in the new towns along the southern border. They seem to have been established in the main during the 1590s, when the state was anxious to win back runaways who had fled to the Cossack lands during or after the *oprichnina*. Their new experience in the martial arts could be put to good use in this vulnerable region. Initially service Cossacks acted as scouts and guides; later on, once they became more settled, they performed military duties of the most varied kind, as did the musketeers. Here, too, a

---

[74] Alekseyeva and Yemelyanov (eds.), *Ist. pesni*, p. 36.
[75] Zagorodsky, *Belgorodskaya cherta*, p. 30.
[76] Anpilogov (ed.), *Novye dokumenty*, pp. 381–2.

high risk was involved: at moments of social tension these men might be tempted to flee back to the Don or Dnieper, much as they or their ancestors had done earlier, or else to turn their weapons against their commanders and make common cause with the oppressed and with invading parties of autonomous Cossacks. This became a general phenomenon during the Time of Troubles. To avoid a repetition of this the authorities tried to avoid concentrating a large number of service Cossacks in any one place. In garrisons on the southern frontier they were usually intermingled with musketeers, soldiers (*soldaty*) etc., and within the Cossack detachments local ex-civilian recruits, who were likely to be more pliable, were added to the original nucleus. A recent student of the Belgorod region in the seventeenth century reckons that no less than three-quarters of all non-privileged servitors were former peasants, townsmen, or vagrants rather than hereditary members of the caste.[77]

By this time the service Cossacks had as a rule lost the right to elect their own atamans. Instead their chiefs were appointed from above, by the Razryad through the intermediacy of the local voivode. They belonged to the privileged servitor class, as did the officers in charge of musketeer units. Simultaneously a natural process of social promotion was at work within the Cossack contingents: atamans, *sotniki,* and others in command positions, who received more generous land allotments than most of their men, were able to augment their holdings and to rise up into the ranks of the provincial gentry, whose military duties and life-style differed but little from their own. Some Cossacks even owned serfs, although this privilege was taken from them towards the mid-seventeenth century. Initially the land allotment norm (*oklad*) for Cossack chiefs was much smaller than that of a privileged servitor: in 1577 it was fixed at 50 quarters, whereas the lowest gentry servitor's entitlement was 100 quarters, and their monetary compensation was a mere one rouble a year.[78] However, in 1589 atamans at Putivl′ received 11 to 15 roubles and their men 3 to 6 roubles; perhaps this was in lieu of remuneration in land, about which nothing is said in the source.[79] By the seventeenth century differentiated scales were in use. In 1630 we hear of 'landed atamans' at Sevsk whose norm ranged from 100 to 200 quarters, according to their grade in the service, and their cash payment from 5 to 7 roubles.[80] Other tables from the 1650s specify fairly similar scales for these senior men, who were thus treated like the humblest provincial gentry, whereas an ordinary Cossack received 16 quarters and 6 roubles (plus a generous allowance of cereals).[81] When considering such figures it has to be remembered that their actual landholdings will have been smaller than their entitlements. At the little border town of Bolkhov in 1646 Cossacks were supposed to have 10 quarters of land and musketeers 7. The

---

[77] Vazhinsky, *Zemlevladeniye,* p. 58.
[78] *AMG* i. 23.
[79] Anpilogov (ed.), *Novye dokumenty,* pp. 128–30; cf. p. 329 and Belyayev, *O storozhevoy . . . sluzhbe,* p. 32 (3–4 roubles in 1594).
[80] *AMG* i. 285.
[81] *DAI* iii. 36; *PSZ* i. 86, 273; Brix, *Geschichte,* p. 486.

exiguousness of their plots will have stimulated holders to augment them by bringing more of the still largely virgin steppe or semi-steppe under the plough: apart from the prospect of economic gain, this would confer improved standing in the service hierarchy. Cossacks were known as rapacious looters, but they will have had even less capital, and probably less leisure, then their petty gentry neighbours in this region.

Speaking very generally, the economic level of lower-grade servitors corresponded to their status in the military hierarchy; but much also depended on chance factors. Ordinary Cossacks often could not afford a horse and had to undergo the humiliation of serving on foot. Those who lost status in this way were obvious candidates for assignment to the new-model forces. Some 20,000 service Cossacks are said to have been transferred in this way, mainly in the crisis years of the early 1650s,[82] but this number seems high: the total for the group in 1651 was around 21,000, but in 1680/1 only 7,000.[83] Enumerated separately in the statistics are the 'Cherkassians' (Ukrainians), who accounted for 2,371 in 1651, 2,966 in 1662/3, but no less than 14,865 in 1680/1.[84] This rise reflects the ambiguous outcome of the war with Poland–Lithuania for the Ukraine. Many Cossacks fled eastwards from the quasi-autonomous territory of the Hetmanate, where social and political conditions were very disturbed, and took service with the tsar. The hetman's forces, which were not under Moscow's control, numbered about 50,000. Thus the service Cossacks formed a foreign body in relation to the general mass of autonomous warriors on the Don and Dnieper. By the time of Peter I's accession the state had won a foothold which could be gradually enlarged during the eighteenth century until it encompassed *all* the Cossacks: a development that not only greatly improved the empire's security in the south but also brought it a valuable addition of cavalry strength.

Two other categories within Muscovy's traditional forces should not be overlooked: the artillerymen (*pushkari*) and the native troops. The former are thought to have comprised about 3,500 men at the end of the sixteenth century and double that number one hundred years later.[85] In the campaign of 1679 the Russian army disposed of 400 cannon, a considerable quantity for that time; already at the siege of Kazan´ (1552) Ivan IV is said to have had 150 heavy or medium-sized artillery pieces.[86] The Tsar´-pushka admired today by countless tourists to Moscow's Kremlin, cast by Andrey Chokhov in 1585/6 and weighing 40 tons, testifies not only to the skill of Russian ironmasters but also to the early tsars' appreciation of the role that artillery could play in building up the country's armed might. The origins of this development date from the

[82] Hellie, *Enserfment*, p. 209, citing *AMG* ii. 1103, 1130; iii. 152.

[83] Chernov, *Voor. sily*, pp. 165, 167. A list for 1662 (Stashevsky, 'Smeta', p. 60) gives 2,329 but it is incomplete, for about 3,500 others were in the Belgorod area alone (ibid., pp. 64–7).

[84] Chernov, *Voor. sily*, pp. 167, 189.

[85] Yepifanov, *Ocherki iz ist. armii*, p. 15; id., 'Voysko', p. 358. In 1651 they numbered 4,245: Chernov, *Voor. sily*, p. 167; cf. Hellie, *Enserfment*, p. 269.

[86] Yepifanov, *Ocherki iz ist. armii*, p. 15; Nasonov *et al.* (eds.), *Ocherki*, p. 451.

1470s, when Aristotele Fieravanti (1415/20–86), the Italian architect and military engineer, came to Moscow; best known for his work on the Kremlin, he also participated personally in Ivan III's campaigns against Novgorod, Tver, and Kazan.[87]

The heavy artillery pieces of the period were difficult to transport—as we have seen, hordes of labourers were drafted for the purpose—and of little use in the field. They were mainly kept in various fortresses, and it was here that the *pushkari* went about their duties. Like the musketeers and service Cossacks they formed a closed corps, in the sense that new recruits were normally drawn from the families of those already enrolled and that they lived in their own settlements (*slobody*). There were even self-contained sub-categories of artillerymen: *zatinshchiki*, who looked after smaller-calibre weapons, and *vorotniki*, or fortress gate-guards. The existence of such social barriers, together with the possession of specialized knowledge, contributed to the development of a certain *esprit de corps*. It may also have mattered that 'whereas the *strel'tsy* and service Cossacks were recruited from various social groups, the artillerymen . . . consisted almost exclusively of townspeople, especially artisans'[88]—although one should guard against anachronistic reasoning here. Guild associations were weak in Russian towns, and the ties formed among artillerymen will have been of a service rather than a professional character. Professionalization was also hindered by the limited facilities for training, the lack of mathematical knowledge, and the diversity of calibres among the weapons which artillerymen were required to maintain and operate.

It is not clear whether social promotion was easier in this branch of service than in others. The officers, as one would expect, held noble rank; some of them deserve to be called specialists, since they served for considerable lengths of time in the Artillery Office (Pushkarskiy *prikaz*), the relevant government department, or in the field as 'commanders of artillery' (*voyevody u naryada*).[89] The master founders were as a rule civilians.

Artillerymen received a cash payment in addition to their small land allotments. These sums increased from about 2 roubles annually in Ivan IV's reign to 5 roubles (plus an allowance of uniform cloth) in that of Alexis[90]— which suggests that in official circles their work continued to be appreciated. They were less likely to be transferred to the new-model forces, which contained no counterpart to their branch as it did for the infantry and cavalry. This organizational continuity lasted into the Imperial era: although artillerymen ceased to form a distinct caste after Peter's reforms, the Artillery Department

[87] Alef, 'Musc. Mil. Reforms', pp. 79–80; Hellie, *Enserfment*, p. 154. Some nationalist historians have advanced large claims for Russia's technical proficiency *vis-à-vis* Western countries in this period, but, as T. Esper observes, 'the arguments supporting such claims . . . are not cogent, if only because such superior weapons would have . . . been copied in other countries': 'Mil. Self-sufficiency', p. 196.

[88] Yepifanov, 'Voysko', p. 357.

[89] Ibid., p. 356.

[90] Hellie, *Enserfment*, p. 157.

remained administratively independent of the War College, much as the Pushkarskiy *prikaz* had coexisted with the Razryad.

The men in all the categories so far discussed were predominantly of Great Russian ethnic stock, with the important exception of the 'Cherkassians' (Ukrainian Cossacks). Western European immigrants served exclusively in the new-model forces, once these had been established; there were few of them in the sixteenth century. Oriental natives, however, played a more significant role in the Muscovite armed forces at this time and contributed a colourful touch to the military scene. The main peoples in question were Tatars from the various formerly independent khanates (Kazan´, Astrakhan´, Sibir´), together with elements from the still independent Nogays and Crimeans, and natives of the middle-Volga region: Mordvians, Mari (Cheremis), and Chuvash; less important were Bashkirs from the Urals approaches, Kabardians from the Caucasus, and Siberian tribesmen. Religious rather than ethnic criteria shaped Russian attitudes towards their eastern neighbours. The tsars did not allow anti-Islamic prejudice to interfere with practical arrangements to improve military security; nor did they promote a sustained missionary effort by the Church. In the early seventeenth century only about one-sixth of Tatar servitors in the Kazan´ region were categorized as 'newly baptized' (*novokreshchentsy*).[91] However, from Ivan III's reign onwards the relatively few dignitaries who took the drastic step of forsaking Islam were handsomely rewarded. The most successful was Sain-Bulat, who for a brief term (1575–6) even occupied Ivan IV's throne as Grand Prince Simeon Bekbulatovich. Many such individuals married Russian noblewomen and their progeny became assimilated into the élite. The Godunov family was one of several that proudly (but probably erroneously) traced its ancestry back to a Tatar notable who had accepted the Muscovite ruler's faith along with his suzerainty.

Whether or not they lost their religious and cultural identity, those Tatars and other orientals who took service with the tsar preserved the social relationships that prevailed within their own milieu. Their chiefs (*tsarevichi*) and princes (*murzy*) brought with them a retinue of dependants who comprised a self-contained military force. In this regard they seem to have been allowed greater freedom than the Russian apanage princes. Only gradually did these forces come under the control of the central bureaucracy: administratively they were subordinate to the Kazan´ chancellery, which had broad territorial responsibilities, rather than to the Razryad. Sometimes, to be sure, the service registers mention officials with Slavic names as commanders of such units, whose functions included political surveillance.[92] But during the sixteenth century Tatar noblemen held many senior military posts. When Ivan IV invaded Livonia in 1558 his army's vanguard was led by Tsarevich Tokhtamysh, who was of Crimean Tatar origin, and the right wing by Tsarevich Kaibulla (or

---

[91] Kappeler, *Russlands erste Nationalitäten*, p. 233; for conferment of rank on converts: Stepanov, 'K voprosu', p. 61.

[92] *RK*, pp. 143, 147, 205; Stepanov, 'K voprosu', p. 62.

Abdullah), who came from Astrakhan.[93] Kaibulla's military career from 1554 to 1565 is well documented: his assignments took him from 'the Swedish lands' in 1555/6 to Livonia, Polotsk, and several other fortified towns along the western and southern borders.[94]

At one point during the Livonian War no less than 6,500 oriental troops descended 'upon the German and Lithuanian land' as part of a cavalry force reputedly 28,000 strong, commanded by the tsar in person.[95] The psychological impact of their depredations was considerable. A contemporary German writer asserted (already in 1561) that they 'behaved tyrannically, according to their customary inhuman cruelty' and even accused them of engaging in cannibalism.[96] Such atrocities, in which the Russian troops cheerfully participated, helped to lead central-European publicists to identify the Muscovites with the Turks as barbarians and natural foes of Christendom.

Several Western observers offered exaggerated estimates of the number of orientals in Russian service. Jakob Ulfeldt, a Danish traveller, claimed to have seen 25,000 Tatars moving towards Livonia in 1578.[97] According to Sir Jerome Horsey 30,000 Tatars took part in the massacres in Novgorod eight years earlier, during the *oprichnina*, and such troops comprised the majority of the forces on the country's western border.[98] Jacques Margeret, the French captain who served in Muscovy during the 1590s, put at 27–28,000 the number of oriental cavalrymen available for action.[99] The real figure was probably only one-third as great, but it cannot as yet be determined accurately.

During the Time of Troubles the subject peoples of the Volga valley rose up and entered the fray. Most of them took the side of the Cossacks and other supporters of the Second Pretender;[100] some, however, backed the beleaguered Tsar Shuysky and later joined the national levy of 1612.[101] The insurgents' aim was to end Russian rule over their territories. Later in the seventeenth century, once the risings had been suppressed and colonization resumed, the conflict acquired more of a social character. The natives who joined the rebel forces of Sten'ka Razin sought to preserve their lands and to reduce the burden of tribute (*yasak*)—or, in the case of those who were servitors, to escape the additional duties now imposed on them.[102] Social differentiation was increasing. At the summit stood a small group of wealthier (and more russified) landowners; below them was a mass of petty-gentry servitors, most of whom had few if any dependants; then there were lower-grade (*po priboru*) men who were

[93] Vernadsky, *Tsardom of Moscow*, i. 94.
[94] *RK*, pp. 150–226 passim s.v. Kaybul.
[95] *DRV* xiv. 351–2; cf. Yepifanov, 'Voysko', p. 343.
[96] Kappeler, 'Deutsche Russlandschriften', p. 14.
[97] Klyuchevsky, *Skazaniya inostrantsev*, p. 94.
[98] Berry and Crummey (eds.), *Rude and Barbarous Kingdom*, pp. 269, 286 (Horsey is not a reliable witness).
[99] Margeret, *L'Estat*, p. 26.
[100] Kappeler, 'Rolle der Nichtrussen', pp. 254–5.
[101] *AI* ii. 145; Vernadsky, *Tsardom of Moscow*, i. 268.
[102] Kappeler, 'Geschichte der Völker', pp. 261–2.

often reclassified as musketeers or serving Cossacks; finally, the bulk of the population consisted of *yasak*-paying peasants and others whose military obligations were only sporadic.[103]

Those with estates normally had to provide their own horses, equipment, and supplies. Only men unable to support themselves received pay or allowances in kind, in which case they were referred to as *kormovye* (literally, 'with food'). The native aristocrats had the best of both worlds, for they retained rights in their ancestral territories but were also initially granted land in Muscovy. As a rule these properties were located along the Oka river line, so that their holders could readily perform their military and diplomatic duties: they were vital in intelligence work.[104] The little town of Kasimov on the Oka, south-east of Moscow, became a kind of Tatar feudal enclave within the Muscovite state. It was named after its first beneficiary, Tsarevich Kasim of Kazan´, who backed Vasiliy II against his rival in the civil war of the 1440s. Its rulers remained Muslim until the 1650s. It was not until 1682, after the death of the last of them, Said-Burgan, that the 'tsardom' (as it was called) was abolished, as part of the military reforms associated with Golitsyn and his group. The declining role of the oriental troops during the seventeenth century[105] is due to two factors: it was evidently thought impolitic to strain their loyalty by committing them extensively to wars fought against Crimean Tatars and Turks; and the tsars now disposed of other units with a higher level of military efficiency. These were the so-called new-model forces, to which we may now turn.

[103] Id., *Russlands erste Nationalitäten*, pp. 213–16, 220; for their service as Cossacks: *DAI* viii. 52 (1679).
[104] Kargalov, *Na stepnoy granitse*, p. 83.
[105] A mere 1,667 native troops were committed to the war with Poland, out of a force numbering 18,700: Chernov, *Voor. sily*, p. 169; id., 'Voor. sily', p. 441; Hellie, *Enserfment*, pp. 270–2.

4

THE NEW-MODEL ARMY AND SOME QUESTIONS OF COST

THE presence of Polish soldiers in Moscow's sacred Kremlin in 1611–12 was humiliating evidence that the traditional armed forces were inadequate for the country's defence. Already under Ivan IV these troops had failed to measure up to the technically more proficient armies of neighbouring European powers. In the seventeenth century the balance tilted further to Moscow's disadvantage. Yet the idea of reform made slow headway, at least until the 1650s. Under Michael Fyodorovich (1613–45), the first Romanov ruler, caution was the watchword. The country's sorry economic condition did not permit any major innovations and the prime concern of its unimaginative leaders was to restore the system as it had existed before the Troubles. Even by mid-century, when the situation had improved, the government shied away from comprehensive measures—partly from inertia, partly for fear of trespassing on vested interests, and partly because a thorough-going 'Westernization' of the military establishment seemed to threaten Orthodox cultural values. Thus the gentry levy, the *strel'tsy* and other traditional forces continued to coexist alongside the more modern 'new-model' or 'new-formation' infantry and cavalry regiments (*polki novogo stroya*) that had since come into being.

This term needs some explanation. Earlier historians generally referred to them as 'regiments of foreign (*inozemskogo*) formation'. This was actually an eighteenth-century neologism[1] and has the defect, to which present-day Soviet writers are particularly sensitive, of emphasizing the role played in these new units by senior officers of foreign extraction, drawn mainly from northern and western Europe. Although these forces were indeed structured on contemporary Western lines, and their nomenclature was German, they need not for that reason be regarded as foreign. The rank-and-file soldiers were of course overwhelmingly Russian, and by the 1660s this was true of the junior officers as well; some Russians were also appointed to positions of command.[2] Moreover, the reform was not just a matter of replacing amateurs by professionals, trained personnel who could teach the men how to handle flintlock muskets and to perform the complicated manœuvres required by the new

---

[1] Kalinychev, *Pravovye voprosy*, p. 44; cf. Hellie, *Enserfment*, p. 350.

[2] Chernov, *Voor. sily*, p. 150. By 1696 they numbered 954, of whom 244 held the rank of lieutenant-colonel or above: Myshlayevsky, 'Ofitserskiy vopros', p. 295. The role of foreign military personnel in Russia cannot be considered in detail here.

linear tactics, which called for strict disciplinary constraints. It also meant substituting for part-time forces regular troops paid and supplied by the central authorities. To be sure, the element of professionalism in the new-model regiments was slight, measured by the criteria of later generations; moreover, the government's lack of resources obliged it to quarter some of these troops in military settlements where they were required to provide for themselves much as the traditional forces did. In this way the distinction between the new and old formations was less marked in practice than it was in principle; nevertheless the distinction was essential since sooner or later the new forces were bound to supersede the old as military technology developed and the power of the state increased.

The reform began somewhat inauspiciously in 1631 when the government of Patriarch Filaret, preparing for war with Poland-Lithuania, took steps to hire a substantial force of western European mercenaries. Although several thousand men were recruited, notably by the Scot Alexander Lesly, their performance in combat was uneven and after the war most of the survivors were discharged. A few hundred, among them Lesly himself, chose to stay in Russia, where they served principally as officers in regiments which, unlike the mercenaries, were drawn from the native Russian population. The infantrymen were known as soldiers (*soldaty*, Ger.: *Soldaten*) and the cavalrymen bore the generic designation of *reytary* (Ger.: *Reiter*); they included lancers (*kopeyshchiki*, from *kop´ye* = lance), while dragoons (*draguny*), who fought on foot as well as on horseback, were considered a separate sub-category.[3] The use of German terms, also for officers' ranks (for example, *kapitan* for captain), indicated the authorities' desire to emulate foreign models closely, although they made some adaptations to suit Russian conditions. During the Smolensk War ten new-model regiments, 17,400 strong, were in service, at which time they comprised about half the total active army. Along with the mercenary units, they were disbanded when peace returned, probably on grounds of expense, but within a few years fresh infantry and dragoon units were formed to fight on the southern border; the *reytary* reappeared later, in the 1650s.[4] Characteristically, an élite element came into being within the new-model forces, just as it did among the musketeers. It consisted of two 'select regiments' (*vybornye polki*) which by the 1670s had between them no less than 10,000 men. One of them, named after Butyrki, then a Moscow suburb where it was quartered, dated its formation from 1642 and was later accounted the most senior regiment in the Imperial army.[5]

The creation of the new-model forces greatly increased the burden of military service for the underprivileged elements of the population. In the

---

[3] Chernov, *Voor. sily*, pp. 139–49; id., 'Voor. sily', pp. 442–4; Hellie, *Enserfment*, pp. 170–2.
[4] Hellie, *Enserfment*, p. 198.
[5] Brix, *Geschichte*, pp. 298–302, 402; Myshlayevsky, 'Ofitserskiy vopros', p. 56; Bobrovsky, 'K kharakteristike', p. 178. The normal regimental size was about 2,000 men: Stashevsky, 'Smeta', pp. 62–4.

sixteenth century men had been recruited according to the amount of land held by owners in various categories, the norm being one for each 100 quarters. This as we have seen left their masters considerable discretion to determine how many of their dependents to send, since the Razryad officials were concerned primarily with the service they themselves rendered personally, and not with that of their untrained followers. In the seventeenth century a new criterion was introduced: the number of peasant homesteads which an owner held, as ascertained by official census-takers. The changeover was gradual: in 1630/1 one recruit had to be furnished for each ten households, while two years later some men were still being taken according to the old system (one per 300 quarters).[6] In 1646 the norm was put at one in twenty, and that year in a symbolic move Tsar Alexis ordered some 30 courtiers who failed to provide such recruits to be fined 20 roubles for each absentee.[7] By 1651 a Swedish agent, Philip von Krusenstjern, was reporting that boys of 14 and 15 were being taken as soldiers; in his view this 'makes it appear that there will be something of a revolt should there be a single misfortune, a severe blow in any one place'.[8] He was perhaps a little over-sanguine, but in 1653 trouble did indeed occur in Kozlov where some two thousand men resisted enrolment as *soldaty*; their alleged ringleader, a provincial gentryman named M. Amosov, was sentenced to be taken round all the local settlements and knouted in each.[9] The affair was, however, of purely local significance.

By the 1660s the authorities were conducting general levies over the whole country except in exposed border areas and the eastern territories. 'Where a father has two or three sons', wrote Grigoriy Kotoshikhin, 'or where three brothers live together . . . one of the three is taken; where there are four sons or brothers, two are taken; and from whomever is found to have more . . . more are taken.'[10] In Novgorod the levy of 1658, of one man per ten households, netted 18,000 recruits, as well as over 10,000 roubles in commutation fees collected from hamlets with less than ten households.[11] In the Perm' area in 1662 the draft took one man in five, although they were used only for local defence purposes.[12] Normally the figure was between one in 20 and one in 50. Three such levies by the Foreigners' chancellery in 1659–61 yielded over 52,000 recruits and 31,000 roubles in cash; several thousand more were taken by other central agencies.[13] It is thought that in all over 100,000 men were taken as recruits during the Thirteen Years War.[14] The authorities required the men to be of a certain age (in one documented case, between 25 and 40) and

[6] *AAE* iii. 222, 225; Brix, *Geschichte*, p. 387.
[7] *AMG* ii. 267; Hellie, *Enserfment*, p. 189.
[8] Forsten, 'Dipl. snosheniya', cccxvi. 329.
[9] Zagorodsky, *Belgorodskaya cherta*, p. 260.
[10] Kotoshikhin, *O Rossii*, p. 133.
[11] *AMG* iii. 504, cited by Hellie, *Enserfment*, p. 195; cf. *PSZ* i. 208.
[12] *PSZ* i. 324; cf. Brix, *Geschichte*, p. 387; Sh., 'Dvoryanstvo', p. 541.
[13] *AAE* iv. 84; *DAI* viii. 40; Lappo-Danilevsky, *Organizatsiya*, p. 392.
[14] Chernov, *Voor. sily*, p. 145; Kalinychev, *Pravovye voprosy*, p. 71.

physically fit; they were to bring picks, spades, axes, and as a rule firearms as well.[15]

Casualty rates among these men were high. 'Many recruits have died and others have fled', a leading general, A. N. Trubetskoy, reported laconically in 1655.[16] Kotoshikhin noted that 'during the course of the Polish war many cavalrymen and soldiers have died of hunger [and] in battles and assaults, [after] laying siege for lengthy periods to various towns'.[17] This was a new development, for hitherto recruits' duties had been mainly of a non-combatant character, such as constructing defence works. Moreover, they had previously served for a short term, usually for the duration of a single seasonal campaign, and then returned to civilian life; but from the mid-seventeenth century onwards, so it appears, they remained under arms for life, much as recruits would do in the eighteenth century. It is not surprising that many of them deserted or turned to banditry. In Thomas Daliel's regiment, stationed at Polotsk, 148 infantrymen deserted during a thirteen-month period in 1659–60 and could not be traced. This was about 10 per cent of his unit's strength. 'The remaining *soldaty* here', wrote the commander, I. B. Repnin, to the tsar, 'envy those fugitives, [in] that they are living in their own homes, and for that reason many are fleeing your service.'[18] Escapees usually returned to their homes, where they concealed themselves with the aid of fellow-villagers and landlords. An idea of the scale of desertions is provided by returns from Kiev for the year 1681/2: out of 3,970 men in the local garrison, 207 (5 per cent) deserted while 116 (3 per cent) died.[19] One year earlier, as part of the reform programme, an amnesty was granted to deserters. Landlords who had sheltered them were allowed to keep them, but if they took men in after the deadline had passed, and were denounced for doing so, they were to forfeit them and two of their 'best' peasants as well, and to pay a five-rouble fine; the men in question were assigned to the southern border.[20] Normally deserters, if caught, were beaten with the knout and returned to service; if they could not be found, their community had to supply substitutes and provide larger sureties for them; in other cases deserters' wives and children were seized as hostages until they gave themselves up.[21] More active forms of opposition were hindered by the tighter disciplinary controls to which men in the new-model forces were subjected. However, in 1661 soldiers in the regiments of W. Bruce and N. von Galen, stationed near Orsha, assaulted their officers and wounded both unit commanders, and *soldaty* were prominent in the 1662 Moscow troubles.[22]

---

[15] *AAE* iii. 222; iv. 84; *DAI* iv. 26; Lappo-Danilevsky, *Organizatsiya*, p. 392.
[16] *AMG* ii. 736.
[17] Kotoshikhin, *O Rossii*, pp. 133–4.
[18] *AMG* iii. 107; cf. [Khilkov] *Sbornik*, 86 (1668).
[19] *DAI* x. 33(iv).
[20] *DAI* viii. 90(ii).
[21] *DAI* viii. 42; Kotoshikhin, *O Rossii*, p. 132; Zagorodsky, *Belgorodskaya cherta*, p. 251.
[22] Bobrovsky, 'K kharakteristike', p. 187.

Soldiers and cavalrymen received an annual payment in cash and grain, on a scale which in theory at least was quite generous: 7¼ to 11 roubles a year.[23] The major expense at this time was officers' pay: foreigners' entitlements were generally about 60 per cent higher than natives', and their annual wage bill came to 210,000 roubles, as against 28,800 roubles for their Russian counterparts.[24] By comparison, the other ranks in 75 regiments of infantry and cavalry cost between 556,000 and 800,000 roubles, according to the pay rate.[25] It was to meet this expense and other growing military costs that the government debased the currency—an expedient which sparked the riots of 1662.

Another device to save money was to recruit male adults in entire communities. The idea was that they would earn their own keep while carrying out routine military duties, and that they would perform these more effectively since they would be defending their own families and property. Two areas were selected for the experiment, which in many respects anticipates the better-known scheme for military settlements introduced by Alexander I (see ch. 12). One was on 'black' land close to the north-western border, in Olonets and Staraya Rusa districts, where from 1649 onwards some 9,000 men were ascribed to service, mainly as infantrymen. From one to three men were taken per household, according to its size, but all their relatives and other residents were registered by name, evidently so that they could serve as replacements.[26] Half of them were stationed in frontier blockhouses, while the other half formed a reserve in the rear. Those on active duty were exempted from taxes, which the reservists had to pay. They were also required to drill, but this obligation had to be reduced (from six times to once or twice a week) since it interfered too much with agricultural work. The military settlements formed a separate administrative district under a commander who had full authority in judicial matters, even those in which neighbouring civilians were involved—whereas elsewhere such cases would be dealt with by elected civilian *guba* elders.[27] The regimental chiefs and many of the officers were foreigners, which doubtless added to the peasants' dislike of the unfamiliar obligations imposed upon them, and they responded in the traditional manner by deserting *en masse*. Six hundred and ninety fugitives were located in various parts of the country.[28] The experiment was a failure, not least because the authorities lost sight of its original rationale and sent the men to fight far away from their homes. In these campaigns they suffered heavy losses and their farms fell into ruin, some being destroyed by Swedish raiding parties. In 1658 a number of these unfor-

[23] Hellie, *Enserfment*, p. 196, citing Stashevsky, 'Smeta', pt. 1, p. 1. There were two rates, of 4 and 6 *den'gi* per day, the former equivalent to 6 roubles a year. This is what soldiers in Sheremetev's army received in 1660: *AMG* iii. 65; cf. ii. 98.

[24] Stashevsky, 'Smeta', pp. 55–6 (our recalculation); the numbers were 1,650 and 638 respectively.

[25] Ibid., pp. 58–9.

[26] *DAI* iii. 65; Pommerening to Queen Christina, Feb.–Mar. 1649, in Yakubov, *Rossiya i Shvetsiya*, pp. 442, 444.

[27] In practice, by ex-military men. See above, p. 41.

[28] *DAI* iii. 82.

tunates petitioned the tsar: 'We, thy slaves, served thee, Great Sovereign, each year in the Lithuanian and German towns and on campaigns without cease, in summer and winter; and while on thy service we became yet more impoverished and in our villages, Sovereign, the arable was not ploughed and our houses emptied, and many of our [kinsmen] live by begging.'[29]

A few years earlier another settlement project had been launched in certain areas along the southern and south-western border. The soldiers concerned here were cavalry rather than infantry. The first mention of such settlers occurs in 1646, in Vyaz'ma district, but the main concentrations were to be found in the strategic Belgorod and Sevsk regions. In 1647 the inhabitants of several villages in Komaritsky sub-district, who had hitherto belonged to the prominent military commander (and boyar) A. N. Trubetskoy, were enlisted as dragoons. In return they were allowed to keep the land they worked and were freed from certain taxes, but received no pay and had to provide their own horses.[30] The Komaritsky dragoons, a force 5,500 strong, seem to have coped more easily with their dual task of farming and soldiering simultaneously—no doubt because they had more land of better quality than the hard-pressed residents of the northern forests. However, the same mistakes were made. In the 1670s they were committed to the campaigns in the Ukraine; their properties were attacked by Tatars and the survivors eventually had to be reclassified as *soldaty*.[31] This occurred about 1680, so that two generations of men will have gone through this experience, exchanging the plough for the sword as and when authority dictated. The failure of these experiments meant that most soldiers in the new-model forces, not being endowed with land, were more clearly dissociated from their civilian environment than the musketeers. Probably fewer of them raised families, so that a smaller proportion of recruits came from within the corps, as distinct from the general population, and probably they suffered proportionately heavier casualties. Both these points admittedly need substantiation.

The new army was not comprised solely of peasant conscripts. It included a good many individuals of provincial gentry background, some of whom volunteered while others were enrolled by force. The latter practice speaks volumes about the real value of social privilege in the Muscovite tsardom and should demolish the misconception that the *dvoryanstvo* constituted a 'ruling class'.

In 1630 two thousand landless gentry servitors were ordered to present themselves in Moscow for enrolment and training as *soldaty*. Only a handful responded.[32] They were promised five roubles a year and a daily allowance, but this incentive was insufficient to overcome their distrust of the 'German colonels' who, the decree specified, were to instruct them; in any case they

[29] *DAI* iv. 146 (p. 394).
[30] Zagorodsky, *Belgorodskaya cherta*, p. 132.
[31] *DAI* iii. 21; ix. 106; Brix, *Geschichte*, pp. 284–5; Chernov, 'Voor. sily', pp. 445–6.
[32] *AMG* i. 267; Myshlayevsky, 'Ofitserskiy vopros', p. 51; Hellie, *Enserfment*, p. 171.

looked on service in the infantry as demeaning. When cavalry units were set up two years later they joined more readily. It is not clear from the sources how much coercion was applied at this juncture, but by 1638 the government had to repeat its first order in a sterner tone; the target figure was doubled, to four thousand.[33] The Ryazan' gentry petitioned for exemption from such onerous duties as constructing the fortified line or long-distance patrolling for intelligence purposes.[34] It is probably in this context that one should set the desperate petition by hungry servitors quoted on p. 49.

Those who were indeed destitute were natural candidates for conscription once the need for their services became urgent. This moment came on the eve of the Thirteen Years War, when privileged servitors not yet enrolled in the traditional levy were assigned to the new infantry regiments, on pain of losing their gentry status and becoming tillers of the soil (*zemlepashtsy*).[35] The men taken were to be 'of good repute and physically strong, desirous to serve and train as soldiers'.[36] The ascription of gentrymen to cavalry units soon became a regular practice: in 1660 1,480 'novices' were sent from the lower Volga region to join 1,726 of their comrades already in the ranks.[37] In 1678, as part of the general reorganization attempted at this time, the government excluded all noblemen who held less than 24 peasant homesteads from the traditional levy and assigned them to the new-model forces—as cavalrymen if they could afford to serve in that way, as infantrymen if they could not.[38] In this manner those who did have some property, and not just those who were landless, were brought within the scope of the conscription policy. They were to draw 24 roubles a year, less one rouble for every homestead they owned. Graduated payments of this kind are also mentioned by Kotoshikhin, writing in the 1660s.[39]

Once enrolled in the new regiments, privileged servitors enjoyed better opportunities, thanks to their social origin, to achieve officer rank, but there were not nearly enough places to satisfy all aspirants; the majority will have had to remain ordinary soldiers. The new-model forces seem to have served primarily as an avenue of downward rather than upward social mobility. Promotion to senior positions was difficult because of the large number of foreigners, whose qualifications were (or were deemed to be) superior; their higher salaries doubtless generated ill feeling. In 1649 2,000 cavalrymen objected to the appointment of a Dutchman as their commander, stating that he was 'unbaptized' and that they had more practical experience themselves.[40] Such animosities were strongest among those from humbler circumstances, whose natural xenophobia was reinforced by the brutal discipline that foreign

---

[33] *AMG* i. 98, 112.　　　[34] *AMG* i. 113.　　　[35] *AI* iv. 70.
[36] Zagorodsky, *Belgorodskaya cherta*, p. 146.
[37] *AMG* iii. 170; cf. *PSZ* i. 280 (1659).
[38] *PSZ* ii. 744 (1678), §§ 7, 12; Sh., 'Dvoryanstvo', p. 206.
[39] Kotoshikhin, *O Rossii*, p. 131.
[40] Pommerening to Queen Christina, 22 Dec. 1649, in Yakubov, *Rossiya i Shvetsiya*, p. 459.

officers imposed; they will also have resented the tsar's heavy reliance on them in times of social crisis, such as the Moscow riots of 1648 or 1662 or the Razin revolt. On the other hand these forces did provide a livelihood, however modest, for thousands of gentrymen who would otherwise have found no employment at all. In 1662/3 at least one-third, and perhaps as many as two-thirds, of the members of this class were serving outside the traditional militia, now as we know in decline.[41] Their only expertise was in military pursuits, and so they needed an alternative to the levy if they were to maintain their social prominence. In this way the new-model forces afforded the gentry a role to which they could readily adapt and prevented them from having to redefine their self-image. For the general health of Russian society it would no doubt have been better if they had been encouraged to do so: to broaden their intellectual horizons, to diversify their interests, and to shake off the constraints of the militarized caste system that cost the country so dear—but this stage would not be reached for another century or so.

In trying to assess the human and economic impact of Muscovite Russia's military effort, one is hampered by the lack of reliable statistics on the size of the armed forces and of the population. The Razryad seldom computed totals of effectives, and the official data for the various elements are incomplete and sometimes contradictory; an added difficulty lies in trying to distinguish those who were actually mobilized for specific campaigns from those who remained in reserve, so to speak.

Foreign observers produced rough estimates based on hearsay, and were sometimes misled by boasting on the part of their official interlocutors. In 1525 D. Gerasimov, an envoy of Vasiliy III in Rome, claimed that his master habitually fielded over 150,000 cavalry, and this information was reproduced by three sixteenth-century Western writers. Five others preferred a figure of 200,000, and two visitors to Muscovy—I. Fabra (1526) and R. Chancellor (1553)—even spoke of 200,000 or 300,000 men of all arms.[42] Margeret reports that in 1598 some foreigners in Moscow believed the army to number half a million, but that he himself had doubts about such a high figure.[43] He was right to be sceptical. The actual figure at the end of the sixteenth century for what one might term the 'active army', excluding recruits, is probably around 110,000, of whom about four-fifths served in the gentry militia and one-fifth in the musketeers or kindred forces. Horsey and Fletcher both came close to this figure,[44] first established in 1891 by the pre-revolutionary historian S. M.

[41] Keep, 'Musc. Elite', p. 211.

[42] Zimin, *Reformy*, p. 446; Berry and Crummey, *Rude and Barbarous Kingdom*, p. 27. The generally reliable von Herberstein reported non-committally (*Moscovia*, p. 173) that the army was said to be 180,000 strong; Klyuchevsky (*Skazaniya*, p. 91) states that he did not give a total figure.

[43] Margeret, *L'Estat*, p. 8. The record for wild guessing must go to Clement Adams, who stated that the tsar never armed less than 900,000 men when preparing for a campaign. Klyuchevsky, *Skazaniya*, p. 90.

[44] Berry and Crummey, *Rude and Barbarous Kingdom*, pp. 180, 271.

Seredonin on the basis of Russian documents. R. Hellie accepts this estimate,[45] but some present-day Soviet writers offer higher figures: for A. A. Zimin the total was 'about 150,000' and for I. A. Korotkov 'up to 300,000'.[46] The former estimate can perhaps be justified if native troops and non-combatants are included.

What relationship did this military force bear to the total population? Estimates of the latter vary even more widely. The Soviet demographer B. Ts. Urlanis thought that the population grew by about 15 per cent in the first half of the sixteenth century, and by 5 per cent in the second. Allowing for territorial changes, he offered the following estimate (millions):

1500	5.8
1550	8.8
1600	11.3[47]

A recent Western student, however, believes that after the mid-sixteenth century the population actually declined and that it may not have recovered its 1550 level until the late seventeenth century.[48] Unfortunately he offers no estimate of the total. A. I. Kopanev, who has studied census registers, puts the figure for *circa* 1550 a little higher than Urlanis, at 9–10 million, and for the late sixteenth century at 11–12 million.[49] If one accepts this estimate, and allows for a balanced sex ratio, one arrives at a military participation ratio among males (all ages) of 2.0 per cent ('active army') and a theoretical maximum of 5.5 per cent. This is high, although of course one has to remember that for most of those involved their participation was episodic.

By the 1680s the armed forces were about twice as large as they had been a century earlier, that is to say at least 200,000 strong, of which a little more than half could be fielded against a foreign enemy. This estimate is based on an (incomplete) list compiled by the Razryad in 1681, which was a year of relative peace.[50] The total given in the source is 164,272 exclusive of 50,000 'Cherkassians' (that is, Ukrainians from the Hetmanate) available as auxiliaries. However, a count of the various items listed produces a figure of 190,938, made up as follows:

1	privileged servitors	19,466
2	dependants of above	21,830
3	musketeers	23,159

[45] Hellie, *Enserfment*, pp. 164, 267.

[46] Zimin, *Reformy*, p. 448; Myshlayevsky, 'Ofitserskiy vopros', p. 13, puts the levy *alone* (including retainers) at 300,000.

[47] Urlanis, *Rost* (1941), p. 190.

[48] Eaton, 'Censuses', p. 3.

[49] Kopanev, 'Naseleniye', p. 245. P. N. Milyukov thought that within the area of the eighteenth-century Russian empire there were 10–11½ million inhabitants in the mid-sixteenth century and 15 million at the end of the sixteenth century: *Essais*, p. 34. Cf. Hellie, *Enserfment*, p. 305.

[50] 'Rospis′ perechnevaya ratnym lyudem, kotorye vo [7]189 g. rospisany v polki po razryadam', in Ivanov, *Opisaniye*, pp. 71–92. The figure is accepted by Brix, *Geschichte*, p. 322;

4	service Cossacks	14,991
5	new-model forces: infantry	78,994
6	new-model forces: cavalry	32,498
		190,938

No figures are offered here for artillerymen, oriental natives, or recruits and dependants brought along by *provincial* gentrymen; those for musketeers and service Cossacks are clearly understated. On the other hand the totals given for all the Moscow *strel'tsy* units and some others are clearly formal 'establishment figures' which exaggerated actual strength. Hellie puts the total complement at 214,600, which is as good a guess as any.[51]

Turning to the individual components, Chernov's estimate of a mere 16,000 for the privileged servitors certainly understates their strength: the total number of *dvoryane* (both sexes, all ages) in 1678 has recently been put at circa 80,000[52] and in the heavily militarized Belgorod region in the late 1690s no less than 54,000 men were on the lists, mostly future 'single-householders'.[53] The *strel'tsy*, as we have seen, were around the 50,000 mark and the other traditional forces approximately 20–30,000; altogether we may say that they comprised about half the total men under arms. The new-model forces will have numbered about 80,000–90,000, two-thirds infantry and one-third cavalry.[54]

This represented a larger proportion of total population than at the end of the sixteenth century. Urlanis, in an educated guess, put this total at 11.5 million persons in 1678,[55] but was probably over-optimistic. The present-day demographer Vodarsky, whose work is more thorough, reckons that there were no more than 9 million individuals living in Muscovy when the census-takers came round in 1677/8.[56] The military participation ratio among males will thus have been of the order of 4.4 per cent.

Not too much should be made of these arithmetical exercises, in view of the scarcity and unreliability of the data. What is clear is that war-like activities absorbed a large proportion of the nation's effort, drained its slender human

Chernov, *Voor. sily*, p. 168; Hellie, *Enserfment*, pp. 226, 269; and by Milyukov, *Gos. khoz. Rossii*, p. 38, who points out that it represents a 2½-fold increase on the figure of 90,000 in 1625–31.

[51] Hellie, *Enserfment*, p. 269 (based on numerous sources but not Ivanov).

[52] Vodarsky, *Naseleniye*, p. 64 n.; cf. id., 'Sluzh. dvoryanstvo', p. 237, where the figure of 30,000 must refer to males only.

[53] Vazhinsky, *Zemlevladeniye*, p. 65; Chernov, *Voor. sily*, p. 171. Chernov's estimate is presumably derived from the 15,825 gentrymen listed by the Razryad as serving in the Belgorod area in 1678 (*DAI* ix. 106); but their 35,000 kinsmen of military age should have been added. As noted in ch. 2, only some 8,000–11,000 privileged servitors took part in the Crimean campaigns of 1687 and 1689.

[54] Yepifanov, *Ocherki iz ist. armii*, p. 9; Kalinychev, *Pravovye voprosy*, p. 45; Filippov, *Uchebnik*, p. 438.

[55] Urlanis, *Rost*, p. 193.

[56] Vodarsky, 'Chislennost'', p. 227; cf. id., *Naseleniye*, p. 192, where the figure of 5.6 million must refer to males only.

and material resources, and slowed its economic development. Hellie offers the intriguing comment that 'the Russian military establishment was much larger relative to the size of the population than in any twentieth-century [developing] country. Modern nations in the 9–10 million population category support armies of from 1,000 to 65,000 men'.[57]

Of the many taxes levied directly and indirectly on the populace in the Muscovite period, only one was specifically geared to military needs. This was the so-called 'musketeers' money' (*streletskiye den´gi*), first levied in cash form in 1615. It was designed to help maintain the Moscow *strel´tsy*, for the provincial units as we know were in principle self-supporting. Payments in kind (cereals) continued alongside this monetary tax during the seventeenth century, and in 1661/2, during the fiscal crisis, an attempt was made to substitute them for the tax. On the other hand, in some provincial areas the *streletskiy khleb* (as these natural dues were known) was commuted into cash payments.[58] Payment, in whatever form, was generally made in three instalments each year; the taxpayers had to take it to the collection point, and sometimes all the way to Moscow, which added to their burden. For this tax, as for others that were levied directly, the unit of assessment was initially the *sokha*, that is the unit of land or other property registered in the cadastre. The size of this varied according to the social status of the owner or holder: ecclesiastical land was taxed at the highest rate, then that of 'black' peasant or urban communities, of service gentry, and of the court (in that order).[59] In the 1630s the 'inhabited area' (*zhivushchaya chetvert´*) and in the 1670s the homestead (*dvor*) were substituted as the basis of calculation. These changes increased the tax yield, but at a heavy social cost. The musketeers' money became, in one historian's words, 'a real scourge for the population' and arrears quickly mounted: in the area administered by the Ustyug office (*chet´*) they were nearly double receipts by 1671.[60] Grain payments rose about fourteenfold between the 1620s and the 1670s;[61] the monetary dues amounted to 0.42 roubles per 'inhabited area' in mid-century and to 2 roubles in the 1670s.[62] In 1681 the assessments were reduced by a third and the administrative arrangements simplified.

One year prior to this modest reform, when an attempt was made to draw up a state budget, anticipated receipts of musketeers' money amounted to 146,951 roubles, or 12 per cent of total anticipated revenue (1,220,367 roubles); actual receipts, however, were over 40 per cent short of what they should have been. More important were the extraordinary levies (*zaprosnye den´gi*), which in 1679/80 amounted to 235,338 roubles (19 per cent of total anticipated

[57] Hellie, Enserfment, p. 370 n. 4.

[58] *AAE* iv. 189; Lappo-Danilevsky, *Organizatsiya*, p. 26; Milyukov, *Gos. khoz. Rossii*, pp. 41, 59.

[59] Lappo-Danilevsky, p. 403.

[60] Milyukov, *Gos. khoz. Rossii*, pp. 59–60, 63–5.

[61] Hellie, *Enserfment*, p. 126; cf. Lappo-Danilevsky, Organizatsiya, pp. 28, 404.

[62] *AAE* iv. 243, 250–1; *AI* v. 48; Chistyakova, 'Volneniya', p. 258.

receipts). Such levies, usually amounting to one-tenth and sometimes even one-fifth of annual income, were imposed seven times during the early years of Tsar Michael's reign and eight times between 1654 and 1680. They fell most heavily on the townspeople, who were occasionally assessed on their capital assets as well as their income.[63] The rest of the state's revenue came from indirect taxes (customs dues and proceeds of the alcohol trade), minor direct taxes, and fees.

Of this money most went on the armed forces, whose costs could not be covered from the revenue sources specifically assigned to the purpose. In the 1679/80 estimates these disbursements came to about 700,000 roubles, or 62.2 per cent of total anticipated expenditure. The Musketeers' chancellery received 250,000 roubles, the Cavalrymen's 110,000 roubles, and the Razryad 82,000 roubles.[64] This may be compared with a figure of 275,000 roubles for military expenditure in the 1630s (when total state disbursements are unknown).[65] In 1663, at the height of the Russo-Polish war, the active army alone (that is, excluding garrison troops) cost more than it did in 1679/80: about 1 million roubles.[66]

Of course much of the military burden on the population cannot be express-ed in monetary terms. Peasants had to perform construction and cartage duties as and when required, and also to supply provisions for the troops. Kotoshikhin, referring to this practice, says nothing about any payment; and Lappo-Danilevsky takes the view that 'usually no compensation was made'.[67] Some commanders did, however, try to fix prices for cereals in the locality under their control when effecting requisitions. Like other European armies at this time, that of the tsar lived to a large extent 'off the land' at home and abroad, although the rudiments of a central supply system existed. From the 1650s onwards low-grade provincial gentry in the south—presumably those who were not mobilized for active service—had to provide grain at the rate of 1 *chetvert'* (= 182 lb.) each of rye and oats per homestead;[68] this was evidently regarded as a tax in kind rather than a commercial operation.

Last but not least, the central treasury kept no account of the payments which the population made to their local commanders, the voivodes, of which part went on their maintenance (and enrichment!) and part on military-oriented as well as civilian projects. The irony was that all this expenditure did

[63] Veselovsky, 'Sem' sborov', p. 87; Stashevsky, 'Byudzhet', p. 413.

[64] Milyukov, *Gos. khoz. Rossii*, p. 75; cf. Stashevsky, 'Byudzhet', p. 417; Ustyugov, 'Finansy', in Novosel'sky and Ustyugov (eds.), *Ocherki*, p. 438; Chernov, *Voor. sily*, p. 179.

[65] Milyukov, *Gos. khoz. Rossii*, p. 36.

[66] Plus over 70,000 quarters (= 6,720 tons) of grain: Stashevsky, 'Smeta', as cited by Hellie, *Enserfment*, p. 227; id., 'Byudzhet', p. 416; for cereal measurements, Hellie, op. cit., p. 371. In negotiations with the Poles in 1656 the Muscovites put their military expenses during the first two years of the war at 1.3 million roubles: S. M. Solov'yev, *Ist. Rossii s drevneyshikh vremen*, Moscow, 1959–64, v (1961), 660.

[67] Kotoshikhin, *O Rossii*, pp. 136–7; cf. *PSZ* i. 139; Lappo-Danilevsky, *Organizatsiya*, p. 410; Brix, *Geschichte*, pp. 430, 551.

[68] Chernov, 'Voor. sily', pp. 452–3; Zagorodsky, *Belgorodskaya cherta*, p. 245.

not buy much in the way of military security, since the quality of Muscovite Russia's vast armed forces did not correspond to their quantity. It would be Peter the Great's principal task to repair this basic defect, but in the process of improving efficiency the burden on the long-suffering population would increase yet further.

II

THE WARRIOR TSAR, 1689–1725

5

PETER'S SOLDIERS

FROM the last decade of the seventeenth century to the third decade of the eighteenth Russian history is overshadowed by the gigantic figure of Peter I (1689–1725), styled 'the Great': this at least has been the general verdict of posterity, as it was of contemporaries. It is commonly agreed also that Peter's military reforms, together with the construction of a navy fundamentally affected, if they did not actually motivate, all the other innovations with which Russia's first emperor was associated: modernization of the institutions of government at the centre and in the provinces, relocation of the capital to St. Petersburg, introduction of the poll tax, encouragement of education on functional lines, and so on.[1] The military reforms were carried out in piecemeal fashion, particularly in the first half of the reign, with little thought for their impact on society as a whole. This was partly due to the pressing exigencies of the war with Sweden (1700–21), which absorbed so much of Peter's attention and grievously overstrained the country's resources; it was also a consequence of the ruler's stormy and impetuous temperament.

The tsar-emperor was a firm believer in the need for government by constraint and in the military as a bulwark of royal power. He was less of a militarist than his principal antagonist, Charles XII of Sweden, in that his obsession with the armed forces was offset by a basic pragmatism and healthy common sense, but prolonged exposure to the service milieu did affect his judgement. 'War is the only delight and passion of this young monarch', the English ambassador remarked in 1704.[2] Later Peter's interests would broaden, but even six years after the great victory at Poltava (1709) he could write to one of his associates, on hearing that his consort Catherine had born him a son and heir: 'I inform you that this night God has given me a recruit with his father's name; may He grant that I shall see him bear a musket.'[3] The conspicuously non-military proclivities of the Tsarevich Alexis, his son by his first marriage, were largely responsible for the tragic conflict between them that ended in the young man's flight abroad, trial on a charge of treason, and eventual death in

---

[1] This view owes much to its eloquent statement by the late nineteenth-century liberal historian V. O. Klyuchevsky, in his lectures on the Petrine period: *Soch.*, vol. 4, abbreviated English translation (by L. Archibald) as *Peter the Great*. Klyuchevsky did not, however, extend to other periods his recognition of 'defence' as supplying the main dynamic of Russian development. The Petrine cult, common to pre- and post-revolutionary Russian (and most non-Russian) writing, has distorted our perception of the period: cf. Cracraft, 'Peter I', 'More Peter'.

[2] Whitworth, 'Doneseniya', *SIRIO* xxxix. 14.

[3] Bychkov, *Pis'ma Petra Velikogo*, p. 40.

prison (1718) after tortures which his father personally authorized. The cruel streak in Peter's nature has to be set against the statesmanlike qualities that have led him to be hailed as a 'genius', not least for his battlefield exploits.

Already at an early age Peter demonstrated an uncommon interest in, and talent for, the military art. Even his toys as a child had a martial aspect. Arbitrarily removed from the centre of power during Sofia's regency (1682–9), the boy was exposed to the influence of irresponsible advisers, among them swashbuckling adventurers from the 'German suburb' whose virtues and vices were typified by his first favourite, François Lefort. He grew into a giant of a man, whose physical strength enabled him to withstand tremendous exertions, at least until his health was undermined by alcoholic excess; he liked to live in the open air and enjoyed all kinds of practical activity. He was justly proud of his skill as a carpenter and as a fancier of several other trades—interests which contrasted strikingly with those of the cloistered, ritualistic early Romanov rulers. The same was true of his preference for simple accommodation and pleasures or the company of those from humble circumstances. Peter deliberately sought to break with Muscovite traditions of governance. He saw himself as the prime exemplar of those norms of social conduct he wanted to encourage among his subjects of all classes: first and foremost, a conscientious attitude towards fulfilment of one's duties towards the state. An obvious manifestation of this was his own 'progress through the ranks' of the armed forces: starting as a bombardier in the Preobrazhensky guards regiment, he rose to become an NCO and eventually a lieutenant-general (while simultaneously acting as Commander-in-Chief throughout!). There was an element of role-playing about this, but it did have a serious educational, or at least propagandist, purpose.

The innovative character of Peter's activities has often been exaggerated, not least in regard to military affairs. His eagerness to assimilate the latest achievements of foreign weapons technology or forms of military organization had been anticipated by Ivan III, Ivan IV, and Alexis. They too had readily accepted Western experts into their service. What was new was the scale of the effort, the consistent determination that lay behind Peter's drive to make Russia a European power—and to do so by defeating her old rival Sweden and gaining a firm foothold on the Baltic seaboard. There was a greater element of rationality in his policies, for he was true to the spirit of his era and shared the general belief that rulers should use their absolute power for predetermined ends, in particular to enhance the strength and prestige of their realms. Such prestige might be obtained by setting up a 'well-ordered police state' (as this concept was then understood), not just by feats of arms; but the military component was assuredly the most important—especially in central and eastern Europe, where the values of the Baroque age acquired a more authoritarian tinge than they did further west. Sweden, Prussia, and some of the lesser German states—not to mention the German-speaking élite of the Baltic provinces, which Russia now annexed—were the principal sources of Western influence on the Petrine empire, rather than Britain or the Netherlands (important though they were for commercial and naval developments); France's turn would come later in the eighteenth century. This point has sometimes been lost sight of by writers dazzled by Peter's well-documented visits to the latter countries (1697–8, 1717).

More important still, the new rational and pragmatic spirit derived from Europe was intermingled with one that had deep roots in Russia's own past. The traditional service-state ethos, which had somewhat weakened towards the end of the seventeenth century, was now mightily reinforced. 'Westernization' did not bring about an easement of the historic bonds that made each of the tsar's subjects, according to his social affiliation, a servant or slave of the Autocrat; on the contrary, it helped the absolutist state to plug some of the loopholes that had appeared in the fabric of universal compulsion and submissiveness. In this sense Peter's reign marks a throwback to the sixteenth century as much as an advance into the eighteenth. It seems to have greatly increased the burden carried by all classes, particularly the lowest—a burden whose rationale lay in an aggrandizement of Russian military power, deemed necessary to achieve supposed 'national objectives'. The reign did not bring any progress towards broader distribution of political power, for Peter, although on occasion willing to devolve administrative responsibilities, was as jealous of his monarchical prerogatives as any of his predecessors had been; and in his treatment of domestic opponents he displayed the arbitrariness and ferocious cruelty one associates more readily with Ivan IV, although Peter's aims were certainly more rational.

Even the principal artefact of the reforms, the standing (regular) army, was not wholly new. As we have seen, during the seventeenth century elements of both the old- and new-model forces had been subjected to mobilization for lengthy periods. Peter's main achievement was to construct an integrated force out of these disparate elements, to impose uniform conditions of service, to institute a system of discipline based on hierarchical principles, to establish military schools, and to bring the troops under centralized administration by the War College in St. Petersburg. Yet Muscovite practices survived like cracks in the walls of the new edifice. They were most evident in the persistence (largely due to the lack of specie) of 'self-maintenance' by troops who in principle were entirely on the state payroll. The eighteenth-century Imperial army might wear European-style uniform and drill according to European manuals, but it remained distinctively Russian—as the society from which it sprang did.

The new army took shape in a long drawn-out process of reshuffle and purge that began almost casually. It is difficult to discern any plans for comprehensive structural change before 1699 at the earliest. This occurred as a response to two problems: first, the need for a better organized, trained force to take on Charles XII's Sweden, once the long desultory war with Turkey had ended; and second, the need to fill the gap left by the martyred *strel'tsy*.

The musketeers were not in themselves a serious threat to Peter's power, as was shown by their role in the crisis of August 1689 (see ch. 3). The victorious Naryshkin faction, however, looked elsewhere for military support. Since 1683 the young tsar had been building up a force, the 'mock' or 'play' (*poteshnye*) regiments, which were clearly designed for use against domestic as well as external opponents. The pleasure-loving regent and her advisers tolerated this menacing enterprise, partly because it kept Peter busily employed at arm's length from the Kremlin. Preobrazhenskoye, a court village near the capital, gave its name to the first guards regiment, which was little more than a motley band until 1687 or even 1692.[4] Its officers were recruited wherever possible from scions of noble or gentry families, as were some of the men; the rest were drawn from their dependants or those of the court. From the start this was conceived as an élite force personally beholden to Peter and ready to do his bidding. Training was supervised by foreign officers from the German suburb; conducted most vigorously during the summer months, it included realistic mock battlefield exercises and embraced all branches of the service, including artillery and engineering (for which Peter entertained a particular interest). By 1687 some *poteshnye* had been relocated in another court village, Semenovskyoe, which gave its name to a guards infantry regiment that claimed second place in seniority throughout the Imperial epoch. By the mid-1690s there were four units, two named after their commanders in the Muscovite tradition, in this royal bodyguard. It carried on the traditions of the two *vybornye* infantry regiments founded in 1642,[5] and—although the proud guardsmen would have been loath to admit it—of the *stremyannoy polk* of Moscow musketeers.

For this corps, with its popular roots, was now cast as the natural enemy of the more privileged *poteshnye*. In the military exercises held after Peter's *coup d'état* the two forces were invariably pitted against each other. The *strel'tsy* were allotted a passive, defensive role and ended up as the losers. The aim of this was as much political as professional: it built up the morale of one formation while weakening that of the other. The first climax came in September 1694, when for several weeks four infantry regiments with cavalry support, commanded by F. Yu. Romodanovsky, engaged six *strel'tsy* units under I. I. Buturlin for possession of a fortress at Kozhukhovo, just outside Moscow, which Peter had built for the purpose. The action was sufficiently lifelike to cause a number of casualties.[6]

---

[4] The Preobrazhensky regiment proudly dated its origins from 1683, which led to an unedifying controversy over the historical justification for the practice: cf. Bobrovsky, 'Poteshnye'; 'Uchrezhdeniye'; P—v, 'Dvukhsotletiye'; Truvorov, 'O vremeni'; for a summing up: Smel′nitsky, 'Proiskhozhdeniye'.

[5] On these see now Rabinovich, *Polki*, p. 24.

[6] Kurakin, 'Gistoriya', p. 67, gives a figure on 24 killed and 15 wounded (including Romodanovsky himself), but this cannot be corroborated; he puts the number of participants at 30,000, but the real figure was only half as great. Kurakin's account and his brief autobiography ('Zhizn′') are, however, valuable since he was the only contemporary Russian writer to express (guarded) criticism of Peter's policies. For a recent study of the manœuvres: Warner, 'Kožuchovo Campaign'.

During the next two years troops of both formations, and others besides, were committed to battle against the Turks at Azov. The strategic city finally fell in July 1696. The 13 *strel'tsy* regiments were given the most dangerous assignments in the siege and sustained heavy losses. Several hundred men were killed in an explosion for which their comrades blamed Lefort, one of the three commanders; he also failed to pay them a bonus they had been promised and, after the fortress had been captured, kept half of them on to do arduous construction work. In June 1697 they set out on the return journey to Moscow but while *en route* were suddenly sent to join a force assembling on the western border, where famine was rife and accommodation desperately short. The men were aggrieved that they had not been permitted to see their families, as was the normal procedure after a campaign.[7]

In March 1698 some 175 *strel'tsy* from four regiments absconded and came to the capital in a body to submit a complaint. In particular they demanded prompt payment of their grain allowance, which had been withheld. When some concessions were made, they tried to exploit the situation—much as in 1682, although the numbers involved were now much smaller. Peter's absence abroad, on his 'Grand Embassy' to western Europe, gave rise to fanciful rumours. It was thought that he might have been killed, and in the popular mind this aroused hopes for the succession of another ruler who would show more respect for tradition—and might even bring about a social utopia such as many commoners secretly yearned for. Sofia, confined in a Moscow convent, was an obvious choice. There is no reliable evidence that, either now or later, she gave any encouragement to the dissident troops;[8] but the belief that she might back them fortified the men's resolve. The petitioners, ejected from Moscow by Semenovsky guardsmen, were allowed to return to their units, where they had the opportunity to spread their views before they were arrested. Fifty of them were promptly freed by their comrades and, as in 1682, this act of defiance inevitably led to others. Having deposed their commanders the mutineers, some 2,200 strong, decided to march on the capital. Most of them seem to have had service grievances uppermost in mind, but political aspirations were articulated more emphatically than in the earlier outbreak—which is not to say that their thinking had become any more sophisticated.

The government reacted with despatch. General A. S. Shein, who was in charge of military affairs in Peter's absence, put together a force of some

---

[7] Ustryalov, *Istoriya*, iii. 152–7, 161; Buganov, *Mosk. vosstaniya*, pp. 363–6; Gordon, *Tagebuch*, ii. 593, 598. The commander on the western border, M. G. Romodanovsky, was a kinsman of their former chief opponent at Kozhukhovo who, as Peter's security adviser, was to become their executioner.

[8] Statements extracted by torture cannot of course be taken at face value, as has lightly been done by pro-Petrine historians: for example, Ustryalov, *Istoriya*, iii. 157–8. Had the evidence been conclusive, the tsar would not have hesitated to execute Sofia instead of merely obliging her to take the veil. Buganov plausibly suggests that the alleged correspondence between her and the rebels may either have never existed or else have been forged by the mutineers (p. 375).

8,000 men, most of them gentry cavalry, and on 18 June soundly defeated the rebels near the Voskresensky monastery, about 50 km. west of the capital. Retribution was exacted at once. Two batches of ringleaders, numbering 56 and 74 respectively, were hanged in public and nearly two thousand men exiled.

News of the rebels' defeat reached Peter at Cracow, on his way back to Moscow from Vienna where he had broken off his tour. He saw matters differently from his principal subordinates: the revolt offered a welcome pretext to destroy the force he so greatly hated. Already in May he had expressed sorrow and anger that Romodanovsky, his security chief, had not launched an investigation into the insubordinate petitioners, adding that such laxity went against earlier decisions—a remark that almost suggests an element of provocation.[9] On his return he lost no time in inspecting and handsomely rewarding the *poteshnye*.[10] At a social gathering on 4 September he suffered a hysterical attack and threatened to kill Shein on the spot; only with difficulty could Lefort calm him down.[11] Ten days later Peter launched a fresh investigation, the object of which was to link the mutiny with political opposition at the highest level. The allegations were widely believed by contemporaries (and later by historians), and although never proven established a pseudo-judicial basis for a wave of terror against the *strel'tsy*.

The main interrogation centre was the headquarters of the *poteshnye* (or *leyb-gvardiya*, as they were now known) at Preobrazhenskoye. This office, the Preobrazhensky chancellery, had been given a security role as early as 1695.[12] The investigators were interested in extracting confessions, not in discovering the actual motives of the accused, whose guilt was taken for granted. In October 1698, and again early in 1699, Moscow was the scene of mass executions, clearly staged with an eye to their deterrent effect. A famous historical painting by Vasiliy Surikov (1881) depicts the victims, bound together and holding lighted candles, being transported by the cartload to gallows erected around the Kremlin wall; the people look on sympathetically while the tsar, accompanied by a bevy of courtiers and foreigners, his new regular troops lined up behind him, watches the proceedings with a wild and ferocious expression. The artist's representation is based on the diary of J. G. Korb,[13] the Austrian secretary of legation, and other primary sources. In the first three-week period no less than 799 men were executed and 193 sentenced to lesser penalties.[14] On the second occasion there were several hundred victims (the exact number is unknown). A mass grave was dug outside the city which contained more than one thousand bodies. Over it a column was erected which bore an inscription

---

[9] *PiB* i. 251; Buganov, *Mosk. vosstaniya*, p. 376.

[10] 'Petrovskaya brigada', p. 255.

[11] Korb, *Tagebuch*, p. 79.

[12] Golikova, *Polit. protsessy*, p. 14.

[13] Korb reported a certain amount of hearsay evidence, but attended at least one of the executions (*Tagebuch*, p. 110). Whether Peter actually took a hand personally in the executions, as Korb states (p. 84), is not certain, but he was definitely among the torturers.

[14] Bogoslovsky, *Petr I*, iii. 118; Buganov, *Mosk. vosstaniya*, p. 404.

detailing the men's crimes—a symbolic gesture which plainly indicates that the repression was as much an act of belated vengeance for the 1682 revolt as a response to the threat of subversion at the time.[15]

Most of those musketeers whose lives were spared found themselves sent to the south, a measure which (as in 1682) had the unintended effect of making people in this sensitive region aware of the events in Moscow. In December 1698 there was disaffection among *strel'tsy* stationed at Belgorod and 60 of these men were taken to the capital for questioning. A few months later trouble broke out in the garrison at Azov where, oddly, the musketeers were urged to revolt by an ex-Preobrazhensky guardsman who had taken religious vows.[16] According to Korb the men hoped for aid from other dissident elements in the steppe lands and even from the Crimean Tatars.[17] They evidently realized that Peter was determined to exterminate them and wanted to die fighting.

Many years later the tsar recalled that after the executions he had so distrusted the rest of the *strel'tsy* corps that 'all their regiments were cashiered [*skasovany*] and [the men] scattered in various towns, wherever they wished to go'.[18] Neither statement is accurate. Recent research has shown that, whatever Peter's intentions may have been, the musketeers survived for some time. The main reason for this was that their services were needed in the European war in which Russia soon became engaged. Thus, of the Azov *strel'tsy* charged with indiscipline only 111 were assigned to other units, while the rest were posted to Smolensk or Sevsk and retained their organizational identity until they were eventually reclassified as *soldaty*. Some saw action in the Baltic theatre. Moreover, in 1702–3 six new musketeer regiments were formed, two of which were sent to join the inter-allied auxiliary corps in Poland and Saxony, where they were all but wiped out at the battle of Fraustadt (February 1706); only a handful managed to fight their way back to the Russian lines.[19]

By this time *strel'tsy* and other troops stationed at Astrakhan', on the south-eastern perimeter of the realm, had risen up in what has been called 'one of the greatest military insurrections in Russian history'.[20] For nearly nine months (July 1705–March 1706) they held the city in their grasp, but they were unable to extend their sway to the Don Cossacks, who were to revolt independently two years later under the leadership of Kondratiy Bulavin. Thus the government was in a position to deal with its enemies separately. Of the 500 Astrakhan' rebels taken to Moscow for indictment, 60 per cent were *strel'tsy*; in all several hundred men were put to death.[21] This was more than a military mutiny and

---

[15] Ustryalov, *Istoriya*, iii. 239–40; Bogoslovsky, *Petr I*, iv. 19–30; Buganov, *Mosk. vosstaniya*, p. 406.

[16] Ustryalov, *Istoriya*, iii. 232–5; Rabinovich, 'Strel'tsy', p. 297: Buganov, *Mosk. vosstaniya*, p. 409.   [17] Korb, *Tagebuch*, p. 123.

[18] [Peter I] *Zhurnal*, i. 3. To Patriarch Dosifey in Constantinople he wrote that 20,000 men had been destroyed: Bogoslovsky, *Petr I*, iv. 173.

[19] Rabinovich, 'Strel'tsy', pp. 285–6; id., *Sud'by*, pp. 11 ff.; *PSZ* iv. 1979.

[20] Rabinovich, 'Strel'tsy', p. 287. Rabinovich's characterization is contested by Golikova, who has since published an excellent detailed study of the rising: *Astr. vosstaniye* (see pp. 28–9).

[21] Golikova, *Astr. vosstaniye*, pp. 306–7.

has to be seen in the context of the Russian state's continuous effort to subdue and integrate the unsettled steppe frontier.

Even after the insurrection had been put down, some *strel'tsy* units remained in being. They are recorded at Kiev and Vyborg in 1710–11,[22] and as late as 1722 a German diplomat speaks of musketeers (here called *Spiessbürger*) mounting guard in the Moscow Kremlin.[23] This may, however, be a misunderstanding; the term *gorodovye strel'tsy* seems to have been applied loosely to groups of armed men whose connection with the musketeers of history was slight or non-existent. Most of the latter were absorbed into the regular infantry, where they were subjected to discriminatory treatment. They could not, for example, volunteer to join, and one who did so, presumably by concealing his origins, was ordered to be 'mercilessly beaten'.[24] Data from 1720–1 on 2,245 officers reveal that only one of them (V. R. Savinikhin) hailed from the *strel'tsy* milieu—and he, characteristically, was detailed to the harsh task of helping to build a canal.[25]

On the surface the privileged elements in Russian society, especially those who had joined the new guards regiments, seemed to have scored a notable victory. The real gainer, however, was the autocratic state, as the rest of Peter's reign would make abundantly clear. For the tsar now proceeded to construct a standing army in which men of all classes were obliged to serve, and the gentry soon found themselves bearing a disagreeably large share of the burden. One near-contemporary observer thought that Peter deliberately manipulated the two groups in order to consolidate his supremacy: 'he had already resolved to wear out and weaken the strel'tsy and the nobility, one corps by means of the other, and to place them on a footing where each would have to depend solely upon his mercy and will.'[26] This interpretation is probably too ingenious, since the tsar acted under pressure of events rather than according to any long-term strategy; but it describes well what actually occurred. Petrine absolutism did indeed rest on the enforced subordination of all the embryonic socio-political interest groups.

The tsar probably entertained for some time the notion of a radical reform and expansion of Russia's military effectives. During his journey to the West he had been able to acquaint himself at first hand with the armies of other powers. Nevertheless the first move did not come until November 1699. It was prompted by the decision to launch an offensive war against Sweden.[27] Peter

[22] Rabinovich, 'Strel'tsy', pp. 279, 286.
[23] Berkhgol'ts (Bergholz), 'Dnevnik,' *RA* (1902), 11, p. 5; the editor (I. Ammon) suggests that they may have been from the Sukharev(sky) regiment, 'the only one to survive', but this was actually disbanded around 1700: Rabinovich, 'Strel'tsy', p. 279.
[24] Vostokov, 'O delakh General'nogo dvora', pp. 17, 28.
[25] Rabinovich, 'Sots. proiskhozhdeniye' pp. 144–5.
[26] J. G. Vockerodt, in Herrmann, *Russland*, p. 26.
[27] Bogoslovsky, *Petr I*, iv. 174–7. For purposes of deception the Turks were publicly identified as the prospective enemy.

did not expect the conflict to be so prolonged; nor could he have foreseen the way his measures would transform the country's armed forces, and ultimately Russian society as well.

An *ukaz* of 8 November called for volunteers from 'all manner of free men'. The response was excellent. The Austrian envoy noted that 'in the taverns the unemployed [*müssige Leute*] are being recruited in large numbers' and attributed this to the rapid rise in prices, 'for otherwise they would have nothing to live from';[28] certainly they will have appreciated the material advantages in prospect. They were promised pay of 11 roubles per annum, which was generous by contemporary standards, and the same supplies of food and clothing as were enjoyed by guardsmen. This measure was no more than a continuation of those used to recruit the *poteshnye*. It did not involve any innovation. Nor did a decree issued on 17 November—at least on the surface. This called for a levy of recruits (*datochnye lyudi*). Such drafts, as we have seen, were a frequent occurrence during the seventeenth century. Only in its particulars did the edict depart from tradition. The obligation differed according to social category: one man was to be provided per 25 households by the clergy and richer merchants; one per 30 households by *dvoryane* in the civil service, widows, retired men, and youths (*nedorosli*); and one per 50 households by those in the armed forces; an extra levy of men with horses (one per 100 households) was imposed upon the metropolitan nobility. The recruits were to be taken from the landowners' household serfs and slaves rather than from the agricultural population; for the same reason the 'black' peasant communities were exempted. Proprietors with less land than the norm could commute the obligation by paying 11 roubles, the equivalent of a soldier's annual pay; the others had also to equip and provision their recruits in the traditional way.[29] The really significant innovation was not stated in the decree, and perhaps was not even realized by its authors: these recruits, unlike their forerunners, would never return to civilian life. They were 'immortals' (a term Peter himself used of them),[30] destined to serve in the army for the rest of their days.

This seems to have come as a shock to the proprietors. By now they had grown accustomed to parting with their men for a season or two, but the prospect of losing their labour for all time led many to try to circumvent the law. They concealed the existence of dependants or skimped on the provisions of those whom they sent, perhaps on a more extensive scale than usual. The five recruiting agencies that had been set up were inundated with petitions: for an extension of commutation privileges, or for men who had previously volunteered to be counted as recruits. There were also petitions by aged or

[28] Pleyer to Emperor Leopold I, 10 Dec. 1699, in Ustryalov, *Istoriya*, iii. 643; Rabinovich, 'Formirovaniye', p. 221.

[29] Text in *Opisaniye dokumentov . . . MAMYu* (21 vols., Moscow, 1869–1916) v (ii). 37–9. Pleyer reported that in practice wealthy nobles might lose up to one-fifth of their domestics (Ustryalov, *Istoriya*, iii. 643). Nearly 30,000 such persons were inspected, of whom 11,500 were enrolled (Mikhnevich, in *SVM* in (1, i, i), app., p. 19; Avtokratov, 'Voyennyy prikaz', p. 230).

[30] *PiB* vi. 2076 (22 Nov. 1707).

crippled recruits who had been submitted in lieu of men who were physically fit. Proprietors disregarded the provision in the decree designed to spare their more productive dependants from the levy; sometimes these men were sent back,[31] which in one case led to a riot. There was a good deal of random violence during the operation, and in the Tula district an official supervising the levy was assaulted by irate civilians.[32]

Peter had hoped to raise a force some 60,000 to 80,000 strong. He obtained about 32,000 men, of whom perhaps a quarter to a third were volunteers. The latter were mostly raised in the Volga region by N. I. Repnin, whereas the men recruited from central Russia by F. A. Golovin and A. A. Weyde (who remained in Moscow) were overwhelmingly conscripts.[33] Cadres could be drawn from the *soldaty* regiments;[34] their numbers had been cut back by the Naryshkin regime in the early 1690s, but 28,000 took part in the Azov campaigns and several thousand must surely have still been under arms in 1698–9. Thirty-two new infantry regiments were formed at that time, and another 39 in 1700.[35] Each was supposed to have about one thousand men, although in fact many were below strength. In readiness for the confrontation with the Swedes they were formed into three divisions, each of nine regiments with 10 companies, equipped and uniformed in European style.

All these units were under the command of foreigners, but it was impossible to draw on this source for the large number of officers now required: each regiment had 36 vacancies at the rank of captain or below, but the three divisions had only 1,137 officers in all, of whom one third were foreign or 'newly baptized'.[36] In May 1700 the authorities began to mobilize Russians to fill the gap. They turned in the first instance to the senior ranks of the service élite. Nobles now once again found themselves required to bear arms personally, and not just to part with their dependants. During the summer nearly one thousand *dvoryane* were assigned as officers to the new regiments, and in 1701 another 8,600 young gentry servitors, who would normally have done duty in the levy, were assigned to 14 new cavalry (dragoon) units.[37] Neither the levy nor the new-model forces were formally abolished: they were silently superseded by units of the new standing army.

Gentry servitors preferred to fulfil their military obligations on horseback even if this meant that some of them had to remain in the ranks.[38] They might

[31] A law to that effect was passed on 23 Dec. 1700: *PSZ* iv. 1820, § 1.

[32] Vostokov, 'O delakh General'nogo dvora', pp. 13–16, 26, 29. Rabinovich, 'Formirovaniye', does not refer to this earlier study.

[33] Rabinovich, 'Formirovaniye', pp. 223, 226–8 (where there is some confusion as to the proportion of volunteers); cf. id., *Sud'by*, p. 6.

[34] Anisimov and Zinevich, *Istoriya*, p. 17.

[35] For details of these see Rabinovich, *Polki*, pp. 26–31, 32–44.

[36] Avtokratov, 'Voyennyy prikaz', p. 240.

[37] Rabinovich, *Polki*, pp. 86–9 (nos. 543–56); id., *Sud'by*, p. 6; id., 'Formirovaniye', p. 234.

[38] No figures are available which could relate rank to social origin *within* units, but it is known that in 1720–1 gentry comprised 71 per cent of cavalry officers as against 52 per cent of infantry officers: Rabinovich, 'Sots. proiskhozhdeniye', p. 139 and below, p. 119.

well have to bear muskets as humble infantrymen, at least in the first years of their careers. During the early part of Peter's reign junior officers, who were more likely to hail from the privileged groups, experienced much the same harsh conditions as their men. Nevertheless it will be convenient to consider officers and soldiers separately here.

At the disastrous battle of Narva (November 1700) the new Russian regiments suffered heavy losses—between 7,000 and 12,000 men—which had to be made good by fresh levies. These were at first raised in haphazard fashion: in 1703, for example, the coachmen (*yamshchiki*) of Moscow and certain other towns were ordered to contribute one recruit for every two households.[39] The authorities lacked accurate demographic data, since no census had been taken since 1678; nor did they as yet have the administrative machinery necessary to conduct another general levy. This became possible only in 1705, when officials of the old Pomestnyy chancellery were called upon to assist those in the newly established Office of Military Affairs; the two bodies then coexisted for several years, the former managing general levies and the latter partial ones.[40]

A decree of 20 February 1705 set the rate at one recruit—it was now that the Western term *rekrut* displaced the old appellation *datochnye lyudi*—per 20 households. Proprietors with less than the norm were to be assessed jointly. Those chosen were to be unmarried youths aged 15 to 20, of good reputation and physically fit (*dobrye i chelovechnye*). Their owners had to hand them over at so-called 'stations' (*stantsii*) in the local town, where they were billeted on the inhabitants and were 'to live peaceably, not harming or imposing upon the townsmen or travellers, and not brawling or engaging in destructive acts'.[41] Enlistment continued throughout the summer of 1705, so that the deadline had to be extended;[42] an earlier threat that proprietors who failed to fill their quota would have it doubled seems to have remained a dead letter. Kurakin states that in fact the system of assessment by households broke down: 'that year they took all (*sic*) the young peasants from Moscow district to be soldiers, and not according to [the number of] households', and the same thing happened in other central areas in 1706.[43] He exaggerated a little, for further levies were indeed raised in this region, and some effort was made to distribute the burden equitably between geographical areas and social classes.

Townspeople, for example, were permitted to hire substitutes if they had none of their own kind to send. Substitutes did not need to be bachelors and—like other recruits—had to bring signed sureties which in their case obliged their hirers to provide a replacement if they deserted or were killed.[44] Later a concession was made to poorer landed proprietors as well. Those with less than 20 households were allowed to pay a commutation fee, assessed at 40 kopecks for each household they possessed (less if they themselves were absent on service).[45]

[39] *PSZ* iv. 1996 (28 Oct. 1704).
[40] Avtokratov, 'Voyennyy prikaz', p. 230.
[41] *PSZ* iv. 2036 (20 Feb. 1705).
[42] *PSZ* iv. 2050 (4 May 1705).
[44] *PSZ*, loc. cit.
[43] Kurakin, 'Zhizn'', p. 272.
[45] *PSZ* iv. 2103, 2104 (28 Apr., 6 May 1706).

However, the authorities' efforts to adjust obligations to resources did not extend very far. Proprietors of all categories had to contribute one recruit on horseback for every 80 households—this in addition to the regular levies.[46] Towards the end of the decade decree was following upon decree in a steady stream. Recipients of the tsar's demands could not anticipate what they would be required to give, which encouraged them to evade his arbitrary and peremptory requests wherever they could. The levy had a demoralizing effect upon everyone involved in it, officials and peasants as well as landowners. The government's goals were unreasonably high—indeed unattainable, as it seemed implicitly to recognize; passive resistance was the natural consequence. A levy at the standard rate, carried out across the whole country, should have yielded about 24,000 men. Those of 1705 did indeed induct 44,500 recruits, but during the next four years only between 11,000 and 15,000 men were taken.[47] In all about 138,000 men are now thought to have been enrolled during the years 1701–9. This figure is a good deal lower than the estimate of 230,000 arrived at by the nineteenth-century military historian Myshlayevsky, to say nothing of Klyuchevsky's guess of 300,000.[48]

After Poltava the pressure eased somewhat and a start was made on the devolution of responsibility for the levy, and for army supply in general, to the new provincial (*guberniya*) administrations. However, early in 1711 the outbreak of another war with Turkey led to near-panic in Peter's entourage. One of the first acts of the Ruling Senate, which in effect took over from the Office of Military Affairs and the now defunct Razryad, was to order proprietors in Moscow to provide one man in three from their household servants; if they had only two such domestics, they were to part with one of them, and if none were fit to be sent they had to pay 30 roubles in lieu—nearly three times the sum that had been demanded in 1699, an increase greater than the rate of inflation.[49] This requirement was additional to the regular levy, which in 1711 was set at one recruit per 10 households. The total yielded was over 50,000.[50] The government was anxious to build up a nationwide reserve of 25,000 recruits, each province maintaining half as many reservists as it did soldiers in the field.[51] However, this measure could not be implemented systematically. From 1713 to the end of Peter's reign there were ten further general levies, at rates ranging from one man per 40 households in 1713 to one per 250 in 1724. These yielded an intake of 153,000 men.[52] In addition a number of partial levies were imposed on specific

---

[46] *PSZ* iv. 2065 (14 July 1705).

[47] Beskrovnyy, *Russkaya armiya*, p. 26; Avtokratov, 'Voyennyy prikaz', pp. 230–2.

[48] Myshlayevsky, *Petr Velikiy*, p. liv (and Mikhnevich, in *SVM* iv (1, i, i). 119); Bobrovsky, *Voyennoye pravo*, ii. 177: 175,000 in 1705–9, without indication of source, and the estimate of 30,000 p.a. which appears to have misled Klyuchevsky (*Peter the Great*, p. 81); he may have included men mobilized for various construction tasks.

[49] *PSZ* iv. 2326, 2355, 2384, 2390 (1 Mar., 30 Apr., 20, 30 June 1711); *DiP* i. 2.

[50] Avtokratov, 'Voyennyy prikaz', p. 233; Beskrovnyy, *Russkaya armiya*, p. 27.

[51] *PSZ* iv. 2338, 2341, 2520, 2533 (16, 22 Mar. 1711, 2, 26 May 1712).

[52] Beskrovnyy, *Russkaya armiya*, pp. 28–9.

areas or social categories. The most unusual of these pressed into army uniform priests and other clergy deemed surplus to the ecclesiastical establishment officially laid down in 1721. Altogether 53 levies, 21 general and 32 partial ones, were raised during Peter's reign; the grand total of recruits must have exceeded 300,000.[53]

This heavy burden fell predominantly on the servile population—including those field workers whom the government had initially tried to protect. 'The army swallowed up the best elements of the village', remarks Beskrovnyy flatly.[54] The wealthier peasant householders might, if their proprietor approved, be able to hire a substitute as townspeople could; but they were forbidden to take fugitives, the most obvious source. If a substitute deserted, the peasant who had hired him was fined, beaten and sent into exile.[55]

Selection was carried out by the landowners (or, if they were absent on service, by their agents), who thereby obtained an important new lever of power over their dependants. The same was true of village and district authorities. In the earlier part of Peter's reign the recruiting officials (*naborshchiki*) were mainly civilian functionaries, but then regular serving officers, seconded from their units for the purpose, took over. They submitted recruits to physical examination, swore them in, and collected their sureties (*krugovye poruki*)—documents whose purpose was to make the men exercise surveillance over one another, and so to hinder defection; if they failed to act as they were supposed to, they were liable to severe punishment.[56] This turned out to be a very crude and inefficient control mechanism. It may even have swollen the desertion rate by giving recruits an incentive to flee *en masse*; at any rate in 1712 the practice of branding recruits in much the same way as common criminals was introduced: the mark of a cross was burned into their left arm and the wound rubbed with gunpowder.[57]

There are also many reports of recruits (and not just deserters) being chained together.[58] One foreign observer states that they were 'taken to Moscow or some other rendezvous, and then on to St. Petersburg or the [field] army, bound together two by two'.[59] Senior officials expressed disapproval of the practice,[60] but it does not appear to have been formally banned; on the contrary, Peter actually issued an order (which has not been published) that recruits should be put in irons while *en route*, adding insouciantly that their escorts should take 'great care' of them.[61] In 1714 the Senate investigated a

[53] Beskrovnyy, however, puts it at 284,187 (in Kafengauz and Pavlenko (eds.), *Rossiya*, p. 347).
[54] Beskrovnyy, *Russkaya armiya*, p. 29.
[55] *DiP* iv (i). 68 (pp. 46–7); cf. *PSZ* v. 2709 (2 Sept. 1713).
[56] *PSZ* iv. 2467 (16 Jan. 1712).
[57] *PSZ* iv. 2456, § 17 (p. 268); *PiB* xii. 5024, § 8; Anisimov and Zinevich, *Istoriya*, p. 21.
[58] 'A te rekruty po se chislo skovany', order to Capt. I. Neyelov in Novgorod (1711), in Shchukin, *Sbornik*, ii. 194.
[59] [Müller], *Nouveaux mémoires*, p. 84.
[60] Dolgorukiy to Chirikov (1712), cited by Beskrovnyy, *Russkaya armiya*, pp. 30–1.
[61] Beskrovnyy, in Kafengauz and Pavlenko (eds.), *Rossiya*, p. 348, citing unpublished archival source.

case where 1,100 recruits had been kept in chains or wooden stocks by order of the governor of Nizhniy Novgorod. Characteristically the senators all but disregarded the abuses inflicted on the men and concerned themselves instead with suspected malfeasance by the governor when hiring carts for their transport.[62]

Recruits probably accounted themselves fortunate if they were despatched to their unit by cart—five men to a vehicle in one recorded instance, eight in another[63]—and did not have to complete the journey on foot. They were supposed to receive some rudimentary training on enlistment, and to be provided by their 'donors' with uniforms, footwear, and provisions; but nothing was done to prepare them for the unaccustomed strain of marching to a destination that might be hundreds of miles away. 'They are moved when the rivers are in flood,' one contemporary noted, 'instead of at the right time, and thus many fall sick and die prematurely.'[64] Escorting officers were under instructions to take the most direct route,[65] but in practice there was often a good deal of superfluous movement. In 1714 a captain Levashev was ordered to take 525 recruits from Archangel to St. Petersburg—by way of Moscow; 1 man died, 4 fell sick, and 40 deserted, which in the circumstances were modest figures.[66]

On reaching his unit the Petrine soldier (like infantrymen in most armies in most ages) continued to spend a lot of his time on the march. The normal practice was to cover 30 versts (about 18 miles) daily, resting every third day;[67] but in the evacuation from Grodno in 1706 troops covered 960 versts in 44 days with only four days' rest.[68] In default of memoir material one turns to army regulations for a few glimpses of the soldiers' daily life. When the signal to set out on the march was given the men were required to appear promptly; 'latecomers and those who sit on the cart carrying effects shall be punished upon the body'. They were to keep in line or else suffer the same penalty. Anyone who disobeyed an order on the march was to run the gauntlet.[69] Discipline was enforced by special cavalry detachments under the *general-geval'diger* or chief of military police.[70] In camp the men were supposed to be accommodated in tents (25 to a tent in the infantry, 16 in the cavalry), arranged in rows with the sutlers (*markitanty*) kept at a distance 'lest the cooking fires cause damage or there be a great stench and mess from the slaughtering of cattle'; latrines were likewise to be situated outside the camp area.[71] In civilian billets three

---

[62] *DiP* iv (ii). 1097 (pp. 877–81).

[63] Avtokratov, 'Voyennyy prikaz', p. 329; *DiP* i. 50 (p. 29).

[64] Petrov, *Russkaya voyennaya sila*, ii. 67.

[65] Avtokratov, 'Voyennyy prikaz', p. 239.			[66] *DiP* iv (ii). 1022 (p. 796).

[67] Peter I to G. P. Chernyshev, in *PiB* ix. 3377 (23 July 1709).

[68] Myshlayevsky, *Petr Velikiy*, p. lxi.

[69] Voinskiye stat'i (Ustav prezhnikh let), §§ 34–6, cited by Myshlayevsky, *Petr Velikiy*, pp. 11–12; Voinskiye artikuly, §§ 76–83 (*PRP* viii. 337–8); Ustav voinskiy, *PSZ* iv. 3006 (30 Mar. 1716), ch. xlviii; Bobrovsky, *Voyennoye pravo*, ii. 580–5.

[70] *PSZ* iv. 3006, ch. xli.

[71] Ibid., ch. xlv, lvi; Bobrovsky, *Voyennoye pravo*, ii. 587, 592.

soldiers were to share a bed or sleeping place, taking turns; they were forbidden to leave the premises after dark except on duty and were supposed to behave properly toward their peasant hosts.[72] The standard term of guard duty seems to have been 24 hours; any offence committed when on guard was punished twice as severely as in normal circumstances.[73] A code of 1706 laid down that soldiers should take good care of their equipment and not wager it in games of chance; they were to refrain from feasting or drinking on Sundays and to display 'Christian charity' towards their comrades, obey orders, respect their superiors, keep silent on parade—and, last but not least, fight the foe 'by day and night, by land or water, wherever military necessity and Our service demands, exhibiting zeal, not fear, sparing no labour in the cause, since God is the giver and sustainer of life'.[74]

The reference to 'labour' was not misplaced. A soldier in Peter's army was as likely to find himself employed on construction tasks as on military operations. One historian writes that 'Russia's great power status was built on the bones of soldiers digging the foundations of St. Petersburg'.[75] This is an exaggeration: the building of the new capital was mainly the work of civilian conscripts, but many of these were former Ukrainian Cossacks (deported in reprisal for Mazeppa's defection to Charles XII) and tens of thousands of them were indeed soldiers. A decree of 1719 called for garrison troops to be sent to the new capital for this purpose 'in lieu of the dragoons'—who must therefore have preceded them; and recruits who had been artisans in civilian life were liable to assignment for work on this gigantic project.[76] Soldiers were used to escort civilian construction workers to the various sites and to prevent them from fleeing while they were employed there.[77] Troops were also engaged in building canals, notably that to bypass Lake Ladoga,[78] and, of course, on various fortification works—for example, at Pskov, Narva, Kiev, Azov, and Taganrog. The last two places were dumping grounds for those who offended against military discipline and were condemned to forced labour. Soldiers assigned to construction work were in practice treated much like the forced labourers who toiled alongside them, not least in regard to pay.[79]

Another form of labour service was that which soldiers performed for their officers. This practice was inherited from the Muscovite period, when it had

---

[72] *Voinskiye artikuly* (*PRP* viii), §§ 85, 88; *PSZ* iv. 3006, ch. lx, § 5; Bobrovsky, *Voyennoye pravo*, ii. 589.

[73] *Voinskiye artikuly*, §26; cf. §§ 36–49 (*PRP* viii. 327, 329–32).

[74] *Voinskiye artikuly* (*PRP* viii), §§ 3, 5–6, 9, 14, 41, 48; cf. *Ustav voinskiy*, preamble (*PRP* viii. 319).

[75] Kersnovsky, *Istoriya*, i. 55.

[76] Luppov, *Ist. stroitel'stva Peterburga*, pp. 85, 88; cf. *PiB* vii. 2323 for an early proposal to this effect. Between 1716 and 1722 40,000 Ukrainian Cossacks were sent to work on canal-building or fortification projects; 30 per cent to 50 per cent of them died. Subtelny, 'Russia and the Ukraine', p. 16.

[77] *PiB* ix. 6389 (1709).

[78] [Peter I] *Zhurnal*, ii. 180 (Oct. 1721).

[79] *SIRIO* xi. 402; *DiP* iv (ii). 1042.

led to manifold abuses and even to mutiny, as in 1682. It was to prove a vexing problem for the authorities throughout the Imperial era. In principle a soldier in the regular army served the tsar alone. But if the state could not or would not pay him an adequate wage, and he could obtain a little extra from private sources, should he not be allowed to come to an arrangement with a superior officer, provided that his services could be spared? The first of many blanket orders condemning the practice was promulgated as early as 1696: officers were not to employ men in their homes, or to have them plough, reap, catch fish, or cut timber on their behalf; instead they were assigned orderlies on a fixed scale according to their rank.[80] These orderlies occupied a kind of limbo between the civilian and military sectors: their masters were responsible for their conduct and provided their uniforms; but in an emergency they were expected to serve and they received pay at a rate half that of a soldier.[81] But in 1710 naval officers were permitted to employ sailors with the sanction of higher authority, and six years later this rule was extended to the army as well. The men were supposed to volunteer for the job (an unrealistic provision in the circumstances); they were not to be given heavy, unhealthy, or humiliating work; the authorities were to be kept informed; and they were to be paid. The rates were at first left to the employing officer's discretion, but in 1724 were fixed at 5 kopecks a day, the same as for peasant labourers.[82] Russia was now at peace; most of the troops had been settled in rural areas, and soldiers formed a ready pool of agricultural labour. Evidently there was no lack of demand among soldiers for civilian work, since they were allowed to complain if men were allotted jobs out of turn. They could also engage in craft activity during their free time—and presumably sell the product. All this showed that the economic life of Peter's standing army preserved more than a trace of an earlier era when self-support had been the rule.

A regular army presupposed regular pay—such as had in fact been issued to soldiers in the new-model forces. Although the historical literature gives a contrary impression, the reign of the tsar-reformer brought no significant progress in this respect and may even have marked a step backwards. The soldiers who enlisted in 1699, as we know, were promised 11 roubles a year, but this wealth turned out to be a mirage, for as much as 5 roubles of the sum might be deducted to pay for uniforms and other items of personal equipment.[83] There was no guarantee that they would get even this. Already in 1700 men were petitioning that they had received nothing, although the money had been given by their proprietors on induction was exhausted.[84] The problem was partly one of inefficient administration: the old *prikaz* structure had been left to decay but nothing better had been put in its place. The Office for Military Affairs,

---

[80] *PSZ* iii. 1540 (8 Feb. 1696), § 12.

[81] *PSZ* v. 2638 (28 Jan. 1713); cf. 2456 (10 Dec. 1711), § 18.

[82] Voinskiye artikuly, §§ 54–5 (*PRP* viii. 333); *PSZ* vii. 4535 (26 June 1724), §10; Bobrovsky, *Voyennoye pravo*, ii. 240–2.

[83] *PiB* xii(ii), p. 282; cf. x. 3571, 4121.   [84] Rabinovich, 'Formirovaniye', p. 231.

set up in 1701 under T. N. Streshnev, was formally responsible for the new regiments, but it had only a rudimentary apparatus and could not collect enough funds to maintain them. It submitted requests for payment to the Ratusha, which had taken over as the main fiscal agency, but could not control what money was actually paid since the Ratusha at first dealt directly with the units concerned.[85] This body resorted to one desperate expedient after another to obtain revenue but could not gather sufficient money to pay the large number of troops that had been raised. Only in 1706 did the Office for Military Affairs assume its proper accounting functions, but even so there was a shortage of copper coin and in practice many units had to live off the land. This was the case with the auxiliary corps sent to Poland and Saxony, which was all but cut off from the Russian command. Patkul's papers contain striking testimony to the plight of these troops who, he complained, 'have no shelter for the winter and must freeze and starve'.[86] Even in Russia itself pay rates were far lower than they were supposed to be. In 1702 infantrymen in Smolensk were to receive 5 roubles a year, but scattered references in official correspondence for 1709–14 show that men were being paid at annual rates of 4, 3.60, and 3.40 roubles.[87] All these rates were lower than that given by the publicist Ivan Pososhkov in his well-known *Book on Poverty and Wealth*, completed in 1724, who tells of a recruit receiving 2 *grivny* (40 kopecks) a month, taking out a knife and committing suicide.[88] In the Semenovsky guards regiment a distinction was drawn between old soldiers and so-called 'nephews' or newcomers, who got 5.70 and 3.20 roubles respectively.[89] Shortly after Poltava Sheremetev reported to the tsar that some men at Chernigov 'are suffering great hardship through the [non-]issue of pay. They did not receive their full amount in June and have had nothing at all for July and August; some detachments have had nothing for several months.'[90] In April 1710 it was Peter's turn to complain to Sheremetev. The troops in West Prussia, he said, 'last drew pay half a year ago' and were 'extremely poor and lacking uniforms.'[91] It is not clear what, if anything, was done.

In 1711, when the first detailed establishment table (*shtat*) for the army was drawn up, pay rates were fixed at 10.98 roubles for an infantryman and 12 roubles for a cavalryman.[92] Nominally this was much the same as in 1699, but it took no account of inflation during the intervening years, which was certainly steep (but unfortunately not quantifiable from the sparse price data available). From this modest sum about half was deducted for uniforms etc.—until 1719, when this practice was apparently done away with[93]—and a few kopecks for

[85] Avtokratov, 'Pervye organy', pp. 165–6.

[86] Erdmann, *Patkul*, pp. 200–2; cf. Bobrovsky, *Voyennoye pravo*, ii. 175–6.

[87] Avtokratov, 'Pervye organy', p. 173; *PiB* ix. 3541; *DiP* i. 129, iv. 1011.

[88] Pososhkov, *Kniga*, pp. 42–4, 50.

[89] Kurakin, *Arkhiv*, iii. 94–5.   [90] *PiB* ix. 3363 (5 Aug. 1709).

[91] *PiB* x. 3620, 3672 (5/6 Mar., 4 Apr. 1710); cf. Bauer to Peter I, in ibid. xii. 5085 (21 Mar. 1712).

[92] *PSZ* iv. 2319 (19 Feb. 1711), pp. 593, 595.   [93] *PRP* viii. 394.

medical supplies.[94] Garrison troops received two-thirds, or usually half, as much as men in the active army.[95] Pay was issued in three four-monthly instalments, the regimental authorities being supervised, at least in theory, by an official of the War Commissariat (the supply organization) known as a *tsal'-komisar* or *tsal'meyster*. If pay did not arrive when due, the men were forbidden 'to cry' about the matter but had to carry on uncomplainingly.[96]

In addition to their pay Peter's soldiers at first received a cash allowance with which to buy foodstuffs. As in the seventeenth century, the assumption was that provisions would normally be available in the locality where troops were stationed at prices they could afford. There were also sutlers, that is, private tradesmen who accompanied the army as it moved about, or at least appeared from time to time in its encampments. This allowance was set at 6 den'gi per day for the volunteers of 1699;[97] but the decree did not state for how long it was to be paid, and it seems to have been viewed by the authorities as a means of attracting men to the colours rather than as a permanent commitment. As for recruits, they were supposed to be provisioned by their former proprietors for the first three months of their service.[98]

The war compelled the government to assume more responsibility for supply matters than it had anticipated, but the administrative breakdown greatly hampered its efforts in this domain. The individual entrusted with full power as commissar-general, Prince Ya. F. Dolgorukiy (1659–1720), was taken prisoner by the Swedes at Narva,[99] and his functions appear to have been taken over mainly by the ubiquitous Romodanovsky.[100] When Dolgorukiy escaped and returned to Russia in 1711, he got back his old job with a still more resounding title ('general plenipotentiary war commissar') and, more importantly, with an experienced deputy, L. Chirikov, and a rudimentary staff.[101] On paper the Commissariat officials had extensive powers *vis-à-vis* field officers in regard to both pay and provisions.[102] But how far did they succeed in coping with their immense tasks?

Hitherto the troops' needs had been met largely by requisitioning. This caused a good deal of distress to civilians, particularly in Poland and the Baltic provinces.[103] Whenever this necessarily arbitrary method did not provide enough, the desperate troops were prone to loot, despite the severe sanctions

---

[94] Anisimov and Zinevich, *Istoriya*, p. 23.

[95] *PSZ* xliii. 2319 (p. 5); iv. 2474 (29 Jan. 1712).

[96] Voinskiye artikuly, § 68 (*PRP* viii. 336).

[97] *PSZ* iv. 1820 (23 Dec. 1700), § 13. There were 200 den'gi to the rouble.

[98] This obligation was not defined until 1705: *PSZ* iv. 2065 (14 July 1705), §7.

[99] Danilov in *SVM* i (1, i, i). 9; *PSZ* iv. 1764; Bobrovsky, *Voyennoye pravo*, ii. 399; *VE* iii. 170–1. Danilov, an official historian, mentions the prince's captivity but then states blandly that in 1703 he was entrusted with greater authority as head of the Office of Military Affairs.

[100] *PiB* iii. 841 (21 June 1705).

[101] *PSZ* iv. 2412 (31 July 1712); Bobrovsky, *Voyennoye pravo*, ii. 402.

[102] *PSZ* iv. 3006, ch. xv, xix.

[103] 'Doneseniya Pleyera', in Ustryalov, *Istoriya*, iv (ii). 563, 580; *PiB* ix. 2991; xi. 4285, 4365; xii (ii). 5388; Myshlayevsky, *Peter Velikiy*, p. li; Bobrovsky, *Voyennoye pravo*, ii. 396; Erdmann, *Patkul*, pp. 171, 200.

taken against those who did so. Foodstuffs often served as a substitute for pay. Referring to some soldiers in Riga in 1710, Peter ordered Sheremetev 'not to give them any money for the moment but have them issued with provisions instead'; in the event all they got was some salt.[104] Another detachment in Germany, which was to be treated similarly, received nothing at all owing to lack of shipping.[105] On the other hand, there is evidence from calmer times of troops getting provisions and a small cash allowance (2 den´gi per day).[106]

Attempts to introduce a more orderly system began by establishing an official ration. Soldiers in the field were to receive each month ¼ chetvert´ (2 puds or 32.8 kg.) of rye flour and ⅛ chetvert´ of groats (*krupa*)—the latter being the basis of the staple item in the soldier's diet, a form of gruel known as *kasha*.[107] According to the English ambassador, in December 1707 the government decided in principle to introduce a system like that in the Habsburg empire, whereby officers and men were allocated a fixed number of rations, varying with their rank.[108] Several years passed, however, before these scales were laid down. In Russia the provisions designed for human consumption were confusingly known as 'portions' (*portsii*), as distinct from *ratsii* which were for horses and other draught animals. In the infantry privates drew one, corporals two, and sergeants three portions, the assumption being that NCOs—and still more officers—had families and servants to support. In wartime each portion was made up as follows: a daily allowance of 2 *funty* (800 grams) of bread, 1 *funt* of meat, 2 *charki* (¼ litre) of wine, and 1 *garnets* of beer, and a monthly allowance of 2 *funty* of salt and 1½ *garntsy* of groats.[109] In the cavalry senior NCOs received the same as their infantry equivalents (as well as rations for their mounts), but corporals and privates received neither. Peacetime rations were calculated on an annual rather than a daily or monthly basis and were less generous.[110] In 1719 the value of the annual portion was put at 5.375 roubles[111]—almost exactly half an infantryman's pay. One is left wondering whether the men actually received these comparatively lavish allocations or whether this was merely a book-keeping operation. Much depended on the administration's ability to raise enough in taxes to buy foodstuffs and to find suppliers with whom to conclude contracts. This was a problem with wide ramifications for Russian society which we shall examine in ch. 6.

[104] *PiB* x. 3783 (21 Aug. 1710), pp. 172, 609.
[105] *PiB* x. 3944 (pp. 299, 706); cf. ix. 3541 (Dec. 1709).
[106] *PSZ* iv. 2533 (26 May 1712); *DiP* iv (ii). 1029 (3 Sept. 1714).
[107] *PSZ* iv. 2034 (18 Feb. 1705). In garrison units the rates were lower: 5 and 3 *chetverti* of flour per annum for married and single men respectively, plus 1½ or 1 *chetvert´* of groats.
[108] Whitworth, 'Doneseniya', *SIRIO* xxxix. 444-5; cf. *PSZ* iv. 2181 (9 Dec. 1707).
[109] *PSZ* iv. 3003, ch. lxviii; cf. iv. 2456, 2612 (10 Dec. 1711, 15 Dec. 1712); Stein, *Geschichte*, p. 75; Bobrovsky, *Voyennoye pravo*, ii. 412-13. Also included was the so-called 'service' (*serviz*) which soldiers in civilian billets received from their hosts: vinegar, firewood, bedding, and 'other usual foodstuffs as available'.
[110] Anisimov and Zinevich, *Istoriya*, p. 23; Petrov, *Russkaya voyennaya sila*, ii. 59.
[111] Bobrovsky, *Voyennoye pravo*, ii. 413 n.

For the moment it is sufficient to note that non-receipt of pay and lack of food were major causes of desertion from the forces, which seems to have been almost as much of a worry for the government at the end of Peter's reign as it had been at the height of the war. Initially the flight from the ranks was on a fairly modest scale, but by May 1703 Pleyer observed ubiquitous notices warning the tsar's subjects against harbouring deserters.[112] He spoke of them as 'having been *discharged* (sic) on the march because they find it so hard to forsake their home, family and [usual] food', which was misleading to say the least. Whitworth was more plain-spoken, and in 1707 reported that 'the soldiers desert in very great numbers; 700 are run away from one regiment of dragoons which was lately sent from here [Moscow] to St. Petersburg, and of the 11 foot regiments now here scarce one has lost less than 200 men, though they were delivered complete about two months ago.'[113] Menshikov wrote to Peter from Akhtyrka in the Ukraine that 'the local people are all running off in various directions, and if I don't stay where I am not a single man of the regiment will be left in this town'.[114]

The military historian Bobrovsky thought that one-sixth of the army's losses to 1709, about 25,000 men, could be accounted for by desertions, but this is no more than a guess which cannot be reconciled with his statement that 'no less than 10,000 men deserted each year' between 1705 and 1709.[115] On the other hand Myshlayevsky probably underestimated the extent of the phenomenon which, on the basis of certain extant records for 1703–6, he put at 3 per cent of recruits and 1.2 per cent of all those under arms.[116] One party of recruits sent to Sevsk in 1709 started out 4,500 strong but lost 410 men, or 9 per cent;[117] and the official who reported this does not seem to have considered such a rate abnormally high. In Repnin's division a check in November 1708 showed 987 men absent of whom 755 were sick and 232 deserters—together about one-quarter of his total effectives.[118] In 1710 the total number of deserters was estimated at 20,000.[119]

The penalty for desertion was, in general, death. As early as 1700 Peter laid down that deserters deserved to be hanged, and this penalty was indeed applied to a soldier named Ivan Alekseyev, who belonged to a unit stationed in Novgorod but was found at Simbirsk; another man who deserted twice was, however, only beaten.[120] The increasing frequency of flight led to sterner measures. In January 1705 it was decreed that every third man recaptured after escaping was to be hanged in public before his comrades, 'so that in future

[112] 'Doneseniya Pleyera', in Ustryalov, *Istoriya*, iv (ii). 608.

[113] Whitworth, 'Doneseniya', *SIRIO* xxxix. 441; cf. 1. 63.

[114] *PiB* ix (ii). note to 2991 (Jan. 1709).

[115] Bobrovsky, *Voyennoye pravo*, ii. 709 and note 739; cf. also Duffy, *Russia's Military Way*, p. 133.

[116] Myshlayevsky, *Petr Velikiy*, p. liv.

[117] *PiB* ix. 2978 (31 Jan. 1709).

[118] *Trudy IRVIO* ii. 32–3

[119] Shendzikovsky, in *SVM* xii (1, i). 113.

[120] *PSZ* iii. 1820, §§ 4, 18; Golikova, 'Iz istorii', p. 273.

they shall not be attracted to flee the service'; the other two men were to be knouted and sent to forced labour for life. This was also the lot of those who surrendered voluntarily, except that in their case the forced labour term was limited to five years, after which they were to be returned to their regiment.[121] To their credit Peter's officials tried to moderate the penalty for desertion: a decree prepared in the Office for Military Affairs (1705) specified that every tenth rather than every third man was to be put to death.[122]

Soldiers who absconded on the battlefield were to be gunned down by their comrades: 'those behind are to fire cannon and muskets at those fugitives without any mercy'.[123] Such draconian penalties do seem to have been applied in practice, especially where the tsar had anything to do with the matter—for Peter used his sovereign prerogative to stiffen penalties imposed by military courts. In 1708 26 Preobrazhensky guardsmen were tried for desertion; six were sentenced to die for crimes they had allegedly committed while on the run; but Peter, when confirming the sentence, extended this penalty to half the men whom the court had sentenced to penal servitude, repeating his familiar refrain: 'and in future those who flee and are caught are to be put to death without any mercy'.[124] In fairness it should be added that this was a crucial juncture in the war.

Later, in 1712, the tsar adopted a gentler tactic of imposing fines on everyone held responsible for the men's escape, from the colonel (1.50 roubles) down to fellow-soldiers (1 kopeck).[125] Sheremetev complained that this measure was ineffective and it had to be abandoned.[126] The Military Statute of 1716 bristled with menacing penalties for insubordination of every kind, and this helped to swell the number of deserters. They were declared outlaws and could be killed on sight by anyone with impunity.[127] By this time whole districts were terrorized by bands of fugitives, sometimes several hundred strong, against whom detachments of troops had to take the field. In Kaluga province a certain Sirotka equipped his followers with uniforms, swords, and muskets, and trained them to mount guard in regular fashion.[128] Many other runaways gathered in Poland, where they escaped 'by whole companies' as they marched homeward from Germany.[129]

Peter was obliged to mix blandishments with outright repression. In 1717 he moderated the penalty—if the gauntlet can be considered an improvement— on men who fled during their first year of service.[130] Two years later a decree

[121] *PSZ* iv. 2019, 2031 (19 Jan., 10 Feb. 1705).
[122] *PSZ* iv. 2065 (14 July 1705).
[123] *PiB* iii. 662 (8 June 1704), § 6.
[124] *PiB* viii. 2739 (pp. 217–26).
[125] *PiB* xii. 5024 (Jan. 1712); *PSZ* iv. 2456 (10 Dec. 1711), § 17.
[126] *PiB* xii (ii), p. 447.
[127] Voinskiye artikuly, § 94 (*PRP* viii. 340–1, 404).
[128] Knyaz'kov, *Iz proshlogo*, ii. 95.
[129] Velyaminov to Repnin, 15 May 1719, cited by Bobrovsky, *Voyennoye pravo*, ii. 709 n. and Rozengeym, *Ocherki*, p. 214.
[130] Peter I to Senate, 23 Nov. 1717, *SIRIO* xi. 356–7; Voinskiye artikuly, § 95 (*PRP* viii. 341, 407).

dealt with some of the abuses which caused recruits to abscond: the failure of their proprietors to supply them with money and provisions for their first months in the service, which henceforth were to be supplied from official sources.[131] An amnesty was also declared, and by October 1720 13,000 men had come back to the fold—although not all these returned of their own free will.[132] Another amnesty was offered to mark the peace of Nystad (1721), which was then extended to all Russian military defectors abroad and the deadline for reporting extended.[133] Those amnestied were, however, required to denounce those who had sheltered them, and severe punishment awaited those who did not do so.[134] A reward of 5 roubles was also offered to anyone who revealed a deserter's whereabouts; if he actually led the authorities to an estate where such individuals were being given refuge, he could hope to receive possession of it—even if he were a mere serf.[135] How many profited or suffered as a result of this measure is not known, but it is clear that in the last years of Peter's reign much of the country was in a state verging on civil war, and it was no accident that within a few days of the emperor's death yet another amnesty was proclaimed, which this time gave deserters almost two years within which to report.[136]

Resistance to Peter's 'garrison state' sometimes took a more active form; as in the seventeenth century, soldiers were to be found among Cossack rebels in the borderlands.[137] But this protest movement should be seen in perspective. The overwhelming majority of men in uniform, whatever their state of mind, served the tsar loyally. Foreign diplomats (as a group, to be sure, superficial observers of the military milieu) were impressed by the discipline of the Russian army. Otto Pleyer, the Austrian envoy, was the most enthusiastic. 'It is most amazing to what perfection the soldiers have been brought in their military exercises; how obediently they fulfil the orders of their superiors and how bravely they fight; one does not hear a word, still less a cry, so zealous are they.'[138] He attributed this in large measure to the personal example of the tsar, who inspired a sense of duty and self-sacrifice among men of all ranks. Certainly, with his simple ways and unaffected manner Peter did have a rare gift for establishing a *rapport* with the common Russian soldier, who was pathetically grateful for the least sign of benevolence on his sovereign's part. Peter also concerned himself intermittently with the health and welfare of the troops. A recent student of the matter concludes that 'on balance, the possibility of getting professional medical attention set the armed forces apart

---

[131] *PSZ* v. 3425, 3443 (24 Sept., 21 Oct. 1719).

[132] Bobrovsky, *Voyennoye pravo*, ii. 710.

[133] *PSZ* v. 3859, 3924, 3926 (29 Nov. 1721, 2, 4 Apr. 1722).

[134] *PSZ* v. 3996 (8 May 1722).

[135] *PSZ* v. 2885, 3445, 3477 (14 Feb. 1715, 30 Oct., 24 Dec. 1719); Bobrovsky, *Voyennoye pravo*, ii. 724.

[136] *PSZ* vi. 4652 (9 Feb. 1725).

[137] Golikova, 'Iz istorii', p. 284.

[138] 'Otto Pleyers . . . Relation' (1710), in Herrmann, *Russland*, p. 121; cf. 'Doneseniya Pleyera', in Ustryalov, *Istoriya*, iv (ii). 540, 542.

from the civilian population and probably improved the servicemen's morale'.[139] They will have attributed the deficiencies to the ill-will or inefficiency of their superiors, retaining a positive image of the ruler.

Moreover, the military ethos was undoubtedly attractive to the more ambitious. Such men took their loyalty oath seriously: each of them had sworn 'to bear appropriate obedience to my commanders set above me in everything touching the well-being and increase of His Tsarist Majesty's forces, state, and subjects . . . and to act in all things as an honest, loyal, obedient, brave, and patient soldier should'.[140] They accepted the official view that a soldier's profession was the most honourable of all, since he risked his life for others in a noble cause. According to the Military Statute 'the term soldier simply means everyone in the army, from the highest general down to the least private'.[141] Supposedly all the tsar's servants were equal in their obligations to him and military rank depended on merit. Thus even the most humbly born could hope for preferment if he displayed sufficient zeal and earned the goodwill of his superiors. He might also hope to win medals and cash gifts which testified to the monarch's appreciation of his services and fortified his self-esteem. These were sources of strength which explain why hundreds of thousands of men reconciled themselves, at least outwardly, to a military despotism from whose effects they suffered more than most.

[139] Alexander, 'Medical Developments', p. 211. In 1712 Peter ordered hospitals to be set up in every province (*PiB* xii. 28; cf. *PSZ* iv. 2477), but seems to have expected the funds for them to be provided locally. Invalid soldiers were treated at Dr. Bidloo's hospital in Moscow, which later became a military institution (Petrov, *Russkaya voyennaya sila*, ii. 65); of its trainees, who numbered a few dozen, most were despatched to the forces, among them Sergey Yevreynov, a soldier's son who by 1736 was heading a field hospital at Azov—the first Russian to occupy such a post (Alexander, 'Medical Developments', pp. 209, 219–20). There were seven provincial institutions, of which that in Kazan´ could accommodate 600 men (Müller-Dietz, *Militärarzt*, pp. 35–6; Rossov, 'Ist. ocherk', p. 377). However, most veterans needing institutional care were sent to monasteries, where they were not always made welcome.

[140] Voinskiy ustav, preamble (*PRP* viii. 320–1).

[141] Yepifanov, 'Voinskiy ustav', p. 174.

6

THE NOBLE SERVITOR
AND THE PETRINE STATE

'ANY man who gets his bread for free, even if only a small amount, will not serve the state usefully or make any effort unless he is compelled to do so, but will try by every device to escape it and live in idleness, which according to the Scriptures is the mother of all evil.'[1] The most remarkable thing about this statement, so characteristic of the tsar-reformer, is that Peter seemed to equate landownership with sloth. Out of uniform, the noble proprietor was seen as a parasite who contributed nothing to the general welfare; neither his entrepreneurial nor his managerial role was of any account. In fact only the wealthiest members of the *dvoryanstvo* (or *shlyakhetstvo*, as it now came to be called, in emulation of the Polish gentry or *szlachta*) could afford to live unproductively from the labour of their dependants. The vast majority took part in agriculture and commerce to the extent that the inexorable demands of state service permitted. It was precisely this historic burden which Peter was set on increasing, with the result that by the end of his reign Russian nobles were more service-oriented, indeed more militarized, than at any time before or since.

State service secured them considerable advantages, both materially and in terms of social prestige. Most of them held officer rank, and in eighteenth-century European armies those who held positions of command needed at least a smattering of education. The Petrine era brought about something of a cultural revolution so far as the country's social élite was concerned, of which we can touch on only those aspects that directly affected military service. The more ambitious noble officers (or would-be officers) went to the new institutions which Peter founded: to garrison schools in the provinces or to specialized establishments for engineers, artillerymen, and naval officers; together these eventually numbered several hundred pupils.[2] Some were sent to study abroad. Others obtained a practical education of sorts through service in their regiments, which for the first time in Russian history might take them to countries such as Poland or Germany—although the psychological effects of these novel experiences were as yet slight. Much more important was the fact that virtually all of them came into contact with foreign or foreign-born

---

[1] *PSZ* v. 2789 (23 Mar. 1714), § 3.

[2] Bobrovsky, *Voyennoye pravo*, ii. 705; *PiB* xii (i). 5024 (27), pp. 22–3, 282–3, 340, 381; Beskrovnyy, 'Voyennye shkoly', pp. 291–4.

officers in the tsar's service. These contacts were often antagonistic, but they did something to enlarge the provincial gentryman's mental horizons. Intellectually—and perhaps even morally, due to changing concepts of honour—the Russian *shlyakhtich* of the 1720s was likely to be a different kind of person from his grandfather who had fought in the gentry levy during the seventeenth-century Cossack wars.

The military talents of this militia were portrayed in most uncomplimentary terms by the publicist Pososhkov, an artisan's son. Some privileged servitors, he averred, could not even load their muskets, let alone shoot straight; they were less concerned with killing the enemy than with returning home safely and would take to the woods *en masse* when the Tatars approached.[3] This statement has often been quoted uncritically: Pososhkov advocated a small highly-trained cadre army, an idea which the tsar rejected in favour of massive forces; but his criticism did contain an element of truth. The militia clearly needed reform if it was to maintain its historical role of helping to protect the steppe frontier; and it was totally unsuited to combat the well-trained armies of Charles XII.

As we have seen in ch. 5, a number of privileged servitors were called up in 1700–1 to form regiments of dragoons; about 13,000 to 14,000 of them were probably under arms at that time.[4] Those rejected on physical grounds were enlisted later—and not necessarily in the cavalry. In the first years of the war the government raised recruits wherever it could find them, with little concern for social distinctions.[5] Those who were of gentry background, provided they displayed a minimum of competence, could expect to become NCOs and officers fairly rapidly; but this was as much a consequence of the high casualty rate as it was of any tenderness for their class origin or personal preferences. Correspondingly, men from non-privileged circumstances could rise up through the ranks, and commissions were sometimes granted on the battlefield to men who showed exceptional merit. This was a time when the army did indeed act as a conduit for the upwardly mobile. But neither Peter nor the members of his entourage made this a policy objective. Their concern was solely with military efficiency. The tsar always insisted that promotion take place in an orderly manner, according to merit: this had been the immediate pretext for his quarrel with Shein in 1698 (see p. 100). The concept of 'merit' was vague, and might mean no more than trouble-free service in a subordinate rank; but primarily it meant technical proficiency. An early disciplinary code laid down that all officers and NCOs were to be tested individually as to their skill in performing complicated manœuvres; 'if someone senior is clumsy and a subordinate does it better, he shall be demoted and the junior man promoted in his

---

[3] 'O ratnom povedenii' (1701), in Pososhkov, *Kniga*, p. 268.
[4] Rabinovich, 'Formirovaniye', p. 234.
[5] For example, *PSZ* iv. 1978 (8 Apr. 1704), 2090 (1 Feb. 1706), 2111–12 (11–13 June 1706), 2197, 2199 (23 Apr., 13 May 1708).

stead'.[6] In this way the fear of some and the zeal of others would combine to advance the interests of the army as a whole.

General inspections offered the best means of weeding out the fit from the unfit. The principle was not new; the thoroughness, and the close interest taken by the sovereign, were. In 1704 Peter held a review of 8,000 nobles in Moscow. After another such parade in 1708 lists were compiled 'of the ranks and names of those fit to be officers and privates'. The tsarevich Aleksey was told to seek out 300 to 500 high-ranking servitors (*tsaredvortsy*, roughly equivalent to the old metropolitan nobility) and to choose some of them to be officers. He replied dutifully: 'I am ordering the young ones to be trained and making them privates, and afterwards shall send them as officers to the regiments listed',[7] adding the pathetic plea: 'where shall I get food for those poor servitors who have neither villages nor estates and say they have nothing to eat?' Such mundane matters had a low priority, especially at this critical moment.

Paradoxically, it was only *after* Poltava that Peter seriously attempted to implement the principle of universal military service by male members of the élite. He concentrated his efforts on adolescents (*nedorosli*). In March 1710 six provincial governors were ordered to carry out 'extremely thorough' inspections of all gentry in their areas: 'list separately those fit for service and bring them with you to Moscow next winter'. The governors would be held personally responsible if any of the young men went into hiding.[8] The results were deemed unsatisfactory, especially as war with Turkey was looming. When he set up the Senate in March 1711, Peter instructed it to hunt down, with the aid of delators, noble boys who had managed to conceal their existence; this was the first occasion that he promised informers half the miscreant's property, the Crown taking the other half.[9] Kurbatov, the governor of Archangel, was particularly zealous in tracking these individuals, who strictly speaking were not deserters (*beglye*) but absentees (*netchiki*); but the means adopted were similar in each case. The headhunt gained in poignancy from the youth of the prey: even boys of 10 were required to register—although only so that they might be sent to school until, at age 15, they were old enough to join the forces. A celebrated edict of 1714 laid down that children of noblemen or clerks who did not study mathematics should be prohibited from marrying,[10] but it is not known how widely this was enforced.

---

[6] Yepifanov, 'Voinskiy ustav', pp. 192–3, citing 'Uchrezhdeniye k boyu'.

[7] *PiB* vii. 2139, 2146 (5, 27 Jan. 1708).

[8] *PiB* x. 3652 (30 Mar. 1710); for other *gubernii* 3991, 4046, 4175 (14 Sept., 17 Oct., 26 Dec. 1710).

[9] *PiB* ix. 4288, 4291; *PSZ* iv. 2337 (13 Mar. 1711); Voskresensky, *Zak. akty*, pp. 36–7. In his journal (*Zhurnal*, p. 328) Peter gave, as the first motive for this action, his desire to purge the officer corps of 'the large number who originated from the common people'; but this was not the reason stated at the time and is probably a later rationalization.

[10] *PSZ* v. 2778 (28 Feb. 1714).

The obligation to denounce those in hiding extended to their relatives, who were to be disgraced if they were senior officers but subjected to 'cruel tortures' if they were of low rank.[11] One notable, V.A. Zhadovsky, reported that a large number of boys were concealed in Kostroma district and was given the job of tracking them down.[12] Nineteen lads were discovered at Tula and no less than 109 at Shatsk.[13] But the penalities imposed were less severe than Peter had wanted. Three noblemen jailed at Yelat´ma were sent to the front without suffering further punishment.[14] Fifty-three men in Kiev province were ordered to forfeit their estates,[15] but it is not clear that they did so. The bureaucratic channels soon became clogged. There was still no machinery for verifying alleged absentees' claims that they had been authorized to stay at home or had been performing some other official errand.[16] There were also cases of resistance with which the authorities found it hard to cope. A clerk and two soldiers, sent to a village near Tula to catch a lad named Sukhotin, who was said to be 'causing damage . . . to many landowners', found he had slipped away two days before they arrived; they tried to arrest his peasants as sureties, but they 'became violent'; the official party had to withdraw after recouping the cost of its journey from Sukhotin's kinsmen.[17]

The hunt for absentees continued throughout the reign, reaching its zenith in 1722 when Peter ordered such youths to be outlawed as if they were bandits; anyone was entitled to slay them at will and their property was to be confiscated.[18] This menacing decree was not easily enforced and did not have the deterrent effect intended. Pososhkov lamented the ease with which gentry servitors could escape the net: one, Zolotarev, allegedly sent a substitute under his own name and meanwhile spent his time terrorizing his neighbours[19]—though this evidence is a little suspect.

Peter realized that he had to make military service more attractive by taking positive measures. Rates of pay for officers, as laid down in the 1711 establishment (*shtat*), were generous, at least by comparison with those of their men. A lieutenant drew 80 roubles a year—over six times as much as a private; a (first) major received 140 roubles, a colonel 300, and a full general 3,120 roubles.[20] (Officers in quarters were supposed to be paid at half rate, as were those in most garrisons.) Guards and artillery officers were treated better, and foreigners better still—at least on paper, for there were complaints, similar to

---

[11] *DiP* i. 14 (13 Mar. 1711); cf. 38, 61, 70 (27 Mar., 16 Apr., 24 Apr. 1711).

[12] *DiP* i. 67 (24 Apr. 1711); cf. 73 (25 Apr.).

[13] *DiP* i. 184, 223 (4 July, 24 July 1711).   [14] *DiP* i. 182 (3 July 1711).

[15] *DiP* i. 201 (16 July 1711), reproduced in Lebedev, *Reformy*, pp. 81–2.

[16] *DiP* i. 223 (24 July 1711); ii. 272 (26 Mar. 1712).

[17] *DiP* iv (i). 76 (22 Jan. 1714).

[18] *PSZ* vi. 3874 (11 Jan. 1722); Troitsky, *Absolyutizm*, p. 133; Klyuchevsky, *Soch.*, iv. 77 (*Peter the Great*, p. 94).

[19] Pososhkov, *Kniga*, pp. 94–5; Klyuchevsky, *Soch.*, iv. 78 (*Peter the Great*, p. 95). The episode apparently took place before 1700.

[20] *PSZ* iv. 2319, pp. 599–602; Mikhnevich, in *SVM* iv (l, i, i). 121 n.; Myshlayevsky, *Petr Velikiy*, pp. 120–1; Avtokratov, 'Pervye organy', pp. 171–2.

those by the soldiers we have already discussed, that they had not been paid and were suffering distress.[21] Documentary evidence suggests that officers sometimes received more and sometimes less than the regulation amounts.[22]

The tsar also ordered that officers were to have precedence over civilian noblemen on all occasions—and should refer to themselves as officers (*ofitsery*) instead of *shlyakhtichi*.[23] This was more important than it may seem, since the idea of *mestnichestvo* remained alive and Peter was anxious to shift the basis of such rivalries from birth to merit; and for him the best criterion of merit was the military rank one had attained. In 1714 he ruled that those gentry servitors 'who do not know the soldier's craft from its fundamentals' should not be appointed officers (which in itself was nothing new); to soften the blow he added that they should serve in the ranks of one of the guards units.[24] This had the result of fostering elitist tendencies within these regiments (a third, consisting of cavalrymen, was added in 1719) and making them something of a noble preserve. Foreign envoys were surprised to find scions of aristocratic families serving as privates in the guards, in the same conditions as those of humble birth.[25] Guards officers enjoyed important material privileges: not only higher pay but also extra rations (*ratsii*) for their mounts, superior accommodation in special settlements (*slobody*), and better medical services.[26] They also held ranks equivalent to those of officers two grades above them in the rest of the army, so that a guards major was on a par with an army (full) colonel.[27] The original rationale for this was that the guards were conceived as training units, from which men would pass out to command units in the field.

Finally, guards officers were close to the sovereign. They enjoyed his special favour and were entrusted with extraordinary responsibilities, as we shall see shortly. These developments were only partly deliberate, and one must be careful not to misconstrue, in the light of the guards' later history, Peter's purposes in the 1714 decree. It is true that in 1723 he ordered all young gentry servitors (and foreigners) to be assigned solely to the guards; but this decree was not published and remained in the archives.[28] The tsar equated artillery service with that in the guards, which suggests that even at the end of his reign professional considerations were more important than social ones. In any case there were simply not enough places in either the guards or the artillery for *every* aspiring young officer. By 1720 only about 6 per cent of officers had begun their service in the guards.[29] Those excluded continued to soldier on in line regiments.

---

[21] *DiP* iv (ii). 1006, 1055.   [22] Cf. *DiP* i. 42, 52, 112.

[23] *PiB* vii. 5024 (8 Feb. 1712), § 21; Troitsky, *Absolyutizm*, p. 42, whose interpretation is preferable to that of Rabinovich.

[24] *PSZ* v. 2775 (26 Feb. 1714); Beskrovnyy, 'Voyennye shkoly', p. 288; Podyapol'skaya, 'K voprosu', p. 186.

[25] Berkhgol'ts (Bergholz), 'Dnevnik', 11, suppl., pp. 20–1.

[26] *PSZ* xliii. 3322 (10 Mar. 1719); Juel, 'Zapiski', p. 71; Müller-Dietz, *Militärarzt*, p. 57.

[27] Troitsky, *Absolyutizm*, p. 109; Glinoyetsky, 'Ist. ocherk', p. 271.

[28] Troitsky, *Absolyutizm*, p. 77.   [29] Meehan-Waters, personal communication.

Another edict that had unforeseen social consequences was designed to prevent the fragmentation of noble estates.[30] Landowners were recommended to bequeath their property to a single heir; those who died intestate had it attributed to their eldest son. A subsidiary aim of this measure was to encourage those sons who were excluded, and inherited only movable goods, to join the service. Later Peter tried to establish the rule that only one third of the males in any noble family should join the civil bureaucracy, 'so that there shall be no shortage of serving men on land or at sea'.[31] Positive inducements of this kind were probably less effective in achieving the ends desired than the standard coercive devices.

The task of organizing periodical inspections and registration of gentry servitors was given first to the Senate, and in 1721–2 to one of its subordinate agencies, the Heraldmaster's Office (*Gerol'diya*), headed by S. A. Kolychev.[32] His instructions required him to 'know', and keep lists of, all such persons by name and by rank, as well as all their male children and the assignments held by each. If this was indeed done—which is uncertain, since this archive had yet to be properly explored—it would have made the control mechanism more thorough and efficient than it had been in the seventeenth century. The *Gerol'diya* inherited the functions and records of the old Razryad. Two innovations were that it devised coats of arms (*gerby*) for noble families and registered separately those who worked their way up into the privileged class by becoming officers.

The principle that promotion to officer rank conferred nobility was enunciated in two decrees of 1719 and 1721 and repeated in article 15 of the so-called 'Table of Ranks' (24 January 1722).[33] The latter was one of the most important pieces of social legislation in Imperial Russian history. It has been the subject of much scholarly discussion, but it is only in recent years, thanks to archival research by a Soviet historian, that it can be evaluated correctly.[34] It is now clear that: (*a*) the ranking system that was destined to govern the lives of civil officials (as well as officers) until 1917 was modelled on that previously existing in the armed forces; (*b*) Peter took account of prevailing sentiment among officers in shaping the reform as it applied to civilians; (*c*) the War College and Admiralty brought their influence to bear in the deliberations held in private before the decree was issued; (*d*) western European influences on the reform, most evident in a preliminary draft compiled by A. I. Osterman, came to be overlaid by native traditions, so that the measure may justly be regarded

---

[30] *PSZ* v. 2789 (23 Mar. 1714), also in Lebedev, *Reformy*, pp. 73–4; for discussion of the wider context, Klyuchevsky, *Soch.*, iv. 87–91 (*Peter the Great*, pp. 106–11).

[31] Voskresensky, *Zak. akty*, 368 (p. 355).

[32] *PSZ* vi. 3877; Voskresensky, *Zak. akty*, 368 (pp. 352–6); Troitsky, *Absolyutizm*, p. 103; *B&E* xvi. 546–7.

[33] *PSZ* v. 3265 (1 Jan. 1719); vi. 3705 (16 Jan. 1721), 3890; Beskrovnyy, 'Voyennye shkoly', p. 287. For an English translation of the Table: Vernadsky *et al.* (eds.), *Source Book*, ii. 344.

[34] Troitsky, *Absolyutizm*, pp. 3–118. Bennett ('Evolution') makes little use of Troitsky's work and is not always accurate.

as a logical outgrowth of earlier Russian practice in harnessing the élite to state service.

Consideration of Peter's reform has been bedevilled by two factors. First, some of the most important provisions were not actually mentioned in the decree, presumably because they were deemed to be self-evident. Second, the phraseology was very confused, such key terms as *chin* and *rang* being used in several different senses;[35] (in the following remarks they are given their generally accepted meaning).

The Table, as is well known, established 14 grades in all branches of state service: military and naval, civil, and court. (In reality there were only 13 grades, but this number was thought unlucky!) These grades, officially known as *klassy*, were arranged hierarchically, the most senior (I) at the top and grade XIV at the bottom. Servitors had the opportunity to climb the ladder from grade to grade, or to transfer from one branch to another at the appropriate level. Since the grades were listed in parallel columns, this seemed to imply that service in any branch at a certain level carried equal status. This was not actually so. Military and naval officers continued to enjoy precedence (here termed *rang* or *predsedatel'stvo*) over civilians in the same grade—unless the latter happened to be princes of the blood. For example, in Grade III a lieutenant-general had precedence over a privy counsellor (*tayniy sovetnik*), his equal in rank; he was senior *both* in status and in rank to a major-general in Grade IV. So too was his wife: there were some complicated rules about daughters' status that need not detain us.

One might have expected the offices or posts (*dolzhnosti*) in the various branches (for example, quartermaster-general) to be listed and placed in some relationship to the classes of persons who were to fill them. This was done in the original draft, based on a Danish model,[36] but in the final version these offices were not even mentioned. Instead office-holders themselves were given a rank (*chin*) appropriate to their class. The significance of this was that it gave the monarch (or whomever else assigned men to jobs) ample freedom of choice. Normally posts at a certain level would be occupied by persons already holding the requisite rank: a brigade commander would be a brigadier. If a vacancy occurred and no other brigadier was available for transfer, a colonel would be appointed and would rise from Grade VI to Grade V on promotion to brigadier. Posts might be occupied temporarily by men of inappropriately high or low rank, but in general promotion was strictly governed by hierarchical principles. One had to possess the requisite seniority (*starshinstvo*).

But how was seniority to be measured? Here the same ambiguity arose as had occurred under the *mestnichestvo* system. There were two kinds of seniority, which in bureaucratic jargon came to be called *vysluga* and *zasluga*. The former carried the connotation of seniority earned by steady service over

---

[35] Shepelev, *Otmenennye istoriyey*, p. 12; Bennett, 'Evolution', p. 6 n.
[36] Troitsky, *Absolyutizm*, p. 66.

a number of years in a particular grade. The latter had the implication of quality rather than quantity of service, that is, of special individual merit, such as valorous exploits in battle. But, to complicate matters further, such merit might be potential rather than actual. The sovereign, as an absolute ruler, could of course appoint anyone to any office, conferring upon him the appropriate *chin* and accelerating his promotion up the hierarchy. So too could those senior individuals to whom such power was delegated by the monarch. There was nothing very surprising about this: a general had to be able to fill a vacancy quickly, which meant rewarding a subordinate who displayed uncommon talent, whether actual or potential. But this loophole opened the way to arbitrary decisions, and thus the apparently rigid ranking system, like its Muscovite predecessor, was really quite flexible. *Vysluga* could indeed be ascertained objectively, by calculating the number of years spent blamelessly in the service; but *zasluga* implied a subjective judgement. Not only was the assessment of merit likely to be partisan; it might also be affected by kinship ties or other links between appointee and appointer. The latter bore full responsibility for his assessment. To be sure, he was supposed to comply with bureaucratic procedures and would normally consult candidates' records (including their personal *attestaty* or *kharakteristiki*—certificates of good conduct signed by superiors and fellow-servitors); but in the eighteenth-century context he was likely to consider their *genealogical* seniority as well.

Place-seeking had been abolished in 1682; aristocracy had not. Peter was suspicious of the old Muscovite *boyarstvo*, but harboured no prejudice against persons of ancient lineage; he was concerned only that they should serve him loyally. Although some of his most celebrated associates, such as Menshikov, were of humble birth, and others were foreigners, the great majority came from the higher reaches of the Russian nobility. So far as army officers are concerned, this fact has been established by recent research. Rabinovich's study of a sample of 2,245 officers (about 53 per cent of the total) in 1720–1 shows that 61.9 per cent were noblemen (*dvoryane*) by birth and only 13.9 per cent from a non-privileged background (former peasants, townsmen, or clergy).[37] Of the former group, 22.6 per cent were from the old metropolitan nobility.[38] These men were concentrated in the upper ranks of the officer corps. The new entrants to the *dvoryanstvo* who had risen up from the ranks, 316 in number in this sample, were overwhelmingly subalterns or else belonged to the so-called 'junior staff' (quartermasters, surgeons, clerks, etc.); only 20 of them had reached the rank of captain and a single one that of lieutenant-colonel. Western research into the *generalitet* (holders of the first four military ranks)[39] confirms that the intake of 'fresh blood' into the nobility was relatively

[37] Rabinovich, 'Sots. proiskhozhdeniye', pp. 138–9. Another 10.6 per cent were former *strel´tsy* or other lower-grade (*po priboru*) servitors; 12.6 per cent were foreigners and 1 per cent of undetermined origin.

[38] Ibid., p. 141, where the misleading term 'feudal aristocracy' is used.

[39] Meehan-Waters, 'Musc. Noble Origins', pp. 31, 40; id., *Autocracy*, pp. 29–37.

limited—less than has hitherto been assumed by historians misled by the apparently radical character of Peter's decrees. It was less extensive than in Sweden, where the same process was under way.[40]

Article 15 of the Table stated (in typically convoluted language) that 'as concerns holders of military rank who are not from the nobility [and] serve up to subaltern rank: when someone receives that aforementioned rank he is a nobleman.' It went on to specify that *hereditary* nobility was meant: any male children born to such an officer once he had been commissioned were likewise ennobled, and if he had any sons born before his commission he could petition for one of them to be included as well. Commoners in the civil service did not have this right: they were granted only 'personal' nobility, as it came to be called, which was not transmissible to their offspring unless they reached Grade VIII, that of 'college assessor' (equivalent to major in the army).[41] In this way those from underprivileged backgrounds who became military and naval officers won an important social advantage over men who rose up through the civil bureaucracy.

However, they were also subject to adverse discrimination, in two ways. First, the outwardly democratic procedure of holding a ballot among all officers of a regiment whenever a vacancy occurred, introduced in 1714, worked against the admission of those of humble birth, although this was not the intention behind the measure.[42] Paradoxically, the fact that the election was held in secret, and was decided by a majority vote (the casting of white rather than black balls for a favourable decision) probably strengthened the influence of the conservative-minded. Secondly, not every officer of underprivileged social origin could expect to be automatically awarded the coat of arms which served as an external sign that he had 'arrived' among the nobility. Article 16 prescribed that these were to be awarded 'according to merit' (*smotrya po zaslugam*), but many commoners will only have been able to demonstrate *vyslugi*. Coats of arms were, however, awarded to civilians whose forefathers had served for at least a century, and such persons were likely to be the progeny of former metropolitan nobles.

This provision may be regarded as a sop to the well-born. They were inclined to look on the Table of Ranks as a potential threat to their position, and some of them may have looked back nostalgically to the days of *mestnichestvo*, when a man's place in society was determined by rules which everyone, the tsar included, had respected. In the discussions behind the scenes they seem to have exerted some informal pressure in this direction, but the personalities involved cannot be identified and their 'lobby' was clearly much weaker than that of the military servitors. The latter's spokesman was Menshikov. The flamboyant Prince of Ingria was Peter's principal favourite and—until 1724,

---

[40] Nordmann, *Grandeur et liberté*, p. 190.

[41] *PSZ* vi. 3890 (24 Jan. 1722), § 11.

[42] Stein, *Geschichte*, p. 72; Petrov, *Russkaya voyennaya sila*, ii. 62; Rozengeym, *Ocherki*, p. 190; Troitsky, *Absolyutizm*, p. 124.

when he fell from grace—president of the War College, the most powerful of the new central government departments (*kollegii*). Menshikov was sensitive about his humble origins, which were held against him by members of the old families, and tried to compensate for this liability by acquiring vast personal wealth, often by unscrupulous means; he was notoriously corrupt and it was this vice that led to his demotion. More to the point, Menshikov's only power base was in the army, particularly in the guards. He was the first Russian politician outside the dynasty to cultivate this source of support in order to build up his standing. It seems to have been his lobbying that secured for guards officers a two-rank seniority over their opposite numbers in the army, as against the one-rank seniority which Peter had originally suggested.[43] Menshikov commanded (nominally at least) a regiment, the Ingermanlandsky, which, like the Butyrsky, enjoyed an elevated status close to that of the three guards regiments proper. This unit was remarkable for the fact that it contained the highest proportion of non-gentry officers (18 out of 56) in the entire army.[44] The prince clearly favoured and protected ambitious plebeian elements whose careers in some respects resembled his own. More than any other member of Peter's entourage, he detested aristocratic ideals and advocated close state regulation of all noble servitors, irrespective of birth. This principle was dear to the tsar as well, but Peter evidently felt it necessary to temporize and did not give in wholly to military pressure.

In the course of the discussion the War College objected to the use in the Table of Ranks of a term for nobility, *znatnost´*, which had aristocratic connotations, and wanted this to be clearly defined; however, it failed to win this point.[45] It was more successful in getting provisions incorporated in the decree that were designed to prevent young nobles who joined the civil service from being promoted straight to high rank, as was very likely to occur given the dearth of administrative talent. This, the army leaders felt, would be 'insulting to military men who earned their rank by performing service for many years under harsh conditions', and accordingly such individuals had to start off as trainees (*kollegii-yunkery* or 'college cadets') without any rank, much like those who served as common soldiers before becoming officers.[46]

The overall result of Peter I's measures was to strengthen the Crown's prerogatives over members of the privileged classes, whose career patterns were regulated from above and, up to a point, 'homogenized'. Unless they happened to be the sole inheritors of a large estate, they were expected to serve for an unlimited term in the armed forces or civil administration; if they chose

---

[43] Troitsky, *Absolyutizm*, pp. 77, 78 n.; Shepelev, *Otmenennye istoriyey*, p. 27; *PSZ* v. 3332.

[44] Rabinovich, 'Sots. proiskhozhdeniye', p. 153.

[45] Troitsky, *Absolyutizm*, pp. 96–7. Rabinovich ('Sots. proiskhozhdeniye', p. 170) suggests, on the basis of a casual instruction by Peter in 1718, that *znatnye* officers were exempt from torture; but this was not a secure legal right. The term *znatnye* also occurs in § 14, where it is employed in a different sense.

[46] An exception was made for those who were particularly well qualified educationally: §§ 13–14; Troitsky, *Absolyutizm*, pp. 106–7.

the civil branch, they suffered diminished prestige and were nevertheless regimented on military lines. Although civil (and court) service was now for the first time plainly differentiated from that in the armed forces, which was a sign of progress towards the creation of a modern bureaucracy, much of the old Muscovite spirit survived. Until 1762/1785 Russian noblemen still lacked any legal definition of their role in society or of their rights. They remained dependants, servitors, constantly at the beck and call of their sovereign or his favourites. For all the Table of Ranks' pedantic insistence on regularity when filling vacancies, those on whom the supreme authority temporarily devolved could quite legitimately staff posts with their own protégés, build up patronage networks, and so turn the system to their advantage. In a sense this was even easier than it had been before, since the administration was now more centralized.

On the surface the Table seems to have driven the last nails into the coffin of *mestnichestvo*, but in fact it allowed it to continue in new guise. The naïve old-fashioned rivalry between genealogically-conscious clansmen over precedence at official functions gave way in the eighteenth century to a more sinister life-and-death struggle between highly rank- and status-conscious officers or officials over jobs, social privileges, and all the other bounties that an omnipotent Autocrat could confer. This was progress of a kind, perhaps, but it was more permutation than innovation. European influences affected the élite's life-style—its language, manners, tastes, and social conduct—but these externals did not greatly change the substance. Its role in society had undergone little improvement. On the contrary: the victory of Petrine absolutism obstructed the process of moral and political maturation on which the privileged classes had embarked in the late seventeenth century. It delayed for fifty years or so the ultimately inevitable weakening of the ties that bound the nobility to the state.

For that state now acquired powerful new instruments of control over those who, by virtue of their Western-style education and exposure to an alien environment, might be tempted to develop aspirations towards autonomous thought. It was able to play on the petty jealousies that kept its functionaries divided, whether these rivalries were based on family connections, economic differences, or segregation by rank. As in an earlier age, it benefited from the amorphousness of the servitor class, and could take action to prevent its members from coalescing against it. In this way the absolutist state preserved its traditional pre-eminence over society.

Last but not least, the autocracy now possessed a powerful means of physical coercion in the shape of the new standing army—a force with which most members of the élite at least had close connections, if indeed they did not actually belong to it. This body of men—the largest in Europe, even if not the best trained—was kept at a high degree of readiness with a view to possible internal emergencies as well as international conflicts. One Western historian recently noted: 'as war became a perpetual activity of the Russian state, so did military service become permanent for its noble classes'.[47] Let us add that this was not a steadily intensifying relationship but rather one that ebbed and flowed as the years went by. Nevertheless the degree to which Russian society was militarized by the end of Peter's reign is remarkable and set a pattern for the future. To comprehend the full impact of the tsar-reformer's policies we have to consider the actions he took to provide for the army's material support.

The Great Northern War led indirectly to a fundamental recasting of the Muscovite administrative and fiscal system. Some of the institutional changes made at this time, such as the introduction of the provinces (*gubernii*) and the poll tax, were destined to endure for generations. The first of these reforms were impromptu responses to military necessity and their unexpected results can to some degree be blamed on external circumstances; but even after 1715, when Peter began to grapple seriously with problems of government, the consequences of his actions were often little short of disastrous. In his concern with long-term ends he overlooked the human factor. Much of the trouble stemmed from the simple fact that his new army was too large and costly for a country with limited resources, so that whatever was done to accommodate its needs was bound to impose unduly heavy burdens on the populace.

Already in the seventeenth century, as we know, the voivode had exercised both military and civil authority within his district (*uyezd*). But command of the local troops was not usually his principal concern unless he were appointed to a frontier area—or unless he were faced with some emergency such as a rebellion. It was different with the governors (*gubernatory*) whom Peter appointed—Menshikov was given charge of Ingria from 1703—since they were preoccupied with military and naval matters, above all the provision of recruits and war supplies. They exercised more power than the officials of the central government, which by 1708 had fallen to pieces. The country was in effect now divided into several satrapies whose chiefs seldom resided in them. The tsar tried to co-ordinate their actions by correspondence, but his attention was fixed elsewhere.[48] The governor of each province was supposed to have a staff: an *ober-komissar* to collect revenue, an *ober-proviant* to receive deliveries in kind, an *ober-komendant* in charge of specifically military affairs, and a *landrikhter* to administer justice. These arrangements suggest specialization of function and even a formal 'division of powers', but in the circumstances it is obvious that these agencies would be dominated by the military element—that is, if they came into existence at all. In practice the hard-pressed governor simply chose a deputy who did whatever his chief demanded of

---

[47] Givens, 'Servitors or Seigneurs', p. 14.

[48] The actual state of affairs is well brought out in Milyukov's classic study of 1892, *Gos. khoz. Rossii*; his main arguments are summarized in Miliukov, A. Seignobos and L. Eisenmann, *Histoire de Russie* (Paris, 1932), i. 328–35, 350–5, 362–9 (Eng. tr. pp. 259–64, 275–9, 285–304). Another fundamental early study, written from a similar viewpoint, is Bogoslovsky, *Obl. reforma*, which can now be supplemented by C. Peterson's excellent *Peter the Great's Admin. and Judicial Reforms . . .* (Stockholm, 1979).

him.[49] At the district level the voivode was replaced by a commandant (*komendant*), but this was little more than a change of name;[50] the only difference was that, in Claes Peterson's words, 'his administration was supervised with the help of military units'—especially those drawn from the guards.

The provinces had scarcely been established when, in January 1710, Peter 'graciously decided to impose state expenditure, for the army, the Admiralty and other disbursements, upon the provinces, so that everyone should know whence he could get a specific amount [of funds]'.[51] This measure gave generals and central officials *carte blanche* to demand from the governors an unlimited supply of resources. The tsar laid down that the needs of the armed forces were to be satisfied first. Some provinces were already spending all their revenue on military purposes and had nothing left for their own requirements. In an effort to equalize the burden a census was undertaken, but it encountered widespread sabotage. Some householders took to the woods, while others bribed officials to overlook their existence. The figures reported were so inaccurate that the government disregarded them and went back to those of the long outdated census of 1678. It was on this basis that the population had to pay for the army: its costs were fixed in the first establishment table (1711) and distributed among the provinces in such a way that each regiment was to be maintained from the revenue collected in a particular fraction (*dolya*) of a province. The fraction was at first conceived as an arithmetical abstraction rather than as an actual territorial unit; it was to consist of 5,536 households, so that there were 146½ *doli* in the country as a whole.[52] On paper at least this was a rough and ready method of sharing out the burden. The central authorities did not try to establish a uniform assessment per household, but left this to be arrived at locally; each community could act as it pleased in distributing its portion of the load, which was to be paid partly in cash and partly in kind, as the military authorities required.

The reform clearly left a great deal to chance; but its principal defect lay elsewhere. Army units were likely to be stationed outside their assigned province,[53] which meant that it would be difficult to convey to them whatever had been collected for their sustenance. The job of liaison was entrusted to so-called commissars (*komissary*)—military officials who occupied an ill-defined position between the central War Commissariat, the local governor, and the regimental authorities. The commissars, hard pressed and untrained for their delicate task, could not ensure a steady flow of money and supplies.

This explains why in 1715 other officials called rural counsellors (*landraty*) were introduced at the level of the fraction, which now assumed the lineaments

---

[49] Milyukov, *Gos. khoz. Rossii*, p. 294, n. 4; Peterson, *Reforms* (see fn. 48) pp. 238–9; Danilov, in *SVM* i. 59.

[50] Bogoslovsky, *Obl. reforma*, p. 47, disagrees.

[51] [Peter I] *Zhurnal*, p. 253; cf. *PSZ* iv. 2247 (27) (27 Jan. 1710).

[52] Klyuchevsky, *Soch.*, iv. 159 (*Peter the Great*, pp. 196–7).

[53] For an example see *DiP* iv (i). 44 (13 Jan. 1714).

of the old territorial division, the district.[54] These men, who replaced the commandants, were as a rule ex-officers of modest means who had been invalided out of the army.[55] Unlike their predecessors (or the commissars) they were supposed to be elected by the local nobility. The term election (*vybor*) should not mislead us. It implied a devolution of responsibility, not a transfer of power, and both in theory and in fact the *landraty* were no more than agents of the governor. Their functions resembled those of Muscovite *okladchiki*, except that the duties which they assigned to their fellow-nobles had to do with military supply, not actual service. Their main job was to supervise and accelerate deliveries, or more concretely to force suppliers to part with their produce on terms acceptable to the army authorities. Unfortunately no information is available as to the nature of these contracts or the prices paid, so that we do not know how far the rural counsellors succeeded in this task. They also organized another census of households, but this had no better result than its predecessor and the data collected were soon rendered obsolete by the adoption of a new system of individual assessment, based on the so-called male 'soul' (*dusha*).

The introduction of the poll tax between 1718 and 1724 was a bench-mark in that long drawn-out process, the degradation of the Russian peasant. It should again be stressed that this had more to do with the state's military policies than with selfishness or greed on the part of the landowning nobility. It needs to be seen in the context of two other changes that were taking place simultaneously. The first of these was the quartering of the army on the rural population, termed by one historian 'a regular assault on their fellow-subjects by over one hundred regiments'.[56] Although the Swedish war had ended Peter was in no mood to demobilize a force on which his regime depended so heavily for support. The second change was the introduction of the sub-province (*provintsiya*) as an intermediate tier in the hierarchy of local government organs, between the *guberniya* and the *dolya* or *distrikt* (as the *uyezd* was now called). Unlike the previous reforms, this was a deliberate effort to remould the administrative structure on rational Western lines, according to the Swedish example. The Russian *provintsiya* was designed as the equivalent of the *landshövdingdöme*. Sweden also seems to have been the model for the quartering of regiments. The Russian reformers knew of the cantonment (*indelta*) system whereby the Swedish Crown assigned land to farmers in return for the obligation to maintain a soldier and his family, and the farmers were allowed to use the soldier's labour when he was off duty.[57] Unfortunately for the *muzhik*, the introduction of this reform did not bring him even the modest advantages enjoyed by the

[54] *PSZ* v. 2879 (28 Jan. 1715); cf. Bogoslovsky, *Obl. reforma*, pp. 48–9; Peterson, *Reforms* (see fn. 48) p. 242.

[55] *PSZ* v. 3003 (22 Mar. 1716).

[56] Klyuchevsky, *Soch.*, iv. 185; cf. vii. 326.

[57] On this system see Nordmann, *Grandeur et liberté*, pp. 87–9. Curiously, Peterson makes only a casual reference to this aspect (p. 268), although he is at pains to emphasize Russia's indebtedness to Sweden for the local government reform.

Swedish peasant. This was partly because of Russia's social and institutional backwardness, and partly because the Swedish system was not applied consistently: in particular, Russia was just now moving *away* from the household tax, which was intrinsically more equitable, to the cruder but more profitable poll tax.

The reason for the change was that the government wanted to increase its revenue in order to maintain the troops properly. The underlying principle was the same as before and breath-takingly simple: to divide total military expenditure by the number of male taxpayers ('souls') and thus arrive at a uniform assessment for the whole country: so many kopecks per individual. Initially Peter held out the prospect that this new tax would *replace* all other state obligations, but this did not happen; there was a certain rationalization of these dues, but the total fiscal burden was much heavier than it had been in Muscovite times—over twice as great, in the estimation of contemporaries.[58]

This is a contentious point, and we shall attempt to substantiate our view below in the context of the state budget. Let us first see what happened in practice 'on the ground'. In November 1718 the tsar issued a laconically-worded decree calling for submission within one year of returns (*skazki*) stating the number of 'souls of the male sex' in each community; on this basis a calculation was to be made as to how many souls would be needed to support a private soldier, allowing for overheads such as regimental and company staffs.[59] Peter greatly underestimated the complexity of this operation. In the first place, those responsible for this third census ran into the same problems as their predecessors: massive concealment of potential taxpayers and lack of administrative staff to detect and deal with defaulters. By the end of 1719 the brigadier in charge of the census, V. N. Zotov, had received only a few statements, and these were inaccurate.

The next step was to send out guards officers with orders to put dilatory officials in irons and to confiscate their property. Governors were instructed to check the data personally and were provided with posses of troops to vet suspect landowners; the deadline had to be extended.[60] The postponement was in part due to the government's decision to include *all* the nobles' dependants, not just their peasants—a far-reaching change whose precise motives are unclear. Possibly the authorities realized that unless this were done the burden on the farming population would be too great, for a pilot project to quarter two regiments in Novgorod province showed that the per capita rate of poll tax would be as high as 97 kopecks.[61] The data on military costs were also found to need revision.[62]

---

[58] Manstein, 'Zapiski', p. 296; Klyuchevsky, *Soch.*, vii. 329; cf. p. 156.

[59] *PSZ* v. 3245 (26 Nov. 1718); Klyuchevsky, *Soch.*, vii. 319; Milyukov, *Gos. khoz. Rossii*, p. 636; Bogoslovsky, *Obl. reforma*, p. 326.

[60] *PSZ* v. 3460 (4 Dec. 1719), 3492 (19 Jan. 1720); vi. 3762 (15 Mar. 1721), 3782 (11 May 1721); Milyukov, *Gos. khoz. Rossii*, p. 638; Bogoslovsky, *Obl. reforma*, p. 327.

[61] Klyuchevsky, *Soch.*, vii. 322, 325 (95 kopecks: figure corrected following *PSZ* vi. 3753 (5 Mar. 1721); cf. *PSZ* vi. 3720 (27 Jan. 1721)); Bogoslovsky, *Obl. reforma*, pp. 355–60.

[62] *PSZ* vii. 4229 (20 May 1723); Klyuchevsky, *Soch.*, vii. 324.

The collection of information, or 'revision' of census data (the word *reviziya* was destined to pass into the language), continued through 1722 and 1723; the terminal date again had to be put off.[63] Not until August 1724, after a number of false starts, could the order finally be given for the troops to move into their 'permanent quarters',[64] and only in the following year were they actually maintained from the poll tax. This was fixed at a rate of 74 kopecks (reduced to 70 kopecks as a public relations gesture on Peter's death). Peasants without private landlords paid an additional 40, and townsmen 50, kopecks. The proceeds accounted for about half total state revenue and went almost wholly on the army.

Each regimental district contained as many taxpayers as were thought necessary to meet its requirements as officially established. For an infantry regiment this worked out at $21,863\frac{7}{8}$ souls, for a cavalry one $60,268\frac{1}{8}$ (at the original 74-kopeck rate).[65] The arithmetical precision was misleading, for it was impossible to delimit the area in which this number of individuals resided, still less to administer it. The regimental districts did not accord with the administrative ones established by the 1719 local government reform, so that there were two overlapping sets of authorities, one military and the other (ostensibly) civilian. In 1722 the War College drew up a schedule setting out the areas where each regiment was to be stationed and which were to maintain it. The officers entrusted with the task of distribution (*raskladka*) were to call on the local gentry to provide assistance, notably in building regimental and company headquarters as well as huts for the men, one *izba* for each two soldiers. (Nothing was said about payment for the materials and labour supplied.) The troops were to be settled in such a way that the soldiers of each company lived within 5 to 10 versts of each other and those of a regiment within 50 to 100 versts. If they had no specially built accommodation, they were to be quartered directly on the peasants.[66]

For this operation the gentry were to elect so-called 'land commissars' (*komissary ot zemli*).[67] These were successors to the *landraty* and had much the same function—except that, having collected the poll tax, they were supposed to hand it over to a military official, also termed a commissar. To add to the confusion, the 1719 reform had set up similarly-named land commissars (*zemskiye komissary*), so that there were actually *three* types of commissar working side by side.[68] Not surprisingly, they came into conflict over access to scarce resources. The civilian officials, who collected dues other than the poll tax,

[63] *PSZ* vi. 3873, 3899, 3901 (11 Jan., 5 Feb. 1722); vii. 4139, 4145, 4294 (9, 19 Jan., 3 Sept. 1723).

[64] *PSZ* vii. 4542 (6 Aug. 1724); Bogoslovsky, *Obl. reforma*, pp. 376-8.

[65] Each infantryman cost 28.40 or 28.5225, and each cavalryman 40.17 or 40.5 roubles. Klyuchevsky, *Soch.*, vii. 327; Milyukov, *Gos. khoz. Rossii*, pp. 664-5.

[66] Bogoslovsky, *Obl. reforma*, pp. 365-7.

[67] *PSZ* vii. 4332 (23 Oct. 1723).

[68] *PSZ* v. 3295 (Jan. 1719), §§ 2, 9; cf. Peter I to Senate, 26 Nov. 1718, in *SIRIO* xi. 374-5. Bogoslovsky (*Obl. reforma*, pp. 404-5) insists on the terminological distinction, but this was probably of little significance in practice.

were only allowed second pickings, as it were, after the two military men had taken their share.[69] Relations between the latter and the regimental authorities were also likely to be strained, since the *komissar ot zemli* was the first to be blamed if supplies failed to arrive in the unit.

Rural Russia now found itself under military occupation. The peasants, and to some extent the landowners too, had a multiplicity of authorities set over them. In more favourable circumstances they might have exploited the bureaucratic rivalries, but this was seldom possible now. At the summit were guards officers invested with special powers, at the base the local colonel, and in between them the various commissars. The guardsmen were 'trouble-shooters' sent out by the emperor or his associates with orders to settle specific problems. In 1724 there were 87 such individuals, only 16 of them officers, on various errands in the provinces.[70] Two years earlier 20 officers and 274 men of the Semenovsky guards regiment were reported to be absent on such missions.[71] Even senior officials trembled at the news of their approach. Land commissars who allowed arrears to accumulate might be dragged around their district in fetters by guardsmen, escorted by NCOs from the local garrison.[72] The voivode of Orel, summoned to the capital for some reason, could not obey because he had been arrested by a mere ensign of the Preobrazhensky regiment. The deputy governor of Moscow, Brigadier I. L. Voyeikov, first resisted these pressures spiritedly but in 1720 was compelled to yield to an energetic sergeant from the same regiment named Yablonsky; thereafter a soldier, P. Pustoshkin, for a time made himself virtual dictator of the former capital and its environs.[73]

Where such potentates were lacking, local affairs were determined largely by the whims of the regimental colonel. He had two sets of instructions, one laying down how he was to deal with revenue matters and the other defining his duties in the preservation of order.[74] The poll tax was to be collected in three instalments during the winter months (December, February, and April). In practice dues were exacted whenever the military authorities thought fit. If the land commissar delayed action on the colonel's requests, the latter was to consult with the governor and replace the elected official by a deputy whom the electors were expected to have chosen in readiness for such an eventuality.[75] This provision vividly illustrates the essentially bogus nature of '*szlachta* democracy' in its Russian adaptation. The colonel was instructed to protect the local inhabitants 'from all manner of impositions and wrongs'. He was not

[69] Bogoslovsky, *Obl. reforma*, pp. 397–403; Peterson, *Reforms* (see fn. 48) p. 287.

[70] Bogoslovsky, *Obl. reforma*, p. 313; see now also Meehan-Waters, *Autocracy and Aristocracy*, pp. 50–4.

[71] V. Aleksandrov, *Gvardeytsy—doverennye lyudi Petra I* (Moscow, 1947)—a rare pamphlet written from a standpoint of uncritical adulation of the Imperial military élite.

[72] Bogoslovsky, *Obl. reforma*, p. 315.

[73] Ibid., p. 316.

[74] *PSZ* vii. 4553–5 (26 June 1724); Rozengeym, *Ocherki*, pp. 194–8.

[75] *PSZ* vii. 4534, §§ 3, 11.

to interfere in relations between serfs and their masters, yet he had an obligation to stop peasants running away: 'and those who flee he shall chase and catch, and having seized them order the landowners to punish them'. Disputes between soldiers and their peasant 'hosts' came before a mixed military—civilian tribunal, but criminal offences were passed to the regular courts. Men might marry local peasant girls, so long as their owners agreed, and the latter were forbidden to keep them back for arbitrary reasons.[76]

Some of these provisions were reasonable, but the situation portrayed in these documents was not. Peter had created, not the 'well-ordered police state' of early eighteenth-century cameralist philosophy, but a pettifogging and brutal despotism which perpetuated old abuses under a veneer of European terminology.

The financial burden which the Petrine army imposed on the Russian people is notoriously difficult to calculate. The chief problem arises from the lack of price data against which to compare the nominal value of the currency. Nor is it known for certain how many men were actually under arms, since as a rule units were below strength, and these units may not have received the entire sum allocated to them by the establishment tables.

Nevertheless these tables must serve as the starting point in any investigation. The 1711 list (effective from 1712) was based on 33 cavalry and 42 infantry regiments in the active (field) army and another 43 infantry regiments as garrison troops; there were a mere 184 men in headquarters staff, including administrative officials.[77] The strength of an infantry regiment in the field army was set at 1,487 officers and men, that of a cavalry regiment at 1,328.[78] Total establishment strength—including the artillery, for whom regular provision was made the following year—and costs are given in Table 1. These estimates covered pay, mounts, and equipment only. Supplies of food and forage, put at 1,260,000 roubles, bring total expenditure to about 4 million roubles[79]—considerably more than the anticipated revenue (for 1711) of 3.2 million roubles. Excluding supplies, the bill for the army and navy together would account for over 90 per cent of total state expenditure, put at 3,008,000 roubles.[80] Some of the regiments provided for were not formed, so that these estimates were not kept to in fact.

---

[76] *PSZ* vii. 4535, §§ 2, 4, 7, 9, 12, 15. On the latter point, cf. Man'kov, 'Krepostnoye pravo', p. 167.

[77] *PSZ* iv. 2319 (19 Feb. 1711), xliii. 2319 (pp. 1–2); Stein, *Geschichte*, p. 65. Prior to this date there had been only 87 regiments; some were dissolved at this time: Avtokratov, 'Pervye organy', p. 171.

[78] *PSZ* xliii. 2319 (p. 4).

[79] Mikhnevich, in *SVM* iv. (l, i, i). 121 n.

[80] Milyukov, *Gos. khoz. Rossii*, p. 234. This was more than during the hectic years 1701–8 (although Milyukov's figure for 1705 is clearly exaggerated); for annual figures see his appendix, pp. 70–140.

Table 1

	Estimated numbers	Estimated cost ('000 roubles, rounded)
General staff	184	91
Cavalry	43,824	765
Guards } Infantry }	62,454	882
Garrison troops	64,769	452
Artillery	3,526	195
Total	174,757	2,385

Sources: *PSZ* iv, xliii. 2319, 2480; *SVM* iv. app. 18, p. 21; Stein, *Geschichte*, p. 66; Solov′yev, 'Kratkiy ocherk' (slight variations).

For the years immediately following, composite figures for military expenditure are not available, since funds were provided by the *gubernii*. Moscow province may serve as an example: its 1716 estimates provided for a total expenditure of 917,000 roubles, of which 771,000 (84.1 per cent) went on military purposes.[81] In the same year Archangel province, which coped better than most with its obligations, was required to devote 79.2 per cent of its expenditure to the armed forces; it actually turned over only two-thirds of the sum requested, but of this 91.3 per cent was military-related.[82] At the end of 1716 governors were directed to send the funds they had collected to the Senate's Military Chancellery.[83] This signified a return to the normalcy of centralized administration.

The War College (as this chancellery soon became) received its funds from another central department, the Shtats-kontora (Treasury), which was responsible for drawing up establishment tables for the entire bureaucracy; revenue collection was supervised by the Kammer-kollegiya.[84] These bodies were directly concerned with the introduction of the poll tax. A new table was now drawn up for the army, which Peter approved on 9 February 1720.[85] In the past nine years the general staff and artillery had expanded, and so had the expenditure on officer's pay and rations; the number of regiments had risen from 118 to 129. Yet the total cost was only a little more than it had been in 1711. This apparent miracle may be explained by the increase in the proportion of garrison troops, who were paid at lower rates, and by the reduction in the proportion of cavalrymen, who were more expensive to maintain. These figures are given in Table 2. This time supplies were included in the estimates, but one should add an undetermined sum for military-related construction, the Ukrainian frontier force (*land-militsiya*), and irregular troops—although these two groups were

[81] Calculated from Milyukov, *Gos. khoz. Rossii*, p. 435. This excludes medical expenditure, most of which was military-related.
[82] Calculated from Milyukov, *Gos. khoz. Rossii*, pp. 464–5, n. 1.
[83] *PSZ* v. 3048 (3 Nov. 1716); Milyukov, *Gos. khoz. Rossii*, p. 498.
[84] Milyukov, *Gos. khoz. Rossii*, pp. 595, 597.
[85] *PSZ* xliii. 3511 (pp. 15–38); Solov′yev, 'Kratkiy ocherk organizatsii', p. 101.

largely self-supporting. For the purposes of calculating the poll tax, Peter rounded off the establishment figures to 4 million roubles: 3 million for the active army and 1 million for the garrison troops. The guards and artillery were maintained from sources other than the poll tax, as was the navy.

Total state expenditure, actual and assigned, in 1720 was probably in the region of 5 million roubles (precise figures are not available),[86] and the armed forces proportion will have accounted for well over four-fifths.

Table 2

	Estimated numbers	Estimated cost ('000 roubles, rounded)[a]
General staff (*generalitet*)	360	163
Guards	5,817	156
Cavalry	39,501	1,389
Infantry and miscellaneous[b]	57,956	1,427
Total active army	103,634	3,135
Artillery[c]	3,526	195
Garrison troops: cavalry	69,869	88
infantry		873
Total regulars	177,029	4,291

[a] Including supplies of food and fodder.
[b] Including 3 grenadier regiments in the cavalry and 5 in the infantry, as well as 1 detached infantry battalion.
[c] Not covered in Table, 1711 establishment figures; actual size ca. 4,000?
Sources: *PSZ* xliii. 3511, p. 36 (Table VI); Stein, *Geschichte*, pp. 81–3; Solov'yev, 'Kratkiy ocherk', p. 227.

The data for 1724, the last full year of Peter's reign, are so contradictory that, although they are often referred to in secondary works, they are best ignored; those for the following year, which have recently been scrutinized by S. M. Troitsky, are more rewarding. Despite the conclusion of peace with Sweden, Russia was still at war, with Persia, and her total effectives, at least on paper, were higher than before. Details are set out in Table 3. This probably overstates the actual number of troops but understates expenditure on military administration and arms production. If total state expenditure in 1725 was a little over 9 million (9,141,000) roubles, the armed forces component was 73.2 per cent—about half-way between what it had been in 1680 (62 per cent) and in the crisis years 1701–8 (80.3 per cent).[87] Post-Petrine leaders did not indulge in such computations, but readily appreciated that military expenditure had risen to an unacceptable level and sought to reduce it.

[86] Milyukov, *Gos. khoz. Rossii*, pp. 661, 663; the total officially recorded, a little under 3 million, is clearly a gross underestimate.
[87] Our calculation; Klyuchevsky, taking the (dubious) 1724 figures, put it at 67 per cent of estimated and nearly 17.5 per cent of actual *revenue* (not expenditure). *Soch.*, iv. 143 (*Peter the Great*, p. 176).

Historians have generally taken a similar view, which for long seemed to be proven beyond all doubt by P. N. Milyukov's detailed research. However, in recent years the former liberal leader has been taken to task by the doyen of Soviet economists, S. G. Strumilin. (Curiously, he does not criticize Klyuchevsky, although his conclusions were much the same as Milyukov's.) Klyuchevsky, taking random data on grain prices, reached a tentative estimate of a 47 per cent depreciation of the rouble between 1680 and 1724, which he expressed in terms of 'contemporary' (1882) roubles as a fall from 17 to 9—a rough and ready index figure which, strange to say, has not been improved on since. In terms of silver content the rouble depreciated by 50.5 per cent, on Strumilin's own showing,[88] which suggests that Klyuchevsky's guess was at least in the right order of magnitude. But until a comprehensive publication of commodity price data is undertaken, any consideration of the actual weight of changes in the tax burden, or indeed of changes in personal incomes generally, is bound to remain highly speculative.

Table 3

	Estimated numbers	Estimated cost ('000 roubles, rounded)
General staff[a]	360	163
Guards	5,817	245
Cavalry	41,674 ⎫	
Infantry	58,754 ⎬	3,840
Garrison troops	69,313 ⎭	
Artillery and engineers	4,526	300
Lower corps[b]	15,000 (?)	330
Ukrainian frontier force	9,150	80
Total regulars	204,140 (?)	4,958
Irregulars	85,000 (?)	177
Military-related medical expend.	-	25
Military-related construction	-	110
	ca. 289,000	5,270
Navy (inc. sea-going troops)	15,000	1,422
Total armed forces	ca. 304,000[c]	6,692

   [a] Not mentioned in Table, 1720 figures.
   [b] *Nizovyy korpus*, a combat and occupation force in the Volga and Persian war theatre.
   [c] Kafengauz (*Rossiya*, p. 70) puts the army's total alone at 318,500, including 210,500 regulars, but gives no justification. Strokov (*Istoriya*, i. 466) estimates that there were 220,000 regular troops, here presumably following Geysman in *SVM* iv (2, 1). 83.
Sources: Stein, *Geschichte*, pp. 91–2; Troitsky, *Fin. politika*, p. 224; *PSZ* xliv (i). 3185, p. 5.

Pre-revolutionary historians thought that state revenue increased 3½ times between 1680 and 1724.[89] They implied that this indicated a steep rise in the tax

   [88] Strumilin, 'K voprosu', p. 183.
   [89] Klyuchevsky, *Soch.*, iv. 143 (*Peter the Great*, p. 177); Milyukov, *Gos. khoz. Rossii*, pp. 659–60.

burden, leading to what Milyukov provocatively called, in the title of one section of his work, 'the ruin of the population'; Klyuchevsky declared that by 1725 'the taxpaying capacity of the peasants had been exhausted'.[90] Against this view Strumilin argues that: (*a*) Milyukov, driven by ideological animus against the Petrine state, exaggerated the strain imposed on national resources; (*b*) he failed to note the benefits that accrued from cessation of grain dues in kind to maintain the *strel´tsy*; (*c*) misreading the census data, he assumed that there had been a great drop in population, whereas actually this was a time of demographic growth; (*d*) economic expansion made higher taxation relatively *less* burdensome than it had been before Peter's reign.

This indictment deserves fuller examination than it can be given here. The first point would require a lengthy digression into all the sources of state revenue; but it is clear merely from the problems encountered in introducing the poll tax that Strumilin exaggerates in declaring roundly: 'there can be no question of any financial crisis in these years'.[91] On the second point, while it is true that this tax fell into abeyance, Peter did not live up to his promise that all such dues, in cash or kind, would be replaced by the poll tax. On the contrary, once the army was quartered among them peasants were under continual pressure to provide a wide range of non-monetary services, especially accommodation and transport. Neither Strumilin nor any other writer offers an estimate of these disbursements. The 1724 Instruction to Colonels fixed payment for military use of peasant horses and carts (5–10 kopecks a day in summer, 4–6 kopecks in winter),[92] but said nothing about any payment for accommodation or other facilities such as the regulation *serviz*. There was also the cost to donors of recruits, estimated by the Senate in 1725 at no less than 100 roubles per man despatched, which many will have passed on to their dependants.[93]

Strumilin's third point has more substance. Since he wrote further research has confirmed his belief that this was an era of demographic expansion. The peasant population (exclusive of recruits) is now thought to have risen from 4.5 to 6.3 million males between 1678 and 1719.[94] In 1724 the taxpaying population of 5.7 million males was more than twice as large as in 1678. But two points need to be borne in mind here. First, those peasants who managed to conceal their existence from the census-takers (and so lead later historians into error) did not pay taxes; if discovered, they could be charged arrears, but this will not have yielded much, and in the interim the burden fell on those who had declared themselves. Second, the doubling of taxpayers was achieved less by natural growth or territorial expansion than by the expedient of including

[90] Milyukov, *Gos. khoz. Rossii*, p. 244; Klyuchevsky, *Soch.*, iv. 145–6 (*Peter the Great*, p. 180).

[91] Strumilin, 'K voprosu', p. 188.

[92] *PSZ* vii. 4535 (26 June 1724), § 3.

[93] Anisimov, 'Iz ist. fiskal´noy politiki', p. 131. It was, however, not always produced: in 1719 nearly 1 million roubles was collected in fines from recalcitrant donors.

[94] Vodarsky, *Naseleniye*, p. 192.

slaves (*kholopy*) and other dependants hitherto exempt. As Klyuchevsky showed, this was a major change for the worse, since it created a single class of bondsmen (*krepostnye*) whose status further deteriorated. This social cost has to be set against the economic gain derived from the fact that ex-slaves now had to earn enough to pay their poll tax. Moreover, this economic stimulus was limited by the way the tax operated. Each community divided up its assessment in such a way that able-bodied farming peasants paid the share of those (for example, domestics, children) who did not work the land, so that the former's obligations were correspondingly increased. On balance Peter's policies may have fostered labour productivity and a growth in GNP; but as yet we cannot quantify this, so that Strumilin's fourth point, which may be valid, remains to be proved.

Whereas Strumilin thought the burden on the peasant taxpayer declined by 15 per cent between 1680 and 1724, a recent Soviet analyst offers the more plausible estimate of a 16 per cent increase; if indirect taxes are included, and inflation allowed for, the demands of the fisc rose at least 2½ times.[95] This is not very different from the doubling of the burden that impressed contemporary observers. One of these thought that 'the tsar's army costs him less than those in other countries'.[96] It was the system whereby taxes were assessed and collected that was mainly at fault, rather than its drain on incomes (it was equivalent to about 12 per cent of the annual earnings of a day labourer)[97]— and this takes us back to the administrative context. Peasant wretchedness was due less to the malignancy of the fisc or to a breakdown of the economy than to the militarization of Russian society. This was a major element in Peter's legacy. Klyuchevsky says at one point that in the measures taken to quarter the army 'we no longer recognize the victor of Poltava'. Alas, today we recognize all too well the gifted and idealistic leader who becomes intoxicated with absolute power and exercises it in tyrannical fashion.

[95] Anisimov, 'Iz ist. fiskal´noy politiki', pp. 135–9. Cf. id., *Podatnaya reforma Petra I: vvedeniye podushnoy podati v Rossii, 1719–1728 gg.*, Leningrad, 1982, p. 278: 2.7 times.

[96] Weber, *Das veränderte Russland*, p. 28; cf. [Müller], *Nouveaux mémoires*, p. 64.

[97] Strumilin, 'K voprosu', p. 185. This estimate is based on the assumption that a taxpayer was responsible for *two* shares at the flat rate. With dues to the landowner, this was 20.5 per cent of income. For other figures on earnings, see id., 'Oplata truda', pp. 54–6.

III

THE IMPERIAL CENTURY, 1725–1825

7

RECRUITMENT AND SERVICE
IN THE RANKS

FOR a century and more after the death of the tsar–reformer the armed forces constituted the principal bulwark of the absolutist regime. It is open to argument how far Imperial Russia remained a 'garrison' or 'service' state, for the relationship between the central power and society at large changed considerably during this long period. Nineteenth-century liberal historians spoke of a process of *raskreposhcheniye* (literally, 'de-bonding'), and the term is not inapt. A perceptive Western critic has recently written that after Peter the traditional social order, based on service to the state, was 'partially dismantled'.[1] Two points need to be stressed in this regard. First, the emancipation process was slow and gradual, interrupted by frequent setbacks and vacillations. It was most sustained during the reign of Catherine the Great (1762–96), but thereafter, under the next three male Romanov rulers, there was something of a reaction. Second, the benefits which this emancipation conferred were distributed unequally. The principal gainers were the privileged elements of society, particularly those nobles (*dvoryane*) who owned much land and many serfs. We shall examine in ch. 10 and 11 what happened to those members of this class who served in the army, primarily as officers, and some of the effects which the 'dismantling' process had on the state itself. In this section we shall be concerned mainly with those who gained least from this transformation: the *nizhniye chiny* or 'lower ranks', that is, the soldiers and NCOs. These men were the principal victims of the 'garrison state' in so far as this still existed.

This statement needs qualification. How can one measure the deprivation to which soldiers in the Imperial Russian army were subject? Two criteria come to mind: the situation of underprivileged civilians, above all various categories of the peasant population, and that of soldiers in other European armies during this period. Unfortunately the sources available do not yet permit a thorough exploration of the parallels, but it can at least be said that the disadvantages of the Russian soldier's condition outweighed the advantages. True, he was spared the threat of starvation which hung constantly over most of his compatriots, since he received pay, food, and various other benefits. He also enjoyed a status which—at least in the eyes of authority—was considerably superior to that of the humble *muzhik*. Each week an infantryman was formally reminded by his commander that he was 'not a peasant but a soldier,

[1] Pipes, *Russia under the Old Regime*, p. 112.

whose title and rank give him preference over that of any previous calling'.[2] Something of this attitude was assimilated by the men concerned, who came to see themselves as professionals whose work was honourable as well as onerous. No doubt they were respected as such by many civilian commoners. On the other hand the serviceman was exposed to a higher risk of sickness and mortality—from disease as much as from enemy action—by the very nature of his duties and life-style; he was largely isolated from the peasant milieu from which he had been forcibly ripped by the act of recruitment; and he was subject to a system of discipline so strict, yet at the same time so arbitrary, that it inured him to violence and brutality while fortifying that spirit of servile fatalism so characteristic of the Russian masses under the old regime.

Limiting ourselves initially to the hundred years that ended with the death of Alexander I (1801–25), we may consider first the soldier's recruitment into the forces and his juridical situation, and then his material (ch. 8) and cultural life (ch. 9). Soldiers did not write memoirs,[3] and where direct evidence of social realities is lacking official records must do duty instead. Fortunately the surfeit of paperwork in the Imperial army that so irritated the more energetic officers yields some useful information.

On few questions are the published materials so plentiful as on recruitment. This is not surprising, for this operation, together with collection of the poll tax, which was related to it, served as the principal point of contact, so to speak, between the autocracy and its subjects. Almost every year, generally in late summer, the sovereign, or the Senate acting in his or her name, would issue a decree ordering that a levy be raised. This *ukaz*, as a rule accompanied by an Imperial manifesto, laid down how many individuals were to be taken from a given number of 'souls', which groups if any were to be exempted, and what procedure was to be followed. Despite several efforts at reform, to be examined shortly, the system remained remarkably resistant to change throughout this hundred-year period and even beyond. It was a very oppressive burden, not only for the men who were enlisted and their families, but also (though in a different sense) for those who provided them, their 'donors' (*otdatchiki*) as they were known in official jargon.[4] The government issued stereotyped injunctions to avoid 'undue burdening of the people' (*lishnogo narodnogo istyagoshcheniya*), but paradoxically precisely those efforts, duplicated at the local level, to ensure that the load was shared fairly did much of the harm. For this task surpassed the modest capacities of the primitive bureaucratic apparatus. It was not just a matter of the human frailties manifested by the officials and officers in charge, nor even of the devious means employed by potential recruits and their donors to evade their unenviable fate. The underlying reason for the misery which recruitment caused

---

2 *PSZ* xvi. 12289, V, § 3 (Instruction to Infantry Colonels, 8 Dec. 1764).

3 With a few minor exceptions: see Keep, 'Pistol', p. 315, n. 5.

4 The terminology employed in recruitment would repay study. Donors might be landowners or, in non-proprietorial communities, chosen representatives of the local population.

was the excessive scale and incidence of the operation; and this in turn was due to Russian rulers' continuous preoccupation, despite the country's backwardness, with the maintenance of an overpoweringly large force—the largest on the European continent. Ostensibly designed to bolster Russia's foreign-policy aims and to safeguard domestic security, it also satisfied a deeper psychological need.

No less than 90 levies were raised during the period 1705–1825. Those imposed up to 1801 yielded an estimated 2¼ million men, and almost 2 million more were called to the colours in Alexander I's reign.[5] Actual intakes were somewhat less than these figures suggest. During the last ten years of this period, when Russia was at peace and four years passed without a levy, the shortfall was 10 per cent.[6] In the 1730s the norm varied from 1 recruit per 98 to 1 per 320 souls, the average 'take' being 1 per 179. Catherine II's local government reform of 1775 led to the establishment of a standard 500-soul recruiting unit. During her reign in peacetime the usual call was for one man to be provided per unit, but the second Russo-Turkish war (1787–91) saw three levies of 5, and one of 4, men from each. The greatest drain occurred in 1812, during Napoleon's invasion, when three levies were called, which took a total of 20 men per unit (not counting those enrolled in the militia).[7]

The scale of each levy was determined after the army authorities submitted an estimate of the gap between actual strength and the establishment figure.[8] This *nekomplekt*, as the gap was called, was filled partly by arrears of men from earlier levies and by internal reassignments as well as by the new intake. The establishment figure, once fixed, seems to have acquired something of a sacramental character. On one occasion Alexander I did challenge his War Minister's figure for the *nekomplekt* as too high, but there is little sign of any sustained effort to adjust military requirements to the country's resources. At the most units might be left deliberately below strength. This procedure was the norm under Catherine II, who doubtless found it a useful way of deluding foreign opinion as to the size of her forces. At the conclusion of hostilities military effectives would normally be reduced, but the end of the Napoleonic Wars were a conspicuous exception in this regard. Only in 1726, when the

---

[5] Respectively 2,271,571 and 1,933,608: Shchepetil′nikov, in *SVM* iv (l, i, ii). 5, 129. Beskrovnyy, who has examined the archives, also gives actual yields for most levies (*Russkaya armiya*, pp. 33–7, 294–7), but sometimes appears to substitute anticipated yields and omits figures for the additional levies of 1731 and 1777–8. The chronological breakdown of his data is as follows: 1726–60: 795,000; 1767–99: 1,252,000; we may put the total for 1725–1801 at ca. 2,150,000. Cf. Aleksandrov, *Sel. obshchina*, p. 245, where the percentage of registered 'souls' taken as recruits is said to have risen from 3.6 per cent in Peter's reign to 7 per cent at the end of the eighteenth and to 8 per cent in the early nineteenth century. For 1801–24 Beskrovnyy's figure (*Potentsial*, p. 72) accords with Shchepetil′nikov's.

[6] Calculated from Shchepetil′nikov (*SVM* iv) p. 132, app. 40.

[7] Shchepetil′nikov (*SVM* iv) pp. 47–68, 132; cf. Keep, 'Russian Army's Response', p. 501.

[8] Shchepetil′nikov (*SVM* iv) p. 3 avers that this was done *after* the Imperial manifesto was issued; but unless some preliminary calculation had been made the manifesto could not have contained a figure for the ratio of recruits to souls, which was kept to when the measure was subsequently implemented.

weak post-Petrine regime committed itself to a programme of demilitarization, was the number of recruits called for in the decree subsequently changed, evidently because of a policy disagreement among those responsible;[9] and in the following year the Imperial manifesto contained no specific figure, this being left to the Senate to determine after checking the poll-tax records.[10] These minor exceptions underline the point that the military authorities were generally able to impose their view of the army's 'needs' upon the monarch and his or her civilian advisers.

Recruitment was initially the responsibility of the various commissars set up in the country areas by Peter I; the provincial governors and district voivodes (who were restored in 1727) exercised a supervisory role. As the army withdrew from its high-profile role in local government (see below, p. 307), a more complicated procedure developed. Reduced to essentials, it involved a joint military–civilian recruiting board, which came to be known as the *rekrutskoye prisutstviye*, in each province. This was constituted afresh for each levy, and was attached to the local fiscal office (Kazennaya palata) once such bodies had been set up in 1775. The chief member of the board was known as the 'military receiver' (*voyennyy priemshchik*). He was a senior military officer appointed by the War College (from 1801: War Ministry) in St. Petersburg. The donors had to appear before the board in person along with those men who had been selected as recruits. The latter were examined as to their physical fitness and, if deemed acceptable, had their heads shaven, took the oath of allegiance, were divided into batches, and were handed over to a 'squad officer' (*partiyonnyy ofitser*) detailed to escort them to their respective units. The donors were given an official receipt (*zachet, kvitantsiya*) for each man handed over. The whole procedure was not supposed to take more than two to three days and had to be completed within two months from the day when the decree ordering the levy was issued.

This bald description does scant justice to the many complex problems which this procedure created. Who was liable to the levy and who exempt? How were recruits chosen? Who might substitute other individuals for those designated, or commute his obligation by a cash payment? Under what conditions might receipts be issued, and how was fraudulent conduct to be dealt with? All these questions evoked furious argument, and a consequent mass of legislation—for everyone knew that the stakes were high: a recruit was unlikely ever to see his family again. Enlistment was literally a life-and-death matter for those liable to it. This element of finality explains why the authorities were, or at least pretended to be, so concerned about equalizing the burden and why those selected so often tried to evade their fate. In some cases they were aided and abetted by their masters or by local officials, while in others they were readily sacrificed to the state's voracious appetite for the lives of its subjects.

9 *PSZ* vii. 4859 (26 Mar. 1726).
10 *PSZ* vii. 5169, 5195 (29 Sept., 3 Nov. 1727).

Let us look at these questions in turn a little more closely. In principle every able-bodied male adult who was *tyaglyy*—that is, liable to pay the poll tax— could be summoned to the colours, whether he was a peasant, a townsman, or even a 'non-registered' ecclesiastic. The system could thus be called one of selective conscription, confined to the underprivileged classes; this limitation distinguishes it from the universal conscription of modern societies, which in a sense it anticipated. Already Peter I had allowed merchants in the senior grade to substitute one of their dependants or a payment in kind for a recruit; and this provision remained in force.[11] In this respect merchants, like priests, were more privileged than the gentry, who were legally obliged to serve until 1762. Another group whose status was somewhat anomalous comprised the 'single-homesteaders' (*odnodvortsy*). At first they were exempted, on the grounds that they were already performing military service (in the Ukrainian *land-militsiya*); but in the late eighteenth century they were gradually assimilated to the category of state peasants, and therefore had both to pay the poll tax and to provide recruits.[12] Similar exemptions were granted to certain people in Siberia who served in local defence forces, artisans in factories producing armaments or other military-related goods, and the drivers (*yamshchiki*) who operated the official postal communications system.

The post-Petrine governments were niggardly in granting such favours. One cannot really call them privileges, since they could be revoked at any time: thus 'homesteaders' were included in the levy of 1730 and drivers in those of 1732 and 1739.[13] So too were certain ecclesiastical personnel suspected of dissident tendencies, although they could send substitutes,[14] and the Old Believers, who in 1738 had to provide more than twice as many recruits as those in other categories.[15] Exemptions from the levy were also used as a bait to tempt Oriental natives into the Orthodox fold.[16]

The state's interest was clearly paramount in all these provisions, and Catherine changed the policy only slightly. In order to entice back Old Believers who had fled to Poland, those who returned of their own free will were exempted from the levy for six years and were also allowed to choose which community they wished to belong to.[17] Refugees (including army deserters) who were discovered by the troops that Catherine sent into Poland and were brought back compulsorily were despatched either to the army or, if unfit, to settlements in Siberia.[18] The latter fate was not so harsh as it might appear, since

[11] For example, *PSZ* x. 7973 (18 Dec. 1739), xiv. 10326 (21 Nov. 1754); but cf. vii. 4845 (5 Mar. 1726), § 2, for a breach of it.

[12] Tkacheva, 'Iz istorii', p. 139; de Madariaga, *Catherine*, p. 101; *PSZ* xx. 14651 (18 Sept. 1777), § 7, xxi. 15723 (3 May 1783), § 5.

[13] *PSZ* viii. 5605 (18 Aug. 1730), 6010 (29 Mar. 1732), x. 7722 (8 Jan. 1739).

[14] *PSZ* x. 7158 (13 Jan. 1737); cf. 7169, 7364 (6 Feb., 7 Sept. 1737).

[15] One recruit per 50 souls as against 1 per 120. *PSZ* x. 7702 (11 Dec. 1738); cf. xiii. 9620 (25 May 1749).

[16] *PSZ* xi. 8236 (11 Sept. 1740), § 14; but cf. xv. 11099 (11 Sept. 1759).

[17] *PSZ* xvi. 11720 (4 Dec. 1762).   [18] *PSZ* xvii. 12507 (10 Nov. 1765).

such settlers enjoyed temporary freedom from the levy—partly because they had to provide for their own defence anyway and partly because the government wanted to build up the population of this remote region.[19]

Catherine's long-term aim was to bring about administrative uniformity throughout her empire,[20] but in practice she permitted various regional particularities to continue in the system of military recruitment and service. In the 1780s the levy was gradually introduced into the newly annexed region of New Russia, but with certain modifications necessitated by differences in its social structure. Many of the farmers here were pioneer settlers. They were given the right to keep one son in each family at home; like the 'homesteaders' they drew lots as to who should serve and remained with the colours for a limited term of 15 years. They were in the main cavalrymen who did duty in the south and formed a local militia rather like the Cossacks. The government also proceeded carefully in White Russia and Poland (eventually residents of a strip 100 versts wide along the western border were given a privileged status in regard to the recruit levy)[21] and in the Baltic provinces, which since their annexation under Peter I had been allowed to pay for the upkeep of the army through general taxation instead of a poll tax; their inhabitants, however, also had to supply the troops stationed in their midst.[22]

This meant that the main weight of the levy continued to fall on the peasants of Great Russia. A hint of regional specialization can be detected in their regard as well, in that men from certain northern areas were frequently sent to the navy rather than the army; but this did not detract from the general principle. Each taxpaying community had to provide its share of the quota. Recruits were chosen by the authorities at the lowest level—the rural commune (*obshchina*), township (*posad*), etc.—who generally acted under the supervision of local landowners and/or district-level officials. Initially the populace worked out its own rules, and these customary practices gradually acquired legal sanction as the state took a closer interest in the proceedings. Tradition dictated that the local elders would select men from the largest (and by implication the most prosperous) families and from any marginal elements (non-*tyaglye*, that is, those who did not work the land or help to bear the community's fiscal obligations). This could be a heavy burden: on the Yaroslavl' estate of M. M. Shcherbatov, a conservative leader prominent in the 1770s, the family of F. Ivanov, which had nine male members of working age, lost four of them in as many levies.[23] Not unnaturally, those with influence in the community, and

[19] *PSZ* xvi. 11860 (11 June 1763), xix. 13475 (16 June 1770).

[20] De Madariaga, *Catherine*, pp. 61, 324; Raeff, 'Uniformity', p. 103, mentions a plan (still unpublished) by R. L. Vorontsov in 1761 which urged the geographical evening out of recruit obligations.

[21] *PSZ* xxvi. 20019 (21 Sept. 1801); xxxi. 24773 (16 Sept. 1810), § 16.

[22] Maslovsky, *Materialy*, ii (ii). 17; *PSZ* xx. 14651, § 7, xxi. 15723, 15846 (Baltic), xxii. 16071 (Kursk), xxiii. 17249 (White Russia). Baltic privileges were restricted by Paul in 1797 (xxiv. 17584) but later expanded again (xxv. 18823, xxx. 22924, 23163).

[23] Aleksandrov, *Sel. obshchina*, p. 250. This recent study, based on votchinal archives, is the first to explore the levy's operation at the local level, and the following passages owe much to this work.

land owners too, sought to extend the coverage to include those less well off, that is, families with at least two members (so-called 'solitaries' with relatives to support were generally exempted), although this meant that they incurred heavier financial obligations, since they had to help pay the dues of those sent and to care for their more indigent dependants.[24] The general (but not universal) trend in the late eighteenth century was to take as the basis the individual household, and eventually all its constituent male members—so in effect anticipating the selective conscription system that would become law in 1874. Those for whom military service would mean the collapse of their precarious economies were granted various financial easements and encouraged to hire substitutes; and since this latter course was beyond the reach of most peasants, complicated accounting arrangements were devised whereby most or all members of the community (and sometimes even several villages) pooled their resources to find the necessary sum, the economically weaker elements borrowing the money. Householders thereby became owners of fractional shares (*doli*) of a (sometimes theoretical!) substitute, and could trade these shares among one another.[25] Selection was often carried out by lot; if a share-owner were nevertheless called on to serve, his share would be returned to his family.

This system enhanced the power of the paterfamilias, who could in practice decide which of his kinsmen should vanish; he might well spare his sons and send cousins or nephews instead.[26] It helped to keep households large, since partition increased the chances of drawing the fatal lot.[27] It may also have kept down the rate of marriage, for although young married men with families stood less chance of being called up, they could not marry without permission of the paterfamilias, and this he might deny to a lad whom he had earmarked as a recruit. These adverse demographic effects, and the tensions that developed within and between households, far outweighed any positive gain which the hiring of substitutes brought by encouraging the circulation of money. There was also the factor that the recruiting system increased peasant indebtedness and contributed greatly to the spread of corruption. Wealthy families might secure favourable treatment by bribing the communal elders (normally elected from their midst), the district clerk, the county police official (*ispravnik*: from 1775)[28]—or even the receiving officer and members of the recruitment board. In 1795 the despatch of 18 recruits from the Perm′ estate of G. A. Stroganov cost the donors 460 roubles, including bribes of 25 roubles to the doctor, 15 to an official of the Kazennaya palata, and smaller sums to officers and NCOs, one of whom marked up the height of undersized recruits.[29] Normally the military men made their views known only if the recruits submitted were clearly unfit, whereupon they would demand replacements and take action against the donors for attempted fraud. The latter,

[24] Ibid., p. 248.   [25] Ibid., p. 269.
[26] Ibid., p. 287.   [27] Ibid., p. 288.
[28] Bolotenko, 'Administration', pp. 383–400; Semevsky, *Krest′yane*, i. 365.
[29] Aleksandrov, *Sel. obshchina*, p. 285.

whether peasants or landowners, had every interest in trying to pass off men whose age or physical condition rendered them unsuitable for service. They also used the levy as a safety valve to rid themselves of villagers whose conduct they found objectionable. These would often be individuals who had offended against the laws of Church or state and were consequently branded as 'trouble-makers'. With our twentieth-century perspective we are prone to label such men automatically as social rebels, and certainly some of them were; but they might simply be unfortunates reduced to indigence by poor harvests or some catastrophe such as their homestead catching fire.

Undoubtedly the recruitment system helped to make many village communities instruments of a clique of powerful householders, and so to subvert its 'democratic' and egalitarian features. Yet it is not as certain as Aleksandrov contends that the recruits despatched were increasingly drawn from the poorer strata of the rural population.[30] The authorities at every level pursued the illusory goal of an absolutely fair distribution of the load between potential donors. This task was complicated *inter alia* by the coexistence within each conscription unit of donors belonging to different socio-economic categories. Let us suppose that one recruit was to be provided for every 100 male souls. Those landowners or communities with precisely that number, or an exact multiple thereof, had an easy task. But those with a fraction of it had to combine their holdings notionally with the 'surplus' of those with more than such a round number. This operation was called the *skladka* (literally, 'putting together').[31] The law also laid down that if in any unit there was an owner with approximately two-thirds of the norm (in this case 70 souls) *he* was to be the donor and all other owners in his notional sub-unit were to compensate him in cash for their shares, the total cost of providing a recruit being fixed separately for each levy. The understanding here seems to have been that the obligation would rotate among the donors in each unit; but since the unit did not cover a fixed geographical area, but varied with each levy,[32] this aim was unrealizable. At first only the poorest landowners were permitted to make their own arrangements by mutual agreement, which meant that they drew lots, but later this provision as we know was extended.

Another complication arose from the patchwork distribution of holdings. What was to be done where a village was owned jointly by several individuals, or where a proprietor held land in several parts of a province or in several provinces? These problems had caused headaches among officials of the Razryad, and their eighteenth-century successors found them almost equally

---

[30] Ibid., pp. 271–3. The very existence of such strata is a contentious matter, since the social pattern of the Russian village was often based on a rotation between 'rich' and 'poor' households in positions of responsibility and influence. We do not yet know precisely why particular landowners or communes changed the method of raising recruits, or indeed whether their decisions were implemented in practice.

[31] First defined in *PSZ* ix. 6490 (24 Sept. 1733), §§ 2–6; cf. xiv. 10326 (21 Nov. 1754), §§ 4–6.

[32] Legally until 1785, but in practice often thereafter as well.

difficult to resolve. The legislators tried, for example, to prescribe limits beyond which a multiple owner might not associate his holdings. What happened in practice, though, as in Muscovy, was that the wealthier owners came to enjoy certain advantages: not just because they were wealthy and so influential, but because the state authorities appreciated that they could best provide the steady flow of recruits required. From the official viewpoint it therefore made sense to allow donors who wanted to deliver their quota directly to the War College in St. Petersburg to do so, especially since such recruits might well be domestic servants rather than field-workers, and so represent less of a drain on agriculture.[33] In this way donors, usually those with substantial means, were spared the wearisome and time-consuming process of the *skladka*; but the local authorities were left with the tricky job of redrawing unit boundaries to take account of their exclusion. Likewise, St. Petersburg residents were permitted, indeed encouraged, to submit recruits at any time, in advance of the next levy, whereupon their quota would be correspondingly reduced; and from the Seven Years War onwards similar privileges were extended to *all* donors, who could present such recruits to their provincial chancellery.[34]

Hand in hand with this liberalization went an extension of the right to substitute, for the recruit designated under the selection procedure, an individual purchased by the donor or donors for the purpose. Such rights were more likely to be exercised by landowners, especially wealthier ones, than urban or peasant communities. Indeed, poll-tax payers (*tyaglye*) were at first expressly prohibited from engaging in such a practice, until the ban was repealed by Peter III (1762).[35] Purchases by communal peasants are authenticated from the 1730s, and later there was a scandalous case involving villagers in Yaroslavl′ province who, with their proprietor's permission, bought the inhabitants of another village, who were regularly despatched to the colours in their stead[36]—as their military slaves, in effect! Sales of substitutes had to be registered with the authorities, and purchasers were not allowed to buy more than one man at a time, to avoid speculation; for the same reason serfs could not be sold within three months of a levy decree, lest such sales be used to camouflage a black market in recruits.[37] Those purchased had to be free men, not individuals ascribed to some taxpaying community; nor could they be fugitives or deserters (although foreigners were acceptable). In a serf-based economy free men were scarce, and accordingly commanded a high price. 'Many a fellow offers to become a recruit for his brothers in the village and receives for this a decent remuneration', wrote one contemporary.[38] This led the authorities to set a maximum price, first fixed at 360 and later raised to 500

---

[33] First mentioned in *PSZ* x. 7394 (6 Oct. 1737); cf. 7435 (16 Nov. 1737), 7936 (1739).

[34] *PSZ* xiv. 10736 (6 June 1757), xvii. 12478 (General Statute on Recruitment, 29 Sept. 1766), 1, § 7, xviii. 13182 (13 June 1768), xix. 13483 (20 July 1770), § 5.

[35] *PSZ* x. 7169 (6 Feb. 1737), xi. 7997 (3 Jan. 1740), xv. 11413 (22 Jan. 1762).

[36] Aleksandrov, *Sel. obshchina*, p. 272.

[37] Semevsky, *Krest′yane*, i. 367–8.

[38] Von Hupel, *Beschreibung*, p. 202.

roubles.[39] In fact the purchase price had already been indirectly determined by officialdom, since the cost of despatching a recruit had been regulated for the benefit of *skladchiki*.

As for monetary commutation, exercise of this right depended on rank, as did the fee payable. In Peter's day merchants had to pay 100 roubles.[40] By the 1730s ecclesiastical owners were required to give double as much, while secular proprietors with 30–70 souls paid only 20–30 roubles.[41] During the Seven Years War, when the provision of recruits lagged behind demand, donors in any category who were in arrears were permitted to make such payments.[42]

The various regulations on substitution and commutation were easily bypassed. Landowners and merchants traded in recruits, passing them off as domestic servants,[43] and built up reserves of them to be used when needed. The main offenders were at first peasant elders or landlords' bailiffs, whose employers were absent on service but had given them *carte blanche* to protect their interests—which in this case coincided with those of their dependants. The natural bonds in a close-knit rural society led people in all walks of life to co-operate against the agents of the distant central *vlast'*. Only fear of delation limited this far-reaching solidarity. Donors would, as noted, submit men who were physically unfit or outside the prescribed age limits, despite the risk of punishment. Another ruse was to inveigle strangers into volunteering in place of one's dependants and to pass them off as such under a false name.[44] In 1774 a knowledgeable observer claimed that, when serving on a recruitment board, he had once been presented with two men so deaf that they could not even hear a cannon being fired.[45] A few years earlier a certain Lieutenant Ukhtomsky of the 2nd Grenadiers was discovered to have bought up numerous runaway peasants in the Vologda area, whom he then sold to donors as potential recruits. In his defence Ukhtomsky asserted that the men had approached him of their own accord and that he had not known their true status, but these patently thin excuses did not save him from court-martial.[46]

Undoubtedly the most frequent source of abuse was the receipt or voucher issued to the donor on acceptance of a recruit. Contrary to the authorities' initial intentions, this became a kind of security paper and might be sold to

[39] *PSZ* xxi. 15721 (3 May 1783); reduced to 400 roubles for landed proprietors on 18 Sept. 1793 (xxiii. 17154)—according to Aleksandrov (p. 272) as a money-raising venture by the Treasury; cf. ibid., pp. 252, 261, 266–7, 283 n.; Semevsky, *Krest'yane*, i. 367–8; *Arkhiv gr. Mordvinovykh*, iv (1902), 39; Martos, 'Zapiski', p. 528, for scattered data on free-market prices; the peak was reached in the late 1810s, when a substitute fetched over 2,000 roubles.

[40] *PSZ* vii. 4550 (17 Aug. 1724).

[41] *PSZ* x. 7169, 7282 (6 Feb., 17 June 1737).

[42] *PSZ* xiv. 10736 (6 June 1757), § 4. Such a law was actually superfluous since a decree of 1754 (xiv. 10326, 21 Nov.), § 10, extended the right to landowners in any category, but it was presumably not widely known.

[43] Aleksandrov, *Sel. obshchina*, pp. 264–5, 270.

[44] *PSZ* xiv. 10326 (21 Nov. 1754), § 11, xix. 13483 (20 July 1770), §§ 7, 10.

[45] Vyazemsky, 'Zapiska', p. 5.

[46] Shchukin, *Sbornik*, ii. 27–30.

another proprietor or community. This practice was due not merely to 'gentry greed' but also to the state's hunger for manpower. Large numbers of such documents were issued to those who presented recruits in advance. The practice caused problems for the authorities too, since receipt-holders could decide when to make use of them, so that officials were unable to foretell what proportion of an intake would be in the form of pieces of paper rather than warm bodies. (By the end of the century the share of vouchers presented in lieu was running at about 5–10 per cent.)[47]

The government tried to use them as an instrument of social policy. In order to give landowners and taxpaying communities an incentive to send peasants to settle underpopulated areas of Siberia, vouchers were awarded as compensation for the loss of their labour power. The first decree to this effect, issued in December 1760,[48] was long interpreted by historians as evidence of the autocracy's supposed subservience to the 'landlord interest', and this view found its way into general textbooks. On closer inspection it is clear that the measure, which did not apply solely to members of the privileged classes, was motivated primarily by concern for state interest. Such settlers had to be fitted out at their donor's expense in the same way as recruits. The decree was one of several designed to promote demographic and economic growth in regions along the empire's eastern border. In a similar vein, Catherine II had officials issue vouchers to proprietors whose fugitive peasants were taken over by the state or whose recruits lost their lives while on service.[49] It is nevertheless also true that the practice reinforced the serf-owner's police powers over his dependants. In theory at any rate he might despatch any of them to be either colonists or soldiers, and receive in exchange a valuable document that saved him from having to provide cannon-fodder at a subsequent levy.

A recruit had to satisfy three crude physical requirements: age, height, and 'fitness'. The age limits were at first (1730) defined at 15 to 30, but in 1754 each was raised by five years. Catherine II lowered the age of acceptance to 17, where it stayed until the era of the Napoleonic Wars. In 1808 it was raised to 19 (but temporarily lowered to 18 in 1811). This 'concession to youth' was offset by extending the maximum limit of age for a recruit to 36 (1806), 37 (1808), and 40 (1812), the 35-year limit being restored after hostilities ended in 1815.[50] In practice recruiting officers interpreted the regulations flexibly and sometimes accepted under-age boys or older men.[51] We need not assume that bribery was involved in every case, for at that time people often did not know

---

[47] Beskrovnyy, *Russkaya armiya*, p. 299.

[48] *PSZ* xv. 11166 (13 Dec. 1760); cf. xvii. 12556 (28 Jan. 1766), xviii. 13019 (28 Sept. 1767).

[49] *PSZ* xxii. 16681 (1 July 1788), xxiii. 16903 (6 Sept. 1790)—these were volunteers recruited during the war with Sweden (Semevsky, *Krest'yane*, i. 602); xxiv. 17623 (8 Dec. 1796).

[50] *PSZ* viii. 5622 (18 Aug. 1730), xiv. 10326 (21 Nov. 1754), § 1, xvii. 12748 (29 Sept. 1766), § 8; Shchepetil'nikov, in *SVM* iv (l, i, ii). 15, 41, 45, 79, 87. In 1811, in a revival of Petrine practice, boys as young as 12 were called up, but they were sent to military orphanages rather than to regiments. *PSZ* xxxii. 25021; Petrov, *Russkaya voyennaya sila*, ii. 318; Shchepetil'nikov (*SVM* iv) p. 154 n.

[51] Vyazemsky, 'Zapiska', p. 6; Keep, 'Catherine's Veterans', p. 390.

their exact age, or wish to state it accurately, and no documentary proof of it was demanded.

The military authorities were concerned as much with a recruit's appearance as they were with his fighting capacity. This was why they were so obsessed with his height. The regulations prescribed a minimum of 2 *arshiny* and 4 *vershki*, equivalent to 5 ft. 3 in. or 1.60 m., 'without shoes'. This was established by the use of measuring rods whose length, to the officials' consternation, might not always be uniform.[52] Height criteria were lowered in 1731 and again (after being restored in the interim) in 1737, when shorter men were to be sent to garrison units or to the navy.[53] Catherine II resorted to the same expedient during the first Russo-Turkish war of her reign,[54] and so did Alexander I from 1805 on: the limit was lowered by half an inch in 1805, 1808, and 1809, one inch in 1806 and 1811, and two inches in 1812.[55]

The net was also cast wider in regard to recruits' physical condition, which was assessed in the crudest manner. During the Seven Years War men were accepted who had two or three teeth missing or suffered from hair loss (evidence of some internal malady).[56] The receiving officers were not medical men, and even when semi-skilled physicians (*lekari*) were added to the recruiting boards they had to work under such pressure that many men were let in who suffered from complaints not visible to the naked eye. This was one reason for the high casualty rate among recruits. It was not until Alexander I's reign, however, that the authorities defined the physical requirements more precisely. Doctors were told to look out for traces of eye disease, consumption, and mental illness, as well as for more obvious deficiencies.[57] But in 1812 these controls once again had to be relaxed: men were accepted who squinted or had six to eight teeth missing (provided that these were not front teeth, for otherwise they could not bite cartridges!); anxious not to leave anything to chance, the authorities laid down that even men who had been castrated were not to be excused.[58] One of the rare soldier memorialists, I. M. Minayev, who was taken as a recruit in 1813 although he was 3½ inches too short, relates that at the medical examination 'the doctor would not believe my words that I was healthy and had all my teeth, but climbed into my mouth as if he were a gipsy'.[59]

Throughout the period members of recruiting boards were on the watch for men who faked illness or maimed themselves in the hope of escaping service. In 1727 offenders in the latter category were ordered to be dealt with in drastic

[52] Cf. for example, *PSZ* xv. 10891 (23 Oct. 1758).

[53] *PSZ* viii. 5768 (4 June 1731), 5914 (20 Dec. 1731: restored), 6004 (22 Mar. 1732), x. 7464 (20 Dec. 1737), xv. 10891 (23 Oct. 1758).

[54] *PSZ* xix. 13483 (20 July 1770), § 13, xix. 13871 (24 Sept. 1772), 14026 (23 Aug. 1773).

[55] Shchepetil'nikov (*SVM* iv) pp. 11, 15, 41, 43, 45, 55.

[56] *PSZ* xv. 10793, 10996 (15 Jan. 1758, 19 Oct. 1759).

[57] *PSZ* xxix. 22282 (24 Sept. 1806); Shchepetil'nikov (*SVM* iv) pp. 152–4; Kruchek-Golubov and Kul'bin, in *SVM* viii. 162.

[58] Shchukin, *Bumagi*, viii. 130–1; Shchepetil'nikov (*SVM* iv) p. 55; *PSZ* xxxii. 25220.

[59] [Minayev] 'Vosp. I. Men'shago', p. 52.

Petrine fashion: one in ten was to be hanged and the rest knouted and sent to forced labour.[60] Münnich, who took charge of the Russian army under the empress Anna Ivanovna (1730–40), evidently thought this a waste of valuable manpower, for in 1730 those who maimed themselves but were still able to hold a rifle or drive a horse and cart were sent to the army.[61] This was also the rule during the Seven Years War and in the first part of Catherine's reign.[62] In 1771 such malpractices were said to be widespread among native peoples of the Volga region, who, 'anticipating a levy, injure their limbs, cut their fingers, poke out or otherwise damage their eyes, knock out their teeth and deform their ears and feet'.[63] Religious and ethnic considerations probably inspired such desperate acts of passive resistance; but the legislators, in true Enlightenment spirit, dismissed such conduct as mere 'barbarism'. A. W. von Hupel, a qualified Baltic-German observer writing in the 1780s, also noted the prevalence of this practice, but did not attribute it to any specific group.[64] He claimed that in Russia recruits showed less dislike of military service than those in other European countries at this time. This optimistic view contrasts with that of a later critic, the Polish democrat J. Tański. 'The time of the levy', he stated, 'is one of crisis and despair for the serfs, even for the most miserable among them. Some prefer death to military service. Often they mutilate themselves by cutting their fingers or pulling out their teeth, or else go into hiding in the forests.'[65] Tański is probably nearer the truth, for there is ample evidence of the persistence of the practice during the first quarter of the nineteenth century.[66] It was a natural response to the increased incidence of levies and the government's failure to humanize the way in which they were raised.

For the recruit the sudden breach with his family and the rural milieu came as a severe psychological shock. Modern sociologists have noted the traumatic effect of unexpected transfer to an unfamiliar institutional environment without adequate explanation of the rationale for the change.[67] This was also recognized instinctively by contemporary observers. C. von Plotho, a Prussian officer who cannot be suspected of sentimentality, describes the sorrowful scenes that occurred when a recruit took leave of his relatives, 'weighed down by the terrible feeling that he will probably never see his wife or children again'.[68] The Frenchman D. de Raymond noted that 'this eternal separation [from his kin] is the most sombre trait in the life of the Russian soldier'.[69] By

---

[60] *PSZ* vii. 5050 (24 Mar. 1727).
[61] *PSZ* viii. 5632 (23 Oct. 1730).
[62] *PSZ* xiv. 10326 (21 Nov. 1754), § 9, xvii. 12748 (29 Sept. 1766), III, § 6.
[63] *PSZ* xix. 13651 (2 Sept. 1771), § 8.
[64] Von Hupel, *Beschreibung*, p. 202 n.
[65] Tański, *Tableau*, p. 158.
[66] For example, *PSZ* xviii. 21442 (7 Sept. 1804), §§ 8–11, xxx. 23286 (28 Sept. 1808), 23759 (1809), etc.
[67] A. Rothacher, 'On . . . Military Socialization,' *Armed Forces and Society* 6 (1979/80), p. 332.
[68] Plotho, *Entstehung*, p. 66.   [69] De Raymond, *Tableau*, pp. 527–8.

the time they were writing military service was at least limited to a fixed term, normally 25 years, but until 1793 it had been indefinite—'so long as one's strength and health allow', as the phrase went. Home leave was all but unheard of for ordinary soldiers—'no furlough sweetens the long parting', in Plotho's words—and they could not even correspond with their families; indeed, until 1800 their kinsfolk might not be officially notified of a man's demise.

Fortunately we have one memoir by a Russian soldier, Pamfil Nazarov, which conveys something of what a recruit felt. 'I became exceedingly sorrowful,' he writes, 'that the time would come for me to leave my mother and brothers, of whom the eldest was married and had a son.' Since his next senior brother was also married, and the youngest was under age, Pamfil was the obvious choice. His grandfather, as head of the household, was called to the village assembly to hear its decision; meanwhile 'bitter tears coursed down my face as I awaited the fateful news'. After bidding farewell to relatives in nearby villages, 'my brothers and their wives and my aged grandfather fell upon their knees before me, pleading that I should volunteer instead of my brothers'. He acceded to their pleas. Several relatives accompanied him to Tver´, the provincial capital, where he underwent medical examination. The sight of several hundred young men as naked as himself 'caused me shame and shyness'. 'The governor called out "forehead!" and this [shaving] was carried out. I was dressed in a garment and taken under guard.' After he had attended his first rollcall parade his relatives were still allowed to see him, but of course they could not accompany him to St. Petersburg, where 'from great sorrow for my parents and from the severity of military [life] I became ill and collapsed several times a day'.[70]

Nazarov may be darkening the colours a little for literary effect, but his account certainly brings us closer to reality than those of some high-ranking Russians or foreigners. A. Lebedev, who witnessed the 83rd levy in Moscow in the summer of 1812, later recalled unsympathetically that 'according to the custom of the time it was accompanied by the obligatory wailing and weeping, which went on the whole morning in front of the recruiting board [office] itself and along all the streets adjoining it'.[71] Sir Robert Wilson, with bluff English heartiness, contended that although 'the day of nomination is passed in general grief, and each family is in unaffected affliction at the approaching separation, ... no sooner is the head of the reluctant conscript shaved, according to military habit ... than the plaints and lamentations cease, and ... revel, with music and dance, takes place until the moment when he is to abandon his native home'.[72]

The recruit's natural sense of alienation was heightened by the shaving of his forehead, that is, the front part of his scalp, and beard. This measure was

---

[70] [Nazarov] 'Zapiski', pp. 530–3.   [71] Shchukin, *Bumagi*, iii. 256.

[72] Wilson, *Sketch*, p. 10. He was taken to task for his sanguine view of the matter by a compatriot: Lyall, *Travels*, i. 140.

introduced by a secret decree in 1738.[73] It evidently replaced the branding ordered by Peter I and served the same purpose. Minayev, whose donor had bribed the barber to spare him this indignity, but in vain, writes that he was 'greatly shaken when I woke up the next day, as it happened opposite a mirror, and saw myself with my forehead shorn.'[74] From 1808 recruits were dressed in an unattractive off-white or prison-grey uniform.[75] This measure, designed as an amelioration, may not have been perceived as such, especially as the material used gave less protection. Hitherto recruits had been required to attend the induction ceremony in regular peasant attire and footwear, which it was their donor's responsibility to provide. These items of clothing were specified in detail and even included a fur coat (*shuba*).[76] Official records do not state what happened to these articles once the soldier had joined his regiment and been issued with a uniform, except that he was not allowed to sell them;[77] probably most items had by then worn out, especially if the recruit had been obliged to cover a great distance on foot—in mid-winter.

He also received from his donor a cash grant and a prescribed quantity of foodstuffs (*proviant*) for this initial period. The receiving officer was supposed to check that these supplies were indeed handed over—for cases came to official notice of donors collecting food for this purpose from their peasants and then keeping it themselves.[78] The cash grant amounted to 1.50 roubles per man. It was taken over by the squad officer, who was supposed to issue it in three monthly instalments, along with the food, which consisted of 6 *chetveriki* of flour, 3 *garntsy* of grits, and 6 *funty* of salt. Each recruit was allocated to an artel, or association of eight to ten men, who among other things learned how to prepare food in common as they would have to do later as soldiers.[79] This arrangement also had a disciplinary aspect, for artel members were bound by mutual guarantee (*krugovaya poruka*). In practice recruits often went short of food, or so at least we are told by a French observer of Catherine's first war with the Turks: 'a poor boy is taken from home, marches for two to three hundred miles, and all he gets for his support is some flour, which is often mildewy, and some milled barley; often he has to sell it or to carry it for more than a fortnight . . . It seems to me that such brave soldiers would deserve to be treated differently.'[80]

The squad officer and the members of the escorting party were supposed to be chosen for their honesty, reliability, and experience. They gave recruits elementary instruction in marching, handling rifles, and so on, but were under

[73] Beskrovnyy, *Russkaya armiya*, p. 39.

[74] [Minayev] 'Vosp. I. Men'shago', p. 53.

[75] Shchepetil'nikov (*SVM* iv) p. 168; *PSZ* xxx. 23275, 23297, § 132, 23848, § 10 (3 Sept., 10 Oct. 1808, 19 Sept. 1809).

[76] *PSZ* vii. 4845 (5 Mar. 1726), § 4, xiv. 10326 (21 Nov. 1754), § 2. The norms were slightly raised in 1757: xiv. 10786 (23 Dec. 1757), § 8.

[77] *PSZ* xxx. 23297 (10 Oct. 1808), § 134.

[78] *PSZ* vii. 4845 (5 Mar. 1726), § 5, viii. 5749 (27 Apr. 1731), § 3.

[79] *PSZ* xiv. 10786 (23 Dec. 1757), II, §§ 4–5.

[80] Warnery, *Rémarques*, pp. 131–2.

orders not to drill them extensively, to employ them on work details, or otherwise to oppress them, for it was realized that such abuses would delay the men's arrival in the unit and make them still more disenchanted.[81] The convoy was seen as a means of accustoming recruits to the military life-style before they were exposed to the full ardours of the service. On the march they were required to cover 20 to 30 versts a day (half that distance in inclement weather), with a rest every third day; they were inspected twice daily and once a week spent the rest period washing their clothes and mending their boots. These rules, like so many others, were not always kept to in practice. Vyazemsky states that the squad officer 'tries to space out the money in his care as is most convenient for himself, and if he is severe into the bargain he tortures the unfortunate recruits with beatings'.[82]

While in the convoy the men had better opportunities for escape than they were likely to have later as soldiers. This is why elaborate rules were devised to ensure that squads kept to the designated route (even if it were rendered unsuitable by flooding etc.), avoided taverns, and were closely supervised when in their billets.[83] If recruits fell seriously ill and had to be left behind, they were supposed to be looked after by army medical personnel. Should their own supplies be exhausted before they reached their destination, they were to be fed at state expense, and the portions of those who died or deserted were distributed as a bonus among the rest.[84]

These rules testify to an awareness on the authorities' part that recruits needed to be treated with a minimum of care, if only because they represented a finite resource. This was no more than a common-sense attitude, based on concern for state interests rather than the influence of Enlightened thought. Yet the principles of the levy were called into question by individual Russians from the start. Already during Peter I's reign, as we have seen, Pososhkov had pleaded for a 'cadre army' that would make up in quality for what it lacked in quantity; but his well-intentioned suggestions were not even considered by the authorities and may even have contributed to his death in prison. Thereafter major wars gave a periodic impetus to reformist ideas. In 1731 Münnich (or, as Soviet investigators insist, the Russian statesman P. I. Yaguzhinsky) put forward a plan for the tax-paying population to be divided into 'companies' of 500 men organized into ten sections, each of which should supply a recruit once in ten years.[85] The scheme is said to have been opposed by self-interested landowners; whether this was the case or not, it would have required con-

---

[81] *PSZ* xiv. 10786 (23 Dec. 1757), II, §§ 6, 30-1, xvii. 12748 (29 Sept. 1766), §§ 2-5.

[82] Vyazemsky, 'Zapiska', p. 5.

[83] *PSZ* xxviii. 21490 (Oct. 1804), §§ 12-13, 19(4), xxix. 22577 (July 1807), xxx. 23297 (10 Oct. 1808), § 53.

[84] *PSZ* xiv. 10789 (23 Dec. 1757), II, §§ 13-14, 17, 21, xv. 10788 (9 Jan. 1758), ch. IX, xv. 10928 (21 Feb. 1759), xvii. 12748 (29 Sept. 1766), II, §§ 7-10, 15-17.

[85] Beskrovnyy, *Russkaya armiya*, p. 34 and in Baranovich *et al.* (eds.), *Ocherki*, p. 300 (not published).

siderable administrative expertise to adjust unit boundaries to demographic changes.

During the Seven Years War P. I. Shuvalov, the leading figure in the military establishment at the time, devised a scheme which, had it been fully acted on, might have turned the Russian army into a territorial militia. He pointed out, as Münnich (or Yaguzhinsky) had done, that the existing system led to a gross waste of manpower, to a high desertion rate, and to uncertainty among donors as to how many men they would have to supply at the next levy. He proposed to divide each province into five sections, each of which would be required in turn to furnish recruits at the rate of 1 per 100 souls. The units were conceived as territorially discrete, since the governors were to delineate their boundaries. However, Shuvalov undermined the impact of this proposed reform by providing that the government might take recruits from more than one section, or even from all of them, in case of emergency.[86] Only part of this scheme (the instructions for implementing the levy) received Imperial assent, and both during Shuvalov's supremacy and thereafter recruits continued to be raised in the traditional manner.[87]

In 1766 Catherine II reissued Shuvalov's so-called 'General Statute' with only minor emendations.[88] Neither she nor the high-powered military commission which she appointed on her accession seems to have envisaged any basic reform. The nineteenth-century military historian D. F. Maslovsky, anxious to detect some sign of progress, claimed that the 1766 statute 'gave legislation on military service greater stability and definition: people could now take comfort in the fact that, when the almost annual manifesto on the levy was issued, its terms would not differ radically from those of the previous one'.[89] But previously there had not been any such radical changes and Catherine, as we know, was soon obliged to increase the quota when war broke out with the Turks. In 1774 A. I. Vyazemsky made the sensible suggestion that recruits should be taken at age 18 and required to serve for only 15 years.[90] He evidently sought, as Pososhkov had, to move towards a smaller but better trained army. However, Vyazemsky did not hold a senior military position and his memorandum received the same fate as his predecessor's (although in this 'enlightened' era at least he suffered no harm).

Both Field-Marshal Rumyantsev and the Tsarevich Paul (Pavel Petrovich) (who opposed his mother's policies on personal and philosophical grounds) espoused the reformist cause. The former was in a position to put through major changes had he wished to, but limited himself to a scheme for permanent recruiting areas, much like those previously adumbrated. Again nothing

[86] *PSZ* xiv. 10786 (23 Dec. 1757), introd., preamble, §§ 1–3.
[87] Beskrovnyy, *Russkaya armiya*, p. 37; Petrov, *Russkaya voyennaya sila*, ii. 152 gives the impression that the measure *was* implemented. For the levies, cf. *PSZ* xv. 10874, 10990 (30 Aug. 1758, 18 Sept. 1759).
[88] *PSZ* xvii. 12478 (29 Sept. 1766).
[89] Maslovsky, *Materialy*, ii (i). 46.
[90] Vyazemsky, 'Zapiska', p. 9.

happened, allegedly because of the lack of barracks.[91] Paul's idea was to introduce foreign mercenaries and a militia system on the Prussian pattern whereby recruits, on completing basic training, would be classified as *kantonisty* and discharged to their homes until required to serve. This, he thought, would have two advantages: first, 'the men will maintain their tie with the land, and their relatives will not, as they do now, fall into despair when they leave to join the service, considering them dead'; second, 'the soldiers, being accustomed to living among peasants, will refrain from excesses when they pass through their villages'.[92] (It was characteristic of Paul to mingle major and minor issues in this way.) But he fought shy of a fundamental reform of the poll-tax system, such as was evidently favoured by his correspondent, General P. I. Panin, and confined himself to the simple notion that levies should be raised at an identical rate each year.[93] Catherine had refrained from demanding recruits in 1762–7 and 1774–5, but Paul's assumption that such irregularities made the levy harder to bear is not convincing. The real need was to match effectives against human resources in a more balanced fashion, and here neither mother nor son showed much imagination. The only gain, and it was a modest one, was the differentiated extension of military service to the non-Great Russian areas, considered above.

When Paul (1796–1801) acceded he introduced a number of measures which shocked contemporaries. Within a matter of days he promulgated with great flourish a new military statute and several other regulations, but none of these brought any alleviation in the recruit's lot. One positive step was to set up a Military Orphanage with places for 800 soldiers' sons[94] who, in the normal course of events, could be expected to follow in their fathers' footsteps and ease the drain on the population as a whole. But the practical results of this measure were less impressive than the emperor hoped. Perhaps the most important change that occurred from the recruit's point of view was a negative one: greater emphasis was placed on drill.[95] Even the principle that levies should be raised annually at a consistent rate was not kept to: during Paul's four-year reign three were summoned, each on a different basis.[96]

Alexander I's principal achievement in this sphere was the establishment of recruit depots (1808).[97] These were designed to cut down on the high rate of losses by habituating men to service conditions more gradually. He also, as we have seen, issued them with sub-standard uniforms. The main object of this

---

[91] Beskrovnyy, *Russkaya armiya*, pp. 299–300, citing A. K. Bayov, *Kurs istorii russkogo voyennogo iskusstva*, v (St. Petersburg, 1909), 30–1.

[92] Paul to P. Panin, 10 May 1778, 'Perepiska', pp. 407–8.

[93] Paul to P. Panin, 14 Sept. 1778, 'Perepiska', p. 416; cf. Barskov, 'Proyekty' and, for a hint of Panin's ideas, Beskrovnyy, *Russkaya armiya*, p. 302.

[94] *PSZ* xxv. 18793 (23 Dec. 1798); see below, p. 203.

[95] *PSZ* xxiv. 17588 (29 Nov. 1797), II, ch. I.

[96] Mikhnevich, in *SVM* iv (I, i). 226; *PSZ* xxiv. 18125 (1 Sept. 1797), xxv. 18646, 19045 (31 Aug. 1798, 23 July 1799)—respectively 3 per 500, 1 per 500, and 1 per 350 souls.

[97] Petrov, *Russkaya voyennaya sila*, ii. 318–19; Shchepetil'nikov (*SVM* iv) pp. 135–50; *PSZ* xxx. 23297 (10 Oct. 1808).

was to ensure greater uniformity and neatness; it was also expected to help in identifying deserters. The measure thus had the ambiguous character typical of so many of Alexander's 'reforms'. In 1813, for instance, the men lost their fur *shuba*, which was replaced by a greatcoat (*shinel'*).[98] One may doubt whether this was a step in the right direction. On the other hand they were now promised an improved diet, with meat or fish according to the season, as well as an issue of spirits three times a week.[99] A more flexible arrangement was introduced with regard to the provisioning of recruits: donors could hand over, in lieu of foodstuffs in kind, a cash sum which varied according to the cost of products in each locality.[100] However, this was difficult to administer, and one wonders how many recruits actually received the hot stew (*privarok*) which their solicitous sovereign prescribed. For Alexander practised the art of public relations: in manifestos he would commiserate with his subjects over the bitter necessity for each fresh levy, yet he did little to better either the juridical or the material condition of those who were called on to soldier in his vast armies—as the survivors of Borodino and Leipzig had every right to expect.

Once allocated to a regiment, there the Russian soldier remained until death (or, more rarely, discharge) supervened. The 25-year service term introduced in 1793 was ostensibly a reward for the troops' loyal conduct during the second Russo-Turkish war of Catherine's reign (1787–91).[101] The privileged servitors had won the same concession half a century earlier (see below, p. 000), but no mention was made of this precedent and it is not certain whether it affected the government's decision. Probably more important were the example of Prussia, where the service term had been reduced to 20 years the previous year,[102] and the positive experience gained with the 15-year term for certain categories of troops in the south. Given the low level of life expectancy among soldiers, the measure may not have made much difference in practice. In 1810 Alexander I contemplated a further reduction,[103] but nothing came of these plans until 1834.

Each soldier's service record (*formulyarnyy spisok*) contained a column for officials to enter the amount of leave he had been granted—but in almost every case these columns were left a pristine blank. The regulations did not prohibit leave; but neither did they provide for it. To be sure, for several years after 1727 and again in 1742 one third of the army was sent home,[104] but it seems that the only men who benefited from this were those from privileged backgrounds who had estates to go to. In the cavalry units in the south, which

[98] *PSZ* xxxii. 25477 (19 Sept. 1813).

[99] *PSZ* xxxii, xliii. 25363 (26 Mar. 1813); Shchepetil'nikov (*SVM* iv) p. 167.

[100] *PSZ* xxx. 23036, 23961 (23 May 1808, 8 Nov. 1809), xxxiii. 26301 (8 June 1816), xliii. 24381 (20 Oct. 1810); Shchepetil'nikov (*SVM* iv) pp. 164, 166, 168.

[101] *PSZ* xxiii. 17149 (2 Sept. 1793), §§ 5–6.   [102] Büsch, *Militärsystem*, p. 46.

[103] Petrov, *Russkaya voyennaya sila*, ii. 319; Tański, *Tableau*, p. 159.

[104] *PSZ* viii. 5492, 6085 (20 Dec. 1729, 3 June 1732), xi. 8642 (18 Oct. 1742); cf. Vyazemsky, *Verkhovnyy taynyy sovet*, pp. 345–6.

were on a militia basis, leave was granted, at least in the 1770s under Potemkin, when one seventh of his newly formed hussars took turns to stay at home.[105] Rumyantsev and the Tsarevich Paul both advocated it for the rest of the troops: the former as part of his plan for a territorial army and the latter because, as he wrote, he had discovered that in practice it did not put up the desertion rate; however, not much seems to have come of their ideas.[106] In the (privileged) Mounted Grenadier regiment in October 1795 one private in three and one corporal in nine were on leave; among officers only captains had a more favourable ratio.[107] However, there may have been special local reasons for this, and the term *otluchka* (absence) could cover errands and work assignments as well as home leave (*otpusk*). A routine monthly report on troops in the First Division in March 1796 suggests that frequency of absence declined according to rank: 41.4 per cent of staff officers, 35.4 per cent of subalterns, 13.9 per cent of cadets, NCOs, and corporals, and 9.4 per cent of privates were lawfully absent at this time.[108]

What often happened in practice, especially under Catherine II, was that regimental commanders, who during her reign wielded almost absolute power over their subordinates' lives, allowed men to go on leave informally, without reporting the fact or entering it in their records, in return for some favour—either a cash 'gift' or, more usually, labour services. Such collusion had been banned already in 1738,[109] but it persisted none the less since it was hard to control and it suited both parties. At the end of Catherine's reign an effort was made to centralize the granting of leave: the War College or commander-in-chief was to issue permission in each case, and forms had to be filled in giving particulars of the man's destination, due date of return, etc.[110]

These rules were further tightened by Paul on his accession: leave had to be taken during the winter months; only a given number might be absent from each unit at any time; and, last but not least, they were not to be paid—which meant that leave would again be limited to the privileged.[111] The emperor regarded private employment of soldiers on leave as a grave abuse. In 1798 a brigadier named Gur'yev was penalized for allowing a private in his unit to overstay his leave, which he had spent on Gur'yev's estate, evidently as a labourer. (Characteristically, the officer merely had to part with an additional recruit.)[112]

Alexander I first allowed leave applications to be granted by (divisional) inspectors,[113] but the wars seem to have led to a reversal of this policy; in any

[105] Dubrovin, *Suvorov*, p. 105.

[106] Dubrovin, *Suvorov*, p. 68; Paul to P. Panin, 10 May 1778, 'Perepiska', p. 408.

[107] TsGVIA, V-UA, f. 1349, d. 300, l. 282.

[108] Ibid., l. 1.

[109] *PSZ* x. 7707 (15 Dec. 1738).

[110] *PSZ* xxiii. 17042, 17158 (Apr. 1792, 31 Oct. 1793).

[111] *PSZ* xxiv. 17588 (29 Nov. 1797), IX, ch. VIII, §§ 5-6, xxiv. 18167 (28 Sept. 1797); Shil'der, *Aleksandr I*, i. 335.

[112] Studenkin, 'Ukazy', p. 508.

[113] *PSZ* xxvii. 20490 (31 Oct. 1802).

case by 1812, as we have seen, well-informed foreign observers were stating flatly that Russian soldiers got no leave at all.[114] It was some time before matters improved in this respect. Not until 1823 did the tsar, now anxious to reduce military expenditure, explicitly permit men to go home for as long as five to six months in the year.[115] In his memoirs Ivan Minayev, who had risen to become an NCO in a guards regiment, states that shortly before this his colonel, a harsh disciplinarian, suddenly allowed him to go on leave for three months. His relatives were surprised to see him. Accompanied by his brother, he went walking in the street to show off his fine uniform: 'at every step people we knew stopped us for a chat and shook their heads [as if to say] "what a fine fellow is he!"'[116] Nine years earlier Minayev had been a reluctant recruit; now he had internalized the military code of values.

Perhaps this soldier's promotion made him something of a special case, for in general it was difficult to rise even to non-commissioned rank, let alone to that of officer. There were few vacancies in the regimental establishment, which set up a promotion block for those who were competent and aspired to better themselves. In 1766 Catherine prescribed that NCOs of gentry background should be promoted ahead of those from humbler circumstances, such as soldiers' children, even if the latter had acquired more seniority.[117] One can readily imagine the sense of grievance that this overt social discrimination created. Advancement was entirely the affair of the unit commander concerned, who sometimes tried to get round the problem by appointing men as 'supernumerary' (*sverkhkomplektnye*) NCOs—which simply meant that they did additional duties without extra pay. One hussar regiment stocked up no less than 198 such supernumeraries before the practice came to light and was prohibited.[118] Some NCOs, mainly gentrymen with private means, got no pay at all until this was permitted in hardship cases.[119] The promotion block problem was not, however, tackled, except in the sense that the army was committed to campaigns which cost many lives, and the ambitious had a chance to step into dead men's shoes.

Non-commissioned officers, especially those of under-privileged origin, were in a difficult situation both socially and psychologically. They were set above the common soldiers yet their rank did not in itself confer any worthwhile privileges. The men generally despised such NCOs, above all when they saw that they were humiliated or maltreated by officers.[120] Not until the 1820s was any serious effort undertaken to improve their educational and professional qualifications. The average NCO tried to compensate for his shortcomings by

---

114 Plotho, *Entstehung*, p. 66; de Raymond, *Tableau*, p. 535.
115 *PSZ* xxxviii. 29398 (2 Apr. 1823), §§ 7–8.
116 [Minayev] 'Vosp. I. Men´shago', p. 58.
117 *PSZ* xvii. 12543 (14 Jan. 1766), I, § 2, n. 1.
118 *PSZ* xxiii. 17376 (29 Aug. 1795).
119 *PSZ* xxv. 18684 (Sept. 1798), xxvi. 20024 (29 Sept. 1801).
120 Shatilov, 'Mysli', p. 368.

adopting a rough manner and sticking to the rule-book, so that his subordinates had to endure a myriad petty tyrannies.[121]

The main change in the Russian soldier's professional duties during this long period was that he had to do more drill and take part in military exercises. Purists distinguished between *ekzertsitsii*, or manœuvres in formation on the parade-ground, which were regulated in detail in military manuals, and *evolyutsii*, or exercises which took more account of the natural features of the landscape and allowed commanders more scope to display initiative.[122] Around 1800 the latter were giving way to the former, due to changes taking place in tactics and armaments. Briefly, the shift from line to column formation meant that men had to perform complex movements promptly, on oral command or at a signal on the drum, while the introduction of more sophisticated (and heavier) weapons called for greater precision in handling and firing.[123] However, the shift was also to some degree the consequence of a mechanistic way of thinking to which both military and political leaders of the age were highly susceptible. One general, extolling the Russian soldier for his patriotic zeal in 1812, remarked casually, but characteristically, that 'as a rule they are but machines'.[124] A whole mental world is revealed by this frank statement: an army was conceived of as a precision tool whose various parts needed to fit together perfectly if it were to function in the proper way. This view accounts for the many regulations (*ustavy*, literally statutes) which laid down in pedantic detail what each man had to do in manœuvres or on the battlefield; for the slightest displacement or delay, it was believed, might endanger the success of the operation and absolute harmony became a supreme goal.

Russian military historians, whether pre-revolutionary or Soviet, have generally blamed the excesses to which this mechanistic spirit gave rise on foreign influences, notably from Prussia, and have hailed those who objected to them as enlightened patriots. This view is anachronistic and exaggerated. The 1755 statute, which laid down many exercises and procedures absent from its predecessor of 1716, was the work of Z. G. Chernyshev and masterminded by P. I. Shuvalov (both Russians). It certainly introduced a more rigid and formal tone, but it was not directly responsible for the army's chequered performance in the Seven Years War. Peter III was a fervent admirer of the great Frederick, but he fell from power before the harmful effects of his Prussian-style changes could make themselves felt. It is significant that the 'patriotic' Catherine II's military advisers, who again were predominantly Russians with considerable professional experience, confined themselves to changes of detail. It was they who, in 1763, standardized drill movements throughout the

---

[121] 'Iz zametok starosluzhivogo': these memoirs, although dealing with a later period, are informative on NCOs' functions and conduct.

[122] Glinoyetsky, 'Nekotorye svedeniya', p. 9.

[123] Menning, 'Origins', pp. 79, 90, 97; id., 'Mil. Institutions'; cf. A. A. Komarov, 'Razvitiye takticheskoy mysli v russkoy armii v 60–rh—90–rh gg. XVIII v.', *Vestnik Mosk. Universiteta*, series 8 (*Istoriya*), 1982, 3, pp. 57–66.

[124] Löwenstern, *Mémoires*, i. 274.

army for the first time. Rumyantsev, and later Suvorov, were noted for their stress on realistic battle training (Suvorov subjected infantry to lateral assaults by squadrons of cavalrymen firing live ammunition!)[125] but this did not lead them to forego the parade-ground. Both leaders also appreciated that rifles could be damaged by excessive burnishing, and that 'smart' tight-fitting uniforms could harm a soldier's health; nevertheless their reforms in regard to dress and equipment did not make a whole world of difference, as nationalist military historians sometimes imply. These measures were of symbolic rather than practical consequence. In short, differences of degree, not of principle, divided protagonists of the so-called 'national school' from those who adhered more openly to foreign military models, as did the monarchs who succeeded Catherine and most of their advisers.

The emperor Paul was the first to stage the gigantic parades that became a regular feature of army life for the next half-century and even beyond. One of the climaxes in this 'paradomania' was the victory march-past on the plain of Vertus east of Paris in 1815, in which 150,000 Russian soldiers are said to have taken part.[126] The outspoken N. N. Murav'yev-Karsky records that 'in Paris the soldiers had more work (*trudy*) than on campaign as there were so many parades while we were there' and that after the battle of Töplitz (modern Teplice, 1813) no less than three parades were held even before the fallen had been buried, so that the stench of corpses spoiled the ceremonial atmosphere.[127] The exaggerated emphasis on drill went hand in hand with petty exactingness in regard to turnout and compliance with regulations. These excesses reached a peak after 1814 during the so-called 'Arakcheyev regime' (*Arakcheyevshchina*: see ch. 12). The purpose was to reinforce discipline, which some alarmist and routine-minded generals feared had been shaken by the troops' wartime experiences. In their view combat 'spoiled' soldiers, whom they valued as much for their appearance as for their effectiveness in battle. Admittedly, they did have some reason for concern, since the men had first been inspired by the patriotic euphoria of the War of 1812 and then, on reaching central and western Europe, had seen something of conditions superior to those in their homeland. However, the threat of indiscipline was tackled in a crude, unintelligent manner which aggravated the troops' natural resentment at the many injustices to which they were exposed.

To understand the situation of rightlessness in which the Russian soldier found himself we have to go back momentarily to the Petrine era. The military statute of 1716, based in its essentials on current Western legislation and practice,[128]

---

[125] Bogdanovich, *Russkaya armiya*, p. 35. At church parades Suvorov had his men remove their hats by numbers: Meshcheryakov, *Suvorov*, i. 92 (Polkovoye uchrezhdeniye, II, § 15).

[126] Bogdanovich, *Istoriya*, vi. 88–92, app. pp. 5–9; von Bradke, 'Avtobiog. zapiski', p. 28.

[127] Murav'yev-Karsky, 'Zapiski', *RA* 1886), 1, p. 34, 2, p. 106.

[128] The more nationalistic Russian and Soviet military historians have minimized the extent of this borrowing, but the close analysis undertaken in 1882–6 by P. O. Bobrovsky (*Voyennoye pravo*) shows that Peter's adaptations concerned only details, not basic principles. The 'debate' on this matter deflects attention from the real question of how the statute was applied in practice.

was introduced at a time when the regular army was still in a formative phase. This to some extent explains (but scarcely justifies) the extremely harsh penalties that it specified for all manner of offences, major and minor: soldiers still needed to be intimidated into giving their superiors the automatic and unthinking obedience characteristic of eighteenth-century armies. On behalf of the statute it may be said that it defined in detail the functions of military office- and rank-holders at every level, the composition and procedure of military tribunals, and the standard penalties for various offences; moreover, in these judicial instances it was allowed to vary sentences according to the specific circumstances of each case, and confirmation by higher authority was provided for. As in Western armies, the court included an auditor whose function was to see that justice was done. Officers were forbidden to punish their men arbitrarily, to beat them cruelly or to injure them on pain of dismissal if they did so repeatedly.[129] Instead they were enjoined to behave in a paternalistic way, treating their subordinates as if they were their children.

It will be noted that the paternalistic principle was compatible with beating as such: only 'cruel' punishment was discouraged. It was hardly reasonable to expect officers to take this general injunction seriously, especially when the law laid down such barbarous penalties for numerous 'major' offences: running the gauntlet (*shpitsruten*, from the German *Spitzruten*) was mentioned in the statute no less than 40 times![130] Furthermore, the auditors had no judicial training or genuine administrative independence. As NCOs or junior officers they were inferior in rank to the court president, so that (as in Prussia) their role inevitably degenerated into a formal one; their assent to a verdict could in practice be taken for granted.

There were many other major deficiencies in the system of military law which Peter established. The accused had no qualified person to help him prepare or present his defence; the trial was held in secret; the preliminary investigation (called *ferger*, from the German *Verhör*) was conducted by the same authorities that held the trial—and they acted as they thought fit, with scarcely any formal regulation; torture could be used to extract a confession; and commanders had wide discretionary power to punish men for minor ('disciplinary') offences without instituting legal proceedings or reporting on the matter to their superiors. Last but not least, men in the armed forces, like all other Russian subjects, were covered by the special procedure that pertained in cases of suspected political crime, which before 1762 at any rate meant that anyone might be denounced and sent for investigation by the dreaded Chancellery for Secret Affairs. This was the successor to Peter's Preobrazhensky prikaz, which as we know had military associations.[131]

---

[129] Voinskiye artikuly, § 33 (*PRP* viii. 328); Yepifanov, 'Voinskiy ustav', p. 203. On the Military Statute in general, see Shendzikovsky in *SVM* xii (l, i). 44–109; Rozengeym, *Ocherki*, 105–85.

[130] Vish, 'Telesnye nakazaniya', p. 136; Shendzikovsky (*SVM* xii) p. 54.

[131] Keep, 'Secret Chancellery'; on weaknesses in the statute see Bobrovsky, *50 let spetsial'noy shkoly*, pp. 4–6.

Those court-martial records that have survived have not yet been studied, so that it is difficult to assess the quality of Russian military justice. The few cases referred to in published sources concern senior officers, and it is an open question whether in Peter's reign ordinary soldiers were affected at all by the new system. By the 1760s at least they were: military courts convened regularly to hear cases involving murder, arson, robbery, and desertion,[132] but most other offences were probably dealt with informally. This augmented the widespread use of physical punishment, and explains why Russian soldiers passed their brief lives in an atmosphere of continual fear and tension.

In other European armies running the gauntlet was an exceptional measure, seen as the equivalent of a death sentence. In Russia it was regularly applied as a means of enforcing discipline, and was prescribed for quite insubstantial offences: appearing late on parade (for the third time), talking or moving in the ranks, or holding one's weapon incorrectly (for the second time).[133] A soldier who stole cash or goods valued at less than 20 roubles had to run the gauntlet once on the first occasion and twelve times on the second; if he dared to do so a third time he suffered mutilation and exile with forced labour—as he did if the sum exceeded 20 roubles, unless his offence was adjudged a capital one.[134] There were also lesser penalties: beating with rods (*batogi*), demotion and transfer, detention in the guardhouse, 'sitting on the wooden horse' and 'standing under the musket'. The last ordeal involved standing to attention for two hours bearing three (or even six) heavy muskets.

It was the gauntlet that typified the military penal system, and however distasteful the matter may be some description of it must be given here. It subjected the victim to the humiliation of a public beating by his peers. Their involvement in administration of the penalty was designed to isolate the miscreant morally from his comrades, who were lined up in two opposing ranks to form a 'street' (*ulitsa*), through which the prisoner, stripped to the waist, staggered along while the men on either side struck him with switches (*prut´ya*) or thongs about one inch in diameter. To prevent him from moving too fast he was preceded by an NCO who held a rifle with the bayonet fixed and pointed to the rear. Any indulgence by his fellow-soldiers was itself construed as an offence, and an officer rode alongside on horseback to ensure that the blows were properly administered; the victim's cries were drowned by drumbeats. Although his back would soon be reduced to a bloody mess, beating continued until he collapsed—and in some cases even thereafter, for his limp body would be placed on a board and carried along.

---

[132] TsGVIA, V-UA, ed. khr. 88 (1763), ll. 15–16. Sentences were regularly reduced on confirmation. In 1759 the government had suspended proceedings against deserters who failed to respond to an amnesty appeal; they were to be summarily knouted and exiled to forced labour. But this decree was not enforced lest it impair the flow of recruits. *PSZ* xv. 10987 (10 Sept. 1759), § 5; TsGVIA, f. 8, op. 5, d. 5, l. 1.

[133] Anisimov and Zinevich, *Istoriya*, p. 26. The authors of this work, writing in 1911, call these penalties 'relatively light'!

[134] *Voinskiye artikuly*, §§ 189, 191 (*PRP* viii. 364–5).

This horrifyingly brutal penalty seems to have been applied even more harshly in Russia than in other European states where it was also on the statute-book, for the number of men constituting the 'street', and thus the number of blows, was higher (usually 1,000 men instead of 200) or else was left to the commander's discretion. Sometimes a sentence prescribed only the number of passes;[135] yet it was common knowledge that several passes could kill a man. Mortality statistics are available in one especially notorious case which occurred in 1819, when Arakcheyev imposed the penalty on some rebellious military colonists at Chuguyev in the Ukraine. Of 52 men so punished, 25 died within ten days.[136] Even so, instances are recorded of soldiers surviving an incredible number of passes. Private F. Moskalev, of the St. Petersburg Grenadiers, who deserted three times in 1786–7, was sentenced to one pass on the first occasion, six passes on the second, and eight on the third, each time through 1,000 men—a total of 15,000 blows. About the same time a soldier in the Irkutsk garrison named Gordeyev deserted no less than six times and received a total of 52,000 blows; on the last occasion he was spared the gauntlet and sent to forced labour instead.[137]

What did soldiers themselves think of corporal punishment? We may gain a glimpse from some verses written in 1803 by Ivan Makarov, a grenadier in the Izmaylovsky guards regiment, who was himself made to run the gauntlet and sent to a line regiment once his literary endeavours were discovered.

> For my country I stand on guard
> Yet my back is beaten hard.
> The stick's the sole reward for me
> Who defends us from the enemy.
> He who beats his men a lot
> Rises straight up to the top
> And is thought extremely keen
> Though a devil he has been.
> He who fails this brutal test
> Has to serve with the rest.[138]

Against this item of evidence may be set a statement by the writer S. N. Glinka, formerly a company commander. A sensitive soul, he resolved not to inflict corporal punishment, but when two soldiers drank themselves into a

[135] Of five men sentenced to run the gauntlet for desertion in 1799, whose records are in TsGVIA, only one had the size of the unit specified: f. 11, op. 6, ed. khr. 33, ll. 12–38.

[136] Vereshchagin, 'Materialy', pp. 158–60. The casualty rate may have been unusually high in this case because the victims included 27 retired soldiers and 15 non-settlers.

[137] Beskrovnyy, *Russkaya armiya*, p. 435.

[138] Ya otechestvu zashchita / A spina moya otbita, / Ya otechestvu ograda— / V tychkakh, palkakh vsya nagrada. / Kto soldata bol'she byot / Tot chin zdes¡ dostayot. / I staratelen, khorosh / Khot´ na chorta on pokhozh. / A kol´ bit´ kto ne umeyet / Nichego ne razumeyet. Gukovsky, 'Soldatskiye stikhi', pp. 143–4. The author was no doubt an educated nobleman who projected his own discontents on to the common soldiers. The other grievances he mentions include strenuous guard duties, lack of medical care, crowded barracks, low pay, and the sorry plight of veterans.

stupor some of their fellows asked him, through their NCO, to have the usual penalty applied because dishonour had been brought upon the regiment. He ordered each of them to be given 15 blows with rods.[139]

Disciplinary controls were intensified whenever the empire was at war and also, of course, depended on the whim of the autocrat and his or her chief military advisers. Both Münnich and Shuvalov were leaders with an authoritarian cast of mind. They set up commissions to revise Peter I's military statute, but with no practical result; as one official historian daintily puts it, 'changes in the application of military law occurred not by legislative action but largely through practice'.[140] In the Izmaylovsky guards regiment in the 1730s soldiers who made mistakes at gunnery trials were beaten with rods 'without any indulgence' (*bez vsyakogo upushcheniya*), although most of them will have been of gentry background; one man was beaten before his entire company for failing to denounce a comrade who falsely claimed to be of noble stock.[141] Chernyshev's 1755 statute is said to have introduced (or perhaps legalized?) the practice of beating soldiers with a cane or baton (*palka*) for mistakes committed on parade, such as dropping a cartridge while loading one's musket.[142] Peter III sought to improve morale by banning rods (*batogi*) and the cat-o'-nine tails (*koshka*)—which probably had the unintended effect of increasing resort to the gauntlet.[143]

The degree to which the penal system was liberalized under Catherine II has generally been exaggerated. Shortly after her accession the empress gradually abolished torture in investigations by civilian agencies, but it persisted in the military until 1782, when a decree was issued prohibiting it.[144] Court presidents were instructed to take their cue from the empress's *Nakaz* of 1766, the penological principles of which were derived from Beccaria. Perhaps for this reason she ordered the decree to remain a secret, only divisional and corps commanders being informed. Some years earlier, to mark her first victory over the Turks, Catherine ordered that men in the ranks should not be whipped, since this was 'a sentence of death' rather than a punishment, but she was careful to add the words *bez suda*, 'unless the court so rules'; whipping therefore continued.[145] Dubrovin claims that 'proceedings began to be taken against [those who ordered] beatings and cruel punishments',[146] but offers no evidence in substantiation. It would be nearer the truth to say that some leading generals, anxious to maintain their standing at court, echoed Catherine's own humanitarian sentiments without, however, either initiating revision of the military statute or erecting effective legal barriers against

[139] Glinka, *Zapiski*, pp. 168, 183.
[140] Shendzikovsky, in *SVM* xii (l, i.) 131-4.
[141] Vish, 'Telesnye nakazaniya', p. 183.
[142] Shendzikovsky (*SVM* xii) p. 152. Text in *VS* 11 (1871), pt. II, ch. IV.
[143] *PSZ* xv. 11467 (9 Mar. 1762); the latter was used in the navy.
[144] *PSZ* xxi. 15313 (1 Jan. 1782).
[145] *PSZ* xx. 14275 (17 Mar. 1775).
[146] Dubrovin, *Suvorov*, p. 107.

arbitrary actions by their subordinates. Regimental colonels in particular enjoyed more freedom than before to determine how the law was applied within their units, and their practice varied greatly.

Characteristic in this respect are S. R. Vorontsov's instructions to his company commanders (1774), which were regarded by other senior officers of 'advanced' views as worthy of emulation and have earned the praise of military historians. 'Do not strike a man for [mistakes in] marching and [rifle] movements,' wrote Vorontsov, 'but unflaggingly teach the men what they have to do . . . It is unbecoming and harmful if a soldier hates his rifle, as he may well do if he is beaten when drilling with it, and comes to look on it simply as an instrument of torture.'[147] Yet in the same document Vorontsov ordered men charged with insubordination to be sent for trial at regimental headquarters because they merit 'the harshest penalties, which cannot be administered at company level'; these penalties were to be carried out in public, 'before the whole regiment, so that others may be dissuaded by the example'. Anyone insulting a sentry was to be killed at once by another soldier, 'and it is up to him whether to kill him with the bayonet or the butt of his rifle'.[148] That such a document could be considered a humanitarian manifesto tells us a lot about the condition of Catherine's army (and later historiography, too).

A. S. Pishchevich, who commanded a cavalry squadron in the second Russo-Turkish war of the reign, claims in his memoirs that for seven years 'I never used the stick, let alone ordered any rogue to run the gauntlet'. Yet he blandly admits that a friend of his beat a dragoon 'so severely that a few days later he died'; an investigation found the officer to blame but Pishchevich persuaded their commander 'to consign the case to oblivion'. He disapproved of what he regarded as laxity by some of his colleagues: 'it takes years to knock a soldier into shape but only a minute to spoil him'. Such a philosophy was probably not untypical of officers in distant provincial stations, such as those on the Kuban´ line where Pishchevich wrote his reminiscences.[149]

Liberal influences percolated slowly, from the top down. The great field-marshals of the age, P. A. Rumyantsev, G. A. Potemkin, and A. V. Suvorov, have acquired a reputation for 'progressive' views that is not wholly deserved, although they certainly displayed more common sense than the martinets of the Gatchina school who succeeded them. Rumyantsev's service regulations (1770) make no provisions for soldiers' rights or welfare (apart from two vague clauses on medical aid).[150] The several dozen court-martial sentences which he confirmed in 1778–80 were not remarkable for their liberalism.[151] Potemkin, certainly more enlightened than most, repeatedly urged senior

---

[147] Glinoyetsky, 'Instruktsiya . . . Vorontsova', p. 39 (§ 5).

[148] Ibid., pp. 34, 42 (§§ 1, 7).

[149] [Pishchevich] *Zhizn´*, pp. 120–1, 147–9.

[150] 'Obryad sluzhby' (1770), in Fortunatov, *Rumyantsev*, ii. 233–51; cf. Suvorov's 'Polkovoye uchrezhdeniye' (1764) in Meshcheryakov, *Suvorov*, i. 73–168, which showed more concern for soldiers' health.

[151] TsGVIA, V–UA, ed. khr. 226 (1778–80).

officers with whom he corresponded to show 'humanity' (*chelovekolyubiye*). To Prince Nassau-Zingen he wrote: 'cease excessive beatings, for it is better to explain to the men what they ought to know'.[152] But this was an admission that, although he had by then been vice-president of the War College for 14 years, this elementary principle had not been enforced. 'Tell your officers', he wrote to General Khvostov, 'that they should treat their men with the greatest mildness and look after their interests . . . Penalties should be moderate and serve to reform, not to injure.'[153] Yet he did not order Khvostov to take proceedings against those who flouted a law that had been on the statute-book since Peter I's reign. The narrow limits to Potemkin's humanitarian sentiment are evident from a phrase in another letter: 'I have ordered punishments to be mild, but if anyone should disobey his commander I shall inflict a penalty equivalent to death'[154]—that is, the gauntlet.

Some of the more conscientious commanders heeded these precepts and repeated them in their own orders, and by the 1790s the atmosphere in many units will no doubt have been more relaxed than before. But when fashions changed at the top, as they did in 1796, the bulk of officers readjusted their thinking accordingly. The reforms which Catherine and her advisers desired had not been placed on a sound legal footing. There is much truth in the observation of G. Gukovsky, a Soviet historian writing before Stalinist neo-nationalism became obligatory:

The story is endlessly repeated . . . of how Potemkin ordered soldiers not to be beaten, or not to be beaten cruelly. Of course this is in itself most remarkable. But it can hardly have had much effect in practice; clearly it was unrealizable given the army's set-up at that time. Soldiers definitely continued to be beaten. If they were sometimes beaten less, this does not mean that there was an easement in their lot, since they were still subject to systematic exploitation.[155]

On his accession Paul at once moved to tighten discipline. His measures were directed principally against senior officers, whom he held responsible, not entirely unjustly, for the abuses that were rife. Soldiers, in so far as they cared about such matters, probably relished the sight of their superiors undergoing the harsh treatment that they themselves had to endure. One of the emperor's first decrees awarded a decoration (the order of St. Anne) to privates and NCOs who had served without fault for 20 years; this automatically exempted them from corporal punishment. Another granted an amnesty to all rankers under investigation for crimes other than murder or the theft of state property.[156] For men in the line flogging with the knout and exile

---

[152] Dubrovin, *Suvorov*, p. 112 (12 Apr. 1788).
[153] Ibid., p. 113 (17 Sept. 1788).
[154] Potemkin to Selevin, 16 June 1788, ibid., p. 114.
[155] Gukovsky, 'Soldatskiye stikhi', p. 122.
[156] *PSZ* xxiv. 17547, 17556 (12, 16 Nov. 1796). Cf. 17576 (22 Nov.), which repeated the standard ban on the private employment of soldiers, only to permit it—as Peter I had done—'with their consent or for payment'; xxiv. 17908 (5 Apr. 1797), § 13.

were to replace the death penalty.[157] But at the same time Paul's new military statutes casually opened the way to greater use of corporal punishment (which, as we know, could easily prove fatal). Running the gauntlet was now expressly made a *discretionary* penalty: a unit commander could order it to be inflicted on soldiers charged with disorderly conduct while on the march. According to some writers it now became the *principal* penalty meted out to privates, since NCOs were more usually punished by reduction to the ranks.[158] The way in which the gauntlet was administered was laid down in pedantic detail. Paul also sometimes revised upwards court-martial sentences passed to him for confirmation, although hitherto (at least since Peter I) the convention had been for the sovereign to mitigate them. Thus an NCO found guilty of forgery, whom the court sentenced to exclusion from his unit, was commanded by the emperor to be flogged.[159]

By these interventions Paul made nonsense of the system of military justice, which for all its defects was at least based on the assumption that courts reached their decisions after conscientious examination of the evidence. Now, as Sokolovsky points out, 'all written documents simply served as material on which the Sovereign based his own personal opinion'.[160] Paul's tyrannical disposition was also apparent in his concern with minutiae: he would, for instance, take pains to specify in *which* prison a convicted soldier should serve his sentence. Distrusting his officials, he closed the auditors' office (Auditorskaya ekspeditsiya) in the War College and set up a new body, called the 'General-Auditoriat', under his personal supervision. This dealt with offences by officers or *dvoryane* in the ranks, while for commoners the War College remained the final reviewing instance.[161]

The new procedure led to endless delays and had to be modified by Alexander I in 1806. Thereafter a man could be made to run the gauntlet only after confirmation of sentence by the brigade commander, who fixed the number of passes (up to three) through a battalion of approximately 500 men. A divisional commander could order six such passes, and commanders-in-chief five through 1,000 men; the death penalty—now restored but rarely enforced—required the assent of the Auditor-General and of the sovereign.[162]

On his accession Alexander I, like Peter III and Catherine II before him, had formally abolished torture throughout his domains and proclaimed an amnesty.[163] The consequences for those within military jurisdiction were less

---

[157] Referred to in *PSZ* xxix. 22322 (18 Oct. 1806).

[158] Shendzikovsky (*SVM* xii) pp. 155–7; *PSZ* xxiv. 17588 (Infantry Field Regulations, 29 Nov. 1796), XI, ch. VI, §§ 2–3. For the cavalry equivalent: xxiv. 17590.

[159] Sokolovsky, 'Iz russkoy voyenno-ugolovnoy stariny', pp. 360–1; cf. Keep, 'Mil. Style', pp. 81–2.

[160] Sokolovsky, 'Iz russkoy . . . stariny', p. 366.

[161] *PSZ* xxiv. 17588 (29 Nov. 1796), IX, ch. IV; xliii. 18308 (5 Jan. 1798).

[162] *PSZ* xxix. 22322 (18 Oct. 1806); cf. xxviii. 20878 (July 1803), strengthening the judicial powers of inspectors. The article in *VE* xiii. 159–60 gives too favourable a picture.

[163] *PSZ* xxvi. 19814, 20022 (2 Apr., 27 Sept. 1801).

striking than might have been expected. 'Merciless' and 'cruel' penalties were prohibited[164]—but the gauntlet was not considered cruel! A doctor now had to be present, who could order the punishment to cease if he thought the victim might expire;[165] but on the man's recovery the beatings recommenced. This was a mixed blessing for the victim—and for the doctor, whose function was scarcely compatible with the Hippocratic oath. The gauntlet was probably inflicted less extensively than it had been under Paul, since sentences were as a rule mitigated on review. This practice became more necessary than ever after 1812, when new field regulations prescribed the gauntlet as the sole corporal punishment for five specified serious offences; since Peter's military statute remained in force, there was an ambiguous legal situation which was not cleared up until 1839.[166]

This ambiguity probably explains the harsh retribution meted out to the rebellious military colonists at Chuguyev in 1819 and to the Semenovsky guardsmen who protested (legally) against excesses by their commander the following year. During Arakcheyev's ascendancy miscarriage of justice became almost as common as it had been under Paul. The Decembrist A. Podzhio (Poggio) records that Major-General Golovin, commander of a guards chasseur regiment, beat to death a private who complained at an inspection about misappropriation of the funds in a soldiers' artel, although such complaints were perfectly proper; on another occasion, before beating a soldier, he had his grave dug in readiness.[167] Such testimony cannot easily be corroborated, but there is no doubt that abuses were widespread, notably striking men for errors committed during drill. Official reports of conditions in the Second Army, stationed in the south of Russia, explicitly acknowledge that this was so. Count Pkheyze, who commanded a brigade, 'personally hits soldiers in the teeth'; Major-General Tarbeyev 'beats whole platoons to excess with his cane'.[168] Such malpractices stood in stark contrast to those in the Russian occupation corps in France (1815–18), where Lieutenant-General M. S. Vorontsov abolished corporal punishment.[169] In 1821 officers of the Izmaylovsky guards regiment freely debated, within earshot of the troops, whether discipline was best maintained by the stick or by persuasion.[170] The more enlightened commanders realized that Russia owed her victory over Napoleon to the long-neglected common soldier. Unfortunately this awakening of social conscience among the officers, which led to the ill-fated Decembrist revolt of 1825 (see

---

[164] *PSZ* xxvii. 20115 (18 Jan. 1802), xxx. 23279 (10 Apr. 1808); Bobrovsky, *50 let spetsial'noy shkoly*, pp. 1–2.

[165] *PSZ* xxvi. 20070 (8 Dec. 1801).

[166] Klugen, 'Neskol'ko slov', p. 193.

[167] Podzhio, *Zapiski*, ed. S. Gessen, in *Vosp. i rasskazy deyateley taynykh obshchestv 1820–kh gg.* (Moscow, 1931), p. 24, cited by Fedorov, *Soldatskoye dvizheniye*, p. 22.

[168] Prokof'yev, *Bor'ba*, p. 72.

[169] Zavalishin, *Zapiski*, p. 109.

[170] Gangeblov, 'Kak ya popal', p. 188.

ch. 11), brought no immediate improvement in their men's plight. Juridically, they were scarcely better off on the expiry of Alexander I than they had been at the death of Peter I a century earlier. This leads one to ask whether the same was true of their material condition as well.

8

THE STRUGGLE FOR SURVIVAL

As in other European armies of the day, in return for his services the Russian soldier received pay, food, a uniform, accommodation, and medical care. These benefits were officially seen as privileges rather than as a legal entitlement. Pay was low by international standards. Count Algarotti, who witnessed Münnich's campaign against the Turks in 1739, noted that in Russia soldiers earned in cash only one-third as much as they did in France or the German states.[1] In common with other contemporary foreign observers, he did not consider this fact in its sociological context, as we might do today, but from the vantage-point of the state economy. Von Hupel remarked approvingly that Catherine's army was cheaper to maintain than those of other rulers, and gave two reasons for this: recruits were obtained by a levy on the native population, and so did not have to be bought as mercenaries did; and the Russian soldier was most economical, 'and that is why his pay is uncommonly small'.[2] To a modern eye von Hupel put the cart before the horse: precisely because the soldier's pay was low he had to limit his consumption to the barest necessities. On the other hand he was less likely than a peasant to suffer hunger through crop failure or indebtedness.

When one attempts to probe into the realities of the troops' material condition several points have to be borne in mind. First, the men's regular pay might be supplemented from other sources, both licit and illicit. Second, pay might be issued after a delay, or not issued at all; this might be due either to bureaucratic incompetence or to corrupt practices, in the commissariat or among officers of the unit concerned. Third, pay was docked at a prescribed rate for medical facilities, but might also be increased by cash bonuses and other rewards granted to men who distinguished themselves in action or otherwise earned the sovereign's favour. Fourth, some account has to be taken of changes in the value of money if one is to ascertain the real worth of a soldier's pay.

Private employment of troops by their superiors had been permitted on certain conditions by Peter's military statute (see ch. 5). Officers were quick to take advantage of the loopholes in the law, which was difficult to enforce. Although the army's establishment tables authorized the provision of batmen or orderlies (*denshchiki*) on a generous scale, the wealthier officers wanted to have more servants, partly because their number was an index of social status, just as in civilian life a landowner's prestige depended on the number of 'souls'

---

[1] Algarotti, *Lettres*, p. 85.   [2] Von Hupel, *Beschreibung*, p. 51.

he possessed. The authorities indulged this vanity up to a point, but were concerned lest too many men be taken off active duty and the army's baggage train (*oboz*) become excessively swollen. (Foreign observers of eighteenth-century Russian armies on campaign were astonished at the large number of horses and carts that accompanied them: although an impediment to mobility, they were essential in the absence of advanced supply bases and units were expected to be as self-sufficient as possible in many items of equipment.) In 1732 Münnich prescribed that officers who owned more than one hundred 'souls' should have no orderlies; instead they were to bring their own (civilian) servants, for whose payment and conduct they were to be responsible.[3] This rule does not seem to have been observed strictly, at least in peacetime. Von Hupel, writing in the 1780s, states that those who dispensed with their quota of orderlies received an additional 10.25 roubles a year, and that this grant was often claimed by junior officers who did not in fact have any civilian servants but instead came to an informal arrangement with one or more men in their company.[4] The government issued a blanket prohibition against taking soldiers 'for private services, such as riding behind [the officer's] carriage, or carrying his cloak or fur-coat, in a word [performing] any domestic tasks'.[5] However, the inspectors who were supposed to ensure that this ruling was observed turned a blind eye to the malpractice.[6]

Some years later S. A. Tuchkov, who made a good career under Paul and was inclined to be critical of conditions in the preceding reign, listed this as one of six major sources of corruption by unit commanders. 'They would take as many men as they wished from the regiment into their service, teach them various trades and appropriate their earnings. In general those [soldiers] who were allowed to perform various jobs for their own benefit [also] had to give part of the money they earned to the regiment.'[7] The same complaint is made by H. von Reimers, whose work (1805) is a panegyric in favour of Paul. Under Catherine, he says, only half the men in an infantry regiment might appear on parade

because its commander, who was its absolute boss, took away 20 or 25 men from each company for his personal requirements, to his estates; alternatively, he would hire them out to private individuals and keep their earnings [as if] by right. These unfortunates would be replaced after a time by other soldiers, but when they came back they were no good at all for drill (*front*), as they were in tatters and had become as rough as peasants.[8]

Von Reimers evidently had a particular case in mind, for he went on to describe a workshop in which over one hundred soldiers were employed; it

---

[3] *PSZ* xliii. 5637 (20 Oct. 1730), pp. 51, 69; xxiii. 17158 (31 Oct. 1793).

[4] Von Hupel, *Beschreibung*, p. 53; cf. p. 35 for another circumstance facilitating private employment, in this case by guards officers.

[5] *PSZ* xxiii. 17158 (31 Oct. 1793); cf. xxii. 15990 (30 Apr. 1784).

[6] Dubrovin, *Suvorov*, p. 19.

[7] Tuchkov, *Zapiski*, p. 9.   [8] Von Reimers, 'Peterburg', p. 445.

produced carriages, sledges, and similar items of excellent quality which were sold in the neighbourhood, the colonel pocketing all the profits.[9]

What these critics overlooked—as have the military historians who have referred to the subject[10]—was that private employment could be of advantage to the soldier as well as to the officer; of the three parties involved in such deals it was the state that stood to lose most, and its defenders were not above shedding crocodile tears on the men's behalf. Of course, officers might abuse the men whom they took, treating them much as if they were their serfs, but excessive maltreatment was likely to come to official notice. It appears that normally soldiers in private employment had some chance of increasing their incomes and that in most cases these mutual arrangements were more than just swindles for the officers' sole enrichment. The practice may also have been beneficial in a more general sense. Soldiers helped farmers bring in the harvest during the short season before the first frost (as their Soviet successors still do today); and officers and men, whose relationship was normally antagonistic or at least coldly distant, will have been brought together in an illicit or semi-licit association against authority, so undermining the legitimacy of the power structure.

The emperor Paul and his German associates like von Reimers instinctively recognized this. Devoted as this ruler was to the principles of absolutism and bureaucratic centralization, he had to tolerate the practice on a limited scale—in garrison regiments, and only for personal services within the unit.[11] Alexander I's policy, on this matter as on so many others, was ambivalent. He first issued a general ban, but when a soldier was accidentally killed while engaged on private work the tsar prohibited employment on 'dangerous' tasks,[12] implying that if there was no danger the practice might continue— which of course it did. Action was taken only when a case came to the emperor's personal notice.[13] During his reign, however, the more enlightened officers began to express open disapproval of the abuses associated with the private employment of soldiers; they did so not only on moral or humanitarian grounds but also because they believed in legality and wanted reforms to make the army more efficient. Major I. S. Zhirkevich[14] notes a case where men at Orel had to go 200 versts to work on land in the Ukraine owned by their commander. Unfortunately he does not tell us whether they were paid, or whether they appreciated the opportunity to return, if only briefly, to a more familiar rural environment where they were at least spared the rigours of the parade-ground. Another memoirist reveals that a company of artillerymen who were

[9] Ibid., p. 446.

[10] Petrov (*Russkaya voyennaya sila*, ii. 244) states that 50,000 soldiers were so employed, that in, about one-eighth of total nominal effectives—but does not give his source; nor does Kersnovsky (*Istoriya*, i. 63), who adds that the practice was particularly widespread in the south of Russia.

[11] *PSZ* xxiv. 17856 (28 Feb. 1797); but cf. 17715 (7 Jan. 1797). The Prussian envoy noted that the men suffered a drop in income as a result of Paul's efforts to restrict it. Schiemann, *Geschichte*, i. 23.

[12] *PSZ* xxvii. 20581, 20865 (7 Jan., 25 July 1803).

[13] *PSZ* xxx. 23864 (29 Sept. 1809), xxxiv. 26732 (15 Mar. 1817).

[14] 'Zapiski', *RS* 13 (1875), p. 573; for other cases cf. Fedorov, *Soldatskoye dvizheniye*, p. 16.

used to keep order at private theatrical performances earned no less than 600 roubles a month.[15] This random evidence does not allow an estimate of the extent to which side earnings from such sources, or else from artisanal activities within the regimental economy, supplemented the soldiers' regular pay.

This was supposed to be issued (apparently in advance) in three instalments during the year, on 1 January, 1 May, and 1 September. Payment was generally more punctual than it had been in Peter's day, although sometimes the money might still fail to arrive, especially when the troops were campaigning in foreign parts.[16] One source claims that this was not too serious a matter for the soldier since he received food and clothing anyway and the money 'serves only for his pleasures';[17] but this view needs qualification. The men might indeed put up patiently with delay that was genuinely due to wartime difficulties (for example, the interruption of communications by enemy action), but it was a different matter where the authorities simply forgot about their existence[18] or held back the money on some pretext or other. A senior officer alleged in 1764 that as much as a third to a half of soldiers' pay might be retained in this way.[19] One purpose of the inspectorate set up by Potemkin was to check such abuses, but it was short-staffed: initially there were only four inspectors.[20] Frequently regimental commanders came to private arrangements with officials in the commissariat or supply departments and built up a sizeable regimental fund, called a 'church chest'.[21] They had some justification for doing so, since they had to provide against sudden contingencies. However, proper accounts were seldom kept and the money might be used for purposes that had nothing in common with soldiers' welfare, such as banners and regalia, musical instruments for the band, and the like.[22] Officers also 'borrowed' money for such purposes from the soldiers' artels as well as from the regimental fund. 'We are short of fat, salt, carts (*povozki*) and horses,' reported a company commander in the Yelizavetgrad musketeers (1790), 'but the recruits' artel has 124 and the old [that is, company] artel has 99 roubles, so I ask the regiment[al commander] whether part of this sum may not be used to buy what the company needs.' Permission was readily granted.[23]

The soldiers' artel was in principle an excellent institution. It often elicited favourable comment from foreign observers. Organized at company level or

[15] Eyler, 'Zapiski', p. 371.

[16] Stein, *Geschichte*, p. 216.

[17] De Raymond, *Tableau*, p. 539. He also argued against more frequent payment on the specious grounds that this would only encourage drunkenness.

[18] This was the fate, two centuries before Voinovich's 'Private Chonkin', of three soldiers in a chasseur regiment who had taken part in the storming of Ochakov (1788) and had been left behind there to guard some stores; over a year passed before they were discovered, 'suffering extreme need, and the state property rotting away due to holes in the roof'. Ya. A. Kastro-Latserda to Pulenbach, 8 June 1790, TsGVIA, V-UA, ed. khr. 16449, 1. 166.

[19] Dubrovin, *Suvorov*, p. 133.

[20] *PSZ* xliii. 16972 (18 June 1791).

[21] Dubrovin, *Suvorov*, p. 134; de Raymond, *Tableau*, p. 536.

[22] Vyazemsky, 'Zapiska', p. 13.

[23] TsGVIA, V-UA, ed. khr. 16449, 1. 138 (19 June 1790), signature indecipherable.

lower, it was ostensibly run by a committee elected at the start of each four-month accounting period. Its operations were supervised by one of the NCOs, the *kaptenarmus*. Each man contributed a certain sum (3 roubles a year in 1812) and the fund was enlarged by adding the money brought in by new recruits, savings from unexpended food allowances, the property of deceased comrades, the proceeds of artisanal activities—and, last but not least, booty (see below, p. 218). Some artels built up a capital fund as large as 800 roubles. The money might be spent on extra food (meat, vegetables) or carts to carry the members' baggage on the march. However, neither the committee nor the supervising NCO actually *held* this money. It remained in the care of the company commander or his nominee and was drawn on as required. This was an open invitation to abuse. While the men themselves as a rule managed their affairs honestly, the same could not always be said of their superiors. The artel system had two major defects. First, it was a simple informal institution, and so a soldier who was transferred or discharged could not easily, if ever, claim repayment of his contributions. Second, it was not genuinely autonomous and could be 'bent' to serve the interests of authority rather than those of its members. There were instances where 'company commanders authorize an advance to the colonel, or in an emergency even give him a present', remarks von Hupel disingenuously.[24]

In this way a soldier could dispose personally of only a portion of his pay. As for the official deductions, everyone in state service, civilians included, had to contribute a sum, determined according to rank, towards the cost of medical care. In 1731 this was fixed at 1 per cent of basic pay for men in the 'lower ranks'; officers paid 1.5 per cent.[25] NCOs, but not privates, also had to pay 1 per cent for hospital expenses.[26] These deductions were made before pay was issued and were non-returnable. The sum was relatively small and according to von Hupel might be donated on the men's behalf by a generously-inclined colonel.[27] Soldiers probably found it more objectionable to be placed on half-pay while they were in hospital, or to be held responsible for the cost of items of equipment they had lost or damaged.[28] Those under judicial investigation were also placed on half-pay.[29] Deductions were also made to cover part of the cost of medals[30]—and originally, as we know, even for uniforms. The latter

---

[24] Von Hupel, *Beschreibung*, p. 150; foregoing also based on Masson, *Mémoires*, iii. 198; de Raymond, *Tableau*, pp. 529, 538; Langeron, 'Russkaya armiya', 4, pp. 148–51; Plotho, *Entstehung*, p. 56; Tański, *Tableau*, p. 210. Duffy (*Russia's Military Way*, p. 130) correctly notes that 'the artel had deep roots in Russian village society, with its peasant meetings and sense of joint enterprise', but does not mention its limitations.

[25] *PSZ* xliii. 5864 (28 Oct. 1731), § 15, Table IV; cf. vi. 3867 (12 Dec. 1721), xv. 10789 (9 Jan. 1758), I, § 7, xliii. 11784 (4 Apr. 1763), p. 14.

[26] Solov'yev, 'Kratkiy ist. ocherk', p. 246.

[27] Von Hupel, *Beschreibung*, pp. 116, 142, 149.

[28] *PSZ* ix. 6852 (24 Dec. 1735), ch. I, § 14, xv. 10789 (9 Jan. 1758), III, §7. The former deduction did not apply to poor officers after 1809: xxx. 23720 (24 June 1809).

[29] *PSZ* xv. 10789 (9 Jan. 1758), II, § 6; Solov'yev, 'Kratkiy ist. ocherk', pp. 247–50.

[30] *PSZ* xxiv. 18225 (27 Oct. 1797).

practice was evidently reintroduced under Münnich, but later in the century units were allocated a separate sum to meet the cost of these items.[31]

On the credit side the soldier received a small sum for meat and salt (87 kopecks per annum in 1731, 96 kopecks in 1763),[32] which was subsequently integrated into his basic pay, as was the 'ration' (now usually in cash) issued to those NCOs who had a horse to maintain. If a unit was sent abroad on campaign, men in the ranks received an additional 3 kopecks a day, which in a full year would have more than doubled their pay.[33] There were also bonuses (or more correctly, *ex gratia* payments) for soldiers who performed some especially meritorious act: for example, seizing an enemy standard in battle, bringing a message with unusual speed, or even doing well at drill![34] From 1807 onward those who won a medal for bravery in the field (men in the ranks had their own division within the Order of St. George) received cash compensation as well: an extra one-third of their annual pay for the first such feat, two-thirds for the second, and double for the third.[35] In 1812 men of the 3rd Infantry Division received 'an unheard-of amount' (not specified, alas) at Alexander I's hands.[36] Finally, certain NCOs who had served 12 years and so were qualified to become officers, but could not be promoted because there was no vacancy for them, received double pay as compensation.[37] In the following analysis we shall disregard these complications and deal with basic pay only.

Pay rates (*oklady*) are given in the establishment tables, although not always in full or with a clear demarcation between the constituent elements; in particular it is not always evident whether the uniform and equipment allowance is included or not. Assuming that it was not, we can say that a private soldier's nominal pay nearly doubled over the course of the century. Rates varied between different arms and categories of service. The pay of an infantryman in the field forces may be taken as the norm. Among those who got more were cavalrymen (especially the heavily armed carabiniers and cuirassiers and the hussars stationed in the south), artillerymen, engineeers, and of course guardsmen; troops in the Ukrainian land-militia and garrison units got less. In the 1730s the rates for private soldiers in the regular forces were as given in Table 1. Among NCOs, a corporal drew approximately 1 rouble more (gross) than a private in an infantry line regiment, an internal garrison regiment, or the guards, but over 3 roubles more in a cuirassier regiment. A sergeant or

---

[31] *PSZ* xliii. 5864 (28 Oct. 1731), Table VI; Petrov, *Russkaya voyennaya sila*, ii. 167; Stein, *Geschichte*, p. 104; von Hupel, *Beschreibung*, pp. 143, 145.

[32] Solov'yev, 'Kratkiy ist. ocherk', p. 240; *PSZ* xliii. 11797 (17 Apr. 1763), p. 23.

[33] Solov'yev, 'Kratkiy ist. ocherk', pp. 253–4 (10 Sept. 1759).

[34] [Shtrandman] 'Zapiski', p. 311; [Minayev], 'Vosp. I. Men'shago', p. 58; N. K. Shil'der, 'Iz vosp. Mikhaylo-Danilevskogo', *RS* 90 (1897), p. 465: in 1817 Alexander I was so pleased with the parade-ground performance of one company of the Horse Artillery that he gave each private 20 and each NCO 50 roubles. Such generosity surprised members of his suite, who recalled that men had received a grant of only 5 roubles for fighting at Borodino.

[35] *PSZ* xxix. 22455 (13 Feb. 1807), § 5; *II PSZ* viii (i). 6611 (6 July 1833).

[36] Yermolov, *Zapiski*, p. 154.

[37] *PSZ* xxx. 23009, 23378, 24015 (10 May 1808, Nov. 1808, Nov. 1809).

Table 1

Gross and Net Annual Pay of Privates, 1730s

Type of unit		Annual pay (gross)[a]	Annual pay (net)
			(roubles and kopecks)
1	Infantryman, field forces	11.85	5.70[b]
2	Dragoon, ditto	12.87	6.70[b]
3	Cuirassier, ditto	14.72	?
4	Artilleryman (bombardier)	14.40[c]	?
5	Engineer (miner)	15.00	?
6	Infantryman, guards	13.37–18.37	?
7	Cavalryman, guards	18.37	?
8	Infantryman, garrison (Baltic)	7.32	[5.23?]
9	Infantryman, ditto (internal)	5.00	[3.20?]
10	Cavalryman, garrison	9.12	[6.25?]
11	Land-militiaman (Ukraine)	6.00	?

Sums to nearest kopeck.

[a] Net pay includes meat and salt allowance, but excludes deductions for medical services and uniform and equipment allowance. For the latter: *PSZ* xliii. 5836 (17 Aug. 1731), p. 119. Grenadiers' allowance was 1–2 kopecks higher.

[b] Source: Mikhnevich, in *SVM* iv (1, i). app., p. 31.

[c] Source: *PSZ* xliii. 2480 (1712). Rates were raised either in or shortly before 1739.

Sources (except where otherwise stated): Solov'yev, 'Kratkiy ist. ocherk', p. 257; *PSZ* xliii. 5864, Table 1.

sergeant–major (*vakhmistr*) earned over three times as much as a private in the engineers, over double as much in the guards, 73 per cent more in the cuirassiers, but only 40 per cent more in an internal garrison unit. When the first hussar units were set up in Elizabeth's reign, consisting in the main of immigrants from the South Slav lands, their pay rates were based on those of their Austrian equivalents; a hussar drew a generous 18 roubles (gross) plus 10.20 to 14.40 roubles for his mount.[38] Artillerymen generally did well under their patron Shuvalov: a bombardier earned 18 roubles (gross).[39] The military commission set up on Catherine's accession, when fixing pay rates, kept to those for the preceding reign—or so at least it stated;[40] there may actually have been a reduction, at least in the artillery and land-militia. Field-force men now got 7.50 to 8 roubles, as did those in Siberian garrison units, but land-militiamen a mere 5 to 5.33 roubles.[41] Men in the Slobodskaya Ukraina did

[38] *PSZ* xliii. 8370 (1 May 1741), pp. 278–9.

[39] *PSZ* xliii. 10689 (11 Jan. 1757), p. 330; but a fusilier earned only 10.90 roubles; cf. p. 366 for those not in the *field* artillery.

[40] *PSZ* xliii. 11735 (14 Jan. 1763), § 22, p. 8; see also pp. 40 ff. for further provisions of this decree and Solov'yev, 'Kratkiy ist. ocherk', p. 244. Duffy (*Russia's Military Way*, p. 130), citing an article in *VS* of 1861, states that pay rates (for infantrymen?) were reduced from the 9 roubles paid during the Seven Years War. Conceivably this decline reflected the loss of the foreign service allowance.

[41] Ibid., pp. 3–4; Vyazemsky, 'Zapiska', p. 13. Some additional data on pay are offered by von Hupel, who also gives the cash value of the uniform and equipment allowance: *Beschreibung*, pp. 143, 153–9, 168–75, 175–8, 193–5. Neither source mentions artillerymen.

even worse, the lowest rate being only 3.75 roubles (1769).[42] On the other hand in 1784, when a new regiment was set up in Tavrida province upon its formation, a private might draw as much as 35 roubles; presumably these were men of privileged background.[43] At this time guards cavalrymen received 24 and ordinary hussars or dragoons from 6 to 11.88 roubles (including a 'ration' of 1.50 roubles where applicable).[44] Some infantrymen and chasseurs (*yegery*) also improved their position towards the end of Catherine's reign. Tables drawn up in 1795 show them earning 9.40 to 9.90 roubles (net?) per annum, but others, both in the field forces and the garrisons, had to be content with the 1763 rates.[45] Senior NCOs now got 35 to 37 roubles, or about six times more than a private, so differentials were increasing.[46]

It is puzzling that these tables do not reflect the award in June 1794 of an across-the-board increase of 2 roubles per annum to men in the field forces, and 1 rouble to those in frontier and garrison units.[47] Was this perhaps not paid until later? At any rate by Paul's accession all field-force men, infantry and cavalry, are listed as earning their previous highest rates, which were still generally in force two years later[48]—when officers' salaries were raised considerably. Alexander I also boosted officers' pay, by an even more significant amount, and this time men in the ranks were not wholly neglected: in the field forces the highest-paid cavalryman received 12 roubles (1801) and the highest-paid infantryman 14 roubles (1811).[49] The base rate was 9.50 roubles, and in internal garrison units 7.50 roubles.[50]

But what could a soldier buy with his roubles? Pending a systematic study of the extensive material in the archives on major commodity prices, such as has long been urged by Soviet scholars, we must be content with those for rye grain that have recently been tabulated by B. N. Mironov.[51] It is true that soldiers did not normally need to buy grain, since this was issued to them; on the other hand, they did consume vodka, which was made from it,[52] and changes in the price of this staple item in the popular diet will have been reflected in those of many other commodities that they did buy. Grain prices varied greatly from

[42] *PSZ* xliii. 13390 (7 Dec. 1769), pp. 132–3.

[43] *PSZ* xliii. 15945 (1 Mar. 1784), p. 210.

[44] *PSZ* xliii. 16376 (10 Apr. 1786), p. 215.

[45] *PSZ* xliii. 17369 (3 Aug. 1795), p. 264.

[46] Ibid., p. 263.

[47] *PSZ* xxiii. 17229 (28 June 1794).

[48] *PSZ* xliii. 19420 (15 May 1799), Tables II, III, pp. 110, 114–15.

[49] *PSZ* xliii. 23603 (22 Apr. 1809), 24729 (16 July 1811), pp. 125, 279; cf. Petrov, *Russkaya voyennaya sila*, ii. 271; Plotho, *Entstehung*, p. 42; Stein, *Geschichte*, p. 288. I stated incorrectly ('Russian Army's Response', p. 511) that nothing was done for them.

[50] *PSZ* xliii. 24703 (3 July 1811).

[51] 'Dvizheniye . . . XVIII v.' (1970), pp. 156–63; 'Dvizheniye . . . 1801–1914 gg.' (1975), pp. 215–57. His decennial figures are based largely on those for *selected* years in each decade. No data are given for the years 1790–5. For the sources used (which are not identified further here), and an evaluation of their reliability: id., 'O dostovernosti', pp. 249–62.

[52] The cost of vodka, which was state-controlled, rose between 1770 and 1811 from 3 to 5–6 roubles a *vedro*: *PSZ* xviii. 13369 (13 Oct. 1769), xxxi. 24168 (Mar. 1810).

one region to another. In the 1740s, for example, the average for all of European Russia was 0.93 roubles (silver) per quarter, but in the central provinces it was 1.25 roubles and in the north-west as high as 2.11 roubles. These differences have been disregarded here, as have those in the purchasing power of various currency instruments (copper, silver, paper assignats).

Table 2 shows that the average price of rye rose nearly 5½ times between the 1710s and the 1800s. Measured on this basis, the pay of soldiers in the field forces deteriorated in real terms over the period. The earnings of an infantryman in a line regiment could buy 11.0 quarters of grain in 1711, 7.1 in 1731, 6.0 in 1763, and 3.6–3.8 quarters in 1796. In the early nineteenth century there was a slight improvement: by 1811 his pay was equivalent to 3.6–5.1 quarters. A cavalryman's pay would have bought the following amounts (in quarters): 12.8 in 1711, 8.4 in 1731, 6.4 in 1763, 4.6 in 1796, and 3.9 in 1801, our last firm date. The decline in purchasing power was less marked for most men in the garrison forces. A daily pound of rye grain (which when baked gave 1⅓ lb. of bread) required 1.37 quarters in a year, or half what a garrison soldier might have purchased with his pay in 1811. In the circumstances he had to count himself fortunate that he was nourished, however imperfectly, by the state.

Food and drink were important to the Russian soldier psychologically as well as physically: preparing, cooking, and consuming food was one of his few leisure activities, and the problem of filling his stomach usually loomed large. His diet consisted largely of grain products, unless he was fortunate enough to be able to supplement his official ration (*payok*) with vegetables or meat obtained (with or without payment) from civilian sources. Providing such additives was, as we know, one of the functions of the artel. Peasants kept pigs and chickens, and soldiers billeted on rural households would join in the feasting when they were slaughtered. Sutlers (*markitanty*) accompanied the army when on the march, but their wares were often too expensive for a mere private's pocket. After a successful engagement enemy cattle might fall into a unit's hands, and in such cases the artel would see to it that the meat was shared out fairly.

By and large the men were left to their own devices, as in Muscovite times. 'No great preparations are made here to feed the soldiers', writes Algarotti. 'They are issued with flour, and as soon as they have pitched camp they dig earthen ovens in which they bake their own bread. When [the authorities] want to give them a treat, they distribute a sort of very hard biscuit which they crumble and boil with salt and some of the herbs they find everywhere.'[53] (At this time the southern Ukraine, which the army was passing through, was still pristine grassland.) Another informant tells us that 'each regiment took along several barrels of beer to cheer up the fatigued soldiers, who throughout the campaign [of 1736] had nothing else to eat but their *proviant* and water'. The

---

[53] Algarotti, *Lettres*, pp. 94, 172.

Table 2

Purchasing Power of Privates' Pay, 1711–1811 (selected years and arms of service)

Date	Arm of service	Nominal annual pay in contemporary roubles	Real value of pay expressed in *chetverti* of rye grain	Price of one *chetvert'* of rye grain in roubles (average for European Russia, 5- or 10- year periods)[a]
1711	Infantryman, field forces	5.70	10.96	
	Cavalryman, field forces	6.66	12.80	
	Intantryman, internal garrison	3.20	6.15	0.52 (1711–20)
	Cavalryman, internal garrison	6.25	12.02	
1731	Infantryman, field forces	5.70	7.13	
	Cavalryman, field forces	6.70	8.38	0.80 (1731–40)
	Infantryman, internal garrison	3.20	4.00	
1763	Infantryman, field forces	7.50	6.00	
	Cavalryman, field forces	8.00	6.40	1.25 (1761–70)
	Infantryman, garrison	3.75–5.33	3.00–4.26	
1796	Infantryman, field forces	9.40–9.90	3.60–3.80	2.61 (1796–1800)
	Cavalryman, field forces	11.88	4.5	
1801	Cavalryman, field forces	12.00	3.88	3.09 (1801–10)
1811	Infantryman (musketeer), field forces	9.50	3.43	
	Infantryman (grenadier), field forces	10–14	3.61–5.05	2.77 (1811–20)
	Infantryman, internal garrison	7.50	2.71	

[a] *Source*: Mironov, 'Dvizheniye . . . XVIII v.'; other data as in Table 1 and subsequent references to *PSZ*.

latter was sometimes kept in disused gunpowder barrels and was unfit to drink. By the time the thirsty and famished troops returned from the Crimea, parties of men had to be sent out to requisition grain from the local peasants, which they had taken the precaution of hiding in underground pits. Each company had a hand-mill with which to grind whatever was found, but often the flour could not be baked owing to lack of fuel. Some soldiers ate it raw and went down with diarrhoea; only one man in five was still fit when the troops returned to base.[54]

Half a century later Pishchevich had a similar tale to tell: cavalrymen *en route* to the Crimea in wintry conditions had no means of baking bread and instead prepared a brew called *salamata* from flour, salt, and water[55]—there is no mention this time of a vegetable content. The author went into raptures at the sight of the men going about their culinary tasks, 'one reaping the grass, others bringing the water or building the fire', and the food tasted good, 'as if cooked under the best conditions'; with such splendid soldiers, Pischchevich averred, Russia could conquer the world, and so he resolved then and there to behave as a model officer. Von Plotho, the Prussian, did not share these Rousseauist sentiments, but was almost as euphoric. The Russian infantryman, he declared admiringly, could do without the costly field bakeries that had been introduced in other armies:

when he gets to his camp or bivouac, he digs a hole in the ground, puts a bast mat in it, pours his flour on top, mixes it with water, heats up a second pit, and so bakes his bread . . . If the Russian has a little salt, or an onion and a cucumber—and some *kvas* or a glass of brandy [sic]—this provides him with a splendid meal.[56]

He does not say whether he tried it himself; most foreigners who did so found the taste highly disagreeable.[57]

The official ration cost the state about 4 roubles per man per annum.[58] It consisted of 3 quarters of flour and 2¼ *chetveriki* of grits,[59] and was issued monthly—presumably to the artel managers rather than to the men individually. A soldier on the march was expected to carry enough food for four days, while supplies for another six days were brought up in carts. The daily issue on the march was 2½ *funty* (ca. 1 kg.) of grain (milled or unmilled) or 1¾ *funty* of *sukhari*. The latter was a kind of biscuit, made by double baking, which kept well but was hard on the teeth and gums and had little taste. The flour contained a good deal of roughage.[60]

---

54 'Turetskaya voyna', pp. 257, 261, 263; cf. 'Prevratnosti sud'by', p. 481.

55 [Pishchevich] *Zhizn'*, p. 37; cf. Richelieu, 'Journal', p. 161.

56 Plotho, *Entstehung*, p. 58.

57 Duffy, *Russia's Military Way*, p. 131.

58 3.88 to 3.95 roubles: von Hupel, *Beschreibung*, p. 144; cf. *PSZ* xliii. 10682 (11 Jan. 1757), p. 330, 13390 (7 Dec. 1769), pp. 132–3.

59 Von Hupel, *Beschreibung*, loc. cit.; Stein, *Geschichte*, p. 247.

60 Von Hupel, *Beschreibung*, pp. 144–5; de Raymond, *Tableau*, p. 539 n.

The ration was ample in carbohydrates but deficient in vitamins. One colonel, passing through Voronezh province in 1769, bought some vegetables for his troops; evidently this was unusual enough for an officer to record the fact in his memoirs.[61] As for meat and fish, Vyazemsky remarked a few years later that they were consumed so rarely as to be 'not worth talking about'. He recommended the introduction of a meat ration of 1 *funt* a week which, he reckoned, would cost the state an additional 1.04 roubles per man per annum.[62] Presumably the 'meat money' of Petrine times, now no longer issued separately, was used for other purposes. Catherine did not respond to the suggestion. To celebrate victory over the Turks, she ordered a modest addition to the ration of grits: half a *garnets* per man.[63] By Alexander I's reign, however, combatant troops were supposed to get 84 *funty* of beef and 20 of salt annually, in addition to their grain ration which remained unchanged.[64]

They also now received a liquor 'portion' of 3 *charki* (³⁄₈ litre), distributed when the men were on campaign or in camp.[65] During the retreat in June 1812 an unexpected allocation of vodka to fatigued soldiers in the 26th Chasseurs had an immediate effect on morale: 'songs could be heard in the ranks . . . and some of the men started up a dance, amusing themselves and cheering the others'.[66] Russian soldiers generally stuck to *kvas*, or native beer, and had a better reputation for sobriety than their officers or most civilians. From 1819 onwards they were not allowed to visit taverns and had to be content with their regulation issue of alcoholic beverages.[67]

The 1716 military statute explicitly exempted troops abroad from observance of religious fasts, but some men insisted on abstaining from meat during Lent. The supply authorities worked on the basis of a 360-day year, so that on major church holidays soldiers will have had to make do with whatever their artel had saved, perhaps supplemented by largesse from their superiors.

How much of what they were allocated did the troops actually get? In the 1780s von Hupel put it at three-quarters.[68] The commissariat services have had such a bad press that their achievement deserves to be put on record. A network of magazines was set up along the main communication arteries, with the idea that troops should not have to march for more than two weeks before reaching a source of fresh supplies. By the early nineteenth century the distance had been reduced to a six- to eight-day march. As early as 1731 there were 14 major provision depots, with a combined storage capacity of 165,000 quarters of grain, and several dozen smaller ones; by 1766 the total number had risen to 135. Stocks were built up by purchases on long-term contract or from *ad hoc* local suppliers, at prices which were determined by the provincial authorities in the light of local market conditions. By mid-century a three-tier

61 Von Shtrandman, 'Zapiski', p. 292.   62 Vyazemsky, 'Zapiska', p. 12.

63 *PSZ* xx. 14275 (17 Mar. 1775), § 3.   64 Petrov, *Russkaya voyennaya sila*, ii. 442.

65 Ibid.; Tański, *Tableau*, p. 209.   66 Antonovsky, 'Zapiski', p. 12.

67 Plotho, *Entstehung*, p. 68; de Raymond, *Tableau*, p. 520; *PSZ* xxxvi. 27814 (25 May 1819).

68 Von Hupel, *Beschreibung*, p. 144 n.

system had come into existence: reserve magazines in grain-growing regions under the control of a central agency, the Proviant-master's section; depots at army (later, divisional) level with enough provisions for one month; and mobile units which could follow the troops on campaign.[69]

A major drawback to efficient management (apart from the ubiquitous rats!) was the tension that developed between officials at various levels. Other conflicts arose between these functionaries and their civilian suppliers, as well as with field officers. Some of the latter believed that official price-setting raised costs and would have preferred a system of direct requisitioning.[70] Landowners complained that the fixed price (*spravochnaya tsena*) was too low and that purchasing agents were under orders to keep it as low as possible. In practice what happened was that each party tried to buy the others' goodwill in an effort to keep the bureaucratic wheels turning. Suppliers would pay magazine supervisors to accept their deliveries; the 'provisions commissioners' tipped the more reliable contractors and the officials who fixed the prices; and field officers might be persuaded to accept produce they knew to be sub-standard.

Regulations issued in 1758[71] prescribed officials' conduct in exhaustive detail, yet there were no effective administrative checks against such abuses. The wide fluctuations in grain prices made it impossible to ensure that the deals concluded locally were above board, and the senior authorities set a poor example. Ya. P. Shakhovskoy, appointed General War Commissar in 1753, was offered a 25,000-rouble bribe by a contractor; he turned it down but admits he was tempted, since he needed the money for his daughter's dowry.[72] No such scruples seem to have bothered his successor, A. I. Glebov, a Shuvalov protégé whose business speculations brought him a large fortune. Under Peter III he rose to become Procurator-General; Catherine II dismissed him from that post, calling him 'a rogue and a cheat', but later permitted him to resume his office (1764), which he held until 1775; he was then again sacked and, after a lengthy investigation, expelled from the state service. Upon his death (1790) the government obtained 157,000 roubles from his sequestered estate, but the money was returned to his heirs by Paul I.[73]

This emperor continued the policy of centralization that had been embarked on in the last years of his predecessor's reign.[74] The supply commissariat was placed under the War College, but this did not lead to much improvement. Paul's choice as departmental head, Major-General P. Kh. Obolyaninov, was unpopular with his colleagues—'his hot temper and crude manner sometimes made relations with him extremely difficult', writes his biographer—and this

[69] Maslovsky, *Materialy*, i. 122, ii. 37–8; Bogdanovich, *Russkaya armiya*, p. 35; Beskrovnyy, *Russkaya armiya*, p. 380. On corruption in the commissariat: Langeron, 'Russkaya armiya', 3, pp. 150–1.

[70] P. Panin to Pavel Petrovich, 12 Jan. 1779, 'Perepiska', p. 762.

[71] *PSZ* xv. 10789 (9 Jan. 1758); cf. xvii. 12459 (24 Aug. 1765).

[72] Shakhovskoy, *Zapiski*, p. 78.

[73] N. Chulkov, 'Glebov, A. I.', *RBS* vi. 341–8.

[74] *PSZ* xxiii. 16959, xxiv. 17750, § 2, 17768, 18010.

personal bitterness became embroiled with bureaucratic intrigue. Some reformers wanted to civilianize the agencies responsible, but this radical idea did not prevail.[75] The troops fighting in East Prussia in the harsh winter campaign of 1806–7 endured famine conditions, even guardsmen being reduced to eating potatoes abandoned by the local peasants.[76] The next year a major scandal broke and Alexander I ordered a thorough purge of the supply administration.[77] The new officials did their best to prepare the army for the trials to come, but in 1812, even before the invasion began, the lack of supplies caused dissatisfaction.[78] 'The armies had to feed themselves from local resources and by bringing up supplies from remote provinces.'[79] Thanks to these measures, by the time they camped at Tarutino, after abandoning Moscow, they had enough—'never did the army live so well', claims one memorialist—but further serious food shortages appeared once they neared the western border in Napoleon's pursuit, and again after they had crossed it.[80] Of the troops fighting in France in 1814 Paskevich later wrote that

the grenadiers shuttling between Nangis and Troyes fed themselves as and how they could, hardly getting a crust of bread, and were completely famished by all the marches and counter-marches. In the morning the soldier leaves his billet hungry, not having eaten the night before; nothing is made ready for him in advance, and when he arrives at his destination he finds nothing there either. How then should he refrain from pillaging?[81]

Even after the war had ended, one general feared that the occupation forces in France would go short because of local crop failures;[82] their home bases were of course far away. But their comrades in Russia faced conditions that were little better. The war had upset agriculture and trade; the government was short of funds; and the old administrative abuses persisted. In 1817 men of the 43rd Hussars complained at an inspection that they were not receiving their full ration and had to take what they needed from the local inhabitants. An inquiry revealed that their company commander had appropriated 689 quarters of flour and 64 of grits, as well as some of the men's pay.[83] It can at least be said that by this time such conduct met with general disapproval and that legal proceedings were more likely to be taken against the culprit than had been the case during the eighteenth century.

[75] D. Mertvyy, 'Zapiski, 1760–1824', *RA* 1867 app. pp. 105–8, 135–8, 229–39; Shil'der, *Pavel*, p. 425; E. Yastrebtsov in *RBS* xvii. 54–7. Curiously, like Glebov, Obolyaninov also had a brief but unhappy spell as Procurator-General (1800–1).

[76] Muromtsev, 'Vospominaniya', p. 68; Kruchek-Golubov and Kul'bin, in *SVM* viii. 143.

[77] Stein, *Geschichte*, p. 330; Petrov, *Russkaya voyennaya sila*, ii. 326.

[78] Shchukin, *Bumagi*, i. 18, ix. 11; cf. Maksheyev, *Voyenno-admin. ustroystvo*, p. 47; Beskrovnyy, *Potentsial*, p. 456.

[79] Petrov, *Russkaya voyennaya sila*, pp. 323–4; Stein, *Geschichte*, p. 301; Beskrovnyy, *Potentsial*, p. 457.

[80] Barclay de Tolly to Kankrin, 25, 27 May 1813, in *VS* 292 (1906), 11, pp. 221–4.

[81] Stcherbatow, *Paskévitsch*, pp. 170–1.

[82] Löwenstern, *Mémoires*, p. 456.

[83] Fedorov, *Soldatskoye dvizheniye*, p. 15.

Deficiencies in clothing were less obvious than lack of food, for commanders paid a lot of attention to their men's external appearance. A study might be written of the military authorities' excessive concern with details of dress, which in the case of some officers became a veritable obsession. This reflected their simple mechanistic view of the army's function. Nothing escaped the attention of these pedants: the cut and colour of uniform cloth, the shape and style of headgear, the positioning of badges and buttons—and, last but not least, the presence or absence of that symbol of masculinity, the moustache. The Russian army had a saying: 'a moustache embellishes a hero, a moustache gives him the proper look';[84] but until 1832 these adornments were restricted to certain favoured categories, such as guardsmen. 'Non-noble grenadiers', ran a typical order to the Izmaylovsky guards regiment in 1736, 'shall henceforth not shave but let their moustaches grow.'[85] Suvorov ruled that his grenadiers' moustaches should be cut level with the lip, leaving a gap of one-sixth of an inch.[86] General Yermolov, proconsul of the Caucasus, believed that facial hair was a useful means of intimidating other people,[87] and he was probably right.

At first commanders were permitted a certain autonomy in matters of dress, but from the reign of Peter III onward the trend was towards conformity and regimentation. Catherine's army was a colourful sight on the parade-ground, for the 1762 military commission introduced a wide spectrum of hues for uniforms that varied according to the arm of service.[88] NCOs would generally buy a uniform of better cloth than that worn by soldiers and pay for their embroidered galloons. Since Peter I's day the cost and expected life-span of each item of clothing and equipment had been laid down in the establishment tables. A tunic was supposed to last for two years, a greatcoat four, and a rifle 20.[89] They were to be inspected each spring and the defective articles replaced. This was no more than common sense, but the principle was applied with a misplaced zeal that caused anguish to every quartermaster—not to mention any soldier who accidentally broke or tore some item and had to pay for a new one. Unlike officers, men in the ranks were meant to wear their uniform at all times.[90] It was ill adapted to the kind of life they led on service and gave inadequate protection against the elements. Pishchevich noted that 'the soldier's thin cloak does not shield him from snowstorms or heavy frost'; and Joseph II, accompanying Catherine on her voyage to the Crimea in 1787, found that 'quite a few men do not have a shirt to their name'.[91] This may have

---

[84] Neizvestnyy, 'Za mnogo let', *RS* 81 (1894), 2, p. 177.

[85] M. P. (contrib.), 'Vyderzhki iz prikazov 1736 g.', *VS* 282 (1905), 4, p. 153.

[86] Meshcheryakov, *Suvorov*, i. 93 (Polkovoye uchrezhdeniye, III, § 15).

[87] Yermolov to Davydov, Jan. 1820, in *VS* 292 (1906), 12, p. 248. However, the arch-disciplinarian Grand Duke Constantine held a contrary view: Constantine to Sipyagin, 4 Feb. 1817. M. D[ubrovin], 'Vel. knyaz'', pp. 114–15.

[88] Von Hupel, *Beschreibung*, pp. 86–92; Shakhovskoy, *Zapiski*, p. 81.

[89] Plotho, *Entstehung*, p. 58; von Hupel, *Beschreibung*, p. 94.

[90] Suvorov allowed soldiers in quarters to wear easy clothes, but prescribed the form they should take: Meshcheryakov, *Suvorov*, i. 143 (Polk. uchrezhdeniye, VI, § 12).

[91] Pishchevich, *Zhizn'*, p. 37; Joseph II to Lacy, 8 June 1787, in *RA*, 1880, 1, p. 370.

been an exceptional situation, since in such newly colonized regions civilian tradesmen were still a rarity. Normally tailoring and repairs were done within the unit, and craftsmanship was of a high standard.

Under Potemkin and Suvorov Russian troops were at least spared some of the ridiculous accoutrements introduced by Peter III, which were unpopular both on practical grounds and because they seemed to symbolize alien 'German' ways. General Khrushchev complained in 1764 that cavalrymen spent hours powdering and braiding their hair and even had to sleep sitting up lest their elaborate coiffure should suffer before they went on parade in the morning.[92] Suvorov's maxim: 'a soldier's outfit should be so:/Up he gets and he's ready to go'[93] was echoed approvingly by Potemkin:

What makes military dress smart to behold is its uniformity and fitness for its purpose. A soldier's tunic should clothe him, not inconvenience him. All extravagance [*shchegol'stvo*] ought to be eliminated, for it is the fruit of luxury and takes a lot of time and money. A soldier has no servants to look after him.[94]

Such common-sense views were no longer in vogue under the militaristic rulers who followed Catherine to the throne. However, the implications of the change have been exaggerated by the more chauvinistic writers. As we have seen, the 'Russian school' differed from the Prussian in style, not in substance. It was tinged with respect for the 'simple Spartan life' and the classical soldierly virtues—values later exemplified by Napoleon. Their consequences for men in uniform would prove just as disastrous as those of old-school conservatives who treated soldiers as if they were inanimate playthings.

Turning to the question of accommodation, we are confronted by a paradox. For a century or so the troops benefited indirectly from the state's inability to build the permanent quarters that Peter I had ordered. Had the gentry co-operated in his scheme, the Russian army would have been even more isolated from the rest of the population than it was. But the emperor's instructions were largely ignored and had to be repealed soon after his death. Landowners were relieved of the obligation to construct barracks on their estates at their own expense,[95] and in the following year the troops (now reduced in strength) were withdrawn altogether from rural districts. This reform dealt a major blow to the Petrine service state and was too radical to last. It was countermanded in 1728 and the army returned; it also continued to collect the poll tax.[96] With the passage of years barracks appeared, first in St. Petersburg (mainly for the guards) and later in Moscow and certain provincial towns, especially in border regions.[97] Those not so housed were billeted on the local

[92] Dubrovin, *Suvorov*, p. 4; cf. Vyazemsky, 'Zapiska', pp. 13–16.

[93] 'Soldatskiy naryad dolzhen byt′ takov / Chto vstal, to i gotov.' Dubrovin, *Suvorov*, p. 70; Bogdanovich, *Russkaya armiya*, p. 21.   [94] Dubrovin, *Suvorov*, pp. 108–10.

[95] *PSZ* vii. 4936 (19 July 1726); Troitsky, *Fin. politika*, p. 131.

[96] Petrov, *Russkaya voyennaya sila*, ii. 124.

[97] *PSZ* viii. 5615, 6171 (4 Sept. 1730, 14 Sept. 1732), x. 7564 (20 Apr. 1738), xi. 8079 (25 Apr. 1740), xvii. 12372 (10 Apr. 1765).

townspeople, who resented the obligation to provide such accommodation (known as *postoy*).[98] Probably only a small proportion of troops were quartered in the towns. Those in country districts, except in the Baltic provinces,[99] were billeted on peasants, as in Peter's day, for most of the year; normally a company would occupy an area comprising several villages or hamlets. They left these quarters for summer training and on campaigns. From 1764 they generally returned to the same area each autumn, instead of being continually relocated; this must have given the soldiers' lives a greater element of stability.

It was, however, less desirable for their peasant hosts (*khozyayeva*), especially in the western provinces where most troops were stationed. For they had to share their already crowded huts with armed strangers, and also provide premises for the regimental and company offices, stores, stables, and the like. All this involved them in considerable expense and inconvenience. Conflicts were frequent. Already in 1724 Pososhkov complained that

soldiers and dragoons behave so roughly in their quarters, and commit such frightful abuses, that their number is beyond calculation. Where they are accompanied by their officers, their conduct is even worse. They brazenly chop wood for their fires and cut down trees if there is none available . . . And for that reason many [peasants] are no longer content to remain in their homes.[100]

Forty years later a senior officer stated that country folk who provided billets looked on soldiers 'as bears who come and go': he even argued that their mutual hostility endangered the empire's social cohesion.[101] He exaggerated, but the idyllic image presented by some military writers of the soldier tenant aiding the farmer's wife as she went about her household tasks and courting her marriageable daughter was equally far from the truth.

The reason why their relations were so antagonistic also explains why the authorities could tolerate such extensive cohabitation without too much fear that the troops might be infected by peasant grumbling and rebelliousness. This reason was that the soldiers were subject to their own military jurisdiction. Run-of-the-mill conflicts with civilians were heard either by the unit commander or by joint courts in which the military element or interest predominated.[102] Russia thus had the equivalent of the Spanish *fuero militar*, although it was less formalized. Confident of support from above, the men naturally identified with the military 'estate' to which they had been ascribed

[98] 'Nakaz Venevskikh zhiteley' [to Legislative Commission of 1767], *SIRIO* 93 (1894), p. 241, § 17; Knabe (*Struktur*, pp. 143–5) offers a detailed study of townsmen's complaints to the assembly on this issue; cf. Hittle, *Service City*, p. 161.

[99] Here nobles were wealthier and may also have welcomed the added security which the troops provided; they built so-called *Quartierhäuser* with stabling as appropriate. Von Hupel, *Beschreibung*, p. 136.

[100] Pososhkov, *Kniga*, p. 44.

[101] Gen. Khrushchev, memorandum of 1764 cited by Dubrovin, *Suvorov*, p. 132. Duffy's picture (*Russia's Mil. Way*, p. 130) is altogether too serene.

[102] *PSZ* vii. 4535 (26 June 1724), §§ 11–12; Meshcheryakov, *Suvorov*, i. 145.

rather than with the peasant milieu from which they stemmed. Suvorov's 'regimental instruction' (1764) prescribed that soldiers in permanent quarters should maintain 'good accord with the civilians (*obyvateli*)', but he also voiced concern lest they 'should grow accustomed to peasant ways of speaking, dressing or reasoning'.[103]

Another factor which separated the two groups was that eighteenth-century rulers abandoned Peter I's concept (imputed rather than stated) that the army should be recruited on a territorial basis, which if implemented consistently might have led men from a particular province or district to combine a feeling of local patriotism with *esprit de corps*. As it was, regiments came to comprise individuals drawn from all parts of the country and were generally not stationed in the area whose name they bore. It is not clear when and why this change occurred. Was it just a by-product of bureaucratic routine or did it—as one later writer suggested,[104] without, however, offering any evidence—stem from a deliberate effort to prevent the aggregation of men with a common civilian background? In any case the result was to weaken such unofficial horizontal bonds as developed between soldiers and civilians. Of course, this schism was not absolute: men who deserted might find shelter in peasant communities, despite the risk of heavy penalties on civilians who proffered such aid.

The state's objective of enforcing hierarchical subordination was also furthered by the construction of barracks, which became much more plentiful during the first decade of the nineteenth century. They were increasingly built and maintained with the aid of funds provided by the central authorities, for which townsmen had previously petitioned in vain.[105] Barracks were unpopular with the men, who enjoyed more freedom when quartered on the rural population. They identified them 'with the service, with everything that makes the soldier's heart miss a beat', as one later commentator put it.[106] Another critic refers to them as damp, crowded, insanitary, and a source of psychological as well as physical disorders.[107] But not until the reform era that followed the Crimean War was any real effort made to grapple with the health problems which these gloomy buildings did so much to aggravate.

Peter I's good intentions in the domain of military medicine were all but frustrated by lack of funds and trained personnel. The establishment tables provided for a doctor in each regiment and several base hospitals, but in practice few posts could be filled and their number was actually reduced in 1731.[108]

---

103 Meshcheryakov, *Suvorov*, i. 141 (Polk. uchrezhdeniye, VI, § 6).

104 Plotho, *Entstehung*, p. 66.

105 *PSZ* xxiv. 18036, 18086, 18664, § 4, 18822, IX, §§ 15–20 (6 July, 11 Aug. 1797, 12 Sept. 1798, 17 Jan. 1799), xxvii. (10 Mar. 1802), xxix. 22020 (10 Feb. 1806: Orel), xxix. 22575 (30 July 1807: Kiev).

106 'Yeger', 'Otryvki iz zapisok unter-ofitsera', *VS* 31 (1863), 6, p. 501.

107 Brant, 'Kazarmennoye raspolozheniye', pp. 77–100; cf. Butovsky, 'O kazarmennoy nravstvennosti', p 138.

108 Kruchek-Golubov and Kul'bin, in *SVM* viii. xlviii.

The few well-qualified doctors, most of whom were foreigners, preferred to stay in the capital, where only senior officers or guardsmen were likely to benefit from their presence. Ordinary soldiers, and indeed their officers too, in line regiments usually had to be content with the ministrations of a barber (*tsyryul'nik*) or medical orderly (*fel'dsher*), who had neither the knowledge nor the facilities to cater adequately to their needs. When troops were sent to fight in the southern steppes, where plague (*chuma*), typhus, and other infectious diseases were rife, the results were often catastrophic. In the 1730s Münnich's armies were decimated by epidemics. Foreigners were struck by the sight of long columns of carts laden with casualties crossing the plain.[109] 'Commonly one third of the sick die', noted one colonel in Russian service; 'there is to each regiment but one head surgeon and his assistant, who are withal not of the most skilful.'[110]

Losses were far heavier in the Seven Years War, although according to one recent student proportionately less than those of the enemy, since the Russians took the trouble to recover their wounded from the battlefield; they also set up mobile field hospitals to give first aid before evacuation to the rear.[111] However, conditions in these establishments may be gauged from a description of the principal army hospital in Moscow by a senior official who visited it in the line of duty:

When we crossed the threshold . . . into the first ward, we were met by . . . a foul stench. Suddenly my eyes made out a multitude of sufferers, some in their last torments, others tossing unconscious from fever or crying out wildly from unbearable pain, yet others trembling with cold and calling for death to relieve them.[112]

It may be characteristic that in this memoir the General War Commissar, whose functions included supervision of the medical services, should have concentrated on his own emotional response to an extreme situation rather than on the practical measures which he took to cope with it: although an educated and humane individual, Shakhovskoy had not been touched by the spirit of the Enlightenment.

By Catherine's reign new intellectual influences did make themselves felt in this sphere. In the Balkan theatre—whence, however, the plague was transmitted to Moscow in 1771 by returning troops, with great loss of life[113]—some unit commanders showed a proper concern for hygienic precautions, and would for example order their men to bathe in vinegar.[114] But medical personnel and facilities were still woefully short. In 1776 the army apparently had a total of 42 doctors or 'staff surgeons' (*shtab-lekari*) and 406 ordinary

---

[109] Kersnovsky, *Istoriya*, i. 74.
[110] Manstein, *Contemporary Memoirs*, p. 171.
[111] Müller-Dietz, *Militärarzt*, p. 40.
[112] Shakhovskoy, *Zapiski*, p. 88.
[113] For a full account of the plague, see J. T. Alexander, *Bubonic Plague in Early Modern Russia: Public Health and Urban Disaster*, Baltimore, 1980.
[114] Glinoyetsky, 'Instruktsiya . . . Vorontsova', p. 34, § 2; Dubrovin, *Suvorov*, p. 74.

surgeons.[115] Vyazemsky complained that regimental field hospitals were allocated a mere 104 roubles (per annum?), even though a unit might have as many as 500 men on its sick list; the 12 carts provided to transport casualties each had space for four men, which meant that any wounded who could walk had to do so; they contracted minor ailments which then turned into incurable diseases.[116] According to one foreign observer the soldiers 'feared the hospital like the tomb'[117]—as well they might, given the cramped unhygienic conditions and the low professional standards of some of their personnel. At Nikolayev in 1789 'there was no one to look after [invalid recruits] but barbers, many of whom got rich from the sick while others took money from the dead'. This was reported by an officer who took their plight to heart. He moved them to a field hospital where, however, 'I lost over 60 men . . . from dysentery and fever, for the air in Kherson was heavy all the time.'[118] Medical knowledge in this era was still at a level where, as one historian puts it, 'it was beyond the power of any individual to stay the appalling mortality'.[119]

Not unreasonably, perhaps, Suvorov disapproved of military hospitals on principle. Assuming command in the southern Ukraine in 1792, he took drastic administrative action to reduce the number of patients, discharging some and moving others to rural areas. His sensible remedies were accompanied by quixotic and arbitrary measures, for the great commander fancied himself as an expert on herbal medicine and liked to prescribe his favourite concoctions. In his view 'drink, food and air' were the three keys to good health; he might have added a fourth, physical intimidation, for he went on: 'whoever neglects his health, [apply] the stick to his superior'.[120] The last remark was made in Russian-occupied Finland, where his troops labouring on a canal construction project in peacetime conditions were dying at a rate of 2.4 per cent per annum.[121] It is unfortunately not yet possible to compare this figure with those for units stationed elsewhere.

At the turn of the century the empire had nine general military hospitals with 5,700 beds, to which may be added the regimental *lazarety*, each of which was supposed to have 45 to 60 beds.[122] In 1802 the army had 422 doctors (over one quarter of all those in the country)—precious few for a force nominally 400,000 strong.[123] During Alexander I's reign there was a considerable expansion: by 1825 there were 95 base hospitals with 29,000 beds and 1,213 doctors

115 PSZ xx. 14839 (19 Feb. 1779). Kruchek-Golubov and Kul′bin (*SVM* viii. xlviii) and Müller-Dietz (*Militärarzt*, p. 59), citing this source, both omit the 120 battalion *lekari*—presumably with good reason.

116 Vyazemsky, 'Zapiska', p. 7.

117 Warnery, *Rémarques*, p. 130.

118 [Mosolov] 'Zapiski', p. 136; cf. Vorontsov, 'Zapiska', p. 489: 'l'affreuse mortalité . . . fait frémir la nature.'

119 Duffy, *Russia's Military Way*, p. 172.

120 Meshcheryakov, *Suvorov*, iii. 74, 126, 223.

121 Ibid., p. 137.

122 Kruchek-Golubov and Kul′bin, in *SVM* viii. lxxvii, lxxxix.

123 Ibid., p. 75.

and surgeons, or roughly four to five times more for double the number of men.[124] The army medical services, hitherto partly controlled by the Interior Ministry, were placed wholly under the military (1805). This logical reform unfortunately did not afford medical personnel adequate protection against bureaucratic arbitrariness, as was necessary if army service were to be made more attractive to skilled doctors; although pay and conditions were improved, in 1806 there were still 17 field and 56 garrison regiments which had no trained medical man at their disposal.[125] Kutuzov's forces in central Europe lost some 12,000 men to disease before the battle of Austerlitz, when they suffered 21,000 casualties in the field.[126] The war of 1806–12 against the Turks had a similarly drastic effect. 'The regiments, reduced to 500 men without having fought an engagement, were pitiful to behold,' wrote Paskevich later with his customary frankness; 'the soldiers, pale and thin, could scarcely carry their rifles and equipment.'[127] Part of the trouble here was the breakdown of the supply services, which left the army dependent on whatever it could requisition locally—and little was to be had in this under-populated area. But conditions were similar in north-eastern Europe during the 1806–7 campaign: at Preussisch-Eylau and Friedland Russian wounded were left on the battlefield to the mercies of the foe. Most froze to death; of those who reached base hospital at Grodno a large number died of starvation.[128]

During the War of 1812 care of the wounded seems to have depended as much on the initiative of regular officers as it did on the official medical services. General M. S. Vorontsov set an example in this respect. On his estate in Vladimir province he set up a hospital where 300 soldiers or NCOs, along with 50 officers, were looked after at his own expense. Although himself wounded and scarcely able to walk, Vorontsov visited the men daily and before they were sent back to their units gave each of them a fresh set of clothes and 10 roubles in cash.[129] Other officers are also on record as having shown the 'fatherly care' for their invalid subordinates that was expected of them.[130] But such acts of charity, however worthy, could not offset the general inefficiency of the medical service, which was overwhelmed by events. The corruption in Moscow military hospitals 'makes one groan', wrote Rostopchin to the tsar.[131] Yermolov, passing through the city as the population fled before Napoleon's advance, heard the cries of thousands of wounded who had been left behind in churches; this, he says, 'caused indignation in the army' at 'the shameful indifference of the capital to [their] unfortunate lot'.[132] Once across the border in

[124] Ibid., pp. 92, 189.

[125] *PSZ* xxviii. 21866 (4 Aug. 1805); Kruchek-Golubov and Kul′bin, op. cit., pp. 79, 82. Petrov (*Russkaya voyennaya sila*, ii. 271) states that the number of trained staff was *reduced*.

[126] Kruchek-Golubov and Kul′bin, op. cit., pp. 239–40; Kersnovsky, *Istoriya*, i. 189.

[127] Stcherbatow, *Paskévitsch*, p. 58.

[128] Kruchek-Golubov and Kul′bin, in *SVM* viii. 242–3.

[129] Shcherbinin, *Biografiya . . . Vorontsova*, p. 66.

[130] Antonovsky, 'Zapiski', p. 174.

[131] Shchukin, *Bumagi*, vii. 419.

[132] Yermolov, *Zapiski*, pp. 98–9.

1813, the troops generally enjoyed more hygienic conditions, but battle casualties were proportionately higher than usual. No less than 22,000 Russians fell at Leipzig, half the combined Allied losses.[133] Among those wounded in this engagement was Pamfil Nazarov. Phlegmatically and without self-pity he describes how, with blood pouring from his leg 'like warm water', he made his way to a village two versts away where a surgeon dressed the wound. The bandage soon fell off. Retying it himself and using his musket as a crutch, he walked for several days until he reached the field hospital, where his injury was left untended for nearly two weeks and his wound became gangrenous. Miraculously he survived and managed to enter Paris with the victors.[134]

Total battle casualties (killed and died of wounds) during this century of Imperial expansion were in excess of ¾ million; if so-called 'sanitary losses' are included, the figure might well be double that.[135] One of Alexander I's officials stated that the army renewed itself in personnel every five to six years[136]—which, if true, was a turnover rate comparable to that in Prussia.

[133] Urlanis, 'Lyudskiye poteri', pp. 161–2.

[134] [Nazarov] 'Zapiski', pp. 536–9.

[135] When contemporary writers referred to military losses they usually meant killed and wounded, and sometimes included prisoners of war and deserters as well. In Europe generally the ratio of killed to wounded was about 1 : 2.4 in the eighteenth century and 1 : 3 in the early nineteenth; of the wounded about 10–12% are thought to have died. Urlanis, *Voyny*, pp. 86–7, 470; B. Abrahamsson, *Military Professionalization and Political Power*, [Stockholm, 1971?], p. 24. Urlanis's statistics should be regarded as no more than educated guesses, and are also inconsistent; nevertheless as a curiosity his figures are tabulated below. For a more sophisticated estimate of post-1825 Russian losses, see Singer and Small, *Wages of War*, pp. 59–75. On the unreliability of official *relyatsii*: Vyazemsky, 'Zapiska', p. 7. Warnery, 'Rémarques', p. 129, confirms the 1 : 10 ratio for wounded who subsequently died. Some scattered data (without indication of source) are in Kersnovsky, *Istoriya*, passim.

wars, campaigns	Urlanis[a]	Urlanis[b]
Russo-Turkish[c]	215,000	200,000
Caucasus, Central Asia	150,000	50,000
Seven Years	120,000	60,000
Russo-Polish	37,000	30,000
Russo-Swedish[d]	25,000	20,000
Pugachev uprising	22,000[e]	600
Russo-French: 1799	7,000	14,000
Russo-French: 1805–7	60,000	
Russo-French: 1812	110,000	100,000[f]
Russo-French: 1813–14	40,000	

[a] 'Lyudskiye poteri', pp. 156–65.

[b] *Voyny*, pp. 55–7, 86–7.

[c] For eighteenth century, but may include war of 1806–12, for which no separate figure is given.

[d] Excludes Great Northern War (U[a]: 100,000).

[e] Apparently includes rebel losses?

[f] Recalculated according to Urlanis's own criteria (360,000 killed and wounded). Beskrovnyy *et al.*, 'Bilan', pp. 133–4, offer a figure of 660,000 for military casualties incurred between 1789 and 1815.

[136] [Obreskov] 'Ob umen'shenii', p. 246. Best, *War and Society*, p. 45, exaggerates.

Losses were particularly high among recruits—proportions of one third to one half were frequently mentioned by foreign writers[137]—but most of these men will surely have deserted, not died. All the same death, not discharge, was the most likely prospect awaiting Russian soldiers. What of the fortunate survivors?

Until the end of the eighteenth century Russia had no 'veteran problem'. Peter I had his old soldiers sent to monasteries.[138] The practice continued,[139] despite occasional grumbles by the religious, until these establishments had their lands secularized in 1764. That year Catherine II set aside 31 towns as places of residence for certain younger and healthier veterans. They were organized into 'detachments of non-serving invalids' and given light duties: guarding armouries, churches, schools, etc. They were not to be sent outside the town to which they were assigned and a sum of 80,000 roubles was set aside for their maintenance.[140] This was a step in the right direction, but the number of places in these units was pathetically small. Over half of them were allocated to officers (695 as against 560 for NCOs and privates); moreover, many of the latter, for instance the 110 guardsmen mentioned, will have been of privileged background. This may have reflected their preponderance among veterans of the Seven Years War. The reform of provincial government in 1775 brought military invalids under civilian jurisdiction, but the emperor Paul characteristically reversed this move.[141] By 1801 the number of non-serving invalids in the lower ranks had climbed to 9,386.[142] This was a respectable growth in absolute terms but represented an infinitesimal proportion of the men who had been inducted into the forces. (Unfortunately no statistics are available for the total number of veterans.)

Throughout the period the official assumption was that the bulk of ordinary soldiers who were no longer fit to serve should be maintained by the communities from which they had been recruited, to which they were supposed to return—as free men rather than serfs. This expectation was unrealistic. Their donors, whether peasant communities or landowners, considered that they no longer bore any obligation towards such ghostly figures who had, as it were, 'returned from the dead'.[143] These men had lost their right to a land allotment and were too old to learn a new trade; unless they could find a new 'protector', they were reduced to begging for alms. We hear of such men 'wandering from

---

[137] For example, [Schwan (?)], *Merkwürdigkeiten*, p. 123; Ami de la Vérité, *Coup d'œil*, p. 90; von Reimers, 'Peterburg', p. 447; de Raymond, *Tableau*, p. 519; cf. Petrov, *Russ. voyennaya sila*, ii. 152 for a 45 per cent loss to one party of recruits in 1754!

[138] *PSZ* vi. 3576 (3 May 1720), vii. 4151 (28 Jan. 1723).

[139] *PSZ* viii. 5337, 5360 (9 Oct. 1728, 17 Jan. 1729), ix. 6321 (10 Feb. 1733), xi. 8354 (26 Mar. 1741), xiv. 10355 (9 Feb. 1755).

[140] *PSZ* xvi. 12060 (26 Feb. 1764); cf. xvi. 11674 (3 Oct. 1762), xliii. 12135, § 10, xliii. 18300, Table VIII; Geysman, in *SVM* iv (2, i). 44-6.

[141] 'Invalidy', *VE* x. 608.

[142] Geysman, in *SVM* iv (2, i). 46.

[143] Neizvestnyy, 'Za mnogo let', p. 122; cf. P. Czap, Jr. in D. Ransel (ed.), *The Family in Imperial Russia: New Lines of Historical Research*, Urbana, Il. 1978, p. 112.

one household to another' much as their predecessors had done in the Muscovite era, and many simply lapsed back into servile status.

It was evidently in order to cope with this problem that the practice grew up of sending men who were due for discharge to (regular) garrison units instead of back to their villages—in other words, of not discharging them at all! The motive was benign: here, in a familiar military setting, they would at least receive half pay and might expect better care than they could hope for as unattached and unwelcome civilians. In 1812 de Raymond wrote that the Russian soldier 'generally serves in the army for as long as he can and then joins a garrison, where he performs ordinary service until he becomes an invalid; he is then put in a monastery where, thanks to a frugal diet, he vegetates for a little while longer.'[144]

In the 1790s the decision as to a man's fate when his 25 years were up was taken at divisional or corps level, on the advice of the regimental commander. The latter would normally take some account of the veteran's marital status—and possibly even of his wishes in the matter. But the authorities' main concern was to dispose of their surplus human cargo as decently and painlessly as could be managed. Catherine ruled in 1795 that if a soldier in a garrison unit or invalid company 'finds relatives or reliable persons who will stand bail for him, take him and keep him at their own expense until his death', he was to be released to their care and given an internal passport.[145] Archival data relating to men in the Yaroslavl´ musketeers regiment who were due for discharge in that year show that 88 men were posted to nearby garrison units whereas 130 (along with 46 who were sick or incapacitated) were sent back to their 'previous domiciles'.[146]

A little later there would have been a third option: institutional care. Five 'invalid homes' existed by 1811, admission to which was confined to those designated as 'completely incapacitated'. Men who were 'partially incapacitated' were either sent to garrison units and invalid companies or else assigned to low-grade civil service jobs.[147] Pensions were paid to invalid NCOs and men after 1815, but by 1825 less than ¾ million roubles had been spent on them—a mere fraction of the sum disbursed on officers' pensions and on administering the schemes.[148]

Among those invalids who were released 'on their own sustenance' (*na sobstvennoye propitanie*), as the decree candidly termed it, were some who had a wife to look after them. Married men also did better materially while in the service, since their wives, if they accompanied them, could earn a little extra money performing menial chores: washing and mending clothes, for example, or perhaps caring for the sick.[149] Our sources unfortunately do not reveal in

---

[144] De Raymond, *Tableau*, p. 527. The last item of information was out of date.

[145] *PSZ* xxiii. 17402 (Oct. 1795).   [146] Keep, 'Catherine's Veterans', p. 396.

[147] Plotho, *Entstehung*, p. 70; cf. *PSZ* xxxi. 24145 (3 Mar. 1810).

[148] Berezhkov, 'Ist. ocherk prizreniya ranenykh', *VS* 137 (1881), 1, p. 50.

[149] *PSZ* xvii. 12543 (14 Jan. 1766), XXV, §3. The latter function was recommended by Potemkin (Dubrovin, *Suvorov*, p. 116), but was probably unusual.

what circumstances a woman who married a soldier (before or after his induction) would opt for army life in preference to remaining in the safer but more solitary[150] environment of her native village. Economic considerations probably weighed more heavily than emotional ones; anyway, the decision will have been made for her by the husband, with other relatives, the landowner and/or village authorities having a say in the matter. The practice of joining the husband's unit seems to have been fairly infrequent, although it dates at least from Peter's reign.[151] A wife could not be accepted there until its commander so ordered; she was subject to military regulations and remained at headquarters when the troops went off to fight; if her husband chose to send her back home, the commander was under instructions to comply with his wishes.[152] It goes without saying that a serving soldier could marry only with his colonel's permission. Von Hupel infers that Russian practice was relatively liberal (compared to that in Prussia, for example), since a commander was glad to have the unit's domestic tasks taken care of in this way.[153] On the other hand, if he had too many womenfolk attached to his unit, this created problems of an administrative and social nature. Their presence probably became less common after 1796, when the tenor of army life became more strained, campaigns and troop movements more frequent, and the turnover of personnel more rapid.

For once the higher authorities do not seem to have interested themselves much in these matters. Potemkin looked at them from the standpoint of demographic growth: the presence of soldiers' wives in the newly annexed southern territories would help the population to multiply, and so a decree was duly promulgated encouraging such migration.[154] One wonders how effective it was. Alexander I's government tried to get soldiers' wives to join their husbands in the Caucasus, evidently with the same aim in view, but acted with typical bureaucratic clumsiness; a number of women sent there from Vil'na died of starvation *en route*.[155]

By this time officials were also becoming aware of the harmful effects of the low reproduction rate among the population at large. Soldiers in particular could seldom marry and beget lawful offspring; however, little was done to change matters.[156] Instead attention was centred on a secondary aspect of the problem. From time to time the idea surfaced that soldiers' sons, being habituated to the military environment and brought up under close supervision during childhood and adolescence, represented a valuable reservoir of

[150] Masson (*Mémoires*, ii. 65) observes that recruits' wives might be encouraged or ordered by their proprietors to remarry—although this would have contravened Church laws.

[151] 'Doneseniya Pleyera', in Ustryalov, *Istoriya*, iv (ii). 564.

[152] *PSZ* xvii. 12543 (14 Jan. 1766), XXV, § 1; xxxiii. 26129 (7 Feb. 1816).

[153] *PSZ* xxxix. 29919 (19 May 1824); von Hupel, *Beschreibung*, p. 109.

[154] *PSZ* xxii. 16130 (14 Jan. 1785).

[155] *PSZ* xxxvii. 28714 (2 Aug. 1820); cf. II *PSZ* i. 283 (27 Apr. 1826). Nicholas I promoted such migration to Siberia as well: ibid. i. 764 (21 Dec. 1826), vii. 5135 (6 Feb. 1832).

[156] Keep, 'Catherine's Veterans', pp. 391-3.

manpower for the forces. If they were encouraged or coerced into following in their fathers' footsteps, might not the burden of the recruit levy be reduced?

Had this been possible, the Russian army would have turned into a self-perpetuating warrior caste, with unforseeable results for the country's social development. However, the idea was just a will o' the wisp, precisely because of the low birth rate in soldiers' families. The number of male children reaching the age of maturity was too slight (at any rate until the 1820s) to make much impact upon recruitment. Nevertheless these boys did receive a rudimentary education (see ch. 9) and this was of considerable importance, given that in Russia generally there was as yet barely any organized primary schooling. It created a group—or caste—of men who were literate and thus able to fill clerical positions in the military administration. They qualified for NCO rank but could not easily attain officer status, and this naturally bred feelings of frustration. The 'soldiers' children' may be regarded as an embryonic sub-intelligentsia, whose descendants would one day show themselves capable of assuming a leadership role in the struggle for revolutionary change. To be sure, this development still lay far in the future, but its roots go back to the early Imperial period.

9

THE MIND IN THE MACHINE

THE idea that Russian soldiers should be educated for their own benefit would have struck most of their superiors as fanciful, to say the least. The training which a recruit received was almost entirely physical: handling weapons and performing evolutions on the parade-ground. It involved little more mental effort than the memorizing of various signals. During his subsequent career in the ranks the soldier was required only to revise this basic knowledge.

It would be quite wrong, however, to visualize the Russian private as an automaton or a moron. Like peasants in civilian life, and indeed people in pre-literate societies generally, soldiers could compensate for their lack of formal instruction by drawing on a rich store of folk wisdom: proverbs, aphorisms, stories, and verse. To some extent this constituted a 'secret language', a mode of communication that was largely beyond the ken of those in authority. It gave those familiar with it assurance and protection against outsiders. The men in the ranks also enjoyed jokes and songs, ribald or otherwise; these were often very different in tone from the officially approved lyrics which they were encouraged to sing on the march. Apart from all this, many recruits brought with them into the service a great deal of practical knowledge which was of vital importance in enabling them to withstand the rigours of army life. In this chapter we shall try to probe the *mentalité* of the Russian soldier, but first we may briefly consider the men who stood out among their comrades because they did receive a minimum of formal instruction.

The garrison school was a creation of Peter I: at least it was he who authorized the setting up of educational facilities in each garrison regiment for the children of serving soldiers. The money was to come from the savings effected when the number of men in the unit fell below establishment strength. However, nothing was done by St. Petersburg to provide premises, equipment, or teachers, and neither officers nor men saw much point in taking the initiative themselves. Except in the Baltic provinces, where the cultural climate was more propitious, those in charge showed little zeal in filling the 3,475 places theoretically available, and whatever tuition was provided seems to have been unattractive. 'Many of those who have learned to read and write', ran an official lament in 1732, 'leave the service and become merchants or artisans, or else enter the homes of men of various ranks [as servants].' To stop this drain on military manpower, boys born to soldiers of non-privileged origin while their fathers were in service were henceforth to be despatched to garrison schools and were then to follow in their fathers' footsteps, 'so that there may be a relief in levying recruits from the people'.[1] The qualifications here were important. Men of gentry background were excluded because they were expected to take a different route: the best of them would enter the Cadet Corps, set up in St. Petersburg at this time (1732) to train potential officers. The ban also extended to the 'single-homesteaders' and other settlers who sustained the Ukrainian land-militia. Boys born to ordinary soldiers before the latter entered service were excluded because such children belonged to the tax-paying communities concerned (or, if they were serfs, to private proprietors); the same applied to those born to men after they had been discharged, although they could be presented for schooling if their fathers wished.

The remaining 'soldiers' children' (*soldatskiye deti*) now officially became the property of the state, and some decrees actually referred to them in these terms: *sobstvennost' voennomu vedomstvu*, or 'property of the military department'. This curious phenomenon was a logical corollary of serf bondage. Clad in military uniform from the tender age of seven, these boys spent their entire brief lives within earshot of the bugle and the drum. The curriculum in a garrison school consisted of reading and writing, singing, arithmetic, artillery and engineering, crafts such as tailoring and carpentry, and—last but not least—drill.[2] Fifteen such establishments were functioning by the mid-1740s, not counting those in the regiments, with a theoretical total of 4,000 places.[3] The first 15-year-old 'graduates' were sent off to their units in 1740, where they served mainly as clerks or mechanics; later some of them became bandsmen, and for this purpose instrumental music was added to the programme at certain schools.

By 1763 the number of pupils had reached 8,755.[4] Growth was assisted by the entry of orphans and illegitimate children fathered during the Seven Years War. The authorities had knowledge of another 752 who were too young to enter school and who either lived with their father in his regiment or, if they had been orphaned, were looked after temporarily by other relatives or foster parents. The first orphanages in Russia date from Catherine's reign. Her government silently tolerated the presence of many soldiers' children 'outside the system', so to speak, because it neither wanted nor could afford to maintain them from state funds. Figures of 10,300 pupils in 1773 and 12,000 in 1797 have been cited, but the latter certainly includes some boys of privileged background as well as a number who were actually being looked after by relatives and were not in school.[5]

---

[1] *PSZ* viii. 6186 (21 Sept. 1732); Shchepetil'nikov, in *SVM* iv (1, i, ii). 174–5. On the whole phenomenon see now Kimerling, 'Soldiers' Children'.

[2] [Rusinov] *Zapiski*, p. 143; Shchepetil'nikov (*SVM* iv) p. 177; *PSZ* ix. 6767, 6849 (9 July 1735, 6 May 1736); Vladimirsky–Budanov, *Gosudarstvo*, p. 187.

[3] *PSZ* xii. 9054 (26 Oct. 1744), p. 249.

[4] *PSZ* xvi. 11816 (14 May 1763); Shchepetil'nikov (*SVM* iv) p. 180.

[5] [Rusinov] *Zapiski*, pp. 166–7; Shchepetil'nikov (*SVM* iv) p. 183. A higher estimate (18,000) was offered by von Hupel: Storch, *Hist.-stat. Gemälde*, i. 459.

Paul I made provision for 8,000 pupils in 63 schools and centralized their administration. They were all considered subordinate agencies of the new Imperial Military Orphanage, an institution which grew out of a school established at Gatchina.[6] Official policy was again dictated by utilitarian rather than charitable aims: not the welfare of the children concerned, as under Catherine, but the interests of the state. The authorities sought to bring *all* soldiers' children within the official net, and altered the curriculum so that greater emphasis was laid on drill and craft subjects. Each Sunday, so the emperor ruled, pupils were to have the military regulations read out to them, 'especially those articles which deal with obedience to orders and the punishments for lack of vigilance on guard duty, cowardice before the enemy, insubordination, theft etc'.[7] One can hardly conceive of a less promising pedagogical approach. These were 'stick academies', as the phrase went, in which pupils were thrashed for the least indiscipline. They also had to perform various services for their superiors, although this practice was prohibited by an Imperial *ukaz* in 1804.[8] The more promising school-leavers now went to serve in military hospitals, and only the less capable ended up in field regiments as NCOs or 'junior staff'.

In 1805 the Senate discovered that over 11,000 soldiers' children (the real number was much higher) had escaped the control system,[9] and once Napoleon had been finally defeated a campaign was launched to round them up. In various parts of the country zealous officials seized boys whose fathers happened to be soldiers or ex-soldiers and without further ado placed them in the schools, or if they were over 15 sent them to the army. In the process they ignored the legal provisions which exempted sons of *odnodvortsy* or boys born when the father was not in service. New rules were drawn up which extended the service liability to, for example, children of landless veterans who 'wandered about idly', or to the illegitimate sons of soldiers' wives.[10]

This toughening of policy was connected with the introduction of the military colonies (see ch. 12), in which all boys, whether born to soldiers or to peasants, became liable to the draft. The term 'military cantonists' (*voyennye kantonisty*) was applied indiscriminately to children in both categories. Pupils in the former garrison schools now came within the purview of Arakcheyev's vast administrative empire.[11] By 1822 the number of pupils in them had risen to over 65,000—a far cry from the modest figure set a century earlier; and there were another 22,000 military cantonists. Some 5,000 lads 'graduated' each year, but half as many (2,446) left their school in a coffin.[12] 'The extreme

---

6 Shchepetil′nikov (*SVM* iv) p. 186 n. The orphanage had two separate sections for the privileged and non-privileged, but some tuition was given in common. Ibid., p. 188.

7 Ibid., p. 190; *PSZ* xxv. 18793 (23 Dec. 1798), § 5 (p. 495).

8 *PSZ* xxviii. 21125 (14 Jan. 1804), § 8; Shchepetil′nikov (*SVM* iv) p. 191 and app. 16.

9 *PSZ* xxviii. 21820 (June 1805); Shchepetil′nikov (*SVM* iv) p. 193.

10 *PSZ* xxxiii. 26376 (28 July 1816); Shchepetil′nikov (*SVM* iv) p. 196.

11 *PSZ* xxxix. 29849 (11 Jan. 1824).

12 Shchepetil′nikov (*SVM* iv) p. 205.

over-crowding', ran an official report, 'not only helps disease to spread among the pupils but causes considerable mortality.' Arakcheyev himself stated privately that before he took over the annual death toll had been 10 per cent and that some children had had to eat bread mixed with sand.[13]

For all this, schooling brought advantages to those pupils who survived it. Statistics show that it helped a soldier to advance in the service. Of 125 men in the Yaroslavl´ regiment known to have been discharged in 1792 and 1795, 17 (13.6 per cent) were described as literate (*gramotu umeyet*).[14] Of 57 veterans classified as physically fit, 11 were literate. Of these seven were soldiers' sons, three sons of clergy (*iz tserkovnikov*), and only one was of peasant stock. Three had risen to join the regimental staff, one had become a sub-ensign, four were sergeants, and one a corporal. The degree of literacy increased with seniority: of private soldiers only one man in 24 was literate, but of corporals one in six, of sergeants four in 14, and of regimental staff three in eight. The educational level reached may not have been high, but it did make a difference to the fortunes of those concerned.[15]

In one cavalry regiment for which data are available the literacy rate was higher: 14 out of 98 veterans (16.6 per cent) who had served their 15-year term. They included a number of Ukrainians who in civilian life were more likely than Great Russians to have access to educational facilities.[16] On the other hand, the Yaroslavl´ regiment soldiers who were of *odnodvortsy* origin had a literacy rate of only 6.9 per cent, less than half that of their social inferiors. This was probably because boys in this category were not admissible to garrison schools, while their parents were too poor to afford a private tutor, as the wealthier gentry could.[17] Among such men, and among common soldiers generally, there must have been a few individuals who taught themselves to read and write. Pamfil Nazarov, who did so in 1816, made rapid progress— 'already by Christmas I could read the psalter and write letters'—and his determination inspired some of his comrades to emulate his example. One of them became a monk—as did Nazarov himself.[18]

How important was religion generally in the Russian soldier's life and outlook? The sources are not forthcoming about such matters, and Nazarov's pious cast of mind cannot be taken as typical. Foreign observers, especially

---

[13] Mayevsky, 'Moy vek', p. 441. Lyall, *Travels*, i. 106, describes the institution in Kiev. The 1,800 boys 'almost all . . . had a squalid, sickly appearance'; they were short of food and slept in damp beds; one in six was ill; but the schooling, on the Lancastrian system, flourished.

[14] Keep, 'Catherine's Veterans', p. 394. This excludes two men who knew German or Polish rather than Russian.

[15] Ibid., pp. 393–4.

[16] TsGVIA, V-UA, ed. khr. 16449 (1790), 11. 142–63.

[17] Keep, 'Catherine's Veterans', p. 395. One historian speaks scathingly of 'the old *odnodvortsy* privilege of being uneducated'; six regimental schools were set up for them in 1752, but they evidently did not make much impact. Vladimirsky–Budanov, *Gosudarstvo*, pp. 128–9, 287–8; *PSZ* xiii. 9972 (13 Apr. 1752).

[18] Nazarov, 'Zapiski', p. 541.

those with democratic or secular sympathies, were prone to exaggerate or misconstrue the Church's influence. If the troops stood their ground under fire, wrote one critical author in 1799, it was because the priests represented the enemy as 'accursed infidels who had to be exterminated' and promised blessings in the hereafter, which the men innocently misinterpreted as meaning an earthly paradise.[19] There was some truth to the first proposition—in 1806 the Holy Synod anathematized Napoleon—but it was less than the whole truth. The soldiers were Orthodox Christian believers in the same sense that the peasants were. That is to say, they enjoyed religious services, especially on campaign when danger threatened, provided that not too much regimentation was associated with them. On the retreat from Smolensk in 1812 the atmosphere in a crowded monastery chapel struck F. N. Glinka as emotionally tense and prayerful.[20] When two priests attached to the 6th Corps were captured, physically abused by Polish soldiers, and then returned to the Russian lines, their sorry appearance 'caused general indignation at such cruel mockery of their sacred office'.[21] This reaction was quite normal. Whatever men might think of individual priests they respected their cloth, just as they did the holy icons that each regiment carried—of St. Nicholas, patron of all soldiers, and of the particular saint who protected the unit concerned. The intensely spiritual character of Orthodoxy helped to reconcile men, in the army as elsewhere, to the prospect of suffering and death. Equally important were the close institutional links between Church and state. Defence of the faith went hand in hand with defence of the 'Fatherland' (*otechestvo*) or 'Motherland' (*rodina*), concepts that struck a responsive chord in the heart of every Russian.

Yet loyal ardour in the cause was not incompatible with an attitude of indifference or scepticism towards those who exercised authority, in the ecclesiastical as in the secular domain. The soldier did not share the belief system of his superiors; he did not, in the jargon of modern sociology, 'identify' with it. His was a folk religion[22]—and a folk patriotism, for that matter—with associations alien to the ways of thought of the educated. The popular world-view was bound up with all kinds of semi-pagan superstitions, and also with chiliastic longings for a 'just tsardom'—beliefs which clergymen and officers strongly disapproved of, in so far as they were aware of them.

One has to beware of anachronism when discussing these matters. In the early modern era men were less self-conscious than they are today, less

---

[19] Ami de la Vérité, *Coup d'œil*, p. 100; cf. Richelieu, 'Journal', p. 169 ('Russian soldiers, happily for them and their Sovereign, have still kept much of that perhaps superstitious piety which doubles men's courage'); also de Raymond, *Tableau*, p. 533; 'Observations sur le militaire', MAE, M et D, Russie 14 (1745-1828), f. 123.

[20] Glinka, *Pis'ma*, iv. 52. His writings may have influenced Tolstoy's memorable portrait of the mass before Borodino in *War and Peace*. Glinka's conduct as a spectator at the battle resembles that of Pierre Bezukhov.

[21] I. P. Liprandi, in Kharkevich, *1812 god*, ii. 5.

[22] On this topic see M. Lewin, 'The Peasant and Religion' (forthcoming) and D. W. Treadgold, 'The Peasant and Religion', in W. S. Vucinich (ed.), *The Peasant in Nineteenth-Century Russia*, Stanford, 1968, pp. 72–107, esp. pp. 102–4.

distrustful of generally accepted values. The idea that by deliberate propaganda men could be persuaded to adopt sentiments which those in authority thought desirable was still in its infancy. In Europe generally it developed under Napoleon; in Russia it began with Catherine II, but still in a relatively benign form. Paul set up a central military chaplaincy,[23] but it cannot be said to have played a major morale-building or ideological role. This came only with Alexander I's Ministry for Spiritual Affairs (1817), and more particularly with Nicholas I (see below, p. 346).

Earlier rulers and commanders would have seen religious and patriotic propaganda among the troops as superfluous. Certainly, in the 1760s Suvorov compiled a catechism for men of the Suzdal´ regiment, which was used as instructional material in a school he established there.[24] But this was not done with the object of manipulating their minds; it was a summary of what Suvorov himself believed, mixed in with common-sense nostrums. It seems to have been accepted as such, if we can believe the *Tales of an Old Soldier* published in 1847 (although this work may have been falsified to make it conform to the official ideology of the Nicolaevan era).[25] According to this source Suvorov urged soldiers 'to love heartily our Sovereign Mother, for she is our first ruler on earth after God' and 'to obey your commanders blindly, not to discuss orders but carry them out!'[26] In the last resort it does not matter much whether this was truly Suvorov's teaching or not. Such ideas were commonplace, and instilling them helped to reinforce the traditional world-view which the soldier brought with him from his peasant past. This outlook was dominated by paternalistic images and metaphors. It had as its key concept the notion of a mighty and all-embracing *vlast´* which ordinary mortals disobeyed at their cost—yet which they were naturally tempted to try to outwit by various ruses and expedients.

In Alexander I's reign writers, some of them officers or ex-officers, began to propagate a distorted and romanticized view of the common Russian soldier. This was linked to the upsurge of national sentiment that followed the victory over Napoleon. Sergey Glinka published in 1822 a collection of moral tales designed to evoke appreciation and emulation of the heroic deeds performed in bygone times. These exploits (*podvigi*) were selected in such a way as to exemplify the characteristics which loyal servants of the autocratic state —especially but not solely in the armed forces—were expected to display: courage, Christian piety, simplicity, indifference to creature comforts,

[23] TsGVIA, f. 11, op. VIII, ed. khr. 18 (1800–1); H. Fil´, 'Religion and the Russian Army', J. G. Purves and D. A. West (eds.), *War and Society in [the] Nineteenth-Century Russian Empire*, Toronto, 1972, p. 26.

[24] Dubrovin, *Suvorov*, p. 73. The text has not survived. In 1794 this catechism (or presumably an updated version of it) was read out daily to troops fighting Polish revolutionaries and included a topical reference to 'French atheists': Kochetkov, 'K voprosu', p. 164.

[25] Kochetkov, 'K voprosu', p. 178.

[26] Dubrovin, *Suvorov*, pp. 73–4. He is also said to have used the phrase 'God is our general': R. K. Dreyling, 'Voinskiy ustav i Suvorov', *Zapiski Russkogo nauchnogo instituta v Belgrade* 3 (1931), p. 345.

generosity towards the unfortunate, and so on. Most of the feats which Glinka cited were by members of the élite, as one might expect—Peter I's life offered ample illustrative material—but the mere fact that ordinary peasants or soldiers could qualify as 'men of honour' was a sign of changing intellectual fashions. The episodes cited sound rather sanctimonious and implausible to the modern ear, but they appealed to contemporaries reared on the sentimentalism of Karamzin and other writers of the age. Thus we learn of an (unnamed) old warrior who, on the retreat in 1812, calmed his grumbling comrades by telling them that their officers knew very well what they were doing ('they are leading us towards the good; they are responsible for us to God and the Tsar; it is our duty to obey and pray; the harder a soldier's task, the greater his glory'), and then gathered the men around him to listen to his stories of earlier campaigns.[27] A soldier could also perform meritorious deeds in routine peacetime circumstances. A certain Komarov, a private in the 2nd Chasseurs, on guard duty in St. Petersburg in 1816, found a wallet containing a large sum of money, handed it in, but declined any reward, saying 'I only did my duty'; he was subsequently made an NCO all the same.[28]

A similar edifying tone is adopted by Glinka's younger brother Fedor, whose memoirs were not published until much later. When recruiting volunteers for the militia in 1807, he allegedly came across invalid veterans who had walked more than a hundred versts to reach the rallying-point. These 'sons of Russian valour, [some] nigh unto the grave, lacking legs or arms, or blind' were told that they had earned their rest, yet they refused to go home. The legless ones were ready to fight in the first rank, carried by their comrades; the blind, not to be undone, demanded that 'those to whom God hath granted eyes may lead us within range of bullet and bayonet . . . We have heard the Sovereign's manifesto, saying that it is time to defend the graves of our fathers. That is why we have come.' The rafters echoed to full-throated hurrahs as Glinka toasted these mighty *bogatyri*.[29]

Such evidence by zealous upper-class patriots is of course suspect. So is that of foreign observers who stemmed from privileged circumstances, often harboured national prejudices, and rarely had the opportunity to observe life in the ranks at close quarters for long. Algarotti praised the Russian soldier for his 'patience in retreat', physical endurance, and loyalty, concluding (like Chancellor 200 years earlier) that 'there is no nation more fitted for war'.[30] Warnery thought that Russian soldiers 'had no equals' in Europe since 'they are always in good humour, even when in the greatest [material] misery'; he admired their practical skill and considered them more valorous than their officers.[31] This indulgent view was closer to the truth than that of the (Baltic?)

---

[27] Glinka, *Russkiye anekdoty*, v. 16–19.
[28] Ibid., v. 154–5.
[29] Glinka, *Zapiski*, pp. 215–17.
[30] Algarotti, *Lettres*, pp. 33, 89, 93.
[31] Warnery, *Rémarques*, pp. 127–8.

German officer who, a few years earlier, claimed that Russian soldiers were naturally servile, lacked all ambition, and were incapable of acting unless they were closely controlled by their superiors.[32]

Curiously 'conservative' views of this kind were echoed by radicals towards the end of the century. The anonymous 'Ami de la vérité' cited above spoke of 'the puerile and rigid subordination' which he had occasion to observe 'hundreds of times' in Russia.[33] Masson believed that acts of courage by soldiers on the battlefield were due mainly to the threat of punishment: 'he fears his officer's cane more than the enemy's cannon; one might say that his cowardice makes him brave'.[34] De Raymond was only slightly more perspicacious in noting that 'Russian troops have a passive courage, a military resignation rather than those *élans de bravoure* inspired by love of glory,'[35] and showed himself to be a poor prophet when he added that 'they are incapable of those supernatural efforts which have so often attended our arms'—this was written just before Napoleon crossed the Niemen!

In fact Russian soldiers were as capable as those in other armies of the age of launching death-defying assaults on enemy positions, especially if they were led by popular and efficient commanders.[36] On the other hand their stoicism and stubbornness did show themselves to best effect in defence. It is reasonable to link this quality to the men's cultural and social background as Orthodox peasants and to Russia's lack of a chivalrous feudal tradition. These traits are exemplified by the conduct of Private Gavrilo Sidorov, hero of the 17th Chasseurs. During the fighting in the Caucasus (1805) he suggested a scheme for transporting artillery across a ditch by means of a makeshift bridge of rifles held up by a dozen broad-shouldered soldiers. The first gun crossed successfully but the second slipped, crushing the unfortunate Gavrilo.[37] It would be superfluous to enumerate, in the manner of regimental historians or of patriots like Glinka, other such *podvigi*; but it is worth noting how many military memorialists, perhaps unconsciously, tended to pick out instances of what de Raymond called 'passive courage'. Ataman Denisov records two occasions, in 1794 and 1799 respectively, when troops he commanded 'held their place' or 'stood without a word' as their comrades fell beside them.[38] Lieutenant Antonovsky extolled the feat of a grenadier who, wounded in the retreat from Smolensk and receiving no medical attention, cut off his own gangrenous arm with his sword and marched on with his unit lest he be left behind among strangers.[39] I. Engel´, a hussar cornet who fought at Leipzig, tells a similar

[32] [Schwan(?)], *Merkwürdigkeiten*, p. 116.
[33] Ami de la Vérité, *Coup d'œil*, pp. 87–9, 99.
[34] Masson, *Mémoires*, ii. 63; cf. Guttin (MAE, M et D, Russie 32 (1800–13), f. 1) who in 1800 allowed also for the promise of material rewards, especially of alcohol.
[35] De Raymond, *Tableau*, p. viii.
[36] Cf. for example Bogdanovich, *Russkaya armiya*, p. 26 (Ochakov); Liprandi, in Kharkevich, *1812 god*, ii. 10 (Smolensk); Yermolov, *Zapiski*, p. 83.
[37] Bobrovsky, *Istoriya 13-go . . . polka*, pp. 149–50.
[38] Denisov, 'Zapiski', 10, p. 383, 12, p. 33.
[39] Antonovsky, 'Zapiski', p. 125.

tale: he came across a soldier who had lost both arms and was being nursed by a comrade. The crippled man said: 'I regret only that I can't smoke my pipe—but what can one say, Your Excellency, it's all God's will.' Engel´ adds that he did not know whether to laugh or to cry.[40] It would be misleading to read too much into these writers' choice of inspiring episodes: they will have remembered those that fitted their own preconceptions of how Russian soldiers ought to behave.

More to the point is the fact that these memorialists have very little to say about the men who served under them. This neglect testifies to the depth of the social gulf between officers and soldiers (including NCOs). If individuals are mentioned, they are seldom identified by name. Officers were supposed to know their men individually, but this was difficult, as guards ensign Venediktov complained, because when they were lined up on parade 'they looked as if poured into the same mould'.[41] The man in the ranks seemed a faceless being, even to officers who fancied themselves as liberals.[42]

A soldier could not afford to be so indifferent towards his officers, whose title, name, and rank he was likewise required to memorize. Privately he might refer to them by nicknames which reflected the place they held on his own scale of values. The official code bristled with references to the paternalistic code of behaviour: for example, the Instructions to Colonels of 1764–6 required them 'to look after their subordinates as fathers look after their children',[43] a principle that was not defined further since to have done so would have demonstrated its limited feasibility. The soldiers interpreted these precepts in their own manner. If an officer showed a spark of human decency, he would be typed as a genuine 'father' (*batyushka*) and his merits praised in an exaggerated fashion, perhaps to point up the contrast between 'good' and 'bad' superiors.

Unfortunately the evidence for the men's attitudes toward their substitute fathers is somewhat suspect. Some so-called 'soldiers' songs' were not spontaneous creations but were written on the men's behalf by their officers. Thus Ya. A. Potemkin (1778–1831), a popular commander of the Semenovsky regiment (1813–19), was the subject of a lament (*plach*) which ended thus:

> I saw him in the heat of battle
> Astride his horse, flying like an eagle.
> In time of peace he was gentle

[40] Shchukin, *Sbornik*, iv. 90.
[41] Venediktov, 'Za 60 let', p. 587.
[42] Captain I. I. Gladilov, speculating idly on what soldiers dreamed about, decided that it must be of parades and marches, and so 'unimaginably sweet'. Apparently oblivious of the contradiction, he went on to describe a conversation he had overheard between two soldiers, one of whom said he had dreamed that his father had died. His comrade thought this a bad omen, but the soldier replied: 'if one's killed, then one's killed, it would be as joyful to me now as if all my sins had been forgiven' (*chtozh ub´yut, tak ub´yut, teper´ tak radostno, kak budto grekhi vse otdal*). This suggests not contentment, as Gladilov fondly supposed, but nostalgia, filial affection, and fatalism. Shchukin, *Sbornik*, vii. 179.
[43] Bogdanovich, *Russkaya armiya*, p. 5; *PSZ* xvii. 12543 (14 Jan. 1766).

> And trained the soldiers with a kindly voice.
> Let us mourn him, O soldiers,
> For our born father is leaving us.[44]

The use of the first person singular in this song marks it as contrived; on the other hand it *might* have been in tune with the men's actual sentiments, especially once Potemkin was replaced by a notoriously cruel commander, Colonel F. E. Shvarts.

It is equally uncertain how many Izmaylovsky guardsmen would have shared the critical views expressed by Grenadier Makarov, who in 1803 complained:

> The officers of our day
> Have become unduly arrogant,
> Setting themselves up as saints
> And treating soldiers like the damned.[45]

More authentic both in style and sentiment are such works as the 'Lament to God by Soldiers in the Crimea', dating from the 1780s, in which the religious motif sounds clearly. God in his heaven is here contrasted with the 'petty earthly divinities' (*zemnye bozhki*, that is, officers), who expect to be praised and worshipped far beyond their merits; this forced, unlawful adulation leads the soldiers to neglect their proper duties towards the Creator, whose protection they invoke against the wrongful authorities' tyranny. A subsidiary theme is the contrast between holy Russia and the pagan country of the former Crimean Tatar khans where they are obliged to serve; they hope one day to leave this barren and dangerous territory and to return to the 'paradise' of their native land.[46] The unknown authors of this lament, which followed ecclesiastical precedents, adhere to the Christian ethic: war and violence are evil, and serve only to gratify the selfish vanity of their commanders. The implications are certainly radical, but not revolutionary. The true believer has to suffer injustice and maintain his faith intact while awaiting Judgement Day, when the sinful will be punished, the powerful humiliated, and the righteous granted life eternal.

Thus we may say that for the Russian soldier of the early Imperial era the ultimate solution to the problem of oppression was a religious Utopia. But he also invoked the protection of the highest earthly authorities against those lower down in the hierarchy. This belief involved him in something of a contradiction. He sensed instinctively that power corrupts; that the mightier a man was, the more likely he was to commit immoral and sinful actions. Yet

---

[44] Kartsov, 'Semenovskiy polk', p. 328.

[45] Gukovsky, 'Soldatskiye stikhi', p. 146. Pushkarev ('Soldatskaya pesnya', p. 430) claims that certain lines of Makarov's ode coincide with soldiers' aphorisms—but this unfortunately proves nothing.

[46] Gukovsky, 'Soldatskiye stikhi', p. 126.

certain outstanding individuals who bore this heavy burden could, in his view, play a redemptive role by interceding for the humble. Such men merited veneration, and a cult developed around them reminiscent of that of saints in the Church. Among the benevolent intermediaries between the Power and the People were, for the peasant, the many pretenders to the throne whose colourful careers enlivened the history of the period.[47] Soldiers attributed a positive role also to certain great commanders. Not of course that anyone dared to impersonate Suvorov in the way that Pugachev claimed to be Peter III; but, along with some other generals of his time, notably Rumyantsev and Kutuzov, he received much the same naïve and quasi-religious adulation. Long after his death soldiers reputedly invoked him thus: 'Appear to us, father, and lead us wheresoever thou wilst, and we are thine to the last drop of our blood.'[48]

An important ingredient in Suvorov's 'magic' seems to have been his ability to communicate his ideas in a form readily comprehensible to the men, with the use of earthy aphorisms and idiomatic phrases (for example, 'knowledge is light, ignorance darkness') which lose much in translation. Together with this went an eccentricity of behaviour and an easy informality that did not, however, signify any readiness to weaken the army's authority structure. Suvorov stood foursquare for maintenance of hierarchical gradations of rank. His devotees accepted this. What they wanted was a genuinely paternalistic leader, a father figure; and Suvorov came as close as anyone to making a reality of this intrinsically unrealistic principle of social organization. Glinka has a veteran recalling fondly that 'none of us was a stranger to Mikhail Ivanovich; he shared his *kasha* with us soldiers'.[49] In their minds a commander's sociability and straightforwardness outweighed his insistence on strict discipline, so long as the rules were applied even-handedly.

It is curious that Suvorov enjoyed greater popularity in the ranks than Potemkin, although the latter was more humane and sparing of the lives of his men.[50] Likewise, Rumyantsev was less benevolent than Peter Panin, but had a higher reputation with the troops.[51] Paskevich claims that a similar aura surrounded General I. I. Michelson (1740–1807), a relatively little-known commander of Russian troops on the Dniester in 1806–7.[52] As with the pretenders, the image was more important than the reality. Suvorov seems to have deliberately encouraged the myth-making by adopting a bizarre style of dress,

---

[47] Peter III and Grand Duke Constantine, both harsh disciplinarians in real life, were popularly regarded as potential 'liberators'. For recent studies of the Pretender myth see Chistov, *Legendy*; Longworth, 'Pretender Phenomenon'; Siegelbaum, 'Peasant Disorders'.

[48] *Rasskazy starogo voina* (1847), as cited by Karayev, *Suvorovskaya 'Nauka pobezhdat''*, p. 29.

[49] Glinka, *Zapiski*, p. 216. Suvorov's first names were actually Aleksandr Vasil´yevich.

[50] Ibid., p. 135; Bogdanovich, *Russkaya armiya*, p. 27.

[51] Von Shtrandman, 'Zapiski', p. 317; Engel´gardt, *Zapiski*, pp. 76, 130.

[52] Stcherbatow, *Paskévitsch*, p. 23. Another popular hero was General Kul´nev who, according to Antonovsky ('Zapiski', p. 88), 'was loved by everyone in the regiment [the 26th Chasseurs] and could serve as a model soldier'; he was killed in battle in July 1812.

accommodation, and conduct—also a useful weapon against highly-placed rivals, as Ségur noted.[53] The manipulative aspect of the myth was of course hidden from rank-and-file soldiers, who had only appearances to go by. Theirs was a Manichean world-view: the forces of good and evil were seen as locked in mortal combat, and the former could prevail only if they had a leader who combined great power (*vlast'*) with the virtues of the common people (*narod*). This surely was the real secret of Suvorov's 'genius', that is to say his ability to inspire an unusual degree of affection and respect.

The heroic deeds of certain great commanders were celebrated in folksong—in stereotyped fashion, as is characteristic of this literary genre. The same motifs, and even the same epithets, continually recur and are applied schematically to different individuals in various historical circumstances. The standard form is for the hero to be absent, or for his qualities to pass unrecognized, until the decisive moment approaches, whereupon he hastens to the scene of action with magical speed, exhorts his warriors to fight bravely, performs feats of valour himself, and either dies in battle or lives to reward his men handsomely on the morrow of victory. This skeleton plot is embroidered with picturesque details which match the specific situation referred to and provide a minimum of historical verisimilitude. Thus *batyushka* Suvorov, before the fort of Bender, tells his soldiers to take up position 'not sparing your white hands'; he assures them, 'smiling gaily', that the foe is weaker than he seems and then cunningly ferries them across the Danube on rafts; wounded, he is carried on a litter to his weeping mother, who at first thinks that her son is drunk, until he tells her that he has been 'filled with lead' by the enemy—who is identified indiscriminately as Turkish, Prussian, or French![54] Similar adventures befall several other great commanders of the period, as they had the chieftains of earlier eras.

It is no surprise to find Russia's autocrats lauded in much the same way. We may suppose that those folksongs which depict the monarch in a military context were current among the troops, although even this elementary point cannot be proven. A frequent motif is the soldiers' lament for a deceased sovereign, whom they implore to return to the world of the living so that good order may be restored to the army and his or her 'orphans' saved from poverty and injustice. Consider the following:

> Without thee thy realm hath grown troubled,
> All the soldiers have deserted.
> Why have they fled?
> Guard duties have become strict
> And changes of the guard rare.

---

[53] De Ségur, *Mémoires*, ii. 12; Duffy, *Russia's Military Way*, pp. 194–5.

[54] Alekseyeva and Yemel'yanov, *Ist. pesni XVIII v.*, pp. 250, 256, 268–9; cf. *Pesni sobr. Kireyevskim*, ix. 307–9, 319–20, 325–6.

> Uniforms are now in green,
> The frosts are chillier yet
> And shoes are worn on unstockinged feet.[55]

This particular example reflects soldiers' sentiments in the immediate post-Petrine era (hence the reference to green uniforms), yet the same metaphors appear in songs that circulated nearly a century later, with Catherine II rather than Peter I as the monarch whose shade is invoked. They implore her to come back to life and witness the sorry condition to which her successors (Paul I is implied in one version, Alexander I in another) have reduced the Semenovsky guards regiment.[56] A lament for Alexander I, couched in the same vein, contains a topical (and uncomplimentary!) reference to the Decembrist insurrection. In this song a sentry plunges his bayonet into the ground and cries:

> Yield, dissolve, damp mother earth,
> Open up, ye boards that seal the coffin,
> Rise up, rise up, right-thinking tsar,
> Our pious Alexander Pavlovich!
> Our army is no longer as it used to be,
> No longer in its former state—
> All the Preobrazhentsy have mutinied.[57]

The Preobrazhensky guards regiment actually remained loyal to Nicholas I in December 1825; in another version the unit is identified, more accurately, as the Horse Guards.[58]

Interpreting material of this kind is a hazardous enterprise, and it would certainly be rash to infer from these songs that the soldiers who sang or spread them really wanted their ex-monarchs to be resurrected from the dead; by extension one may doubt whether they were even monarchists in an educated man's understanding of the term. Like religious doctrines, concepts of political obligation were given a peculiar twist in the thinking of common people. They venerated the ruler as a person but were incapable of visualizing the monarchy as an institution and harboured strong suspicions of whomever or whatever stood between the monarch and his or her loyal subjects. This view remained implicit rather than explicit, for it was dangerous to express it too openly, and its partisans had neither the leisure nor the intellectual gifts necessary to develop it into a full-blown theory. Nevertheless it emerges quite plainly in a Cossack song about Peter I and the 'treacherous boyar' Gandzherin—although this motif goes back to the sixteenth century—and in the

---

[55] *Pesni sobr. Kireyevskim*, viii. 292; cf. Alekseyeva and Yemel'yanov, *Ist. pesni XVIII v.*, p. 155.

[56] Alekseyeva and Yemel'yanov, *Ist. pesni XVIII v.*, p. 287; cf. Domanovsky *et al.*, *Ist. pesni XIX v.*, pp. 111–15. The post-1820 context would suit the theme better.

[57] Domanovsky *et al.*, *Ist. pesni XIX v.*, p. 127.

[58] *Pesni sobr. Kireyevskim*, x. 201.

highly critical verses that circulated about Arakcheyev, who is blamed for having 'destroyed all of Russia' and taken away one-third of the soldiers' pay.[59]

The emperors and empresses are uniformly depicted in a favourable light as hospitable, generous, and caring; but these *topoi* are compatible with a certain scepticism about their fitness to wield the sacred power entrusted to them. This critical undertone comes into the open in the lionization of Pugachev or in the support for Grand Duke Constantine, seen (wrongly) as a rival to his brother Nicholas in 1825; in one version Constantine even has the guards regiments fighting on his side.[60] The songs also tell us something about the soldiers' attitude towards the empire's institutions. One or both of the tsar's brothers (not identified) is smuggled by a loyal sentry into the Senate, where he finds a treacherous officer threatening the emperor's life; they promptly despatch the miscreant and then discuss whether they should or should not burn down this centre of subversion.[61] This was a curiously distorted reflection of the Northern Society members' hopes that the Senate, the supreme judicial body in the country, might legalize their *coup* and help turn Russia into a constitutional monarchy.

Support for an idealized autocracy went hand in hand with national chauvinism. As is only natural, soldiers' songs contain plenty of uncomplimentary references to the country's historic enemies, with the Muslim peoples stirring fiercer hatreds than Europeans. A ditty about the second Russo-Turkish war of Catherine's reign has the soldiers celebrating the fall of Ochakov and (rather prematurely) the fact that 'all the Turks have come beneath our power'.[62] In another song a wounded soldier staggers home after having received three blows from 'the Turkish tsar' (or, in another variant, 'a young Frenchman') but gloatingly informs his anxious mother that he had cut off his assailant's head (indeed, that he had done so with a bayonet, which would have required considerable dexterity).[63] As a rule, however, the folklore material contains little glorying in martial violence for its own sake. Such motifs are found rather in the stirring verses that were occasionally made up on the men's behalf by bellicose officers.[64]

Russian soldiers behaved with moderation towards prisoners of war and the civilian population of the lands in which they fought—or so at least official sources and memoirs would have us believe. In Europe generally at this time relatively civilized standards prevailed in warfare, at least until the paroxysms of the Napoleonic era, and Russia's leaders were anxious to demonstrate their

[59] Alekseyeva and Yemel'yanov, *Ist. pesni XVIII v.*, pp. 106, 305; Domanovsky *et al.*, *Ist. pesni XIX v.*, pp. 150 ff.

[60] Domanovsky *et al.*, *Ist. pesni XIX v.*, p. 148; cf. Chistov, *Narodnye sots. utopii*, pp. 196 ff.

[61] Domanovsky *et al.*, *Ist. pesni XIX v.*, p. 129. In Moscow a rumour circulated that a soldier stationed at Taganrog had saved Alexander I from assassination by substituting himself for him: N. K. Shil'der, 'Pokhoronnyy god', *RS* 90 (1897), p. 22.

[62] *Pesni sobr. Kireyevskim*, viii. 255.

[63] Ibid., pp. 118–19.   [64] For example, Glinka, *Pis'ma*, iv. 22–3.

enlightenment before critical Western opinion. There were of course exceptions. In 1812 Yermolov earned a bad reputation for tolerating or encouraging atrocities—especially against Poles, for whom he harboured great contempt—and his attitude found some emulators in the officer corps. This was a time when nationalist sentiments were coming to the fore. The soldiers, on the other hand, says one observer,

remained good and loyal [that is, observed the regulations on this score], for the Russian is by and large generous towards his vanquished foes. [He] will kill without remorse in the *mêlée*, but I have seen him share his bread and brandy with one who has surrendered although he would unhesitatingly have massacred him a minute earlier.[65]

Engel´ describes an incident after the battle of Leipzig when one of his men willingly agreed to part with some of his rations for a wounded French grenadier saying: 'Why should I not give him bread? After all the French are men just as we are.'[66]

The regulations referred to by Löwenstern went back to Peter the Great's military statute. This prescribed heavy penalties for killing prisoners, who were declared to be the property of the tsar and not of those who captured them; soldiers were also under orders to spare non-combatant civilians (who were, however, defined in such a way as to exclude males of military age unless they were clergy).[67] Similar instructions were issued by Rumyantsev and Suvorov.[68] But to what extent were these well-intentioned rules enforced?

There seem to have been three circumstances in which Russian troops behaved with unwonted licentiousness and cruelty. The first occurred during the early years of the Seven Years War, when there was a relaxation of discipline that may have owed as much to administrative inefficiency as to the ill-will of particular commanders (Fermor had a better reputation than Apraksin in this regard). One historian speaks disparagingly of the troops' 'Asiatic' behaviour.[69] The well-known memorialist A. T. Bolotov was in 1757 a sub-lieutenant in an infantry regiment stationed in East Prussia where, he states, soldiers in the main force 'mercilessly laid waste all the villages around' and earned for Russia 'ill fame throughout the world'; he summarizes Prussian accounts of outrages against civilians and remarks cautiously: 'one cannot

[65] Löwenstern, *Mémoires*, i. 295. Benkendorf states that peasant guerillas rather than soldiers were responsible for the numerous atrocities committed against French prisoners and stragglers during Napoleon's retreat from Moscow ('Zapiski', Kharkevich, *1812 god*, ii. 110–13), but those by Cossacks are well authenticated.

[66] Shchukin, *Sbornik*, iv. 90–1.

[67] *PSZ* v. 3003 (Voinskiy ustav, 22 Mar. 1716), §§ 104–5, 114. The first Petrine codes allowed units to keep prisoners taken in minor engagements: Myshlayevsky, *Petr Velikiy*, p. 36 (Voinskiye stat´i, § 99).

[68] Dubrovin, *Suvorov*, pp. 69, 91, 102; Sukhomlin, *Suvorovskiy sbornik*, p. 160.

[69] Bogdanovich, *Russkaya armiya*, p. 4. Duffy (*Russia's Military Way*, pp. 75, 83) compares the Russians favourably with the Prussians but remarks that 'the Cossacks gave a lead in rapacity and vandalism to even the best regiments'.

guarantee that our Kalmyks and Cossacks did not commit such atrocities in some places, especially on the flanks.'[70]

The Poles also suffered greatly from depredations by the Russian army as it passed through their territory during this conflict, and it was they who were the victims of the second major exception. Some Russian leaders developed a prejudice against the inhabitants of this country for its political and military weakness, even though this was due in no small measure to their own interference in its internal affairs. Their attitude (which contrasted with that of the late Muscovite era) communicated itself to the troops, who soon learned from experience that they could wreak their will on the all but defenceless civilian population of the Commonwealth without fear of reprisals and that their superiors would condone acts of violence, especially where these were misrepresented as motivated by religious zeal. Ancient animosities against Catholics and Jews could camouflage crimes whose purpose was simply to fill the pockets or gratify the lust of those who perpetrated them. After the second partition of Poland (1793) the men who took up arms under Kosciuszko in defence of their country's sovereignty were treated as rebels. Several hundred Russians had been surprised and slaughtered by the insurgents in their initial assault, and a desire to avenge the loss helped to provoke a number of outrages. The war took on a guerilla character, and as always this increased the hatred on both sides. The final storming of Praga, the key to Warsaw, in October 1794 led to a particularly ugly massacre.[71] Cossack troops seem to have been mainly to blame, but they had probably been given a green light by higher authority. Suvorov, after capturing the city, broke with eighteenth-century convention by allowing his forces to loot it for several hours. The event entered Russian military folklore:

> Our Suvorov gave us freedom
> To take a walk for just three hours.
> Let's take a walk, lads,
> Our Suvorov has ordered it.
> Let's drink his health . . .

[70] Bolotov, *Zhizn´ i priklyucheniya*, i. 490–2; cf. a report to Empress Elizabeth by General Sibilski, a Saxon in Russian service, of 14 Nov. 1757, which was leaked and published in Danzig the following year, and is quoted by Bil´basov in *ZhMNP* (Jan. 1887), ii. 161–2. The Kalmyks were accused of cannibalism and Russian officers themselves acknowledged that they 'spread fear and horror'. The Soviet historian Belikov (*Kalmyki*, pp. 84–9) puts a favourable gloss on their behaviour.

[71] 'They're all dogs, they have fought against us, let them perish', one soldier is said to have exclaimed as he split open his victims' skulls with a hatchet: de Madariaga, *Catherine*, p. 447. Engel´gardt (*Zapiski*, p. 177) saw heaps of mutilated bodies 'of dead and dying soldiers, [civilian] inhabitants, Jews, monks, women and children'. According to one authority 3,000 Polish soldiers were drowned in the Vistula and total casualties among the insurgents were over 13,000; of 4,000 civilians who took up arms only 80 survived: Sukhomlin, *Suvorovskiy sbornik*, pp. 249–50. Bezborodko put the number at 20,000 killed and 10,000 wounded (de Madariaga, loc. cit.) but Kersnovsky, *Istoriya*, i. 140, and *B&E*, xlviii. 934, give lower figures: 10,000 killed and wounded. The Polish historian Th. Morawski, *Dzieje narodu polskiego*, Posen (Poznań), 1877, v. 420–1, states that few were saved from 15,000 insurgents.

Long live Count Suvorov!
Thou livest by the truth
And leadest us soldiers justly![72]

The third area where the rules of war were not observed was the most important: the campaigns against Muslim powers. The four Russo-Turkish wars of
this period were fought with a savagery that had few parallels in other European theatres. This may have been partly due to a desire to avenge the humilia-
tions of the 'Tatar yoke', which left lasting traces in the Russian folk memory,
and partly to popular prejudice against the Muslims as 'infidels' (*basurmany*),
as they were called. It was widely believed that the Ottomans took no
prisoners, and certainly those Russians whom they did capture had an unenviable fate: in 1808 Paskevich found that even officers had been put to work on
the galleys in chains.[73] This practice may explain why some Turkish prisoners
also had to serve in Russian galleys in the Baltic during the war of 1788–90
against Sweden,[74] but in general Ottoman subjects captured by the Russians
probably fared rather better—too well, in Paskevich's opinion. Nevertheless
as late as 1828 one-third to one-half of a party of 12,000 Turkish prisoners
perished within a few days as they were being marched back from the Danubian
principalities under the supervision of a Cossack general named Yefremov.[75]

Suvorov also had much to answer for. At Ochakov in 1788 and two years
later at Izmail his conduct foreshadowed that in Warsaw in 1794: he gave his
men the run of the town after it had been taken. On the first occasion 10,000
and on the second 30,000 enemy troops are said to have been killed,[76] and the
men also took many coins which they 'exchanged by the hatful'.[77] The
rampage became common knowledge throughout Europe and adversely
affected Russian prestige.[78] Cossack atrocities against Crimean Tatars are
documented by Shtrandman, who states that they 'mutilated everyone in their
path, not excluding women and children'.[79] The atmosphere in this region
after the peace of Kuchuk-Kainardji in 1774 (which gave Russia indirect

[72] *Pesni sobr. Kireyevskim*, ix. 326. This item is not reproduced in modern Soviet collections!
Suvorov's conduct at Praga is represented as humane by Kochetkov, 'K voprosu', p. 160.

[73] Stcherbatow, *Paskévitsch*, pp. 30–1.

[74] Tuchkov, *Zapiski*, p. 34.

[75] Von Hansen, *Zwei Kriegsjahre*, pp. 200–7; 'Vospominaniya neizvestnogo o turetskom
pokhode 1828 g.', Shchukin, *Sbornik*, vi. 270; but cf. P. P., 'Vosp. kaval. ofitsera', pp. 98, 126.

[76] Bogdanovich, *Russkaya armiya*, pp. 27, 30. Civilian casualties may account for the differing
estimates. Kersnovsky (*Istoriya*, i. 133) states that at Izmail 34,000 men were killed and 6,000
taken prisoner. *B&E* xxiv. 850 puts the casualties at 23,000, de Madariaga (*Catherine*, p. 415) at
26,000 and 9,000 prisoners. Cf. also Duffy, *Russia's Military Way*, p. 188.

[77] Mosolov, 'Zapiski', p. 139. For a graphic description see Richelieu, 'Journal', pp. 175–84.

[78] Ami de la Vérité, *Coup d'œil*, p. 149. Löwenstern claims (*Mémoires*, i. 64) that Suvorov later
regretted the bloodshed, which was allegedly imposed on him by 'the impetuosity of his troops',
but Masson more plausibly suggests the reverse (*Mémoires*, ii. 67; cf. iii. 133).

[79] Von Shtrandman, 'Zapiski', p. 306. During the second invasion of the Crimea (1778) troops
under General de Balmen burned most of Kaffa (Kefe) and slaughtered all the Tatars in the town:
Fisher, *Crimean Tatars*, p. 66; id., *Russ. Annexation*, p. 94, where the number of victims is put at
600.

control of the khanate and foreshadowed its annexation in 1783) may be sensed from the following incident. In 1778 ensign N. Rachkovsky of the Illyrian Hussars, *en route* from Bensug to Kiprili with four guns, got drunk, handed over command of his unit to an NCO, and stayed behind with two hussars, a Cossack, and three Kalmyks. They came across three Tatars, of whom 'they beat two with whips and then took them to a hollow some way from the town and shot with a pistol'; the Cossack thereupon killed the third man and 'committed tyranny' on their corpses, 'driving his pike into their chests'. The crime was dealt with by regular military judicial procedures, both Suvorov and Rumyantsev advocating death sentences, but the final decision on the case is not known.[80] In fairness it should be added that after their incorporation into the empire the Tatars were treated by the authorities with relative liberality.[81]

The campaigns which Russia fought in Transcaucasia during the early nineteenth century were likewise characterized by great ferocity. The soldiers approached Persians, and later the non-Christian peoples of the Caucasus, with preconceptions formed during centuries of warfare against Tatars and Ottomans. The annals of the long struggle against the Caucasian mountaineers are filled with tales of massacre and looting. In 1816 one general (Delpozzo) promised his troops that 'the wives, children, cattle and [other] things they capture shall be their property'; and thirty years later another senior officer reported that 'all booty became the property of the unit concerned'.[82] This was a colonial war in which terroristic measures were deemed necessary and legitimate; Peter I's regulations on the disposal of loot were not suspended but instead were tacitly ignored. Native adversaries were seen in the same light as domestic insurgents such as the followers of Pugachev, and treated accordingly.

Even with regard to the peaceful civilian population of the empire's heartland Russian soldiers sometimes behaved like occupiers. Many a landowner had cause to rue the day when troops were quartered on his property. The men's contempt for the servile population was often reinforced by their unhappy experiences in rural billets which we have already noted. A French diplomat put this point succinctly. On enlistment, he wrote, the peasant recruit became

a new being who no longer has anything in common with the village he has left. The army becomes his fatherland and his family. [The soldiers'] common fate and the reciprocity induced by the service create that proud fraternity we have had ample occasion to observe.[83]

[80] TsGVIA, V-UA, ed. khr. 226 (1778–80), 11. 49–49ᵛ.

[81] De Madariaga, *Catherine*, pp. 364–6. Fisher (*Crimean Tatars*, pp. 70–80) gives a severer judgement.

[82] Potto, *Utverzhdeniye*, iii. 68 (Kabarda, 1804), 75, 156 (Chechnya, 1805, 1816); cf. von Klaproth, *Reise*, i. 398–9 (Kabarda, Yerevan, 1804–5), 571 (Cherkessia); Murav'yev [–Karsky], 'Iz zapisok', *RA* (1895), 3, p. 320; A. I. Gagarin, 'Zapiski o Kavkaze', *VS* 288 (1906), 3, p. 320.

[83] Bois-le-Comte to Montmorency, 5 Sept. 1822, MAE, M et D, Russie 40 (1821–2), f. 160; cf. 'Mémoire sur la situation de la Russie' (1845), ibid., 43 (1835–48), f. 222ᵛ: 'the soldier is no longer of the people but constitutes a nation apart'.

The peasants for their part by and large looked on the members of this 'proud fraternity' as alien oppressors. The rift persisted even in 1812, when (so we are led to believe by historians) the general upsurge of patriotism extended to commoners. We have a frank and percipient statement to this effect from the pen of A. Chicherin, a young lieutenant who in November 1812 decided to study a village (Krasnaya Slobodka) in Smolensk province where he happened to be stationed. The population, he thought, could be divided into four groups. One, which 'mercilessly refuses [us] its hospitality', comprised people whose hearts had been hardened by the bitter experiences they had undergone. A second category consisted of those 'tortured by fear', who 'try to hide from the sight of their liberators'. A third group were still paralysed by shock, and only the fourth 'has at last been infected by the idea of liberty'—by which he meant that they were well disposed towards their compatriots in uniform. As an example of the latter type he mentions a peasant who, although reduced to destitution by Cossack requisitioning, uncomplainingly shared his last crust of bread with Chicherin's soldiers.[84]

Looting was a problem for the authorities even when the army was defending Russian soil. Barclay de Tolly had 15 soldiers hanged for robbing a church on the retreat to Smolensk: significantly, the case was referred to him by the tough-minded Yermolov.[85] Rostopchin reported to the tsar that Russian troops pillaged Moscow before the enemy arrived to do the same,[86] but his evidence is not always reliable. In general peasants and others with produce to spare were treated high-handedly. They were supposed to be paid for whatever the troops took from them, but this rule, like so many others, was not always observed. In 1812 especially, when funds were short and the administration disorganized, vouchers (*kvitantsii*) might be issued in exchange for goods. They could be redeemed later—that is, if the recipient survived and could make good his claim; the sum repaid was, however, often less than the cost of the produce.[87] Some useful data are contained in the reports which the bailiff of an estate near Vitebsk sent to his master, M. S. Vorontsov. The property suffered exactions by soldiers of both armies in turn. After the war was over the bailiff estimated the total damages at over 110,000 roubles, of which foreign troops were responsible for 57,181 roubles (52.6 per cent) and Russians for the remainder; the enemy had issued vouchers worth 17,999 roubles, whereas the Russians did so for only 4,405 roubles (8.4 per cent as against 31.4 per cent). Only the latter vouchers were of course now redeemable, but there were far fewer of them. When the bailiff complained to an officer about the behaviour of men of the Narva infantry regiment, he was cursed and threatened.[88] (One is left wondering whether these grievances had anything to do with Count Vorontsov's liberal leanings!)

[84] Chicherin, *Dnevnik*, pp. 49–50.
[85] Davydov, *Zapiski*, p. 29; cf. Yermolov, *Zapiski*, p. 38.
[86] Shchukin, *Bumagi*, vii. 422; cf. i. 97.
[87] Zhuravsky, 'Stat. obozreniye', 12, p. 313.
[88] Shchukin, *Bumagi*, iv. 286–306.

If such was the fate of a Great Russian aristocrat, one can imagine the treatment meted out to Poles, Jews, and other civilians whose loyalty was considered doubtful. In one (unidentified) western district where the Polish-speaking population was unsympathetic, a Russian subaltern later wrote: 'wherever we found that landowners had supplies of grain, wine and cattle, we took them for vouchers, not bothering to calculate the exact number of men we had but only whether [the goods] would be in our way if we were pursued'.[89] Once the armies had entered central Europe, they acted in similar fashion if Russia's allies failed to deliver supplies. N. N. Murav'yev, who later achieved fame as a general in the Crimean War, was with a guards unit in Bohemia in 1813 when this situation arose:

Our men lost patience [he writes] and, despite the orders of their commanders, gave battle to the armed [Czech] peasants and the Austrians; [at Otendorf, on the Saxon border] our guardsmen robbed everything without mercy . . . took away cattle, money and women's headgear, let the stuffing out of pillows—this was always the first thing a soldier did in a raid—and in short looted this unfortunate village thoroughly.[90]

Lieutenant Chicherin's description of the Russians' behaviour in Saxony may be considered a classic. The average villager, he states,

greets the [Russian] soldier amicably, following the goodness of his heart and offering him a glass of beer. Suddenly a group of men force their way into his house. His wife runs off to fetch some milk and the table is laid. Then our barbarians see a cow, grab it and drag it off. She prays for pity, but other soldiers climb through the windows, make their way up to the attic, dig about in the trunks and take whatever they find. The column has already passed through the village by the time the soldiers catch up with it, dragging along their loot.

Then a fresh party of soldiers arrives. They tear the straw off the roof of the cottage, leaving its owner seated on a pile of boards surveying the loss of 20 years' hard work.

The column forms up and marches off. It has been here for only one night, but has reduced a prosperous village to complete beggary. Our allies are left cursing us . . . The misfortunes that have befallen our own fatherland have so hardened our hearts that no one thinks it shameful to take whatever he needs without payment. Each man competes with the other in robbery and boasts of it.[91]

By the time the Russian army reached France, Chicherin had been killed in action. Murav'yev picks up the story. The proprietor of Brienne-le-Château owned a valuable library and natural history collection. 'Our soldiers set to

---

[89] Antonovsky, 'Zapiski', p. 12; for earlier excesses see Langeron, 'Russkaya armiya', 4, pp. 151–3.

[90] Murav'yev [-Karsky], 'Zapiski', *RA* (1886), 1, pp. 10, 16; for abuses in Saxony: [Svechin?], 'Iz dnevnikov russkogo ofitsera o zagranichnom pokhode 1813 g.', *RA* 1900, 7, p. 293.

[91] Chicherin, *Dnevnik*, pp. 187–8. Paskevich records that after the battle of Leipzig he could not sleep for the noise of soldiers fishing corpses out of the river and robbing them of valuables. Stcherbatow, *Paskévitsch*, p. 164.

work on it; some officers who turned up out of curiosity saw the disorder and chased the men away, but were themselves attracted by the books and minerals.' Murav'yev acknowledges frankly that he himself could not resist 'a few novels which . . . I read at night and then, to save the extra weight, used as fuel for the stove'.[92] In this instance the men did not have the excuse of hunger, although in their defence it should be added that other armies behaved in like fashion; according to Murav'yev the Prussian troops took more than the Russians did.

Looting was a particular scourge in the Balkans, where there was no civil government infrastructure to protect the population against the troops' ravages, but on the contrary the local notables enthusiastically joined in their exactions. A recent student of the problem states that 'when the various plans for logistical support broke down, the army often simply took what it needed'.[93] The military leaders issued ferocious orders against looters—in 1810 Kamensky II ordered culprits to be given 12,000 blows with the stick for this offence[94]—but such violent measures were neither effective nor justified, given the fact that official supply policy was based on much the same arbitrary principle. The population of the 'liberated' areas was expected to maintain the Imperial armed forces in lieu of providing men themselves.[95]

The Russian soldier certainly made a vital contribution to the empire's expansion. Yet he scarcely constituted a stable element in maintaining order in the annexed regions since he lacked the cultural prerequisites for such a function. He was indifferent, if not actively hostile, to ethnic groups whose ways differed from his own. The very fact of conquest seemed to show that they were inferior, and so reinforced his prejudices. This chauvinistic outlook was seldom articulated, and in this it differed from the nationalism that was now gaining currency in educated circles. It ensured that conflict rather than co-operation became the hallmark of social interaction at the lowest level between the various nationalities that made up the empire.

Was the outlook of the Russian soldier maturing? Many foreign critics thought so. The anonymous author of a memorandum written for the French government in the late 1790s argued that

wars have taught him that everywhere he can live better than in his native land; his prejudices are gradually disappearing and desertion has begun to spread. Besides this the troops do not obey so blindly as before, dare to criticize orders by their superiors, and often refuse to carry them out.[96]

Another contemporary was still more sanguine: the soldiers had become less staunch in battle and fought only because 'they now have cannon trained on

---

[92] Murav'yev [-Karsky], 'Zapiski', *RA* (1886), 5, pp. 86–8.
[93] Jewsbury, 'Russian Army's Role', p. 151.
[94] Petrov, *Russkaya voyennaya sila*, ii. 272.   [95] Stcherbatow, *Paskévitsch*, p. 35.
[96] 'Observations sur le militaire', MAE, M et D, Russie 14 (1745–1825, Forces militaires), f. 123.

their backsides'.[97] (Incidentally, this practice, although kept an official secret, can be authenticated from other sources during the war of 1812, when it seems to have been Yermolov's idea; called 'the chain', it is said to have 'caused many thousands to remain in the ranks of the brave'.[98] But this was of course not the sole reason for the troops' loyalty.)

Foreign observers were right in their estimate that military morale was changing, although they overestimated the pace at which this was occurring and its practical effect. Russian soldiers would still fight stoutly for Tsar and Fatherland for another century or so. The main evidence of change is the desertion rate. Flight from the colours was the easiest way for a soldier to register dissatisfaction with his lot. It was a gesture of passive protest, under-taken at great personal risk, in a situation where more active measures, such as an act of collective insubordination, would have been so fraught with danger as to be impracticable. Desertion was not just a means of self-help but also a blow against the absolutist military system, in the same sense as the flight of peasants to the borderlands was a silent indictment of serfdom.

The authorities took the desertion problem seriously and developed a whole range of measures to deal with it which can only be touched on briefly here. Naturally there are no comprehensive statistics as to its extent; the scattered evidence suggests that the rate fell under Catherine II but rose again thereafter. In 1732 there were said to be 20,000 fugitives, equivalent to 10 per cent of total effectives.[99] The proportion was only one tenth as great (200 out of 20,000) among Russian forces in Finland over a ten-month period in 1792,[100] and it was probably higher in this region than in other parts of the empire at the time. In the Vologda infantry regiment 30 men deserted in one month during the peaceful year of 1779,[101] but in the entire First Division only 38 did so during March 1795.[102] Both units were stationed in frontier areas (Kuban´, Kiev) and the season was the same. In two months of 1812 the police chief at Dorogobuzh, a small town in western Russia, had 17 cases brought to his notice by the staffs of six regiments stationed nearby;[103] but he would not have been informed of those absconders whom the military authorities had already caught. Higher figures are reported from another unit, the Yekaterinburg regi-ment (140 men in one month),[104] but they mean little unless we know what the normal rate of wastage was. Fortunately composite figures are available for the Second Army, stationed in south-western Russia, for three successive peacetime years, 1819–21. They show a desertion rate of 1.3 per cent, 1.5 per cent, and 1.6 per cent respectively[105]—significantly less than in 1732. It was

[97] Ami de la Vérité, *Coup d'œil*, p. 101.

[98] Mayevsky, 'Moy vek', p. 254; cf. Löwenstern, *Mémoires*, i. 273.

[99] Petrov, *Russkaya voyennaya sila*, ii. 151; Kersnovsky, *Istoriya*, i. 63.

[100] Meshcheryakov, *Suvorov*, iii. 137.   [101] Von Shtrandman, 'Zapiski', p. 273.

[102] TsGVIA, V-UA, fond 1349, d. 300 (1796), l. 1.

[103] Shchukin, *Bumagi*, i. 1–76, esp. pp. 19, 21, 40, 59, 73. For desertion from the Lithuanian Ulans: ibid., ix. 3 ff. Desertion rates were high among militiamen, especially in the Baltic: Voyensky, *Akty . . . 1812 g.*, ii. 265, 274.   [104] Semevsky, *Polit. i obshch. idei*, p. 125.

[105] Kiselev to Zakrevsky, 5 Apr. 1822, *Pis´ma*, *SIRIO* lxxviii (1891). 102.

also lower than that in other European armies, but since the latter included large numbers of mercenaries this is not surprising. The Russian rate must be considered high given the fact that this was a conscript army, nationally and socially homogeneous, and that penalties were so severe.

Deserters who were caught generally faced the gauntlet, and might be executed if their offence was carried out in aggravating circumstances.[106] As a rule sentences were commuted. For example, I. Chernoy, a dragoon in the Valuyki regiment, serving in the Ukrainian land-militia, deserted for the second time in June 1762, adopted a false name, and stole one rouble and some 'belongings' (*pozhitki*). A court martial sentenced him, on the basis of the military statute and a decree of 1759, to the knout, facial mutilation, and forced labour for life in Siberia. The sentence went up for confirmation to Lieutenant-General Lachinov, who substituted a penalty of four passes through a gauntlet of 1,000 men. This was reduced by the higher confirming authority (Lieutenant-General Olits) to three passes, followed by service in a garrison unit—also in Siberia, but in a better location than the notorious silver mines of Nerchinsk.[107]

Men who fled tended to do so in small groups, as this enhanced their chances of survival. Before quitting they often took weapons and ammunition, together with some money or other valuables which they could exchange for food. To wear peasant dress was no guarantee against detection. S. Pletenets, who deserted from the Yelizavetgrad mounted musketeers in June 1790, encountered a search party; for some reason he 'took off his hat, and so Kernyut [Pidsakov, chief of the search party], seeing his shaven head, declared him to be a fugitive'.[108] It was helpful to acquire a false internal passport, although if a man were discovered bearing one this aggravated his offence. It was often hard for the authorities to establish the identity of a suspected deserter without going to the length of confronting him with his erstwhile comrades. To be sure, his physical features (*primety*) were described in his papers, and in the search orders, but only in vague terms. On the other hand the searchers had all the resources of the civilian administration at their disposal as well as posses of troops. Most deserters were probably recaptured without much effort after a few days of liberty. They were wholly dependent on their wits and on the goodwill of petty officials, tavern-keepers, and the like, who might well be tempted by the prospect of a reward if they turned them in.[109] It was therefore an advantage to would-be deserters if their units were stationed close to the frontier.

---

[106] Voinskiye artikuly, §§ 94–100 (*PRP* viii. 340-3).

[107] TsGVIA, V-UA, ed. khr. 88 (1763), ll. 15 ff. Cf. the case of Stepan Odintsev (Apr. 1779) in ibid., ed. khr. 226, ll. 62-3.

[108] TsGVIA, V-UA, ed. khr. 16449 (1790), ll. 139 f.

[109] This was 5 roubles under Peter I, but was doubled in 1732 and again in 1797. *PSZ* viii. 6024 (17 Apr. 1732), xiv. 10737 (7 June 1757), xv. 11405 (16 Jan. 1762), xxiv. 18244 (15 Nov. 1797), § 5; xxvi. 19270 (9 Feb. 1800).

Investigators invariably questioned those they caught as to the exact route they had taken and how they had kept alive. A man might typically reply that he had eaten vegetables growing in the fields and had laid up in woods by day or empty houses at night.[110] The purpose of this questioning was to discover and punish any civilians who had given him food or shelter, as well as to ascertain whether he had committed any robberies while on the run. Captured deserters were also asked several *pro forma* questions, such as whether they had received their pay and had intended to abscond temporarily or for good. Courts martial observed such juridical formalities but did not bother to probe the accused's motives more broadly.

Occasionally local authorities organized round-ups of suspected fugitives. Catherine II disapproved of the practice. In 1795 she wrote to M. M. Izmaylov, the Moscow commander-in-chief, declaring that the reason why men fled was that 'they do not get their due, are beaten cruelly, and made to dig ponds [for their officers] and to drink wine in the taverns [to increase the lease-holders' revenue]'. She ordered those detained to be asked what specific grievances they had—but refrained, perhaps out of respect for legal procedure, from saying whether they were to be set free.[111]

Her successors were less squeamish. They did not return to the early eighteenth-century (and Muscovite) practice of sending out special investigators (*syshchiki*), which Catherine had abandoned,[112] and they continued the long-standing habit of granting amnesties. But Paul imposed penalties on unit commanders whose men deserted—and made these officers responsible for paying the reward to the delator.[113] In 1811 Alexander I ordered soldiers who had fled to the Cherkessians (in the Caucasus) and were recovered to be summarily executed, presumably as traitors.[114] He set up a permanent security force, called the Internal Guard (*Vnutrennyaya strazha*), one of whose chief tasks was to apprehend deserters. By 1817 he became worried that the large number of military convicts who had been sent to the Orenburg line or to Siberia 'are corrupting fine young recruits' in those areas, and ordered them to be kept in their units instead.[115] The normal penalty for deserters was still the gauntlet: one to three passes through 500 men for the first offence, six for the second, and five passes through 1,000 men for the third, fourth, or fifth offence.[116]

---

[110] Cases of A. Nikolayev and V. Poletayev (Aug. 1799), TsGVIA, f. 11, op. 6, ed. khr. 33 (1799), ll. 23, 36ᵛ.

[111] Vorontsov, 'Zapiska', *AKV* x. 385.

[112] For the practice: *PSZ* xiv. 10650 (19 Nov. 1756), § 10; for its repeal xvi. 11672 (2 Oct. 1762); cf. xvi. 11919 (12 Sept. 1763).

[113] PSZ xxiv. 17588 (9 Nov. 1796), IX, ch. VI, § 1 (p. 90); xxiv. 17590 (9 Nov. 1796), ch. 38, § 1 (p. 184); xxv. 18913 (Mar. 1799).

[114] *PSZ* xxxi. 24704 (3 July 1811), § 15 and accompanying 'Instruktsiya', § 10.

[115] *PSZ* xxxiv. 27091 (13 Oct. 1817).

[116] See above, p. 173. Under Paul there were many discretionary sentences: TsGVIA, f. 11, op. 6, ed. khr. 33.

It was Alexander I, too, who took stern measures to close the western border to defectors, whether military or civilian. In the eighteenth century Poland had been the favourite sanctuary; others were Moldavia, the Crimea, and the Don, although after the collapse of the Pugachev insurrection the last area was no longer safe. Already Peter I had established a so-called 'cordon' along the Polish border, which his successors maintained in being.[117] However, it seems to have been fairly easy to evade the patrols that manned it. In the 1750s a number of disgruntled South Slav immigrants serving in the new military settlements in the Ukraine simply slipped across the frozen Dnieper by night, taking their uniforms and ammunition with them.[118] Catherine II tried, not without success, to induce deserters (and other fugitives) abroad to return to Russia by promising them advantageous conditions,[119] but the cordon evidently remained in existence until the last days of the Polish-Lithuanian Commonwealth, for Mosolov recalls that he served in it in 1791.[120] After Kosciuszko's insurrection a number of ostensibly 'Polish' soldiers who had been integrated into the Russian army were discovered to be Russians after all. They were sentenced to the gauntlet or the knout and, if they survived that penalty, posted to units stationed in remote parts of the empire.[121] The same fate generally awaited those who were recovered from refuges in Moldavia or the Caucasus, although at first many of them were settled in New Russia.[122]

With Poland's disappearance from the European map Austria and Prussia became the most likely sanctuaries, but their governments, bound to Russia by common dynastic and political interests, were unsympathetic to defectors from that country. In 1810 the emperors Alexander and Francis signed a convention on the reciprocal return of fugitives (some Austrian deserters having previously been accepted into the Russian army), and later a similar agreement was reached with the elector of Saxony, who was also grand duke of Warsaw.[123] After the defeat of Napoleon the former arrangement was renewed and other conventions concluded with Prussia and France.[124] The last of these agreements was motivated by the fact that already by 1814 some 6,000 men, among them 'senior NCOs decorated with crosses and medals', had deserted from two corps that fought in France.[125]

---

[117] *PSZ* vii. 4489, 4695 (3 Apr. 1722, 19 Apr. 1725), xii. 9448 (30 Oct. 1747); cf., for the Crimean border, viii. 5842 (27 July 1731).

[118] Pishchevich, *Zhizn'*, p. 418.

[119] *PSZ* xvi. 11618 (19 July 1762), xvii. 12396 (11 May 1765).

[120] Mosolov, 'Zapiski', p. 141.

[121] Beskrovnyy, *Russkaya armiya*, pp. 435–6, citing archival sources.

[122] 6,130 fugitives (including some civilians?) were returned from the Danubian Principalities between 1782 and 1802 (excluding the war years 1787–91): Grosul, *Dunayskiye knyazhestva*, pp. 25–7; Semenova, *Rossiya i osvob. bor'ba*, p. 85; Druzhinina, *Sev. Prichernomor'ye*, p. 65.

[123] *PSZ* xxx. 23295 (9 Oct. 1808), xxxi. 24282, 24522 (1 July 1810, 15 Feb. 1811); cf. xxvi. 20049 (9 Nov. 1801).

[124] *PSZ* xxxiii. 25874 (5 June 1815), 25986 (8 Nov. 1815), additional articles (p. 342), 26266 (13 May 1816: Prussia), xxxiv. 26751 (24 Mar. 1817: Prussia), xxxviii. 29115 (14 July 1821: Austria); cf. also P. S. Squire, 'Metternich and Benckendorff, 1807–34', *SEER* 45 (1967), pp. 135–62, esp. p. 147. [125] Murav'yev [-Karsky], 'Zapiski', *RA* (1886), 2, p. 119.

The risk of this 'iron curtain' policy was that it bottled up frustrations which might explode in organized violence. During the period we have been considering troubles of this kind were rare. The infrequent exceptions emphasize the soldiers' general docility. It is now known that among those jailed for political offences in the early 1790s there were more men in uniform (about 200) than any other class of Russian subject,[126] but the implications of this fact should not be exaggerated. Disaffection, where it occurred, usually had its roots in some ethnic, regional, or 'corporatist' grievance. This was the case with those land-militiamen who sympathized with Pugachev's revolt—an insurgency which originated in the government's encroachment on the liberties of the Yaik and Don Cossack 'hosts' on the empire's south-eastern border.[127] It was also the case with the Don Cossacks who were sent to the Caucasus in 1794 for holding 'dubious gatherings and conclaves'[128] and their Polish contemporaries who, having been inducted into the Russian army, came out in sympathy with Kosciuszko's revolt.[129]

Those disturbances that on the face of it seem to have been protests against service conditions likewise had a marked regional flavour. There was trouble among militiamen (*opolchentsy*, that is, members of the national levy) at Dubosary in the Ukraine in 1807 when, instead of being disbanded at the end of hostilities as they had been led to expect, they found themselves drafted into regular army units.[130] Rather similar in nature, but more serious, were the riots which broke out among militiamen at Insar, Saransk, and Chembar (Penza province) in the autumn of 1812. The men concerned belonged to the 1st, 2nd, and 3rd Cossack infantry regiments, and a consciousness of their rights as Cossacks played a significant part in their action, as well as their understandable indignation at the authorities' needlessly violent attempts to 'restore order'. At Chembar a Colonel Dmitriyev fired on a crowd which refused to disperse. The Insar men (and perhaps the others too) held that they could not legally be sent to fight away from their own locality because they had not been sworn in (which was true); furthermore, a militia unit in neighbouring Tambov province had been disbanded for administrative reasons, and they suspected that they were being discriminated against. They were nevertheless ordered to move off and the 'ringleaders' arrested. Thereupon the men promptly released them (much as the *strel'tsy* had done in 1682 and 1698), seized some liquor at gun-point, and for two days and nights ran amok in the town, breaking into houses and stealing property valued at some 8,000 roubles.[131] The stated motive for this *pogrom* may well have concealed sentiments of a more political

---

126 Dzhedzhula, *Rossiya i . . . burzh. revolyutsiya*, p. 171.
127 Beskrovnyy, *Russkaya armiya*, p. 452.
128 TsGVIA, f. 801, op. 62/3, ed. khr. 304 (1798); Svatikov, *Rossiya i Don*, pp. 234–9.
129 Meshcheryakov, *Suvorov*, iii. 299, 308, 312, 327.
130 Tuchkov, *Zapiski*, p. 279.
131 Shchukin, *Bumagi*, iv. 156–76; Beskrovnyy *et al.*, *Nar. opolcheniye*, pp. 380–6. There is some doubt about their fate; from the published sources it seems that the Chembar men were punished but the Insar ones pardoned. About 250 men were involved in all.

character, perhaps involving Ukrainian autonomist sympathies as well as concern for Cossack rights. In any case it is doubtful whether the action may be properly categorized as a mutiny.

The first real mutiny in the Imperial Russian army seems to have occurred at Chuguyev (Slobodskaya Ukraina) in 1819. It will be examined in chapter 13, since it involved the military settlers. We may also leave for later discussion the celebrated protest staged in the following year by men of the Semenovsky guards regiment in St. Petersburg against excesses by their commander, Colonel Shvarts. The latter was a nominee of Arakcheyev, the principal architect and commander-in-chief of these colonies. As we shall see, even these disturbances were relatively minor affrays which did not threaten the security of the absolutist state or the military system that was its principal bulwark.

On the whole the Russian soldier remained a submissive cog in the vast machine of which he formed part—remarkably so, in view of the deprivations and injustices to which he was subjected and the lack of any effective procedure for settling grievances. He was reasonably well integrated into his martial environment, even though he might not share its prevailing values and beliefs. Psychologically and culturally, as well as from a legal and social aspect, soldiers comprised a distinct caste with its own *mores* and life-style. They had lost touch with their civilian origins, yet shared the peasants' fundamental world outlook, particularly their faith in a religious Utopia. This faith implied a radical restructuring of the existing socio-economic and political order and posed a latent threat to the absolutist regime; but its ulterior significance would not become apparent until the twentieth century. In the meantime these hard-pressed men found solace in the hope that divine or monarchical justice would set the world aright.

IV

GENTLEMEN TO OFFICERS

10

BIRTH OF THE
MILITARY INTELLIGENTSIA

How could the Russian soldier of the early Imperial era hope to escape his sorry plight? Mutinous acts could at best win short-term local easements and generally called forth draconian reprisals. The alternative was to await a change of heart among his superiors. Reformist ideas were in the air, particularly during the reign of Alexander I. But in Russia the state power did not work together with enlightened elements in the officer corps, as it did in Prussia after Jena. The tsarist empire emerged victorious from the Napoleonic Wars and there was no sense of a national emergency that required drastic solutions. Such a mood was not engendered until 40 years later, when Russia suffered major reverses during the Crimean War. To be sure, Alexander I was sincerely concerned for his soldiers' welfare, but unhappily the measures he took did little to improve their lot and in some respects even worsened it. The military settlements, to be examined in ch. 12, were introduced under the aegis of state paternalism, not of liberalism, and their main purpose was to buttress the autocratic power. They were opposed with good reason by liberal-minded officers as well as by many civilian administrators, and after 1815 the reform movement in educated society was driven underground. Guards officers in particular were active in setting up masonic lodges and secret societies. Political programmes were drawn up and plots hatched. Finally, in December 1825 a few bold spirits took the desperate step of insurrection. The so-called 'Decembrists' ended their lives on the gallows or were sent into Siberian exile. The new tsar, Nicholas I (1825–55), devoted himself to maintaining the status quo, in the army as elsewhere. During his reign, to be considered in ch. 14, the old military system by and large survived, with all its well-known faults, until the 'great reforms' of the mid-nineteenth century.

The insurgents of 1825 left behind them an attractive myth that has powerfully shaped all writing on the subject. For a century or so historians and publicists looked on them as martyrs for the cause of progress, sacred to later generations of the intelligentsia. They were viewed as heroic 'forerunners' whose noble ideals deserved respect and emulation. Apart from the writers' own preferences the nature of the sources available led them to favour a biographical or ideological approach to the study of 'Decembrism'. Not until the twentieth century were archival materials made accessible and published. Yet the traditional interpretation has lived on in Soviet historiography, although with certain changes of emphasis necessitated by Marxist–Leninist doctrine. From the 1930s onward the nationalist element in the 'Decembrists'' outlook was singled out for more positive treatment than their liberalism, and their intellectual debt to the West was played down.[1] Only in recent years have some Western historians begun to question the canonical view.[2] The first step in demystifying the officers' reform movement is to place it in its proper military-service context and to treat it as an early instance of Praetorianism.[3] This task will be attempted in ch. 11. First we have to examine the milieu in which the movement developed.

During the eighteenth century most Russian officers continued to visualize their situation as servitors of the Crown in terms of personal and family advancement: that is to say, they combined loyalty to the autocrat with concern for their own interest and that of their immediate kin group; some of them were also conscious of belonging to an informal patronage network. This 'traditional' thought pattern may be contrasted—in theory—with a more 'modern' one in which officers see themselves, and are seen by others, primarily as members of a corporation: an individual regiment, a branch of service (cavalry, artillery), or the 'officer corps' as a whole. The latter term is inappropriate in the Russian context during our period, although it is sometimes used for the sake of convenience. 'Corporatism' and a sense of professional loyalty were certainly developing, but initially at least the social climate was not favourable to the growth of horizontal ties. They became possible only as a consequence of four major changes, which in the main may be associated with the enlightened rule of Catherine II. These were: (*a*) the abolition of compulsory state service by noblemen (1762, confirmed in 1785); (*b*) the assignment to the *dvoryanstvo*, by the administrative reforms of 1775/85, of a definite role in the social and cultural life of the provinces; (*c*) the victories won in successive wars against Prussians, Poles, and, above all, Turks, which heightened Russian army officers' self-esteem; and (*d*) the expansion of the military colleges, known as 'cadet corps', and the broadening of their curriculum to include civil as well as professional subjects.

As a result of these changes, and other factors too, by the 1790s Russian nobles, not least those in military uniform, had acquired a taste for the fruits of European culture and had even begun to acquire political ambitions. Politicization was accelerated by the often traumatic experience which officers of all ranks, but especially the senior men, went through during the brief reign of

---

[1] This viewpoint was taken to an extreme by Prokof'yev, *Bor'ba* (1952), who turned the Decembrists into proto-Zhdanovists—but did draw attention to their views on military subjects. The standard Soviet work, richly documented, is Nechkina, *Dvizheniye dekabristov*.

[2] Mazour, *First Russ. Revol.*, provides a good narrative account but the interpretation is now somewhat outdated. Raeff, *Decembrist Movement*, is more thoughtful; Lincoln, 'Re-examination', discusses the traditional approach and makes useful suggestions for further research.

[3] On this see now A. Perlmutter, *The Military and Politics in Modern Times*, New Haven and London, 1977, esp. pp. 89–114, who is however mainly concerned with twentieth-century manifestations of the phenomenon.

Paul, and then by the brutal manner in which it was terminated in the *coup d'état* of 11 March 1801—in which more officers were involved than had been the case in any of the several eighteenth-century 'palace revolutions'.

Peter III's 'charter of liberties' (1762) was certainly a landmark in the history of the *dvoryanstvo*, but its impact should not be exaggerated. The state took measures to protect its interests and to ensure a continued supply of officers.[4] As two recent writers put it, 'the hallowed tradition of a service nobility . . . , by now crumbling in the West, had been upheld in Russia'.[5] Indeed, the problem for the authorities was not a shortfall but rather an over-abundance of young men with high ambitions but poor qualifications for positions of command. This was the reason for the presence of large numbers of supernumeraries (*sverkhkomplektnye*), especially in the guards or in other favoured regiments. These men usually stayed at home until an opportunity arose for them to secure military employment, although some actually followed their units into the field in the hope of winning preferment more quickly. When casualties were heavy, as they were during the Napoleonic Wars, the pressure became less acute.

The existence of supernumeraries, and also the official practice of maintaining the armed forces below establishment strength in peacetime—at a level which was not made public—make it difficult to ascertain just how large a proportion of *dvoryane* continued to serve after 1762. One cannot simply set the number of officer vacancies in the *shtaty* against the figure for male noblemen (recently put at 108,000, of all ages, in 1782).[6] W. Pintner believes it to have been a mere 27 per cent (including civil servants) in 1800, but agrees that his estimate needs refinement.[7] We need to know the length of time served, at various junctures, by nobles in different income groups. The proportion of servitors was certainly significant, and must have been greater among the mass of impoverished gentry than among the (relatively few) aristocrats. The latter might don uniform largely for reasons of social prestige, but for the former state service was almost a *sine qua non*. It was the only way of earning a living and supporting one's family in conditions markedly superior to those of one's serfs. For such men the right to apply for discharge papers—which applied only in peacetime and was beset by wearisome bureaucratic formalities—seems to have been important less for material than for psychological reasons. It was a symbol of gentry privilege *vis-à-vis* commoners, to whom it was denied, rather than a tangible opportunity. Unless such officers or NCOs were wounded or fell sick, sheer economic necessity obliged them to soldier on until they had completed the regulation term of 25 years. This term had been set by a decree

---

[4] *PSZ* xv. 11444 (18 Feb. 1762); Kalachov, *Materialy*, i. 38; Dukes, *Catherine and Nobility*, pp. 42–5; Jones, *Emancipation*, pp. 27–34, 277; Raeff, 'Peter III', pp. 1291–4; Rexhauser, *Besitz-verhältnisse*, p. 50.

[5] Kamendrowsky and Griffiths, 'Trading Nobility', p. 217.

[6] Kabuzan and Troitsky, 'Izmeneniya', p. 158.

[7] Pintner, 'Russia as a Great Power', p. 35.

of 31 December 1736, issued on the outbreak of war with Turkey, which had a propagandist intent and was not implemented until after the end of hostilities four years later.[8] During Catherine's reign the settled troops served for only 15 years, but were then classified as reservists; the 25-year term, as we know, was extended to men in the 'lower ranks' in 1793.[9]

Most officers seem to have begun their service as rank-and-file soldiers, as Peter I had intended, although for those who were well connected this was often just a formality. They might be enrolled in a regiment while still in infancy and granted leave until they had completed their studies. Thus P. M. Volkonsky (1776–1852) was enlisted as a Preobrazhensky guardsman on the day of his baptism; at the age of 16 he wanted to see active service, got himself posted to another unit, and within a matter of weeks was an ensign; two years later he had been appointed adjutant in his own regiment.[10] It should, however, be noted that such laxity was more characteristic of Catherine's reign than it was of those of her successors, and also that it was more usual in the higher reaches of society than among provincial gentrymen who had no aristocratic patron.

Patronage was important in finding a vacancy precisely because of the abundance of supernumeraries, which made for fierce competition. Even those who had the necessary *svyazi* ('ties', the customary euphemism) could not always afford to take up the appointment offered—say that of adjutant to a prominent general, which was one of the quickest routes to the top.[11] Senior officers tried to assist the impecunious, but had to put the interests of the service first. General Kiselev wrote frankly to a friend in 1828, in regard to a member of the Tolstoy family, that 'I have done all I could, placing both his nephews in the best regiment and recommending them to their commanders as if they were my kin', but adding that for some reason they had failed to make the grade.[12] Another contemporary states that in the guards regiments new appointments took effect from 1 January each year, and so at the end of December 'the secretary would be pestered with questions: "Will my son get in?", "Has my nephew been put on the list?" and so on.'[13] Such pressure by civilian relatives was scarcely possible, however, once the neophyte had received his commission.

The psychological importance of this step is underlined by A. N. Martos, who in 1809 was promoted sub-lieutenant after a mere six weeks in the ranks (and an examination in his speciality, engineering): 'everyone who has obtained his first officer rank and a sword knows that there is scarcely any pleasure on

---

[8] *PSZ* ix. 7142 (Eng. tr.: Vernadsky *et al.*(eds.), *Source Book*, ii. 381); on its erratic implementation, Manstein, *Zapiski*, p. 186; Troitsky, *Russkiy absolyutizm*, p. 142.

[9] *PSZ* xxiii. 17149 (2 Sept. 1793), § 6.

[10] Volkonsky, 'Rasskazy', p. 177; cf. von Hupel, *Beschreibung*, pp. 28, 101 n.; Engel'gardt, *Zapiski*, p. 59; Mosolov, 'Zapiski', pp. 125–6; Dolgorukiy became an ensign at the age of 12: Dolgorukov, 'Otryvki', p. 290. Advancement in the military is discussed briefly by Floyd, 'State Service', pp. 63–6.

[11] Pishchevich, *Zhizn'*, pp. 22–6; cf. Löwenstern, *Mémoires*, i. 7–13; Stcherbatow, *Paskévitsch*, pp. 7–10.

[12] Kiselev to Zakrevsky, 2 Sept. 1828, 'Pis'ma', p. 159.

[13] Glinka, *Zapiski*, p. 136.

earth to compare with this reward'.[14] Subsequent advancement up the hierarchy of *chin* depended mainly on seniority, although it could be accelerated
where a man displayed unusual merit—or where he had unusually good connections: Paskevich was a major-general at 28, and two sons of Field-Marshal
M. F. Kamensky (1738–1809) reached that rank at the ages of 26 and 22.[15] For
the average subaltern what mattered most was his relationship to his colonel,
who controlled what was written in each of his officers' testimonials (*attestaty*).
These essential documents were supposed to be signed by the candidate's comrades before they were seen by his superiors, but a contemporary tells us that
in practice junior officers would sign whatever their commander wanted for
fear of receiving a bad testimonial themselves.[16] It might take 15 years to reach
the rank of captain and another 10 years to become a major.[17]

These long delays were due partly to social discrimination. The promotion
ladder might be blocked artificially, so to speak, by the arrival in line regiments
of young officers, usually of privileged background, who had transferred from
the guards on completion of their training there or from personal choice; in
such circumstances they qualified for a two-grade advancement. Then there
were ex-officers who had been discharged to civilian life but returned—perhaps,
as in 1812, from patriotic motives—and got back their old rank, or even a higher
one. The reason for this was that on retirement an officer who had served for
at least one year in his current rank (five years in the case of colonels) was raised
by one grade;[18] furthermore, seniority gained while serving in the civilian
branch might be taken into account when a man rejoined the army. Thus
L. A. Naryshkin, who returned to the colours in 1812 after five years at court,
was promoted from lieutenant to captain.[19]

All this inevitably created a good deal of discontent. On the other hand
everyone benefited when there were promotions *en masse* to mark a victory on
the battlefield or even some event in the life of the court. On such occasions
ambitious junior officers would try to ensure that they came to the notice of
the top-level decision-makers.[20] They might even complain that comrades with
less seniority had been promoted ahead of them[21]—evidence that the old
Muscovite tradition of *mestnichestvo* was slow to die.

The survival of the traditional service-state mentality explains why in the
Imperial era officers displayed what seems an extravagant concern with matters

[14] Martos, 'Zapiski', p. 306. Normally two years' service in the ranks was now required before
a commission: Muromtsev, 'Vospominaniya', p. 69.

[15] Stcherbatow, *Paskévitsch*, i. 81; *RBS* viii. 423, 439.

[16] Rzhevsky, 'O russkoy armii', p. 361; *PSZ* xvi. 11625, 11769 (24 July 1762, 3 Mar. 1763); von
Hupel, *Beschreibung*, pp. 95–104; Vorontsov, 'Zapiska', p. 487; Sazonov, 'Attestaty', *VE* iii. 247–9.

[17] Plotho, *Entstehung*, p. 75; von Hupel, *Beschreibung*, p. 103.

[18] For example, *PSZ* xxvii. 20358 (3 July 1802).

[19] 'Vosp. L. A. Naryshkina', Kharkevich, *1812 god*, ii. 151.

[20] 'Prevratnosti sud'by', p. 501; von Shtrandman, 'Zapiski', pp. 82, 287; Mosolov, 'Zapiski',
p. 129; Dolgorukov, 'Otryvki', pp. 290, 326.

[21] TsGVIA, V-UA, f. 1349, d. 300 (1796), 11, 19–20, 23 (petitions by Capt. D. R. Kossovsky
and V. A. Kuz'min).

of status and rank. It was in this way that they defined their self-image and their relationship to those above and below them. The really important step on the ladder was that from captain to major, which raised one from subaltern (*ober-ofitser*) rank to that of 'staff officer' (*shtab-ofitser*). Appointments at this level and above were, at least in theory, made by the sovereign,[22] with whom staff officers could therefore claim to have entered into a direct personal relationship. The political implications of this were considerable, as we shall see in a moment.

Officers' service conditions were far superior to those of their men. They could expect to be granted leave, normally limited to a period of 29 days, if they could be spared from their unit. A quota system operated, and during the eighteenth century decisions on such matters were gradually decentralized. Engel'gardt notes that in Potemkin's forces 'almost all the colonels went on leave for the winter' of 1789, so that their regiments had to be commanded by majors.[23] The rules were tightened up later.[24] Junior officers, to be sure, might be too poor to afford the journey home, but if they were lucky a kindly superior might come to their rescue by sending them on some official errand.[25] Figures for 1796 show that—as in the ranks—the frequency of leave was highest among the most senior officers and lessened steadily as one went down the hierarchy.[26]

It was also the wealthy and well-connected who were most likely to put in for transfer to another unit—perhaps in order to serve alongside a kinsman, or even (although this motive could not be openly stated) to escape an antagonistic relationship with the colonel. In the late eighteenth century such transfers occurred so frequently that efficiency and morale suffered, since it was impossible for officers who were continually on the move to get to know their men or to identify with their unit.[27]

Materially, those at staff-officer level and above were well looked after. Even a lowly lieutenant's earnings were a multiple of those of a private. In 1748 the difference was 16.7:1 (slightly less, 15.1:1, in 1763), but by 1839 it had reached 37.1:1.[28] These ratios should be regarded only as rough approximations. A statistically acceptable index of officers' incomes would require accurate information on the inflation rate and the fluctuating value of the paper *assignat* roubles in which troops were paid during most of this period.[29]

[22] Petrov, *Russkaya voyennaya sila*, ii. 156; von Hupel, *Beschreibung*, p. 58.

[23] Engel'gardt, *Zapiski*, p. 96. [24] *PSZ* xxvi. 20042 (1 Nov. 1801).

[25] Dubrovin, *Suvorov*, p. 133; E. Shchepkina, foreword to [Vasil'yev] *Dnevnik*, p. v; von Hupel, *Beschreibung*, pp. 108, 127.

[26] TsGVIA, V-UA, f. 1349, d. 300, l. 1: 41.1 per cent of staff officers, 35.4 per cent of subalterns, 13.9 per cent of NCOs, and 9.4 per cent of privates.

[27] Levanidov to Rumyantsev, 30 Dec. 1794, in ibid., l. 2; *PSZ* xxiii. 17119 (Apr. 1793); Rzhevsky, 'O russkoy armii', p. 360; von Hupel, *Beschreibung*, pp. 104, 128; Duffy, *Russia's Military Way*, p. 148.

[28] MAE, M et D, Russie 14 (1745–1828), f. 17ᵛ; Solov'yev, 'O pensiyakh', p. 307; Lebedev, *Russkaya armiya*, pp. 70–6.

[29] The annual (average?) stock exchange quotations are given by Shtorkh, 'Materialy', pp. 812 ff.

The purchasing power of officers' pay seems to have improved, even though the nominal rates in silver currency were in the same order of magnitude. During the early years of Catherine II's reign an infantry colonel in the field army drew 600, a lieutenant-colonel 460, and a major 310–390 roubles; after the return to metal, in 1839, the figures were 575, 430, and 375 roubles respectively.[30] A further difficulty here is that of estimating the value of allowances. Officers drew 'rations' in cash on a scale that varied according to rank: in 1763 an infantry colonel drew 17 'rations' together worth 91.80 roubles, roughly equal to one-sixth of his pay. They also, as we know, enjoyed the 'free' services of orderlies (*denshchiki*); and unit commanders received so-called 'table money', which amounted to 3,000 roubles for a regimental chief. There were wide differentials between the better-paid officers in special forces such as artillery, grenadier, or guards units and the less well-paid who did duty in provincial garrisons.

On the other hand, whatever their station, they had obligations—for instance, to maintain horses and items of clothing and equipment, the cost of which would normally be deducted from their pay at source.[31] These burdens were heavy, especially in privileged units, where it is impossible to distinguish between those that were functionally necessary and those that were imposed merely by social convention. As in other armies of the period, wealthy officers with private means might actually spend more than they earned in the service. A. A. Blagovo, a guards lieutenant who noted down pedantically all his expenditure, spent 285 roubles in 1740, which must have been considerably more than his pay; ten years later, when he was evidently living in retirement on his estate, he spent 741 but earned 1,034 roubles.[32] A Cossack major-general, A. K. Denisov, states in his memoirs that in the early 1800s his salary was inadequate to keep him in his lofty station, so that he 'went short even of necessities'; but this was partly because he had purchased an estate and incurred a debt of 50,000 roubles—a predicament from which he was rescued by two comrades.[33] Many officers ran up huge debts from gambling, which was part of the accepted life-style.[34]

At the other end of the spectrum were genuinely impoverished officers who had to support themselves and several relatives wholly from their pay. Such men were often dependent on the charity of their fellows or the colonel; the latter could, if he chose, draw on the unit's reserve funds for this purpose. Some commanders made a regular practice of entertaining their subordinates. Lieutenant-General F. M. Num(m)sen, inspector of cavalry in Livonia, who

[30] *PSZ* xliii. 11735 (14 Jan. 1763), and for 1795 and 1811 rates xliii. 17369, 24729; Stein, *Geschichte*, pp. 219, 244 (1798, 1801); MAE (as cited in n. 28), f. 117.

[31] von Hupel, *Beschreibung*, pp. 131, 148; Stein, *Geschichte*, p. 199.

[32] 'Pamyatnaya knizhka', *Shchukinskiy sbornik*, ii. 440, iii. 93.

[33] Denisov, 'Zapiski', pp. 244–9.

[34] Löwenstern, as a major in temporary retirement, won and lost about half a million roubles in 1810: *Mémoires*, i. 155–62; cf. Mosolov, 'Zapiski', p. 173; Glinka, *Zapiski*, pp. 13, 137.

also headed a cuirassier regiment in that region during the 1790s, held a weekly feast for his officers. They sat down to table at 2 p.m. and did not rise until midnight. 'It was a real orgy; one had to drink until one dropped', one of the participants recalls.[35] These occasions were useful up to a point as a means of reinforcing service loyalties and maintaining control. Needless to say, they were hardly feasible when a unit went to the front, and excessive indulgence in alcohol might on occasion have harmful results on the battlefield.[36]

The real problem here was that even junior officers who were economical and abstemious could not accumulate enough savings to tide them over a campaign, when they would have to acquire equipment and a stock of food. In consequence they often went as hungry as their men—even more so, according to one memorialist who broke the taboo on complaining in print about material wants.[37] The future general A. A. Zakrevsky told his biographer that in 1802, when he was an ensign stationed in Lithuania, he was lodged for some time in a filthy henhouse and lived solely off eggs—which in later years he would cook tastefully for his friends.[38]

To make ends meet junior officers would often pool their limited resources, in a manner not too different from that of a soldiers' artel. Sometimes they would even mess together with their men. When Catherine II heard of such expedients she expressed concern, perhaps because she feared that fraternization of this kind would undermine discipline.[39] Practices such as this lead one to qualify the conventional image of junior officers being separated from their men by an all but unbridgeable gulf. Despite the difference in pay rates and the nobility's growing class-consciousness the gap was often narrower than it might be in civilian life, where the relationship was one between master and serf.

Scattered data on officers' private incomes suggest that few had large estates —although no doubt their personal service records (*formulyarnye spiski*) do not tell the whole story.[40] Of 14 officers stationed in Moscow in 1764 who were in line for promotion, and whose records were therefore submitted to the governor, one who bore a princely title had 450 souls, three others had between 14 and 18 souls, and the remainder apparently had no property.[41] A century later, when the first systematic investigations were undertaken into officers' material conditions, using the same type of records, only 16 per cent were found to own land. The statistician responsible suggested that this figure ought to be doubled(!) to allow for deliberate understatement, so that not too

[35] Löwenstern, *Mémoires*, i. 25.
[36] Tarlé, *Campagne de Russie*, p. 115; Hansen, *Zwei Kriegsjahre*, p. 39.
[37] Von Stork, *Denkschrift*, p. 45.
[38] Drutsky-Sokolinsky, 'Biogr. zametka', pp. i–ii.
[39] Pishchevich, *Zhizn´*, p. 38; Vyazemsky, 'Zapiska', p. 20; Dubrovin, *Suvorov*, p. 9; cf. Eyler, 'Zapiski', p. 337.
[40] Zayonchkovsky, *Prav. apparat*, p. 11, has shown that this was true of the records of civil officials.
[41] Shchukin, *Sbornik*, vii. 375–9.

much should be made of it.[42] Cavalry officers were wealthier than their infantry counterparts, as one would expect.

In the eighteenth century the autocrat would still reward his or her meritorious servitors with grants of land and peasants, as Muscovite rulers had done. The best-known instances concerned men in privileged units who were close to the court, such as the grenadiers who hoisted the empress Elizabeth (1741–61) to the throne, or the troops from Gatchina whom Paul, on his accession, incorporated into the guards.[43] This archaic practice ceased under Alexander I, but both he and his successors continued to make lavish gifts of ornamental weapons, jewellery, or cash, and sometimes even paid off their officers' private debts. 'I consider it my duty to serve Him to the last drop of my blood', wrote N. I. Krivtsov to his mother in 1815, after the tsar had given him 25,000 roubles for this purpose.[44] In 1817 Martos, then a captain, was presented with a ring which he soon afterwards sold for 2,000 roubles.[45] I. A. Baratynsky, a favourite of Nicholas I, received an *annual* bonus of 2,000 silver roubles from 1834, which was doubled in 1846, and a lump sum of 4,300 roubles in 1845.[46] Another notable recipient of Imperial largesse was P. K. Essen, military governor of St. Petersburg from 1830 to 1843.[47] Such grants—and personal pensions, too—were often tied to the award of medals, which might be emblazoned with diamonds, or to membership of chivalric orders; these were of course matters that fell within the sovereign's prerogative.[48] Medals were also awarded to entire units. As the Polish critic Tański observed perceptively, 'ces sortes de récompenses collectives sont d'une bonne politique, elles entretiennent l'esprit de corps'.[49] The emperor's 'fount of honour' had a material aspect which meant a great deal to potential beneficiaries and helped to keep them loyal, even though the arbitrary way in which awards were often made might engender irritation and cynicism.[50] Curiously enough, the political implications of this largesse have yet to be studied. Presumably the prospect of royal favour affected the behaviour of senior officers more than it did that of their subordinates, but this is only a hypothesis.

Russian officers did not form a closed caste, but they were of course drawn overwhelmingly from the ranks of the privileged, as was the case in other

[42] L. Il'yashevich, 'Zhenatye ofitsery', *VS* 34 (1863), p. 422.

[43] For a routine instance, to a colonel who performed well against Pugachev (1777): Shchukin, *Sbornik*, i. 142–3; Manstein, *Zapiski*, p. 243; Chicherin *et al.*, *Istoriya Preobr. polka*, ii. 581; Volkonsky, 'Rasskazy', p. 186; Shil'der, *Pavel*, pp. 565 ff.

[44] *Shchukinskiy sbornik*, iii. 275.

[45] Martos, 'Zapiski', p. 534; cf. Denisov, 'Zapiski', p. 615; Dolgorukov, 'Otryvki', p. 326; Fabritsius, in *SVM* vii. 113, n. 1.   [46] *RBS* ii. 495.

[47] Shepelev, *Otmenennye istoriyey*, p. 34.

[48] *PSZ* xxiv. 17908 (5 Apr. 1797); Drutsky-Sokolinsky, 'Biogr. zametka', pp. viii–ix; Sazonov, 'Ordena', *VE* xvii. 143–5.   [49] Tański, *Tableau*, p. 176.

[50] Mosolov, 'Zapiski', p. 134; Modzalevsky (ed.), *Arkhiv Rayevskikh*, i. 98; Engel'gardt, *Zapiski*, pp. 122, 141.

armies at this time. Noble status conferred important advantages as regards entry into the officer corps and subsequent promotion prospects, and it also mattered a great deal which family one came from. Most officers of the period took this discrimination for granted and expected it to continue. The law provided that non-noble NCOs could be promoted after four, eight, or twelve years' service, according to their social origin: the three categories comprised respectively the sons of (non-noble) officers, clergy, and commoners.[51] Such individuals automatically became noblemen, although once they left the service their status was only that of personal, as distinct from hereditary, nobility. During Catherine's reign there seems to have been a trickle of under-privileged entrants, although no statistics are available. A. S. Pishchevich, who in the early 1790s served as a squadron commander in the Astrakhan´ Dragoon regiment, recalls in his memoirs that on leaving this unit, stationed on the distant Kuban´ line, he recommended his efficient sergeant-major, Z. N. Popov, for promotion; after a year's delay Popov was duly made an ensign and took up duty as regimental quarter-master.[52] In every case such decisions were taken by higher authority and were no mere formality, at least after 1796. Paul insisted that all his officers should be nobles, in this emulating his hero Frederick the Great.[53] Alexander I laid it down in 1803 that commoners who were promoted to officer rank should serve in (less prestigious) administrative capacities such as auditors or commissariat officials.[54] This ruling presented a problem, since there were far more qualified candidates than there were vacancies. A way out was found by giving those denied such promotion financial compensation, in the shape of double pay.[55] But at the same time the qualifying term was extended to 20 years for clerks and other auxiliary personnel, who were precisely those most likely to be literate and to have some administrative experience. Nicholas I made literacy an absolute requirement[56] but otherwise kept the system as it was (see ch. 14). Ex-commoners so promoted tended to identify strongly with the existing order, although in the long term their presence did represent a challenge to noble predominance. Their fellow officers referred to them contemptuously as 'bourbons',[57] but do not seem to have perceived them as a serious threat.

They were much more concerned about the influx of foreigners—many of whom were actually their non-Russian or non-Orthodox compatriots, above all Baltic Germans. This resentment went back to the reign of Peter I, who had appointed a large number of such officers to senior positions. In 1722 13 out of

---

[51] *PSZ* xvii. 12543 (14 Jan. 1766), I, § 2; von Hupel, *Beschreibung*, p. 100; Maslovsky, *Materialy*, i. 46.
[52] Pishchevich, *Zhizn´*, pp. 154–5.
[53] *PSZ* xxiv. 17534 (8 Nov. 1796), 17588 (29 Nov. 1796), V, §§ 2, 4, 7.
[54] *PSZ* xxviii. 20914 (27 Aug. 1803).
[55] *PSZ* xxx. 23009, 23378, 24015 (10 May 1808, Nov. 1808, Nov. 1809).
[56] *II PSZ* iii. 2198, 2311 (31 July, 29 Sept. 1828); v (i). 3686 (31 May 1830).
[57] Neizvestnyy, 'Za mnogo let', Feb. 1895, p. 123; 'Iz zametok starosluzhivogo', p. 295.

49 generals (26.5 per cent) were of non-Russian stock.[58] During the 1730s Anna Ivanovna, worried about the security of her regime after the tumultuous events surrounding her accession, encouraged the appointment of foreign officers, especially to the new guards regiments which she founded,[59] and one of them, Field-Marshal B. C. von Münnich (Minikh), became commander-in-chief. Nationalistic historians have often misrepresented her reign as a time when Russia groaned under an 'alien yoke'.[60] In doing so they have projected back into this era attitudes that did not become current until later in educated circles, as Russian national consciousness developed.[61] The empress Elizabeth helped to foster this myth by presenting her own rule as a return to the 'national' principles that had allegedly guided Peter the Great. In 1742 chauvinistic sentiment among guardsmen led to some violent incidents. Later the Seven Years War against Prussia naturally fostered antagonism towards officers of German background in Russian service.[62] However, one should be careful not to exaggerate the significance of this. The prevailing spirit was still cosmopolitan rather than nationalistic. The non-Russians did not form a homogeneous or isolated group in the army or in noble society generally. Many of them assimilated without much trouble into the Russian milieu, spoke the language, attended the same schools as Russians, and shared the same service ethos; religious differences were ceasing to be of much account.

Where there was hostility, this was often due to clumsy and irresponsible action by the autocrat. Thus on his accession Peter III arbitrarily changed sides in the war with Prussia, so nullifying the gains achieved at such cost and making it appear as if the heavy casualties had been suffered in vain. He also took a number of other measures that might have been expressly designed to offend his subjects. The military men among them were particularly incensed by the favouritism overtly shown toward the emperor's personal guard, recruited from his duchy of Holstein, and by the introduction of Prussian-style uniforms and drill manuals.

These grievances gave a powerful stimulus to the *coup d'état* of 28 June 1762. Yet this remained a purely dynastic affair, the work of a few dozen courtiers and guards officers. It would be wrong to think of Catherine II being hoisted to power on the crest of a wave of national sentiment—even though she was not averse to presenting herself in this light for propagandist effect. At the

---

[58] Peter I to Senate, 11 Jan. 1722, *SIRIO* xi (1873), 440–2. For data on the ethnic composition of the officer corps in 1700: Rabinovich, 'Formirovaniye', pp. 225, 228–9; and for contemporary opposition to non-natives: Pososhkov, *Kniga*, p. 255.

[59] Keep, 'Secret Chancellery', p. 179.

[60] For a more balanced evaluation see A. Lipski, 'The "Dark Era" of Anna Ivanovna: a Reexamination', *American Slavic and East European Review* 15 (1956), pp. 477–88.

[61] On the latter topic see H. Rogger, *National Consciousness in Eighteenth-Century Russia*, Cambridge (Mass.), 1960.

[62] On the 1742 incidents: Manstein, *Zapiski*, pp. 251, 254–6; Wich to Carteret, 24 Apr. 1742, *SIRIO* xci. 464; Chétardie to Amelot, 12 July 1742, *SIRIO* c. 280; F., 'O sostoyanii', p. 9; [Schwan(?)], *Merkwürdigkeiten*, pp. 115–17, 215–17.

beginning of her reign 41.3 per cent of 402 staff officers and above in active service whose names have been recorded were non-Russians. The proportion was highest among lieutenant-generals (63.7 per cent) and lowest among first majors (34.3 per cent)—not counting the field-marshals, all of whom were Russian.[63] Catherine tightened up the procedure for admitting candidates from abroad and made a point of filling the leading posts with Russians. Those who bore German names often gave the empire excellent service: F. W. Bauer, for example, was responsible for re-establishing the General Staff in 1770.[64] But it was around this time that a nationalistic mood began to make itself felt, for reasons that had less to do with the actual alien 'presence' than with the general trend of ideas. There was a natural reaction against the cosmopolitanism of Catherine's court.[65] In a memorandum which he evidently wrote 'for the drawer' Lieutenant-General S. M. Rzhevsky (1732–82) made 17 fundamental criticisms of conditions in the army. In the last of these he exclaimed: 'Why do we need such a multitude of foreign officers?' and went on to allege that many of them were professionally incompetent ('valets and teachers dressed up as servitors of the Crown') and that they oppressed worthy native sons, who were forced to take less prestigious jobs in the civil administration.[66] To this conservative spokesman the only rightful place for *dvoryane* was in the armed forces, occupying the positions of command to which he thought they were entitled by birth and tradition. A purge of foreigners, he might have added, would have also helped to alleviate the supernumerary problem. For chauvinistic arguments of this kind were most likely to appeal precisely to unemployed and semi-educated scions of the gentry—not least those adolescents whom one writer termed 'super-supernumeraries'.[67]

Most would-be officers had only a brief and unsystematic domestic education. A few attended regimental or garrison schools[68] or, later in the century, a private college set up at Shklov, near Smolensk, by Major-General S. G. Zorich, an amiable but notoriously unprincipled officer with court connections.[69] Another notable 'nursery' for future officers was the boarding school (*pension*) attached to Moscow University. The professional-military educational institutions for which Peter I had laid the groundwork were slow to develop. A major step forward was taken in 1732, when the so-called Nobles' Land Cadet Corps was established in St. Petersburg. It was modelled on the

[63] Lebedev, *Russkaya armiya*, pp. 4–69; conveniently tabulated by Duffy, *Russia's Military Way*, p. 147.

[64] *PSZ* xvi. 12014 (14 Jan. 1764); Duffy, *Russia's Military Way*, p. 146.

[65] Walicki, *History*, pp. 14–34; de Madariaga, *Catherine*, p. 540.

[66] Rzhevsky, 'O sostoyanii', p. 361.

[67] Von Hupel, *Beschreibung*, p. 43.

[68] Denisov, 'Zapiski', p. 22; Mosolov, 'Zapiski', p. 126.

[69] Glinka, *Zapiski*, p. 138; Pishchevich, *Zhizn'*, p. 28. On Zorich, whose real name was Nerazić, see Helbig, *Russische Günstlinge*, pp. 275–9; Tuchkov, *Zapiski*, pp. 150–7; *RBS* vii. 466–7.

Ritterakademien in Prussia and other European states. Münnich's role in its foundation was reflected in the provision that a quarter of its 360 places should be reserved for non-native (in effect, Baltic German) entrants, who were likely to be better prepared for the instruction offered. Students received a basic general education for the first two years and then concentrated on military-related subjects. On graduation they were accorded a rank (and a job) that supposedly reflected their scholastic proficiency. Most were assigned to the field forces as ensigns.[70] During the Seven Years War, at the behest of P. I. Shuvalov, similar facilities were set up for artillerymen and engineers and the Cadet Corps was expanded. The latter's budget, fixed at 63,000 roubles in the 1730s, had risen to 200,000 roubles half a century later, when the student body numbered 600. By the end of the eighteenth century, however, only 985 men had graduated out of the 2,186 admitted.[71]

During Catherine's reign 'foreigners' were limited to 100 places and some entrants were accepted from the under-privileged classes. In the curriculum the emphasis was shifted towards more general subjects, in an effort to broaden the pupils' intellectual horizons and to fit them for service outside the armed forces as well as within them. The atmosphere became more humane and culti-vated—indeed, almost excessively remote from reality, in the view of some contemporaries. S. N. Glinka, who studied at the college under Lieutenant-General F. Ye. fon-Angal't, director from 1786 to 1794 and noted for his broad-mindedness, remarks ironically that some of his fellow cadets 'who left after completing a classical education collapsed under the weight of their learning when they encountered ordinary officers; in despair they took to Bac-chus' cup and so were prematurely lost to the service'.[72] The instruction was coloured by Rousseauist ideas and cultivated elevated moral sentiments, including patriotism. One German observer thought that family bonds would suffer from the excessive importance attached to implanting 'love for the Fatherland'.[73]

It is hard to overestimate the psychological impact of the educational experi-ence which young men went through in the Cadet Corps and other select insti-tutions. Induction into them, as many memorialists record, was a traumatic experience soon eased by the forging of strong personal ties; these were often kept up after graduation and could help men in their subsequent careers. In this way informal associations were created which cut across divisions of rank and softened their asperities. F. N. Glinka, brother of the man just mentioned,

[70] *PSZ* viii. 5811 (28 Aug. 1731), xliii. 5881, 6050 (18 Nov. 1731, 12 May 1732); Stein, *Geschichte*, p. 107; Petrov, *Russkaya voyennaya sila*, ii. 153.

[71] Beskrovnyy, *Russkaya armiya*, p. 450. For the corps' budget in the late eighteenth century, see the relevant entry in Dolgorukov, *Khronika*.

[72] Glinka, *Zapiski*, p. 100; he adds that others were inspired to imitate the feats of classical heroes on the battlefield.

[73] Von Hupel, *Beschreibung*, p. 40. For a recent critical view of the instruction given in the corps, see M. J. Okenfuss, 'Education and Empire: School Reform in Enlightened Russia', *JGOE* 27 (1979), p. 59.

went to war in 1812 as a humble lieutenant and was greeted cordially on his first assignment by former associates who were now colonels; touched by their friendship, he looked back nostalgically to his schooldays, 'when each of us loved to contemplate how we might be useful to the Fatherland'.[74] This was more than just a loyalist platitude: the term *otechestvo* was coming to acquire an emotional nuance it had lacked before, and to vie with the established notion of personal loyalty to the autocrat. The studies which these officers undertook might not make for intellectual profundity or even impart knowledge of much immediate professional relevance; but they did lead them to question and debate contemporary issues, within the limits of propriety, and to develop a new sense of their own worth as individuals. The schools created nothing less than a new class: the military intelligentsia.

This useful term, recently coined by Soviet scholars, needs clarification. Taken literally, it refers to those officers who acquired, along with their education, broader cultural (and in some cases political) interests: a prefiguration, so to speak, of the later civilian intelligentsia. But such a definition does less than justice to those educated officers—perhaps the majority—who were preoccupied with professional matters and, if pressed, would have defined their political views as conservative and monarchist. Two points need to be made here. First, Russian officers preserved much of the traditional service mentality. Second, the critical attitude which some of them adopted was moral, not political, in origin. The cultural awakening of the late eighteenth century did not destroy the old gentry ideal of service, but rather gave it a new focus: the nation, as an entity distinct from the monarch. Naturally, these 'officer-intellectuals' took the view that they themselves were the best judges of the nation's true interests: it is an anachronism to speak of them as democrats, but they might with justice be termed nationalists. As nationalists they implicitly rejected conventional ideas about the legitimation of power and the natural order in society. Respect for hierarchy of rank remained, but the criterion was now personal merit rather than seniority, aristocratic lineage, wealth, or even the sovereign's accolade. Merit was assessed according to ethical criteria. Those who exercised power were expected to be responsible and virtuous, in their private as well as in their public lives. The virtuous man should be brave, truthful, honest, just—and above all, earnest; he was to abandon frivolous pleasure-seeking for an appreciation of the arts and sciences; to use the classical imagery in vogue, Minerva was to be the ally of Mars. One cultivated stoicism in the face of adversity and showed loyalty to kinsmen and comrades, but analysed their strengths and weaknesses of character as severely as one's own, and drew upon literary models for inspiration in shaping one's conduct.[75]

This credo may strike a modern social critic as naïve, but in the Russia of 1800 it was revolutionary. It explains why the tepid humanism of the young

[74] F. N. Glinka, *Pis'ma*, iv. 29.
[75] For stimulating elaborations of this theme, see Raeff, *Origins*, and Lotman, 'Dekabrist'.

Alexander I could be interpreted as heralding a new age of righteousness, or why young officers caught up in the new mood should condemn abuses within the army that had hitherto been taken for granted, such as building up a private fortune at the expense of one's men or subjecting them to gross physical cruelty. Corruption seems to have reached a peak in the last years of Catherine's reign, when a regimental commander could expect to make a profit of several thousands of roubles a year.[76] Physical violence was probably most widespread later, during the so-called Arakcheyev regime (ca. 1815–25), which will be discussed in ch. 12.

The reign of Paul exemplified many of the evils which the military intelligentsia would try to combat. Like his father, the emperor was a fervent admirer of Frederick the Great, but in seeking to emulate him succeeded in adopting only the externals of his by now somewhat tarnished military system. While still tsarevich, Paul set up a 2,400-strong élite force on his estate at Gatchina. Prussian methods of instruction were employed and many of the officers were of German stock. There was a striking parallel here not only with Peter III's Holsteiners but also with the young Peter I's private army over a century earlier. No sooner had Catherine died than these 'Gatchina men' (*Gatchintsy*) were brought to the capital, handsomely rewarded (for no apparent merit), and enrolled in the guards. Ostensibly, their task was to train their officer comrades in the intricacies of Prussian drill and tactics, so that they in turn might be sent out to instruct the line regiments. The revised army regulations which Paul lost no time in promulgating—predictably modelled on those of Frederick—were to be enforced throughout the Russian army. The brusque, tactless way in which these changes were effected caused a great deal of offence, as did the emperor's insistence that all officers on the active list, however senior in rank or feeble in health, should demonstrate proficiency in the new parade-ground skills to his own satisfaction.

The underlying purpose of all this was to assert the monarch's personal control over the armed forces by tightening discipline and enforcing strict hierarchical subordination. Paul doubted the loyalty of officers or functionaries who had enjoyed Imperial favour under the previous administration, and especially the military bureaucrats entrenched in the General Staff and War College. The former was dissolved and replaced by another, less effective, body; the War College survived, but with diminished powers. Instead the emperor relied heavily upon the inspectors. They were strengthened, notably by an infusion of *Gatchintsy*, and sent out to review the divisions in the field. They also supervised the regimental 'chiefs' (*shefy*), who were another Pauline innovation.[77] These officers, who held general's rank, were conceived as intermediaries between the autocrat and the units they nominally commanded,

---

[76] See Tuchkov, *Zapiski*, p. 9, Langeron, 'Russkaya armiya', 4, pp. 160–1, and sources cited in Keep, 'Pistol', pp. 313–14.

[77] *PSZ* xxiv. 17720 (9 Jan. 1797), xxv. 18470, 18725 (8 Apr., 31 Oct. 1798).

which were renamed after them. The abolition of territorial designations for regiments[78] was a reversion to seventeenth-century practice and led to much confusion, not least because there was a rapid turnover of personnel at senior level. The upper echelons of the officer corps were swollen by an influx of freshly-appointed generals—'promotion went very rapidly for those with strong nerves', one of them recalled later[79]—while a purge was conducted of those identified as protégés of Potemkin or P. A. Zubov, favourites of Catherine who were blamed for the 'slackness' that Paul detected in the armed forces. In all 340 generals and 2,261 staff officers were discharged during his reign. Many of them were soon rehabilitated, but such acts of monarchical clemency only confirmed the general impression that the country was in the grip of an irresponsible and arbitrary tyrant.[80]

From the start the emperor's military reforms met with antagonism. Nostalgia for the easy-going ways of the recent past was mingled with chauvinism and concern for one's personal career prospects. There was a good deal of sullen grumbling. Some critics poked fun at the ruler's foibles.[81] Others, more pertinently, invoked the law to protect their rights. A certain Captain Hoffmann, menaced with discharge because he had been kept in detention, which in his superiors' eyes 'dishonoured' him and rendered him unfit for further service, requested an inquiry 'according to the laws' and was duly vindicated by the Military Commission. Paul, however, overruled the commissioners and reprimanded them.[82] In what may be seen as a mass gesture of protest, no less then 3,500 officers, about one-quarter of the entire officer corps, tendered their resignation from the service during his reign.[83] We do not know what the normal rate of discharges was, but it is fair to assume that this action, coming on top of the purge, must have had a serious destabilizing effect.

Some officers, and many more soldiers, deserted. This called forth repressive measures reminiscent of those adopted by Peter I. Like the great tsar, but with less justification, Paul encouraged delation. In at least one case that has been documented he took action on the denunciation of a captain by a private.[84] Punishments became more severe, and were sometimes revised upwards when they were submitted to the sovereign for confirmation.[85] Even noblemen might be flogged, after revocation of their noble status in order not to infringe too blatantly the privilege accorded to them in 1785. All this engendered an atmosphere of fear and suspicion which led some officers to take to the path of conspiracy.

---

78 *PSZ* xxiv. 17587 (29 Nov. 1796), § 1; xxiv. 17720 (9 Jan. 1797).

79 Sablukov, 'Iz zapisok', col. 1903.

80 On Paul's military policies see now Duffy, *Russia's Military Way*, pp. 202–8; of the earlier literature the following are informative: Petrov, *Russkaya voyennaya sila*, ii. 242–65; Lebedev, 'Preobrazovateli'; Volkonsky, 'Rasskazy', pp. 179–87; Vorontsov, 'Zapiska', pp. 474–87.

81 Lebedev, 'Preobrazovateli', p. 583; Dzhedzhula, *Rossiya*, p. 183.

82 Vish, 'Telesnye nakazaniya', p. 141.	83 Beskrovnyy, *Russkaya armiya*, p. 433.

84 [Igel'strom], 'Arkhiv', p. 485; [Mosolov] 'Zapiski', p. 149. But he also ordered an officer to be dismissed for delation: Sokolovsky, 'Iz pyli arkhivov', p. 288.

85 Sokolovsky, 'Iz voyenno-ugolov. stariny'; Vish, 'Telesnye nakazaniya', 10, pp. 139–41.

This move from passive to active opposition may be said to mark the beginning of Russian Praetorianism as a social phenomenon. (The term 'Praetorians' was sometimes used, especially by foreign writers, in regard to the guards detachments involved in earlier palace *coups*, but incorrectly since these military interventions had next to no social resonance.) In 1797 several dozen officers, all of intermediate rank (captain to colonel), came together in an informal circle in which the central figure was A. M. Kakhovsky, a colonel who had been dismissed from a senior post and was living on his estate in Smolensk province.[86] The local gentry had long been exposed to Polish–Lithuanian cultural influences and had a certain tradition of autonomous action; they were also closely connected by kinship and service ties. Many officers in this circle belonged to the St. Petersburg Dragoon regiment, which was stationed in the area. Its chief, Major-General D. Tarakhanov, and his successor gave them what protection they could. Kakhovsky was also related to Yermolov, who already demonstrated the wilfulness and independence of spirit for which he would later, as a successful general, be renowned. Members of the group discussed the writings of the *philosophes* and ventilated freely their disgust at Paul's tyrannical regime. Some even spoke of regicide. The authorities learned of the circle's existence and in January 1799, after a lengthy investigation, at least 17 men were sentenced to terms of prison or exile. The sentences would have been stiffer but for the covert support which the conspirators obtained from highly-placed sympathizers, among them an official of the Secret Expedition. At this time patronage relationships were very important to all those threatened by persons in authority. S. I. Mayevsky, a junior officer discharged on political grounds, was aided by a General Essen, who appointed him to his staff.[87] M. T. Kachenovsky, later a noted scholar, but at this stage in his career a mere subaltern, was arrested for some minor fault but freed by the intercession of Lieutenant-General A. Z. Durasov.[88]

The dissidents naturally sought to give their movement an ideological colouring. They did not have to look far. Foreigners, especially of German stock, were prominent at court and in the army's upper ranks. It is by no means certain that Paul was more generously disposed towards them than Catherine had been, but this was irrelevant. So was the fact that native Russian officials shared the responsibility for some of the emperor's most disagreeable acts: Rostopchin, for instance, helped to edit the 'Prussian' military statute of November 1796. The aliens were an easy target for anyone wishing to discredit the ruling group.

This patriotic spirit found expression in a veritable cult of Suvorov. He came to be seen as embodying a 'national school' of martial arts diametrically opposed to that of the current military establishment. There was some

[86] Snytko, 'Novye materialy'; Dzhedzhula, *Rossiya*, pp. 184–5.

[87] Mayevsky, 'Moy vek', p. 132.

[88] Glinka, *Zapiski*, p. 173; *RBS* viii. 577; cf. the experiences of Mosolov, who lacked such a patron, recounted in his 'Zapiski', pp. 149–54.

substance to this view—the ageing field-marshal did not hide his contempt for the new army regulations and was soon banished to his estate—but his partisans, who needed an inspirational figure as leader, absolutized the difference between him and his critics. In so doing they helped to build up a myth which has exercised a lasting influence on Russian military historiography and has only recently been called in question.[89] Involuntarily Suvorov became a focus for disaffected officers, eighteen of whom, on resigning their commissions, accompanied the fallen field-marshal to his estate, where they were later arrested as a security risk.[90] Colonel Kakhovsky, who had served on Suvorov's staff, is said to have urged him to effect a *coup*, a suggestion which he reportedly turned down out of humanitarian considerations. The story is uncorroborated[91] and does not ring true.

Instead Suvorov took the course followed by many of his fellow officers of lower rank: recalled to active duty in 1799, he gladly left the oppressive atmosphere of his homeland for the battlefields of central Europe, where he could expect to win further laurels. His exploits in the campaign of 1799–1800—the Adda, Novi, and the epic crossing of the Alps—raised his prestige to even greater heights, but on his return, physically ailing, he was in no position to lead the dissidents even had he wanted to. Their nationalistic spirit was reinforced by the disappointing performance of Russia's Austrian ally during the campaign, and by Paul's astonishing turn towards an accommodation with Bonaparte.[92]

The general malaise found expression in the formation of a new conspiratorial network. Unlike its predecessor, this drew its support primarily from guards officers stationed in St. Petersburg and was headed by several highly-placed dignitaries. They included N. P. Panin, who held major-general's rank but was a civilian (and diplomat), and above all General P. A. von der Pahlen (Palen), who as military governor of St. Petersburg had charge of security matters in the capital. According to N. A. Sablukov, a colonel in the Horse Guards loyal to Paul, 188 persons were privy to the plot (in its second phase).[93] Sixty-eight individuals have been positively identified: 50 of them were in the armed forces, all but six in the guards.[94] The majority—34 of the 61 whose age is known—were young men in their 'teens or twenties; at least 20 are thought to have harboured some personal grudge against the tsar.

[89] Duffy, *Russia's Military Way*, p. 234, notes justly that both Suvorov and his predecessor Münnich were 'creative members of the cosmopolitan European military community'.

[90] *RBS* xx. 59.

[91] It originated with Yermolov, whose memoir has yet to be published in full: Snytko, 'Novye materialy', p. 112.

[92] For a recent analysis of this policy switch which demonstrates its rationality, see O. Feldbaek, 'The Foreign Policy of Tsar Paul I, 1800–1: an Interpretation', *JGOE* 30 (1982), pp. 16–36.

[93] 'Zapiski', p. 87; cf. [Bartenev] 'Graf Panin', p. 409.

[94] Kenney, 'Politics of Assassination', pp. 128–31; cf. also Zubow, *Paul I*, pp. 314–15. For an early list: M. A. Fon-Vizin, 'Obozreniye proyavleniy politicheskoy zhizni v Rossii' [1835], in Semevsky *et al.*, *Obshchestvenniya dvizheniya*, i. 133.

Among the plotters were the generals in command of the Preobrazhensky and Semenovsky regiments (P. A. Talyzin, L.(?) I. Depreradovich), the Horse Guards (F. P. Uvarov), and the Keksgol'm infantry regiment (N. I. Verderevsky), to name but the most prestigious units. A recent student of the *coup* observes that those involved in it were 'the cream of the officer corps'.[95]

Paul got wind of what was afoot and to avoid exposure the conspirators had to act in haste. On the night of 11 March 1801 they sent a posse of guardsmen to the fortress-like Mikhaylovsky Palace in order to depose the emperor. In what seems to have been an unpremeditated act he was assassinated.

Was this no more than another palace revolution? The participants' elevated social status and their lack of a political programme might suggest as much, yet this conclusion would be too simple. The number of activists was greater than in the *coups* of 1725–62, and they had the backing of a movement of opinion in educated society, not least among the military intelligentsia. Young officers greeted the news of Paul's demise—officially but implausibly attributed to a fit of apoplexy—with enthusiasm. Two of the conspirators, the brothers Generals Platon and Valerian Zubov, went to the lengths of securing control of the two cadet corps, and made use of the informal links among the students for their own political purposes.[96]

On the other hand the affair cannot confidently be labelled 'Praetorian' since those who carried it out wanted *less*, not more, military intervention in public life. They stood for a return to normality, to the leisurely ways of government characteristic of Catherine's last years. In this sense the *coup* was a retrograde phenomenon. On social issues its partisans were conservative: they do not seem to have thought of improving the lot of the underprivileged. Their constitutional ideas were vague. They intended to establish a regency council under Grand Duke Alexander (who was privy to their plans), and a document to this effect was prepared by D. P. Troshchinsky, a civilian member of the group. They did not question the principle of monarchy, or even autocracy. Another paradox is that they had to soft-pedal their nationalistic sentiments, since a vital role in the plot was played by von der Pahlen, a Baltic German aristocrat. Opposition to Paul's military policies occupied a significant place in their thinking, but blended in with other concerns which at the time seemed even more important. The conspirators acted largely from motives of self-preservation, and may have wanted to forestall the emergence of a broader movement, within the officer corps and educated society generally, which they feared might get out of control.

[95] Warner, 'Political Opposition', p. 160.   [96] Ibid., p. 159.

11

THE PRAETORIAN OPTION

ON his accession Alexander I introduced a number of measures designed to heal the breach that had begun to open between government and 'society'.[1] The army was among the beneficiaries of this thaw. Officers who had been discharged were transferred to the retired list, and so in effect rehabilitated.[2] One edict granted a formal pardon to 115 persons of rank who had been kept under surveillance or arrested by the Secret Expedition; of these 58 were officers or ex-officers, and of the 41 commoners 7 were soldiers.[3] Some of Paul's unpopular changes to military uniform were countermanded. Characteristically, his equally unpopular army regulations remained in force until 1811–12, when they were quietly superseded rather than annulled. Regiments got their old territorial names back. Something was done to improve the supply system, and educational facilities were expanded.[4] Still more important, new pay scales were announced, which brought a colonel's salary from 900 to 1,040–1,250 roubles a year, according to the arm of service. Captains received a minimum increase of 17.7 per cent and ensigns one of 18.0 per cent—in paper money, the value of which was rising at this time.[5] Officers' future material prospects were also catered for. In 1803 the government introduced a pay-related pension scheme, with benefits proportionate to length of service.[6] Last but not least, the military build-up, which between 1802 and 1805 added about 50,000 men to the army's strength, provided extra vacancies for supernumerary officers and so eased their discontents.

All this—and the burgeoning national consciousness—helps to explain why the army responded with apparent relish to the war of the Third Coalition. The mood changed after Austerlitz, a defeat for which the tsar bore some of the responsibility. There was once again understandable dissatisfaction at the performance of Russia's central European allies, first Austria and then Prussia. The grim winter war of 1806–7 sparked a lively debate about strategic issues, in which the qualifications of individual leaders, especially the commander-in-chief L. L. Bennigsen (who was German-born), were freely called into question.

---

[1] McConnell, 'Alexander I's Hundred Days'.

[2] *PSZ* xxvi. 19782 (13 Mar. 1801).

[3] *PSZ* xxvi. 19784 (15 Mar. 1801).

[4] *PSZ* xxvi. 19809, 19826 (31 Mar., 9 Apr. 1801), xxvii. 20224 (9 Apr. 1802); Stein, *Geschichte*, pp. 232, 246.

[5] *PSZ* xxvi. 19926 (24 June 1801); Stein, *Geschichte*, p. 244; Petrov, *Russkaya voyennaya sila*, ii. 262.

[6] *PSZ* xxvii. 20631, 20770 (23 Feb., 21 May 1803); cf. Solov'yev, 'O pensiyakh', p. 304.

Those officers who were able to maintain contact with kinsmen or friends in the capital cities shared their sense of outrage at the treaty of Tilsit, and again the tsar took much of the blame.[7]

In the noble *fronde* of 1807–12 concern over the economic effects of Napoleon's Continental System merged with distrust of the bureaucratic spirit behind Speransky's reforms. It was basically a civilian phenomenon, for two main reasons. First, the armed forces were kept busy fighting Turks, Persians, and Swedes, and in 1809 also had to march about in a mock war with the Austrians; at one moment four campaigns were in progress simultaneously. Officers in the field were unable to follow closely events or rumours in distant St. Petersburg. Second, there was a high rate of intake into their ranks during these years, both to make up for losses and to command the new units that were constantly being formed.[8] By 1812 there were about 2,000 more officers on strength than there had been nine years earlier.[9] Some of the younger men were channelled into the expanding network of military schools. The best known of these, called the 'Noblemen's regiment', was founded in 1807. Young *dvoryane* flocked to join it; by 1812 it had 2,000, and three years later 3,000, cadets who on graduation automatically received ensign rank.[10] Cadet schools were also opened in such provincial towns as Tambov and Tula.[11] In these 'stick academies' life was very tough and there was little opportunity for political scheming, but they probably did have some impact on the pupils' minds.

The more privileged strata of the nobility had better educational prospects. The Page Corps (founded in 1802) and the celebrated lyceum at Tsarskoye Selo (1811) prepared men for both the civil and military branches of state service. Would-be officers could also attend a training institution known as the Column-Leaders' Corps, set up in 1811 as a private venture, and there were several other specialized schools.[12] Here, too, the cadets suffered a good deal of material hardship and discipline was enforced with rod and fist. Nevertheless they developed a sense of fellowship which helped them to withstand these trials and encouraged solidarity in the face of acts of injustice. The first known instance of this dates from 1813, when a popular cadet in the Page Corps name Arsen'yev, abetted by several comrades, resisted 'execution' (as a public flogging was termed). The affair was judged sufficiently serious to be referred to the tsar, who decided that the alleged ring-leader should receive 30 lashes of the whip.[13]

---

[7] Shil'der, *Aleksandr I*, ii. 168–70, 209–11; Pypin, *Obshchestvennoye dvizheniye*, pp. 122–3; Predtechensky, *Ocherki*, pp. 217–22.

[8] For the expansion see Stein, *Geschichte*, pp. 251–2, 258, 261, 267, 281; Prokof'yev, *Bor'ba*, p. 48.

[9] Beskrovnyy, *Potentsial*, p. 81.

[10] Gol'mdorf, 'Dvoryanskiy polk', pp. 797–8.

[11] Beskrovnyy, *Potentsial*, p. 124.

[12] Nechkina, *Dvizheniye*, i. 102, 443; Beskrovnyy, *Potentsial*, pp. 126, 130.

[13] Gangeblov, 'Yeshche iz vospominaniy', p. 188; cf. Venediktov, 'Za 60 let', pp. 260, 270; Skaryatin, 'Iz vospom. molodosti', pp. 21–2; Kolokol'tsov, 'Preobrazh. polk', p. 284.

The schools also stimulated a professional spirit among their more successful pupils, who after they had graduated naturally sought to update their knowledge and to spread it among their less well-endowed fellow-officers. In 1809 M. A. Fon-Vizin, a lieutenant in the Izmaylovsky guards regiment (and a nephew of the celebrated writer), helped to set up an informal circle to study military history. The group included Major P. A. Rakhmanov, of the (substitute) General Staff, a remarkable mathematician who founded at his own expense Russia's first military periodical, *Voyennyy zhurnal*. This published articles with a patriotic emphasis on current and historical themes. Not only Suvorov and Potemkin were singled out for praise, but even the tenth-century Prince Svyatoslav, portrayed as 'the first Russian hero in name and deed'.[14] The implication here was that the 'national school' had developed strategic and tactical doctrines that were superior to those of aliens. According to one participant in these gatherings, they discussed the democracy of ancient Athens in a manner too free for the taste of their regimental commander, who packed them off to serve in war-torn Finland.[15] Officers such as these had no subversive intent, but their superiors, who looked on their activities with ill-concealed suspicion and harassed them, accelerated the drift towards political opposition. The episode was a harbinger of what would become almost commonplace after the Patriotic War of 1812 and its sequel.

By this time a growing minority of Russian officers spent their leisure moments in more cultured fashion than had been customary hitherto. Already in the 1790s the traditional pastimes—carousing, gambling, and pursuing the fair sex—no longer seemed fitting to men of honour, who instead patronized the theatre or, if stationed in some dismal provincial garrison town, put on amateur dramatic productions themselves.[16] Around 1793 S. A. Tuchkov, then a subaltern in Moscow, joined a literary and cultural association, the 'Free Russian Society for the Propagation of the Sciences'; when posted to the capital he was admitted to a similar group.[17] Such activities were scarcely possible under Paul, but when a new wind began to blow after 1801 they regained popularity. In 1809–11 Muromtsev, a subaltern in the Izmaylovsky regiment, went to the theatre 'almost every Sunday' and, through a dramatist friend with whom he shared an apartment, was introduced to the Russian Literary Assembly, where he heard Krylov read his fables. The group met at the house, 'not far from our barracks', of the esteemed poet (and former minister) G. R. Derzhavin, who had himself spent 15 years in the army.[18]

When such officers went off to fight in 1812 they tried to sustain an interest in the finer things of life, so far as front-line conditions allowed. Such 'cultured' pursuits gave them spiritual strength when they were confronted

---

14 Prokof'yev, *Bor'ba*, pp. 50–1; *RBS* xv. 512–17.

15 Muromtsev, 'Vospominaniya', p. 71; Semevsky, 'Fon-Vizin', p. 2.

16 Pishchevich, *Zhizn'*, pp. 87, 133; Eyler, 'Zapiski', p. 335.

17 Tuchkov, *Zapiski*, pp. 19–20, 43.

18 Muromtsev, 'Vospominaniya', pp. 69, 81; on Derzhavin, see Wortman, *Legal Consciousness*, p. 98.

with death and devastation on an unprecedented scale—on Russian soil, invaded from the west for the first time in a century. The younger Glinka notes that of an evening he and his comrades would gather at the billet either of General M. A. Miloradovich or of their colonel 'in order to read, draw, talk, and joke'; these impromptu soirées were 'distinguished by our commander's kindliness and by an agreeable informality'.[19] Active service attenuated the rigid social conventions that normally governed communication between officers of different rank. A. I. Antonovsky, a subaltern in the 26th Chasseurs, found it surprisingly easy to make contact with people in other units, who would sometimes share their last crumbs with a stranger; after experiencing one such act of charity, he vowed that he would never forget 'this most noble trait'.[20]

The recently published diary of another lieutenant, A.V. Chicherin of the Semenovsky regiment, is particularly revealing on the *mentalité* of the military intelligentsia during the war. Illustrated with sketches from his own pen, it has an authenticity lacking in more sophisticated 'literary' accounts. The author was killed in action at the age of 20, so fulfilling his ambition 'to give my life for the heart of my Fatherland'.[21] The young Chicherin's ardent patriotism is accompanied by an equally sincere humanistic sentiment, expressed in such simple but moving phrases as 'man is born to live among people like himself', or that it is everyone's duty 'to make others happy' and 'to try to be useful'.[22] A casual mention of the social contract reveals the ultimate source of these ideas. Our diarist is familiar with Rousseau and carries Swift's *Gulliver's Travels* in his knapsack. His reading leads him to reflect on the contrasting destinies of officers and men in the ranks. Initially he tries to convince himself that social privilege does have some rational basis in natural disparities of character; but a few days later, struck by the sight of his soldiers trying to catch some sleep in a waterlogged bivouac, he exclaims pathetically: 'if only I could share with them the comforts I enjoy!'[23] Later he makes a practice of visiting the wounded, doing his best to cheer them, and handing out what little food or money he can spare. The men's gratitude reinforces his sentiments of charity and paternalistic concern.[24]

Of particular interest is Chicherin's emotional response to the horrors of warfare. On first perceiving soldiers dying without any medical care, he wants 'to turn aside, perhaps with a sigh, and seize the least excuse to forget'; but not long afterwards he finds that he cannot get used to the heaps of frozen corpses and begins to question the morality of war.[25] Other writers, too, initially seemed content with an aesthetic concern for their own sensibilities; but as time passed they developed compassion for the innocent victims of the struggle, respect for

[19] Glinka, *Pis'ma*, iv. 241–2.
[20] Antonovsky, 'Zapiski', p. 45.
[21] Chicherin, *Dnevnik*, p. 14.
[22] Ibid., pp. 35–6.
[23] Ibid., pp. 21, 26.
[24] Ibid., pp. 133–6.
[25] Ibid., pp. 48, 67, 130.

those who tried to relieve suffering, and contempt for those on either side who committed deliberate acts of barbarism.[26]

Chicherin discusses freely the merits of individual commanders, but retains an implicit faith in the monarch. There is no hint in his diary of any critical evaluation of the empire's institutions. He was surely not alone in responding to his experiences on an ethical rather than a political plane. Did these officers' attitudes change once they had crossed the Russian border into Poland, Germany, and finally France? The question is controversial, as we have noted, and it is worth stressing the point that Russian officers were not entirely strangers to central Europe. Their experience went back at least as far as the Seven Years War; later many had a chance to savour foreign amenities in occupied Poland or in the Danubian principalities. Often their impressions had been unfavourable, due in part to national or religious prejudice, but with time attitudes changed. In 1805 F. N. Glinka described enthusiastically the prosperity of the Austrian countryside on seeing it for the first time, and noted the 'free rights' enjoyed by merchants and peasants.[27]

In 1813 Chicherin was unimpressed by Poland ('the peasants here', he wrote, 'live together with their cattle . . . [and] everything speaks of poverty and ignorance'), but the German states presented a more agreeable picture. The towns were well built, with public fountains decorating the squares. Even the poorest peasants had horses fit to draw a carriage; and our diarist recognized that this relative prosperity had something to do with the superior political and administrative arrangements under which they lived.[28] At Bunzlau he came across a throng of cheerful, well-dressed farmers standing in front of the town-hall, and to his surprise discovered that they were there in order to pay their taxes. And yet

the love I bear my fatherland burns like a pure flame, elevating my heart. . . . Here we continually see the achievements of civilization, for they are evident in everything—in the manner of tilling the fields, building houses, and in [popular] customs—yet never, not even for a minute, would I wish to settle under an alien sky, in a land other than that where I was born and where my forefathers were laid to rest.[29]

Ensign Nikita Murav'yev adopted a haughty attitude towards the burghers of Hamburg whom he met, since they seemed to him unduly concerned with the prompt payment of bills and similar mundane matters.[30]

Thus Germany produced a complex and contradictory impact on the minds of the more sensitive Russian officers. What they saw there elicited respect, even admiration, and yet their prevailing emotions were shame and envy. The

---

[26] Murav'yev[-Karsky] 'Zapiski', *RA* 4 (1886), p. 49, 5 (1886), p. 97; Löwenstern, *Mémoires*, i. 328–9; Antonovsky, 'Zapiski', p. 200.

[27] Glinka, *Pis'ma*, i. 6, 19, 54, 179.

[28] Chicherin, *Dnevnik*, pp. 104, 108, 176–7, 264 (his anti-Polish sentiments may derive from injuries suffered by his family during Kosciuszko's revolt).

[29] Ibid., pp. 155, 177.

[30] Druzhinin, *Murav'yev*, p. 71.

experience augmented their malaise about the direction of affairs at home without offering a satisfactory model for change. This mood was later to be given a philosophical foundation by the intellectuals of the 'marvellous decade' (1838–48), who became obsessed with Russia's backwardness *vis-à-vis* 'the West'. The problem was not perceived in such terms by the men of 1813–14, who saw themselves as heroes liberating Napoleon's unwilling subjects from a hateful tyranny.

France, too, produced a preponderantly negative impression, if one may go by the published sources. Memories of earlier cultural ties had receded, and there was now an understandable antagonism towards a country that was associated mainly with revolution, imperial expansion, and invasion by the Grande Armée. 'Paris is a nice town', wrote one officer; 'it is a bit like Moscow, [which] is smaller but more populous. There a family has an entire house, whereas in Paris one finds a family behind each window. In short, there's nothing to be envious about except perhaps the ladies [*madamy*].'[31] What impressed this writer most was the zoo, which boasted 'an enormous elephant'. Another observer, probably of higher rank, who like many *dvoryane* had learned French in his youth from a private tutor, recorded opinions that were only a little more favourable. On crossing the border he found the inhabitants dirty, impoverished, and ignorant. 'Where is that *douce France* of which our tutors had told us, I wondered.' Perhaps it lay ahead, in the capital? But Paris disappointed him too: life was expensive and the people unfriendly. As a professional soldier he was more taken by the Artillery Museum and the Invalides than the Louvre, where he inspected the paintings from a sense of duty rather than for pleasure.[32] Likewise Krivtsov, who was introduced to Chateaubriand, Madame de Staël, and other leading celebrities, found the city 'poor, dirty, and unbearable' but then went on to criticize the excess of luxury.[33] His attitude might be illogical, but it was quite understandable psychologically: the visitors from the east poured scorn on the very temptations they found hard to resist and sought to escape: 'the city is very grand, rich, and jolly, but I would much rather leave it as soon as I can and, praise be to God, come home'.[34]

Admittedly, letters to relatives written by survivors of an arduous campaign cannot tell the whole truth. In a more positive vein S. I. Mayevsky later declared that his education had not really begun until, aged 33, he arrived in the French capital, for it was there that he learned to appreciate the finer things of life.[35] However, he was of Polish extraction—and did not put pen to paper until 1831, by which time attitudes towards the West were changing. Even less valid as evidence is the oft-cited remark by the 'Decembrist' I. D.

---

[31] I. Ikonnikov to I. S., 24 Apr. 1814, in *Shchukinskiy sbornik*, i. 411.
[32] Murav'yev[-Karsky], 'Zapiski', pp. 110–17.
[33] *Shchukinskiy sbornik*, iii. 273.
[34] I. Danilov to his wife, 1. Apr. 1814, in ibid., iii. 297.
[35] Mayevsky, 'Moy vek', p. 282.

Yakushkin to the effect that 'a year in Germany, followed by several months in Paris, could not but change the views of any thinking Russian youth: in such a tremendous environment each of us matured a bit'.[36] This was written in 1854.

Some Russian officers stayed on in the small occupation force that was stationed in France from 1815 to 1818. These troops were kept in isolation from the French public, to minimize the risk of intellectual contagion, but the experiences which its officers gained may have been more important in shaping opinion. The commander, Lieutenant-General M. S. Vorontsov, was in practice allowed considerable autonomy. He set up schools at which soldiers were taught to read and write by the then fashionable 'Lancastrian method' (mutual instruction on a voluntary basis). He also ordered officers under his command to abstain from inflicting corporal punishment.[37] This humanitarian move was not solely due to Vorontsov's own relatively enlightened views: public floggings, it was realized, would impair Russia's standing in Western eyes. However, the experiment worked well, and when these men and their officers returned home they suffered a rude shock.

It was generally expected that with the coming of peace the tsar would once again take up the cause of reform, so consolidating the national unity that had led Russia to victory. These hopes were quickly shattered. Instead Alexander I, now in a mystical mood and obsessed with the threat of revolution, opted for reactionary policies at home and abroad. The educated public became disenchanted. So long as the war was in progress the emperor's domestic critics had suppressed their doubts about the quality of his leadership, but now the *fronde* reappeared with new vigour. The army's prestige had never stood higher, and discontented civilians began to eye it as a potential agency for change. Suggestions in this vein were well received by many thoughtful officers, who could resume contact with civilian relatives or acquaintances and had ample opportunity to form their own opinion of the country's plight. Few of them as yet envisaged political action, but they were readier than before to discuss their grievances, and from this it was but a step to the setting up of informal organizations.

The officers' approach to broader issues was heavily coloured by their professional discontents. To men who had proved in action their mastery of the military art it was humiliating that they should now be required to adhere pedantically to every detail of army regulations. The authorities placed more emphasis than ever on turnout and drill, almost as if they hoped to quash dissent by busying the troops with parade-ground exercises. As before, those who failed to meet these exacting standards were subjected to harsh and arbitrary disciplinary measures. All these excesses were attributed, rightly or wrongly, to

[36] Yakushkin, *Zapiski*, p. 8; cf. Fon-Vizin in Semevsky *et al.*, *Obshchestvenniya dvizheniya*, i. 182–3, written in the 1830s.
[37] Zavalishin, *Zapiski*, p. 109. Vorontsov's regulations were first published in *VS* 5 (1859), 2, pp. 495–502, 5, pp. 75–8. On Lancastrian schools see J. C. Zacek in *SEER* 45 (1967), pp. 343–68.

the excessive influence wielded by Alexander's favourite, A. A. Arakcheyev. The latter's remarkable unpopularity was due not merely to his personal short-comings, or even to his exceptional position: he was also seen as an administrator, a 'chair-borne general' who had failed to distinguish himself during the war yet presumed to bully those who had. In truth Arakcheyev became something of a scapegoat. Although ethnically Russian, he was a 'Gatchina man' and so could readily be identified with the aliens in the army's upper echelons (and at court) who were an obvious target for nationalistic resentment. Critics also held that the tsar was too generous towards his non-Russian (especially Polish) subjects, and that he spent too much time on European affairs, which necessitated his presence abroad, instead of settling the serious problems that beset his own long-suffering people.[38]

In this way the army's injured pride merged with a now greatly enhanced Great Russian national consciousness. This sentiment seems to have been more important than the constitutionalism and the concern for social reform that were stressed by earlier historians, particularly those who wrote in the late Imperial era. 'Decembrism' was less a political ideology than a state of mind. This fact was reflected in its chequered organizational history. We shall consider this in the light of the participants' military situation and experience.

The first groups to take shape were officers' artels, that is, associations of friends in the same unit who would share living expenses and enjoy each other's company when the day's work was done. One of these, in the Izmaylovsky guards regiment, is said to have possessed a well-stocked library (presumably distinct from that of the unit—for several guards regiments now possessed such facilities).[39] Another artel, in the Semenovsky regiment, at one time had as many as 20 members.[40] A third group, which developed out of this one, emerged in 1814 among officers of the General Staff. It acquired a high-sounding name, the 'Holy Artel', which reflected its members' masonic connections. It included at least two, and perhaps three, brothers: sons of a remarkable but little-studied individual, Major-General Nikolay Nikolayevich Murav´yev (1768–1840). It was he who founded the Column-Leaders' school referred to above. He did so with the aid of two other senior members of his clan: Mikhail Nikitich Murav´yev (1757–1807), who as Alexander I's ex-tutor and a former curator of Moscow University had considerable leeway in educational matters, and Nikolay Mikhaylovich Murav´yev, who offered the premises. No less than 24 future 'Decembrists' attended this school, among them three of Nikolay Nikolayevich's four sons (Aleksandr, Nikolay, and

---

[38] Shil´der, *Aleksandr I*, iv. 92–6; McConnell, *Alexander I*, p. 153; N. M. Karamzin, 'Opinion of a Russian Citizen' (1819), translated in J. L. Black, *Essays on Karamzin*, The Hague and Paris, 1975, pp. 193–6.

[39] Gangeblov, 'Kak ya popal', p. 190; Zavalishin, *Zapiski*, p. 50; for the library in the guards general staff, set up by Sipyagin: D[ubrovin], 'Vel. Knyaz´,' p. 102.

[40] Yakushkin, *Zapiski*, p. 9; Nechkina, 'Svyashch. artel´', p. 166; id., *Dvizheniye*, i. 121.

Mikhail) and Nikita, son of Mikhail Nikitich.[41] The significance of these apparently obscure genealogical details will become evident shortly.

In November 1816 Aleksandr and Mikhail, respectively a lieutenant-colonel and captain (?) in the guards, obtained the tsar's permission to set up in the General Staff, where they were both employed, an organization to promote military education—the cause with which their family, like Fon-Vizin's circle before it, had been so closely identified. Known as the 'Society of Military Men Who Love Science and Literature' (pompous titles were in vogue), it resumed publication of *Voyennyy zhurnal* with F. N. Glinka as editor. In the first year of operation its activities cost the sizeable sum of 55,000 roubles[42]—presumably borne, at least in part, by the Treasury. Aleksandr Murav´yev seems to have looked on this legal organization as useful cover for a clandestine one which came into existence about this time. Paradoxically, the latter is better known to historians than the former. It is generally referred to as the 'Union of Salvation' (*Soyuz spaseniya*), although its unwieldy alternative title, the 'Society of True and Loyal Sons of the Fatherland', gives a better idea of its ideological tone. It had some 30 members, all guards officers, at its peak. They took an oath to observe its statute, a document of which the text has not survived; it was evidently patterned on the masonic model and contained programmatic references to constitutional government and the ending of serfdom. When the Guards Corps moved to Moscow for several months in August 1817, Aleksandr Murav´yev, who conveniently was quartermaster, arranged to secure quarters where members of the group could meet and exchange ideas. Differences soon arose. Aleksandr Murav´yev himself favoured a military *coup*, but neither this course nor the assassination of the tsar, which was also mooted, won general support. The moderates—among them Mikhail Murav´yev—felt that acts of terrorism would discredit their enterprise. They favoured instead a covert propaganda campaign among their fellow officers and their civilian associates. Partly because of these tensions, and partly for security reasons, it was decided to disband the organization and to prepare a new statute which would serve as a rallying-point for those who wished to continue clandestine activity.[43]

The radicals set the tone in the new society, which came into being early in 1818. The 'Union of (Public) Welfare' (*Soyuz [obshchestvennogo] blagodenstviya*: again there is some ambiguity about its title) ostensibly had cultural and charitable rather than political aims, but most of its leaders saw this simply as

---

[41] Druzhinin, *Murav´yev*, p. 59; Nechkina, *Dvizheniye*, i. 102–3, 443; id. (ed.), I. S. Kalantyrskaya *et al.* (comps.), *Iz epistolyarnogo nasledstva dekabristov: pis´ma k N. N. Murav´yev-Karskomu*, i., Moscow, 1975, which contains letters exchanged by members of this clan. The relatively liberal atmosphere of the Column-Leaders' school is described by Basargin, *Zapiski*, pp. 245–76.

[42] Prokof´yev, *Bor´ba*, pp. 274–6; Gabayev, 'Gvardiya', p. 161; Beskrovnyy, *Potentsial*, p. 217.

[43] Yakushkin, *Zapiski*, pp. 13–14; Nechkina, 'Soyuz spaseniya' and *Dvizheniye*, i. 141–84; Druzhinin, *Murav´yev*, p. 92; Mazour, *First Russ. Revol.*, pp. 66, 69; Luciani, *Société*, p. 164.

a *ruse de guerre*, designed to throw enemies off the scent and to assuage the misgivings of neophytes. Once associated with the society, initiates could gradually be familiarized with its ulterior purposes and, if they accepted them, be given positions of responsibility. The new statute, modelled on that of the German *Tugendbund*, provided for a directing nucleus, or core organization, called the *Korennyy sovet*. The significant point about the elaborate hierarchical structure of the society is that it was designed to ensure that power remained in the founders' hands. It held little promise of democratic control.[44] Such principles, or the lack thereof, would prove attractive to later generations of Russian revolutionaries as well.

In the more proximate future it set the pattern for both the regional societies to which the Union of (Public) Welfare gave way in 1821, after another bogus dissolution. By this time some 200 individuals, mainly guards officers, are thought to have been associated with the organization. The radical leaders decided that the time had come to purge it of those who showed vacillating tendencies.[45] The latter predominated in St. Petersburg, whereas the radicals held sway among the 'southerners', whose most active cell was at Tul'chin (Podolia province), headquarters of the Second Army.

Before examining the consequences of this split, we may pause to consider certain factors that vitally affected the operations of all clandestine groups during this period. The first is the key role played by highly-placed 'patrons'. The publication of *Voyennyy zhurnal* was made possible by General N. M. Sipyagin, the chief of staff, who gave the enterprise his blessing. A professional soldier to his finger-tips, Sipyagin was promoted with unusual speed, rising from captain to major-general within a mere two years, when he was in his late twenties. This rapid ascent may help to account for his quasi-liberal views, for which he was posted away from the general staff in 1819. (He was succeeded by two noted 'hard-liners': A. Kh. Benkendorf, later head of Nicholas I's gendarmes, and then P. F. Zheltukhin.) Sipyagin had a genuine interest in military education—after his dismissal from the staff he set up an officers' school at his own expense—and evidently sympathized with what his subordinates were doing, although he did not identify himself with them and it is not clear how much he even knew, or wanted to know, about their clandestine activities.[46] Another patron was Ya. A. Potemkin (1778–1831), a distant relative of the field-marshal, who was both an adjutant to the tsar and commanding officer of the Semenovsky guards regiment until 1819, when his political reliability came under suspicion and, like Sipyagin, he was sent off to the provinces, where he was given command of a division.[47] His officers were

---

[44] 'Doneseniye', p. 284; 'Zakonopolozheniye', in Semevsky *et al.*, *Obshchestvenniya dvizheniya*, i. 547–76, esp. III, §§ 1, 9 (p. 557); for an English translation of this document, see Raeff, *Decembrist Movement*, pp. 69–99.

[45] Druzhinin, *Murav'yev*, p. 104; Nechkina, *Dvizheniye*, i. 304–42. Mazour (*First Russ. Revol.*, p. 83) attributes this step to the moderate elements alone.

[46] Sipyagin is a little-known figure: see M. Kochergin's brief biography in *RBS* xviii. 508–10.

[47] *RBS* xiv. 686–8; Nechkina, 'Svyashch. artel'', p. 166.

sorry to see him go (as were his men, especially once he had been replaced by the notorious Shvarts: see below, p. 298), for he had looked benignly on their social gatherings and had sometimes even attended them. General Yermolov, as commander of the Caucasian Corps, was powerful enough to tolerate political activity by liberal-minded officers, some of whom had been sent to this distant frontier area as a punishment. When passing through Moscow in September 1821, he warned his former adjutant, Fon-Vizin, that the tsar knew of his conspiratorial activities.[48] His attitude was ambivalent, as was that of several other generals, notably those stationed in the provinces. The principal activists were colonels and others of medium rank. Many had served on such generals' staffs during the recent campaigns. Some owed their appointments to their protection; a few were connected to them by family ties. Thus V. P. Ivashev, a prominent 'southerner', was the son of a former aide-de-camp to Suvorov who had been involved in Paul I's assassination, and N. N. Deprera-dovich was the nephew of another of these military conspirators.[49] These links suggest a certain 'dissident tradition' in which age, rank, and kinship were all important factors. Five generals, notably M. F. Orlov, joined the Union of (Public) Welfare, but the senior men generally kept out of anything subversive and were useful to the societies mainly through the influence they wielded in high places as tacit opponents of Arakcheyev and the extreme militarists.

There were also many family links among the activists. The Murav'yev clan has already been mentioned. It was distantly connected to the Murav'yev-Apostols, who provided two leaders of the 'southerners' in 1825, as well as to N. P. Panin, who had been so prominent in the 1801 *coup*.[50] Two sons of General N. N. Rayevsky, a hero of 1812, were associated with the clandestine circles, and his two daughters married other activists, M. F. Orlov and S. G. Volkonsky (both of them generals). There were several pairs of brothers and one group of four siblings, the Bestuzhevs.[51]

A full-scale prosopographical study of the movement has yet to be under-taken, but preliminary studies, Western and Soviet, reveal a good deal about the participants' background. W. B. Lincoln's analysis of the 289 men who were sentenced by the Supreme Criminal Court shows that 85.7 per cent of those for whom data are available had fathers in state service (38 per cent of whom had been in the army) and that 87 per cent had served in the army themselves; 73 per cent were still in military uniform in December 1825.[52] Of

---

[48] Yakushkin, *Zapiski*, p. 65; Fon-Vizin in *VD* iii. 74; Nechkina, *Dvizheniye*, i. 353, ii. 110–12, 148.

[49] Kenney, 'Politics of Assassination', p. 133 (P. N. Ivashev); Nechkina, *Dvizheniye*, ii. 219–20, 333, 348; Prokof'yev, *Bor'ba*, pp. 106–7.   [50] [Bartenev(?)], 'Panin', p. 432 n.

[51] Lotman, 'Dekabrist', p. 66; Orlov, *Kapitulyatsiya Parizha*, p. 274 (for Rayevskys); Kleinschmidt, *Geschichte*, pp. 323–34, 346–51 (for Murav'yevs, Bestuzhevs); Fedorov, *Sold. dvizheniye*, p. 86 (for Vadkovskys).

[52] Lincoln, 'Re-examination', esp. pp. 359, 366–8 (tables); cf. Prokof'yev, *Bor'ba*, pp. 98–101. A more recent Soviet study is Lur'ye, 'Evolyutsiya' (unpublished: see p. 11 of his dissertation abstract).

the 579 men officially listed (in 1827) as having been involved in the affair[53] 78.8 per cent were serving officers. The term military intelligentsia is certainly appropriate in their regard, for 'of the 166 Decembrists for whom we have the necessary information, 147 (88.5 per cent) had some sort of formal institutional education'.[54] Nearly one third had seen action. Age data are available for 254 officers sent for trial; they indicate that 70.2 per cent were 30 years old or less. The breakdown by rank is as follows:

rank	'involved'	sentenced
generals	17	7
staff officers	115	52
junior officers	315	192
total armed forces*	447	251

* includes navy and retired.
Sources: Prokof´yev, *Bor´ba*, pp. 99–100; Lincoln, 'Reconsideration', p. 368.

The importance of the colonels relative to their total number is striking: 68 were 'involved', of whom 26 were sentenced. There was also a relatively high proportion of staff officers (in the normal sense of this term); actual or former guards officers accounted for 46.5 per cent of the members of the Southern and 69 per cent of those of the Northern Society.[55] The differential reflects the fact that these privileged units were stationed mainly in St. Petersburg (and Warsaw) rather than on the empire's south-western perimeter.

One task that awaits historians is to reconstruct the Russian army's 'order of battle' in the early 1820s and to identify all the leading personnel and the location of each unit. Only once this is done can firm conclusions be drawn as to the extent to which the armed forces had been affected by dissent and conspiratorial activity. Despite the large claims sometimes made, it would seem that its scale was modest—and anyway below the 'threshold' necessary for a successful Praetorian-type revolution.

One major problem confronting conspirators in the Russian army of the 1820s was that of communication. Several hundred miles separated their two main centres, St. Petersburg and Tul´chin. This made it impossible to create an effective nation-wide organization and impeded settlement of the personal and political differences bound to arise in any clandestine body. 'Technical' military considerations also crucially affected the fate of the various secret

[53] 'Prikosnovennye k delu': the term is vague and the data need verification. This includes nine men not listed in the *Alfavit dekabristov*, on which these computations are based, but not another 20 who were indicted later: Beskrovnyy, *Potentsial*, pp. 225–6. The *Alfavit* was published in *VD* viii.
[54] Lincoln, 'Re-examination', p. 359.
[55] Ibid., pp. 362–3.

societies. Units were periodically relocated or called out on manœuvres. Officers might be transferred, go on leave, or apply for discharge. This turnover made it hard to maintain contact.[56] Army life did provide malcontents with an organizational structure to which they could adapt their own; moreover, officers often had a good deal of leisure time, and manœuvres might afford cover for conspiratorial meetings; but these advantages were more than offset by the heightened risk of exposure. Correspondence was subject to interception and any hint of unconventional behaviour aroused immediate suspicion.

Alexander I revived the practice of internal espionage within the army, which he had allowed to lapse earlier in his reign. In January 1821 he accepted a proposal by General I. V. Vasil'chikov, commander of the Guards Corps, to set up a secret military police force (distinct from the Internal Guard) to exercise surveillance over troops stationed in and around the capital. It was allotted a staff of only 15 and a modest budget (40,000 roubles),[57] but it could call on the services of *ad hoc* informers who were rewarded in other ways. In May 1821 the authorities received valuable information from M. K. Gribovsky, a (civilian) librarian in the Guards General Staff and a key member of the Union of (Public) Welfare; under heavy pressure he not only betrayed his comrades but even helped to set up the surveillance system over them.[58] Two other informers, Captain A. I. Mayboroda of the Vyatka infantry regiment and I. V. Shervud (Sherwood), an NCO in the 3rd Ukrainian Ulans, reported on the Southern Society and enabled the authorities to effect a major *coup* by arresting its leader, Colonel P. I. Pestel', on the eve of the ill-fated insurrection of 14 December 1825.[59]

Colonel Pestel' had played a key role in the movement almost from its inception. Born to a family of Smolensk *szlachta*—his father became governor of Siberia—and educated first in Germany and then at the Page Corps, he entered the Litovsky guards regiment as an ensign and fought in the campaigns of 1812–14; he was severely wounded at Borodino. Subsequently (1817) Pestel' became adjutant to Field-Marshal P. Kh. Wittgenstein, commander-in-chief of the Second Army, and in September 1821, aged only 28, reached colonel's rank.[60] This swift promotion testified to his remarkable intellect, drive, and organizational talent. Pestel' gained a sound grasp of military affairs and was also unusually well-read in contemporary political literature, from which he

[56] Two examples must suffice. At the crucial Moscow conference of January 1821 the 'southerners' were represented by the moderate Burtsev rather than their radical leader Pestel' because the former qualified for leave in that city and so could go there without attracting attention: Semevsky, 'Fon-Vizin', p. 29. Nikita Murav'yev, the 'northerners'' leader, took a year's leave in 1820–1 to attend to his family affairs, and after getting his old job back (through protection) absented himself again in 1824–5: Druzhinin, *Murav'yev*, pp. 114, 120–1, 147.

[57] Shil'der, *Aleksandr I*, iv. 548–50 (cf. 203–15); Volkonsky, 'Arkhiv', pp. 656, 660; cf. Monas, *Third Section*, p. 46.

[58] Yakushkin, 'S'yezd', p. 601; Volkonsky, 'Arkhiv', p. 661; Nechkina, *Dvizheniye*, i. 90, ii. 28.

[59] *VD* iv. 8–17, 38–40; Mazour, *First Russ. Revol.*, p. 181.

[60] *VD* iv. 6–7; a biography of Pestel' in English is forthcoming.

derived strong republican convictions. Other dissident officers were impressed by his erudition and earnestness, but were also somewhat afraid of his headstrong dictatorial temperament. One major who served under him was reminded of Napoleon, and even the poet Kondratiy Ryleyev, who shared Pestel''s republican views, considered him 'not a Washington but a Bonaparte'.[61] There was a streak of ruthlessness behind his idealism, and he was contemptuous of those associates whom he deemed faint-hearted or dilettantish. From a twentieth-century perspective Pestel' appears irresistibly as a prototype of Lenin; indeed, it has become commonplace to describe *Russkaya pravda*, the programmatic document which he compiled, as the first manifesto of 'Russian jacobinism'.[62]

Pestel' was largely responsible for the streamlining of the first secret societies: revolutionary centralism was to be the order of the day. 'The main thing', he said in evidence later, 'was that there should be no divisions or intrigues, for they could ruin everything.'[63] His posting to Second Army headquarters at Tul'chin inadvertently removed him from the centre of affairs. He promptly set up an organization there which had several subordinate cells, and this bore the imprint of his own strong personality. The 'southerners' endeavoured to impose a republican programme on their comrades in the north, and in November 1819 Pestel' returned to the capital for six months. He was successful in his aim, but it was a paper victory. The 'northerners', unhappy at the prospect of violence, began to favour a schism which, when it finally came about, after a conference in Moscow in January 1821, took a form of which Pestel' and the radicals disapproved.

These differences prevented the dissidents from reacting to a major provocation by the authorities, the dissolution of the Semenovsky guards regiment after the alleged 'mutiny' in its ranks (October 1820: see below, p. 298). The setback led to a loss of morale among the conspirators in the capital. In 1821-2 the Guards Corps was sent to the Vil'na region for 15 months. The move was made in part for domestic security reasons: to remove potential trouble-makers from St. Petersburg. It was not until the autumn of 1822, when the corps had returned, that Captain Nikita Murav'yev and several former associates in the defunct Union of (Public) Welfare agreed to set up a new cadre group, which came to be known as the 'Northern Society'.[64] It turned out to be a quiescent body, whose members devoted themselves mainly to theoretical discussions. Murav'yev was the principal architect of a constitutional charter designed to counter Pestel''s extreme republicanism. He hoped that some future tsar, if not Alexander I himself, might be persuaded to endorse it. One possible scenario which he and his comrades envisaged was that the dissidents might force a new ruler's hand by refusing *en masse* to take the oath of allegiance unless he did so. This tactic has been criticized as politically naïve. It can

---

[61] Lorer, *Zapiski*, p. 70; Basargin, *Zapiski*, pp. xxxvii–xxxviii, 15–16; 'Doneseniye', p. 293.
[62] Text in *VD* vii. 113–209; Eng. tr. (abbreviated) in Raeff, *Decembrist Movement*, pp. 124–56.
[63] *VD* iv. 87.   [64] *VD* i. 320.

be understood only against the background of the protest movement which was developing in the army at the time, in which the secret society members were to some extent involved.

It will be recalled that in Paul's reign malcontents had inundated the authorities with discharge applications. In September 1820 the same step was taken by officers of the Izmaylovsky regiment,[65] and the next year their comrades in the Novorossiysk Dragoons 'went sick' in a body to publicize their resentment at the unduly severe punishment of an NCO for some trifling fault.[66] So far as is known these were both spontaneous acts which owed nothing to any clandestine group, but in May 1822 a similar incident involved two captains in the Litovsky regiment, N. N. Pushchin and P. A. Gabbe, who did have clandestine connections.[67] They acted in a more decisive fashion, actually rebuking their commander in public, yet their protest, like the others, was an impromptu affair. The same was true of the 'Norov incident' (March 1822), which differed in that the victim was not a soldier but an officer, Captain V. S. Norov of the Chasseurs guards regiment and a former member of the Union of (Public) Welfare. When Grand Duke Nicholas sharply reprimanded him without due cause, his comrades took the view that he had been personally insulted and ought to 'receive satisfaction'. Nicholas neither could nor would appear on the duelling-ground—Russian history might have taken a different turn had he done so—and accordingly about 20 officers put in for transfer to a line regiment. Six of them, including Norov, were arrested, and after a period in detention had their request granted by way of punishment.[68]

Each of these incidents was in itself of minor consequence, but the conspirators evidently felt that a significant protest movement was under way. It seems to have subsided once the Northern Society was formed, perhaps because its members wanted to husband their resources until the organization had consolidated its strength. By 1825 it had built up its position in several guards regiments (Moscow, Horse, Finland, Izmaylovsky, and First Grenadiers) as well as in the naval infantry (*morskoy ekipazh*). However, these units comprised only a fraction of the entire corps, which had 13 regiments, each of 3,000 men, plus a few smaller detachments.[69] Moreover, all the units just listed, elements of which participated in the insurrection of 14 December, were in one of the two infantry divisions, which was under the nominal command (*shefstvo*) of Grand Duke Michael. The other, subordinate to Nicholas, resisted the 'revolutionary contagion'. Nicholas was not popular personally, so that the reason for this may simply be that he exercised closer control over his senior officers, and that they in turn followed his example.

[65] Volkonsky, 'Arkhiv', pp. 648–9; Gangeblov, 'Kak ya popal', pp. 186–7; Chernov, 'Iz istorii', p. 95.

[66] Fedorov, *Soldatskoye dvizheniye*, pp. 174–5.

[67] Ibid., pp. 176–8; Beskrovnyy, *Potentsial*, p. 223.

[68] N. Polivanov, 'N. S. Norov, dekabrist, 1793–1853', *RA* 37 (1900), 1, pp. 273–304; *VD* viii. 138; Nechkina, *Dvizheniye*, i. 374; Fedorov, *Soldatskoye dvizheniye*, p. 175.

[69] Gabayev, 'Gvardiya', pp. 164–72; Lavrov, 'Diktator', p. 191.

Wittgenstein, commander of the Second Army in the south, was set in a different mould. The liberal V. F. Rayevsky wrote later that, despite his non-Russian background, 'he was loved and respected by all'.[70] He left administration largely to his chief of staff, General P. D. Kiselev. Both men may be categorized as 'patrons'. Later Kiselev became a loyal (and effective) minister of Nicholas I, but at this time he played along with the dissidents. He allowed his house to be used as a conspiratorial meeting-place and replaced a number of the more objectionable regimental commanders by men of his own choice.[71] One of these individuals was Colonel I. G. Burtsev, a secret society member, who represented the 'southerners' at the 1821 Moscow conference. He disapproved of Pestel´'s radicalism and according to some accounts tried to exclude his rival from the Southern Society.[72] Whether this was so or not, Pestel´ retained control of the organization, aided by his dual responsibilities as a staff officer at army headquarters and CO of the Vyatka infantry regiment. This unit was based not far away at Lintsy, an estate belonging to a Polish landowner, Prince Eustachy Sanguszko. Some other properties in the region were owned by Russian officers. They offered convenient conspiratorial venues, as did the fairs which officers attended in the line of duty (mainly to purchase horses) as well as the annual manœuvres that were held in anticipation of war with the Turks. The Southern Society was able to set up two subordinate cells, one at Kamenka (Major-General S. G. Volkonsky, Colonel [retired] V. L. Davydov), and the other at Vasil´kov (Lieutenant-Colonel S. I. Murav´yev-Apostol, CO of the Chernigov regiment).[73] The latter was a former officer of the Semenovsky guards regiment who bitterly resented its disbandment, which had caused him to be transferred to a unit of the line.

The 'southerners' did more than their comrades in the north to win their men's sympathy, by humane treatment and setting up schools, and were better at conspiratorial technique. A concern for secrecy came naturally to Pestel´, who was preoccupied with the preparation of a draft republican constitution. This, as is well known, envisaged a provisional revolutionary dictatorship, in which Pestel´ clearly expected to play the principal role. Most Northern Society members found this prospect unpalatable. They had an opportunity to ventilate their objections in the spring of 1824, when Pestel´ was again sent to the capital on a mission. His draft (still incomplete) of *Russkaya pravda* did not win their approval. There is some evidence, however, that certain leaders (Colonel S. P. Trubetskoy and Lieutenant E. P. Obolensky) may have subsequently moved toward a more radical position.[74] The ideological breach was not

---

[70] [Rayevsky] 'Vospominaniya', p. 84.

[71] Lorer, *Zapiski*, p. 78; Yakushkin, *Zapiski*, pp. 36, 536-9; on Kiselev see Leyev, 'Doreformennaya armiya' (based on his papers but uninformative as to his opinions).

[72] Yakushkin, *Zapiski*, pp. 36, 161; Mazour, *First Russ. Revol.*, pp. 84, 98.

[73] The group at Kishinev, headquarters of 16th division, was no longer of great consequence. Luciani, *Société*, pp. 171-3.

[74] *VD* i. 107-32; Druzhinin, *Murav´yev*, pp. 139-43; Mazour, *First Russ. Revol.*, pp. 119, 121, 128-9.

absolute (as is sometimes implied), for Pestel' himself, disenchanted at the cool reception given to his ideas, was moderating his stand—at least for tactical reasons. He later told investigators that he had feared the disagreements would weaken the movement.[75] Testimony given under pressure is of course suspect, but there is reason to believe that Pestel' was telling the truth, for he named several associates in the vain hope of earning the authorities' indulgence. His account of the group's tactical plans is also plausible: they saw the former Semenovtsy as a potential nucleus of supporters, who would back a *coup*; this the conspirators hoped to bring off in the summer of 1826, when the tsar was due to attend manœuvres in the south.

Did they intend to assassinate him? The investigators insisted that they did, and the evidence on this score, although inconclusive, cost Pestel' his life. Certainly he had no objection on principle—his writings are explicit on the matter—but one must emphasize the point that the plotters, for all their elaborately detailed schemes concerning Russia's future, were remarkably pragmatic, indeed light-hearted, about the methods they intended to employ to attain their goals. If required to decide promptly, they would probably have opted for violence on grounds of expediency. Had they been given time for reflection, they might well have rejected terrorism.

An obsession with ultimate ends, to the neglect of means, was characteristic of revolutionary movements in this era. Another sign of immaturity was the mystification with which the Russian conspirators, like those elsewhere, liked to surround their activities. They would, for example, exaggerate their own strength in order to impress initiates or rivals, and perhaps just to keep up their spirits. In the long run such fraudulent practices were counter-productive. The harm they could do was particularly evident in the negotiations held in August–September 1825, during army manœuvres, at Leshchin (a village near Zhito-mir), between leaders of the Southern Society and those of another group, the 'Society of United Slavs', which had come into being independently.

This organization grew out of a circle led by two sub-lieutenants in the 8th Artillery Brigade, the brothers P. I. and A. I. Borisov. It consisted almost wholly of subaltern officers (the only senior man was a major) and by this time had 51 members, probably more than were in the Southern Society. The latter, especially Lieutenant-Colonel S. I. Murav'yev-Apostol and his close friend, Sub-Lieutenant M. R. Bestuzhev-Ryumin, were eager to bring about a merger—but only on their own terms. They recognized that the United Slavs' links with Polish patriots and other activists abroad could prove valuable, but they were also alarmed by the more militant tendencies of the United Slavs. These differences were important, but should not be inflated.[76] Each group approached

---

[75] *VD* iv. 92; confirmed by Lorer, *Zapiski*, p. 79.

[76] Historians have tended to interpret the difference ideologically, so confusing the matter. Nechkina's 1927 monograph, *Obshchestvo ob'yedinennykh slav'yan*, represented the group as 'democrats' opposed to an 'aristocratic' military *coup*: cf. B. E. Syroyechkovsky *et al.*, notes to Gorbachevsky, *Zapiski*, p. 310. This is the principal source on the negotiations between the two bodies. His evidence is judiciously evaluated both in this edition and by Luciani, *Société*.

programmatic and tactical questions from a slightly different standpoint, due not least to the fact that they were divided by military rank as well as social background.

There was also a jurisdictional angle: Murav′yev-Apostol, as CO of the Chernigov regiment, had misgivings about allowing another clandestine society to make converts among his men. Both groups were agreed that it was desirable to recruit NCOs and soldiers, but the United Slavs attached a higher priority to this task and could claim to have scored some success. The Southern Society leaders wanted to limit such propaganda to the most receptive elements, especially ex-Semenovtsy, and thought that even they could not be brought to understand the conspirators' ulterior purposes. 'For them such formulas as republican government or equality of classes [that is, human rights] would be the enigma of the Sphinx', said Murav′yev-Apostol to a United Slav activist (Sub-Lieutenant I. I. Gorbachevsky) on 15 September; whereas his interlocutor wanted 'to explain, with the necessary tact, all the advantages of a revolution and to reveal to them gradually all the society's secrets [that is, its aims] but not its actual existence'.[77] The discussion became heated, with exchanges of threats and accusations—one of the Borisov brothers questioned the need for a provisional military dictatorship in the Pestel′ mould—but the quarrel was patched up.[78] In retrospect it is clear that both groups stood foursquare in the Praetorian tradition: they sought to use military force to secure political changes that would benefit the army and the wider society of which it formed a part.

Alexander I's unexpected death at Taganrog on 19 November 1825 left a dynastic vacuum which would seem to have offered the dissident officers a golden opportunity. For nearly three weeks of confusion neither Constantine nor Nicholas, the late tsar's brothers, would take the throne, each considering the other to be the rightful ruler.[79] Unfortunately for the conspirators neither claimant was sympathetic to their aspirations. The best chance to impose their own ideas came on 27 November, when news of Alexander's death reached St. Petersburg, but officials administered the oath of allegiance to Constantine promptly, before any protest could be staged.

The Northern Society, caught totally unprepared, was unable to improvise any realistic plan. Its members conferred, wrote leaflets and spread rumours, but not until 9 December, faced with the prospect that Nicholas might succeed, did they contemplate immediate action. By this time the future emperor had learned of what was afoot and could take counter-measures. The officers knew that this was so, and prepared their action in a mood of despair and romantic readiness for self-sacrifice. 'We shall die, oh, how gloriously shall we die!',

---

[77] Luciani, *Société*, p. 192; Gorbachevsky, *Zapiski*, pp. 29–30.
[78] Luciani, *Société*, p. 189; Gorbachevsky, *Zapiski*, p. 23.
[79] On the crisis: B. E. Syroyechkovsky (ed.), *Mezhdutsarstviye 1825 g. i vosstaniye dekabristov v perepiske i memuarakh chlenov tsarskoy sem′i*, Moscow and Leningrad, 1926.

exclaimed Ensign A. I. Odoyevsky, a noted poet. Their civic heroism, as one historian puts it, was tinged with oriental fatalism.[80]

The northerners' plan, such as it was, called for secret society members in those units that had been most extensively 'penetrated' to bring their men out on the fraudulent pretext that the oath to Nicholas was illegal. This, it was hoped, would encourage other regiments to follow their example, and create conditions in which the insurgent leaders could impose their constitutional designs on the Senate.[81] The scheme might just conceivably have worked—if the cadres had been as resolutely committed to the cause as the organizers hoped. But this was not the case. Of the Moscow regiment only four companies (671 men in all) were induced to join the movement. This was less than a quarter of the unit's total strength. In the First Grenadiers the proportion was higher (over 40 per cent), but significantly only two of the insurgent officers were members of the society; one (Lieutenant N. A. Panov) happened to be the adjutant and the other officers obeyed him more or less mechanically. In the naval infantry there was a good turn-out (approximately 1,100 men out of a possible 1,280), but only one officer (Lieutenant A. P. Arbuzov) belonged to the conspiratorial network.[82] The Finland regiment remained neutral, although Lieutenant Obolensky, a prominent member of the society, was serving in it.[83] Colonel Trubetskoy, hurriedly named provisional dictator, took fright and abandoned his post, and there were several other notable defectors. Altogether the rebels had an estimated 30 officers, all but one of them subalterns, and 2,850 soldiers. They found themselves confronting a government force potentially about three times as strong.[84]

Even so odds were not so unfavourable as it may seem. Morale was uncertain in both forces. On the insurgent side most soldiers did not know what was expected of them. Typically, the rebel chiefs had made no arrangements to feed their men, who were left standing for hours to no apparent purpose on the wintry Senate Square. The leadership shown on the government side was not much better, but Nicholas and his staff were under less compulsion to act quickly. They first tried to persuade the rebels to surrender peacefully. These talks failed, as did a cavalry charge. With dusk falling the mood of the civilian onlookers became uncertain. Artillery was brought up, and after a final warning the cannon opened fire.[85]

The insurgents fell or fled—and were quickly rounded up, along with a number of spectators. Exact casualty figures are unknown, for many of the bodies of those killed were thrust beneath the ice of the Neva. One estimate puts insurgent losses at 70–80, including 13 fatalities.[86]

[80] Mazour, *First Russ. Revol.*, p. 184.

[81] Zavalishin, *Zapiski*, pp. 190–1.   [82] Gabayev, 'Gvardiya', pp. 175–9.

[83] Lieutenant E. A. Rozen led two and a half companies to a bridge across the Neva where they halted and merely observed the action. For his biography: G. R. Barratt, *Rebel on the Bridge*, London, 1975.   [84] Gabayev, 'Gvardiya', p. 181.

[85] Ibid., p. 186; Mazour, *First Russ. Revol.*, pp. 175–80. For a view from the government side: Fel'kner, 'Zapiski' (not used by Mazour).   [86] Gabayev, 'Gvardiya', p. 191.

A comparable number were killed or injured in the second insurrection, staged in the south independently by elements of the Chernigov regiment under the leadership of S. I. Murav´yev-Apostol. Since there is an excellent recent account of this uprising,[87] we need not consider it here, merely noting that its tragic outcome was even more predictable than that of the rising in the capital.

Why did the 'first Russian revolution' fail? This question would be keenly debated, especially in opposition circles, over the next century. Gradually a consensus developed that the reason lay in the Decembrists' reluctance to involve the *narod* (common people) in their action, and that this attitude could be explained by their social exclusiveness. Their aims, so the argument ran, were noble and progressive, but their conduct was not sufficiently 'democratic'; Russia could be freed only by a revolution of the masses, not by a *coup d'état* engineered on their behalf by disenchanted elements of the upper class.

Advocates of this view seldom asked themselves whether joint action by officers and men was feasible, given the conditions in Alexander's army, or how much participation by soldiers would have been necessary for success. The whole 'Decembrist movement' from 1814 on—itself a term of questionable accuracy—was seen outside its armed–forces context, and in this way the thrust of historical inquiry became skewed. Today we should have learned (although myths die slowly) that military *coups* may indeed be successful, at least in the short term, and that mass uprisings are likely to produce repressive authoritarian regimes. In other words there is no necessary correlation betweeen a revolutionary movement's social comprehensiveness and the quality of its result. The latter will be determined rather by the state of the society that is overturned. When examining the Russia of 1825 we cannot but be struck by its unreadiness for a successful revolution, even of the limited Praetorian type.

In the tsarist empire progressive-minded officers faced even tougher obstacles than their counterparts did in Naples, Piedmont, or the Iberian peninsula, to say nothing of the German states. The power of the monarchy was still absolute, its hold over the machinery of government as yet unweakened, its image untarnished by military defeat. By and large the *dvoryanstvo* believed that the maintenance of serfdom was essential to their own and the country's well-being. The educated élite was wafer-thin and unused to organization; and the mass of the people, being generally illiterate, could scarcely be expected to comprehend the conspirators' aims, let alone support them actively. Soldiers, it is true, were more amenable than peasants to propaganda, or to what is now called 'political mobilization'; but the 'Decembrists'' ideas on army reform— they envisaged a conscript force on the French revolutionary pattern along with various material alleviations[88]—would probably not have satisfied the rank and file, even if they had known of them and been able to voice their

[87] Luciani, *Société*, pp. 228–51; cf. Mazour, *First Russ. Revol.*, pp. 181–202, 248 (casualties).
[88] Prokof´yev, *Bor´ba*, pp. 109–78.

opinions. Their attitude towards their officers' efforts on their behalf was necessarily ambiguous (see further below, p. 300).

Moreover, the service milieu set very narrow limits to what could be achieved in trying to bridge the gulf. The authorities treated as seditious even efforts by honest officers, such as M. F. Orlov and V. F. Rayevsky, to take judicial action against corrupt or cruel subordinates whose arbitrary conduct contravened military law—although it might have been said that by instituting proceedings against them they were actually upholding the existing command structure. In Alexander's army the very idea of legality was suspect to the authorities, who hypocritically ignored the laws in force when it suited them. We have already seen that informal horizontal contacts were difficult to sustain over great distances, and that the surveillance system was as thorough as contemporary techniques permitted.

Another obstacle was the formality that normally governed relations between officers of staff and subaltern rank. In an effort to counter this the secret societies developed an alternative hierarchical system, based on personal and ideological loyalties, and to some extent managed to enforce it. Since *esprit de corps* was feebly developed in the Russian army, there does not seem to have been much rivalry between different arms of service, although officers in line regiments harboured a certain distrust of those in the guards. The collapse of the Northern Society's leadership at the hour of decision should be seen as 'a failure of the colonels' as well as one of aristocrats, in the sense that junior officers like Captain A. Bestuzhev or Lieutenant Panov found themselves in command of larger forces than they were trained to handle. The role of civilians in the clandestine organizations, especially in the north, is also significant. The poet (and official) Ryleyev was second to none in political commitment and also demonstrated considerable organizational talent, but his civilian status prevented him from taking decisive action on the Senate Square and may explain why he left the scene prematurely. It is a curious fact that those rebel leaders who resorted to armed violence were civilians (P. G. Kakhovsky, W. Küchelbecker [V. K. Kyukhelbeker]) rather than officers; this may explain why the latter did not emulate their example.

Russia's Praetorians showed a good deal of ingenuity in camouflaging their intentions and took readily to conspiratorial methods of struggle. But some of them became obsessed with 'technique': secret meeting-places, false identities, code-words, and the like. As already noted, deliberate deception made it hard to establish relations of comradely trust, and the intrigues between members of the two regional societies led a number of activists to abandon the cause in disgust. The issues that divided them were as much moral as political, and there were faults on both sides. So far as the political aspect is concerned, it is obvious that despite much endeavour programmatic unity was not achieved, although the parties were not really far apart. Their views of the future order ranged from the 'authoritarian' (N. Murav´yev) to the 'autocratic' (Pestel´)—to use Perlmutter's terminology for different types of Praetorian rule. This need not have mattered much if the principal conspirators had been agreed on tactics, but this was not the case. The idea of seizing power was not firmly established in their minds, although they probably had sufficient physical means to take this crucial step—if not to hold on to power once they had seized it.

Their indecisiveness may best be explained in terms of the Russian political culture, shaped as this was by the idea of patrimonial and paternalistic monarchy. Even those who were prepared to commit regicide were probably monarchists at heart, for all their professed republicanism. They sought to manipulate the tsardom, as the symbol of national unity, and to influence its policies in a direction that would cater to the military interest, which they identified with the general weal. The readiness with which a number of activists first approached Alexander I with their reform proposals and then confessed their errors to his successor in the hope of receiving a royal pardon suggests that the myth of autocratic benevolence was still strong among these officers, just as it was among the populace at large—although in the case of their confessions we have to make allowance for the severe psychological strain induced by defeat, arrest, and detention in harsh physical conditions.

The historical literature on the 'Decembrists' implies that, had they triumphed, Russia would have entered upon a radiant future of indefinite duration. It is perhaps not superfluous to suggest that a Praetorian victory in 1825 might have had very different results. On one side of the speculative equation the revolutionaries would have benefited from such factors as the army's historically predominant role and high prestige in society, the weakness of civilian government institutions, the fragmentation of opinion within the élite, and the low level of political awareness among the masses. On the other hand, even if they had secured the co-operation of a royal figure-head, their new order would surely have evoked considerable resistance from traditionalists in all classes; nor would the empire's national minorities have taken kindly to Pestel´'s plans for a unitary state. Could the military have pushed through their reform programme, and preserved their cohesion, in the face of administrative obstruction and popular opposition?

The example of Spain is instructive. Don Rafael del Riego's successful rising in 1820 (which greatly impressed Russian liberals)[89] led to civil war and foreign intervention, and was followed by a restoration of absolutism. Geography and *Realpolitik* might have spared Russia another foreign invasion, but she could scarcely have escaped the other consequences. Successful Praetorian *coups* generally lead in the long run only to a limited injection of fresh blood into the élite. But here speculation should cease.

---

[89] De Madariaga, 'Spain and the Decembrists', p. 145; cf. M. V. Nechkina, 'Dekabristy vo vsemirno-istoricheskom protsesse', *VI*, 1975, 12, pp. 3–18 (Eng. tr.: *Studies in Soviet History* 15 (White Plains, NY, 1977), pp. 32–62).

None of the above gainsays the fact that the insurgents' aims were by and large beneficent, or that their defeat was a tragedy. Russia had to endure Nicholas I's 30-year 'freeze' before, in the wake of the Crimean War, their ideas would be revived—this time by a reform-minded government as well as by elements in educated society.

V

THE MILITARY SETTLEMENTS

12

THE ARMY TAKES TO THE COUNTRYSIDE

THROUGHOUT Europe the bitter experiences of the French revolutionary and Napoleonic Wars accelerated the trend towards professionalism among the military. Russia was no exception. Already by the late eighteenth century a distinction had emerged within the privileged class between those who served the state as officers in the armed forces and those who did so in the civilian bureaucracy. Gradually men in each category came to see themselves as belonging to separate, although inter-related, groups. The process gathered speed after 1801, and again after the victory over Napoleon. Nevertheless there was also a powerful countervailing trend, so that the two sections of the establishment never became entirely divorced from one another.[1] The Romanov rulers relied heavily on military officers, serving or retired, to staff those administrative posts that called for expertise in the arts of coercion. This was particularly true under Nicholas I. Frightened by the Decembrist revolt, the 'iron tsar' took firm measures to reassert control over the army and to make it once again a wholly dependable instrument of the Crown. It was given broad responsibilities which considerably undermined its professional effectiveness, as the Crimean War amply demonstrated. Meanwhile the process of 'civilianization' was continuing apace in the lower echelons of the bureaucracy, and this prepared the way for qualitative changes in the nature of the regime after Nicholas I's death in 1855.

It is against this background, which will be examined more closely in ch. 13, that we must consider a particular phenomenon which exemplifies better than any other the military's predominance in Russian civil society during the early nineteenth century: the military settlements (or 'colonies', as they are sometimes misleadingly called). It is important at the outset to correct two common misapprehensions about these settlements. First, the grandiose and contentious scheme set up by Alexander I after 1816, and entrusted to his favourite Arakcheyev, was a modification of arrangements that had existed for a hundred years or so in the southern border areas and which had been reasonably successful in achieving their more limited objectives. Second, Nicholas I reverted in some respects to the earlier pattern during the first years of his reign, and it was in this modified form that the settlements survived until the 1860s. Each phase deserves to be evaluated separately, with an objectivity that was unfortunately often lacking in earlier accounts.[2]

---

[1] Pintner, 'Evolution', seems to exaggerate the extent of this development.

[2] After their disbandment the settlements became, for many critically-minded publicists and historians, and later even for official writers, a symbol of the failings of the discredited

Although ultimately abandoned, the settlement project affected the lives of several hundred thousand of the tsar's subjects. Its historical significance lies in the fact that it was the first major effort in modern times to carry through a programme of social and cultural change under military auspices. It may be seen as an early experiment in state-sponsored social engineering, such as many authoritarian regimes have attempted in our own day.

The post-Petrine rulers inherited a long, exposed border along the southern perimeter of the empire that could not be defended, still less pushed further forward into the fertile steppe, by conventional methods alone. The regular troops stationed in the area had to be supplemented by elements of the local population, whose way of life was to some degree militarized and who therefore were accorded a special semi-privileged status. The outer ring of this defence system was formed by the various Cossack hosts (*voyska*), notably those on the rivers Dnieper and Don. The hosts gradually lost the last vestiges of their former autonomy and came under the central authorities' control. It was exercised in the main through a pliable upper class of landowning officers, known as 'elders' (*starshiny*), most of whom eventually became integrated into the Russian nobility.[3]

The Cossacks are less relevant to our theme than the farming settlers who made up the inner ring. In return for rather shaky official recognition of their rights to the land they worked, and for certain other privileges, such as a measure of tax relief, they were obliged to perform specified military duties on a selective basis. As the frontier moved south, so too did the servicemen who protected it. They lived under a military administration patterned on that which had originated in the Belgorod area during the late seventeenth century (see above, p. 36). During the Imperial era this system was extended: first to the territory of the former Hetmanate and to the so-called Slobodskaya Ukraina to the east; then further south to the province of New Russia (Novorossiya); and finally to the Caucasus. As each area became pacified it was brought under the regular machinery of provincial government, broadly similar to that prevailing in the empire's heartlands, and the bulk of the inhabitants adopted a civilian life-style. The process was not yet complete by the end of our period—or indeed even by 1917, when the Imperial regime collapsed. This was partly because the ethnic make-up of the Caucasus region was even more complex than it was in the south European steppe.

'Nicolaevan system' as a whole. This led to unbalanced treatment of the subject, on a limited source basis, and the few attempts to defend it lacked credibility. In recent years Western scholars have attempted a re-assessment: see Pipes, 'Colonies', and especially the work of A. D. Ferguson. Of his thorough dissertation, 'Russian Military Settlements, 1810–1866' (Yale, 1953) two excerpts have been published, cited here as 'Land-militia' and 'Settlements, 1825–66'. While indebted to both historians for valuable insights, the present writer finds some of their conclusions excessively 'revisionist'.

[3] Menning, 'Mil. Institutions'; id., 'Emergence'.

The treaty of Adrianople (1713) pushed Russia's frontier in the south-west back to a line above the great bend in the river Dnieper. To bolster defences in this region Peter I called into being a force known as the Ukrainian land-militia. This took shape slowly, and by the 1720s numbered about 9,000 men, organized into five regiments, each of ten companies. Those who served in it were in the main 'single-homesteaders' (*odnodvortsy*), offspring of the lower-grade old-formation troops who had performed a similar role in the Muscovite era. They were joined by veterans of the new regular army, which also provided command personnel.[4] The state contributed arms and munitions, equipment, and horses, and paid a salary equivalent to that of garrison troops, but for the rest of their supplies (food, clothing, etc.) the militiamen were expected to support themselves. This was asking a great deal. To be sure, land was plentiful, but they had few other resources; apart from the risk of hostile attack and the vagaries of the climate, they were obliged, like Muscovite gentrymen earlier, to perform service assignments which took them away from their plots during the summer months when their presence there was most necessary. In fact much of the farming had to be done by their relatives or other dependants, the latter known as *pomoshch(n)iki* (literally, 'assistants'). Average yields were extremely low: two- to three-fold for most grains,[5] and hunger was seldom far away. In principle militiamen were required to take turns in bearing arms, and to do so only between the ages of 15 and 30. But during Anna's reign they were mobilized *en masse* for the war against the Turks, and each homesteader was also under orders to supply one labourer to help build yet another fortified line along the border. This was a major construction enterprise, 800 versts long with forts spaced at 10-verst intervals, and although strategically effective it claimed the lives of many of its builders. During the 1730s the number of land-militia regiments was doubled, but only half of the men in them were actually settled. Even in those that were many soldiers still lacked proper housing—still less a farm—and had to subsist in temporary shelters. Not surprisingly, desertion was rife. Once the war was over the new government had to reduce the land-militia's effectives once again and to come to the survivors' aid.[6]

Evidently disappointed at the performance of this force, from 1751 onwards the authorities turned to another source of military manpower: immigrants from south-eastern Europe, mostly Serbs (or other South Slavs), of whom many had gained relevant experience on the Austrian *Militärgrenze*.[7] These men, who comprised six regiments, served on terms similar to the Ukrainian land-militia, from whom they soon began to draw reinforcements. They also

---

[4] *PSZ* v. 2643 (2 Feb. 1713), vi. 4131 (12 Dec. 1722), vii. 4223 (14 May 1723); Solov'yev, 'Kratkiy ist. ocherk', pp. 315–18; Stein, *Geschichte*, pp. 71, 92; Ferguson, 'Land-militia', pp. 141–2.
[5] Rabinovich, 'Sel. khoz. odnodvortsev', p. 142.
[6] *PSZ* viii. 6055 (12 May 1732), ix. 6315 (27 Jan. 1733), xi. 8787, 8801 (28 Sept., 7 Oct. 1743), xliii. 5680, 5778 (22 Jan., 15 June 1731); Bulcke, *Manstein*, p. 78; Yevstaf'yev, *Vosstaniye*, pp. 30–1.
[7] [Rusinov] *Zapiski*, pp. 116–20; Stein, *Geschichte*, p. 150; for the diplomatic background see H. L. Dyck, 'New Serbia and the Origins of the Eastern Question . . .', *RR* 40 (1981) pp. 1–19.

had to withstand rigorous conditions, as is plain from the memoirs left by one of their officers, a rough-hewn Serbian captain, S. S. Piščević (Pishchevich). During his first year on the steppe (1754) he lived 'like a shipwrecked sailor on a desert island' and survived on a diet of garlic, onions, and boiled grass, occasionally seasoned with a few berries; 'everywhere there was weeping and sobbing', he wrote, for those wholly dependent on their pay found that after deductions for uniforms and equipment they had nothing left for daily needs.[8] Nevertheless their settlements—in this case the term 'colonies' is certainly appropriate—managed to survive, although their military quality was adjudged unsatisfactory and after troubles broke out they were brought under closer control (1763); this meant a greater infusion of Cossacks and Ukrainian militiamen.

The militia itself was scaled down at this time, but was not actually disbanded until 1769.[9] Even then the change seems to have been rather superficial: the units were turned into regular dragoon and infantry regiments, but the men continued to maintain the homesteads they possessed. Catherine II, as we know, sought to introduce greater administrative uniformity in the empire's borderlands, but she was wise enough to proceed slowly. The Ukrainian line of the 1730s had now lost its usefulness as the settlers rapidly spread southwards into New Russia, which was established as a separate province in 1764. Over the next decade the successes achieved in the war of 1768–74 against the Turks revolutionized the problem of Imperial defence in this quarter. Potemkin, who was placed in supreme charge, favoured the creation of units of mobile light cavalry, known as hussars and lancers (*pikinyery*), whose strength rose from 3,000 to 10,000 by 1776.[10] Although classed as regular troops, some of them at least were settled in the region. Their term of service was fixed at 15 years and they were given higher rates of pay. Had this not been done, it would have been impossible to recruit large numbers of ex-militiamen and Cossacks into their ranks.

From an ethnic point of view these formations were predominantly Ukrainian.[11] One soldier had to be provided from each plot (*uchastok*), measuring 26 to 30 dessyatines, on which a modest land tax was payable; settlers were allowed to acquire more land if they could afford to buy and work it.[12] In theory this land belonged to the state, as did the original plot, but in practice there were few obstacles to its acquisition as private property, especially by senior officers. Most of the territory in the region, however, remained open steppe for many years to come, since it would have been impossible for the settlers to have cultivated the enormous area assigned to each

---

[8] [Pishchevich] *Izvestiye*, pp. 189–90.

[9] *PSZ* xviii. 13175 (10 Oct. 1768); Dubrovin, *Suvorov*, p. 38; Kersnovsky, *Istoriya*, i. 105.

[10] *PSZ* xx. 14552 (24 Dec. 1776).

[11] Druzhinina, *Sev. Prichernomor'ye*, pp. 54, 63; Auerbach, *Besiedelung*, pp. 67, 69; P. V. Zavadovsky to S. R. Vorontsov, 3 Mar. 1775, in *AKV* xxiv (1880), p. 146.

[12] Druzhinina, *Sev. Prichernomor'ye*, pp. 58–60.

military unit. For example, the Black Hussar regiment (so named from the colour of its uniform), stationed along the Polish border, was allotted approximately a quarter of a million dessyatines,[13] comprising 16 of the 70 districts (*okruga*) into which Yelizavetgrad sub-province (*provintsiya*) was divided. Of these districts more than two-thirds (52 out of 70) were reserved for military use. The figure was similar (108 out of 140 districts) in the sub-province named after the empress, Yekaterinoslav.[14] Each district was supposed to measure between 15,000 and 20,000 dessyatines, that is, approximately 40,000 to 50,000 acres.

Unfortunately nothing is known of the agricultural activities in which these soldier-farmers engaged. They seem to have been more closely supervised than the old land-militiamen had been, but this control was exercised at a regimental rather than a regional (still less national) level and was probably not too oppressive. On the other hand the scope allowed to individual initiative encouraged abuses (most notably, the private employment of soldiers) and, at least in the eyes of some officers, undermined discipline. Would these disadvantages be outweighed by the assurance that the men would be adequately fed from the stocks which each unit could build up? Before such questions could be answered a new war broke out with Turkey (1787–91) and the military authorities' attention was diverted into more familiar channels. The soldier-farmers of New Russia were deeply involved in this struggle, which upset their regiments' fragile economies and cost them much loss of life, as the two earlier conflicts had done.

The war did, however, bring the Russian empire a further extension of territory in the south-west, the potentially rich and all but empty lands between the rivers Bug and Dniester. Initially known as the 'Ochakov region [*oblast'*]' (and then attached to the Yekaterinoslav sub-province of New Russia), it soon came to share in the rapid growth of the whole area, thanks to the development of the port of Odessa. Another Cossack host was established in the region, named after the river Bug, and a considerable area of land was assigned to military settlement. Each man in the ranks was entitled to a plot of 25, each subaltern officer 50, and each staff officer 120 dessyatines.[15] The 'Odessa division' was soon disbanded on the orders of Paul I; it was reconstituted in 1803.[16] At the turn of the century over two-thirds of the population around Tiraspol' on the Dniester consisted of military settlers;[17] nevertheless one cannot say that this region became heavily militarized, as was the case in the area immediately to the north-east. Nor, for other reasons, did the Crimean peninsula. It was the territory lying between the rivers Bug and Dnieper that became the heartland of military settlement in south Russia (see Map 2).

[13] Auerbach, *Besiedelung*, p. 33.
[14] Ibid., pp. 32–3; Bartlett, *Human Capital*, p. 113.
[15] *PSZ* xxii. 16605 (14 Jan. 1783), § 3; Bartlett, *Human Capital*, pp. 135–6.
[16] *PSZ* xxvii. 22872 (28 Apr. 1803); Lobachevsky, 'Bugskoye kazachestvo', p. 601.
[17] Druzhinina, *Yuzhnaya Ukraina*, p. 86.

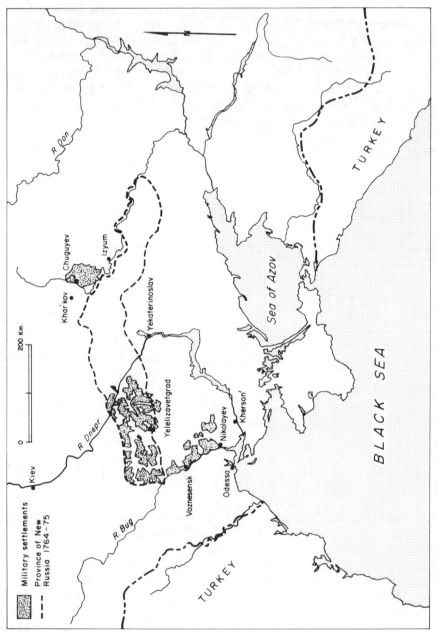

Map 2. Southern Russia, showing areas under Military Settlement

In 1784 military settlers accounted for a sizeable proportion of the population of Yekaterinoslav governor-generalship (*namestnichestvo*). Of 352,000 male taxpayers 160,000 were categorized as military settlers (*voinskiye poselyane*) and another 2,000 as 'settled soldiers' (meaning veterans); this was equivalent to 46.0 per cent. They were distributed unevenly, with the heaviest concentrations on either bank of the Dnieper above the rapids. This figure excludes 19,000 'single-homesteaders', who in 1787 were reclassified as state peasants; they too had military obligations and some of them were even turned into Cossacks.[18] In 1788 a number of ecclesiastical peasants, and even 4,000 'surplus clergy', were likewise assigned the status of military settlers, as were some privately-owned serfs.[19] By 1801, within slightly different territorial boundaries, the percentage of 'militarized settlers' (Druzhinina's term) had declined to 33.6 per cent: in round figures, 152,000 males out of 452,000.[20] A quarter-century later (1827) a further diminution had taken place, to 27.4 per cent: 195,000 out of a total male population that had now risen to 712,000.[21] The trend to civilianization was slow but unmistakable.

Russia's successes in the south during Catherine's reign suggest that the settlement system proved its worth in conventional military terms: it provided men and (presumably) supplies for troops who had to fight in a theatre remote from major centres of population and resources. Whether the settlers achieved their economic objectives is less certain—one modern authority states firmly that 'despite heavy initial subsidies, the regiments never attained the degree of self-support for which the Imperial authorities had . . . hoped'[22]—but contemporaries could plausibly blame the shortcomings on external factors that had disrupted orderly management.

It does not appear that any official investigation into the merits of these policies was undertaken during the reigns of either Paul or Alexander I, despite—or perhaps because of—the fact that high-level opinion about them was divided. This lapse was to prove a serious defect when the idea was taken up again after the peace of Tilsit in 1807, and on a much greater scale after 1816—with other areas of the empire in view, and for motives that differed considerably from those of the eighteenth-century pioneers.

Already in 1778, while still tsarevich, Paul had praised the Prussian 'canton' system, which he saw as a superior alternative to general recruitment. He suggested that one-quarter to one-third of the men in each regiment could be released from active duty during the winter months. Both the soldiers and the state, he thought, stood to benefit: the men's morale would improve and the

[18] Druzhinina, *Sev. Prichernomor'ye*, pp. 158, 187.

[19] *PSZ* xxii. 16605, 16607, 16646, 16650 (8, 14 Jan., 19, 25 Apr. 1788); Druzhinina, *Sev. Prichernomor'ye*, pp. 127, 189.

[20] Druzhinina, *Yuzhnaya Ukraina*, p. 70. These include 31,500 Cossacks but exclude the former 'single-homesteaders'—and the *regular* troops stationed in the area.

[21] Druzhinina, *Yuzhnaya Ukraina*, p. 167.

[22] Menning, 'Mil. Institutions', p. 16.

authorities could give proper supervision and care to their children and to veterans. Each army—there were to be four of them—would have a reserve from which regiments could draw reinforcements as and when required.[23]

Some enthusiasts attached special importance to the last point. The soldiers' male offspring would be so numerous, and so well adjusted to the military environment, that they could in time supply all the army's needs; in this way the burdensome levy system could be done away with. Potemkin dreamed of 'an inexhaustible flow of warriors in lieu of recruits'.[24] Advocates of this utopian view did not bother their heads with demographic projections, or even ask themselves whether the armed forces' vast intake was really necessary. It was in a similar spirit of insouciance and vague benevolence, combined with a very real concern for state interest, that Alexander I approached the question of military settlements.

From 1802 onwards, as we know, the army rapidly increased in size, partly to make up for the unprecedentedly heavy casualties suffered in the first encounters with Napoleon (1805-7). By 1808 the armed forces were absorbing 56.1 per cent of total state expenditure, as against 40.2 per cent five years earlier.[25] The need for economy was self-evident. Several thoughtful military leaders shared the tsar's anxiety about the demoralizing effect of the levy system. The institution of recruit depots in 1808 (see ch. 7) was clearly no more than a palliative. In the same year Lieutenant-General M. A. Obreskov suggested the creation of a reserve, to be made up of men who had completed seven years' active service,[26] but nothing came of the idea. No better success attended N. S. Mordvinov, Minister of the Navy and a dogged framer of reform proposals, who in 1810 advocated that certain troops be set aside to produce food for the rest.[27] Instead Alexander turned to Arakcheyev. In June of that year he visited his friend's estate at Gruzino (Novgorod province), which was run on strict military lines and had the reputation of a model establishment. The visit convinced the tsar that Arakcheyev's disciplinarian methods were suited for general application. A scheme was taking shape in his mind for a *nation-wide* system of military settlements, and his former War Minister seemed the logical person to run them.[28] Characteristically, Alexander was most impressed by the superficial features of the arrangements at Gruzino: 'the order that prevails everywhere, the cleanliness, the construction of roads and plantations, the symmetry and smartness we saw on every hand'.[29] His idea was to cover Russia

[23] Paul to P. Panin, 10 May, 14 Sept. 1778, 'Perepiska', pp. 407, 413; Barskov, 'Proyekty', p. 119.

[24] Potemkin, *Bumagi* (Sbornik voyenno-ist. materialov, 6, 1893), p. 120, as cited by Druzhinina, *Sev. Prichernomor'ye*, p. 127.

[25] Keep, 'Russian Army's Response', p. 521.

[26] Bogdanovich, 'Ob umen'shenii', pp. 245-51; Yevstaf'yev, *Vosstaniye*, pp. 35-6.

[27] *Arkhiv gr. Mordvinovykh*, 4 (St. Petersburg, 1902), pp. 13-15; Yevstaf'yev, *Vosstaniye*, p. 36; Shchepetil'nikov, in *SVM* iv (I, i. ii), pp. 93-7.

[28] Shil'der, *Aleksandr I*, iv. 24; Yevstaf'yev, *Vosstaniye*, p. 37; Jenkins, *Arakcheev*, pp. 143-6.

[29] Grand Duke Nicholas Mikhaylovich, *Correspondance de l'Empereur Alexandre Ier avec sa sœur, la Grande Duchesse Catherine*, St. Petersburg, 1910, pp. 32-3.

'with a veritable network of Gruzinos, hundreds of villages which the army would make as neat, orderly and elegant as the estate of Arakcheyev'.[30] Henceforth this simple-minded but extravagant concept would guide official thinking about the military settlements and obscure their essential purposes, which were to save money by making the troops more self-sufficient in regard to food supply and to improve their condition. After the harrowing experiences of the great campaigns of 1812–14 the tsar became still more obsessed with the idea. The soldiers' sufferings aroused his humanitarian sentiments and he came to see the settlement scheme as a personal moral obligation which he ought to fulfil at any cost. This attitude communicated itself to members of his entourage. Arakcheyev himself was one of several senior officers who, eager to curry favour with the ruler, suppressed their initial doubts as to the project's feasibility and devoted all their energies to implementing it.

For some zealots in high places the scheme would not only improve the empire's military posture but also transform its cultural life. One of Arakcheyev's correspondents contended that, unlike regular recruits whose martial virtues had been debased by serfdom, the settlers, 'born to the military calling, will drink in its spirit with their mothers' milk; . . . they will have the chance to develop their innate talents, [and so] this class will bring forth great men like Lomonosov and Menshikov. No longer will those endowed with natural genius be swallowed up by the plough.'[31] Such sentiments might have seemed dangerously revolutionary to Alexander I or Arakcheyev, both firm upholders of serfdom in the empire's heartlands; but they too had an exaggerated notion of what the reform could accomplish. If soldiers became farmers and farmers soldiers, might not Russia's social and geopolitical problems be solved at a single stroke?

The deeper implications of these ideas were not lost on foreign observers. A French diplomat noted in 1818 that the reform would strengthen the autocratic state by making it less dependent on the gentry for the provision of recruits.[32] One of his compatriots, writing some years later, reckoned that it would enable Russia to pursue a more adventurous foreign policy.[33] In a similar vein liberal-minded Russian officers feared that the settlers might form a militarized caste which the government could use to crush internal dissent.[34] Such apprehensions were not entirely groundless. It was no coincidence that the informer who denounced Pestel´ belonged to a settled regiment. In general, however, the Praetorians tended to believe that the experiment was bound to fail. It was one of their principal grievances against the regime. Pestel´ thought it misconceived in principle and noted correctly the shaky economic calculations

---

[30] Pipes, 'Colonies', p. 207.

[31] Mel´gunov, *Dela i lyudi*, p. 284.

[32] 'Exposé des forces militaires de la Russie . . .' [1818], MAE, M et D, Russie 26 (1808–20), f. 192ᵛ; cf. H. H. de Dreux-Brezé, 'Notes recueillies . . . sur les colonies militaires . . .' [1826], ibid., Russie 29 (1807–27), f. 199.

[33] De la Rue to Maison, July 1834, ibid., Russie 37 (1831–52), f. 139ᵛ.

[34] Zavalishin, *Zapiski*, p. 98.

on which it was based.[35] Some critics expected it to end in bloody catastrophe. In 1820 a civilian official termed the settlers 'new *strel'tsy* who in time will lead Russia to revolution . . . the fire will start in these accursed settlements; already now a single spark would suffice to set everything ablaze'.[36] This was an alarmist view, although as we shall see presently soldiers and peasants alike did put up strong resistance to the scheme. The settlers' revolutionary potential was a source of hope to some dissident officers, but they were unable to make use of it.[37]

More typical was the concern expressed by an officer of conservative leanings to the effect that soldiers and peasants who received an education, yet were denied the right to own property, were likely to revolt.[38] Many senior officers opposed the scheme on professional grounds—and not just because they associated it with the tsar's unpopular favourite. Commenting in 1817 on some draft regulations compiled by Arakcheyev, Barclay de Tolly prophesied that if soldiers turned their hand 'from the rifle to the plough or sickle, their military spirit can be expected to vanish completely'. I. I. Dibich (von Diebitsch) reckoned that 'a century of uniformity in thought' would be required for success.[39] Both these men were experienced generals—of Baltic German extraction—who took a common-sense view. Other conservatives were more self-interested. A. Ya. Storozhenko, a senior staff officer, thought it wrong for commoners to be educated at the state's expense and feared that the settlers' agricultural produce would compete preferentially with that of private landowners.[40]

Alexander I knew that his scheme was unpopular and suspected the critics' motives. This was one reason why it was introduced gradually and almost by stealth—although this only stimulated fears about its ulterior purposes and helped to spoil the chances of achieving its ends. The clearest statement of what the tsar intended was not made until 1821, by which time implementation of the project was well under way. It came in a formal charter (*gramota*) issued to the Ukrainian Ulan regiment—not a general decree (*ukaz*):

to ease [the peasants'] transition to the military estate and to make [the soldiers'] service less burdensome . . . We have formed the irrevocable intention to settle each regiment on the land, within a certain district, and to provide that its intake shall be drawn exclusively from the inhabitants of that district.[41]

Before we can evaluate the military settlements as they existed in reality, and not just in the official mind, some idea must be given of their territorial extent

---

[35] *VD* vii. 162 (Raeff, *Decembrist Movement*, p. 152).
[36] N. M. Longinov to S. R. Vorontsov, Oct. 1820, 'Iz pisem', p. 364; cf. pp. 404–5.
[37] Mazour, *First Russ. Revol.*, p. 45; Fedorov, *Soldatskoye dvizheniye*, p. 69.
[38] Shchepetil'nikov, in *SVM* iv (I, i, ii), app. 15; Ferguson, 'Settlements', p. 205.
[39] Shchepetil'nikov (*SVM* iv), p. 108 (full text in *VS* (1861), 6, pp. 335–63); cf. Yevstaf'yev, *Vosstaniye*, pp. 45–51; Ferguson, 'Settlements', p. 142.
[40] Storozhenko, 'Iz zapisok', pp. 455, 475–6; Pipes, 'Colonies', p. 217.
[41] *PSZ* xxxiv. 26803 (18 Apr. 1817); cf. xxxiv. 26843 (8 May 1817), xxv. 27512 (26 Aug. 1818).

and principal characteristics. Later we shall discuss the reaction of the men concerned and the modifications which Nicholas I made to the system.

A beginning was made in 1810, when one battalion of an infantry regiment, the Yelets Musketeers, was settled in former Polish territory that was now part of Mogilev province. More than 4,000 state (that is, non-proprietorial) peasants resident there had to sell off their possessions and move to Yelizavetgrad in New Russia. About half of them are said to have perished *en route*.[42] Construction of the settlement had scarcely started when the area was overrun by Napoleon's troops; the surviving buildings were then taken over by the local peasants, who had to be ejected by the musketeers when they returned. Soon two regiments were quartered permanently in the region, which however remained the smallest of the four widely separated settlement areas.[43]

In 1816 the organizers turned their attention to Novgorod province. Why they chose it is not clear. Memories of the seventeenth-century precedent may have been a factor; probably more important was its proximity to the capital, and particularly to Gruzino. The swampy terrain was unsuited to agriculture, but typically this point was overlooked when the first 19 villages were assigned to the grenadier regiment that bore Arakcheyev's name. In the north-west the residents (officially termed *korennye zhiteli* or 'natives') were not expelled but turned into settlers—that is, militarized. Several months elapsed before they were told of their impending fate, and for a time even the civil governor was kept in the dark. By 1818 several adjacent districts along the river Volkhov and west of Novgorod had also been taken over to accommodate five more grenadier and cuirassier regiments, and elements of two other divisions were settled across Lake Il'men around Staraya Rusa. The authorities tried to make the territory compact by buying up some civilian properties in the area.[44]

This problem loomed much larger in the settlements established from 1817 onwards in the former Slobodskaya Ukraina. Designed for cavalry units, they were administered from Chuguyev, a small town south-east of Khar'kov, where many officers descended from Ukrainian land-militiamen had acquired property over the years. Arakcheyev and his aides (Lieutenants-General I. O. Vitt [de Witt] and Linasevich) decided to expropriate them in the interests of uniformity, but the compensation offered stood in no relationship to the properties' real value. This led to grumbling and eventually to active resistance (see ch. 13). Even shabbier treatment was meted out to 135 Chuguyev residents who were deported, much like the Mogilev peasants before them. These harsh measures nullified the main advantage which Alexander I had

---

[42] Mel'gunov, *Dela i lyudi*, p. 278; von Bradke, 'Avtobiogr. zapiski', p. 51.

[43] Shchepetil'nikov (*SVM* iv) pp. 98–9; Fabritsius, in *SVM* vii. 504–11; Lykoshin, 'Voyennye poseleniya', pp. 87–8; Petrov, 'Ustroystvo', p. 89; Yevstaf'yev, *Vosstaniye*, p. 63.

[44] *PSZ* xxxiii. 26389 (5 Aug. 1816); Shchepetil'nikov (*SVM* iv) pp. 99–100 (with map); Dubrovin, *Sbornik*, v. 70–3, 84; Kartsov, 'O voyennykh poseleniyakh', 2, pp. 146–54, 3, pp. 82–3; Tański, *Tableau*, p. 119.

hoped to derive from the fact that the local people, as he thought, 'still retained their martial spirit'.[45]

The same mistake was committed in the south-western settlements, where the militia tradition had never been interrupted. These were scattered across the steppe in a great semicircle, from the Yelizavetgrad area westward to the river Bug and then downstream almost to Nikolayev; the administrative centre was located at Voznesensk (see map). They were set up in 'old military villages'[46] whose inhabitants (especially the ex-Cossacks) knew their rights and resented the enforced change of status. Trouble broke out as soon as the project was initiated in 1817, and morale was not improved when, four years later, General Vitt decided to force the pace of development. Aware of the area's rich agricultural potential, he offered handsome incentive payments to any regimental commander who managed to make his unit self-sufficient in food and fodder grains within three years—an unreasonably brief term.[47]

Alexander I was planning other settlement areas in Yaroslavl' province and in Volhynia when he died. At that time Arakcheyev's organization, the Separate Corps of Military Settlements, reportedly controlled 160,000 soldiers (including nearly 4,000 officers).[48] Two military writers state that this was almost one-third of the Russian army's entire strength, which if so implies that this was only about half as large as it should have been according to the establishment tables (approx. 900,000).[49] The settlers comprised 20 regiments each of infantry and cavalry, located respectively in the forest and steppe zones, plus sundry artillery, engineering, and transportation units.[50] Arakcheyev claimed that there were also nearly as many (154,000) children, termed 'cantonists', and 8,000 invalids; if one accepts these figures, and adds in the 374,000 peasants who had by then been brought within the system,[51] the reform encompassed about ¾ million persons.

They were divided into several categories. In each settled regiment only a quarter of the men became farmers (*khozyayeva*) with a homestead of their

[45] Shchepetil'nikov (*SVM* iv) p. 118; Petrov, 'Ustroystvo', pp. 111, 138–44, 232–7; Vereshchagin, 'Materialy', p. 149; Kartsov, 'O voyennykh poseleniyakh', 3, pp. 88–90.

[46] *PSZ* xxxiv. 26800, 27195 (16 Apr., 24 Dec. 1817); Kabuzan, *Zaseleniye Novorossii*, pp. 66–7; cf. pp. 209, 226 for population tables which, however, evidently exclude the farmers (*khozyayeva*) and other dependants who also lived under military rule. For a vivid description (1822): Lyall, *Travels*, i. 144–52.

[47] Dubrovin, *Sbornik*, v. 60–1, 69; Shchepetil'nikov (*SVM* iv) p. 117; Kartsov, 'O voyennykh poseleniyakh', 3, p. 95; Yevstaf'yev, *Vosstaniye*, pp. 76–7.

[48] Shchepetil'nikov (*SVM* iv) p. 114; Fabritsius (*SVM* vii) p. 591 and app. p. 103.

[49] Petrov, *Russkaya voyennaya sila*, ii. 339; Kartsov, 'O voyennykh poseleniyakh', 3, p. 112. For lower contemporary estimates: Pontcarré, 'Rapport sur les colonies militaires' [1824] and La Ferronays to de Damas, 22 Apr. 1827, in MAE, M et D, Russie 27 (1819–27), ff. 67f., 217: 67–70,000. (Excerpts from this despatch are in Schiemann, *Nikolaus I*, ii. 415–22.) Tański (*Tableau*, p. 120) estimates the number (in the south alone) at 47,000.

[50] Lykoshin, 'Voyennye poseleniya', p. 88; Kartsov, 'O voyennykh poseleniyakh', 3, p. 112; Fabritsius (*SVM* vii) pp. 269ff.

[51] The latter figure (both sexes) was given by Chernyshev in an official report of 1850: 'Ist. obozreniye', *SIRIO* xcviii. 420. Arakcheyev's would deserve closer scrutiny: the number of children seems too high and may refer to all family members, since soldiers' wives are not listed separately.

own. The other troops were either active soldiers or reservists. In peacetime they lodged with their farmer comrades, assisting them with the field work. When they went off on campaign their families and property were entrusted to the farmers, who 'shall look after it all and keep it as safe and calm [sic] as they would themselves'.[52] Regulations such as these expressed the ideal of a military community run on patriarchal lines. Soldier-farmers were to be selected for their high moral standards and the respect they enjoyed among their fellows. Wherever possible they were to be married men who had gained some experience of agriculture before joining the service. If not enough qualified soldiers were available, settlers were recruited from the local civilian population, the rest of whom earned their living as labourers.[53]

Last but not least, the soldier-farmer was to have 'a perfect knowledge of drill movements and everything pertaining to the parade-ground'. He was exempt from active duty in the field, but had to be fit, martial in bearing and of smart appearance—and how else in Alexander's army could this be achieved except by frequent bouts of drill? Exercises were suspended for six weeks during the harvest season and in October, a month set aside for building and repair work around the settlement.[54] In 1826 certain Novgorod settlers were drilling three times a week, and in the south General Vitt ordained that 'each farmer, together with his assistant and cantonists, shall stand to attention before his home whenever the commander rides by'.[55] Characteristically, firearms training received minimal attention, perhaps because the authorities feared that the weapons might be turned against them.[56]

Settlers were required to wear uniform, even when engaged on construction work, and were liable to disciplinary penalties if they failed to keep it clean. Their caps bore the number assigned to each rural district (*volost'*), considered the equivalent of an infantry company.[57] Not everyone resented such regimentation: when Nicholas I changed the rules some settlers at Romny (Poltava province) begged to be allowed to keep their uniforms, which they preferred to normal peasant attire.[58]

The reaction may have been similar to the accommodation provided. In place of the random scattering of tumbledown huts found in most Russian villages, each settlement consisted of 64 square wooden buildings (called *svyazi* or 'links'), painted in identical colours and arranged in eight symmetrical rows, with the company office in the middle. The barrack-like aspect aroused misgivings among some upper-class visitors, but the settlers themselves

---

[52] *PSZ* xxxiv. 26942 (27 June 1817); Petrov, 'Ustroystvo', p. 224.

[53] Petrov, 'Ustroystvo', pp. 225–8. In the Novgorod area one-third fell into the latter category: ibid., p. 222.

[54] Lykoshin, 'Voyennye poseleniya', p. 92.

[55] Petrov, 'Ustroystvo', p. 204.

[56] Ibid., p. 221; Lykoshin, 'Voyennye poseleniya', p. 92; Kartsov, 'O voyennykh poseleniyakh', 3, p. 102; Ferguson, 'Settlements', p. 191.

[57] Petrov, 'Ustroystvo', pp. 130, 203.

[58] Storozhenko, 'Iz zapisok', p. 454.

probably appreciated the improved sanitation: farm animals, for instance, were kept in separate sheds. On the other hand, their living quarters were very cramped: an area of 9 by 16 *sazhens* (66 square metres) had to be shared by four families of farmers and their lodgers. Each pair of families pooled their household resources—an interesting adaptation of the artel principle.[59] The settlers had to build their homes themselves (perhaps with the aid of a military labour battalion), as well as workshops, guardhouses, exercise-halls, administrative offices, and so on—not to mention houses for senior NCOs (who were not allotted homesteads) and officers. All this imposed a heavy burden.

Still more onerous was the construction work that had to be done to improve communications (roads, canals) and to facilitate the agricultural and other economic activities which each unit carried on. The Russian soldier was certainly no stranger to physical labour, but in the settlements there was far more of it than usual and he received precious little reward. The normal wage was 25 kopecks a day, half the usual rate at the time for hired civilian workers, and from this trivial sum a portion was deducted for food. Often, it seems, the men received no more than a ration while their pay went straight into the artel fund, or even into that of the settlement, on the specious grounds that this capital existed for the soldiers' own benefit. Labourers who were remunerated on a piecework basis had to meet high norms. In Novgorod in 1826 each man was expected to dig a trench 15 *sazhens* (32 metres) long in one day.[60] The officials who fixed these targets were under pressure from above to provide quick results and knew that no questions would be asked if they ignored regulations. The administration took the view that military labour was a valuable but under-exploited resource. 'Soldiers could do amazing things for the state's benefit', wrote V. P. Kochubey to Arakcheyev, 'so long as they are kept under reasonable and effective surveillance and work according to a well thought-out plan.'[61] He was convinced that in the Novgorod settlements, which he had just visited, this was indeed the case.

Most of the work was of course agricultural. The farms were expected not only to meet the army's own requirements but also to yield a surplus for sale. Civilian output levels were to be exceeded by enlarging the sown area, improving techniques, and developing communications. In so far as these plans were designed to encourage a spirit of initiative among the settlers, they were quite sensible; but nowhere were they set down coherently, and narrow limits were set to free enterprise in practice. When some farmers suggested setting up an industrial plant the idea was turned down as premature.[62] Produce

[59] Bois-le-Comte to La Ferronays, 24 July 1821, MAE, M et D, Russie 27 (1819–27), f. 41; Lykoshin, 'Voyennye poseleniya', pp. 93–4; Petrov, 'Ustroystvo', pp. 154–6; Yevstaf'yev, *Vosstaniye*, pp. 70–1.

[60] Petrov, 'Ustroystvo', pp. 116, 121–3, 203; Yevstaf'yev, *Vosstaniye*, p. 66, Kartsov, 'O voyennykh poseleniyakh', 3, p. 107, claims that on construction projects soldiers' food was better than usual, but offers no evidence that this was so.

[61] Kartsov, 'O voyennykh poseleniyakh', 3, p. 87.

[62] Ibid., p. 112.

had to be sold according to contracts drawn up in advance and vetted by the military authorities, who built up an elaborate bureaucracy for the purpose. Few members of the divisional or regimental committees had the necessary business experience or understood the elementary rules of accountancy. While endeavouring to control petty details they distributed grants and loans as much for their psychological as for their economic effect, which they were unable to estimate accurately. On one occasion the tsar authorized expenditure of 658,000 roubles to give each of the northern settlers a minimum of five cows— a measure that could still be hailed 70 years later as evidence of monarchical generosity.[63] Naturally, the money sometimes did good, but such acts set a poor example to those officers who had to decide whether or not to extend a loan to an individual settler.[64]

Another major weakness of the development programme was that settlers lacked full legal title to their land and were in effect tenants for life of the state, rather like the *pomeshchiki* of Muscovite times. To have conceded this right would have undermined serfdom by establishing a sizeable class of property-owning peasants.[65] A settler could pass on his holding to a son or son-in-law (or could adopt a soldier as an heir if he had no children);[66] but this was a duty, not a right, and implied a transfer of service obligations as well. Even the movable property of a settler was not protected, for the interests of the unit as a collective took precedence over those of individuals. The authorities reasoned that in the last resort all a soldier-farmer's wealth—land, buildings, stock, tools, and in some cases even articles of furniture—had been 'given' to him by the government, and so could rightfully be taken away.

As so often in Russia, authoritarianism and egalitarianism went hand in hand. The land allotments were distributed among the settlers in the same way as was done in most peasant communities. The norms were relatively generous, at least in the south where arable was plentiful, and something was done to reduce the intermingling of strips that was the bane of communal agriculture.[67] Yet in 1826 Dibich found that 'the soldier-farmers are scarcely able to feed their own families; . . . agriculture has been completely neglected and everything has been done for appearance's sake instead of for genuine

[63] Ibid., 4, p. 94.

[64] Petrov, 'Ustroystvo', pp. 135–7. In 1822 a 200-rouble ceiling was imposed on such loans. Interest was usually charged at 5 per cent (Ferguson, 'Settlements', p. 184), but officers in the settlements who had access to a separate loan fund paid no interest whatever on loans—which could reach as much as two-thirds of their annual salary: Petrov, p. 135.

[65] Pipes, 'Colonies', p. 211, assumes that this was indeed the government's intention, but the cavalry settlement regulations are explicit on this point: 'soldiers in settled squadrons . . . will turn into their property [*sobstvennost´*] all they manage to acquire by working the land and raising cattle' (Petrov, 'Ustroystvo', p. 224). Civilians who brought land into the system were allowed to keep it, but this did not affect the general principle. Like other classes of the tsar's subjects, the farmers lacked any clear definition of their rights. Shchepetil´nikov justly observes (*SVM* iv, p. 107) of the settlers that 'everything they had could become someone else's property'.

[66] Petrov, 'Ustroystvo', p. 229.

[67] Storozhenko, 'Iz zapisok', p. 455; von Bradke, 'Avtobiogr. zapiski', p. 39; Shchepetil´nikov (*SVM* iv) p. 116; Ferguson, 'Settlements', p. 164.

effect'.[68] This was not a wholly impartial view, but it contained a good deal of truth. One reason for the settlers' poverty was that their grants were phased out too soon, before the farms were firmly established, in the interest of registering a profit. Although they were exempt from taxation and received many favours denied to ordinary peasants, the settlers had to bear a greater economic burden. This was contrary to the government's intention and resulted from its chronic inability to calculate costs and benefits. The paradox was all the greater in that the inhabitants of the military settlements enjoyed a degree of social security that was far in advance of the time.

These measures embraced medical care, education, and provision for orphans, invalids, and veterans. By 1820 there was at least one hospital in each infantry settlement and one for every two of cavalry; each battalion had its para-medical personnel (*fel'dshery*); medicines were supplied free of charge.[69] Foreign visitors were impressed. A French diplomat who toured the settlements in Kherson province noted that in the hospital at Petrikovka each patient had a bed of his own, and that wives could stay there to look after the men.[70] Yet a doctor in the northern settlements recorded that fever, dysentery, and scurvy were rife. He attributed this mainly to poor diet and overwork.[71] Casualties were particularly heavy in military-labour battalions. Lieutenant-Colonel N. I. Panayev, who supervised construction work in the Novgorod area, wrote that 'if one man in ten died, this was not considered a high mortality rate'; only if it rose to one in eight was an inquiry held, and even so those responsible were not punished.[72]

The authorities were more interested in raising the birth rate. Midwives—still a rarity in the Russian countryside—were provided, one for each regiment, and initially at least married couples qualified for a 25-rouble grant.[73] Arakcheyev ruled that marriages should take place by mutual consent, but in practice some commanding officers would draw up lists of prospective partners, much as landowners were wont to do with their serfs. Tales of 'colonels distributing brides like sheep' are probably exaggerated,[74] but there is no doubt that the authorities interfered on an unwarranted scale in settlers' private lives. Official expectations that such measures would generate a self-perpetuating flow of soldiers were soon shown to be naïve. Instead recruits from the general levy had to be assigned to the settlements to make up their numbers.[75]

68 Shchepetil'nikov (*SVM* iv) pp. 115–16.
69 Dubrovin, *Sbornik*, v. 58; Ferguson, 'Settlements', pp. 186–7.
70 Dreux-Brezé, 'Notes recueillies . . .' (1826) [see fn. 32], f. 187.
71 Yevropeus, 'Vosp.', p. 226.
72 Panayev, 'Rasskaz', pp. 66–7.
73 Petrov, 'Ustroystvo', p. 213.
74 Kartsov, 'O voyennykh poseleniyakh', 2, p. 154.
75 Shchepetil'nikov (*SVM* iv) pp. 116, 119; N. [V.] Putyata, 'Yeshche neskol'ko slov o voyennykh poseleniyakh', *RA* 1874, 1, 4, col. 1046; Storozhenko, 'Iz zapisok', p. 466.

All children were classified as 'military cantonists' and became legally the property of the regiment in which their fathers served. Those aged seven or under lived with their parents (or, if orphaned, were placed in the care of soldier-farmers). When they turned eight they donned uniform and went to the school established in each district, where NCOs instructed them in the three Rs and the Scriptures. Some of these teachers were trained. After four years' schooling the boys formally entered the regimental reserve; the classroom was supplemented by the parade-ground and the curriculum acquired a more military flavour.[76] 'Drill is as necessary as study', the tsar ruled.[77] In the Bug settlements 'each boy learned the military statute with the aid of a wooden sabre and carbine, [seated] upon a wooden horse, and there were sometimes wooden cannon as well'.[78]

This training, which continued until the age of 18, was more intensive than anything available to civilian commoners, but its quality can only be guessed at. On the positive side the boys learned useful craft subjects; but they were also subjected to a good deal of bullying, and the discipline was unduly severe. The administrators sought to produce a caste of thoroughly dedicated young soldiers. Up to a point they succeeded. The defects—brutality, arrogance, narrowness of vision, formalism, lack of initiative—were characteristic of Russia's 'military culture' as a whole.

Unfortunately it was officers with this limited mind-set who were called on to manage the settlements, and here lay their gravest failing. From the start Arakcheyev insisted that they should be run as an independent organization. The civilian authorities had no jurisdiction whatever within the areas that were taken over; all administrative functions, including the maintenance of public order, were exercised solely by army personnel. An astonished contemporary remarked that 'no one can enter those parts of the country . . . without a special pass made out by some military authority'.[79] No outside agency, whether military or civilian (least of all the Council of Ministers, which rubber-stamped any relevant papers submitted to it), could supervise the operations of the sizeable bureaucracy which Arakcheyev built up. The Separate Corps had no fewer than 3,678 officers, including 28 generals, on its staff,[80] and was organized, as one would expect, on strictly hierarchical principles without any real input from below. In theory peasants and others could submit complaints, but if they were deemed to be unsubstantiated punishment swiftly followed.[81]

For all his ferocity Arakcheyev was not cast in the mould of a modern dictator. He was no more than a henchman of his sovereign, and towards the

[76] Petrov, 'Ustroystvo', pp. 109–10; Tański, *Tableau*, pp. 124–5; Ferguson, 'Settlements', pp. 188–9.
[77] *PSZ* xxxvii. 28765 (29 Sept. 1821), § 10.
[78] Lobachevsky, 'Bugskoye kazachestvo', p. 605.
[79] Von Stork, *Denkschrift*, p. 77.
[80] Shchepetil'nikov (*SVM* iv) p. 114; Beskrovnyy, *Potentsial*, p. 37.
[81] Lykoshin, 'Voyennye poseleniya', p. 97.

end of Alexander's reign there were signs that the favourite was losing his grip. He attempted to devolve responsibility for decision-making, but this only blurred the lines of authority and encouraged the regional commanders to take liberties, whereupon their subordinates did likewise. Many of the senior officers, notably Generals P. A. Kleynmikhel' (Kleinmichel), Arakcheyev's chief of staff, and Vitt, were of Baltic German extraction, but it would be quite wrong to blame 'aliens' for the abuses that occurred, as some historians have done.[82] Two factors are more relevant: (*a*) settlement officers lacked specialized training in agriculture or farm management—indeed, there was a belief in military circles that this was unnecessary;[83] (*b*) once appointed to the Separate Corps, they generally made their careers entirely within it, and so were looked askance at by their fellows in line regiments. The latter resented the fact that settlement officers received a bonus of 50 per cent on top of their regular pay.[84] Actually half this sum was deducted during the first four years of service to create the capital for a special officers' loan fund, and the money could not be reclaimed on transfer. As the years went by it became ever harder to secure such a posting, or even a discharge. This limitation on officers' mobility lowered their morale.

From a moral point of view the settlement officer was placed in a difficult position. He had to keep in his superior's good graces by expressing confidence in the scheme, whatever his inner thoughts might be. Daily he was tempted to behave hypocritically and dishonestly. The more conscientious (and prosperous) tried to leave, while others joined for the sake of the bonus. The evils of absolutism in the administrative domain were here reproduced in microcosm. Those in subordinate positions of authority were under constant pressure to produce results, yet knew that their actions could not easily be controlled. This opened the way to bureaucratic abuses, notably misappropriation of state funds and cruelty towards inferiors. In the Polotsk regiment, settled in the Mogilev region, several company commanders sold surplus grain on their own account and withheld their men's pay—the latter a common offence in line units as well. Two brother soldiers named Trusov conspired with two senior NCOs to exploit some soldiers' labour; fearing exposure, they killed another NCO named Grigor'yev and beat another settler so severely that his distraught wife died in childbirth. These facts were reported by two privates, one of whom was the best farmer in his district, and an investigation was launched which confirmed their account. The brigade commander, however, had the *informants* court-martialled! They were sentenced to run the gauntlet five and six times respectively through 500 men. The verdict was upheld by the

[82] For example, Kersnovsky, *Istoriya*, ii. 278: 'a German idea, transposed by the gauntlet into the clay soil of Novgorod'.

[83] Von Bradke, as a 20-year-old sub-lieutenant, was put in command of 7,000 men engaged on construction work, although—as he told Arakcheyev frankly—he had no experience of civil engineering and could not distinguish rye from oats: 'Zapiski', p. 36.

[84] Fabritsius (*SVM* vii), app. p. 269.

regional commander, Major-General Yefimovich. When the case came to Arakcheyev's notice in 1821 he belatedly tried to see that justice was done. But he was powerless against the tsar. Alexander happened to know the brigade commander personally and simply ordered him transferred to another post.[85] With such dereliction of duty at the top it is not to be wondered at that subordinates ignored or defied the law.

Three years later a major on Vitt's staff was charged with stealing no less than 230,000 roubles. According to the investigating officer the sum was really almost twice as large and the regional commander himself was a party to the fraud. 'Everyone from Count Vitt downwards', he wrote later, 'tried to cover up the frequent misdeeds . . . and abuses, for each saw that his superior wanted to punish only those who made mistakes involuntarily [and not the actual culprits].'[86] Or, to be more precise, higher authority exercised close supervision over external formalities and trivial details while neglecting matters that vitally affected the functioning of the system.

It may seem unfair to evaluate the settlements as they existed in 1825, when the scheme was still in its initial phase and had over thirty more years to run. However, Nicholas I's modifications are best considered separately, and since Arakcheyev lost his command within weeks of Alexander I's death[87] this date does constitute something of a landmark.

'Une pensée libérale dans un corps despotique'[88]—this was one contemporary's lapidary verdict, which it would be hard to improve on. The main errors may be listed, in order of importance, as follows:

   (i) over-administration by personnel of inferior quality;
   (ii) unrealistic and excessively ambitious planning;
   (iii) poor choice of sites, especially in the north;
   (iv) unnecessarily harsh discipline and petty regimentation.[89]

These failings had a common denominator: disregard of the human factor.

Can one attempt a closer analysis of the costs and benefits? Unfortunately Pipes's statement in 1950 that the financial information is insufficient for a reliable estimate[90] still holds good. Arakcheyev reported expenditure of 13.8 million roubles during the quinquennium 1818–23, explaining that earlier allocations had gone unrecorded.[91] He also claimed that two-thirds of this was

---

85 Petrov, 'Ustroystvo', pp. 163–8.

86 Storozhenko, 'Iz zapisok', pp. 447–8, 471–3.

87 For details see Ferguson, 'Settlements', pp. 211–13 and 'Settlements, 1825–66', p. 110.

88 Dreux-Brezé, 'Notes recueillies . . . [see fn. 32], f. 202.

89 This judgement accords broadly with that of Pipes, 'Colonies', pp. 215–19, except that we cannot accept his contention that 'the military colonies were a planned rational society' fundamentally alien to the psychology of the Russian peasant, for whom 'the ultimate reward for his labours is the prospect of leisure'. It was precisely the *ir*rationality of the Prussian-style military discipline imposed on them that caused resentment, and with good reason.

90 Pipes, 'Colonies', p. 210.

91 Petrov, 'Ustroystvo', pp. 247–8.

covered by 'savings', but this was false reckoning since it involved simply a book-keeping transfer from one disbursing agency to another.[92] His former figure corresponds roughly with his original estimate of 350,000 roubles as the cost of settling one battalion;[93] but it is not consistent with his calculation one year later of a total outlay of 10.8 million roubles.[94] Confusion arose in part from a failure to distinguish between capital and current expenditure, and both sums are certainly too low, especially when administrators' salaries are included. On the other hand it would be misleading to equate costs with the capital accumulated in the various settlement funds, which in January 1825 totalled 20.9 million roubles,[95] for some of this was generated locally or came out of the men's own pockets. But this may give us an approximate order of magnitude, whereas a French estimate (1826) of 34.3 million roubles is perhaps on the high side.[96]

What did the government get for its money? Here we are entirely in the dark, since there are no figures on the amount or value of the settlements' output. Nor do we know how much was sold on the market or delivered to the troops. Even in the less impoverished south such deliveries accounted for only half the army's requirements in 1827.[97] Ferguson (who did not use the French papers) holds that by that year 'enough self-support was being achieved to save the state treasury almost as much money as was being put into the project',[98] but this seems uncertain. How much was normally paid to the army's supply contractors, and what did the government lose in tax revenue? Officials were loath to discuss such questions. Their attitude was much like that of landowners at the time who believed that their serfs' unpaid labour brought them nothing but clear profit.[99]

Yet curiously economic advantages, real or supposed, seem to have loomed larger in the planners' minds than defence considerations. This was the reverse of the situation on the Austrian *Militärgrenze* (to say nothing of the Prussian *Landwehr*). The Polish critic Tański noted that 'there is a big difference between this [Russian] code and the one which governs the regiments on the Austrian border. There at least one finds the rudiments of natural and civil law, whereas in Russia the will of the bosses [*chefs*] constitutes the law.'[100] The military settlements turned into a caricature of their founder's benevolent intentions. They produced, not a force of self-reliant reservists, but a mass of helots toiling under the lash of a self-serving military bureaucracy. This effort

---

[92] Storozhenko, 'Iz zapisok', p. 469.

[93] Petrov, 'Ustroystvo', p. 219; cf. p. 175.

[94] Ferguson, 'Settlements', p. 180.

[95] Ibid., p. 176.

[96] 'Etat de frais pour les colonies militaires', Mar. 1826, MAE, M et D, Russie 27 (1819–27), f. 78.

[97] La Ferronays to de Damas, 22 Apr. 1827, ibid., f. 220ᵛ.

[98] Ferguson, 'Settlements', p. 182.

[99] Confino, *Domaines*, pp. 265–70.

[100] Tański, *Tableau*, pp. 134, 151; for other comparisons, Marmont, *Voyage*, i. 226 and (for the eighteenth century) Ferguson, 'Land-militia', pp. 151–8.

'to make the native inhabitants and the soldiers a single whole'[101] created a strange form of agrarian militarism. In the twentieth century Russian (and especially Ukrainian) farmers would recall it as an awesome precedent.

[101] M. Speransky (1825), in Kartsov, 'O voyennykh poseleniyakh', 4, p. 145.

13

RESISTANCE, REPRESSION, AND REFORM

THE soldiers and peasants on whom the government sought to confer the economic and social benefits associated with the military settlements were quick to manifest their distaste for the scheme. Their first step was to petition for redress of grievances. These pleas were usually disregarded and the plaintiffs punished. Opposition then took a more drastic turn. Some settlers or their dependants fled; others committed suicide; a few raised the flag of revolt. Nevertheless this resistance remained episodic and, in the last resort, ineffectual. The local authorities sometimes lost control of the situation, but the government was never put at risk. Under Nicholas I the disturbances gave an added urgency to ideas of reform, but cannot really be said to have instigated them. What worried officials most was the prospect that the dark warnings uttered by the scheme's conservative opponents seemed to be taking shape. Soldiers were prominent in initiating the rebellions in the settlements. If the whole army were placed on this basis, as originally intended, might not the troops ignite a massive insurgency among the state peasants that could spread to millions of privately-owned serfs as well?

In discussing these acts of resistance it is important to distinguish between the settlements in the forest and steppe zones. In the former area disturbances were 'few and minor', at least during Alexander's reign.[1] The most serious trouble arose in the south, on the river Bug and in the Slobodskaya Ukraina. In Nicholas I's reign the roles were reversed, for in 1831 the Novgorod settlements were the focal point of unrest. It was the government's good fortune that the four regions were too far apart for their residents to make contact easily, let alone concert acts of protest.

In the Novgorod area matters were complicated by the fact that several peasant communities were made up of religious dissenters (Old Believers), who traditionally paid extra taxes in lieu of military service. When they were incorporated into the settlements in 1817 they were required to shave their beards, in their eyes an act of blasphemy. Troops were sent against them. In self-defence they took to axes and pitchforks, but to no avail. Their spokesman, an army clerk named Filipp Mikhaylov, was arrested and made to run the gauntlet; 11 other men were transferred elsewhere.[2] These were mild penalties by the standards of the day, and when disturbances broke out in a neighbouring district the

---

[1] Ferguson, 'Settlements', p. 193.

[2] Martos, 'Zapiski', pp. 530–2, 535–7; Petrov, 'Ustroystvo', pp. 147, 240–2; Fedorov, *Soldatskoye dvizheniye*, pp. 27–8; Yevstaf′yev, *Vosstaniye*, pp. 82–7.

next year Arakcheyev again responded with relative moderation.[3] Nevertheless the incidents left a painful impression. Four years later some dissenters passed on their grievances to a visiting diplomat, who was moved by their plight.[4] They particularly resented assignment to regiments that were named after foreign (non-Orthodox) rulers, the King of Prussia and the Emperor of Austria.

In the south both Old Believers and Dukhobors found themselves conscripted. An appalling judicial massacre took place at Zybkaya (Kherson province) in 1821, when a group of dissenters was forced to run the gauntlet. At least nine men succumbed at a public beating while their womenfolk watched, urging them on to die bravely as martyrs for their faith.[5]

In the Bug settlements trouble broke out as soon as they were established in 1817. It was rooted in social rather than religious grievances. The men believed that their rights as Cossacks had been guaranteed in perpetuity by the Crown under Catherine II. This was also the view of one of their officers, Captain Barvinsky, who was branded as the ringleader in the subsequent investigation. Ninety-three men faced charges, of whom 64 were sentenced to death. On review Arakcheyev mitigated the penalties; two of those convicted were transferred to service in Siberia—Barvinsky's fate is not known—while the rest were freed with a warning.[6] Disturbances recurred the following spring, when the tsar was due to visit the area. The authorities tried to prevent the men from presenting a petition to him, although earlier complaints submitted through regular bureaucratic channels had been ignored. A soldier raised the matter on parade and was struck in the face by an officer. At once there was general uproar, which rapidly spread to other units in the region. This time 30 men were indicted, of whom three eventually ended up in Siberia.[7]

Arakcheyev acted in a harsher spirit in 1819, when a similar commotion broke out in the Slobodskaya Ukraina. The reasons for his change of behaviour are unclear. He may simply have lost his temper. Alternatively he may have become alarmed by disturbances that were occurring at this time among the Don Cossacks and have decided that a show of force was required to prevent a general revolt in the southern borderlands. In the Chuguyev area, as on the Bug, there was common ground between officers and ordinary soldiers. The former were aggrieved at the inadequate compensation offered to them for confiscated property. An ex-captain whose brother was senior adjutant of the 2nd Ulan Division drew up a petition calling for the military settlements to be abandoned. This probably encouraged some of the men to act. On 27 June a party of soldier-

---

[3] Kartsov, 'O voyennykh poseleniyakh', 3, p. 91.

[4] Bois-le-Comte to De la Ferronays, 24 July 1821, MAE, M et D, Russie 27 (1819–27), ff. 38–40 (also in 40 (1821–2), ff. 6 ff.).

[5] Storozhenko, 'Iz zapisok', p. 464. The incident was also told to Dreux-Brezé when he arrived in the area in 1826: 'Notes recueillies . . .', ibid., Russie 29 (1807–27), ff. 184–5.

[6] Petrov, 'Ustroystvo', pp. 146, 239–40; Bogdanovich, *Istoriya*, v. 358–64; but cf. Storozhenko, 'Iz zapisok', p. 452 and Fedorov, *Soldatskoye dvizheniye*, p. 29, for a different version.

[7] Petrov, 'Ustroystvo', pp. 148–9, 242–4; Yevstaf'yev, *Vosstaniye*, pp. 88–9.

farmers refused to reap hay for their unit's horses because they needed to work on their own plots instead. The protest was backed by reservists—retired Cossacks, some of whom were elder kinsmen of the initiators. The movement spread to an adjacent district (that of the Taganrog Ulan regiment) and menaced the town of Khar'kov. The rebels burned down three buildings and killed an NCO who refused to join them.

The authorities at first reacted dilatorily, hoping to quell the protest by persuasion rather than force, but then brought up two loyal regiments. On 2 August arrests began. In all over two thousand persons, including settlers' wives and children, were taken into custody. Open-air camps had to be set up as there was not enough room in the local jails. A military tribunal sentenced 275 individuals to death, while others were punished by informal disciplinary measures. Arakcheyev, who came down to take charge of the judicial proceedings, substituted mass public beatings for the death penalty. Of the 52 persons who ran the gauntlet (up to 12,000 blows), 25 died (see above, p. 168). Those awaiting their turn were promised a pardon if they repented. The tactic succeeded, for three-quarters of those sentenced to corporal punishment were sent into exile instead. Among them were several dozen active and retired officers.[8] The affair was soon a topic of conversation in the capital.[9] It helped to turn public opinion against the government, and Arakcheyev in particular. It was not generally known at the time that the tsar had explicitly approved his conduct.

The troubles in the military settlements must be seen in the context of the growing disaffection within the army generally during the last years of Alexander I's reign. This was rife among men in the ranks as well as their officers. Most of the disturbances occurred in provincial garrisons and were dealt with in secret, so that contemporaries knew little about them. Disproportionate attention was aroused in educated society by the so-called 'mutiny' in the Semenovsky guards regiment in October 1820. This incident occurred in one of the armed forces' most senior and prestigious units, which was stationed in the capital and therefore had 'high visibility'. Liberals and conservatives were both tempted to jump to the conclusion that sedition was rampant at the very centre of the military establishment. This was not so, as is evident when one examines the matter closely. Strictly speaking, there was no 'mutiny' but only a legitimate peaceful protest.[10] Its significance lies in the authorities' panic-

---

[8] There is a good account in Fedorov, *Soldatskoye dvizheniye*, pp. 43–71; cf. Vereshchagin, 'Materialy'; Yevstaf'yev, *Vosstaniye* pp. 90–1; Petrov, 'Ustroystvo', pp. 149–52, 244–5.

[9] Oksman *et al.*, *Dekabristy*, p. 27; Turgenev, *La Russie*, i. 315.

[10] Wieczynski ('Mutiny', p. 172) correctly terms it a 'non-violent demonstration of protest' against the regiment's unpopular new commander, Colonel F. E. Shvarts, and a 'trivial matter'—but uses the conventional term 'mutiny' in the title of his article. To his account four points should be added: (*a*) Shvarts, in addition to other provocative acts, limited the soldiers' earnings from off-base labour, on which they had come to depend; (*b*) some men believed (wrongly) that Shvarts was Jewish, and chauvinistic prejudice heightened their antagonism; (*c*) the rank-conscious officers resented their guards unit being taken over by a mere army colonel, quite apart from his defects of character; (*d*) some of them criticized Shvarts within earshot of their men.

stricken response, which took the spectacular form of disbanding the regiment overnight. The alleged ringleaders were sentenced to the gauntlet, followed by exile to the Siberian mines, while the rest of the men were dispersed among other units, most of which were located in the south, where they formed a reservoir of potentially subversive elements; as we know, the officers in the secret societies tried to make use of their disaffection.

It is now clear, thanks to recent Soviet research, that apart from this affair there were at least 15 other collective protests by soldiers between 1820 and 1825.[11] When Grand Duke Constantine wrote privately that 'the men in the ranks are ceasing to obey their superiors'[12] he was exaggerating, but they were indeed less willing than usual to put up passively with corrupt or unjust actions by their superiors. This attitude was more widespread in the south, as one might expect. Distance from the capital was a factor here, as was the presence of many of the men who had served in France under Lieutenant-General Vorontsov. They also had the sympathy and goodwill of several enlightened senior commanders, among them some of the 'patrons' whose role was discussed in ch. 11. Major-General M. F. Orlov, who headed the 16th Infantry Division stationed in Moldavia, tried to apply the law in an even-handed manner—conduct so unusual that it cost him his position (1823). He sent for court-martial officers who committed acts of brutality or peculation, but even so could not prevent all those who submitted complaints lawfully from being punished.[13] One of the his associates, Major V. F. Rayevsky, wrote later that this was a general practice,[14] but fortunately there were exceptions. Thus in June 1823 a company of the Tobol´sk infantry regiment protested against cruelty on the part of their lieutenant, Pertsov, by stepping forward in a body during a parade held by the corps commander, General I. V. Sabaneyev; there is no record of their being punished for doing so, and Pertsov was posted to another division.[15] Protests in guards units seem to have been handled less severely. One should not assume that every complaint was necessarily justified. In one unit penalties were imposed for misconduct and drunkenness by a lieutenant, A. V. Usovsky, who later became an active member of one of the secret societies; he was evidently just trying to enforce the regulations in a reasonable way.[16]

This incident shows how difficult it was for Praetorian officers to find a common language with their men. Their tactics were on the whole sensible: to

None of this, needless to say, exonerates him from responsibility for unpardonable conduct. Wieczynski's sources may be supplemented by Engel´gardt, *Zapiski*, pp. 232-7; Kartsov, 'Semenovskiy polk'; Chernova, 'Iz istorii', pp. 56-68; V. I. Rachinsky, 'O besporyadkakh . . .' [1852], in *Shchukinskiy sbornik*, i. 157-69; Fedorov, *Soldatskoye dvizheniye*, pp. 72-160.

[11] Fedorov, *Soldatskoye dvizheniye*, pp. 161-73; on the 'Kamchatka regiment affair' cf. also Orlov, *Kapitulyatsiya Parizha*, p. 296.

[12] Fedorov, *Soldatskoye dvizheniye*, p. 164.

[13] Ibid., pp. 165-8; *RBS* xii. 358-9.

[14] 'O soldate' (c. 1822), reproduced in Oksman *et al.*, *Dekabristy*, p. 22.

[15] Fedorov, *Soldatskoye dvizheniye*, pp. 170-1.　　　　[16] Ibid., p. 172.

win the soldiers' confidence by behaving in exemplary fashion, and then to spread their ideas in casual conversations with those whom they felt they could trust. The message was one of restraint until the 'appointed hour'. The agitation, conducted on a man-to-man basis, did not have any significant impact until the summer of 1825; then it made some headway, especially in the south, but was soon nullified either by betrayal or by the conspirators' premature and fateful decision to act. How did the soldiers respond? Even the most sympathetic seem to have retained a certain prudent scepticism towards these approaches from above. This was quite understandable: after all, if the plot failed it was they who would suffer the heaviest penalties, and the risk of exposure was enhanced by the lackadaisical attitude which many secret society members took towards security. In the event some 2,400 men were sent to the Caucasus for their part in the two insurrections of December 1825, of whom nearly 200 first had to run the gauntlet.[17] During the investigation those soldiers who were questioned naturally tried to play down the extent of their participation in the movement, and this has to be allowed for when evaluating their evidence. Nevertheless Private F. N. Anoychenko was probably telling the truth when he acknowledged that, as he had understood it, the conspirators were planning 'a revolt (*bunt*) against the tsar's power' and that he had held back from sharing this information with his comrades 'from fear lest someone might see me and tell the authorities'.[18]

Nicholas I's purge of the army, coupled with the customary expectation that the accession of a new ruler would lead to improvements, helped to reduce manifestations of discontent among both officers and men. The outbreak of two major wars, against the Persians and the Turks, followed in 1831 by a campaign against Polish rebels, also diverted soldiers' attention from their own grievances. Even so in 1829 military settlers in Slobodskaya Ukraina mounted one of the best organized, but least known, protests: at Shebchinka men of the Serpukhov Ulans, many of them former 'single-homesteaders', offered stout resistance to the troops sent to restore order in their village. This was stormed, at the cost of over 100 casualties among the defenders; 50 men were put on trial.[19]

By comparison the great uprising which broke out two years later in the north-western settlements was less rational in its aims and less self-controlled; indeed it displayed archaic and savage features reminiscent of the seventeenth-century *strel'tsy* outbreaks. Typically, the mood of violence gave way rapidly to one of contrition. The revolt suggests that the settled soldiers were coming to share peasant ways of thought and action; the artillerymen are said to have shown themselves particularly vindictive.[20]

[17] Beskrovnyy, *Potentsial*, pp. 231–2; Odintsova, 'Soldaty—dekabristy'.

[18] *VD* vi. 215–19; Fedorov, *Soldatskoye dvizheniye*, pp. 189–90, gives a more positive evaluation.

[19] Yevstaf'yev, *Vosstaniye*, pp. 93–4; Beskrovnyy, *Potentsial*, p. 234.

[20] Ushakov, 'Kholernyy bunt', p. 152. A full account of the uprising is given by Yevstaf'yev, *Vosstaniye*, pp. 113–202.

To be sure, the situation in Novgorod in July 1831 was extraordinary. An epidemic of cholera, which had started in Transcaucasia three years earlier, was sweeping through the empire's northern and central provinces. It was the first appearance of the disease, for which there was no known cure. It struck suddenly, painfully, and almost always fatally. In St. Petersburg 600 victims were dying each day and the residents were fleeing in droves. Officials imposed quarantine measures and ordered buildings to be fumigated and wells purified. The purpose of these precautions was, however, not properly explained, and as they seemed to have no effect contempt for the authorities soon turned to dark suspicions that the sickness must be their fault. Were not the health workers perhaps actually poisoning the wells? Assaults on them were reported, first in the capital and then in its surroundings.[21]

Refugees transmitted news of these stirring events to the inhabitants of the north-western settlements, who were already seething with resentment at their economic and other woes: heavy work norms, overcrowding, niggling regulations, and sadistic disciplinary controls. The 'punishment book' of the Duke of Mecklenburg Grenadier regiment for December 1830 (which happens to have been published) shows that heavy sentences were administered for trivial offences at a rate of about eight a day.[22] Orthodox clergy had been proselytizing the dissenters, and some officers contributed to the disaffection, perhaps unwittingly, by dissociating themselves from the disagreeable orders they had to execute.[23] The epidemic was in truth something of a pretext, as a French diplomat noted: 'the soldiers and peasants . . . took the troubles caused by the cholera as a favourable opportunity [to revolt]'.[24]

The disease had yet to strike the area of the settlements when violence began near Staraya Rusa on 10/11 July, in a military-labour battalion which consisted in part of locally recruited peasants.[25] These men, who had not been inducted into the forces, were however less militant than the uniformed soldiers, particularly the teen-aged 'cantonists'.[26] They seized officers and others in authority and either lynched them on the spot or hauled them off to face a makeshift trial. When some of them confessed to the fantastic charges, this was taken as corroboration that the rumours were true. Simple-minded monarchism and xenophobia were mingled with ancient superstitions. Some rebels claimed to be implementing a decree by the tsar and sent messages to St. Petersburg in this sense—although Panayev reports hearing one group exclaim

[21] The standard account in English of the epidemic is R. E. McGrew, *Russia and the Cholera, 1823–1832*, Madison and Milwaukee, 1965; on the military settlements see pp. 120–1.

[22] Some examples: absent from roll-call (private): 10 blows; stealing stockings (private's wife): 50 blows; unlawful sex (private's wife): 50 blows; quarrelling (veterans): 50 blows; stealing 2 bags of oats (private): 150 blows; 9 days' absence without leave and drunkenness (private): 200 blows. *Shchukinskiy sbornik*, iv. 29.

[23] Panayev, 'Rasskaz', p. 67.

[24] De la Rue to Maison, July 1834, MAE, M et D, Russie 37 (1831–52), f. 141^v.

[25] Gribbe, 'Kholernyy bunt', p. 522.

[26] Ushakov, 'Kholernyy bunt', pp. 154, 159; Kartsov, 'O voyennykh poseleniyakh', 4, p. 104.

'we need no tsar'.[27] There was also a tale that the authorities had been bribed by the Poles with five million roubles—a curious echo of Nicholas I's initial belief that Polish revolutionaries were responsible.[28]

Few of the north-western settled districts escaped the contagion. The active battalions were away fighting in Poland, and few reliable troops were available. Some officers, including Lieutenant-General A. A. Eyler (Euler), who was in charge of the Novgorod colonies, seem to have lost their heads. But it was only a question of time before order was re-established. The tsar's adjutant-general, A. F. Orlov, master-minded the repressive measures, and Nicholas arrived in person to hear the settlers' pleas for forgiveness. After appropriate religious services had been held the men were marched off, 'chained to an iron bar in groups of ten';[29] some of them had been duped into believing that they could expect a pardon. The military-labour battalion in which the trouble had started was confined in the fortress of Kronstadt and every man court-martialled. In all over 3,600 individuals of both sexes were tried and punished, of whom 119 died from the effects. The rebels had taken nearly two hundred lives. It was the gravest outbreak of popular violence in the empire since Pugachev's uprising half a century earlier.

The nature of the reprisals will come as no surprise. The only novelty was the scrupulous care taken by the tsar in prescribing personally the exact number of blows that were to be administered to each culprit—with whip, knout, or the thongs used in the gauntlet ritual. A soldier in the Astrakhan' Grenadier regiment, a loyal unit selected for the grim task, records that loaded cannon were placed at each corner of the square lest the men disobey their orders, and that the general in charge, P. F. Danilov, urged them to show no mercy. 'The groans and weeping of the victims, the thunder of horses' hooves, the clank of chains and the heart-rending beat of the drums—all these sounds intermingled and hung in the air . . .' Of the men from the King of Prussia regiment one lost an eye and two or three victims' entrails spilled to the ground. 'I saw enough horror in two hours to last me a lifetime'.[30] The liberal *émigré* N. I. Turgenev compared the massacre with Peter I's execution of the *strel'tsy* in 1698.[31] The parallel was not inapt—yet these rebels, unlike their forerunners, could claim to have won a victory of a kind.

It was clear to Nicholas I that the settlement system would have to be reformed, if only to improve the regime's security. To a group of Novgorod landowners he said: 'I know, gentlemen, that you were bothered during this affair, but

[27] Panayev, 'Rasskaz', p. 78.

[28] For the superstitions: Panayev, 'Rasskaz', p. 79; Kartsov, 'O voyennykh poseleniyakh', 4, p. 97.

[29] Panayev, 'Rasskaz', p. 127.

[30] Yevstaf'yev, *Vosstaniye*, pp. 224–34; in English, Ferguson, 'Settlements, 1825–66', pp. 114–15. *RBS* vi. 81 represents Danilov as humane and mild. On the repression generally, cf. Schiemann, *Nikolaus I*, iii. 150–3; Curtiss, *Russian Army*, pp. 282–5.

[31] Turgenev, *La Russie*, i. 319.

I shall reform [the settlements] and organize them in such a way that this could never occur again.'[32] Hitherto he had confined himself to relatively minor administrative changes designed to dismantle the settlements' top-heavy bureaucracy and to bring them under his own direct control. Now 'there was a complete separation of the military from the economic personnel in each district'.[33] Although both groups remained under military jurisdiction and much of the old system continued in being, a big step was taken towards civilianization. To understand this apparent contradiction, we must look at the reforms a little more closely.

The settlements in the north-west underwent the most substantial changes. The relevant decrees were issued in November 1831 and March 1832,[34] as a result of which these settlers were redesignated 'farming soldiers' (*pakhatnye* or *pakhotnye soldaty*). Essentially three things happened: (*a*) their functions were redefined; (*b*) a purge was carried out; (*c*) the administration was in part civilianized. In their new status they no longer had to undergo military training, perform guard duty, shave their heads, or wear uniform; but they were still required to produce foodstuffs and provide quarters for the active troops; the latter might belong to any regiment stationed in the locality, instead of being allotted to them permanently as before.[35] They were made subject to the general recruit levy and had to pay a high rent (*obrok*) of 60 roubles a year.

On the second point, only those settlers who initially had been selected from among state peasants were considered reliable enough to become 'farming soldiers'. Those who had previously been soldiers were either transferred to regular units or discharged; those who wished to stay on their farms could do so only as state peasants, not as 'farming soldiers'.

On the third point, the existing districts (*okruga*) were retained, but the regimental and company (*volost´*) committees became semi-civilian bodies. That is to say, they were still under the authority of army officers at district level and above. If an offence was committed, it was dealt with by a military tribunal. The chief post was held by a general who had been associated with the settlements in this area since their origin. As one foreign visitor put it, the settlers became 'peasants rather than soldiers, although constantly subject to the orders of their generals and colonels'.[36] Another observed that, although the active soldiers and the farmers were placed under separate administrations, the brigade commander had the final word.[37] The districts were no longer associated with particular regiments but bore numbers instead. The economic infrastructure was maintained, and indeed developed. Military administrators

[32] Ferguson, 'Settlements, 1825–66', p. 115. The following paragraphs owe much to this article.
[33] Ibid., p. 117.
[34] II *PSZ* vi(ii), 4927 (8 Nov. 1831), vii. 5251 (25 Mar. 1832), summarized by Ferguson, 'Settlements', pp. 227–31; id., 'Settlements, 1825–66', pp. 116–19.
[35] In 1841, for instance, guardsmen were involved: Pajol to de Dalmatie, 4 Oct. 1841, MAE, M et D, Russie 37 (1831–52), f. 196ᵛ.
[36] Ibid.
[37] Marmont, *Voyage*, i. 204.

continued to watch over a large variety of enterprises: stud farms, forests, granaries, flour-mills, brickworks, loan funds, and so on. Moreover, they were still supposed to supervise the inhabitants' social and cultural life—for example, their hygienic conditions—although it appears that in practice there was a good deal less interference than before. Arakcheyev's 'breeding pro-gramme' in particular was silently relegated to limbo, and the authorities now behaved much as they did in villages inhabited wholly by (civilian) state peasants: that is to say, they concerned themselves almost exclusively with exacting taxes and keeping order, while neglecting their supposed welfare functions.

In short the inhabitants forfeited the 'privileges' they had enjoyed as settlers, but their overall burden was reduced. One may suppose that they perceived this as an amelioration. Their land allotments were enlarged[38] and other improvements carried out, so that their incomes were probably higher than those of peasants in most neighbouring districts (although there is no hard information on this point).

The settlers in Mogilev and Vitebsk provinces were transferred to 'farming soldier' status in 1836. They were required to pay rent at only half the rate of their fellows in the north-west, since they had not participated in the distur-bances.[39]

In the southern settlements, which had also remained calm in 1831, the government saw less reason to carry through a major reform. Their in-habitants had provided a large amount of grain (to say nothing of manpower) for the armies fighting in the Balkans in 1828–9,[40] and their economic outlook seemed relatively rosy. In effect they now reverted more or less to the eighteenth-century pattern, with manpower obligations much like those of Cossacks. Active soldiers and reservists were no longer required to work in the fields—although in practice they seem to have done so.[41] The farmers (*khoz-yayeva*: the old terminology was retained in the south) had to do three days' labour a week on lands from which all the harvest and profits went to the state.[42] On the other three days they could work for themselves; they were free to engage 'assistants' as before and to sell any surplus so obtained. These arrangements placed them in a situation rather like that of serfs on private estates in the region. In both cases the three-day norm might be exceeded in practice; the main difference was that the settlers' surplus went straight into the army's granaries instead of to a landlord.

[38] Chernyshev, 'Ist. obozreniye', p. 420.

[39] II *PSZ* xi(ii), 9626 (21 Oct. 1836); Ferguson, 'Settlements', p. 235.

[40] Lobachevsky, 'Bugskoye kazachestvo', pp. 609–10; Ferguson ('Settlements, 1825–66', p. 112) accepts a figure given informally by Vitt to Marmont, which was probably inflated for effect.

[41] II *PSZ* xxxii(i), 31920 (4 June 1857), § 67; cf. Ferguson, 'Settlements, 1825–66', p. 119.

[42] Ferguson, 'Settlements, 1825–66', pp. 119–20; Dussieux, *Force et faiblesse*, p. 61, states that in practice less was demanded, but the reverse was also true.

Other important pursuits in this region were horse-breeding (until 1844, when the stud-farms were abandoned as unprofitable)[43] and livestock-raising. De la Rue, who visited the area in 1834, noted that the Kherson settlements could supply 45,000 head of cattle to other provinces where there was a famine—but that the stricken areas included the Chuguyev settlement district, whence an entire division had to be temporarily evacuated at a cost of 1.4 million roubles.[44] Another visitor, an Austrian officer very favourable to the scheme, produced figures for Kherson province which, examined critically, reveal that by this date the expansion of the livestock herd had done no more than keep pace with the rise in population.[45]

The total herd of cattle and sheep in the military domains increased by 58.6 per cent and 53.4 per cent respectively between 1826 and 1850.[46] Presumably the state did well out of this. What the individual settler gained is less obvious. In the latter year there were, in eight districts of the former Slobodskaya Ukraina, 1,800 settlers and twice as many persons curiously designated 'non-farmers' (dependants?); taken together, half of them had no cattle at all, and income levels were stated to have declined since the 1820s because agricultural expansion had failed to keep up with population growth.[47] In the Bug settlements a system of labour norms was introduced around this time which, as enforced by unsympathetic young cavalry officers, added considerably to the farmers' burdens. A local priest described their situation as if reciting a litany: 'If a man fails to fulfil his quota, he is beaten; if he works too fast and leaves [grain in the stubble], he is beaten; if he gets tired and lets the grain stand a while, he is also beaten.'[48]

By the end of Nicholas I's reign over 1 million dessyatines had been added to the territory under military rule, which covered nearly 3½ million dessyatines (3.76 million hectares). The expansion affected new areas. In 1837 five districts were set up in Kiev and Podolia provinces on land confiscated from 'disloyal' Polish proprietors. The civilian population here numbered 56,000. In order to make room for the settlers, nearly 13,000 of them were compelled to move to other areas.[49] This forced migration resembled the one undertaken in 1810 (to look no further back), except that, so far as is known, it did not lead to heavy casualties. Simultaneously other regions were established in the Caucasus, but they never became a major undertaking.[50]

In 1850 the War Minister reported that there were 713,000 'residents' (*zhiteli*) in military settlements, nearly twice as many as in 1826.[51] This figure

[43] Chernyshev, 'Ist. obozreniye', p. 422.

[44] De la Rue to Maison (July 1834) [see fn. 24], ff. 143, 145.

[45] Marmont, *Voyage*, i. 227. The duke, who was a friend of General Vitt, was too easily deceived by appearances, but gives a useful description of the settlers' life (pp. 199–204).

[46] Calculated from data in Chernyshev, 'Ist. obozreniye', p. 422.

[47] Stolypin, 'Ob uprazdnenii', pp. 767–8.

[48] Lobachevsky, 'Bugskoye kazachestvo', p. 624.

[49] II *PSZ* xiii(ii), 10775a (6 Dec. 1837) [in xii. app.]; Ferguson, 'Settlements, 1825–66', pp. 120–1. [50] II *PSZ* xii(i), 10576 (10 Oct. 1837); Ferguson, 'Settlements, 1825–66', p. 120.

[51] Chernyshev, 'Ist. obozreniye', p. 420.

evidently refers to settlers and dependants, but excludes the military element (active troops, reservists, and cantonists)—as does the slightly higher figure (730,000) given by a Soviet historian.[52] How large was the military element? According to a contemporary foreign source there were 24 cavalry regiments in the southern settlements (Kherson and Khar'kov provinces only), with 160 active and 104 reserve squadrons, making a total of 51,000 men.[53] To these must be added the artillerymen and other support troops, the regiments stationed in other settled areas, soldiers' wives and children (cantonists), and officers. The grand total of persons within the system must have exceeded one million.

The comprehensive programme of military and other reforms instituted after the Crimean War put an end to this state within a state, which by then was generally recognized as an anachronism. The immediate motive seems to have been as much moral as economic. The settlements had a bad reputation for corrupt practices, as had the entire system for supplying the troops in the Crimea. The Russian army was about to reduce its swollen effectives and to change its mode of recruitment and pattern of service (see ch. 15). This logically involved a move by the military away from economic self-sufficiency towards reliance on the civilian market in meeting requirements for grain and other commodities. Between 1856 and 1858 the 'farming soldiers' in the north and west were turned into 'apanage' (*udel*) or Crown peasants. The southern settlers were harder to dispose of. They did not become state peasants until 1866, but in the interim their labour obligations were gradually reduced and the administrative structure civilianized.[54] The more pious among them attributed these changes to miraculous intervention by their patron saint.[55]

As part of this process the military surrendered, in 1860, its control over seven sizeable towns, including Uman', Yelizavetgrad, and Chuguyev, which had served as headquarters or bases.[56] This act passed almost unnoticed amidst the other momentous changes of the era, yet it might be seen as symbolic. It marked the close of a long but waning tradition whereby the military had exercised first a preponderant, then a significant, influence over local government, and indeed in the administration of the empire generally. It is appropriate to

[52] Beskrovnyy, *Potentsial*, p. 37.

[53] Dussieux, *Force et faiblesse*, p. 61. Marmont (*Voyage*, i. 197, 209) offers two totals of 32,400 and 36,000 men for the five divisions in Kherson and Khar'kov provinces only (1834). Kohl, who travelled through southern Russia in 1840, put the military element in these settlements at 60,000: *Reisen*, i. 26. In 1854 there were 75,000 men in active units stationed in the settlement districts and 'various settlement units': Bogdanovich, *Ist. ocherk*, ii. app. 34. The same table shows a total of 761,000 soldiers and an almost identical number of 'general population'; but the tenth revision (1858) put the total number of military settlers at 1,119,000 (572,000 males): J. Blum, *Lord and Peasant in Russia . . .*, Princeton, 1960, p. 503.

[54] Ferguson, 'Settlements, 1825-66', pp. 123-4; for relevant legislation, Amburger, *Geschichte*, pp. 325-6.

[55] Lobachevsky, 'Bugskoye kazachestvo', p. 626.

[56] II *PSZ* xxxv. 36415 (19 Dec. 1860); Chernyshev, 'Ist. obozreniye', p. 420; Kabuzan, *Zaseleniye Novorossii*, p. 68.

consider this tradition in the following pages, for the underlying reason why the military settlements had become obsolete by mid-century was this: they were out of step with the trend towards professional specialization. A modern state needed to be ruled by officials, not by officers.

During the eighteenth century the Russian army beat a slow retreat through the empire's institutions of government. Not until the first decade of Alexander I's reign was there a decisive shift away from the employment in civil posts of serving officers (or those who had just resigned their commissions). Even so much of the Imperial administration continued to wear a martial look right down to the Reform era. Apart from simple inertia—a force always to be reckoned with in Russian history—there were four main reasons, which were mutually reinforcing, for this state of affairs. First, the armed forces were the only available source of manpower, given the fact that the gentry preferred to join the armed forces and that the higher levels of the civil service, like the officer corps, were all but closed to commoners. Second, the various military academies produced a fair crop of officers with at least a smattering of general as well as professional education; the universities and other civilian higher schools, which developed only after the 'cadet corps', yielded better trained men, but at first far too few of them. Third, the tasks of government were for a long time seen as predominantly coercive in nature, and therefore individuals with a military background seemed to be well suited to perform them. Fourth, the army needed to renew its commanding personnel every so often in order to remove 'dead wood' and maintain efficiency; and it faced an additional problem in the presence on its rolls, at least in peacetime, of large numbers of supernumeraries. Few of those who retired or were excluded on grounds of age, wounds, or incompetence, or who fell victim to one of the periodical economy drives, had an assured private income. If they were not to die in poverty they had to be found jobs they could handle which would provide them with a reasonable income.

In the course of the eighteenth century more and more officers transferred from military to civilian service (and sometimes back again). Indeed, this almost became the normal career pattern. As the taste for civilian employment grew, ambitious young noblemen would put in a spell with their regiment and then, having obtained some experience of the wider world, would apply for discharge and appointment to a civil-service position—with the statutory promotion on completion of the minimum service term. Except in wartime such requests were as a rule freely granted, since the state's broader interests were well served by them, even though the army suffered from the high turnover rate, and such transfers led to many complaints about unjustified advances in rank (see ch. 10).

The employment of men with a military background in the bureaucracy was the most obvious way, but not the only one, in which the army's influence was brought to bear upon the administration. Some branches of the economy (mining, road transport) were run on military lines and with much assistance by army personnel. Large areas of the empire, notably sensitive border regions that had recently been annexed and were populated largely by ethnic minorities, were placed under what was essentially a system of military government. The following summary remarks can do only partial justice to a large topic.[57]

We may concentrate on local government, since in a vast empire with poor communications it was the district (*uyezd*) and provincial (*guberniya*) authorities that were most likely to come into contact with the tsar's subjects. Significantly, it was precisely such officials, rather than those at the centre, who tended to have military backgrounds and to approach their civil tasks in an unimaginatively mechanistic or disciplinarian spirit. Only gradually were they superseded by men with a broader education and outlook.

Peter I's successors relaxed his unduly coercive and militarized system of provincial government. In 1727/8 they also abolished, ostensibly on grounds of expense, the *provintsiya* as an intermediate level of local administration, and from then until 1775 rural Russia was ruled much as it had been in the seventeenth century. In the district the chief figure once again became the voivode or commander. He had broad police, fiscal, and judicial powers. These were not clearly distinguished from those of his superior, the governor (*gubernator*), so that neither the latter nor the officials of the procuracy could ensure that his actions conformed to the law, or even to the central authorities' wishes. The voivodes had a well-deserved reputation for corrupt practices; they were grossly underpaid and as before were tacitly expected to 'feed' themselves at the inhabitants' expense.[58]

In our context the important point is that eighteenth-century voivodes were almost invariably former staff officers (usually colonels).[59] They executed their functions with the aid of the garrison troops stationed in their district (which they commanded). Soldiers were used to quell minor disorders, put down banditry, catch fugitive peasants, enforce collection of taxes (especially arrears), and so on. In 1727 military officers were removed from poll-tax collection, but this experiment lasted only five years; thereafter two to three officers would normally be detailed for such work at the provincial, and one at

[57] Despite the Soviet taboo on study of Imperial Russian militarism, pioneering work has been done on the bureaucracy by S. M. Troitsky and others which sheds light on our subject. Still more useful is the contribution made by several Western students of the civil service, notably W. McK. Pintner, H.-J. Torke, R. Wortman, and J. P. LeDonne. None of these scholars, however, has yet tackled the military aspect *per se* and its importance is generally underrated. Quantified studies of the civil service rest on analysis of career records *(formulyarnye spiski)*, and in the absence of similar data for officers the following survey is necessarily somewhat impressionistic.

[58] The classic study is Yu. V. Got'ye, *Istoriya oblastnogo upravleniya v Rossii ot Petra I do Yekateriny II*, 2 vols., Moscow/Moscow and Leningrad, 1913–41, who provides numerous examples; see esp. i. 86–9, 107–9. For the first moves: Vyazemsky, *Verkhovnyy taynyy sovet*, pp. 339–42.

[59] In Siberia, however, he might sometimes be an illiterate ex-Cossack or even a former serf—or so the government complained: PSZ x. 7730 (12 Jan. 1739); Troitsky, *Russkiy absolyutizm*, p. 136.

the district, level.[60] In the principal towns an officer of the local garrison was appointed 'police-master'; he too had a small squad of soldiers at his beck and call, which apparently was distinct from the force available to the voivode.[61]

Figures for 1755 show that, of 836 provincial officials in the first three grades for whom data are available, 532 (63.6 per cent) entered on this stage of their career either directly from the armed forces or after attending military or naval schools; for those in 'middle-ranking positions', numbering 294, the figure was as high as 250 (84.0 per cent).[62] A survey taken in 1773 showed that of 365 voivodes and assistants (holding ranks VI and VIII) only 58 had never served in the military, whereas 163 (57.2 per cent) had spent more than 20 years in the forces.[63] During the latter part of Catherine II's reign the situation improved: the range of educational opportunities expanded, and so did the number of provincial civil-service jobs. Of a larger sample of 1,520 provincial officials who entered before 1794, 533 (35.1 per cent) were ex-military, although the proportion was still as high as 73 per cent among those in the 'middle-ranking' category.[64]

The reforms of 1775–85 defined local officials' functions more precisely, with some regard to the principle of separation of powers; a number of posts were filled by candidates of the local gentry instead of being government appointments; and a new office of governor-general or *namestnik* was established. The governor-general had authority over several (usually two) provinces, each of which continued to be administered by a governor, now assisted by several executive bodies. At the district level the rural police chief (*ispravnik*) became the most important official.[65] Although an elected functionary, this successor to the voivode seems to have exercised his powers in much the same way. He was still likely to be a former officer who had received no specialized training for his new job. Such men regarded their posts as 'a sinecure rather than a challenge'[66] or as welcome relief after the rigours of campaigning against the Turk. It was precisely at this moment (1774) that the government was confronted with an efflux of officers from the armed forces—the second in a dozen years. One need not leap to the conclusion that this was the principal motive for the reform, but it was certainly a contributory one. Data are available for 105 men who in 1788 held either of two provincial-level posts that carried economic and judicial responsibilities respectively. Seventy-eight of them had previously served in the armed forces, and 23 had

[60] Troitsky, *Russkiy absolyutizm*, p. 172; Petrov, *Russkaya voyennaya sila*, ii. 171.

[61] Yeroshkin, *Istoriya gos. uchrezhdeniy*, pp. 121–2.

[62] Troitsky, *Russkiy absolyutizm*, pp. 276–8; cf. Pintner, 'Evolution', p. 210 for slightly different figures.

[63] Givens, 'Nobiliar Career Patterns', pp. 115–17.

[64] Pintner, 'Evolution', pp. 211–12. The data are not exactly comparable, because the later figures contain no rubric for direct entrants from educational institutions. They do not support Pintner's statement that 'the pattern of 1755 holds until the end of the eighteenth century'.

[65] For discussion of the reforms see de Madariaga, *Catherine*, pp. 277–91, 296, 583–5; LeDonne, *Ruling Russia*.

[66] Givens, 'Nobiliar Career Patterns', p. 117.

done so for more than 20 years.[67] The proportion will probably have been even higher among rural police chiefs.

For the senior echelons of the provincial administration biographical sources are more plentiful, so that one can put some flesh on the bare statistical bones. Nearly all the 77 governors appointed after 1775 were military men. The Russian countryside experienced what J. P. LeDonne has called 'an invasion of the major-generals'.[68] This may seem paradoxical since, as we have suggested, Catherine's intention was to reduce the military's role rather than to expand it. One has to take into account the improved quality of the individuals selected and the greater control that was henceforth exercised over them—especially by the *namestniki* as direct agents of the Crown and close confidants of the ruler. These dignitaries were appointed principally for their all-round *savoir-faire*— and not simply for their expertise in the arts of coercion or just to keep them occupied, as was so often the case lower down the hierarchy. Of 30 governors-general who came fresh to the field of provincial administration, exactly half (15) were generals who had proved themselves on the battlefield. Of the others nine bore military rank but 'were truly civilians' (their experience had been in police work), and the remainder 'belonged to the higher ranks of the civil bureaucracy'. Most of the military men had had some exposure to civil administration prior to their appointment to this prestigious position.[69]

Closer examination shows that these governors-general were stationed either in the two capitals or in those borderland areas where they might need to use their military skills.[70] The cities of St. Petersburg and Moscow (along with Kiev) had been ruled by governors-general from time to time earlier in the century;[71] now the office became permanent. St. Petersburg was placed under a field-marshal, A. M. Golitsyn (1783), and then one of his close associates, General Ya. A. Brius (Bruce), until 1791, whereupon it passed into the hands of an individual with mainly police background (N. P. Arkharov). Moscow was run in turn by 'one of those political generals who abound in the Russian army' (V. M. Dolgorukov), by a senior commander whose reputation dated back to the Seven Years War (Z. G. Chernyshev), and by Brius. At the time of the French Revolution the man currently in this office was another elderly general, P. D. Yeropkin, who was thought too lax and replaced by 'a known hard-liner', A. A. Prozorovsky. The latter, who had served with Dolgorukov, doubled as commander-in-chief of the troops in the region. His predecessors seem to have done so as well.[72]

[67] Ibid., p. 124; cf. Wortman, *Legal Consciousness*, p. 77, for the biography of one such official, P. I. Prityupov.

[68] LeDonne, *Ruling Russia*, MS.

[69] LeDonne, 'Catherine's Governors', pp. 21, 23, 25.

[70] De Madariaga, *Catherine*, p. 358 (Rumyantsev, Chernyshev, Repnin).

[71] Amburger, *Geschichte*, pp. 369–70, 382, 384; the holder sometimes bore the title of 'commander-in-chief'.

[72] LeDonne, 'Catherine's Governors', pp. 22–3; Amburger, *Geschichte*, pp. 382, 385; *RBS* xv. 7. *PSZ* xx. 14392 (7 Nov. 1775), IV, §§ 89–90 prescribed (rather vaguely) the proper relationship between governors-general and military commanders.

It would be tedious to follow the pattern of appointments through the various border provinces. We may simply note that three regions in the southeast in which the population had shown some sympathy for Pugachev (Astrakhan´, Ufa and Simbirsk, and Orel and Kursk) were ruled by generals, as was Khar´kov, which from 1788 formed part of Potemkin's 'empire'. Field-Marshal Rumyantsev was put in charge of the so-called 'old' Ukraine (Chernigov, Kiev, Novgorod-Seversk) from 1781 to the end of Catherine's reign. By contrast, the former Polish provinces of Polotsk and Mogilev were treated gently: from 1782 they were ruled by a civilian-oriented individual, P. B. Passek.[73]

In the last years of the Catherinian era the government of the empire seemed to be running down in bureaucratic routine, and her successor had some grounds for attempting a shake-up. His brief but trend-setting reign brought a concentration of power at the summit. It also witnessed a move towards militarization. This involved three main changes: entrusting army personnel with certain definite responsibilities within the civil administration; promoting an element of professionalism instead of relying so heavily on the aristocratic élite; and improving public servants' ethos by inspiring them with the military values of discipline, obedience, and efficiency.[74] This did not mean that the armed forces took control of the country. Paul wanted the military and civilian authorities to keep strictly within their respective spheres of competence, which he sought to define more clearly, and to work together amicably in 'a joint effort to advance the Sovereign's affairs'.[75] The idea was quite sensible, but unfortunately Paul was his own worst enemy. His brutal and arbitrary behaviour made even his reasonable measures seem obnoxious to broad segments of élite opinion, and so his reforms did not take shape as he desired.

In the local government sphere the Pauline spirit made itself felt in the sudden appearance of a new official: the military governor (*voyennyy gubernator*). In effect this functionary superseded the governor-general (*namestnik*), whom the emperor saw as a regrettable innovation of his mother's. Military governors were appointed in the two capital cities and in eleven provincial centres which were evidently chosen for their key geographical location.[76] Although they were supposed not to interfere in the business of their civil counterparts, some military governors were soon given supervisory powers over them, and even over the civil administrators of *neighbouring* provinces.[77] Characteristically, civil governors were permitted to send only 'communications', not 'orders', to military governors, but nothing was said about messages

73 Amburger, *Geschichte*, pp. 371–2, 394, 397, 403.
74 Keep, 'Paul I', p. 3 (Ragsdale (ed.), *Paul I*, p. 92).
75 *PSZ* xxv. 18400 (25 Feb. 1798); cf. Sokolovsky, 'Iz istorii . . . stariny', p. 358.
76 Amburger, *Geschichte*, p. 375 n. The office of *namestnik* was not explicitly abolished and the term 'governor-general' continued to be used. On the St. Petersburg chiefs: 'Iz zapisok A. F. Voyeykova', *Ist. sbornik . . . v Londone*, ii. 123; Shil´der, *Pavel*, pp. 357, 393, 436.
77 Amburger, *Geschichte*, p. 374.

in the reverse direction.[78] In most jurisdictional conflicts the men with arms at their disposal will probably have got the better of the argument—especially where they commanded the police.[79] On the other hand, when P. S. Meshchersky, the Kazan′ military governor, used troops to maintain the town's piped water supply, he was reprimanded on the grounds that he had exceeded his competence, for soldiers were supposed to be used only to *build* such facilities.[80]

Delicate distinctions of this kind were naturally very difficult to enforce. The officials concerned sought to expand their police powers to the maximum limit. In 1798 the St. Petersburg military governor (then P. A. Palen) was given the right to confirm decisions of the civil courts and to manage a ramified network of police inspectors and sub-inspectors, who were appointed 'masters' (*khozyayeva*) of their districts. They were instructed to deal with disturbances of the peace 'in a mild and non-violent (*tikhiy*) manner',[81] but were left to find out in practice how far they could really go. Other statutes sought to lay down the powers of junior military officials such as town commandants (a reversion to the Petrine precedent) and town majors (*plats-mayory*). The former had the privilege of reporting personally to the sovereign.[82]

Paul's unhappy reign with its violent end is significant in administrative history because it showed that bureaucratization and militarism were insufficient, indeed literally fatal. Unfortunately this was not the lesson learned by his two successors. Both Alexander I and Nicholas I by and large walked in their father's footsteps, although they did not emulate his provocative excesses.[83] Alexander's reformist intentions were noble but his practice was often very different—as his biographers have consistently noted, and as we have seen in regard to various issues of major concern to the troops. In the realm of local government he tilted the balance between the military and civilian element in favour of the former. This shift was not entirely deliberate, but in part a response to the Napoleonic challenge; however, the process began before the external threat materialized. In 1801 Alexander ordained that military governors should automatically have control of the police apparatus and set up new jurisdictions for them in western frontier areas.[84] Military influence did not wane when the wars ended in 1814, although this time there was no general rush of demobilized officers into the civil service, as had been the case after earlier conflicts, since the army's strength was maintained at a high level.

[78] *PSZ* xxv. 18400 (25 Feb. 1798).

[79] Certain military governors were accorded the title of 'chiefs for civil affairs' (*nachal′stvuyushchiye po grazhdanskoy chast′yu*): cf. *PSZ* xxiv. 17778 (1 Feb. 1797), xxvi. 19609 (18 Oct. 1800). The St. Petersburg city police was placed under the military governor, but then transferred to his civilian counterpart: xxiv. 18296 (28 Dec. 1797), xxvi. 19671 (30 Nov. 1800).

[80] *PSZ* xxiv. 17878 (18 Mar. 1797).

[81] *PSZ* xxv. 18663 (12 Sept. 1798), VI § 20; for the Moscow counterpart see xxv. 18822 (17 Jan. 1799); Yeroshkin, *Istoriya gos. uchrezhdeniy*, p. 136.

[82] [Rusinov] *Zapiski*, p. 113; *VE* xiii. 68; *PSZ* xxiv. 17777 (1 Feb. 1797).

[83] This point is developed in our 'Mil. Style'.

[84] *PSZ* xxvi. 19866 (11 May 1801), 20004, § 3, 20005, §§ 4, 5 (both 9 Sept. 1801).

In 1816 a new official appeared in the two capital cities: the military governor-*general*.[85] Both St. Petersburg and Moscow remained under military rule throughout the reign, and so did most border areas.[86] The strategic location of the north-western region (Vil'na, Grodno) explains why the supreme office here was held by such prominent soldiers as L. L. Bennigsen and M. I. Kutuzov; and much the same was true of the western region.[87] The Baltic provinces and the Ukraine ('Little Russia') were granted civilian rulers, probably in order to appease the local ethnic-minority élites.[88] In the south-east the Orenburg region remained consistently under military government, as did the Caucasus, but in Siberia, which presented few security problems, civilians exercised control (expect over a strip of territory along the southern perimeter).[89]

Alexander I also found it necessary to strengthen the military force at the disposal of the provincial authorities. In the eighteenth century this had consisted in large part of men unfit for active duty, who were buttressed by regular units during major insurgencies such as the Pugachev revolt. In 1796–7 regulars were employed to quell several minor affrays as well. Typical was their response to unrest among the peasants of Radogoshch (Orel province). Field-Marshal N. V. Repnin and General (D. P.?) Gorchakov brought up a hussar regiment with artillery support and burned down the village, killing or injuring some 150 persons.[90]

The normal procedure in such cases was for the civilian officials of the district (or the local landowners) to report the outbreak of 'trouble' to the civil governor, who had the right to summon military assistance.[91] Alexander I seems to have abandoned (at least in the heartland of the empire) the vindictive practice of destroying entire villages in reprisal for rebellious acts, and to have ordered the culprits to be tried by the civil courts instead. But his successor found this altogether too permissive and had them court-martialled. Officially such proceedings were to be instituted only when force had been used against the troops;[92] but this proviso was not an effective safeguard against abuse, since any tribunal would accept the military authorities' version of events. Civilian offenders were liable to the same stringent penalties that were meted out to soldiers who infringed army discipline.

It was inconvenient, and on occasion actually counter-productive, to divert regular forces from their normal duties to suppress rural unrest. This was one reason why in 1811 the tsar set up the Internal Guard (*Vnutrennyaya strazha*)—

[85] *PSZ* xxxiii. 26496 (30 Oct. 1816).

[86] Amburger, *Geschichte*, pp. 382, 385; *VE* vii. 124; *B&E* xvii. 50.

[87] Amburger, *Geschichte*, pp. 392, 394 (N. N. Khovansky was a *military* officer: see *RBS* xxi. 380).

[88] Amburger, *Geschichte*, pp. 389, 398; this liberalism did not apply to Kiev itself, New Russia, or the Don.

[89] *PSZ* xxvii. 20938 (16 Sept. 1803)—on Orenburg; Amburger, *Geschichte*, pp. 403–4, 406.

[90] Dzhedzhula, *Rossiya*, pp. 166–9.

[91] *PSZ* xxiv. 17801 (12 Feb. 1797), xxx. 23076 (10 June 1808). The procedure became more complex later: Luig, *Geschichte*, p. 45.

[92] LeDonne, 'Civilians', pp. 174, 180.

although the immediate motive for this step was the threat of foreign invasion:
the frontier guards were reorganized on military lines at the same time. In 1816
the Internal Guard became a separate corps, similar to that set up for the
military settlements. It was divided into eight (later eleven) regional commands, each under a general, and was headed by an adjutant-general to the
emperor (E. F. Komarovsky). Apart from 'put[ting] down acts of insubordination and riotous behaviour', the men performed a wide range of other
police and para-military tasks: escorting and training recruits, hunting
deserters and fugitive serfs, and guarding state buildings.[93] Among these
buildings were prisons; these soldiers also kept watch over the detainees,
whether military or civilian, who were sentenced to serve in the 'detention
companies' (*arestantskiye roty*) set up in 1823.[94] Ordinary convicts came within
their purview as well until the establishment of the celebrated convoy (*etap*)
system of escorting prisoners to Siberia, which was run mainly by local
Cossacks.

By Nicholas I's reign the Internal Guard numbered about 145,000 men, not
counting gendarmes (*zhandarmy*).[95] The latter were not, as is usually thought,
an invention of 'the gendarme of Europe'. They had precedents in Paul's
private army at Gatchina (1792–6) and in the Russian occupation force in
France, where in 1815 a dragoon regiment was converted into one of gendarmes. At first given a military police role, by 1817 it had acquired power
over civilians as well. 'Gendarme divisions' were set up in the two capital
cities, and detachments in 56 other towns. The gendarmes provided the muscle,
so to speak, for the Internal Guard: they had to meet higher physical standards
and were more mobile.[96] Nicholas elevated and expanded this force. The gen-
darmerie became a separate corps (1827) and was placed under an ostensibly
civilian agency, the blandly named Third Department of HIM's Own Chancery.
Its functions included internal espionage and are sufficiently well known to
need no discussion here.[97] We may simply note that most of its officers and
men were drawn from the armed forces; they had to be tall, 'of good-looking
appearance' (*blagovidnoy naruzhnosti*), and able to ride a horse and to meet
relatively demanding criteria as regards intelligence, morality, and general
character.[98]

Such requirements were in accordance with Nicholas I's conviction that the
armed forces constituted a repository of virtue. Even more than Paul and
Alexander I he was an enthusiastic advocate of the military way of life and
devoted much attention to parade-ground skills (see ch. 14). 'Military trifles

---

[93] *PSZ* xxxi. 24704 (3 July 1811), xxxii. 25329 (2 Feb. 1813), xli. 30571 (31 Oct. 1825);
Dubrovin, *Sbornik*, v. 32–8; *VE* vi. 443–4; Yeroshkin, *Istoriya gos. uchrezhdeniy*, pp. 191–2.

[94] *VE* iii. 18.

[95] Bogdanovich, *Ist. ocherk*, i. 18.

[96] *VE* x. 355–7.

[97] II *PSZ* iv. 3199 (27 Sept. 1829), xi(i), 9355 (1 July 1836); LeDonne, 'Military Justice', p. 186.
Two standard works on the subject are Monas, *Third Section* and Squire, *Third Department*.

[98] II *PSZ* x(i), 7993 (25 Mar. 1835), xi(i), 9355 (1 July 1836), VII, §§ 98–110.

concern you more than they should,' his mother wrote to him in 1814, adding that he ought to show more regard for the common soldier's welfare, 'which is often neglected and sacrificed to elegance of dress, useless drill, and the personal ambition and ignorance of [their] chief[s].'[99] Unfortunately the future emperor ignored this sensible advice, or at least interpreted it in a highly idiosyncratic manner. Once he had become tsar, Nicholas surrounded himself with a 'military household' (*voyennyy dvor*) of impressive dimensions—in 1853 the Imperial suite included 45 generals and 48 colonels[100]—from which he drew most of his advisers; but among these men there were few with genuine talent.[101] He utilized his personal adjutants (*fligel'-ad'yutanty*) or aides-de-camp as top-level trouble-shooters, in much the same way as Peter I had employed his guards officers (see ch. 6)—but with far less justification, since in the intervening century Russia had after all developed a rudimentary bureaucratic structure.

As a contemporary later recalled,

It was almost impossible to make a career except by serving in the armed forces: all the senior offices in the state—ministers, senators, governors—were given over to military men, who were more prominent in the Sovereign's eye than officials of civilian agencies. Apart from this, it was taken for granted that every senior person should have had a taste of military discipline.[102]

The writer exaggerated, but only slightly. Let us examine an official handbook for 1853.[103] In that year (which saw hostilities in the Balkans and so may not be wholly typical) only 12 provinces of European Russia were left under the control of civilian governors (see table and Map 3). In 14 others this official was subordinate either to a military governor in his province or else came under a (military) governor-general with responsibility for several provinces. In two cases the same man held both offices. In the remaining 23 provinces the highest civilian official was only a vice-governor and the military predominance was even more overwhelming. The typical military governor was a nobleman in his fifties who had entered the army directly from some prestigious educational institution, had seen action, had been closely associated either with the tsar personally or with a leading general, and had gained some experience of police work on transfer to the civil service.

The composition of the central government under Nicholas I has been more thoroughly studied. Of the 52 men appointed to ministerial positions during his reign 32 (61.5 per cent) held the rank of general or admiral; three more had been colonels, and only ten had never served as officers; most of those who

---

[99] Dubrovin, *Sbornik*, v. 79; Lincoln, *Nicholas I*, p. 60.

[100] *Pamyatnaya knizhka na 1853 g.*, St. Petersburg, [1853], pp. 150–3.

[101] Polievktov, *Nikolay I*, p. 323; Curtiss, *Russian Army*, pp. 46–53.

[102] Shcherbatov, '12 let molodosti', p. 87; cf. M. A. Korf, unpublished diary for 1848, cited by Zayonchkovsky, *Prav. apparat*, p. 42.

[103] *Adres-kalendar'. Obshchaya rospis' vsekh chinovnykh osob v gosudarstve, 1853*, St. Petersburg, [1853], pt. 2.

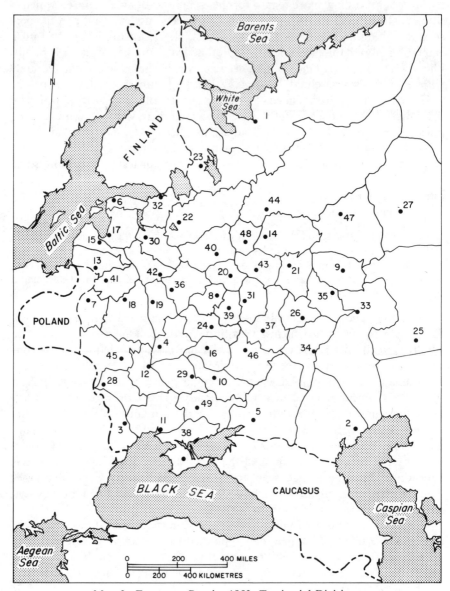

Map 3. European Russia, 1853: Territorial Divisions

had done so had seen action in the field.[104] A study of the Senate reveals a similar picture: the ex-military contingent was 67 per cent in 1846—16 per cent less than it had been 20 years earlier.[105] One former colonel who reached the Senate in 1845 observed that 'in Russia it is the general fashion to look on a senatorial appointment as a relaxation after many years of hard work'.[106]

The fundamental point, though, is that the armed-forces background of those who held senior appointments was no longer characteristic of the civil service as a whole. Pintner's study of personal service records shows that, of entrants to central agencies in the top five ranks, the proportion with previous military experience fell to 25 per cent in 1815–34 (as against 34 per cent in 1795–1814); by 1855, he concludes, the military had 'ceased to be predominant in numbers even at the top, where they were once most heavily concentrated' and 'the overwhelming majority of minor officials in the provinces was composed of lifetime civil servants'.[107] These men were as a rule better educated than their ex-military colleagues, and the differential between them was growing wider.

What this meant in terms of outlook is still not entirely clear. The general cultural level of provincial civilian officials was notoriously low,[108] but one cannot automatically write off all ex-officers as more ignorant or brutal than their civilian counterparts. After all, liberal and nationalist ideas had first struck root in their milieu. But under Nicholas I officers with such views were deemed potentially disloyal; if they obtained responsible posts in the civil administration they had to keep their sentiments to themselves or else risk a great deal of unpleasantness. The experiences of I. I. Venediktov are instructive in this regard. As a military cadet around 1850 he acquired what he describes cautiously in his memoirs as 'new sentiments', and instead of joining a guards regiment on graduation opted for a post in the Ministry of the Interior. He found that the road construction department was managed on military lines: 'I beheld row upon row of tables, behind which were innumerable officials. Right in front a stern-looking gentleman sat bowed over some papers. To one side lay huge sealed bundles, each bearing a label. These were birch rods designed for administering disciplinary punishments [to the clerks].' The ministry's atmosphere was painfully similar to the one he had sought to avoid.[109]

Probably most officials with a military background were 'men of the old school' who applied mechanically the norms of conduct they had learned in

[104] Lincoln, 'Ministers', p. 313; id., *Nicholas I*, p. 164.

[105] Wortman, *Legal Consciousness*, p. 57; for the State Council, see W. B. Lincoln, 'The Composition of the Imperial Russian State Council under Nicholas I', *CASS* 10 (1976), pp. 369–81 and D. Field, in *Kritika* 15 (Cambridge, Mass., 1979), p. 124.

[106] Von Bradke, 'Avtobiogr. zapiski', p. 289.

[107] Pintner, 'Evolution', pp. 212, 214.

[108] It is a cliché to cite Gogol' on this point; see now the scathing comments in the same spirit of Zayonchkovsky, *Prav. apparat*, pp. 143–60.

[109] Venediktov, 'Za 60 let', p. 128.

Civilian/Military Rule in Provinces, * 1853

Province	CIVILIAN GOVERNOR ONLY (no military presence)	CIVILIAN GOVERNOR SUBORDINATE TO — Military governor	Governor-general as 'overlord'	Governor-general as military governor	CIVILIAN VICE-GOVERNOR ONLY — Power exercised by: as mil. governor	Governor-general and subordinate mil. governor	Military governor invested with civil power	Military governor by default
1 Archangel								
2 Astrakhan'		×ᵃ						×ᵃ
3 Bessarabian oblast'								
4 Chernigov						×	×ᵈ	
5 Don Cossack Host land						×		
6 Estlyand			×					
7 Grodno							×	
8 Kaluga						×	×ᵉ	
9 Kazan'							×ᵉ	
10 Khar'kov			×					
11 Kherson		×ᵇ,ᵍ				×	×	
12 Kiev						×	×	
13 Kovno	×							
14 Kostroma								
15 Kurlyand				×				
16 Kursk	×							
17 Liflyand				×				
18 Minsk			×					
19 Mogilev		×ᶠ			×(?)			
20 Moscow								
21 Nizhniy Novgorod								×
22 Novgorod								×
23 Olonets	×							
24 Orel						×	×ᵈ	
25 Orenburg							×ᵈ	

26 Penza
27 Perm'
28 Podolia
29 Poltava
30 Pskov
31 Ryazan'
32 St. Petersburg
33 Samara
34 Saratov
35 Simbirsk
36 Smolensk
37 Tambov
38 Tavrida
39 Tula
40 Tver'
41 Vil'na
42 Vitebsk
43 Vladimir
44 Vologda
45 Volynia
46 Voronezh
47 Vyatka
48 Yaroslavl'
49 Yekaterinoslav

Notes:

a Naval officer
b Civilian governor's office held by military officer
c Military governorship vacant
d Cossack host
e 'Administrator of civil part [of province]'
f Military governor-*general*
g Acting appointment
* European Russia excluding Poland, Finland and Caucasus

the army. Wortman points out that they 'had not received legal training and regarded the law as little different from other commands, requiring no special respect or understanding'.[110] Such an outlook set them apart from the growing number of professional bureaucrats who had been trained in the elements of jurisprudence and were impregnated with a new ethos, one that put less emphasis on reverence for authority and more on fidelity to abstract ideals. Individuals of this type were, like Venediktov, reluctant to enter the armed forces, since they found its *mores* uncongenial, and those who did so usually resigned their commissions within a few years. Of the chief procurators, that is, officials in the Senate who were principally responsible for law enforcement, only 10 per cent had military experience in 1856, as against 36 per cent thirty years earlier, and their average length of service in the forces had declined from eleven years to eight.[111]

Civilianization was a slow process, to be sure, but an ineluctable one. European intellectual influences had long since been percolating into the Russian élite, and the ideologues of 'official nationalism' could offer no credible alternative philosophy. Moreover, 'men of various ranks' (*raznochintsy*) were gradually ousting *dvoryane* from their established positions in the official world. The days of the service state were numbered as surely as those of serfdom. The army was a major bulwark of conservatism, but in 1854–5 the war brutally exposed its deficiencies, as it did the shortcomings of the Nicolaevan system as a whole. It placed reform inexorably on the agenda. The army's pervasive presence in Russian society, which the military settlements epitomized, stood revealed as an impediment to maintenance of the empire's great-power status. In the next quarter-century the topical question was to be: would the reformers be allowed to complete their task? But the underlying, less obvious problem was whether the autocratic order could survive such an effacement of the military, on whose coercive power Russia's government had rested for so long.

110 Wortman, *Legal Consciousness*, p. 92.   111 Ibid., p. 57.

VI

TOWARDS A MODERN ARMY, 1825–1874

14

MARKING TIME

THE Emperor Nicholas I exemplified the militaristic spirit that came so naturally to the Romanovs.[1] His natural sympathy for legitimist principles, his aversion to the ideas of nationalism and liberalism that were coming to the fore elsewhere in Europe, were fortified by the experience of the Decembrist revolt that marred his accession. The tsar exaggerated the dangers that threatened his empire's security, and sought to reinforce it by applying simple military solutions to complex problems. His fears were played on by officers of the Third Department and others in his entourage. In the first months of the reign the armed forces were subjected to a minor purge. This was followed by measures of administrative centralization. Several leading posts were entrusted to members of the ruling dynasty, while the emperor's personal adjutants, already referred to, played an important role as extraordinary inspectors and controllers.

Less defensibly, Nicholas maintained the tradition set by his immediate predecessors of taking an inordinately close interest in the minutiae of military service: staff tables, uniforms, decorations, and above all drill. It was no rarity, a contemporary noted, to see 40,000 men on parade in St. Petersburg—indeed the capital's main square had room for more than twice that number. The tsar was a past master in judging the finesse and precision of their movements as he took the salute. Reputedly he had memorized and could imitate vocally each of the bugler's calls.[2] There was something almost sensual about his infatuation with the parade-ground. From Voznesensk, where he attended manœuvres in 1837, he wrote to his wife: 'I don't think there has ever been anything more splendid, perfect, or overwhelming since soldiers first appeared on earth.' At one emotional moment during the spectacle 'tears welled up, he placed his hand on his heart, raised his eyes to Heaven and prayed aloud: "O Lord, I thank Thee that Thou hast given me such power. Grant me the strength never to abuse it."'[3]

Not sparing himself in the execution of his royal duties, Nicholas expected equally high standards of his subordinates. He once spotted some men of the Izmaylovsky regiment marching in disorderly fashion along a country road. The major-general in command was summarily despatched to the guardhouse for a week and the case published in daily orders to the entire Guards Corps to

[1] This theme is explored further in our 'Mil. Style'.
[2] Bismarck, *Russische Kriegsmacht*, pp. 12, 30, 37; von Haxthausen, *Kriegsmacht Russlands*, p. 119.
[3] Schiemann, *Geschichte*, iii. 327–8.

achieve the desired exemplary effect.[4] The tsar's obsession with outward show, hierarchical subordination, and mechanical compliance with commands came to be emulated by many of his officers. It led them to neglect more substantial matters likely to affect the army's performance in the field. Manœuvres remained formal affairs at which little attempt was made to simulate battle-field conditions. The troops were seldom given instruction in marksmanship, for commanders set little store by firepower, preferring the cold steel of the bayonet. There were some grounds for their attitude, since the smooth-bored muzzle-loaders issued to Russian infantrymen were of little use in action; but other European armies of the day were introducing guns with rifled barrels that had much greater accuracy and range. The same was true, *mutatis mutandis*, of the artillery. The Russian military authorities were slow to adjust to these technical innovations, just as they were to the tactical changes associated with them,[5] although their efficacity had already been demonstrated during the campaigns against Napoleon.

Yet Nicholas's army had ample opportunity to acquire combat experience. Successful wars with Persia (1826–8) and Turkey (1828–9) brought the empire added power and prestige. The Caucasian tribes proved harder to conquer than St. Petersburg expected. Fired by religious zeal and ethnic loyalties, the Chechen, Ingush, and other peoples of the region made the most of their excellent defensive positions. They offered fierce resistance to the Russian troops who made their way up the narrow valleys, taking hostages and burning villages or crops as they advanced. The long drawn-out Caucasian War was expensive in blood and treasure. It tied down large bodies of men at a time when the regime faced a greater threat from the rising tide of nationalism in central Europe. The insurrection which broke out in Warsaw in November 1830 was followed by several months of fighting between regular troops and bands of guerillas, who won a fair measure of popular support in the empire's western provinces as well as in ethnically Polish territory. The European revolutions of 1848 prompted the tsar to declare a state of emergency and to call up more troops, although he already had more men under arms, poised to strike, than any other ruler. In the following year Nicholas intervened to help the Habsburgs put down the rebellious Hungarians. The campaign brought Russia little glory and led indirectly to the materialization four years later of a much greater threat. Britain and France, alarmed at what they took to be expansionist moves against Turkey, drifted into war on the latter's behalf. Austria seemed likely to join the allies. Wisely, the Russian government decided to withdraw the troops it had sent into the Danubian principalities, but then unexpectedly found itself facing an allied expeditionary force on its own soil, in the Crimean peninsula. The 'Eastern War', as the Russians called it, strained the empire's resources so severely as to rule out the prospect of victory. The

[4] Sokolovsky, 'Russkaya gvardiya', pp. 44–5.
[5] For details see now Beskrovnyy, *Potentsial*, pp. 102–16.

two-and-a-half-year struggle cost about half a million soldiers' lives—three-quarters as many as during the whole period from 1789 to 1815.[6]

Was Nicholas's reign then one of military disaster, brought on by his own misguided policies? This was the view taken by some critics after his death, when policy matters could be discussed in public with greater freedom. There was a natural tendency to cast the tsar as scapegoat, much as Stalin would be nearly one hundred years later. 'Magnificent, but all a mistake': Nikitenko's celebrated assessment of the reign should not blind one to its positive achievements, even if the overall judgement cannot but be negative. It is true that these accomplishments were often the work, not of the tsar personally, who was fond of shelving awkward decisions, but of subordinates who had to overcome obstruction in high places. On the whole this was a period of marking time—which is not a synonym for immobility, but implies an accumulation of energy in preparation for a new step forward.

There is no doubt that Nicholas sincerely loved his troops, and that his efforts to better their lot were not so fruitless as his brother's had been. He and his aides also gave a great deal of thought to various improvements in military administration which at least pointed the way towards more substantial changes in the following reign. It is a paradox of the Nicolaevan era that the efforts made to preserve and consolidate existing structures actually laid the groundwork for them to be dismantled. This was as true in the military domain as it was in the field of general social and economic policy. The liberal *émigré* N. I. Turgenev dismissed the tsar's principal measures in the sphere of military reform as mere palliatives.[7] He was right, but only in the short term. Their implications went deeper. Moreover, a new generation of experienced and well-educated officers was rising to the surface. It would be stretching a point to call them liberals, but they were critical of the arbitrariness and chaos that lay hidden beneath the apparently orderly exterior of military life. They sensed that reforms were essential, even if only to ensure the monarchy's survival. Though slighted under Nicholas's heavy hand, these 'cadres' were able to implement much of their programme after 1855.

For the tsar the men in the ranks were 'the subject of Our constant heartfelt aspirations',[8] but this did not mean that they were treated humanely, as responsible individuals with natural rights. Concretely, three things were done on their behalf. First, the recruitment system was modified, and the terms of service alleviated, in order to build up a trained reserve. Second, various steps were taken to improve the troops' material well-being, and also that of their dependants. Third, the quality of the officers set over them was improved by

---

[6] Bogdanovich, *Ist. ocherk*, i. 173–4, as revised by Bestuzhev, 'Krymskaya voyna', p. 196; cf. Curtiss, *Crimean War*, p. 471 and, for the earlier figure, Beskrovnyy *et al.*, 'Bilan démographique', p. 134. A contentious preliminary study of Crimean War casualties was Obruchev, 'Iznanka', 2, pp. 429–76, esp. pp. 436, 459.

[7] Turgenev, *La Russie*, p. 308.   [8] II *PSZ* xi(i), 9141 (7 May 1836).

extending the network of military schools and tightening administrative controls. However, these organizational measures were not reinforced by any substantial change in the system of military justice. In practice soldiers remained subject to arbitrary treatment by their superiors, who could inflict barbaric penalties for trivial faults. This was a conspicuous black spot on Nicholas's record as a military leader. His reluctance to remedy these well-known abuses made the task of later reformers more difficult than it need have been.

For most of the reign the army's paper strength was around 800,000; after 1848 another 100,000 men were added to meet the supposed revolutionary threat, and in 1853 Russia's land forces numbered some 1.1 million; they had grown to over 1½ million by the time the Crimean War ended, exclusive of the militia.[9] Great efforts were made to keep to establishment norms, but one authority estimates the peacetime shortfall at about 20 per cent.[10] Whatever the exact figure, it was clearly enormous: 'the [official] view seemed to be that one could never have enough', was Turgenev's acid comment.[11]

Nicholas was keen to reduce the heavy drain on the empire's human and financial resources. He also knew that only a relatively small proportion of his troops could be fielded in time of war. Other European powers, notably Prussia, had adopted a system of keeping down the size of their active forces and building up a reserve of trained manpower which could be called on in an emergency. The tsar sought to emulate them. The problem was magnified by Russia's vast distances and poor communications, which made mobilization of reservists a laborious task, as well as by bureaucratic inertia. Gentry landowners, too, were content with the existing system, not least because it offered them a convenient means of ridding their estates of undesirables. They (and other donors) could still send them to the army whenever they wished, without waiting for the next levy, and receive a voucher in exchange.[12] During the 1840s the number of vouchers offered in lieu of recruits, for whatever reason, ran at about 10 per cent of the anticipated intake.[13] The government approached the matter in its usual cautious fashion. Instead of establishing a truly separate reserve force, with its own source of manpower and organizational structure, it simply required each active unit to set aside reserve battalions, composed of

[9] Maksheyev, *Voyenno-stat. obozreniye*, p. 217; von Bismarck, *Russische Kriegsmacht*, p. 82; Bogdanovich, *Ist. ocherk*, i. app. 5. The later figures are for 'listed strength' and therefore more accurate than the earlier establishment totals. Some 360,000 men were in the militia (*opolcheniye*): Beskrovnyy, *Potentsial*, p. 80. Bestuzhev's figure of c. 2 million men in the armed forces in 1856 ('Krymskaya voyna', p. 194) includes the navy.

[10] Kersnovsky, *Istoriya*, ii. 292. For a contemporary estimate of 30 per cent: von Haxthausen, *Kriegsmacht Russlands*, p. 37. French diplomatic sources estimated the real shortfall in 1840 at 18.2 per cent: 'Nomenclature générale de l'armée russe . . .', MAE, M et D, Russie, vol. 37 (1831–52), ff. 251–2.

[11] Turgenev, *La Russie*, p. 299.

[12] II *PSZ* vi(i), 4677 (28 June 1831), IV, § 324. If landowners did not claim a voucher for them, they were exempted from paying for their outfitting and provisions: III, § 189. On arrival at their unit such recruits were assigned to non-combatant duties: V, § 432.

[13] Beskrovnyy, *Potentsial*, p. 79; Polievktov, *Nikolay I*, p. 330. For legislation on vouchers: II *PSZ* vi(i), 4677, IV, §§ 321 ff.

selected old soldiers with a given number of years' 'faultless' service to their credit, who were sent on what was termed 'unlimited leave'. These men had to report annually for a spell of training to refresh their skills, but their military value was low. Only some 210,000 such men were available when they were needed to strengthen the forces in the Crimea[14]—too few to make any real difference. Thus the idea, although sound, was not pushed to its logical conclusion. Most historians have taken the view that to have done so would have undermined the edifice of serfdom, since the presence in the countryside of large numbers of ex-soldiers legally exempt from bondage would have created an unacceptable security risk.[15] There is, however, no hard evidence that worries on this score determined government policy, and gentry resistance to reform in this area has probably been exaggerated.

Thus the manpower for both the active army and the reserve continued to be provided in the main by the traditional recruit levy. A volunteer system was also in operation, but it chiefly concerned certain annexed territories (Finland, Georgia); and some 35,000 men were transferred to the Imperial forces from the Polish army when this was disbanded after the 1830–1 revolt.[16] The levy gave the army an average annual peacetime intake of about 80,000.[17] In all over two million men were conscripted between 1826 and 1850; the last years of the reign, which witnessed the heavy impositions of the Crimean War period, brought the figure almost to three million.[18]

In 1834 Nicholas sought to reduce the damage done by frequent levies, and to cut down administrative costs, by carving the European part of his empire into two zones of roughly equal population, each of which was to provide recruits in alternate years.[19] That year the annual intake (three men per 1,000 male 'souls') was drawn mainly from the northern zone, as was that of the following year; the first one to come wholly from the southern zone was summoned in 1837. Two years later the zonal boundary was redrawn so that it ran from north to south,[20] and from then on levies were generally raised alternately in the eastern sector (which included Moscow) and the western (which included St. Petersburg). The populace probably welcomed these measures, if only because they reduced the amount of official interference in their lives, and thus the opportunities for extortion. But they did not enjoy a much greater degree of security, since the planned norm of five men per thousand was frequently exceeded. Moreover, levies from both 'halves' (as the zones were called) were still taken in 1836, 1840, and no less than three times in 1854–5—at varying

[14] Beskrovnyy, *Potentsial*, p. 77.

[15] Polievktov, *Nikolay I*, p. 331.

[16] Verzhbitsky, *Revol. dvizheniye*, p. 150; those implicated in the revolt were, however, sent into exile.

[17] Curtiss, *Russian Army*, p. 234.

[18] Chernyshev, 'Ist. obozreniye', pp. 330–1; for 1851–5 Beskrovnyy (*Potentsial*, pp. 78–80, recalculated) offers a figure of 886,182; cf. Bogdanovich, *Ist. ocherk*, i. 170, app. 12 (the figures are hard to reconcile).

[19] II *PSZ* ix(i), 7317 (1 Aug. 1834); Beskrovnyy, *Potentsial*, pp. 77–8.

[20] II *PSZ* xiv. 12513 (8 July 1839).

rates.[21] The territorial divisions did not survive the test of war and were later abandoned.

Under Nicholas I the state authorities assumed a more active role in the recruit selection process. This was based, as before, on methods which the peasants themselves had devised to share out the burden so that their lives should suffer the least dislocation. One may doubt whether increased bureaucratic regimentation made their choices more equitable: indeed, the reverse may well have been the case, given the poor quality of local officialdom.[22] The Recruiting Statute of 1831[23] was essentially a recapitulation of earlier edicts on the subject, but it did specify in greater detail how the ranking lists (*ocherednye spiski*) of men liable to conscription were to be drawn up.[24] These arrangements were needlessly complicated. For conscription purposes each province was divided into sections (*uchastki*) whose boundaries often overlapped those of the regular administrative units. The inhabitants of each section elected an elder (*starosta*), who had the task of ensuring that the levy was conducted properly. But the government did not ensure that this peasant nominee could stand up to pressure from local police officials or members of the recruiting board. He was subordinate to other functionaries and it was they, not he, who drew up the actual list.

This ranged all families in a section in order of size, with the largest at the head, so that those best able to spare men of working age should be called on first; households with a single male, or for which the loss of an able-bodied worker would spell economic disaster, were exempted. The lists were to be revised every three years to ensure that all changes in family size were registered; allowance was made for differences in age structure and where two families were similarly composed they were to cast lots to establish their relative standing in the list. Within each family single men were to precede those who were married and older bachelors younger ones; where all were married, the choice fell first upon the childless, and if all were fathers the matter was decided by the grandparents, by mutual consent or by casting lots. The law-makers left nothing to chance, and took steps to prevent the dissolution of extended families as a device to evade conscription.[25]

Unfortunately, social reality took little account of these precise and logical schemes. Senators on inspection tours and provincial governors reported that communities failed to keep ranking lists or that recruits were simply nominated by local officials, who enriched themselves handsomely in the

[21] Petrov, *Russkaya voyennaya sila*, ii. 425; Haillot, *Statistique militaire*, p. 316; Beskrovnyy, *Potentsial*, p. 78.

[22] Bolotenko, 'Administration', pp. 373–439. The following paragraphs owe a great deal to this study.

[23] II *PSZ* vi(i), 4677 (28 June 1831).

[24] This procedure had been defined in an earlier code of 1810 (Beskrovnyy, *Potentsial*, p. 71), but does not seem to have been implemented.

[25] Bolotenko, 'Administration', pp. 382–3; II *PSZ* vi(i), 4677, III, §§ 90–136, esp. §§ 99, 101–3, 112, 115, 130.

process.[26] The recruiting boards, too, earned a bad reputation for venality. In Simbirsk one military receiver habitually took money for turning away healthy recruits or accepting those with physical defects, and at one levy collected about 8,000 roubles—which he soon gambled away at cards.[27] The most profitable source of gain was the larger and wealthier families, who could afford to bribe officials to accept a recruit from some family lower down on the list. At Astrakhan´ in 1836 40 families managed to evade their responsibilities in this way; and in Volhynia that year a clerk set up a bogus recruiting board of his own, at which he inducted two brothers, the elder of whom was a mere nine years old.[28] The cost to the populace was heavy, since in addition to bribes they had to supply a sum of money, fixed at 33 roubles, to cover each recruit's food, clothing, and transit expenses.[29]

Such malpractices make it hard to credit Lieutenant-General Bismarck's confident assertion that 'the abuses which used to take place when recruits were inducted, which caused heavy losses among them, have vanished, thanks to the emperor's concern'.[30] Yet the picture was not entirely bleak. Nicholas sent his aides-de-camp to the provinces as overseers, and from 1838 onwards gradually introduced a simpler system which put the emphasis on the casting of lots among all men aged 20–21 in each section. By 1848 this procedure had been introduced among state peasants in 34 provinces, and in 1854 was made general among them; some serf proprietors also went along with it.[31] Drawing lots, although apparently less equitable, made it harder for the wealthier peasants to cheat. It also meant that the army inducted more younger men, who could hope to return to civilian life in middle age, when they were still able to earn their living, rather than as worn-out or disabled veterans.

The authorities also tightened the rules governing substitution and exemption. Since hired men made poorer soldiers an effort was made to reduce their number by offering would-be volunteers an opportunity to enlist directly, in return for a monetary reward.[32] The state's policy was not entirely consistent, since one noblewoman of enlightened views, who ordered substitutes hired for all her conscripted peasants, was officially commended for her pains;[33] it was presumably felt that the proprietress's personal interest in her scheme would limit the scope for abuse.

---

[26] Bolotenko, 'Administration', pp. 390, 392.

[27] Stogov, 'Ocherki', p. 643; Bolotenko, 'Administration', p. 411; cf. Tański, *Tableau*, p. 157: 'everything is venal there'.

[28] Bolotenko, 'Administration', pp. 413, 415.

[29] Ibid., p. 421; II *PSZ* vi(i), 4677 (28 June 1831), II, §§ 184–91; viii. 6362 (1 Aug. 1833).

[30] Von Bismarck, *Russische Kriegsmacht*, p. 84.

[31] Beyrau, 'Leibeigenschaft und Militärverfassung', p. 206; II *PSZ* xxix. 28331 (9 June 1854); Petrov, *Russkaya voyennaya sila*, ii. 423; von Haxthausen, *Kriegsmacht Russlands*, p. 69.

[32] Petrov, *Russkaya voyennaya sila*, ii. 424; for the abuses: 'Rapport sur l'armée de terre de la Russie' [Oct. 1852], MAE, M et D, Russie, vol. 37 (1831–52), f. 353ᵛ; Bolotenko, 'Administration', pp. 396–9.

[33] Von Haxthausen, *Kriegsmacht Russlands*, p. 70.

As regards exemptions a certain irony was involved. J. S. Curtiss remarks nicely that Nicholas 'sought in various ways to lighten [the burden of military service], in part by compelling additional categories of people to submit to it'.[34] Precisely so: these groups consisted mainly of ethnic and religious minorities that had hitherto escaped, such as Jews. Their privileged situation did not accord with the desire for uniformity that animated administrators in the Nicolaevan era, and its abolition was calculated to appeal to chauvinistic sentiments among the masses. Jews were now conscripted in the same way as other subjects of the tsar, except that their communities formed separate sections in each province.[35] It was only a small step from segregation on practical grounds to overt discrimination, in the army as elsewhere. The spirit of official policy is conveyed by a decree of 1832 that Jewish soldiers should not be promoted to non-commissioned rank unless they had demonstrated valour in battle.[36] The military establishment took the view that the Jews' distinct life-style made them unsuited for all the rigours of the service. This was the ostensible rationale behind the ruling that Jewish recruits might be taken at the tender age of 12,[37] and then assigned to cantonists' battalions for a six-year training period designed to remould their minds and bodies.

The lot of these boy soldiers was harsh indeed. They were generally treated even worse than Russian cantonists were. In his memoirs Aleksandr Herzen records that, when on his way to exile in Vyatka in 1835, he came across a party of children aged only eight or nine who were being driven to Kazan'; their well-disposed but powerless escorting officer expected that half of them would die of exhaustion or hunger before they reached their destination.[38] The law prescribed that Jewish soldiers should be free to profess their religion, but this right was usually ignored in practice and in 1843 a wave of forced conversions began.[39] A sympathetic (Russian) former boy-soldier states that the life of those who resisted this pressure was 'worse than forced labour', since they incurred hostility at every level in the military hierarchy. He tells of one Berko Finkelstein, a 15-year-old boy who remained true to Judaism and was subjected by his company commander to a succession of sadistic tortures—being made to stand barefoot on a hot stove or hung upside down by his heels—yet refused to recant. Subsequently Finkelstein became a model soldier, where-

---

[34] Curtiss, *Russian Army*, p. 234.

[35] II *PSZ* ii. 1330 (26 Aug. 1827); iii. 2045 (22 May 1828). Other decrees simply applied to Jewish soldiers the regulations generally in force: for example, viii(i), 5987 (Feb. 1833); xiii(ii), 11386 (3 July 1838).

[36] II *PSZ* vii. 5428 (12 June 1832).

[37] In practice some of them were as young as eight. S. M. Dubnow, the eminent Jewish historian, discerns anti-Semitic bias in this (*History of the Jews in Poland and Russia* . . . [1916], reprinted New York, 1975, ii. 19, 23), but as we know Russian cantonists faced a similar fate; the latter were, however, in the military caste and not recruits from the civilian population.

[38] A. I. Herzen, *My Past and Thoughts*, tr. C. Garnett, revised by H. Higgins, London, 1968, i. 219.

[39] Ginzburg, 'Mucheniki—deti', p. 56.

upon his commander remarked: 'Now there's a Yid for you!'[40] The comment suggests an underlying ambivalence towards the victim not unknown among anti-Semites elsewhere.

During the Crimean War Jews were required to provide recruits at higher rates than non-Jews, and although their communities resisted the levy more actively than most nearly 30,000 were taken.[41] A liberal-minded officer who witnessed their conscription in Bessarabia was distressed at the sight of mothers desperately clinging to their children as soldiers tried to drag them away. But two of his men reacted differently: 'They don't ask us when taking our children. Are the Jews any better than we are? Let there be one line for everyone.'[42]

Recruits from other national minority groups, such as Latvians, also suffered from discriminatory practices, if in a less extreme form. They might for instance be beaten for disobeying oral commands that were given in Russian, which they could not understand.[43] Old Believers and religious sectarians, some of whom held pacifist convictions, were also brought within the scope of the levy. They were generally assigned to units fighting in the Caucasus, and were denied leave or discharge unless they converted to the state Church; otherwise they were left in peace so long as they did not actively propagate their beliefs.[44] In his memoirs of the 1830s General Murav'yev-Karsky recalls seeing a party of sectarian recruits (probably Dukhobors) being taken from Tambov to the Caucasus. One of them, asked about his beliefs, said: 'Why should I risk my life to kill another man who has done me no harm?' He added that before being conscripted the members of his group had been severely punished for their dissident opinions, but had refused to recant.[45]

The induction procedure remained basically unchanged under Nicholas I, although the 1831 statute laid it down in greater detail.[46] One minor but symbolic step forward was taken in 1849, when the archaic practice of shaving each man's scalp, as if he were a convict, was finally done away with.[47] After 1831 those who tried to avoid the levy by maiming themselves or simulating illness were punished a little less harshly than before.[48] Recruits also received increased food allowances, longer rest periods on the march, and more

---

[40] Fedorov, 'Igrushechnaya armiya', pp. 166–7.

[41] Bogdanovich, *Ist. ocherk*, i. app. 11–12.

[42] Neizvestnyy, 'Za mnogo let', pp. 141–2.

[43] Gribbe, 'Kholernyy bunt', p. 514; also cited in Curtiss, *Russian Army*, p. 239.

[44] II *PSZ* v(ii), 4010 (20 Oct. 1830), §§ 2, 6; vii. 5120 (29 Jan. 1832); cf. ix(i), 6730 (17 Jan. 1834).

[45] Murav'yev[-Karsky] 'Zapiski', *RA* (1886), 11, p. 331.

[46] II *PSZ* vi(i), 4677 (28 June 1831), III, §§ 214 ff. A graphic eye-witness account of this was given by an English clergyman who visited Russia in the late 1830s: the Revd R. L. Venables, *Domestic Scenes in Russia* . . . , London, 1839, pp. 189–94 (also cited by Bolotenko, 'Administration', pp. 407–10).

[47] II *PSZ* xxv(ii), 23149 (1 Apr. 1849).

[48] Bolotenko, 'Administration', p. 429; cf. von Haxthausen, *Kriegsmacht Russlands*, p. 72; Tański, *Tableau*, p. 158.

appropriate clothing. As a result of such measures, so War Ministry statisticians maintained, the death rate among recruits went down, but these claims
require critical scrutiny.[49]

Relatives had good reason to take leave of their sons and brothers with the
customary weeping and wailing. Haxthausen admits that each levy caused
'mourning and horror' in the villages; he was shown a milestone on a road
leading out of Moscow which marked the point at which recruits had to part
from their kin.[50] Soldiers' wives as a rule lost all contact with their husbands: a
field postal service did exist during the Crimean campaign, and at least some
men in the ranks had access to it.[51] Their wives had the same status in the
peasant community as widows, who were generally made unwelcome by their
in-laws; unless they remarried, they might be forced into vagrancy or prostitu-
tion simply to keep alive.[52] Any children born to them within a certain length
of time (two years, according to Haxthausen) after their husband's departure
were automatically classified as cantonists and were taken away from them on
reaching school age, so that the infants' mothers had no incentive to care for
them. However, in 1838 single male children born to soldiers prior to their
recruitment were declared exempt from the levy, and in the same spirit the
wives of wounded soldiers, and soldiers' widows, were permitted to keep one
son at home.[53] With cold but impeccable logic the decree referred to such boys
as 'given' to their mothers by the state, whose property they indeed were
according to the law.

On the other hand, those soldiers' wives who were allowed to accompany
their husbands to their regiments might enjoy conditions that won the admiration of foreign observers. 'In barracks', a French officer reported, 'one often
finds a row of rooms occupied by married soldiers, who may stay for several
years in the same room . . . In St. Petersburg these establishments are almost
elegant, the families' beds being separated by curtains, with a common space
beyond. This could happen only in Russia.'[54]

The same writer was also enthusiastic about the benefits which autocratic
paternalism supposedly conferred on soldiers' children. 'Many things in

---

[49] Expressed in percentage form, these figures were 0.21 per cent (1826–35) and 0.057 per cent
(1835–50): Chernyshev, 'Ist. obozreniye', p. 331. Curtiss accepts these data (*Russian Army*, pp.
238–9), but it is clear that the true figure for recruit mortality was not 2,324, as stated here, but
much closer to 146,894, the figure given on p. 328, where (perhaps to disguise the fact) deceased
recruits are lumped together with those soldiers who died while being sent to civilian agencies. The
rate was therefore about 6 per cent.

[50] Von Haxthausen, *Kriegsmacht Russlands*, pp. 72, 76.

[51] Neizvestnyy, 'Za mnogo let', p. 52; N., 'Vyderzhki iz soldatskoy zhizni', *VS* 34 (1863),
p. 158.

[52] II *PSZ* xii(i), 10425 (6 July 1837), §§ 28–30; Curtiss, *Russian Army*, pp. 236–7; Bolotenko,
'Administration', pp. 430–1. P. Czap notes in D. L. Ransel (ed.), *The Family in Imperial Russia
. . .*, Urbana, 1978, p. 206 that many soldiers' wives acted as foster-mothers to foundlings.

[53] II *PSZ* xi(i), 9761 (6 Dec. 1836); xii(ii), 10725 (21 Nov. 1837); xiii(ii), 11794 (29 Nov. 1838);
xiv. 11947 (18 Jan. 1839).

[54] 'Rapport sur l'armée de terre de la Russie' [Oct. 1852], MAE, M et D, Russie, vol. 37 (1831–
52), f. 370ᵛ. A less euphoric view of conditions for families in barracks is given by N. A. Mombelli
in his diary: *Delo petrashevtsev*, i. 243–4.

Russia seem barbaric at first sight', he wrote, 'but on closer inspection turn out to be necessary and even philanthropic: such is the case here.' He conceded that the education received by boys in 'this little army of 25 battalions, 20 squadrons, and 5 batteries' deprived them of a natural family environment.[55] Or, as a compatriot put it less squeamishly, 'a barracks serves them as cradle and the regimental banner as their country.'[56]

The number of soldiers' children was swollen by the expansion of the military settlements. It reached 196,000 in 1830, 223,000 in 1842, 295,000 in 1850, and 378,000 in 1856.[57] Of these 23,000 (1831), 36,000 (1842), and 41,000 (1850) were unofficially reported to be in school—not counting those who received a simple general education in the first two grades.[58] On completing their schooling a few more gifted pupils became military topographers, but the majority were posted straight to a regiment, where they could expect to be promoted fairly swiftly to NCO rank; others became craftsmen, bandsmen, or medical orderlies.

An impression of what life was like for a cantonist can be gleaned from the memoirs of D. V. Fedorov, son of a soldier in the Bug Ulans stationed at Voznesensk in the 1840s. At the age of eight he was seized by two soldiers and dragged screaming from his home. Taken to another province, he first joined a gang of boys who ran about in rags and begged or stole their food. Later he received tuition for several hours each day, the rest of the time (except for two hours' leisure in the evening) being taken up with drill or physical training. The curriculum included Russian, religion, history, geography, and arithmetic as well as specialized military subjects. All except the last were taught mechanically, with plentiful application of the cane and other familiar aids to classroom discipline. Notwithstanding this experience the author was one of the few who managed to rise to officer rank.[59] Soldiers' children did at least obtain some instruction, unlike those of the great mass of peasants, but it can scarcely be deemed adequate preparation for command responsibilities.

From the viewpoint of men in the ranks the change that mattered most was undoubtedly the reduction in their term of service. The first harbinger of this came in 1827, when those with 22 years to their credit (20 in the guards) were allowed to apply for discharge; if they chose to stay on they received the equivalent of six months' pay as a bonus and double pay for the rest of their term; and if they served for five more years they qualified for a pension.[60] There was an important qualification: such individuals had to have served 'without fault' (*besporochno*); and as matters stood a good-conduct badge

[55] 'Rapport', ff. 369v–71.

[56] Haillot, *Statistique militaire*, p. 363.

[57] Kimerling, 'Soldiers' Children', p. 114.

[58] Haillot, *Statistique militaire*, p. 328; Tański, *Tableau*, p. 318; von Haxthausen, *Kriegsmacht Russlands*, pp. 58–60.

[59] Fedorov, 'Igrushechnaya armiya', pp. 160–3; another personal account is cited by Curtiss, *Russian Army*, pp. 240–1.

[60] II *PSZ* ii. 1315 (22 Aug. 1827); cf. i. 109 (30 Jan. 1826).

could be lost for the least mistake. Potential applicants for discharge seem to have been deterred by the uncertainties facing them in civilian life. In 1832 it was laid down that each soldier discharged prematurely (for whatever reason) was to be issued with a passport entitling him 'to live wherever he wishes in Russia, in any town or district'.[61]

These edicts prepared the way for the reform of July 1834 mentioned earlier, which reduced the general term of active service by five years, which were to be spent in the reserve instead. The break came after 15 years for soldiers of good conduct in so-called cadre units. All these reservists were considered to be on 'indefinite leave' until the allotted time-span had expired; only after that did they become genuine veterans—'on pure discharge', as the decree put it with unconscious humour.[62] Men on indefinite leave came under the civilian authorities, but were handed over to the military if they committed some offence.[63] They had to dress neatly, shave, and report for an inspection parade (*sbor*) each summer. This probably did not constitute a burdensome obligation, unless it involved a long journey.[64] Much more arduous was the task of re-establishing themselves in civilian life. In most cases their modest savings scarcely sufficed to buy tools and stock. Only in an emergency might they receive a small grant.[65] Those who settled in a community of state peasants did better, at least on paper: they received a land allocation and an annual cash grant, and if they were developing new territories were also exempt from most taxes. All this again was conditional on good conduct.[66]

The tsar had confidently hoped that reservists would be 'a constant example to their [civilian] compatriots in exact observance of the legally prescribed order'.[67] But this was scarcely possible if they remained impoverished outsiders without close ties to their community. On the other hand, it does not seem that they went to the opposite extreme, as some over-anxious conservatives feared at the time, and as some radical historians have supposed, to the point of assuming a leadership role in peasant revolts—although there were indeed a few instances of this, as we shall see presently. In the 1830s about 15,000 men were leaving the active army annually under this scheme. This was too few either to constitute a security threat or to stabilize the countryside, let alone build up an adequate reserve.

The state considered that its responsibilities to its soldiers ceased once they had been discharged, unless they either had exceptionally long service records or had been wounded (from 1847, those injured in accidents joined the latter

---

[61] II *PSZ* vii. 5294, 5524 (15 Apr., 27 July 1832).

[62] II *PSZ* ix(i), 7373–4 (30 July 1834); cf. ix(ii), 7620 (6 Dec. 1834). The arrangements differed slightly in the two zones: von Haxthausen, *Kriegsmacht Russlands*, p. 82.

[63] II *PSZ* xiv. 12166 (23 Mar. 1839), § 226 n.

[64] Verzhbitsky, *Revol. dvizheniye*, p. 39 dissents, but neglects to note that men with 20 years' service were excused this obligation. The requirement was rescinded to mark Alexander II's coronation: II *PSZ* xxxi. 30892 (26 Aug. 1856).

[65] II *PSZ* xiv. 12859, 12958 (7 Nov., 7 Dec. 1839).

[66] II *PSZ* xvi. 14464 (16 Apr. 1841), § 8.

[67] II *PSZ* ix(i), 7373 (30 July 1834).

group).[68] If veterans were living at home, cared for by relatives or left to their own devices, they qualified for an annual pension or a once-and-for-all grant. A select few were accommodated in one of two homes for old soldiers in St. Petersburg and Moscow.[69] Such residents did not qualify for a pension, whereas those in invalid companies did (and received pay at a reduced rate as well). Between 1825 and 1854 less than 13,000 veterans in all received pensions. The total amount expended on them came to 232,000 (silver) roubles, equivalent to 44 per cent of that expended on pensions and grants to invalid officers, who were only 18 per cent as numerous.[70] On paper pension payments ranged from 50 roubles a year for a lightly wounded private in an invalid company to 200 roubles a year for a severely crippled (*uvechnyy*) NCO living at home.[71] The capital from which these payments were made, along with those to officers, was augmented by about 20 million silver roubles during the reign.[72] Pensions were a favour, not an entitlement. It is not clear whether all the discharged wounded received them (or fractions of the designated sums). In 1854, when war casualties were on the rise, pensions expenditure was less than half a million silver roubles, compared with an overall military budget of 178.6 million.[73] The total number of veterans must have been in the hundreds of thousands—one foreign source offers an estimate of 660,000[74]—but it is not known how many of them were wounded or injured.

Another form of veterans' aid was assignment to the internal security forces as prison guards, escorts, etc., or to government officers as messengers.[75] Again, no statistics are available of the number so employed, who if wounded drew full army pay. The cost of this assistance, which no one bothered to calculate, ought to be added to pensions expenditure to arrive at a true overall figure. It may be said, however, that only a modest step forward had been taken towards providing veterans with adequate social security.

Before indicting the government for its meanness one must remember that military expenditure was already cripplingly high and that money still played a

68 II *PSZ* ii. 1592 (6 Dec. 1827), § 38; iv. 3333 (12 Dec. 1829); Berezhkov, in *SVM* xiii(i), 94.

69 The Chesme home in St. Petersburg, set up in 1830, had space for 400 men (and 16 officers), but this total was not reached until some years had elapsed; the Izmaylovsky home in Moscow attained this total in the 1840s, but in 1850 its capacity was reduced to a mere 100 veterans from the ranks: Berezhkov, in *SVM* xiii(i), 121–2. The homes were financed from interest on a capital sum which, after several private bequests as well as allocations by various state bodies, reached 1 million roubles by 1855. A third home, founded by Paul I, now catered for veteran sailors only.

70 Ibid., p. 129. These data are incomplete and do not lend themselves readily to analysis by recipient's rank. The figure of 232,000 roubles may exclude once-and-for-all grants and payments to soldiers' dependant siblings (cf. p. 94) and widows (cf. II *PSZ* x(i), 8154 (23 May 1835); xiii(ii), 11546 (20 Sept. 1838)), but these expenditures were probably quite small. On the other hand an additional 180,000 roubles were spent between 1825 and 1854 on officers' families, and 884,000 roubles on the care and schooling of their orphaned children.   71 Ibid., p. 117.

72 Ibid., p. 129, and app. 8 (the figures are hard to reconcile).

73 Ibid., p. 129; id., 'Ist. ocherk', p. 58; *Min. finansov, 1802–1902*, i. 628.

74 'Mémoire sur la situation de la Russie' [Dec. 1845]. MAE, M et D, vol. 43 (1835–48), f. 226ᵛ.

75 II *PSZ* ii. 1428 (Sept. 1827); v(i), 3505 (25 Feb. 1830); vi(i), 4282 (22 Jan. 1831); vii. 5131 (4 Feb. 1832); viii(i), 5981 (16 Feb. 1833).

limited role in the economy. Cash was seen as a luxury compared with such basic necessities as food, lodging, and medical care. Officials therefore felt that they had done their duty by catering to these essential wants.

This attitude helps to explain why Nicholas did not increase soldiers' pay. Its real value, so far as can be ascertained, continued to fall. When the paper *assignat* was replaced by the silver rouble in 1839, an infantry private (musketeer) drew 2.70 and a sergeant 4.05 roubles per annum.[76] Those sent on active service to the Caucasus or abroad received a supplement. As before, a soldier would normally have his pay docked before issue, but might earn a little extra from casual awards—Nicholas continued his brother's habit of making donations to men who did well at drill—or from outside work. Soldiers employed on officially approved construction projects got 40 (paper) kopecks for a job that normally required one day's labour, and sometimes a larger food ration as well.[77] This work, which at its peak (1843) involved men from 28 regiments, was often physically arduous and unhealthy.[78]

A great deal of the men's energies was directed to maintenance of their unit's internal economy. The artel came into its own here, especially on campaign. During the Crimean War resourceful soldiers in one detachment bought and slaughtered a bull; they stored the meat in special pits filled with salt water and made footwear from the hide, which they sold on the local market or to other units; 30 per cent of the proceeds went to the former leather-workers who ran the operation, while the rest was divided up among the men. They are said to have appreciated the additional income and not to have resented the work involved.[79]

Such practices were important in varying the soldiers' diet, which seems to have improved during this period. The cereals ration remained the same, but meat was supposed to be issued to men in all units, not just a privileged few, at a rate equivalent to 95 grams a day.[80] Seasonal variations were important, as was geographical location. In the poorer rural areas men often went hungry in the spring, as did the peasants on whom they were quartered.[81] On campaign the meat issue might be doubled and vegetables added—it was now that potatoes and beetroots made their appearance in the Russian soldiers' traditional stew, which the Prussian general Bismarck claims to have tasted and enjoyed on several occasions.[82] Alternatively, monetary payments might be

---

[76] II *PSZ* xv. 14116 (12 Dec. 1840), p. 1258; Tański, *Tableau*, pp. 206–7; cf. Curtiss, *Russian Army*, p. 254. Officers' pay was, however, raised appreciably: Chernyshev, 'Ist. obozreniye', pp. 356–7. At this time a musketeer drew 1/88th as much as a lieutenant, 1/114th as much as a captain, and 1/186th as much as a colonel. See also figure 2.

[77] II *PSZ* ix(i), 6700 (4 Jan. 1834); x(i), 8210 (2 June 1835).

[78] Il'yashevich, 'Stat. issled. smertnosti', p. 397; Curtiss, *Russian Army*, p. 248.

[79] Lenovsky, 'Ocherki iz byta voysk', *VS* 6 (1859), pp. 465–6.

[80] Chernyshev, 'Ist. obozreniye', pp. 345–6; Petrov, *Russkaya voyennaya sila*, ii. 442; Yezersky, in *SVM* iii(ii), 35.

[81] Il'yashevich, 'Stat. issled. smertnosti', p. 374.

[82] Von Bismarck, *Russische Kriegsmacht*, p. 127.

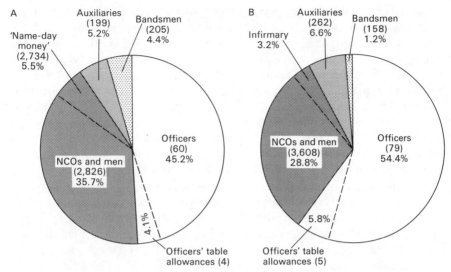

Fig. 2. Distribution of Regimental Funds (Pay etc.) according to 1840 establishment tables. A. Preobrazhensky Guards Regiment. B. Line Infantry Regiment.

made in lieu of the meat and liquor ration in order to give the men an incentive to provide for themselves.[83]

Booty was often a valuable source of foodstuffs, especially in the remote Persian and Balkan theatres. In the latter case a levy of supplies 'produced a general outcry' among the inhabitants, and during the Polish campaign efforts to requisition food met with such strong local opposition that little was secured.[84] In the brief Hungarian campaign supply arrangements worked better: some produce was received from the Austrians and the bulk of the army's needs were met either from magazines set up close to the frontier or by requisitioning at fixed rates.[85] This was the first time that rail transport was used to feed the troops. In less developed territories such as the Danubian principalities, where the Russian army again found itself in 1853, there was little to requisition, the men went short, and private contractors had to be brought in.[86] This procedure meant that results were unpredictable and that opportunities for corruption multiplied. The abuses reached scandalous proportions during the Crimean War. One entrepreneur who contracted to provide 10,000 puds of beef bouillon delivered less than one-tenth of that amount and was later put on trial.[87]

[83] K. L. N., 'Vosp. o dunayskoy kampanii', p. 183; Lenovsky, loc. cit.; Tański, *Tableau*, p. 209.

[84] Kiselev to Zakrevsky, 5 Oct. 1828, in 'Pis'ma', *SIRIO* 78 (1891), p. 161; Maksheyev, *Voyenno-admin. ustroystvo*, pp. 48–50; cf. V. Aratovsky, 'Rasporyazheniya po prodovol'stviyu deystvuyushchey armii v 1848 g.', *VS* 82 (1871), 12, pp. 88–91, 113–16, 124–5.

[85] Maksheyev, *Voyenno-admin. ustroystvo*, p. 51.

[86] Neizvestnyy, 'Za mnogo let', p. 118.

[87] Zatler, *Opisaniye rasporyazheniy*, i. 105–6.

The Crimean theatre posed an almost unfair test of the army's supply system, since the peninsula produced little except cattle and wine, and the roads in the south were so bad that trains of ox-drawn carts crossing the steppe from the nearest magazines took ages to reach their destination. Some supply bases were destroyed by enemy naval action. The Russian troops made matters worse by looting, which cost the local Tatars one third of their herds; the natives sold the rest for whatever they could get and fled in panic, leaving the country around Sevastopol' all but deserted.[88] Various units sent out purchasing units of their own which outbid each other, so driving up prices further. Yet some officials, trained to carry out orders unquestioningly, insisted on adhering to totally unrealistic fixed prices.[89] General F. K. Zatler, an experienced but tactless administrator, was placed in charge. He embarked on a series of desperate expedients which gave ammunition to his many critics. Mutual recriminations and jurisdictional struggles raged at the top, while in the besieged city of Sevastopol' soldiers went without biscuit for ten days at a stretch.[90] Eventually Zatler got them some, a feat that occasioned one of those ambivalent ditties that Russian soldiers were so fond of:

> General Zatler
> got us the biscuit,
> what a fine fellow is he!
> He issued an order
> to tighten our belts
> and oh, how our stomachs do ache![91]

'The food was of very poor quality', writes a recent historian of the campaign, 'and it was impossible to cook it properly. The rations contained much salt meat, which caused terrible thirst. The local drinking water was brackish and, since little or no fresh water was brought in . . . there was much digestive disease.'[92] In the circumstances it is surprising that the soldiers' morale held up as well as it did.

The authorities now showed greater concern than before over the effects which unwholesome diet, overstrain, and epidemics had on soldiers' health. Simultaneously advances in medical knowledge were making it possible to heal more of the wounded and sick. Nicholas devoted a great deal of attention to the state of military hospitals, paying surprise visits and summarily punishing those responsible for inadequacies, such as dirty linen.[93] Unfortunately inspec-

---

[88] Ibid., i. 44, 77.

[89] Ibid., i. 47 n., 84, 354.

[90] Ibid., i. 116; Pirogov, *Sevast. pis'ma*, p. 56.

[91] 'A Zatler general / sukhariki dostavlyal / bol'no khoroshi, bol'no khoroshi! / On izvolil prikazat' / nam, chtob dietu soblyudat' / Bryukho zabolit, bryukho zabolit!' Neizvestnyy, 'Za mnogo let', p. 119. There are less complimentary versions.

[92] Curtiss, 'Sisters of Mercy', p. 466.

[93] Yezersky, in *SVM* iii(ii), pp. 13–14 (Moscow, 1830).

tors often concentrated on superficial aspects, for instance whether the statutory number of officers were on duty in the orderly room.[94] Nevertheless statistical controls were considerably improved and by 1851 the number of military hospitals had almost doubled, from 95 to 189.[95] The Medical-Surgical Academy, the chief institution in the field, turned out about 50 well-qualified doctors a year in the first decade of the reign, and 60 to 70 at its end.[96] One of its finest teachers was the celebrated surgeon (and later pedagogue) N. I. Pirogov (1810–81), first holder of the chair of hospital surgery; in 1846 he founded an anatomical institute which he also directed. Pirogov combined theory with practice in exemplary fashion. In 1848 he went to the Caucasian front to improve medical services in the field and spent nine months there, enduring the harshest conditions. During the six-week siege of the village of Salta he performed no less than 800 operations. It was at this time that he pioneered the use of ether as an anaesthetic.[97] His achievements were much appreciated by the men, once they had overcome their initial misgivings. Pirogov had to fight a harder battle against prejudice in the military establishment.

During the war with the Turks of 1828–9 the Russian army's medical services were overwhelmed by an epidemic of plague (*chuma*). One doctor later recalled seeing 500 carts laden with supplies held up for a week at a quarantine station because the drivers could not afford to bribe the official in charge to let them through. One field hospital, although well equipped materially, had only one doctor for 400 patients, largely because the medical personnel themselves had been stricken by the disease.[98] Another memorialist blamed 'the exclusive use of biscuit and salt meat' for the spread of scurvy, and noted that the doctor in his unit, who for some reason lacked the regulation surgical equipment, had to extract bullets with his pocket-knife.[99] Dysentery and typhus took a heavy toll in the army. 'An invisible enemy, more redoubtable than the Turks, reduced it to a shadow', wrote a contemporary French observer.[100] In 1829 almost three-quarters of the Russian troops were afflicted by disease, and nearly half of the force died—an astonishingly high proportion; total casualties have been put at over 118,000.[101] Shortly afterwards another 93,000 men died during the eight-month Polish campaign.

Even in routine peacetime conditions losses among the troops were very heavy. In the 1840s[102] 37.4 men died out of every thousand taken to hospital.

[94] Sokolovsky, 'Russkaya gvardiya', pp. 55–6.

[95] Chernyshev, 'Ist. obozreniye', p. 361; Yezersky (*SVM* iii(ii)) p. 34 n.

[96] Beskrovnyy, *Potentsial*, p. 138.

[97] N. I. Pirogov, *Otchet o puteshestvii po Kavkazu* . . . , Moscow, 1952, pp. 10, 16–27; *VE* xiii (1915), 433. On Pirogov's influence see Frieden, *Russian Physicians*, pp. 5–11.

[98] Zeydlits, 'Vosp. o turetskom pokhode', pp. 423, 427.

[99] Von Hansen, *Zwei Kriegsjahre*, pp. 78, 93, 138.

[100] AMG F. G¹45. 'Situation présentant l'effectif . . . de l'armée russe' (unnumbered, undated).

[101] Curtiss, *Russian Army*, pp. 248–9; cf. Urlanis, 'Lyudskiye poteri', p. 165 (125,000); cf. Chernyshev, 'Ist. obozreniye', p. 371; Yezersky (*SVM* iii(ii)) p. 37.

[102] More precisely 1841–52, excluding the so-called 'war years' 1848–9.

Making allowance for those who passed away in their unit *lazarety* (where ordinary soldiers were more likely to remain),[103] the mortality rate was probably twice that of other European armies—although less than that of the British army in India.[104] Losses in the active army were just as high as those in invalid commands, although these consisted of veterans; only gendarmes had a significantly lower rate.[105] In the Caucasus the toll was proportionately nearly twice as great as in Lithuania, but battle casualties accounted for only one in eleven of these deaths.[106]

Figures for those who fell sick are less reliable, since many cases will have gone unreported; but they make it clear that disease was prevalent. In the first 25 years of Nicholas's reign 16 million cases were treated in base and field hospitals, which means that on average two-thirds of the soldiers were referred to them once a year.[107]

In the campaigns of 1853–5 the Russian army did not suffer such serious proportionate losses as in 1828–9, although the overall toll was again fearsome. In the Crimea the authorities, caught by surprise and not expecting such a high casualty rate, were slow to respond to the emergency situation which soon developed. 'The scenes I witnessed will remain in my memory all my life', wrote a guards officer who was present at the battle on the river Alma.

More than one hundred wounded were lying, groaning terribly, in pools of blood around a cart; some were suffering so badly that they besought me to finish them off; others, stricken with thirst, asked me as a favour to give them a drop of water, but there was none to be had.[108]

Pirogov, who arrived in Sevastopol' in November, found 'over 2,000 wounded, all mixed up together, lying on dirty mattresses soaked with blood'. He set to work at once, performing operations for ten days running, ten hours a day—although his role was supposed to be purely supervisory.[109] The regular medical staff were overwhelmed by events and displayed little initiative. Even Pirogov, who soon found himself heading a team of capable and energetic doctors, could make but a modest contribution to solving the problem, which again was in large measure one of supply. 'There is not an extra mattress to be had, no decent wine or quinine bark, nor even acid, in case typhus develops', he wrote in March. 'There are no tents and few horses or carts. No one knows where to put the wounded, for all the nearby hospitals are already overfull.'[110]

---

103 Yezersky (*SVM* iii(ii)) p. 27.

104 Il'yashevich, 'Stat. issled. smertnosti', pp. 363–4, 388, 405. Von Haxthausen (*Kriegsmacht Russlands*, p. 101) rightly, as we now know, criticized some contemporary Western estimates as too high; however, those for 1840–1 in MAE, M et D, Russie, vol. 37 (1831–52), ff. 251–2 were too low.

105 Il'yashevich, 'Stat. issled. smertnosti', p. 374.

106 Ibid., pp. 391–3.

107 Chernyshev, 'Ist. obozreniye', p. 374.

108 Dubrovin, *Mat. dlya ist. Krymskoy voyny*, ii. 474.

109 Pirogov, *Sevast. pis'ma*, pp. 5, 17–18, 31, 67.

110 Ibid., p. 97.

The only bright spot was the presence of several dozen volunteer female nurses, who toiled heroically, cheering the men and acting as a check on corrupt officials.[111] Some of them accompanied wounded who were evacuated to the rear on long journeys over appalling roads in uncovered ox-drawn carts.[112] In the eight months from March to October 1855 no less than 88,000 wounded or sick were transported from Sevastopol´ to base hospitals in the interior, and another 113,000 got as far as Simferopol´.[113] This was a considerable feat, even if conditions in the latter city were appalling: water was short and relief funds were misappropriated by hospital staff, two of whom were subsequently put on trial.[114] In 1855 23 per cent of hospital patients there died.[115] At Nikolayev the mortality rate that year stood at 14 per cent, but in the first months of 1856 it soared to 43 per cent, largely because of overcrowding, poor food, and inadequate sanitation.[116] In besieged Sevastopol´ itself the medical services had almost completely broken down by the end of 1855 as typhus, scurvy, and other infections took their toll—of doctors and nurses as well as of the exhausted troops.

Contemporary writers, and later historians too, have been prone to blame the catastrophe wholly on administrative short-comings, underestimating the 'objective' difficulties stemming from the necessity to wage war in such a location. Nevertheless there was a good deal of bureaucratic incompetence, intrigue, and corruption. Too many senior officers held to the view that soldiers were bound to suffer anyway and that concern on their behalf was a mark of weakness. Pirogov came up against bigoted functionaries who pestered him with requests for data on the number of cures he had effected while ignoring material deficiencies for which they themselves were largely responsible. 'Is this a time for establishing mortality rates,' he exclaimed, 'when patients are crowded together like sardines and no one cared about their shelter when they fell sick or were wounded?'[117] Unfortunately a preoccupation with paper formalities while disregarding reality was characteristic of Nicholas I's administration, in the army as elsewhere. Many of the successes achieved in health care were the result less of the system than of those who found ways of bypassing it.

Leo Tolstoy, an artillery subaltern during the Crimean campaign, captivated the literary public, and officers in particular, with his *Sevastopol´ Sketches*, in

111 Curtiss, 'Sisters of Mercy', gives an excellent account of their work. The organization which despatched them stood under the patronage of the enlightened Grand Duchess Helen and was the forerunner of the Russian Red Cross. Previously care had been provided by male nurses: Yezersky (*SVM* iii(ii)) p. 20; cf. II *PSZ* iii. 1888 (21 Mar. 1828).

112 Curtiss, 'Sisters of Mercy', p. 98.

113 Zatler, *Opisaniye rasporyazheniy*, i. 2-3 n.

114 I. S. Lebedev, 'Ranenyy Sevastopolets o poryadkakh v Simferopol´skom gospitale 1855-6', *RA* 1912, 2, 256.

115 Yezersky (*SVM* iii(ii)) p. 38 n.

116 Ibid.; Curtiss, *Crimean War*, p. 468.

117 Pirogov, *Sevast. pis´ma*, p. 99; cf. p. 113.

which he offered a vivid portrayal of front-line conditions, and also hinted cautiously at the corruption and inefficiency that marred the army's performance.[118] To many military men the outcome of the war seemed to vindicate critical sentiments which they had hitherto been obliged to keep to themselves. After the harsh punishments meted out to the Decembrists and their sympathizers, the tsar instituted strict controls over the army's internal life. Gendarmes reported regularly on the officers' mood and employed agents-provocateur to expose those whose unorthodox behaviour or casual talk suggested political unreliability.[119] Under such conditions there could be no question of continuing the political activity that had characterized the last decade of Alexander I's reign. Dissent was silenced, but not eliminated. In a paradoxical way Nicholas's repression encouraged a maturation of thought within the army, as it did in Russian society generally, even though no one could express their ideas freely. Like their civilian counterparts, the military intelligentsia of the preceding era had been captivated by grand designs for radical change; now the spirit was different. Most officers remained loyal conformists, at least in their outward behaviour, but there was an enlightened minority—rationalists, if not precisely liberals—whose common-sense views derived from practical experience; they were more reflective, pragmatic, and above all aware just how far they could safely go.

It was partly a matter of generations, as one contemporary pointed out. Using 'Aesopian language' to make his point without alarming the censor, he stated that in the late 1820s the older officers, 'who had fought against Napoleon' (*scilicet*: had survived the purge), patronized newcomers to their regiments, seeking to develop their 'sense of honour' and reproving them gently for such moral shortcomings as 'boasting, excessive self-indulgence, or indignation against the general understanding'; the younger men, with few exceptions, treated them with respect and 'put knowledge of the service ahead of everything else'.[120] The natural response was to relinquish any overt interest in public affairs and to concentrate on professional matters.

Much depended on potential dissenters' physical location, rank, educational background, and social origin. To begin with the first point: in the Caucasian Corps, to which some 60 officers and 2,400 soldiers implicated in the Decembrist revolts were despatched, the authorities tacitly tolerated a certain latitude of thought. The commander in chief, Yermolov, had himself been among the movement's 'patrons' and for that reason had an uneasy relationship with Nicholas: 'I trust him least of all', the tsar had written in 1825.[121] In 1830 he

---

[118] B. Eykhenbaum, *Lev Tolstoy* (Leningrad, 1928), i. 241; V. Shklovsky, *Lev Tolstoy*, Moscow, 1963, p. 214; L. N. Tolstoy, *Pol. sobr. soch.*, iv (1935), 3–120.

[119] For example, Private Ippolit Zavalishin, brother of the Decembrist, denounced 80 of his comrades at Orenburg in 1827: Verzhbitsky, *Revol. dvizheniye*, pp. 90–4; cf. the case of a self-proclaimed radical, N. P. Sungurov, in ibid., pp. 103–7, who in Moscow in 1831 denounced several Polish officers who planned to join the rebels.

[120] P. P., 'Vosp. kaval. ofitsera', p. 90.

[121] Nicholas to Dibich, 12 Dec. 1825, *RS* 35 (1882), p. 196.

replaced him by his favourite, I. F. Paskevich, who tightened controls over the exiles but also made use of them on his campaigns. This gave some men the chance, by performing deeds of valour, to win back their commissions and even to reach senior positions, although they were kept under close surveillance.[122] In the 1830s it became the fashion in St. Petersburg society for officers to put in for postings to the front. Such volunteers were often mere careerists who returned to safety as soon as they had seen action or qualified for preferment. One guards officer who arrived in 1837 was at first shocked by the informality he found in the Caucasus, but gradually learned to appreciate the greater freedom that officers enjoyed there. 'I have to admit that in this respect the Caucasus is of enormous benefit to our young officers', he wrote. 'The St. Petersburg milieu spoils people . . . [and] encourages all those petty passions and vices which so disfigure contemporary society: egoism, vanity, intrigues, boasting'; in the Caucasus, on the other hand, officers broadened their outlook and learned to judge each other according to their character instead of their rank.[123] It is of course not unusual for men at the front to feel morally superior to 'paper-pushers' in the rear, especially if the latter are as far removed from the scene of action as they were here.

Service on the frontier had its negative side, too. It stimulated chauvinistic sentiments and brutality, especially towards the native peoples of the region, as well as moral lapses such as intemperance or dishonesty. 'I saw company commanders who were so drunk that they could not keep their seat on horseback when fording streams; they fell in and had to be fished out by their men', wrote one disgusted senior officer after a tour of inspection. On parade no one dared to speak up about such shortcomings, yet 'there wasn't a company that would not have had 20 complaints to make about their pay or equipment', since this was systematically held back by officers on one pretext or another.[124] Service in the Caucasus was not popular. Officers taking parties of troops there 'hoped to return as soon as they had delivered them, and the soldiers said openly that they were being led to the slaughter and that this justified acts of violence on their part against the inhabitants'.[125]

The prospect of duty in Poland or the western provinces, where most troops were stationed, was only slightly less disagreeable. Subaltern officers resented the coolness with which, for a mixture of social and political reasons, they were received by the relatively wealthy Polish or polonized landowners.[126] If sent to the Danubian principalities they might even be greeted with contemptuous oaths.[127] In Great Russia too life in a provincial garrison was unsatisfying to anyone with cultivated tastes. The improvement that had occurred in the

---

122 Beskrovnyy, *Potentsial*, p. 236.

123 N. S. Martynov, 'Guasha: otryvok iz zapisok', *RA*, 1898, 2, pp. 317–18. Martynov was the duellist who killed the poet Lermontov, but this does not diminish the value of his observations.

124 A. I. Gagarin, 'Zapiski o Kavkaze', *VS* 288 (1906), 3, pp. 24–5.

125 Murav'yev[-Karsky] 'Iz zapisok', *RA*, 1895, 3, p. 320.

126 P. P., 'Vosp. kaval. ofitsera', pp. 90–1.

127 K. L. N., 'Vosp. o dunayskov kampanii', p. 180.

late eighteenth century was not sustained. At Poltava in the 1820s most officers amused themselves by hunting, playing cards or billiards, drinking punch, or visiting the local brothel.[128] There were few books—our serious-minded informant, a Baltic German, owed his education to a chance copy of Brockhaus's *Encyclopedia*—and those who wanted to better themselves received little encouragement from comrades or superiors.[129]

The cultural blight was least marked in the capital. The formalism for which St. Petersburg was noted, and the tight administrative controls, were offset by the presence of several military educational establishments where enlightened views survived *sub rosa*, and the well-connected could mix freely in aristocratic society. Free-thinkers were more likely to be found among the upper and middle strata of the nobility. The cadet schools preferred men with this background, and could afford to choose since there were always more candidates than vacancies. On the other hand, the Russian *dvoryanstvo* was losing its taste for military service. One reason for this was the spread of education: rising cultural standards engendered a desire for greater personal independence. Another was the draconian discipline that was enforced in these establishments, which deterred the more sensitive souls from entering them, unless their families were so poor that this was the only way ahead. In the 1830s, according to recent calculations, only some 10 per cent of *dvoryane* were in the armed forces, which was certainly a significant decrease.[130]

Nicholas I wanted to keep the schools, and the officer corps, a noble preserve, and also to ensure that all officers were properly educated.[131] He failed on both counts. In 1840–3 a system of examinations was introduced which all candidates for commissions had to take.[132] Nine new cadet schools were added during the reign and four others raised in status.[133] They produced 17,754 graduates, of whom (by 1850) 14,415 had become officers. The army as a whole had about 2,000–2,500 vacancies each year. The cadet corps could fill less than 600 of them; but of those who passed out 38 per cent joined the guards or engineers rather than line regiments, which received only about one-sixth of their requirements from this source.[134]

The rest were either so-called *yunkery* or NCOs promoted from the ranks. *Yunkery*—only the name was Prussian—were successors to the supernumeraries (see above, p. 233): gentry sons who volunteered for service with a regiment as sergeants and were commissioned after a specified term, normally two years.[135] Their educational attainments were very low, since they received no

---

[128] Von Hansen, *Zwei Kriegsjahre*, p. 22.   [129] Curtiss, *Russian Army*, pp. 194–9.

[130] Kabuzan and Troitsky, 'Izmeneniya v chislennosti . . . dvoryanstva', pp. 153, 159, 164.

[131] Floyd, 'State Service', pp. 213–16; II *PSZ* v. 3457 (1 Feb. 1830); viii. 5982 (16 Feb. 1833).

[132] Floyd, 'State Service', pp. 255–6; II *PSZ* xv(i), 13176 (18 Feb. 1840); xvii(i), 15716 (4 June 1842); xviii(i), 16523 (9 Feb. 1843). For a description: Milyutin, *Vosp.*, p. 89.

[133] Beskrovnyy, *Potentsial*, p. 125; Polievktov, *Nikolay I*, p. 332.

[134] 'K ist. voyenno-uchebnoy reformy', p. 352; Floyd, 'State Service', p. 216.

[135] For those who had attended university the term was reduced to six months, and for those with degrees to three months. II *PSZ* iv. 2874 (18 May 1829); Curtiss, *Russian Army*, p. 187; Floyd, 'State Service', pp. 213–14.

formal training while in the regiment, and the little knowledge they had came from their pre-service schooling. Finally, there were the 'bourbons', likewise NCOs promoted from the ranks.[136] These were generally former cantonists and tended to keep apart from their comrades; they comprised 7 per cent of infantry officers and 5 per cent of those in the cavalry.[137]

It is not possible to estimate precisely how many entrants to the officer corps came from non-noble backgrounds, which included the category of *razno-chintsy*, or 'men of various ranks'. One estimate for the 1850s puts it at 15 per cent, the remainder being either hereditary (50 per cent) or 'personal' (35 per cent) nobles.[138] Personal nobility was conferred on volunteers or (non-noble) officers' sons. The high proportion of officers in this group can be partly explained by a decree of 1845 which was designed to purge the state service generally of men with lower-class backgrounds and inadequate education.[139] Ostensibly prompted by the great expansion that had taken place in the bureaucracy and the armed forces since Peter I's day, this edict made an important change in the Table of Ranks. Henceforth hereditary noble status was conferred only on those who reached 'staff officer' rank, that is major to colonel, instead of on mere ensigns as hitherto. However, the Crimean War mitigated the socially select character of the officer corps which the government was so eager to foster. In 1853–5 12.1 per cent of new officers were promoted from the ranks, while another 60 per cent or so were former volunteers or *yunkery*.[140] In this way a significant number of *raznochintsy* certainly did enter the officer corps.

Did this influx have a political impact? It is tempting to assume that it did, but the radicalization of officer opinion characteristic of the first years of Alexander II's reign seems to have been most evident among men who had been through (or even were still in) the cadet schools. The same was doubtless true of covert dissenters during the Nicolaevan era. Such individuals had a social weight and intellectual potential denied to ex-commoners, who for understandable reasons tended to be politically timid, since they did not want to risk the privileged status they had so painfully acquired.

The cadet schools were entrusted to the charge of Nicholas's younger brother Michael, a stern disciplinarian, aided by the unpopular General Ya. I. Rostovtsev. Even in the General Staff Academy, founded in 1832 and subsequently named after the tsar, which was so to speak the *pièce de résistance* in the machinery of élite military education, the teaching was uninspiring. Dmitriy Milyutin, who studied there in 1835–6, wrote later that the director,

---

136 Neizvestnyy, 'Za mnogo let', p. 120.
137 'K ist. voyenno-uchebnoy reformy', p. 354.
138 Neizvestnyy, loc. cit.; Floyd, 'State Service', p. 247.
139 II *PSZ* xx. 19086 (11 June 1845); Floyd, 'State Service', p. 272.
140 'K ist. voyenno-uchebnoy reformy', p. 355, where the second figure is put at 69.2 per cent; but this is too high, since the total for both categories is 72 per cent: Bogdanovich, *Ist. ocherk*, i. app. 20.

I. O. Sukhozanet, was 'severe, demanding, and pernickety'; he missed no opportunity to display his power and was both hated and feared by the students.[141] A great controversy raged as to whether students in the academy, who were experienced junior officers, should be required to do drill. General Henri Jomini, the Swiss strategist then in Russian employ, advised against it, but the decision went against him.[142] In the Guards Sub-Ensigns' school drill periods were extended to three hours a day when Nicholas acceded to the throne, and the tsar himself used to attend zealously; the first parade was held at 6.30 a.m. and the last from 7 to 8 p.m.[143] An orderly officer supervised the cadets' conduct closely day and night, and inspectors attended many of the lectures. The scale of penalties for defaulters ranged from a reprimand (private or public) to detention in the school jail (*kartser*) on a diet of bread and water for a term of up to a month.[144] But at least from this school no one who committed some minor offence was sent off to serve in the ranks, as happened in most other élite establishments, where there was also more corporal punishment.[145]

The cadets' behaviour was seldom exemplary, and the better connected among them would sometimes deliberately flout the rules and so provoke the authorities into taking disciplinary action against them. Yet it is also clear that the excessively strict internal regime sparked dissent and protest. In one case a cadet sentenced to be flogged seized a knife and cut his own throat, and in another suicide attempt a little later a boy jumped down a stairwell.[146] The cadets, we are told, felt sympathy for those subjected to corporal punishment and disgust at its use[147]—yet they were too cowed to protest collectively, as they had done before and would shortly do again. Nicholas's administrative methods—'a system of terror', Milyutin called it[148]—forced men to suppress their grievances; later several of them would ventilate their frustrated anger and guilt in memoir accounts of their experiences.[149] Nevertheless these memoirs are more trustworthy than the bland account of a casual visitor such as Lieutenant-General Bismarck, who was impressed by 'the great cleanliness, ample and healthy food . . . and truly fatherly care that is apparent even in the least details'.[150]

Paternalism also took the form of heavy emphasis on religious and patriotic values. At the Guards Sub-Ensigns' school students learned about 'the Russian God' created by the theorists of Official Nationalism, and worshipped before

141 Milyutin, *Vosp.*, pp. 115–21.
142 Polievktov, *Nikolay I*, p. 328.
143 Potto, *Ist. ocherk Nikol. kaval. uch.*, pp. 22, 24.
144 Ibid., pp. 14, 24.
145 Odintsov, 'Posmertnye zapiski', p. 305; Neizvestnyy, 'Za mnogo let', pp. 180, 184–5.
146 Neizvestnyy, 'Za mnogo let', p. 186.
147 Ibid., p. 188; cf. Odintsov, 'Posmertnye zapiski', p. 302.
148 Milyutin, *Vosp.*, p. 120.
149 One exception was D. G. Kolokol'tsov, who endured injustice in the Guards Sub-Ensigns' school but praised the harsh methods employed: 'Preobrazh. polk', p. 284.
150 Von Bismarck, *Russische Kriegsmacht*, p. 14.

an icon which bore the names of their teachers. In a typical passing-out address Grand Duke Michael declared that 'the inseparability of Tsar and Fatherland is our strength, before which our enemies will ever crumble and subversion fade'.[151] Up to a point this propaganda was effective. Many cadets developed an almost embarrassingly effusive love for their sovereign, who was liable to be mobbed if he appeared in their midst.[152] In the long run, however, this simple bond of personal loyalty provided inadequate social support for autocratic rule. It engendered a rigid pattern of thought and conduct among officers that left them at a loss when circumstances changed. One modern historian notes that the 'militarization' of life in the cadet schools involved 'an intellectual *dressage* that inculcated submissiveness and made men function in a ritualistic rather than an efficient manner'.[153]

Perhaps its most serious consequence was to hinder the development of a sense of legality, such as was emerging at this time among civilian members of the élite. This explains the prevalence of corrupt practices among officers once they reached their units and sank into the torpid routine of regimental life; it also accounts for their passivity in the face of injustice and brutality. It is no doubt true that 'those military leaders with opposition tendencies were at best restricted to working within the limits of individual units . . . and could not hope to influence government policy in regard to the armed forces as a whole';[154] and certainly many acts of passive resistance will have gone unrecorded. Nevertheless more could have been done in an informal way to protect the juridical status of the officers themselves and their men.

It is anachronistic to speak of a 'revolutionary movement' in the Russian army at this time.[155] Yet the evidence which Soviet historians have painstakingly accumulated shows that nonconformist sentiments survived and occasionally led to acts of resistance. In the early years dissidence mainly took the form of reading or circulating forbidden verse by Pushkin or Ryleyev—as in the cadet school at Kaluga, for example.[156] In 1830 a staff captain, S. I. Sitnikov, distributed political writings of his own through the mail under a pseudonym. The technique was amateurish, as was his appeal to the addressees that they should support a 'democratic Slavic—Polish army' which had no existence in fact.[157] However, this was the beginning of a 'Polish phase' in military

---

[151] Potto, *Ist. ocherk Nikol. kaval. uch.*, pp. 8, 37, 62, 69. Indoctrination in the army is also treated by Curtiss, *Russian Army*, pp. 256–71. The chaplaincy budget accounted for a mere 23,000 roubles in 1840, or 0.03 per cent of total military expenditure. II *PSZ* xv(ii), 14131 (1840), p. 1458. For the term 'Russian God' see A. I. Gagarin, 'Zapiski o Kavkaze', *VS* 288 (1906), 3, p. 29. For an example of contemporary propaganda: [General] I. N. Skobelev, *Perepiska i rasskazy russkogo invalida*, 2 pts., St. Petersburg, 1844 (4th edn., first published under a different title in 1833).

[152] Von Bismarck, *Russische Kriegsmacht*, p. 151; Potto, *Ist. ocherk Nikol. kaval. uch.*, pp. 48, 78.

[153] Beyrau, 'Formation', p. 309.

[154] D´yakov, *Osvobod. dvizheniye*, p. 208.

[155] Verzhbitsky, *Revol. dvizheniye*: an informative work, but the author plays down the role of Poles and other non-Russian ethnic groups.

[156] Ibid., p. 99.

[157] D´yakov, *Osvobod. dvizheniye*, p. 215.

opposition, stimulated by the revolt in November 1830 and then by the incorporation in Russian units of men from the formerly independent Polish Army. The rebels enjoyed some sympathy among officers who hailed from the western provinces with their polonized nobility. Many of the latter served together in the Lithuanian regiment.[158] There were numerous desertions: one list of such offences (which has not been published) contains 49 names and another 27;[159] we have neither a total figure nor a breakdown by rank, but it is safe to assume that almost all those concerned were from the western provinces.

During the 1830s some Polish ex-officers who had been sent into exile, like their *émigré* comrades, continued to plot the restoration of their country's independence and won the sympathy of Russians serving in the armed forces. One such was an ensign of aristocratic background, V. Urusov, stationed at Astrakhan'. In 1834 he joined a Pole named Janiszewski in a plot to seize control of the town—or so at least the authorities, who got wind of the scheme in time, alleged.[160] Four years later another young Russian officer, A. P. Kuz'min-Karavayev, who had been educated in the Noblemen's regiment and was then a sub-lieutenant in an infantry regiment, conceived the bold plan of freeing from captivity in Vil'na one of the leading Polish prisoners: Szymon Konarski, an ex-captain in the Polish army who had later become an under-cover agent of the *émigré* organization Młoda Polska. Kuz'min-Karavayev, together with several other junior officers and NCOs, held a number of clandestine meetings on an estate near Zelva in Grodno province. The escape plot was betrayed by another prisoner; Konarski was executed; and eleven of his sympathizers, including Kuz'min-Karavayev, were court-martialled and sentenced to terms of Siberian exile.[161]

In the 1840s the government once again found itself facing dissent among officers stationed in the capital. Several of them frequented literary evenings attended by officials, students, and others at which the conversation turned to sensitive matters such as serf emancipation. At least three distinct groups existed, but there were links between them and historians have customarily treated them together under the label 'Petrashevtsy'. M. V. Butashevich-Petrashevsky was not a military man but one group of his associates did gather around N. A. Mombelli,[162] a young guards lieutenant, and had a strong military flavour: of the 43 men known to have attended his Monday gather-

---

[158] Verzhbitsky, *Revol. dvizheniye*, p. 147.

[159] Ibid.; Beskrovnyy, *Potentsial*, p. 238.

[160] Verzhbitsky, *Revol. dvizheniye*, p. 153; Fedosov, *Revol. dvizheniye*, pp. 143–4. On Konarski see S. Kieniewicz in *Polski słownik biograficzny*, Warsaw, Cracow, and Wrocław, xiii (1967/8), 477–9.

[161] Verzhbitsky, *Revol. dvizheniye*, pp. 160–72; for his subsequent fate: A. F. Smirnov, in A. I. Herzen (Gertsen), *Sobr. soch.*, xv (Moscow, 1958). 320.

[162] Mombelli (1823–91) had studied in the Noblemen's regiment. His diary shows that he developed a perceptive understanding of the nature of absolutist rule, but that his behaviour was eccentric. Although a strong critic of corporal punishment (of which he gives a graphic eye-witness description), he gave his own batman 50 strokes of the lash for being drunk, but then repented of his action: *Delo petrashevtsev*, i. 243, 251–2, 258.

ings, 33 were officers and 20 of them were in his own unit, the Moscow regiment, which had been prominent in the events of December 1825.[163] One member of this group, Captain F. N. L'vov, taught chemistry at the Pavlovsky cadet corps. In another group which met at the home of an official named S. F. Durov there were two guards subalterns, Lieutenants N. P. Grigor'yev of the Mounted Grenadiers and A. I. Pal'm of the Chasseurs, who were graduates of the Page Corps and the Noblemen's regiment respectively. Its most celebrated member, Fedor Dostoyevsky, had been educated as a military engineer and had reached lieutenant's rank before retiring to civilian life in 1844.[164] Grigor'yev composed an effective piece of agitational literature, *A Soldier's Chat*, for distribution among the troops.[165] No approach was, however, actually made to the soldiers; nor did circle members try to set up secret cells in their units or contemplate a military *coup*. Such tactics had been discredited by the Decembrists' failure, and these men were in any case more moderate in their views. As humanitarian idealists they hoped to spread their message by non-violent means.

Despite this they were treated as dangerous criminals. As is well known, Dostoyevsky was one of those subjected to the terrible psychological ordeal of a mock execution, being pardoned at the last moment; Mombelli and Grigor'yev were each sentenced to 15, and L'vov to 12, years of forced labour in the Siberian mines.[166] In all 280 men were investigated and 122 of them tried in secret. This unduly repressive action helped to ensure that the Russian public remained tranquil in the revolutionary year 1848. There were some mutterings of dissatisfaction in the army, however, and in one incident which alarmed Nicholas some officers of the 2nd Cavalry Division drank a toast to the cause of French liberty.[167] An investigation revealed that they were from the western provinces, and the matter was settled by a few transfers.

Rather more serious was the disaffection among the troops sent to Hungary in 1849. As in 1831, a number of men deserted. One group of over 60 defectors is reported to have fought on the insurgents' side.[168] Their action seems to have been prompted by service grievances rather than political motives, but these certainly existed too. The antagonism that the more nationalistically-inclined officers felt towards Germans in command positions in their own army naturally carried over to the Austrians. By upholding dynastic legitimism in the Habsburg lands Nicholas seemed to be acting contrary to Russian interests, while the Hungarians were admired for their bravery, cheerfulness,

[163] Verzhbitsky, *Revol. dvizheniye*, pp. 202, 222; D'yakov, *Osvobod. dvizheniye*, pp. 52–3; cf. Mombelli's evidence in *Delo petrashevtsev*, i. 383.

[164] Verzhbitsky, *Revol. dvizheniye*, p. 217.

[165] Ibid., pp. 212–14.

[166] Beskrovnyy, *Potentsial*, p. 241; cf. Leykina, 'Mombelli'. Grigor'yev went insane. See A. F. Voznyy, *Politseyskiy sysk: kruzhok petrashevtsev*, Kiev, 1976, p. 44.

[167] Verzhbitsky, *Revol. dvizheniye*, pp. 239–44; D'yakov, *Osvobod. dvizheniye*, pp. 247, 261.

[168] Verzhbitsky, 'Sochuvstviye peredovykh ofitserov'; id.' *Revol. dvizheniye*, p. 251; Averbukh, *Revol. i nats.-osvobod. bor'ba*, p. 323.

self-confidence, and high standard of military organization. A spirit of chivalry that transcended national boundaries was involved as well. An eye-witness later recalled that 'the antipathy towards the Austrians was transmitted from the officers to the soldiers, who were well disposed towards the Hungarians, fraternized with them freely, walked around with them arm in arm, and went drinking with them in the taverns'.[169] A staff captain named A. Gusev prepared an appeal in which he urged his comrades and subordinates to change their allegiance.[170] He and seven other officers were hanged as traitors; another eight men were exiled to Siberia. Once again it seems that most who took the insurgents' part were from the western or south-western (that is, Ukrainian) provinces, where 1848 gave a fillip to nationalist sentiment among the educated classes.

There was less trouble during the 'Eastern War', partly because Slavophil and Pan-Slav ideas had an impact on officer opinion. The campaigns could plausibly be represented as waged in defence of national and common Slav interests against the Turks, backed by aggressive Western powers and half-backed by 'faithless' Austria. A major security threat[171] arose only after the end of the war, when it became clear that to continue Nicholas I's harsh policies would gravely strain military morale. Maintenance of discipline in the armed forces now became part of a much broader and more complex problem, the renovation of the empire's political and social order.

[169] Alabin, 'Russkiye v Vengrii', p. 102; Averbukh, *Revol. i nats.-osvobod. bor'ba*, pp. 319–23.

[170] Verzhbitsky, *Revol. dvizheniye*, p. 249. Beskrovnyy (*Potentsial*, p. 242) states that Gusev actually delivered his appeal, but Fedosov (*Revol. dvizheniye*, p. 262) maintains that his intentions were discovered and forestalled by the authorities.

[171] A relatively *minor* threat arose from would-be recruits to the militia, who hoped by volunteering to win release from serfdom.

15

AN AGE OF REFORM

THE changes brought about in Russian society during the reign of Alexander II (1855–81) spelled the end of the traditional service state. This was their effect: it was not the express aim of those responsible. Their basic purpose was to maintain and strengthen the autocracy, whose continued existence they deemed essential to the empire's survival. A new tsar, they hoped, would push through major institutional innovations, overriding objections from the nobility and co-opting its more progressive members in the great task of national renewal.

The reforms were master-minded by a small group of enlightened officials who had attained senior positions under Nicholas I. At that time, although they enjoyed the protection of certain members of the ruling family, they could do little to implement their ideas. After 1855 they had new opportunities. Alexander II was more open-minded than his father, despite the military education he had received, which instilled in him the by now customary enthusiasm for the parade-ground.[1] The reformers could hope to persuade him that decisive action was necessary in the monarchy's own interest as well as that of the country, and that public opinion, which had received a psychological shock from defeat, would welcome the government's initiative. *Glasnost'* (literally, 'publicity') was a key term in the reformers' vocabulary. By this they meant opening up issues of current concern to discussion in the salons and in the press. Such a debate, they believed, could be kept within 'safe' limits and provide a channel for communication between officials and qualified persons outside the government. Although the reformers did not say so explicitly, they also expected the pressure from below to counteract the tsar's natural ambivalence.

Unfortunately Alexander's lack of self-assurance and anxiety to preserve his Imperial prerogatives led him to pursue an inconsistent course. He was not above playing some ministers off against others. Bitter factional struggles ensued. They were fought out in various official bodies, notably in the many *ad hoc* commissions set up to formulate policy options. Leading politicians engaged in a veritable 'war of memoranda' submitted for the monarch's approval; their contents were occasionally leaked to the public, and journalists manipulated, with the object of bolstering the contestants' position in these high-level disputes.

---

[1] Wortman, 'Power and Responsibility'. In 1858 Alexander conducted 17 Imperial inspections, and in 1861 13: *VOVM 1858*, p. 58; *1861*, p. 51.

This explains why the 'Great Reforms' (as they rather grandiloquently came to be called) were not planned or executed systematically. Rather they came about piecemeal, like those of Peter I, and their scope was often subsequently curtailed by administrative action. On occasion the tsar intervened with decisive effect to move matters forward (or else, especially in his later years, backward), but he did not issue any coherent statement as to what his goals were. The resulting confusion has encouraged historians to step in and supply logical, but necessarily speculative, interpretations of their own.

Controversy has arisen in particular over the relationship between serf emancipation, the key measure, and changes in the military domain. In 1966 A. J. Rieber suggested that 'the military reform provided the decisive impetus for freeing the serfs', although he admitted that the evidence in favour of this view was only circumstantial.[2] The diplomatic historian Winfried Baumgart has gone further: 'the abolition of serfdom was . . . not an end in itself but was subordinate to the military reform, [for] the army was still the most important pillar of the autocracy as embodied under Alexander II'.[3] The last part of this statement may well be correct; nevertheless this interpretation takes liberties with chronology and distorts the actual relationship between the two measures. Military concerns were certainly important to the framers of the peasant reform, but it was carried through for a variety of motives, the most important of which were the need to increase Russia's productive forces and to maintain political stability in the countryside.[4]

The military benefits that could be expected were strongly urged by Major-General D. A. Milyutin (1816–1912) in a memorandum submitted as early as March 1856,[5] but this document has to be placed in its contemporary political context. Milyutin, who as Alexander's War Minister from 1861 to 1881 became the architect of the military reforms (to be discussed presently), was one of the most dynamic of the 'enlightened bureaucrats' in the circle patronized by the Grand Duchess Helen (Yelena Pavlovna). A convinced abolitionist, he seized the opportunity to advance this idea formally; in view of its sensitivity he could do this best in his capacity as a member of a commission on army reform. It does not follow that he considered this a self-sufficient reason for abolition, or that his arguments played a significant part in the decision to proceed with emancipation.

Nor was the government forced to free the serfs because of the threat of peasant revolt, notably the outbreaks in the south of Russia in 1854–5 among men

[2] Rieber, *Politics of Autocracy*, p. 29; id., 'Alexander II: a Revisionist View', *Journal of Modern History* 43 (1971), pp. 42–58.

[3] Baumgart, *Peace of Paris*, p. 200 (Ger. edn., p. 249).

[4] See T. Emmons, *The Russian Landed Gentry and the Peasant Emancipation of 1861*, Cambridge, 1968, pp. 48–50; id., 'The Peasant and the Emancipation', in W. S. Vucinich (ed.), *The Peasant in Nineteenth-Century Russia*, Stanford, 1968, p. 44; A. A. Skerpan, 'The Russian National Economy and Emancipation', in A. D. Ferguson and A. Levin (eds.), *Essays in Russian History: a Collection Dedicated to G. Vernadsky*, Hamden, Conn., 1964, p. 164.

[5] 'Mysli o nevygodakh . . .', cited by Zayonchkovsky, 'Milyutin: biograf. ocherk', p. 17; Miller, *Miliutin*, p. 22; Beyrau, 'Leibeigenschaft und Militärverfassung', p. 210; not yet published.

who volunteered for the militia in the hope of winning their liberty. The authorities suppressed the disturbances in their usual clumsy and brutal way without much ado. On the other hand, serfdom was indeed a hindrance to any restructuring of the army into a relatively small active (cadre) force and a large trained reserve—the reform which Nicholas I had tinkered with and which Milyutin would eventually force through. Was it an *insuperable* obstacle, as many writers have assumed? There was nothing to prevent the tsar from ending the custom (nowhere clearly established in law and widely disregarded in practice) of freeing ex-servicemen. Dietrich Beyrau is surely right in stating that a 'more than marginal military reform . . . would also have been possible even under serfdom'.[6] Whether this is so or not, once the tsar had publicly placed emancipation on the agenda in March 1856, abolitionists could sell their cause to conservatives by stressing the military advantages to be gained: more prosperous and self-reliant peasants would make soldiers more able to comprehend orders, handle modern equipment, and take the initiative on the battlefield—aptitudes that were now essential, as the Crimean War had abundantly shown.

As for military reform, this was now generally seen to be inevitable. The war had cost Russia dear in men, money, and equipment, and had revealed grave administrative shortcomings. The casualty toll has already been referred to. In a memorandum of January 1856 Milyutin estimated the drain on civilian labour at 800,000 men.[7] Particularly grave were the financial repercussions of the war. In 1854–6 the War Ministry's budgeted expenditure reached 652 million roubles, an increase of 237 per cent on the previous three-year period.[8] Unpublished documents show that the true figure was nearer 800 million roubles.[9] The result was a deficit which according to one official military source totalled 651 million roubles—coincidentally a figure almost identical with that for expenditure and 468 per cent greater than that in the previous triennium.[10] Baumgart puts it at eleven times higher than pre-war figures, but this is an exaggeration.[11] In that year (1857) the leading economist of the day estimated the 'financial burden' of the war at 566 million roubles,[12] but this in turn seems to be too low.

Whatever the exact figure, the economy drive undertaken over the following years succeeded in eliminating the deficit by 1862—with the result that a modern sceptic would expect: the way was clear for a further increase in

---

[6] Beyrau, op. cit., p. 211; but cf. p. 206.

[7] Bestuzhev, 'Iz ist. Krymskoy voyny', p. 206 and fn. 1.

[8] *Min. finansov*, i. 628, 636–7; Beskrovnyy, *Potentsial*, p. 483. Combined military and naval expenditure, expressed as a percentage of total state expenditure, was as follows: 1853: 36.2 per cent; 1854: 51.9 per cent; 1855: 51.4 per cent; 1856: 42.0 per cent. For lower near-contemporary unofficial estimates: Bliokh, *Finansy*, ii. 4–5, 8–9, 16–17, 25–6.

[9] Bestuzhev, 'Iz ist. Krymskoy voyny', p. 208.

[10] Maksheyev, *Voyenno-stat. obozreniye*, p. 203.

[11] Baumgart, *Peace of Paris*, p. 73.

[12] Beyrau, 'Leibeigenschaft und Militärverfassung', p. 194 n., citing the unpublished memoirs of another minister, A.V. Golovnin.

military expenditure.[13] The armed forces bore their share of the savings made in the intervening period, for their expenditure in 1857–61 fell by 13.7 per cent of that in 1854–6 while civilian expenditure grew by 76.2 per cent.[14] Forestt Miller, who relies on Bliokh's statistics, gives a contrary impression, stating that 'the army [had] no effective programme for reducing its size in peacetime'.[15] This is unfair, for although the War Minister did indeed resist pressure by his colleagues for economy, troop strength was significantly reduced. In 1856 the militia was disbanded, as were several Cossack units; 421,000 regulars were sent on indefinite leave, many of them before their term had expired, and another 69,000 crossed off the lists altogether. By temporarily desisting from recruit levies and reducing the service term (see below, p. 375) the army's strength was brought down from 1.7 million in 1856 to less than 1 million in 1858, and to 850,000 in 1859.[16]

One reason why military expenditure failed to drop as rapidly as troop strength was that the authorities launched a programme of re-equipping the forces with modern weapons. By 1859 each infantryman and most cavalrymen had been issued with a rifle, which is said to have made such soldiers 'masters of the field' against foes less well armed; the artillery also received guns (of bronze, later of steel) which had a longer range and were more efficient.[17] In 1859 7.5 million roubles was spent on what were delicately termed 'special objects', and the following year this sum nearly doubled.[18]

A great deal of attention was given to improving the army's administration. The need for this had been urged in the first report submitted to the tsar, on 4 June 1855, by the commander-in-chief of the Guards and Grenadier Corps, Lieutenant-General F. V. Ridiger (Friedrich Rüdiger). His age, seniority, and battle honours (and perhaps also his Baltic German background) allowed him to speak more freely than his colleagues were yet prepared to do. He blamed the abuses primarily on the excessive centralization of authority, which over-burdened subordinate agencies and deprived unit commanders of initiative, and secondarily on inadequate training. There was too much emphasis on drill at the expense of firing practice, and the entire military educational system, for men as well as officers, needed overhauling. Army regulations should be revised and—the most delicate point—officers' qualifications for their posts reviewed.[19] In July 1855 a commission was set up to examine these and other

---

[13] *Min. finansov*, i. 636; Beskrovnyy, *Potentsial*, p. 483; Bliokh (*Finansy*, ii. 91) puts the 1862 deficit at 11.9 m. roubles.

[14] Calculated from *Min. finansov*, loc. cit.

[15] Miller, *Miliutin*, pp. 27–8.

[16] Bogdanovich, *Ist. ocherk*, i. 121–58, app. 5, 15; *VOVM 1858*, pp. 1–3; Kersnovsky, *Istoriya*, ii. 395.

[17] Zayonchkovsky, 'Milyutin: biograf. ocherk', p. 30; Kersnovsky, *Istoriya*, ii. 397; Beskrovnyy, *Potentsial*, pp. 144, 155; II *PSZ* xxx. 28998 (30 Jan. 1855); xxxiii. 33257 (5 June 1858); xxxiv. 34599 (10 June 1859).

[18] Bliokh, *Finansy*, ii. 58.

[19] N. A. Danilov, in *SVM* i. 382; app. pp. 33, 39; Zayonchkovsky, *Voyennye reformy*, pp. 64–6; *RBS* xvi. 171.

ideas, and once peace had been concluded a purge got under way. Senior generals who held sinecures were obliged to retire.[20] One of the main targets was the Internal Guard. This unpopular force was placed under another Baltic German general (V. F. von der Launitz) and subjected to a thorough reorganization, which proved to be but a prelude to its abolition in 1864. An investigation revealed that 16,400 men, or 11.5 per cent of its strength, were corrupt and that criminal offences were six times more frequent in the corps than they were in line units. Most of the men were formally pardoned, reclassified as Cossacks, and sent in batches to settle the coastal region recently annexed from China; they were allowed to take their wives and received grants to help them start a new life.[21]

The supply administration was another obvious candidate for the reformers' zeal. Some of the more conspicuous suspects were prosecuted: 776 officers (not all in the commissariat) were charged with 'offences against the service' in the seven years 1855–61.[22] A contemporary military critic noted that this 'campaign against the *intendanty*' left untouched a number of the major culprits, among them a guards colonel who, having accumulated a sizeable fortune by various manipulations, on retirement built himself a manor-house with 70 rooms.[23] Still, the opportunities for malfeasance were reduced. Purchasing arrangements were revised to ensure that the army obtained the bulk of the cereal products it consumed at public auctions instead of from individual suppliers under long-term contracts.[24] At unit level commanding officers were deprived of responsibility for economic matters, which initially produced an improvement—or so at least one infantry subaltern noted. No longer, he claimed, could a CO keep fewer horses or order more ammunition than officially prescribed, or delay the issue of new uniforms to his men—all devices that had been widely used for self-enrichment. Companies now received their allocations of firewood, boots, and underclothing, along with their pay, directly from the supply authorities instead of through regimental headquarters. Most striking here is the frankness with which the writer reveals details of previous abuses and his naïve trust in the efficacy of such elementary remedial measures.[25]

In general the reformers, high and low, placed too much confidence in mere administrative changes. There was certainly a need to decentralize the top-heavy military establishment, but this came to be seen as something of a panacea, or as a substitute for more sweeping measures that might disturb conservatives. Nor was the army leadership of one mind. The War Minister, N. O. Sukhozanet, dragged his feet on organizational reforms, just as he did

[20] II *PSZ* xxxi. 30792, 30831 (28 July, 8 Aug. 1856).

[21] II *PSZ* xxxiv. 33163 (18 May 1858); Bogdanovich, *Ist. ocherk*, i. 144, ii. 444–8; *VOVM 1858*, pp. 50–3; *1861*, p. 63; *VE* vi. 443.

[22] Bogdanovich, *Ist. ocherk*, ii. app. 32.

[23] Neizvestnyy, 'Za mnogo let', *RS* 83 (1894), 10, pp. 69–80.

[24] *VOVM 1858*, p. 103; *1864*, p. 22; *1870*, p. 22; Bogdanovich, *Ist. ocherk*, ii. 147–59.

[25] Apolev, 'Ocherki', pp. 1–40; cf. Bogdanovich, *Ist. ocherk*, ii. 172.

on curbing military expenditure.[26] His appointment in 1856 was apparently designed to appease the right-wingers, for it would have been more logical if the tsar had entrusted the job to A. I. Baryatinsky, his chief confidant in military matters. But Baryatinsky was appointed viceroy of the Caucasus, where the war was about to be stepped up; and he took his protégé Milyutin with him as acting chief of staff. The latter had his eye on a senior post in the ministry and was frustrated at Sukhozanet's uncooperative attitude.[27] While he was absent from St. Petersburg the drive for reform slackened. On the other hand, while in the war zone Milyutin had the chance to set up military districts, to which power within the Caucasian Army could be devolved; many of the worst abuses were remedied and subordinate officers encouraged to show greater initiative; several hundred men were sent on courses to learn the use of the new weapons, as well as gymnastics, grammar, and arithmetic.[28] The defeat and capture of the formidable *imam* Shamil in 1859 seemed to vindicate his methods, which he was more certain than ever should be extended to the whole empire.

On the strength of these successes Baryatinsky put Milyutin forward for the job of War Minister, but a year passed before he was appointed Sukhozanet's deputy. The older man still refused to give him anything important to do, and it took another year of bureaucratic intrigue before the minister was shunted off to take charge of the restless Poles; thereupon Milyutin succeeded him, first *de facto* and then *de jure* (May, November 1861).[29] Similar controversy would attend his direction of the ministry over the next 20 years. Conservatives resented him as a 'desk general' who lacked 'a soldierly heart'[30]—although he had in fact been wounded in action. Milyutin faced criticism from the left, too, although in the nature of things this was less sustained or articulate. In a curious way the two groups of opponents reinforced each other.

The new minister lost no time in preparing a lengthy memorandum which he presented to the tsar on 15 January 1862.[31] In this he amplified the ideas he had advanced six years earlier. The army's efficiency was to be improved by eliminating wasteful and expensive practices. Transition to a relatively small cadre force, supplemented by a large reserve, would require a major devolution of authority to new military districts (*okruga*). Their chiefs' job was to mobilize these reserves when needed and to administer all the regular troops stationed within their area; they were also to replace military governors and the commanders of corps (the largest tactical unit, which was to be abolished). This highly contentious measure need not be considered further here,[32] except to

---

[26] Kersnovsky, *Istoriya*, ii. 397. For a sensitive appreciation of his ministry see E. W. Brooks, 'Reform in the Russian Army, 1856–1861', *SR* 43 (1984), pp. 63–82.

[27] Zayonchkovsky, 'Milyutin: biograf. ocherk', p. 18.

[28] Rieber, *Politics of Autocracy*, pp. 62–8; Miller, *Miliutin*, pp. 29–32; II *PSZ* xxxiii. 32939 (1 Apr. 1858); xxxiv. 34782 (31 July 1859).

[29] Zayonchkovsky, *Voyennye reformy*, p. 49; id., 'Milyutin: biograf. ocherk', p. 19.

[30] Kersnovsky, *Istoriya*, ii. 398.   [31] Danilov, in *SVM* i. app. pp. 70–183.

[32] [Milyutin] 'Voyennye reformy', pp. 21–35; for a full analysis, see Miller, *Miliutin*, pp. 34–66, 79–87; Jones, 'Administrative System' in *MNERSU* ii (1980), 108–17.

note that historically the *okruga* were somewhat reminiscent of the pre-Petrine *razryady*. The idea of building up a trained reserve had been in the air for decades; nevertheless Milyutin's programme heralded a veritable revolution in military affairs—indeed in Russian society as a whole. Universal (but selective) conscription held out the prospect of a democratic citizen army on the French model—this in an autocratic empire where the mass of the people had yet to become fully-fledged citizens. In such armies officers and men performed their duty out of a conscious loyalty to the nation-state, an abstract entity, rather than from a natural awe of the personal authority invested in an absolute monarch and his appointees. Conscription also implied that soldiers should be educated and properly looked after, and that they had rights as human beings which should be protected by the military judicial system.

Such ideas could not be spelled out fully, even in a confidential memorandum to the tsar. Both Alexander II and Milyutin were half-afraid of them. They wanted above all to consolidate the monarchy, whereas a conscript army would undermine it. Thus from the start the reform effort suffered from an underlying ambiguity and its implementation was bound to be half-hearted.

Nothing illustrates this ambiguity better than the controversy that surrounded the reformers' efforts to introduce an element of *glasnost'* into the shaping of military policy. The establishment of a new professional journal, outside the jurisdiction of military censorship, had been recommended to the tsar by Ridiger in 1855.[33] The idea was particularly dear to the heart of Milyutin. In June 1856 he sent a memorandum to the deputy War Minister, A. A. Katenin, in which he deplored officers' literary tastes, or lack thereof; the new periodical, he suggested, should accustom them 'painlessly' to the habit of reading by combining general educational matter with information of a more limited and official character; and its price should be low. He clearly had in mind the successful journal *Morskoy sbornik* ('Naval Miscellany'), published under Admiralty auspices with the patronage of the enlightened Grand Duke Constantine Nikolayevich.[34] Another year elapsed before the idea was taken up by senior officers of the Separate Guards Corps, who held that either police or military censorship would unduly restrict the journal's scope and that they themselves would ensure it did not go too far. Alexander concurred. Early in 1858 he abolished the Military Censorship Committee[35] and then approved a scheme which allowed the guards staff to choose the editors of the prospective *Voyennyy sbornik* ('Military Miscellany'). Major-General A. P. Kartsev turned to none other than N. G. Chernyshevsky, the country's leading radical journalist.[36]

[33] Danilov, in *SVM* i. app. p. 40. There already existed a periodical, *Voyennyy zhurnal*, published by the Committee on Military Education, and a newspaper, *Russkiy invalid*, but both were narrow in scope and dry. For a fuller account of the following episode, Keep, 'Chernyshevsky' (forthcoming); Koz'min, 'Chernyshevsky'; Makeyev, 'Chernyshevsky—redaktor'.

[34] Lincoln, *Vanguard*, pp. 146–8; Beyrau, 'Leibeigenschaft und Militärverfassung', p. 198.

[35] II *PSZ* xxxiii. 32819 (1 Mar. 1858).

[36] Kartsev was then Chief Quartermaster of the Guards Corps. For his biography see E. W.

He was probably attracted as much by Chernyshevsky's professional experience as by his political views. He may also have thought that any undue radicalism on his part would be checked by the two assistant editors, Lieutenant-Colonel V. M. Anichkov and Captain N. N. Obruchev, both of whom were general staff officers as well as professors at the Military Academy. In fact all these men already knew each other well from the St. Petersburg military colleges, at one of which Chernyshevsky had been briefly employed as an instructor.

Voyennyy sbornik made a great impact and its circulation soon leaped to 6,000, three times that expected by the authorities. Officers were invited to submit contributions which, as selected and edited, took a tone critical of the military establishment. In one of the first articles Obruchev questioned the privileges enjoyed by guardsmen, advocated a militia system, and suggested that in civilized European states the armed forces' role was declining. Other writers dealt with such sensitive issues as corruption, corporal punishment, and the need 'to raise the soldier's image in his own eyes so that he may appreciate his own worth'.[37] All this was strong meat for the traditionalists. *Russkiy invalid* complained that the editors of the new journal were guided by 'speculative concepts'. The authorities clearly could not permit two organs of military opinion to contradict one another, and the military censor, Colonel L. L. Shturmer (Stürmer), had his own axe to grind. He submitted an adverse report to the tsar. Kartsev asked Chernyshevsky to refute his allegations, but the journalist did not help his case by intemperate language and pedantic explanations which, like Shturmer's charges, avoided the real issue at stake: were the malpractices referred to typical, and if so what legal and administrative steps should be taken to overcome them? The upshot was that, after seven issues had appeared, Chernyshevsky had to resign; the journal was allowed to continue under a new editor who had a military background, and was made subject to dual censorship. It still was able to publish much interesting material, and from 1862 became a mouthpiece of Milyutin's administration. The War Minister made a point of dissociating himself from alleged 'subversives' such as Chernyshevsky; Obruchev, who in 1861–2 helped to found a revolutionary organization called Land and Liberty, made his peace with the authorities and, as an official of the Military Education Committee, became one of Milyutin's closest collaborators. His change of heart was apparently in part a response to the 1863 Polish insurrection, which produced a rightward shift in Russian public opinion.

In the late 1850s the Polish cause had won considerable support among 'advanced' Russian youths, including those who wore military uniform.[38] It

Brooks in *MERSH* xvi (1980), 44–7. Many writers (for example, Makeyev, 'Chernyshevsky—redaktor', p. 65) attribute the decision to Milyutin, but he was no longer in the capital.

[37] N. Obruchev, 'O vooruzh. sile i yeyo ustroystvo'; D. S., 'Zametki komandira strelkovoy roty', in *VS* 1 (1858), pp. 16–56, 113–19.

[38] This subject has been closely investigated in recent years by Soviet scholars, notably V.A.

was taken up vigorously by the liberal *émigré* Aleksandr Herzen, and copies of *Kolokol* ('The Bell') reached St. Petersburg and other cities where military colleges were located.[39] Disciplinary rules in these establishments had been somewhat relaxed in 1855 and the cadets allowed to take an interest in the progress of the war; they could also mix more freely with university students. It was not long before they set up informal discussion groups at which the talk turned to political and social questions. Young activists established mutual support funds (*kassy*), libraries, and eventually even clandestine presses on which agitational material could be printed. This 'technological advance' distinguished the dissidents of this generation from their forerunners in 1816–25. They were more impetuous and sometimes displayed a streak of bitterness, even though the underlying mood was still one of idealism. As before, it was but a short step from the salon to the conspiratorial 'society', with all its paraphernalia of pseudonyms and secret meeting-places. The administration was better placed than before to meet the challenge, since it was prepared to co-opt young radicals, on fairly generous terms, as well as to repress them.

In St. Petersburg the new spirit first made itself felt at the General Staff Academy, where entry requirements were liberalized during and after the war. One of those admitted in 1857 was Zygmunt Sierakowski, a 31-year-old Pole from Volhynia who, as a university student under Nicholas I, had been arrested for trying to leave the country without permission and sent to serve as a private in the Orenburg corps, on the empire's south-eastern border. Here he had risen to commissioned rank and now, on entering the academy, was promoted to captain. He soon became the focus of a group of like-minded men who met daily either in the apartment of his friend, Lieutenant Jarosław Dąbrowski, or in some other convenient location. As many as two hundred individuals associated with this circle have now been identified,[40] of whom some 50 to 70 may be regarded as core members. It was an informal association with little organizational structure: 95 per cent were servicemen, four-fifths of them subalterns and only 2 per cent majors or above; most were in their mid-twenties. One-third (34 per cent) were Orthodox by religious affiliation; 22 per cent hailed from the empire's 'internal provinces' but 53 per cent

D'yakov and I. S. Miller, and we now know much more about the individuals and organizations involved. However, care is needed in handling the official interpretation of the movement, which stresses either (Great) Russian paramountcy or, slightly less debatable, the sense of international brotherhood among revolutionaries from all ethnic groups within the empire.

[39] Herzen's first appeal to Russian troops in Poland was written in March 1854, but it was not until 1861–2 that issues of *Kolokol* and leaflets published by the Free Russian Press in London began to circulate at all widely in the army: Verzhbitsky and Frumenkov, 'Rasprostraneniye "Kolokola"'; D'yakov, 'Gertsen, Ogarev i Komitet russkikh ofitserov v Pol´she', *RSR* iii. (1963), 3–30. For a breakdown of this material: Radchenko, *Kolokol . . . sistemat. rospis´*, items nos. 882–959, 1979–2035.

[40] Leykina–Svirskaya and Shidlovskaya, 'Pol´skaya revol. organizatsiya', pp. 19-21; D'yakov, 'Peterburgskiye ofitserskiye organizatsii', pp. 273, 337; for a list see G. V. Bogdanov and V.A. D'yakov in *Vosstaniye 1863 g. i russko-pol´skiye svyazi 60-kh gg.*, Moscow, 1960, pp. 489–637. Cf. also Smirnov, 'Sierakowski'.

from Lithuania or White Russia, 15 per cent from the Ukraine or the south-west, and 8 per cent from the Congress kingdom.[41] At their evening gatherings they would break up into small groups to exchange news, read books and journals, or discuss various current problems. A surviving photograph shows ten earnest young men, most of them in uniform, and one holding a book to symbolize their intent.[42]

Shortly afterwards smaller circles came into being at the Engineering and Artillery academies. Their members were on average a few years younger, but there was a certain amount of overlap.[43] The engineers, some 60 strong, had a higher concentration of Russians (and Baltic Germans) than the General Staff Academy group; the artillerymen were mostly ethnic Russians or Ukrainians, 75 per cent of the members stating their religion as Orthodox. At the latter institution a leading role was played by two professors, both colonels aged about 40: S. A. Usov, editor of the pro-reform *Artilleriyskiy zhurnal*, and P. L. Lavrov, who would eventually become one of Russia's best-known socialist theorists; at that time he could be termed a liberal.[44] A combination of legal and clandestine activity was characteristic of dissidents in this relatively easy-going era. The teachers at the various military colleges had a circle of their own; among those who attended these gatherings were Anichkov, assistant editor of *Voyennyy sbornik*, and M. I. Dragomirov, later one of Russia's leading strategists.[45]

At a lower level groups were formed in the Konstantinovsky Cadet Corps, which trained officers for the artillery, and in the First Cadet Corps, which was conveniently situated next to the university.[46] Also important was the riflemen's training regiment at Tsarskoye Selo, just outside the capital: the course there lasted only one year, so that a number of men who picked up advanced political ideas while in training subsequently transmitted them to units in the provinces.[47] In one Moscow military college the mood was such that 'we knew Chernyshevsky by heart and swore by his name'—or so at least one cadet later claimed; he and his friends belonged to a secret society to which neophytes were admitted after rites performed with daggers and a human skull, in the best Romantic tradition, but they also had their own printing-press.[48]

In the autumn of 1860 a minor incident at the Engineering Academy alerted the authorities to the security problem. A student named Nikonov, asked to apologize for 'inappropriate' remarks he had made about his superiors, refused to do so and faced expulsion. More than one hundred of his comrades rallied

41 D'yakov, 'Peterburgskiye ofitserskiye organizatsii', pp. 278–9, 348–9, 352.
42 Smirnov, *Revol. svyazi narodov*, pp. 156, 161.
43 D'yakov, 'Peterburgskiye ofitserskiye organizatsii', pp. 281, 349, 352.
44 Ibid., pp. 282–3, 295.
45 Ibid., p. 286.
46 Ibid., pp. 286, 295.
47 Ibid., pp. 284–5.
48 Ashenbrenner, 'Vospominaniya', p. 5; Figner, 'Ashenbrenner', p. 193.

to his support. Eleven of them yielded under pressure, but 115 were indeed relegated at their own request, with the proviso that they might apply for readmission after two to three years.[49] The penalty was mild—and indirectly helped to spread dissent to provincial centres. Cadets in other institutions remained quiescent and the participants' aims were very modest; the affair owed much to chivalrous sentiment and scarcely menaced the autocracy. Perhaps the most significant feature was that a similar protest had been staged the year before by Polish students at Warsaw's new Medical-Surgical Academy.[50]

The situation in the Congress kingdom was by this time becoming more and more acute, and in February 1861 five men were killed in a clash between troops and demonstrators. Although the authorities tried to appease public opinion, further violence followed and the movement soon began to spread into Lithuania and White Russia; both regions were placed under some form of martial law. It was in these promising circumstances that Dąbrowski left St. Petersburg for Warsaw, where he was appointed quarter-master of an infantry division[51]—a post that provided excellent cover for revolutionary activity. He became the leading light in the patriots' Warsaw organization, which soon developed into a National Central Committee (KCN).[52] He was also the key figure in developing a conspiratorial network among Polish and Russian dissident officers stationed in Poland and beyond its borders. A total of three to four hundred men are now known to have had contact with this organization, which came to be called the Committee of Russian Officers in Poland.[53] One of its most important links was with Vil'na, where Captain Ludwik Zwiezdowski, who had belonged to the General Staff Academy circle, was now adjutant to the military governor, General V. I. Nazimov[54]—another strategic post. Ties were also maintained with Kiev (Lieutenant F. P. Warawski), Moscow (H. Kieniewicz), and St. Petersburg, where the parent organization, now somewhat enfeebled, was run mainly by two subalterns, W. W. Pogożelski and P.-E. J. Jundziłł, who were studying at two of the military academies in the city.[55]

The security authorities soon managed to intercept the dissident officers' correspondence and in February 1862 a member of the organization, Lieute-

[49] D'yakov, 'Peterburgskiye ofitserskiye organizatsii', p. 292; cf. *Kolokol* 92 (15 Feb. 1861), p. 777.

[50] Leslie, *Reform and Insurrection*, pp. 82–3.

[51] Smirnov, *Revol. svyazi narodov*, p. 206; Kukiel, 'Military Aspects', p. 377.

[52] Kieniewicz et al., *Vosstaniye*, i. 511–13; Wandycz, *Lands of Partitioned Poland*, pp. 169–70; Leslie, *Reform and Insurrection*, p. 146.

[53] For a list of members, see D'yakov, 'Alfavitnyy spisok . . .', *RSR* iii (1963), 34–82; cf. Kieniewicz et al., *Vosstaniye*, i. 477–86.

[54] Leykina–Svirskaya and Shidlovskaya, 'Pol'skaya revol. organizatsiya', p. 27; Smirnov, *Revol. svyazi narodov*, p. 213; Amburger, *Geschichte*, p. 392.

[55] Leykina-Svirskaya and Shidlovskaya, 'Pol'skaya revol. organizatsiya', pp. 34, 38; D'yakov, 'Peterburgskiye ofitserskiye organizatsii', pp. 312, 332; there was also a civilian circle led by J. Ogryszko.

nant W. Kapliński (V. T. Kaplinsky), was arrested in Warsaw. In June two subalterns and an NCO were hanged in public. This brought an attempt on the life of the acting viceroy, and at several places comrades of the executed men staged commemorative religious services. Milyutin ordered a purge of 'all officers . . . who exhibit moral depravity and exert a harmful influence on their comrades and subordinates'.[56] Several hundred men were discharged while others were posted to areas in the interior. Regimental libraries were combed for subversive material. In Vil'na and St. Petersburg commissions of investigation were set up, but the officials who manned them displayed little energy and considerable respect for legal forms. For instance, thanks to Nazimov's intervention on his behalf, Zwiezdowski was simply transferred to another staff job in Moscow, where he was able to continue his revolutionary agitation.[57] On the other hand, in August 1862 the authorities scored a coup by arresting Dąbrowski, although they did not discover his key role; his successor on the KCN, Lieutenant Zygmunt Padlewski, lacked his drive and organizational talent.

In November 1862 Padlewski and a comrade, A. A. Potebnja, held talks in St. Petersburg with the leaders of a shadowy Russian civilian organization, Land and Liberty. Potebnja, a russified Ukrainian and an ensign in the Shlisselburg infantry regiment, had been through the Konstantinovsky Cadet Corps (where he had first met Dąbrowski) and the Tsarskoye Selo riflemen's school; it was he who had shot and wounded the acting viceroy, General Lüders.[58] The nucleus of Land and Liberty included at least two senior officers, Obruchev and Lieutenant-Colonel A. D. Putyata, but most of its members were students,[59] and its two representatives at the talks were both civilians: A. A. Sleptsov and N. I. Utin. Confronted by the more experienced military activists from Poland, they conceded that their organization was still in its infancy and had little influence. Nevertheless an agreement was concluded on 23 November which contained a phrase to the effect that, if insurrection broke out in the Congress kingdom, the KCN 'counts on an efficacious diversion by its Russian allies to prevent the tsarist government from sending fresh troops to Poland'.[60] A good deal of wishful thinking was involved here, since the Russian society lacked the means to undertake any such action; an element of self-deception can also be discerned in the provision that the dissident *Russian* officers stationed in Poland should form a body of their own, which the

---

[56] Miller, 'Russko–pol'skiye revol. svyazi', p. 138; Smirnov, *Revol. svyazi narodov,* pp. 210–13; Leslie, *Reform and Insurrection,* p. 144.

[57] Smirnov, *Revol. svyazi narodov,* p. 214.

[58] Leykina–Svirskaya, 'Potebnja', p. 98.

[59] Venturi, *Roots of Revolution,* p. 269; D'yakov, *Peterburgskiye ofitserskiye organizatsii,* pp. 333–4.

[60] Text in Venturi, *Roots of Revolution,* pp. 271–2; Panteleyev, *Vospominaniya,* pp. 319–20; Miller, 'Russko-pol'skiye revol. svyazi', p. 143.

KCN would pay for. Although Land and Liberty did not provoke the Poles into premature action, as one Polish historian later asserted, misunderstandings were bound to arise: the two parties were unequally matched and there was a latent dichotomy between military and civilians; in the background loomed the vexing problem of the destiny of the ethnically mixed borderlands.

In the event the officers were able to give more help to their civilian friends than vice versa, since they arranged to evacuate a clandestine printing-press which was threatened with exposure from St. Petersburg to an estate in Vitebsk province.[61] When insurrection broke out in Warsaw on 22 January 1863 and the KCN transformed itself into a provisional national government, Land and Liberty could do little more than issue a leaflet which bore the sensational title 'Polish Blood is Flowing, Russian Blood is Flowing'; a student at the General Staff Academy obtained a military map which was passed to the insurgents, and some officers (notably Dąbrowski) were assisted in escaping from captivity. Between 40 and 50 volunteers were despatched from the interior provinces to join the insurgents, but this was done by Poles in the capital rather than by Land and Liberty.[62] Sleptsov toured the Volga region in the hope of stirring up a peasant revolt, but achieved nothing. In Kazan´ two Polish officers distributed a bogus Imperial manifesto 'abolishing' military service and instructing peasant soldiers to leave their units; but the instigators of this affair, which has received far more attention than it warrants, were soon arrested after being betrayed by a student.[63]

In Poland itself and the western provinces several hundred officers and soldiers deserted, as they had done in 1831, and some subalterns brought their entire detachments over to the insurgents; but the rebellion was doomed to failure from the start and the government forces never lost the initiative. Although local resistance by small bands of partisans continued into 1864, the authorities were able to bring in reinforcements (there were over 360,000 soldiers in Poland by the end of 1863) and to mount the campaign of repression indelibly linked with the names of Generals F. F. Berg and M. N. Murav´yev. Sierakowski and Padlewski were among those taken captive and executed. According to official figures, in 1863–5 67 officers and 422 men were charged with anti-state offences; 30 officers and 161 men were executed, and 107 officers and 1,918 men were exiled to Siberia (for crimes of all categories).[64] Military courts heard 26,200 cases in 1864, almost double as many as in 1862.

The opposition movement in the armed forces between 1856 and 1864 was broader in extent and more determined than that of Alexander I's last decade,

---

[61] It was run by I. G. Zhukov, an ex-captain discharged for spreading revolutionary propaganda among the troops: Venturi, *Roots of Revolution*, p. 274; D´yakov, op. cit., p. 318; Smirnov, *Revol. svyazi narodov*, p. 218.

[62] Leykina–Svirskaya and Shidlovskaya, 'Pol´skaya revol. organizatsiya', pp. 45–7.

[63] Venturi, *Roots of Revolution*, pp. 303–15; B. P. Koz´min, *Kazanskiy zagovor*, Moscow, 1929; Leykina–Svirskaya, in *RSR* i (1960), 423–49.

[64] Bogdanovich, *Ist. ocherk*, iv. 518, app. 57, 75, 77–8; Milyutin, in his annual report, gave different figures: *VOVM 1864*, app. vi, pp. 7, 12; 3,193 civilians were sent to the army as a penalty: Bogdanovich, iii. app. 47.

which is much better known. Its vigour was partly due to the fact that Russia had been defeated in the field; another factor was the greater role played by Poles, Ukrainians, and others who either had or were acquiring a consciousness of their national identity. The conspirators also benefited from the presence of *émigré* leaders who commanded considerable moral authority: Herzen's *Kolokol* in particular was able to serve as a practical co-ordinating centre as well as a publishing outlet for locally produced material. Socially, the movement lacked the aristocratic flavour that had characterized 'Decembrism', at least in the north. Most activists were from the lower provincial gentry and held subaltern rank. They made up for their relatively limited experience of active service by their common schooling in the military college network which Nicholas I had built up in the interim. The men of this generation were more professional in outlook and also had closer ties with like-minded civilians. Finally, they were more familiar with the social theories of the day, even though their understanding of them might be superficial—as was to be expected, given the empire's educational backwardness. This shortcoming may have contributed to their failure; but more important was the imbalance of forces (the insurgents were outnumbered by about 40 to 1) and certain avoidable mistakes. If there was a 'revolutionary situation' in the tsarist empire at this time, as Soviet historians insist, it was one that the radicals of the day, Poles as well as Russians, were in no position to exploit. In the later 1860s and 1870s the opposition movement struck deeper root, but it was carried forward mainly by civilian intellectuals and the role of the military element declined.

One effect of the revolutionary ferment that culminated in the 1863 insurrection was to arouse misgivings among conservatives in the military establishment as to the wisdom of proceeding with fundamental reforms. Milyutin was compelled to postpone his plans to introduce conscription, since even his decentralization measures ran into heavy weather. So far as men in the ranks were concerned, the main improvements initially came in the areas of justice and education, which we may examine in turn.

   Alexander II's celebrated dictum, 'May justice and mercy reign in the courts', could not easily be applied to the armed forces. The principles underlying the judicial reform of 1864, which was modelled on western European practice, were officially extended to the military domain 'to the extent compatible with the needs or advantage of the service'. This formula, approved by the tsar in September 1862, was clearly ambiguous. How could the new laws 'maintain and if possible strengthen military discipline and hierarchical subordination (*chinopochitaniye*)' and simultaneously 'secure the person of each [soldier] from arbitrariness and injustice by his superiors'?[65] This required a veritable revolution in attitudes, which the reformers at least deserve credit for

---

[65] Bogdanovich, *Ist. ocherk*, iv. 478–9.

trying to bring about. Before the new military statute (which replaced that of 1839) and penal code received Imperial assent in June 1867 they were thoroughly vetted by several expert commissions and state agencies, and senior commanders were also invited to express their views. Unfortunately it is not yet possible to distinguish the contribution of the various elements of the military public from that made by Milyutin and his close associates. Bogdanovich's semi-official account extols the War Minister's role and is less than just to his forerunner, Sukhozanet, or to Senator I. Kh. Kapger, whose drafts of a penal code (1860) and other legislative acts foreshadowed much that was to come. Nevertheless it is probably true that without Milyutin's drive the reform would not have gone as far as it did.

Perhaps the most important change for the soldiers was the legal definition of offences for which disciplinary penalties could be imposed. Although Nicholas I had taken a step in this direction in 1839, when military laws were codified, in practice (as Milyutin noted in a report to the tsar) such offences had been decided in an arbitrary manner; the number of strokes administered 'depended entirely on the personal whim of one's superior'.[66] In 1859 the maximum was set at 200 and a written order was normally required. On 6 July 1863 Alexander II approved a set of regulations whose provisions were developed in subsequent legislation (April 1865, July 1869): for instance, an NCO in sole charge of a detachment could confine a man to his quarters for 24 hours, a sergeant-major could do so for 48 hours, and a company commander for eight days.[67] A commanding officer could sentence a man to any of the penalties listed, the most severe of which was 50 strokes with rods (*rozgi*).[68] But the main point was that corporal punishment was henceforth to be the exception rather than the rule. It could be administered only to persons placed in a special category. Such men were termed—rather oddly, but in conformity with Prussian precedent—'punished' (*shtrafovannye*). In the Russian historical context this meant that most soldiers were now legally in a situation similar to that which their officers had enjoyed since 1762.[69] The 'punished' were envisaged as a small class of hardened offenders who would serve their term in their units, performing labour tasks, or else, in the most serious cases, in detention companies or jails. The reformers shared the current Western enthusiasm for imprisonment as a reformatory measure, and allowed for rehabilitation once a certain period had elapsed.[70] While in his unit a man could be placed in its punishment cell (*kartser*) for up to five days, or in a so-called 'dark cell' for up to eight days. But the most usual penalties were

---

[66] *VOVM 1864*, app. vi, p. 21; Kudryavtsev, 'O distsiplinarnom ustave 1875 g.', p. 91.

[67] II *PSZ* xxxviii. 39830 (6 July 1863), V; Bogdanovich, *Ist. ocherk*, iv. 463.

[68] II *PSZ* xxxviii. 39508 (17 Apr. 1863), § 7; Bogdanovich, *Ist. ocherk*, iv. 458.

[69] The parallel should not be pushed too far, since this right was not granted to them as a social estate (*sosloviye*); but even after 1762/1785 a nobleman could forfeit his privileged status and so become liable to corporal punishment or other severe sanctions.

[70] II *PSZ* xli. 43451 (2 July 1866); xliii. 45878 (20 May 1868).

fatigues and extra turns of duty.[71] A soldier so penalized had the right to complain, and even to choose someone to present his case; his superiors were obliged to hear him out patiently and to satisfy valid objections; but if a man alleged that his legal rights had been infringed he had to complain formally at an inspection parade, which was bound to be an intimidating experience.[72]

Those whose offences were serious enough to warrant court-martial could also expect to be treated less harshly than before. Nicholas I had not been totally indifferent to the fearsome penalty of running the gauntlet: in 1830 he laid down a limit of 6,000 blows and four years later halved that figure; but the rulings were not publicized, lest discipline be undermined, and in practice they were not regularly enforced.[73] To mark his coronation Alexander II is said to have reduced the number of blows to 1,000 and to have reserved the penalty solely for 'serious disobedience and impertinence'.[74] In the ensuing discussion attitudes towards its abolition became something of a talisman. Advocated by Kapger as well as Milyutin, its 'complete elimination' was announced by the tsar on 17 April 1863 'as a fresh example of paternal concern and to raise morale'. Characteristically, this elevated sentiment was followed by a provision that offenders could still be given up to 200 blows with rods—in public—until such time as sufficient prisons were built. This penalty could be inflicted only by court order on men in the 'punished' category.[75] A contemporary writer noted that conservatives offered less resistance to this reform than they did to the easing of disciplinary penalties.[76]

We need not explore here the whole range of penalties, extending from reprimands and fines to exile with forced labour and capital punishment, but a word must be said about imprisonment. The detention companies first set up in 1823 had grown into a major institution under Nicholas I, who made provision for 55 companies with up to 13,750 detainees. Prisoners of all categories were lumped together indiscriminately; with heads shaven and their legs often in fetters, they did construction work and drilled in their 'spare time'.[77] These units, 'schools of dissolution' as one writer called them, were replaced in the reform era by so-called correctional companies, in which the emphasis was shifted from labour to rehabilitation. The authorities prescribed in elaborate

---

[71] Bogdanovich, *Ist. ocherk*, iv. 462–3, and for the 1869 revisions p. 468; cf. also Kudryavtsev, 'O distsiplinarnom ustave 1875 g.', p. 92.

[72] II *PSZ* xxxviii. 39830 (6 July 1863), VII, §§ 63 ff.; Bogdanovich, *Ist. ocherk*, iv. 469.

[73] Klugen, 'Neskol′ko slov', p. 199; cf. Keep, 'Military Style', p. 77; Vish, 'Telesnye nakazaniya', 11, p. 117.

[74] Klugen, loc. cit. (not in *PSZ*).

[75] II *PSZ* xxxviii. 39506, 39508 (17 Apr. 1863); Bogdanovich, *Ist. ocherk*, iv. 456–7. Birching procedure was as formalized as that of the gauntlet had been, men of the victim's company being obliged to watch as the blows were administered an an NCO counted each one aloud; there was no longer a provision for a medical officer to be in attendance, but instead the escort had to 'watch vigilantly to prevent any breach of order on his [the victim's] part': II *PSZ* xliii. 45892 (23 May 1868).

[76] Shatilov, 'Mysli', p. 364.

[77] A.V. Tavastshern, 'Arestantskiye roty', *VE* iii (1911), 18–19 and more fully in *SVM* xii. 306–33; Afanas′yev, 'Distsiplinarnye bataliony', p. 117.

detail how inmates were to be housed, fed, and even taught to read.[78] There were to be 16 such establishments, with room for 6,800 detainees; but the facilities promised did not all materialize in practice and there was serious overcrowding in some centres. By 1879 the number of detainees had fallen to 2,200; some men were returned to their units but others were sent to perform forced labour or transferred to military prisons, which were usually located in old fortresses.[79]

These changes were accompanied by new procedural rules designed to ensure that the accused received a fair trial. Hitherto military tribunals, expected to keep strictly to the book, had lacked the capacity to come to an independent decision. Their verdicts were passed upward for review to various administrative agencies and even, through the Auditor-General, to the tsar. Decisions were inordinately delayed or taken in ignorance of the facts. The reformers were keen to cut down the paperwork as well as to improve the quality of justice. Henceforth courts were to conduct proceedings orally and to allow the accused to defend himself—through an advocate if the case were heard above regimental level. The procurator, an official new to the military domain, conducted the preliminary investigation and supervised the legality of the trial. Only if he challenged the verdict, or if the accused appealed, was the case to go for review. Efforts were made to give procurators legal training.[80] There is evidence that they took their duties professionally. In 1878 one of them stood up to a powerful official, saying: 'Your Excellency, you have no power to alter a statute.'[81] But there was an acute shortage of qualified officials—in 1867 one post in 14 was unfilled—and the Military Justice College at this time produced a mere 22 graduates a year.[82] Since the courts frequently had to make do with untrained officers, and old habits died hard, far too many verdicts continued to be referred upwards.[83]

The jurisdiction of tribunals at every level was now carefully defined. This had the happy consequence of removing from their purview many civilians who hitherto had been subject to military law: ex-soldiers, foresters, vagrants, smugglers, and sometimes disobedient peasants.[84] Now men faced military proceedings 'only for crimes constituting a direct breach of military service duties'[85]—a formula which excluded, say, offences by off-duty reservists. However, as always there was a loophole: military justice took precedence over civilian 'in places under sole jurisdiction of the army authorities'. This

---

[78] Bogdanovich, *Ist. ocherk*, iv. 489–91; Tavastshern, in *SVM* xii. 385–425.

[79] Bogdanovich, *Ist. ocherk*, iv. 498–501; Afanas'yev, 'Distsiplinarnye bataliony', p. 127.

[80] Bogdanovich, *Ist. ocherk*, iv. 501–8; II *PSZ* xli. 43473 (9 Aug. 1866).

[81] Mordvinov, 'Iz zapisok', p. 857 (1878); for a similar case F. N. Platonov in *IV* 124 (1911), p. 508; neither, however, involved soldiers' rights.

[82] Bogdanovich, *Ist. ocherk*, iv. 502, 505; iii. app. 54. About half that number passed through another institution, the Military Judicial Academy, on which see [Bobrovsky] *50 let spetsial'noy shkoly*, pp. 56 ff.; II *PSZ* xliii. 45666 (30 Mar. 1868).

[83] Bogdanovich, *Ist. ocherk*, p. 511.

[84] Ibid., ii. 420; on this question see LeDonne, 'Civilians'.

[85] Bogdanovich, *Ist. ocherk*, iv. 484.

meant not only barracks and bases but also the large areas of the empire under 'enhanced protection', where the military were thus given a fairly free hand with the local civilian population. A decree issued during the Polish revolt laid down that even in peacetime persons accused of major disciplinary or security offences could be tried by field court-martial, which was to pass sentence as if the country were at war.[86] The 1869 statute was still more specific. In an emergency serving officers could be substituted for court presidents or procurators; procedural safeguards were to be applied only 'so far as possible'; and civilians could be judged 'for crimes detailed either in an Imperial decree or in proclamations by the Commander-in-Chief'[87]—who thus acquired quasi-dictatorial powers.

That miscarriages of justice could occur under such a system goes without saying. One particularly tragic episode has recently attracted attention. In 1866 Private Vasiliy Shabunin, of the 65th Moscow infantry regiment, a chronic alcoholic, was charged with striking his company commander, a Polish captain named Jasiewicz; he confessed his guilt and was duly sentenced to death under an article of the old statute. The unit was stationed near Leo Tolstoy's estate, and the writer agreed to take up the man's defence. His plea for mercy failed to convince the court, and an attempt to intercede with the emperor also went awry—circumstances which weighed heavily on Tolstoy's conscience for the remainder of his days.[88] It is clear from the file on this case, which Kerr summarizes, that Milyutin had the case tried by field court-martial because he wanted to secure a conviction, and that the testimony was doctored to make it seem that Shabunin had committed his offence without any provocation. This occurred shortly after an attempt on the tsar's life. Alexander II and several of his ministers panicked. In 1866 military courts sentenced 18 men (including four civilians) to death, as against seven in 1865, and three in 1867.[89]

Although overall statistics on military offences in the reform era are available, there has been no systematic examination of law enforcement in this (or any other) period, and the individual cases that are known may not be typical. It appears that even in combat zones formal complaints (*pretenzii*) were handled better than before. Under Nicholas I officers accused of misconduct by their men and found guilty were at the most transferred, whereas the complainant was invariably punished! But in 1858 Captain Gedrymowicz of the Apsheron infantry regiment, stationed in the Caucasus, severely beat several subordinates; after complaints were filed he was tried and given two months' detention, *no* action being taken against the men.[90] There was a trend towards a more even-handed approach and milder penalties. In 1863 12 NCOs

---

[86] Ibid., p. 457; II *PSZ* xxxviii. 39506 (17 Apr. 1863), § 7.

[87] Ibid., pp. 487–8.

[88] Kerr, *Shabunin Affair* (but cf. H. McLean in *RR* 42 (1983), p. 194); P. A. Sergeyenko, 'Delo Shibunina [sic]', *Zvezda*, Moscow, 1978, 11, pp. 158–63.

[89] *VOVM 1867*, app. ix, p. 18; for other figures: Bogdanovich, *Ist. ocherk*, iv. app. 78.

[90] D'yakov, 'Soldatskoye dvizheniye', p. 79.

and 55 privates in the crack Yamburg Ulans made a collective protest. The tsar reversed an obviously biased verdict by a lower court and placed the blame on the negligent commanding officer.[91] Another case, in 1865, involved men of the 108th Saratov infantry regiment. When a captain started to beat a sergeant-major on parade the men broke ranks, surrounded the officer and were on the point of seizing his drawn sword when a civilian policeman intervened. The three 'ringleaders' were sentenced to six years' forced labour—but the captain was cashiered.[92] This verdict, though scarcely equitable, represented an advance on earlier practice. Milyutin's reforms of military justice do not deserve all the praise sometimes heaped on them,[93] but they pointed in the right direction, and his successors had a hard time trying to turn the clock back.

The same could be said of the War Minister's efforts to encourage literacy and basic education among soldiers, with the object of fitting them to become NCOs—and officers. Not that anyone envisaged radically upsetting existing officer selection procedures: this would have aroused stiff opposition within the nobility, and in any case substitute cadres were not yet available. It was rather a matter of bridging the cultural gap between officers and men in the ranks and humanizing the general atmosphere. 'An army', Milyutin had once written, 'is not merely a physical force, a mass that serves as an instrument in military operations, but also an association of individuals endowed with intelligence and sensitivity.' These moral qualities needed to be respected and nurtured by commanders, who should learn 'how to manage their men'.[94]

This meant a change in training methods, with more emphasis on marksmanship and personal fitness, to be developed by gymnastics, along with instruction in the three Rs, scripture, and military subjects. This was a novelty —at least for soldiers drawn from regions other than the Baltic. The first such schools were set up in guards and grenadier regiments in 1857. Contributors to *Voyennyy sbornik* initiated a lively discussion on teaching methods and other practical matters. The early enthusiasts had exaggerated expectations of what could be achieved. The instructors were usually NCOs who lacked qualifications for the job; there were no proper textbooks and the reading material consisted either of army manuals or of cheap Western novels in translation. Some soldiers would have preferred the New Testament, but copies were in short supply; other critics suggested, quite sensibly, using the works of contemporary Russian writers. The real problems, though, were time and money. The courses were given on winter evenings, after an 11-hour

---

[91] Ibid., pp. 82–4.

[92] Ibid., p. 85.

[93] E. Lampert writes that 'by bureaucratizing the whole system [the reform] turned the Russian army . . . from a penal establishment into one of the most enlightened institutions of nineteenth-century European military history': *Sons Against Fathers: Studies in Russian Radicalism and Revolution*, Oxford, 1965, p. 47.

[94] Zayonchkovsky, *Voyennye reformy*, pp. 49–50.

working day, and the cost was frequently met from the sums which units set aside to buy extra food. Soldiers could hardly be expected to react positively; nor was there any guarantee that they would be promoted if they learned to read and write.[95]

The most fruitful experiments were conducted in the Ukraine, a region which had played a similar pioneering role in Russia's general educational development two centuries earlier. A central school, with a broadened curriculum, was set up in Khar'kov (1865) to train officers and NCOs as teachers.[96] The experience gained here and elsewhere was taken into account by War Ministry planners. In July 1867 they issued an instruction designed to systematize the scattered educational initiatives by bringing them under closer bureaucratic control. All soldiers were henceforth to be taught, and shortly afterwards it was ruled that all NCOs had to be literate; a 'pedagogical detachment' (*uchebnaya komanda*) was set up in each regiment.[97] However, the financial provision made for these schools was inadequate—10 kopecks per man per year from central funds—and results fell far short of those officially claimed. One expert who visited 18 units in 1870 found that 'the soldier can scarcely cope with the technique of reading . . . in a book he sees only the letters, not understanding what they mean, and he cannot relate what he has read'.[98] This was clearly the fault of the under-qualified instructors rather than the men. Bobrovsky proposed limitations on class size, more intensive tuition, and a pedagogical approach designed to encourage oral and written self-expression. But to many officers of the old school all this seemed an expensive and possibly dangerous luxury.

In 1868 the proportion of literate soldiers was officially put at 27.7 per cent, but the real figure was closer to 20 per cent.[99] By 1892 the percentage had more than doubled, to 54 per cent. Since the literacy rate among *recruits* during the same period climbed faster, from 9 per cent to 34 per cent,[100] it is an exaggeration to claim, as Milyutin's recent biographer does, that the Russian army became 'the school of the nation' *a la française*.[101] Nevertheless educational standards were higher among soldiers than they were among peasants. Sappers and gunners had an appreciable lead over infantrymen and cavalrymen (in that order), as one might expect. After the 1874 reform, when literate soldiers returned home on completing their term of active service, they doubtless helped to stimulate the peasant's thirst for knowledge, even if they could not quench it, as one zealous writer had initially hoped.[102]

[95] Bobrovsky, 'Vzglyad na gramotnost'', pp. 278–93.

[96] P.V., 'Organizatsiya tsentral'noy shkoly gramotnosti v Chuguyeve', *VS* 89 (1873), 1–2, pp. 151–63.

[97] Bogdanovich, *Ist. ocherk*, iii. 124; Bobrovsky, 'Vzglyad na gramotnost'', pp. 296; (1871), 52; Zayonchkovsky, *Voyennye reformy*, p. 215.

[98] Bobrovsky, op. cit., p. 60.   [99] Zayonchkovsky, *Voyennye reformy*, p. 211.

[100] Bobrovsky, op. cit., p. 282; Kurochkin, 'Odinochnoye zaklyucheniye', p. 285; Bogdanovich, *Ist. ocherk*, iii. app. 49; cf. Syrnev, *Vseobshchaya voinskaya povinnost'*, p. xxix.

[101] Miller, *Miliutin*, pp. 91, 141.

[102] S. N., 'O gramotnosti v voyskakh', *VS* 4 (1858), 7, pp. 2, 5, 10.

The army authorities were quite understandably more concerned with improving officers' education. A full account of this reform exists in English,[103] so that it need not be discussed here: suffice it to note that Milyutin tried to do away with the exclusive cadet schools, which had given so much trouble in the first years of Alexander II's reign (he described their influence as 'noxious') and were clearly not cost-effective. He wanted future officers to obtain their general education in a civilian institution—thereby reducing the military's traditionally heavy involvement in this field—and then to undergo a brief period of professional training in a so-called *yunker* school. This scheme shocked conservatives in the military establishment, and in the event the cadet corps survived in disguise as military *gimnazii*. There were 12 of them, supplemented by four specialized colleges (*uchilishcha*) and three others.[104] The *yunker* schools, which numbered 16 by 1874, remained inferior in status and had limited budgets: training here cost only one-tenth as much per man as it did in the higher schools.[105] Yet it was the *yunker* schools that continued to supply the bulk of the officer intake.

In this way the reformers' purpose was largely thwarted. Nevertheless the new system did permit a certain democratization of the officer corps. More NCOs were commissioned after passing the examination that was now made obligatory.[106] They comprised 48 per cent of all new officers in the quinquennium 1866–70,[107] but it is not known how many of these NCOs were commoners by origin.[108] The problem, as always, was the lack of vacancies. The reformers insisted that those who qualified—the term was still 12 years (10 in the guards)—could be commissioned only if a place existed. Deserving NCOs who could not be promoted were given certain privileges and extra pay (100–150 roubles p.a.), which could be converted into a pension when they retired, as they were now encouraged to do.[109] One successful 'bourbon' (see above, p. 240) has left memoirs which suggest that he was a man of limited intellect, completely engrossed in barrack routine. 'In 32 years,' he wrote, 'I have grown so accustomed to the service and love it so much that sometimes I feel I was born into it.'[110]

Although class barriers were not easily overridden, there were signs of a new spirit in relations between officers and men. As was always the case in Russia, those in positions of authority adjusted their attitudes to conform to those at

[103] Miller, *Miliutin*, pp. 92–141; Stein, 'Offizier', pp. 393–6.
[104] Maksheyev, *Voyenno-stat. obozreniye*, pp. 222 ff.
[105] *VOVM 1870*, pp. 49, 52–3; Miller, *Miliutin*, p. 135.
[106] II *PSZ* xli. 42994, 43302 (10 Feb., 14 May 1866).
[107] Bogdanovich, *Ist. ocherk*, iii. 188, 194–5, app. 56–7.
[108] In 1861 5.8 per cent of officers then serving had been promoted from the ranks: Miller, *Miliutin*, p. 95. P. Brant put the proportion higher, at 9 per cent in the infantry and 8 per cent in the cavalry: 'Proizvodstvo nizhnikh chinov', p. 475. For the regulations: II *PSZ* xxxiv. 34884 (8 Sept. 1859), II, § 2. There was a sudden influx of 2,141 ex-NCOs (67 per cent of new entrants) in 1864, when the rules were relaxed, but later the proportion from this source declined.
[109] II *PSZ* loc. cit., III, §§ 2–6; xxxviii. 39758 (19 June 1863).
[110] 'Iz zametok starozhilogo', p. 295.

the top. Most younger and better educated officers identified with the reform movement. On being posted to a unit they would try, at least initially, to carry out their duties humanely and to abstain from traditional abuses. Paternalism, not comradeship, was still the watchword; but it was characteristic that officers should now venture into print with edifying stories about individual soldiers whom they knew.[111] Writers in *Voyennyy sbornik* drew attention to the plight of officers' servants (*denshchiki*), who drew lower rates of pay (normally 2.10 roubles p.a.) and sometimes stole their master's effects or took to drink.[112]

The economy drive prevented any general increase in soldiers' pay—or that of officers either, although they had their disability pensions raised by approximately 33–55 per cent.[113] The question of the men's pay seems to have been too sensitive for *Voyennyy sbornik* even in its most outspoken phase. But the reformers did at least eliminate compulsory deductions for artels and other purposes, which had given rise to many 'misunderstandings' in the past.[114] Men were encouraged to open personal savings accounts instead. The distinction between the men's own funds and those of their unit was still not always adhered to in practice: in 1869 soldiers in the Aleksopol' infantry regiment had 964 roubles deducted from their savings for the privilege of being transported to camp by rail.[115] More than ten years later there were still complaints that *artel'shchiki* showed favour to their friends or connived with local tradesmen to feather their own nests.[116] The problem was not one that could be corrected simply by tighter controls, or even by raising cultural standards. It was bound up with the men's quite natural anxiety to make some money on the side to satisfy their elementary needs, especially for food.

Rations were increased for those serving in Poland during the insurrection— evidently to prevent them drawing unfavourable comparisons with the local inhabitants' diet. In most areas of the empire the allowance designed to give each man a daily hot dish, called 'stew money' (*privarochnye den'gi*), was also raised. But it was not until 1871 that the basic ration was improved.[117] In practice

---

[111] N., 'Vyderzhki iz soldatskoy zhizni', *VS* 34 (1863), 11–12, pp. 139–68; 35 (1864), 1–2, pp. 289–305.

[112] M. N., 'O zamene denshchikov . . .', *VS* 31 (1863), 5–6, pp. 407–18.

[113] II *PSZ* xxxi. 30891 (26 Aug. 1856); Bogdanovich, *Ist. ocherk*, ii. 462–3. *Kolokol* noted that many wounded officers did not receive the pensions due to them: 1 Dec. 1862, p. 1254. New pay scales issued in 1863 (II *PSZ* xxxviii. 40229, 40425, 6 Nov., 24 Dec.) left privates' pay rates unchanged. In 1861 pensions and grants paid to other ranks amounted to 9.7 per cent of those paid to officers, but in 1864 they rose to 22 per cent: *VOVM 1858*, p. 69; *1864*, p. 8.

[114] II *PSZ* xxxviii. 39758 (19 June 1863), § 2; Martyanov, 'Obyazatel'nye vychety iz zhalovan'ya nizhnikh chinov . . .', *VS* 29 (1863), 1–2, pp. 113–24. Conservatives frustrated an effort to transfer responsibility for managing the latter funds to an independent committee of officers, fearing that this would undercut the authority of the CO: Bogdanovich, *Ist. ocherk*, iv. 202–24.

[115] Zayonchkovsky, *Voyennye reformy*, p. 219 n.

[116] Butovsky, 'O kazarmennoy nravstvennosti', pp. 136–7.

[117] II *PSZ* xl. 41790, 42470 (11 Feb., 15 Sept. 1865); *VOVM 1861*, p. 118; Bogdanovich, *Ist. ocherk*, iv. 144–6; Petrov, *Russkaya voyennaya sila*, ii. 443. Some units were able to maintain kitchen gardens, and tinned food made its appearance around 1871: *VE* xiii. 122.

it may have mattered more that soldiers now had a better chance of receiving their deserts. In the supply field decentralization could produce tangible results, since the officials at district level were in closer touch with suppliers. They were now given greater latitude in purchasing provisions; the central authorities continued to draw up long-term contracts with reliable civilian merchants, but did so mainly to meet the needs of troops stationed in grain-deficient regions.[118]

There was also an improvement, though not a dramatic one, in the provision of medical aid. Milyutin placed military hospitals under the army's chief medical authorities, which could be expected to take a more professional attitude than commissariat officials; within each hospital, too, doctors were given more power *vis-à-vis* administrators. The average size of these establishments was reduced, which made them more manageable, and they were relocated so as to share out resources between different regions more equitably. A reserve of staff and equipment was built up in readiness for future emergencies. In *lazarety* the amount of money spent per patient more than quadrupled, whereas in military hospitals it rose by only a quarter; in this fashion the gap, without any publicity, was narrowed between officers and men.[119] At the lowest level a network of medical posts (*okolotki*) was established which by 1870 catered for half the total number of cases treated. The capacity of the *lazarety* increased, and so did the ratio of doctors to potential patients: from 1:474 in 1861 to 1:367 ten years later.[120] But the War Ministry's zealous statisticians obscured the fact that the total number of medical personnel grew by only 5 per cent, and that there were twice as many orderlies (*fel'dshery*) as there were doctors. Graduates from civilian medical schools still found army life unattractive. The Medical-Surgical Academy greatly improved its teaching and nearly doubled its annual number of graduates (the average for the nine years 1862–71 was 129). By 1867 its student body passed the one-thousand mark; however, 40 per cent of the students left before they had completed the course.[121]

In 1868–70 the average mortality rate among serving soldiers (including reservists) was 1.92 per cent—considerably lower than it was for under-privileged civilians, and probably below what it had been at the start of the decade.[122] Hospital mortality rates, at 39.1 per thousand in 1868–70, were actually *higher* than in the 1840s, but this reflected the fact that more serious cases were now admitted for treatment instead of being written off as incurable. Both 1864 and 1866 were bad years for the troops' health, the medical

---

[118] *VOVM 1864*, p. 22; Bogdanovich, *Ist. ocherk*, iv. 148–52, 155, 162–3.

[119] Bogdanovich, op. cit., iv. 385, 394, 445–7 (respectively from 7¼ to 32 and from 45 to 53 kopecks per man per day).

[120] II *PSZ* xxxiv. 34935 (9 Oct. 1859); S. I. Yezersky, in *SVM* iii (ii), 104; *VOVM 1861*, p. 222; for number of effectives ibid. pp. 1–4; Bogdanovich, *Ist. ocherk*, iii. app. 38.

[121] Bogdanovich, op. cit., iv. 427–9; for slightly different figures: Frieden, *Russian Physicians*, p. 39, and for the improvements pp. 56–7.

[122] From Bogdanovich's appendices 38 and 71 it can be seen that in 1862–4 2.01 per cent of effectives died, but since these earlier data included non-serving Cossacks they are not exactly comparable.

authorities reporting 'unfavourable hygienic conditions' in the west and 'miasmatic swamp vapours' in the Caucasus.[123] In the latter year a cholera epidemic claimed the lives of 5,388 men, about one-third of those who caught the disease.[124] In general epidemics accounted for 70 per cent of cases hospitalized and for 57 per cent of all military deaths.[125] Strikingly, in Turkestan the chance of dying in 1868–70 was 2.7 per cent, not much greater than in St. Petersburg (2.5 per cent) or Moscow (2.0 per cent).[126] The excess in Central Asia was attributable not just to the war against the khanates but to mismanagement of the traditional kind. 'Men became excessively fatigued by [having to] march long distances in the summer heat, from 10 a.m. until evening, without the necessary rest stops, so that when pitching camp for the night they often refused to eat supper.'[127]

The statisticians also collected data on morbidity, but their figures need adjustment to take account of men discharged for incapacity or chronic sickness.[128] Another problem is that more soldiers were now treated for minor ailments and so found their way into the records. Thus not too much significance should be read into the fact that the proportion of officers and men reporting sick rose from 69 per cent in 1862–4 to 100 per cent in 1868–70.[129] The important point is that they were more likely than before to receive some kind of beneficial medical care—even though army doctors were still looked down upon by their fellow officers, since Pirogov's recommendations for an improvement in their status were not acted on.

Outside the medical field the authorities manifested their newly discovered concern in a host of other ways, ranging from an improved supply of footwear to the introduction of canteen facilities, which cannot be considered here. Figures for 1866 show that, of a total military budget of 116.6 m. roubles, 71.5 m. were spent on pay and allowances, clothing, food, and medical services; by twentieth-century standards equipment and munitions cost surprisingly little, whereas administration accounted for a sizeable 13.4 m. roubles.[130] These data do not reveal how equitably this expenditure was broken down between officers and men, but both groups benefited from the more relaxed and humane atmosphere. Last but not least, soldiers knew that the impending move to conscription would mean that their service terms would be shortened and equalized with those of their superiors.

In one of several favours granted to mark his coronation Alexander II promised that, barring unforeseen emergencies, no recruit levy would be raised for three

123 *VOVM 1864*, app. vii, pp. 9, 11.
124 *VOVM 1867*, app. v, p. 14.
125 Bogdanovich, *Ist. ocherk*, iv. 437, app. 73.
126 Ibid., iv. app. 72; his interpretation of these data (p. 442) is questionable.
127 *VOVM 1870*, app. vi, p. 40.   128 Ibid., p. 67.
129 Calculated from Bogdanovich, *Ist. ocherk*, iii. app. 38; iv. app. 71.
130 Calculated from Maksheyev, *Voyenno-stat. obozreniye*, p. 210; for a long-term view of the latter question, see W. Pintner, 'The Burden of Defense in Imperial Russia' (forthcoming in *RR*).

years.[131] In 1859 a minor war scare led to the call-up of some reservists, but the earlier concession was repeated.[132] The active service term for new recruits was fixed at 12 years instead of 15; those currently serving had to complete their 15-year assignment before transfer to the reserve (where the terms were *not* reduced).[133] In 1868 the period of active service was further reduced to 10 years.[134] In the interim levies had resumed. Of the 1.2 million men enrolled into the army between 1862 and 1870, over 800,000 were recruits taken by a procedure little different from the traditional one, which Milyutin himself characterized (in his unpublished memoirs) as 'barbarous'.[135] The only significant modification occurred in 1868, when it was ruled that substitutes, now known as *zamestiteli*, could no longer be hired privately, but only through the authorities; the assumption was that they would normally be veterans or men due for transfer to the reserve.[136] The practice whereby donors could send men to the army as punishment was terminated in 1864.[137] As the army's effectives declined, men in the older age brackets were the first to be discharged.[138]

In 1863 reservists of different categories already accounted for 44 per cent, and recruits for only 33 per cent, of the active army's intake, which that year swelled greatly to face the rebellious Poles and the possibility of foreign intervention on their behalf.[139] This provided further graphic evidence of the usefulness of a reserve system, even though in practice the mobilization did not go too smoothly. Milyutin wanted an active service term of only seven to eight years[140] and put forward a revised scheme for a recruitment statute based on the principle that burdens should be borne equitably by members of all classes—that is, for selective conscription. This contentious proposal was passed to a commission headed by a civilian official, N. I. Bakhtin, which proved incapable of solving such weighty questions.[141] Meanwhile another commission, under General P. A. Dannenberg, was examining, in a critical spirit, the issue of army structure and the proposed reserve system. Neither body was under the War Minister's control, and he had to compromise. Edicts issued in August 1864 laid down that unit strength should vary according to a standard determined mainly by the state of national military preparedness (that is, wartime, advanced peacetime, peacetime, and cadre strengths).[142]

---

131 II *PSZ* xxxi. 30877 (28 Aug. 1856).

132 II *PSZ* xxxiv. 34339 (7 Apr. 1859).

133 II *PSZ* xxxiv. 34884 (8 Sept. 1859), §§ 1–2.

134 II *PSZ* xliii. 45876 (20 May 1868).

135 Zayonchkovsky, *Voyennye reformy*, p. 82; figures in Bogdanovich, *Ist. ocherk*, iii. app. 47.

136 II *PSZ* xliii. 46002 (18 June 1868); Zayonchkovsky, *Voyennye reformy*, p. 83.

137 Bogdanovich, *Ist. ocherk*, iii. app. 47; for the practice as engaged in by the Imperial court: II *PSZ* xxxiii. 33619 (15 Oct. 1858).

138 II *PSZ* xl. 41749, 42776 (31 Jan., 15 Dec. 1865).

139 Calculated from Bogdanovich, *Ist. ocherk*, iii. app. 47.

140 Zayonchkovsky, 'Milyutin: biograf. ocherk', p. 26.

141 Miller, *Miliutin*, pp. 184–7; Zayonchkovsky, *Voyennye reformy*, p. 82.

142 Zayonchkovsky, 'Milyutin: biograf. ocherk', pp. 75–6. Cavalry units, stationed mainly in the western provinces where they performed police duties, remained at wartime strength. Cf. II *PSZ* xxxix. 41165–7 (6 Aug. 1864).

In 1869 Milyutin returned to the charge. By this time the number of reservists (533,000) had doubled since Nicholas I's day and was nearly three-quarters of total strength.[143] This was, however, still inadequate—particularly in the light of Prussia's successes against the Second Empire. Sedan was almost a second Sevastopol' for the Russian military establishment. On 21 November 1870 the tsar announced his intention 'to extend direct participation in military conscription . . . to all classes in the empire'.[144]

Before the 'Milyutin reform', as it may properly be called, was promulgated on New Year's Day 1874 three years elapsed that were marked by bitter struggles in government circles, with echoes in the press.[145] The first paragraph of the conscription statute ran: 'the defence of throne and fatherland from foreign foes is a sacred duty of every Russian subject'.[146] The entire male population, 'without distinction of class (*sostoyaniye*)', was liable for military service. This did not, and could not, mean that every conscript would be treated equally; but the privileges that were accorded were no longer based on class origin but on educational qualifications. This criterion favoured the upper classes, of course, but its purpose was to cater to state interests by ensuring an adequate supply of trained NCOs and officers. Everyone who was selected served for a total of 15 years before being relegated to the militia (*opolcheniye*); but those with educational qualifications served a shorter period in the active army before being transferred to the reserve. For the wholly unschooled the two terms were six years and nine; for men with higher education they were six months and 14½ years; and there were three intermediate categories.[147] Students in certain designated educational establishments, as well as business men whose interests might be jeopardized by call-up, could apply for deferment but were not exempt.[148]

In practice army recruits after 1874 still fell into one of two basic categories: conscripts in the literal sense and 'volunteers' (*vol'noopredelyayushchiyesya*): the clumsy term literally meant 'those who freely determine [their fate]' and accurately described their situation.[149] After registration, which had to be effected between the ages of 16 and 20, the former remained in their communities until they received their call-up notices; the latter could volunteer at any time between their 17th birthday and two months before they were due for conscription; they could join at any time of the year and (normally) choose their preferred unit or formation.[150] Anyone with at least two years' schooling could volunteer, but in practice this was the route most favoured by men with

---

[143] Miller, *Miliutin*, pp. 192–3 (strength from Bogdanovich, *Ist. ocherk*, iii. app. 38).

[144] Miller, *Miliutin*, p. 195.

[145] For discussions in English, ibid., pp. 195–227 and, more recently, Bauman, 'Debates'.

[146] II *PSZ* xlix. 52983 (1 Jan. 1874), I, § 1. Milyutin's first draft omitted any reference to 'throne' or 'subject': Zayonchkovsky, 'Podgotovka', p. 173.

[147] II *PSZ* xlix. 52983 (1 Jan. 1874), IV, § 56; Kursakov, *Spravochnaya knizhka*, p. 39.

[148] II *PSZ* xlix. 52983 (1 Jan. 1874), IV, §§ 52–3.

[149] For the differences between these volunteers and the *okhotniki*, cf. Kursakov, *Spravochnaya kniga*, pp. 28–32.

[150] II *PSZ* xlix. 52983 (1 Jan. 1874), XII, § 174; Kursakov, op. cit., p. 10.

higher scholastic attainments—and from privileged backgrounds. This was because only as many volunteers could be accepted as there were vacancies; and unit COs naturally preferred to take the pick of the crop. Having joined the forces, volunteers had to serve at the front, not as auxiliaries;[151] but on the other hand they enjoyed certain important advantages. They did not have to mess together with conscripts if they could afford not to do so, and could live in 'free quarters' instead of barracks; they wore a distinguishing badge and were exempt from labour duties; finally, COs were enjoined 'to supervise their life-style and material conditions', which was virtually an invitation to accord them preferential treatment.[152] Last but not least, men in the first three educational categories (whether they were volunteers or conscripts) enjoyed swifter promotion to NCO and officer rank. Under pressure from the conservatives Milyutin had to accept a proviso whereby men in the third category, on becoming officers, had to serve a further three years before acquiring gentry status.[153] This discrimination was clearly based on socio-political rather than professional considerations. Concessions such as this were necessary to make the reform palatable to members of the privileged classes, whose enthusiasm for military service was in any case waning.

For conscripts in the new army there was much that was familiar. The minimum height requirement was lowered by 1½ *vershki* (6.6 cm.) but measured in the time-honoured way. There were privileges on family grounds for the only sons of widows or incapacitated fathers, the only brothers of orphans, the younger brothers of men already serving, and so on.[154] Such individuals might still be called up if the quota could not be filled by men without such privileges. Among the innovations, besides the shorter term of active service, were improved pensions (36 roubles p.a.) for men incapacitated while on service and an explicit mention of the civil rights (for example, to ownership of property) which they retained as soldiers.[155] Once relegated to the reserve men had few duties in peacetime: a maximum of two six-week training periods, and those who held government jobs were spared mobilization. Once in the militia their obligations were even fewer: in a national emergency only men in the first of two categories were liable to be called up to reinforce the reservists, and no one over 40 had to serve at all.[156] These significant alleviations offset the fact that the incidence of service was now higher than before.

Figures for the first decade after the reform show that 27 per cent of men deemed liable to conscription were actually called up.[157] These two million individuals were overwhelmingly (85 per cent) peasants; gentry accounted for

[151] II *PSZ* xlix. 52983 (1 Jan. 1874), IV, § 58; XII, § 175.

[152] Ibid., XII, §§ 176–80; Kursakov, *Spravochnaya kniga*, pp. 19–20.

[153] II *PSZ* xlix. 52983 (1 Jan. 1874), XII, § 181; Kursakov, *Spravochnaya kniga*, pp. 22–3; Zayonchkovsky, 'Podgotovka', p. 195.

[154] II *PSZ* xlix. 52983 (1 Jan. 1874), VI, § 45.

[155] Ibid., III, §§ 25–30, 33.

[156] Ibid., V, §§ 36, 38.

[157] Syrnev, *Vseobshchaya voinskaya povinnost'*, p. xii.

less than 1 per cent (this figure evidently excludes volunteers).[158] Those with duly certified educational qualifications numbered a mere 35,000 or 1.7 per cent—but another 411,000 (20.2 per cent) were literate, and their share was rising. Deferments on educational grounds were in the range of only two to three thousand a year.[159] A surprisingly high 51.8 per cent of men liable to conscription claimed privileges on family grounds; the proportion of men in these categories who were called up was small: 1.7 per cent (35.6 per cent if one includes childless married men).[160]

The government succeeded in its primary purpose of building up a large reserve. In 1876, when war broke out again with Turkey, its size exceeded ¾ million; ten years later, despite combat losses, it had doubled.[161] However, this force was less well trained than the reformers had anticipated. The Russian army had modernized its structure but it still lagged behind the forces of potential European adversaries organizationally, technically, and psychologically. In an age of intensifying nationalism and imperialist rivalry these were serious shortcomings. Moreover, instead of the reform drive being carried forward with vigour, backed by commensurate changes in other areas of public life, after 1881 an effort was made to reverse it. With this 'counter-reform', as contemporaries called it, the Russian empire entered upon a period of decline that ended in revolution.

Were the seeds of its collapse sown in the Milyutin era, when the service state was dismantled? It is easy, but facile, to blame Russia's failure to meet the challenge of the modern world on the egoism of her social élite, or of certain groups within it. Russian conservatives faced a very real problem: how to hold together a rapidly fragmenting society at a time when absolutism by divine right, the traditional source of political legitimacy, was losing credibility. Throughout its history tsarism had been intricately bound up with the notion of universal state service. The privileged classes had won a measure of freedom from it in the eighteenth century; now, a hundred years later, similar if less extensive rights were granted to commoners. These measures destroyed the intellectual and moral justification for such service. Logically, the old bureaucratic and militaristic state order should have given way to one based on the principle of free contract, oriented to economic growth, in which political power would be freely and openly bargained over by competitive, autonomous social groups. But such a prospect did not seem either practical or attractive to nineteenth-century Russians, whatever their station in life. Only a few intellectuals embraced Western values eagerly. Instead officials, gentry landowners, and even most of the intelligentsia launched into a self-destructive struggle to redefine the state order in accordance with abstract principles of one kind or

---

158 Ibid., pp. 76–7.
159 Zayonchkovsky, 'Podgotovka', p. 198.
160 Syrnev, *Vseobshchaya voinskaya povinnost'*, pp. xix, 115.
161 Zayonchkovsky, 'Podgotovka', p. 199; Kersnovsky, *Istoriya*, ii. 404.

another, regardless of their applicability to the concrete circumstances Russia faced.

In this contest the political establishment enjoyed superior material strength but the intelligentsia had the more plausible ideas. The armed forces were generally perceived, and perceived themselves, as a principal bulwark of conservatism. They were an obvious target for revolutionaries and anti-militarists, many of whom dreamed of abolishing the centralized state apparatus altogether and entrusting the people's security to a democratic militia. Conservatives dismissed such notions as irresponsible and utopian, not entirely without reason. But they went too far in an opposite direction, identifying democracy with anarchy and the destruction of 'the foundations (*ustoi*) of Russian life', as the current phrase went. They cast themselves as the natural guardians of state interest, equating this with the interest of the 'Russian nation' and, implicitly, all the tsar's subjects. National chauvinism went hand in hand with the maintenance of social privilege, resistance to institutional change, and repressive measures against autonomous bodies such as the judiciary, local government organs, the universities, and the press. They saw to it that defence expenditure was still allocated a large share of the state budget: 50 per cent in 1885, 56 per cent in 1913.[162] The army's needs were no longer determined simply by agreement between the autocrat and his War Minister, but after debate in the State Council; but in this as in other senior government bodies there continued to be a high proportion of members with service backgrounds. Yet after the 'Great Reforms' one could no longer say that the Russian empire was a military or militaristic state, and the armed forces had ceased to be the preferred career option for members of the social élite.

Within the army strong emphasis continued to be placed on discipline and respect for rank. This was accompanied by successful efforts to maintain the officer corps as a noble preserve. Formally, non-nobles who passed through the military schools had the same rights as others to a commission, but no major change occurred in the social composition of the officer corps before 1914.[163] The traditional arms of service were still favoured over the more technical ones, and welfare measures frequently disparaged as likely to 'soften the troops' moral fibre'. Among officers an ascetic Spartan spirit came into vogue. It was linked to a cult of simple paternal relations towards the men, to a concern with ceremonial, and above all to an unreflective glorification of the empire's martial traditions: the 1880s and 1890s were the great age of military historiography in Russia. Writers on supply problems characteristically insisted on the army's right to requisition what it needed from the inhabitants of occupied areas in wartime, rather than on the need to build up an effective

---

[162] P. R. Gregory, *Russian National Income, 1885–1913*, Cambridge, 1982, p. 138.
[163] Stein, 'Offizier', pp. 422–3; P. Kenez, 'A Profile of the Prerevolutionary Officer Corps', *Calif. Slavic Studies* 7 (1973), pp. 121–33.

organization of depots in advance.[164] Maladministration and corruption in the rear echelons continued to plague the Imperial Russian army so long as it existed. The cadet corps encouraged the growth of a caste spirit, most in evidence among guards officers (although their historic privileges *vis-à-vis* line officers were now curtailed). Those at the summit of the hierarchy still did best materially and enjoyed high prestige in polite society. In 1905 Russia had no less than 1,673 general officers (145 of them in full rank), and a hostile critic estimated that their maintenance cost the state 10.8 million roubles a year— twice that of the medical services.[165]

One consequence of these reactionary tendencies was that the social gulf between officers and men, which Milyutin had tried to bridge, grew wider again. Every effort was made to insulate the army from civilian influences—not least because it was often called on to help put down civil disorders. By and large officers accepted this. One infantry major, describing military life at this time, compared his regiment to a monastery:

Each community has its own rules and view of life. Each is exclusive and constitutes an organic entity . . . In each one withdraws up to a point from the outside world and becomes wholly absorbed in one's chosen group, which for the lonely pilgrim on this earth replaces house, friends, children, and in a way even his beloved wife. A man inclined towards contemplation chooses a monastery. More active, energetic types make their home in a regiment.[166]

It was not until the revolutionary year 1905 that politics suddenly burst in upon the cloistered, self-sufficient world of these military professionals. But the soldiers were less isolated. The vast majority of them now spent only a brief term (four years from the turn of the century) with the colours before returning to civilian life, which despite all its manifold hardships at least spared them the bullying to which they were still exposed in the ranks.[167] The men's material position remained precarious, with pay still only three to four roubles per annum until 1905, when it was belatedly increased.[168] In these cir- cumstances it is not surprising that, in contrast to the situation a hundred years earlier, 'subversive' influences should have penetrated the Russian army from the bottom up. When it collapsed in 1917 it was the committees formed at company or regimental level that were the most revolutionary.[169]

*

[164] Maksheyev, *Voyenno-administrat. ustroystvo*, p. 111; id., *Snabzheniya: organizatsiya i taktika ikh na voyne*, St. Petersburg, 1898, p. 4.

[165] N. A. Rubakin, 'Voyennaya byurokratiya v tsifrakh', *Russkaya mysl'*, 1907, 1, p. 51.

[166] A. von Drygalski, *Unsere alten Alliirten. Scenen und Typen aus dem Friedensleben der russischen Offiziere*, Berlin, 1894, p. 197.

[167] Corporal punishment for men in the 'punished' category remained on the statute books until 1904, and in practice was never wholly eliminated. One conservative wanted the number of permitted strokes to be tripled: Kudryavtsev, 'O distsiplinarnom ustave 1875 g.', p. 101.

[168] Stein, 'Offizier', p. 477.

[169] A. Wildman, *The End of the Imperial Russian Army: the Old Army and the Soldiers' Revolt, March–April 1917*, Princeton, 1980.

What was the legacy of the old army to the new? The Bolsheviks set out to make a complete break with the policies of the 'feudal' and 'imperialist' past, but it was not long before their rudimentary militia was superseded by a regular force. During the civil war of 1918–20 Trotsky's Red Army (RKKA) proved its worth as an essential bulwark of the revolutionary dictatorship. In the mid-1930s it was converted into a fully professional body in which many of the old Imperial traditions were revived: officers' ranks and insignia, strict discipline, specialized military schools (some of them named for Suvorov) and so on.

But this army was a very different phenomenon from its predecessor. The Soviet soldier received a modern technologically-oriented education and his loyalty to the regime was carefully nurtured by a ramified network of political officers. The official ideology might acquire a strong patriotic flavour, but its purpose was to serve the interests of the ruling party, which was committed to a supranational cause. To that end it mobilized all the country's human and material resources on a scale undreamed of by the tsars. This was not really militarization, even if the agitators often used military terminology in their rhetoric; the Communist party remained in sole charge. The new order which Stalin created took from Imperial Russia's heritage whatever could help to substantiate and legitimate its power, but it was not erected directly on its foundations. It had a different *raison d'être*. Even so the old service state, which in its four hundred years of existence had taken so much from the Russian people and given so little in return, set an awesome precedent. Perhaps its principal legacy was psychological. In the USSR men responded to the call of the central *vlast´* in a generally stolid and submissive spirit that their forbears would have found all too familiar.

BIBLIOGRAPHY

This bibliography is limited mainly to works cited by short titles in the footnotes. Wherever possible, collectively edited works and those issued by institutions are entered under the name of the principal editor or contributor.

ABBREVIATIONS

AAE	*Akty sobrannye v bibliotekakh . . . Arkheograficheskoy ekspeditsiyey Imperatorskoy Akademii nauk*, 4 vols., St. Petersburg, 1813–28
AE	*Arkheograficheskiy yezhegodnik*, Moscow, 1957–
AI	*Akty istoricheskiye sobrannye i izdannye Arkheograficheskoy komissiyey Imperatorskoy Akademii nauk*, 5 vols., St. Petersburg, 1841–2
AKV	*Arkhiv knyazya Vorontsova*, 40 vols., Moscow, 1870–95
AMG	*Akty Moskovskogo gosudarstva: Razryadnyy prikaz, Moskovskiy stol, 1571–1664*, ed. N. A. Popov / D. Ya. Samokvasov, 3 vols., St. Petersburg, 1890–1901
AMGF	See archive sources
B&E	*Entsiklopedicheskiy slovar' Brokgauz i Efron*, ed. I. V. Andreyevsky *et al.*, 41 vols., St. Petersburg, 1890–1904
CASS	*Canadian-American Slavic Studies*, Montreal/Pittsburgh/Tempe, Ariz./Irvine, Calif., 1967–
Chteniya	*Chteniya v Imperatorskom Obshchestve istorii i drevnostey rossiyskikh*, 256 vols., Moscow, 1846–1916
CMRS	*Cahiers du monde russe et soviétique*, Paris, 1959–
CSP	*Canadian Slavonic Papers*, Ottawa/Toronto, 1959–
DAI	*Dopolneniya k Aktam istoricheskim*, 12 vols., St. Petersburg, 1846–72
DiP	*Doklady i prigovory Pravitel'stvuyushchego Senata*, ed. N. F. Dubrovin, N. V. Kalachov, 6 vols., St. Petersburg, 1880–1901
DRV	*Drevnyaya rossiyskaya vivliofika . . .* , 2nd series, ed. N. I. Novikov, 20 vols., Moscow, 1788–91, repr. The Hague, 1970
FOEG	*Forschungen zur osteuropäischen Geschichte*, Berlin, 1954–
IA	*Istoricheskiy arkhiv*, 8 vols., Moscow, 1955–62
IS	*Istoriya SSSR*, Moscow, 1957–
IV	*Istoricheskiy vestnik*, 150 vols., St. Petersburg, 1880–1917
IZ	*Istoricheskiye zapiski*, 108 vols. to date, Moscow, 1937–
JGOE	*Jahrbücher für Geschichte Osteuropas*, Stuttgart/Wiesbaden, 1953–
KiS	*Katorga i ssylka*, Moscow, 1921–35
KS	*Kievskaya starina*, 94 vols., Kiev, 1882–1906

LN	*Literaturnoye nasledstvo*, 94 vols. to date, Moscow, 1931–
MAE	See archive sources
MERSH	*Modern Encyclopedia of Russia and the Soviet Union*, ed. J. L. Wieczynski, Gulf Breeze, Fla., 1976–
MNERSU	*Military-Naval Encyclopedia of Russia and the Soviet Union*, ed. D. R. Jones, Gulf Breeze, Fla., 1978–
PiB	*Pis´ma i bumagi Petra Velikogo*, 12 vols. to date, St. Petersburg and Moscow, 1887–
PRP	*Pamyatniki russkogo prava*, 8 fascs., Moscow, 1952–61
PSZ	*Polnoye sobraniye zakonov Rossiyskoy Imperii*, Ist series, 45 vols., St. Petersburg, 1830
II PSZ	*Polnoye sobranie sakonov Rossiyskoy Imperii*, IInd series, 55 vols., St. Petersburg, 1830–84
RA	*Russkiy arkhiv*, ed. P. I. Bartenev, 55 vols., Moscow, 1863–1917
RBS	*Russkiy biograficheskiy slovar´*, 25 vols. (incomplete), St. Petersburg, 1896–1918, repr. New York, 1962
RH	*Russian History/Histoire russe*, Pittsburgh, 1974–
RK	*Razryadnaya kniga 1475–1598 gg.*, ed. V. I. Buganov, Moscow, 1966
RR	*Russian Review*, Stanford/Cambridge, Mass., 1941–
RS	*Russkaya starina*, 176 vols., St. Petersburg/Petrograd, 1870–1918
RSR	*Revolyutsionnaya situatsiya v Rossii v 1859–1861 gg.*, ed. M. V. Nechkina *et al.*, 8 vols., Moscow, 1960–79
RV	*Russkiy vestnik*, 306 vols., St. Petersburg, 1856–1906
SEER	*Slavonic & East European Review*, London, 1922–
SIE	*Sovetskaya istoricheskaya entsiklopediya*, ed. Ye. M. Zhukov, 16 vols., Moscow, 1961–76
SIRIO	*Sbornik Imperatorskogo Russkogo istoricheskogo obshchestva*, 149 vols., St. Petersburg, 1867–1916, repr. Nendeln, 1971
SR	*Slavic Review: American Quarterly of Soviet & East European Studies*, Seattle/Colombus, Ohio/Stanford, 1945–
SVM	*Stoletie Voyennogo ministerstva, 1802–1902*, ed. D. A. Skalon *et al.*, 13 vols. in 21, St. Petersburg, 1902–11
TsGVIA	See archive sources
VD	*Vosstaniye dekabristov*, 14 vols., ed. M. N. Pokrovsky *et al.*, Moscow, 1925–76
VE	*Voyennaya entsiklopediya*, ed. K. I. Velichko *et al.*, 18 vols., St. Petersburg/Petrograd, 1911–15
VEv	*Vestnik Yevropy*, St. Petersburg/Petrograd, 1866–1916
VI	*Voprosy istorii*, Moscow, 1945–
VOVM	Russia. War Ministry. *Vsepoddanneyshiy otchet po Voyennomu ministerstvu*, St. Petersburg, 1858–[1916]
VS	*Voyennyy sbornik*, 254 vols., St. Petersburg/Petrograd, 1858–1916
V-UA	See archive sources

W&S   *War and Society*, Duntroon (Australia), 1983–
ZhMNP   *Zhurnal Ministerstva narodnogo prosveshcheniya*, St. Peters-
           burg/Petrograd, 1834–1917

UNPUBLISHED SOURCES

Archives

France. Ministère des Affaires Etrangères (MAE). Mémoires et documents
    Russie 14. 1745–1828
    Russie 20. 1790–1791
    Russie 26. 1808–1820
    Russie 27. 1819–1827
    Russie 28. 1821–1834
    Russie 29. 1807–1827
    Russie 30. 1735–1759
    Russie 32. 1800–1813
    Russie 35. 1778–1828
    Russie 36. 1826–1832
    Russie 37. 1831–1852
    Russie 40. 1821–1822
    Russie 43. 1835–1848
France. Ministère de la Guerre, Vincennes (AMGF)
    C^{2}287. Campagne de Russie. Papiers Belliard
    G^{1}45. Notes diverses sur l'armée russe, 1854–1856
USSR. GAU. TsGVIA (Tsentral'nyy Gosudarstvennyy Voyenno-istoricheskiy arkhiv)
    fond 8, opis'.1/89, ed. khr. 1806. 1759–1760. Court-martial proceedings
    f. 11, op. 3, ed. khr. 1443. 1744–1802. Drafts of miscellaneous decrees
    f. 8, op. 5, d. 5. 1759. Decree on punishment of deserters
    f. 8, op. 5, ed. khr. 315. 1776. Court-martial proceedings (Capt. T. Pavlov, Butyrsky infantry regiment)
    f. 11, op. 6, ed. khr. 33. 1799. Court-martial proceedings
    f. 11, op. 8, ed. khr. 1. 1793–1796. War College reports on personnel matters
    f. 11, op. 8, ed. khr. 8. 1794–1795. Field-Marshal Rumyantsev's reports on insubordinate Polish soldiers
    f. 11, op. 8, ed. khr. 18. 1800–1. Reports of Senior Field Chaplain P. Ozeretskovsky
    f. 801, op. 62/3, ed. khr. 26. 1797. Court-martial proceedings (Pte. K. Yelyakov, Ryazhsk Musketeers)
    f. 801, op. 62/3, ed. khr. 77. 1797. Court-martial proceedings (Lieut. P. Machikhin)
    f. 801, op. 62/3, ed. khr. 117. 1797. Court-martial proceedings (Pte. F. Czechowicz, Murom Musketeers)
    f. 801, op. 62/3, delo 168. 1798. Court-martial proceedings (Ensign D. Konstantinov, Azov Musketeers)
    f. 801, op. 62/3, ed. khr. 304. 1798. Court-martial proceedings (Don Cossacks I. Korotkov *et al.*)
    Voyenno-uchenyy arkhiv (V-UA), chast' I, delo 87. 1762. Investigation into rumours in Semenovsky guards regiment

V-UA, ed. khr. 88. 1763. Auditor's journal for Land-militia Corps

V-UA, ed. khr. 226. 1778–1780. Journal of outgoing orders, confirmations, etc. of Lieutenant-General Auditor's Expedition

V-UA, ed. khr. 16449. 1790. Papers of Yelizavetgrad Mounted Musketeer regiment

V-UA, f. 1349, d. 300. 1796. Gen. Levanidov's reports on state of forces in First Division

Theses and unpublished papers

Bauman, R. F., 'The Debates over Universal Military Service in Russia, 1870–1874' (Yale, 1982).

Bolotenko, G., 'The Administration of the State Peasants in Russia, 1825–1838' (Toronto, 1979).

Brown, P., 'Muscovite Government Bureaux', 120 pp.

Bulcke, I., 'C. H. von Manstein, 1711–1756: sein Beitrag zur Russlandkunde im 18. Jhd.' (Munich, 1965).

Eaton, H. L., 'Early Russian Censuses and the Population of Muscovy, 1550–1650' (Urbana, 1970).

Ferguson, A. D., 'Russian Military Settlements, 1810–1866' (Yale, 1953).

Floyd, J. L., 'State Service, Social Mobility and the Imperial Russian Nobility, 1801–1856' (Yale, 1981).

Givens, R. D., 'Servitors or Seigneurs: the Nobility and the Eighteenth–Century Russian State' (Berkeley, 1975).

Hellie, R. F., 'Muscovite Military Slavery', 18 pp.

—— 'The Muscovite Provincial Service Elite in Comparative Perspective', 32 pp.

Menning, B. W., 'A. I. Chernyshev: a Russian Lycurgus', 42 pp.

—— 'Military Institutions and the Steppe Frontier in Imperial Russia, 1700–1861', 29 pp.

—— 'The Origins of the Modern Russian Military Tradition: the Eighteenth–Century Army', 123 pp.

—— 'Russia and the West: the Problem of Eighteenth–Century Military Models', 28 pp.

Pintner, W. McK., 'Russia as a Great Power, 1709–1856: Reflections on the Problem of Relative Backwardness, with Special Reference to the Russian Army and Russian Society' (Kennan Institute Occasional Paper, 33.) Washington, 1976.

Rexhauser, R., 'Besitzverhältnisse des russischen Adels im 18. Jhd.: historische Fragen, methodologische Probleme' (Erlangen, 1971).

Warner, R. H., 'The Political Opposition to Tsar Paul I' (New York, 1977).

PUBLISHED SOURCES

Afanas'yev, V., 'Distsiplinarnye bataliony i roty v ryadu voinskikh nakazaniy, soprya-zhennykh s lisheniyem svobody', *VS* 194 (1890), 7, pp. 108–42.

Aksenov, K., *Severnoye obshchestvo dekabristov: k 125-letiyu vosstaniya 14-go dekabrya 1825 g.*, Leningrad, 1951.

Alabin, P. V., 'Russkiye v Vengrii v 1849 g.: iz pokhodnykh zapisok', *RS* 35 (1882), pp. 91–112.

Alef, G., 'Aristocratic Politics and Royal Policy in Muscovy in the Late Fifteenth and Early Sixteenth Centuries', *FOEG* 27 (1980), pp. 77–109.

—— 'The Crisis of the Muscovite Aristocracy: a Factor in the Growth of Monarchical Power', *FOEG* 15 (1970), pp. 15–58.

—— 'Muscovite Military Reforms in the Second Half of the Fifteenth Century', *FOEG* 18 (1973), pp. 73–108.

Aleksandrov, V. A., *Sel'skaya obshchina v Rossii: XVII–nachalo XIX v.*, Moscow, 1976.

—— 'Streletskoye naselenie yuzhnykh gorodov Rossii v XVII v.', in Aleksandrov *et al.* (eds.), *Novoye*, pp. 235–50.

—— *et al.* (eds.), *Novoye o proshlom nashey strany: pamyati akademika M. N. Tikhomirova*, Moscow, 1967.

Alekseyev, M. P. and Meylakh, B. S. (eds.), *Dekabristy i ikh vremya: materialy i soobshcheniya*, Moscow and Leningrad, 1951.

Alekseyev, Yu. G., '15-rublevyy maksimum po sluzhiloy kabale: sluzhba s zemli i feodal'naya renta', in Nosov, N. E. *et al.* (eds.), *Issledovaniya po sotsial'no-politicheskoy istorii Rossii: sbornik statey pamyati B. A. Romanova*, Leningrad, 1971, pp. 110–17.

Alekseyeva, O. B. and Yemelyanov, L. I. (eds.), *Istoricheskiye pesni XVIII v.*, Leningrad, 1971.

Alexander Aleksandrovich [Grand Duke] (contrib.), 'Pis'ma imperatora Aleksandra I-go i drugikh osob tsarstvuyushchego doma k F. Ts. Lagarpu', *SIRIO* v (1870), 1–121.

Alexander, J. T., 'Medical Developments in Petrine Russia', *CASS* 8 (1974), pp. 198–221.

Algarotti, F., Count, *Lettres du Comte Algarotti sur la Russie . . . avec l'histoire de la guerre de 1735 contre les Turcs*, London, 1769.

Amburger, E., *Geschichte der Behördenorganisation Russlands von Peter dem Grossen bis 1917*, Leyden, 1966.

Un Ami de la Vérité (pseud.), *Coup d'œil sur l'état actuel de la Russie envisagé sous les rapports physique, moral, économique, politique et militaire, ou: les Russes tels qu'ils sont*, Lausanne, 1799.

Anderson, P., *Lineages of the Absolutist State*, London, 1974.

Andolenko, C. R., *Histoire de l'armée russe*, Paris, 1967.

Anisimov, N. V. and Zinevich, M. K., *Istoriya russkoy armii: epokha Petra Velikogo, 1699–1762* [sic] *gg.*, Chuguyev, 1911.

Anisimov, Ye. V., 'Iz istorii fiskal'noy politiki russkogo absolyutizma pervoy chetverti XVIII v.: podvornoye nalogooblozheniye i vvedeniye podushnoy podati', *IS* 1983, 1, pp. 127–39.

Anpilogov, G. N. (ed.), *Novye dokumenty o Rossii kontsa XVI—nachala XVII v.*, Moscow, 1967.

Antonovsky, A. I., 'Zapiski', in Kharkevich, *1812 g.*, iii. 1–207.

Apolev, M., 'Ocherki khozyaystva armeyskogo pekhotnogo polka', *VS* 8 (1859), 7, pp. 1–40.

Ashenbrenner, M., 'Vospominaniya: shestidesyatye i semidesyatye gody', *Byloye*, St. Petersburg, 1907, 4, pp. 1–20, 5, pp. 106–23, 6, pp. 78–96.

Auerbach, H., *Die Besiedelung der Südukraine in den Jahren 1774–1787*, Wiesbaden, 1965.

Averbukh, R. A., *Revolyutsiya i natsional'no-osvoboditel'naya bor'ba v Vengrii, 1848–1849*, Moscow, 1965.

Avrich, P., *Russian Rebels, 1600–1800*, New York, 1972.

Avtokratov, V. N., 'Pervye komissariatskiye organy russkoy regulyarnoy armii, 1700–1710 gg.', *IZ* 68 (1961), pp. 163–88.

—— 'Voyennyy prikaz: k istorii komplektovaniya i formirovaniya voysk v Rossii v nachale XVIII v.', in Beskrovny *et al.* (eds.), *Poltava*, pp. 228–45.

Azadovsky, M. K. (ed.), *Dekabristy: novye materialy*, Moscow, 1955.

Babkin, A. (ed.), 'Documents inédits sur l'armée russe de la fin du XVIIᵉ siècle', *CASS* 11 (1977), pp. 287–305.

Babkin, V. I., 'Organizatsiya i voyennye deystviya narodnogo opolcheniya v Otechestvennoy voyne 1812 g.', in Beskrovnyy *et al.* (eds.), *1812 g.*, pp. 134–63.

Baranovich, A. I. *et al.* (eds.), *Ocherki istorii SSSR: period feodalizma: Rossiya vo vtoroy polovine XVIII v.*, Mowcow, 1956.

—— *Ocherki istorii SSSR: period feodalizma: XVIII vek: vtoraya chetvert'*, Moscow, 1957.

Barskov, Ya. L., 'Proyekty voyennykh reform tsesarevicha Pavla I', *Russkiy istoricheskiy zhurnal* I (Petrograd, 1917), 3–4, pp. 104–45.

[Bartenev, P. I.?], 'Graf N. P. Panin: biograficheskiy ocherk', *RA* 46 (1909), 2, pp. 405–44.

Bartlett, R. P., *Human Capital: the Settlement of Foreigners in Russia, 1762–1804*, Cambridge, 1979.

Basargin, N. V., *Zapiski*, ed. P. E. Shchegolev, Petrograd, 1917.

Baumgart, W., *The Peace of Paris, 1856: Studies in War, Diplomacy and Peacemaking*, tr. A. P. Saab, Santa Barbara and Oxford, 1981.

Baumgarten, G., *Sechzig Jahre des Kaukasischen Krieges, mit besonderer Berücksichtigung des Feldzuges im nördlichen Daghestan im Jahre 1839*, Leipzig, 1861.

Belikov, T. I., *Kalmyki v bor'be za nezavisimost' nashey rodiny, XVII—nachalo XIX v.*, Elista, 1965.

Belov, E. A., 'Moskovskiye smuty v kontse XVII v.', *ZhMNP* 249 (1887), pp. 99–146, 319–66.

Belyayev, I. [D.], *O storozhevoy, stanichnoy i polevoy shuzhbe na pol'skoy ukraine Moskovskogo gosudarstva do tsarya Alekseya Mikhaylovicha*, Moscow, 1846, reprinted Ann Arbor and London, 1980.

Belyayev, I. S. (ed.), *Arkhiv sela Voshchazhnikova*, fasc. I: *Bumagi fel'dmarshala B. P. Sheremeteva*, Moscow, 1901.

Bennett, H. A., 'Chiny, ordena and Officialdom', in Pintner and Rowney, *Russian Officialdom*, pp. 162–89.

—— 'Evolution of the Meanings of *Chin*: an Introduction to the Russian Institution of Rank Ordering and Niche Assignment . . .', *California Slavic Studies* x (1977), 1–43.

Berezhkov, D., 'Istoricheskiy ocherk prizreniya ranenykh', *VS* 137 (1881), 1, pp. 36–58, 138 (1881), 3, pp. 37–55.

Berkhgol'ts (Bergholz), F. W. von, *Dnevnik kammer-yunkera Berkhgol'tsa, vedyennyy im v Rossii v tsarstvovaniye Petra Velikogo s 1721 do 1725 g.*, tr. I. Ammon, supplement to *RA*, 1902–3.

Berry, L. E. and Crummey, R. O. (eds.), *Rude and Barbarous Kingdom: Russia in the Accounts of Sixteenth-Century English Voyagers*, Madison, Milwaukee, and London, 1968.

Besançon, A., *Education et société en Russie dans le deuxième tiers du XIXe siècle.* (Civilisations et sociétés, 40.) Paris, 1974.

Beskrovnyy, L. G. (comp.), *Khrestomatiya po russkoy voyennoy istorii*, Moscow, 1947.

—— *Ocherki po istochnikovedeniyu voyennoy istorii Rossii*, Moscow, 1957.

—— *Ocherki voyennoy istoriografii Rossii*, Moscow, 1962.

—— (ed.), *Polkovodets Kutuzov*, Moscow, 1955.

—— *Russkaya armiya i flot v XVIII v.: ocherki*, Moscow, 1958.

—— *Russkaya armiya i flot v XIX v.: voyenno-ekonomicheskiy potentsial Rossii*, Moscow, 1973.

—— (ed.), *Stranitsy boyevogo proshlogo: ocherki voyennoy istorii Rossii*, Moscow, 1968.

—— (ed.), *Voprosy voyennoy istorii Rossii*, Moscow, 1969.

—— 'Voyennye shkoly v Rossii v pervuyu polovinu XVIII v.', *IZ* 42 (1953), pp. 285–300.

—— *et al.* (eds.), *Narodnoye opolcheniye v Otechestvennoy voyne 1812 g.: sbornik dokumentov*, Moscow, 1962.

—— *et al.* (eds.), *Poltava: k 250-letiyu Poltavskogo srazheniya*, Moscow, 1959.

—— *et al.* (eds.), *1812 g.: k 150-letiyu Otechestvennoy voyny: sbornik statey*, Moscow, 1962.

—— *et al.* (eds.), *Voprosy istorii khozyaystva i naseleniya Rossii XVII v.: ocherki iz istoricheskoy geografii XVII v.*, Moscow, 1974.

——, Kabuzan, V. M., and Yatsunsky, V. K., 'Bilan démographique de la Russie en 1789–1815', *Annales de démographie historique* 2 (1965), pp. 127–34.

Best, G., *War and Society in Revolutionary Europe, 1770–1870*, London, 1981.

Bestuzhev, I. V., 'Iz istorii Krymskoy voyny 1853–1856 gg.', *IA* 8 (1959), 4, pp. 204–8.

—— 'Krymskaya voyna i revolyutsionnaya situatsiya', *RSR* iii (1963), 189–213.

Beyrau, D. 'La Formation du corps des officiers russes au XIXe siècle: de la "militaris-ation" à la "professionalisation" [abstract], *CMRS* 19 (1978), pp. 309–10.

—— 'Von der Niederlage zur Agrarreform: Leibeigenschaft und Militärverfassung in Russland nach 1855', *JGOE* 23 (1975), pp. 191–212.

Bil′basov, V. A., [review of Maslovsky, D. F., *Russkaya armiya v semiletnuyu voynu*], *ZhMNP* 251 (1887), pp. 146–85.

Billington, J. H., *Fire in the Minds of Men: Origins of the Revolutionary Faith*, New York, 1980.

Bismarck, Count von, *Die kaiserlich russische Kriegsmacht im Jahre 1835, oder: Meine Reise nach Sankt–Petersburg*, Karlsruhe, 1836.

Blagovo, A. A., 'Pamyatnaya knizhka poruchika leyb-gvardii Semenovskogo polka A. A. Blagogo, 1739–1740', in *Shchukinskiy sbornik* ii (1903), 385–455, iii (1904), 44–94.

Bliokh, I. S., *Finansy Rossii: XIX stoletiye: istoriya—statistika*, 4 vols., St. Petersburg, 1882, ii.

Bobrovsky, P. O., 'Besedy o voyennykh zakonakh Petra I-go Velikogo', *VS* 191 (1890), 1, pp. 5–28, 209–22.

—— (comp.), *Istoriya 13-go leyb–grenaderskogo Erivanskogo Ye. V. polka za 250 let, 1642–1892*, Paris, 1942.

—— 'K kharakteristike voyennogo iskusstva i distsipliny v voyskakh XVII i nachala XVIII stoletiya', *VS* 201 (1891), 9–10, pp. 5–27, 177–96.

—— 'Mestnichestvo i prestupleniya protiv rodovoy chesti v russkom voyske do Petra I-go', *VS* 184 (1888), 12, pp. 241–69.

—— 'Petr Velikiy kak voyennyy zakonodatel′', *VS* 175 (1887), 5, pp. 5–29, 6, pp. 145–64, 176 (1887), 7, pp. 5–26.

—— 'Poteshnye i nachalo Preobrazhenskogo polka', *VS* 248 (1899), 7–8, pp. 3–34, 237–69.

[——], *50 let spetsial′noy shkoly dlya obrazovaniya voyennykh zakonovedov v Rossii, 10 noyabrya 1832–1882* . . . , St. Petersburg, [1883].

—— *Voyennoye pravo v Rossii pri Petre Velikom*, 3 pts., St. Petersburg, 1882–98 (pt. 2, 'Artikul voinskiy . . .').

—— 'Vzglyad na gramotnost′ i uchebnye komandy (ili polkovye shkoly) v nashey armii', *VS* 76 (1870), 12, pp. 279–310, 78 (1871), 3, pp. 41–87, 4, pp. 283–97.

Bogdanovich, M. I. (ed.), *Istoricheskiy ocherk deyatel′nosti voyennogo upravleniya v Rossii v pervoye 25-letiye . . . imperatora Aleksandra Nikolayevicha, 1855–1880 gg.*, 6 vols., St. Petersburg, 1879–81.

—— *Istoriya tsarstvovaniya imperatora Aleksandra I i Rossii v yego vremya*, 6 vols., St. Petersburg, 1869–71, repr. Ann Arbor and London, 1980.

—— *Russkaya armiya v vek imperatritsy Yekateriny*, St. Petersburg, 1873.

Bogoslovsky, M. M., *Oblastnaya reforma Petra Velikogo: provintsiya 1719–1727 gg.*, Moscow, 1902, repr. The Hague and Paris, 1970.

—— *Petr I: materialy dlya biografii*, 5 vols., Moscow, 1940–8, repr. The Hague and Paris, 1969.

[Bogoyavlensky, S.?], 'Streletskiye golovy i sotniki pri Ivane IV', *Chteniya* 1910, 4, 4, pp. 13–15.

Bolotov, A. T., *Zhizn′ i priklyucheniya Andreya Bolotova, opisannye samim im dlya svoikh potomkov*, Moscow and Leningrad, 1931, repr. Newtonville, Mass., 1973.

Bradke, E. F. von, 'Avtobiograficheskiye zapiski', *RA* 1875, 1, pp. 13–53, 257–94.

Brant, P., 'Kazarmennoye raspolozhenie voysk i vliyaniye yego na zdorov′ye nizhnikh chinov', *VS* 30 (1863), 3–4, pp. 77–100.

—— 'Proizvodstvo nizhnikh chinov v ofitsery', *VS* 31 (1863), 6, pp. 473–88.

Brix, M. R., *Geschichte der alten russischen Heeres-Einrichtungen von den frühesten Zeiten bis zu den von Peter dem Grossen gemachten Veränderungen*, Berlin, 1867.

Buganov, V. I., '"Gosudarev razryad" 1556 g. i reformy 50-kh gg. XVI v.', *IS* 1957, 5, pp. 220–31.

—— '"Gosudarev razryad" pervoy poloviny XVII v.', *Problemy istochnikovedeniya* 8 (1959), pp. 361–71.

—— 'K izucheniyu sostava "Gosudareva dvora" XVI v.', in V. T. Pashuto *et al.* (eds.), *Obshchestvo i gosudarstvo feodal′noy Rossii: sbornik statey, posvyashchennyy 70-letiyu akademika L. B. Cherepnina*, Moscow, 1975, pp. 55–61.

—— 'Letopisnye izvestiya o moskovskom vosstanii 1682 g.', in Aleksandrov *et al.* (eds.), *Novoye*, pp. 310–19.

—— *Moskovskoye vosstaniye 1662 g.*, Moscow, 1964.

—— *Moskovskiye vosstaniya kontsa XVII v.*, Moscow, 1969.

—— 'O sotsial′nom sostave uchastnikov moskovskogo vosstaniya 1662 g.' *IZ* 66 (1960), pp. 312–17.

—— 'Obzor spiskov razryadnykh knig posledney chasti XV—nachala XVII v.', *Problemy istochnikovedeniya* 6 (1958), pp. 152–219.

—— 'Opisaniye spiskov razryadnykh knig XVII v.', *AE* 1972, pp. 276–82.

—— *Razryadnye knigi posledney chetverti XV—nachala XVII v.*, Moscow, 1962.

—— 'Sokraschennaya redaktsiya razryadnykh knig 1550–1636 gg.', *Problemy istoch-nikovedeniya* 9 (1961), pp. 270–9.

—— 'Sokraschennaya redaktsiya razryadnykh knig 1559–1605 gg.', *AE* 1957, pp. 88–101.

—— (comp.), *Vosstaniye 1662 g. v Moskve: sbornik dokumentov*, ed. A. A. Novosel´sky, Moscow, 1964.

—— and Kazakevich, A. N. (comps.), *Vosstaniye moskovskikh strel´tsov: 1698 god: materialy sledstvennogo dela: sbornik dokumentov*, Moscow, 1980.

—— and Savich, N. G. (comps.), *Vosstaniye v Moskve 1682 g.: sbornik dokumentov*, Moscow, 1976.

Büsch, O., *Militärsystem und Sozialleben im alten Preussen, 1713–1807: die Anfänge der sozialen Militarisierung der preussisch-deutschen Gesellschaft*, Berlin, 1962.

Bushnell, J., 'Peasants in Uniform: the Tsarist Army as a Peasant Society', *Journal of Social History* 13 (1979–80), pp. 565–76.

Butovsky, N., 'O kazarmennoy nravstvennosti i o vnutrennem poryadke v voyskakh: zametki rotnogo komandira', *VS* 149 (1883), 1, pp. 125-38.

Bychkov, A. F. (ed.), *Materialy Voyenno-uchenogo arkhiva Glavnogo shtaba*, vol. 1, St. Petersburg, 1871.

—— *Pis´ma Petra Velikogo, khranyashchiyesya v Imperatorskoy publichnoy biblioteke i opisaniye nakhodyaschikhsya v ney rukopisey, soderzhashchikh material dlya istorii yego tsarstvovaniya*, St. Petersburg, 1872.

Chechulin, N. D., *Goroda moskovskogo gosudarstva v XVI v.*, St. Petersburg, 1889, repr. The Hague and Paris, 1969.

—— *Ocherki po istorii russkikh finansov v tsarstvovaniye Yekateriny II*, St. Petersburg, 1906.

Chernov, A. V., 'Obrazovaniye streletskogo voyska', *IZ* 38 (1951), pp. 281–90.

—— 'Vooruzhennye sily', in Novosel´sky and Ustyugov (eds.), *Ocherki*, pp. 439–53.

—— *Vooruzhennye sily russkogo gosudarstva v XVI–XVII vv.: s obrazovaniya tsentra-lizirovannogo gosudarstva do reform pri Petre I*, Moscow, 1954.

Chernov, S. N., 'Iz istorii bor´by za armiyu v nachale 20-kh gg. XIX v.' [1929], in id., *U istokov russkogo osvoboditel´nogo dvizheniya: izbrannye stat´i po istorii deka-brizma*, Saratov, 1960, pp. 179–260.

[Chernyshev, A. I.], 'Istoricheskoye obozreniye voyenno-sukhoputnogo upravleniya s 1825 po 1850 god', *SIRIO* xcviii (1896), 299–447.

Chernyshevsky, N. G., 'Zamechaniya na doklad o vrednom napravlenii vsey russkoy literatury voobshche i "Voyennogo sbornika" v osobennosti, sostavlennyy g. voyen-nym tsenzorom polkovnikom Shtyurmerom', in id., *Polnoye sobranie sochineniy v 15 tomakh*, vol. 5: *Stat´i 1858–9*, ed. V. Ya. Kirpotin *et al.*, Moscow, 1950, pp. 441–91.

Chicherin, A., *Dnevnik, 1812–1813 gg.*, ed. L. G. Beskrovnyy, Moscow, 1966.

Chicherin, A., Dolgov, S. and Afanas´yev, A., *Istoriya leyb-gvardii Preobrazhenskogo polka, 1683–1883*, 4 vols., St. Petersburg, 1883.

Chistov, K. V., *Russkiye narodnye sotsial´no-utopicheskiye legendy*, Moscow, 1967.

Chistyakova, Ye. V., 'Moskva v seredine 30-kh gg. XVII v.', in Aleksandrov *et al.* (eds.), *Novoye*, pp. 301–9.

—— 'Volneniya sluzhilykh lyudey v yuzhnykh gorodakh Rossii v seredine XVII v.', in Ustyugov *et al.* (eds.), *Russkoye gosudarstvo*, pp. 254–71.

Clarkson, J. D., 'Some Notes on Bureaucracy, Aristocracy and Autocracy in Russia, 1500–1800', in Ritter, G. A. (ed.), *Entstehung und Wandel der modernen Gesellschaft: Festschrift für H. Rosenberg zum 65. Geburtstag*, Berlin, 1970, pp. 187–220.

Confino, M., *Domaines et seigneurs en Russie vers la fin du XVIIIᵉ siècle*, Paris, 1963.

Corvisier, A., *Armées et sociétés en Europe de 1494 à 1789*, Paris, 1976.

Cracraft, J., 'More "Peter the Great"', *CASS* 14 (1980), pp. 535–44.

—— 'Peter I "the Great"', *MERSH* 27 (1982), pp. 224–35.

Crummey, R. O., *Aristocrats and Servitors: the Boyar Elite in Russia, 1613–1689*, Princeton, 1983.

—— 'Crown and Boyars under Fyodor Ivanovich and Michael Romanov', *CASS* 6 (1972), pp. 549–74.

—— 'Origins of the Noble Official: the Boyar Elite, 1613–1689', in Pintner and Rowney, *Russian Officialdom*, pp. 46–75.

—— 'Peter and the Boyar Aristocracy, 1689–1700', *CASS* 8 (1974), pp. 274–87.

—— 'The Reconstitution of the Boyar Aristocracy, 1613–1645', *FOEG* 18 (1973), pp. 187–220.

—— 'Reflections on Mestnichestvo in the Seventeenth Century', *FOEG* 27 (1980), pp. 269–81.

Curtiss, J. S., *The Russian Army under Nicholas I, 1825–1855*, Durham, NC, 1965.

—— 'Russian Sisters of Mercy in the Crimea, 1854–1855', *SR* 25 (1966), pp. 84–100.

—— *Russia's Crimean War*, Durham, NC, 1979.

Danilov, N. N., 'Vasilij Vasil'evic Golicyn, 1682–1714', *JGOE* (old series) 2 (1937), pp. 539–96.

Davydov, D. V., *Zapiski . . . , v Rossii tsenzuroy nepropushchennye*, London and Brussels, 1863.

Degtaryev, A. I., 'Dokhody sluzhilykh zemlevladel'tsev v I–oy polovine XVI v.: po materialam Novgorodskogo i Starorusskogo uyezda Shelonskoy pyatiny', *Problemy otechestvennoy i vseobshchey istorii*, fasc. 3, Leningrad, 1976, pp. 86–90.

Demeter, K., *Das deutsche Offizierkorps in Gesellschaft und Staat, 1650–1945*, 2nd edn., Frankfurt, 1964.

Demidova, N. F., 'Byurokratizatsiya gosudarstvennogo apparata absolyutizma v XVII–XVIII vv.', in Druzhinin *et al.* (eds.), *Absolyutizm*, pp. 206–42.

—— 'Gosudarstvennyy apparat Rossii v XVII v.', *IZ* 108 (1982), pp. 109–54.

[Denisov, A. K.] 'Zapiski donskogo atamana Denisova, 1763–1841', contrib. A. P. Ch[ebotarev], *RS* 10 (1874), pp. 1–45, 11 (1874), pp. 379–409, 601–41, 12 (1875), pp. 27–49, 237–71, 457–80.

Dolgorukov, S. N., *Khronika rossiyskoy imperatorskoy armii: iz raznykh svedeniy sobrana*, St. Petersburg, 1799.

Dolgorukov, Yu. V., 'Otryvki iz zapisok . . .', in Dolgorukov, P., *Skazaniya o rode knyazey Dolgorukovykh*, St. Petersburg, 1840, pp. 287–337.

Domanovsky, L. V., Alekseyeva, O. B., and Litvin, E. S. (eds.), *Istoricheskiye pesni XIX v.*, Leningrad, 1973.

[Doneseniye] 'Materialy dlya istorii za pervuyu polovinu XIX v.: I. Doneseniye sledstvennoy komissii Ye. I. Velichestvu', *RA* 19 (1881), 2, pp. 277–332.

Dovnar-Zapol'sky, M. V., *Idealy dekabristov*, Moscow, 1907.

Drutsky-Sokolinsky, D. V., 'Biograficheskaya zametka o zhizni grafa Arseniya Andreyevicha Zakrevskogo', *SIRIO* lxxiii (1890), i–xvi.

Druzhinin, N. M., *Dekabrist Nikita Murav'yev*, Moscow, 1933.

—— *et al.* (eds.), *Absolyutizm v Rossii, XVII—XVIII vv.: sbornik statey k 70–letiyu so dnya rozhdeniya . . . B. B. Kafengauza*, Moscow, 1964.

—— and Syroyechkovsky, B. E. (eds.), *Ocherki iz istorii dvizheniya dekabristov: sbornik statey*, Moscow, 1954.

Druzhinina, E. I., *Severnoye Prichernomor'ye v 1775-1800 gg.*, Moscow, 1959.

—— *Yuzhnaya Ukraina v period krizisa feodalizma, 1825-1860 gg.*, Moscow, 1981.

—— *Yuzhnaya Ukraina v 1800-1825 gg.*, Moscow, 1970.

Dubinskaya, L. G., 'Pomeshchich'ye i votchinnoye zemlevladeniye Meshcherskogo kraya vo II–oy polovine XVII v.', in Pavlenko *et al.* (eds.), *Dvoryanstvo*, pp. 120–34.

Dubrovin, N. F., *A. V. Suvorov sredi preobrazovateley Yekaterininskoy armii*, St. Petersburg, 1886.

—— (ed.), 'Bumagi grafa Arseniya Andreyevicha Zakrevskogo', *SIRIO* lxxiii (1890).

—— *Materialy dlya istorii Krymskoy voyny i oborony Sevastopolya*, 3 fascs., St. Petersburg, 1871-2.

—— (ed.), *Sbornik voyenno–istoricheskikh materialov*, fasc. 3, St. Petersburg, 1893.

—— (ed.), *Sbornik istoricheskikh materialov, izvlechennykh iz arkhiva Sobstvennoy Ye. I. V. kantselyarii*, fasc. 5, St. Petersburg, 1892.

[——] 'Velikiy knyaz' Konstantin Pavlovich v somneniyakh i otritsaniyakh sovremennykh yemu poryadkov: iz perepiski yego s N. M. Sipyaginym' [signed N. D.], *RS* 101 (1900), pp. 91–123.

Duffy, C., *Borodino: Napoleon Against Russia, 1812*, London, 1972.

—— *Russia's Military Way to the West: Origins and Nature of Russian Military Power, 1700-1800*, London and Boston, 1981.

Dukes, P., *Catherine the Great and the Russian Nobility: a Study Based on the Materials of the Legislative Commission of 1767*, Cambridge, 1967.

Dussieux, L., *Force et faiblesse de la Russie au point de vue militaire: études géographiques et statistiques*, Paris, 1854.

D'yakonov, M. A., *Ocherki obshchestvennogo i gosudarstvennogo stroya drevney Rusi*, 4th edn., St. Petersburg, 1912.

—— *Vlast' moskovskikh gosudarey: ocherki iz istorii politicheskikh idey drevney Rusi: do kontsa XVI v.*, St. Petersburg, 1880, repr. The Hague and Paris, 1969.

D'yakov, V. A., 'Alfavitnyy spisok chlenov ofitserskoy organizatsii, vozglyavyaemoy Komitetom russkikh ofitserov v Pol'she i lits, kotorye mogli by byt' svyazany s etoy organizatsiyey', *RSR* iii (1963), 34–82.

—— 'Chislennost' i sostav uchastnikov osvoboditel'nogo dvizheniya v russkoy armii v 1856-1865 gg.: opyt istoriko–sotsiologicheskogo issledovaniya', *IS* 1970, 1, pp. 27–43. (Eng. tr.: *Studies in Soviet History* 9 (1970/1), pp. 195–230.)

—— 'Gertsen, Ogarev i Komitet russkikh ofitserov v Pol'she', *RSR* iii (1963), 3–33.

—— *Osvoboditel'noye dvizheniye v Rossii, 1825-1861 gg.*, Moscow, 1979.

—— 'Peterburgskiye ofitserskiye organizatsii kontsa 50–kh—nachala 60–kh gg. XIX v. i ikh rol' v istorii russko–pol'skikh revolyutsionnykh svyazey', in Khrenov, I. A. (ed.), *Iz istorii klassovoy bor'by i natsional'no-osvoboditel'nogo dvizheniya v slavyanskikh stranakh* (Uchenye zapiski Instituta slavyanovedeniya, 28), Moscow, 1964, pp. 268–369.

—— *Revolyutsionnoye dvizheniye v russkoy armii v yego vzaimnosvyazi s pol'skim osvoboditel'nym dvizheniem 1856-1865 gg.*, Moscow, 1966.

—— 'Soldatskoye dvizheniye v 1856-1865 gg.', *RSR* v (1970), 71–89.

—— and Miller, I. S., *Revolyutsionnoye dvizheniye v russkoy armii i vosstaniye 1863 g.*, ed. M. V. Nechkina, Moscow, 1964.

—— and Smirnov, A. F., 'Protest 106 ofitserov', *RSR* i (1960), 224–37.

Dzhedzhula, K. E., *Rossiya i velikaya frantsuzskaya burzhuaznaya revolyutsiya kontsa XVIII v.*, Kiev, 1972.

[Engel'gardt (Engelhardt), L. N.], *Zapiski L'va Nikolayevicha Engel'gardta, 1766–1836*, Moscow, 1868.

[Englishwoman] *The Englishwoman in Russia: Impressions of the Society and Manners of the Russians at Home*, By a Lady Ten Years Resident in that Country, New York, 1855, repr. New York, 1970.

Erdmann, Y., *Der livländische Staatsmann Johann Reinhold von Patkul: ein abenteuerliches Leben . . .* , Berlin, 1970.

Esper, T., 'Military Self-sufficiency and Weapons Technology in Muscovite Russia', *SR* 28 (1969), pp. 185–208.

—— 'The Odnodvortsy and the Russian Nobility', *SEER* 45 (1967), pp. 124–35.

Essen, N. N. (contrib.), 'Semenovskaya istoriya 1820 g.: vospominaniya odnogo iz ofitserov polka', *Dela i dni* 1 (Petrograd, 1920), pp. 113–21.

Evans, J. L., *The Petraševskij Circle, 1845–1849*, The Hague and Paris, 1974.

Eyler (Euler), A. A., 'Zapiski', *RA* 18 (1880), 2, pp. 333–99.

Eymontova, R. G. (comp.), *Dvizheniye dekabristov: ukazatel' literatury, 1928–1959*, Moscow, 1960.

F., *O sostoyanii russkoy armii v Semiletnyuyu voynu*, Leipzig, 1863.

Fedorov, A. V., *Obshchestvenno-politicheskoye dvizheniye v russkoy armii 40-kh— 70-kh gg. XIX v.*, Moscow, 1958.

—— *Russkaya armiya v 50-kh—70-kh gg. XIX v.*, Leningrad, 1959.

Fedorov, D. V., 'Igrushechnaya armiya: iz byta yuzhno-russkikh kantonistov', *IV* 78 (1899), 10, pp. 148–72, 11, pp. 545–75.

Fedorov, V. A., *Soldatskoye dvizheniye v gody dekabristov, 1816–1825 gg.*, Moscow, 1963.

—— 'Vosstaniye voyennykh poselyan v Chuguyeve v 1819 g.', *IZ* 52 (1955), pp. 305–24.

Fedosov, I. A., *Revolyutsionnoye dvizheniye v Rossii vo vtoroy chetverti XIX v.: revolyutsionnye organizatsii i kruzhki*, Moscow, 1958.

[Fel'kner, V. I.] 'Zapiski general-leytenanta V. I. Fel'knera: 14-oye dekabrya 1825 g.', *RS* 2 (1870), pp. 202–30.

Ferguson, A. D., 'Russian Landmilitia and the Austrian Militärgrenze: a Comparative Study', *Südostforschungen* 13 (Munich, 1954), pp. 139–58.

—— 'The Russian Military Settlements, 1825–1866', in: Ferguson, A. D. and Levin, A., *Essays in Russian History: a Collection Dedicated to G. Vernadsky*, Hamden, Conn., 1964, pp. 109–28.

Figner, V. N., 'Mikhail Yul'yevich Ashenbrenner, 1842–1926', *KiS* 32 (1927), pp. 192–201.

Filippov, A. N., *Uchebnik istorii russkogo prava*, pt. I, 4th edn., Yur'yev [Tartu], 1912.

Fisher, A. W., *The Crimean Tatars*, Stanford, 1978.

—— *The Russian Annexation of the Crimea, 1772–1783*, Cambridge, 1970.

394 *Bibliography*

Fletcher, G., *Of the Russe Commonwealth* [1591], in Berry and Crummey (eds.), *Rude and Barbarous Kingdom*, pp. 87–246.
—— ibid., ed. A. J. Schmidt, Ithaca, New York, 1966.
Forsten, G. V., 'Diplomaticheskiye snosheniya Shvetsii i Rossii vo vtoroy polovine XVII v., 1648–1700', *ZhMNP* 315–17 (1898).
Fortunatov, P. K. (ed.), *P. A. Rumyantsev*, 2 vols., Moscow, 1953.
Frieden, N. M., *Russian Physicians in an Era of Reform and Revolution, 1856–1905*, Princeton, 1981.

Gabayev, G. S., 'Gvardiya v dekabr'skiye dni 1825 g.', in Presnyakov, *14-go dekabrya*, pp. 155–206.
Gajecky, G., *The Cossack Administration of the Hetmanate*, 2 vols., Cambridge, Mass., 1978.
Gangeblov, A. S., 'Kak ya popal v dekabristy i chto za tem posledoval', *RA* 1886, 6, pp. 181–280.
—— 'Yeshche iz vospominaniy . . .', *RA* 1886, 10, pp. 167–202.
Gessen, S. [Ya.], *Arakcheyevskaya barshchina: istoricheskiye zarisovki iz epokhi voyennykh poseleniy*, Moscow, 1932.
Ginzburg, S. M., 'Mucheniki—deti: iz istorii kantonistov—yevreyev', *Yevreyskaya starina* 13 (Leningrad, 1930, repr. Tel Aviv, 1972), pp. 50–79.
Givens, R. D., 'Eighteenth-Century Nobiliary Career Patterns and Provincial Government', in Pintner and Rowney (eds.), *Russian Officialdom*, pp. 106–29.
Gleason, A., *Young Russia: the Genesis of Russian Radicalism in the 1860s*, New York, 1980.
Glinka, F. N., *Pis'ma russkogo ofitsera o Pol'she, avstriyskikh vladeniyakh, Prussii i Frantsii, s podrobnym opisaniyem Otechestvennoy i zagranichnoy voyny s 1812 po 1815 g.*, 8 pts., Moscow, 1815–16.
Glinka, S. N. (ed.), *Russkiye anekdoty—voyennye, grazhdanskiye i istoricheskiye, ili: Povestvovaniye o narodnykh dobrodetelyakh Rossiyan drevnikh i novykh vremen*, 5 pts., Moscow, 1822.
—— *Zapiski*, St. Petersburg, 1895.
Glinoyetsky, N. P., 'Instruktsiya rotnym komandiram za podpisaniyem polkovnika grafa [S.R.] Vorontsova, 1774 yanvarya 17 dnya', *VS* 82 (1871), 11, pp. 33–46.
—— *Istoricheskiy obzor Nikolayevskoy Akademii General'nogo shtaba*, St. Petersburg, 1882.
—— 'Istoricheskiy ocherk razvitiya ofitserskikh chinov i sistemy chinoproizvodstva v russkoy armii', *VS* 174 (1887), 4, pp. 266–90.
—— 'Nekotorye svedeniya ob obuchenii russkikh voysk vo vtoroy polovine proshlogo veka', *VS* 82 (1871), 11, pp. 5–32.
Golikova, N. B., *Astrakhanskoye vosstaniye 1705–1706 gg.*, Moscow, 1975.
—— 'Iz istorii klassovykh protivorechiy v russkoy armii', in Beskrovnyy *et al.* (eds.), *Poltava*, pp. 269–85.
—— *Politicheskiye protsessy pri Petre I: po materialam Preobrazhenskogo prikaza*, Moscow, 1957.
Golitsyn, N. S., 'Russkiye soldaty v prusskoy sluzhbe, 1713–1817', *RS* 66 (1890), pp. 125–32.
Gol'mdorf, G. M., 'Dvoryanskiy polk, 1807–1859: prazdnovaniye 75-oy godovshchiny dnya yego osnovaniya', *RS* 34 (1882), pp. 797–802.

Golovine (Golovin), I., *Russia under the Autocrat Nicholas the First*, 2 vols., London, 1846.

Golowin (Golovin), I., *Russland unter Alexander II*, Leipzig, 1870.

Gorbachevsky, I. I., *Zapiski: pis'ma*, ed. B. E. Syroyechkovsky *et al.*, Moscow, 1963.

Gordon, P., *Tagebuch des Generals Patrick Gordons während . . . seines Aufenthaltes in Russland vom Jahre 1661 bis 1699*, [ed.] M. A. Obolensky and M. C. Posselt, 2 vols., St. Petersburg and Moscow, 1849–52.

Got'ye, Yu. V., *Ocherk istorii zemlevladeniya v Rossii*, Sergiyev Posad [Zagorsk], 1915.

—— *Zamoskovnyy kray v XVII v.: opyt issledovaniya po istorii ekonomicheskogo byta Moskovskoy Rusi* [1906], 2nd rev. edn., Moscow, 1937.

Gozdavo-Golombiyevsky, A. A., 'Istoriya Razryadnogo arkhiva, 1711–1812', *Opisaniye dokumentov i bumag khranyashchikhsya v Moskovskom arkhive Ministerstva yustitsii*, 5 (Moscow, 1888), pp. 1–152.

Gribbe, A. K., 'Kholernyy bunt v Novgorodskikh voyennykh poseleniyakh', *RS* 17 (1876), pp. 513–36.

Gribovsky, V. M. (comp.), *Pamyatniki russkogo zakonodatel'stva XVIII st.: posobiye dlya izucheniya istorii russkogo prava*, St. Petersburg, 1907.

Grosul, G. S., *Dunayskiye knyazhestva v politike Rossii, 1774–1806*, Kishinev, 1975.

Grosul, V. Ya., *Reformy v dunayskikh knyazhestvakh i Rossiya, 20–e—30–e gg. XIX v.*, Moscow, 1966.

Gukovsky, G., 'Soldatskiye stikhi XVIII v.', *LN* 9–10 (1933), pp. 112–52.

Gulevich, A., *Voyna i narodnoye khozyaystvo Rossii*, St. Petersburg, 1898.

Gvinchidze, O. S., *Brat'ya Gruzinovy*, Tbilisi, 1965.

Haillot, C. A., *Statistique militaire et recherche sur l'organisation et les institutions militaires des armées étrangères*, i. Paris, 1846.

Hansen, H. von, *Zwei Kriegsjahre: Erinnerungen eines alten Soldaten an den Feldzug der Russen gegen die Türken 1828 und den polnischen Aufstand 1831*, Berlin, 1881.

Hassell, J., 'Implementation of the Russian Table of Ranks during the Eighteenth Century', *SR* 29 (1970), pp. 283–95.

Haxthausen, A., Freiherr von, *Die Kriegsmacht Russlands in ihrer historischen, statistischen, ethnographischen und politischen Beziehung*, Berlin, 1852.

Helbig, G. A. W. von, *Russische Günstlinge* [1809], repr. Stuttgart, 1883.

Hellie, R. F., *Enserfment and Military Change in Muscovy*, Chicago and London, 1971.

—— 'The Petrine Army: Continuity, Change and Impact', *CASS* 8 (1974), pp. 237–53.

—— *Slavery in Russia, 1450–1725*, Chicago and London, 1982.

Herberstein, S., Freiherr von, *Moscovia*, tr. W. von den Steinen, introd. and ed. H. Kauders, Erlangen, 1926.

Hermann, B. F. J., *Statistische Schilderung von Russland in Rücksicht auf Bevölkerung, Landesbeschaffenheit, Naturprodukte, Landwirtschaft, Bergbau, Manufakturen und Handel*, St. Petersburg and Leipzig, 1790.

Herrmann, E. (ed.), *Russland unter Peter dem Grossen: nach den handschriftlichen Berichten Johann Gotthilf Vockerodts und Otto Pleyers* (Zeitgenössische Berichte zur Geschichte Russlands, 1), Leipzig, 1872.

Hittle, J. M., *The Service City: State and Townsmen in Russia, 1600–1800*, Cambridge, Mass., 1979.

Holderness, M., *New Russia: Journey from Riga to the Crimea by Way of Kiev* . . . , London, 1823, repr. New York, 1970.

Hupel, A. W. von, *Beschreibung der russisch-kaiserlichen Armee nebst andern kürzern Aufsätzen* . . . (Der nordischen Miscellaneen 5. und 6. Stück), Riga, 1782, repr. Hanover-Döhren, 1972.

[Igel'strom] 'Arkhiv grafa Igel'stroma', pt. II. 'Ukazy Pavla Petrovicha', contrib. D. A. Tolstoy, *RA* 1886, 12, pp. 480–96.

Il'yashevich, L., 'Statisticheskoye issledovaniye smertnosti v nashey armii', *VS* 29 (1863), pp. 359–412.

Istoricheskiy sbornik Volnoy Russkoy tipografii v Londone, [ed. A. I. Herzen], 3 bks., bk. 2, London, 1860, repr. Moscow, 1971.

Ivanov, P. (comp.), *Opisaniye Razryadnogo Arkhiva s prisovokupleniem spiskov so mnogikh khranyashchikhsya v onom lyubopytnykh dokumentov*, Moscow, 1842.

'Iz pisem N. M. Longinova k grafu S. R. Vorontsovu', *RA* 1912, 1, pp. 481–547, 2, pp. 30–66, 161–205, 336–416.

'Iz zametok starosluzhivogo', *VS* 46 (1874), 3–4, pp. 295–303.

Izyumov, A., 'Zhiletskoye zemlevladeniye v 1632 g.', *Letopis' istoriko-rodoslovnogo obshchestva v Moskve* 8 (31–2), 3–4 (1912), pp. 26–163.

Jenkins, M., *Arakcheev: Grand Vizier of the Russian Empire: a Biography*, London, 1969.

Jewsbury, G. F., *The Russian Annexation of Bessarabia, 1774–1828: a Study of Imperial Expansion*, Boulder, Colo. and Guildford, 1976.

—— 'The Russian Army's Role in the Danubian Principalities, 1806–1812', *South-eastern Europe* 2 (Pittsburgh, 1975), 2, pp. 145–53.

Jones, D. R., 'Administrative System and Policy–making Process', *MNERSU* ii (1980), 34–169.

Jones, R. E., *The Emancipation of the Russian Nobility, 1762–1785*, New York, 1973.

Juel, J., 'Zapiski Yusta Yula, datskogo poslannika pri Petre Velikom, 1709–1711', tr. Yu. N. Shcherbachev, *RA* 1892, 3, 5, 7–11 *passim*.

'K istorii voyennoy-uchebnoy reformy imperatora Aleksandra II-go, 1856–1870', *RS* 54 (1887), pp. 345–66, 693–712.

Kabuzan, V. M., *Izmeneniya v razmeshchenii naseleniya Rossii v XVIII—pervoy polovine XIX v.: po materialam reviziy*, Moscow, 1971.

—— *Zaseleniye Novorossii (Yekaterinoslavskoy i Khersonskoy guberniy) v XVIII—pervoy polovine XIX v., 1719–1858 gg.*, Moscow, 1976.

—— and Troitsky, S. M., 'Izmeneniya v chislennosti, udel'nom vese i razmeshchenii dvoryanstva v Rossii v 1782–1858 gg.', *IS* 1971, 4, pp. 153–69.

Kafengauz, B. B., *Rossiya pri Petre I*, Moscow, 1955.

—— and Pavlenko, N. I. (eds.), *Ocherki istorii SSSR: period feodalizma: Rossiya I–oy chetverti XVIII v.: preobrazovaniya Petra I*, Moscow, 1954.

Kahan, A., 'The Costs of "Westernization" in Russia: the Gentry and the Economy in the Eighteenth Century', *SR* 25 (1966), pp. 40–66.

Kalachov, N. V. (ed.), *Materialy dlya istorii russkogo dvoryanstva*, 3 fascs., St. Petersburg, 1885–6.

Kalinychev, F. I., *Pravovye voprosy voyennoy organizatsii russkogo gosudarstva vtoroy poloviny XVII v.*, Moscow, 1954.

Kamendrowsky, V. and Griffiths, D. M., 'The Fate of the Trading Nobility Controversy in Russia: a Chapter in the Relationship Between Catherine II and the Russian Nobility', *JGOE* 26 (1978), pp. 198–221.

Kappeler, A., 'Die deutschen Russlandschriften der Zeit Ivans des Schrecklichen', in Kaiser, F. B. and Stasiewski, B. (eds.), *Reiseberichte von Deutschen über Russland und von Russen über Deutschland*, Graz and Cologne, 1980, pp. 1–23.

—— 'Die Geschichte der Völker der Mittleren Wolga (vom 10. Jh. bis in die zweite Hälfte des 19. Jh.) in der sowjetischen Forschung', *JGOE* 26 (1978), pp. 222–57.

—— *Ivan Groznyj im Spiegel der ausländischen Druckschriften seiner Zeit: ein Beitrag zur Geschichte des westlichen Russlandbildes*, Bern and Frankfurt, 1972.

—— 'Die Rolle der Nichtrussen der Mittleren Wolga in den russischen Volksaufständen des 17. Jhds.', *FOEG* 27 (1980), pp. 249–68.

—— *Russlands erste Nationalitäten: das Zarenreich und die Völker der Mittleren Wolga vom 16. bis 19. Jahrhundert* (Beiträge zur Geschichte Osteuropas, 14), Cologne and Vienna, 1982.

Karasev, A., 'Kazn´ brat´yev Gruzinovykh 27-go oktyabrya 1800 g.', *RS* 7 (1873), p. 573.

Karayev, G. N., *Suvorovskaya 'Nauka pobezhdat´' v svete peredovoy sovetskoy voyennoy nauki: stenogramma publichnoy lektsii, prochitannoy v Leningrade v 1950 g.*, Leningrad, 1950.

Kargalov, V. V., *Na stepnoy granitse: oborona 'krymskoy ukrainy' russkogo gosudarstva v pervoy polovine XVI v.*, Moscow, 1974.

—— 'Oborona yuzhnoy granitsy russkogo gosudarstva v pervoy polovine XVI v.', *IS* 1973, 6, pp. 140–8.

Kartsov, P. P., 'Leyb-gvardii Semenovskiy polk v tsarstvovaniyakh Pavla I-go i Aleksandra I-go', *RS* 38 (1883), pp. 311–32.

—— 'O voyennykh poseleniyakh pri grafe Arakcheyeve', *RV* 206 (1890), 2, pp. 139–71, 207 (1890), 3, pp. 82–113, 4, pp. 75–116.

—— 'Perventsy imperatorskoy rossiyskoy gvardii v ocherkakh istorii ikh boyevoy i mirnoy zhizni', *RS* 40 (1883), pp. 663–92.

Keep, J. L. H., 'Bandits and the Law in Muscovy', *SEER* 35 (1956–7), pp. 201–22.

—— 'Catherine's Veterans', *SEER* 59 (1981), pp. 385–96.

—— 'Chernyshevsky and the *Military Miscellany*' (forthcoming).

—— 'L'Élitisme militaire en Russie à la fin du xviiie siècle: le témoignage du comte de Langeron', *Slovo* 3 (Paris, 1980), pp. 165–76.

—— 'From the Pistol to the Pen: the Military Memoir as a Source on the Social History of Pre–Reform Russia', *CMRS* 21 (1980), pp. 295–320.

—— 'The Military Style of the Romanov Rulers', *W&S* 1 (1983), pp. 61–84.

—— 'The Muscovite Elite and the Approach to Pluralism', *SEER* 48 (1970), pp. 201–31.

—— 'Mutiny in Moscow, 1682: a Contemporary Account [by H. Butenant]', *CSP* 23 (1981), pp. 410–42.

—— 'Paul I and the Militarization of Government', *CASS* 7 (1973), pp. 1–14, repr. in Ragsdale (ed.), *Paul I*, pp. 91–103.

—— 'The Russian Army's Response to the French Revolution', *JGOE* 28 (1980), pp. 500–23.

—— 'The Secret Chancellery, the Guards and the Dynastic Crisis of 1740–1741', *FOEG* 25 (1978), pp. 169–93.

Kenney, J. J. Jr., 'The Politics of Assassination', in Ragsdale (ed.), *Paul I*, pp. 125–46.

Kerr, W., *The Shabunin Affair*, Ithaca (New York) and London, 1982.

Kersnovsky, A. A., *Istoriya russkoy armii*, 3 pts., Belgrade, 1933–5.

Kharkevich, V. (ed.), *1812 god v dnevnikakh, zapiskakh i vospominaniyakh sovremennikov: materialy Voyenno–uchebnogo arkhiva Glavnogo shtaba*, 3 fascs., Vilna, 1900–4.

[Khilkov, G. D.], *Sbornik knyazya Khilkova*, St. Petersburg, 1879.

Khoroshkhin, M. P., *Kazach'ya voyska: opyt voyenno–statisticheskogo opisaniya*, St. Petersburg, 1881.

Kieniewicz, S. *et al.* (eds.), *Vosstaniye 1863 g.: materialy i dokumenty: russko-pol'skiye revolyutsionnye svyazi*, 2 vols., Moscow and Wrocław, 1963.

Kimerling, E., 'Soldiers' Children, 1719–1856: a Study of Social Engineering in Imperial Russia', *FOEG* 30 (1982), pp. 61–136.

Király, B. K. and Rothenberg, G. E. (eds.), *War and Society in East Central Europe During the Eighteenth and Nineteenth Centuries*, i. New York, 1979.

Kirilov, I. K., *Tsvetushcheye sostoyaniye Vserossiyskogo gosudarstva* [1726–7], Moscow, 1977.

[Kiselev, P. D.], 'Pis'ma Pavla Dmitrievicha (vposledstvii grafa) Kiseleva k Arseniyu Andreyevichu (vposledstvii grafu) Zakrevskomu', *SIRIO* lxxviii (1891), 1–178.

Klaproth, J. von, *Reise in den Kaukasus und nach Georgien unternommen in den Jahren 1807 und 1808*, 2 vols., Halle and Berlin, 1812, repr. Leipzig, 1970.

Kleimola, A., 'Boris Godunov and the Politics of Mestnichestvo', *SEER* 53 (1975), pp. 355–69.

—— 'The Changing Face of the Muscovite Aristocracy: the Sixteenth Century: Sources of Weakness', *JGOE* 25 (1977), pp. 481–93.

—— 'Military Service and Elite Status in Muscovy in the Second Quarter of the Sixteenth Century', *RH* 7 (1980), pp. 47–64.

—— 'Status, Place and Politics: the Rise of Mestnichestvo During the Boiarskoe Pravlenie', *FOEG* 27 (1980), pp. 195–214.

—— 'Up Through Servitude: the Changing Condition of the Muscovite Elite in the Sixteenth and Seventeenth Centuries', *RH* 6 (1979), pp. 210–29.

Kleinschmidt, A., *Russlands Geschichte und Politik dargestellt in der Geschichte des russischen hohen Adels*, Cassel, 1877.

[Klenk, K., van] *Posol'stvo Kunraada fan-Klenka k tsaryam Alekseyu Mikhailovichu i Fedoru Alekseyevichu*, St. Petersburg, 1900.

Klugen, L., 'Neskol'ko slov o telesnom v russkikh voyskakh nakazaniyakh po pravilam voyennoy distsipliny', *VS* 9 (1859), 9, pp. 191–210.

Klyuchevsky, V. O., *Istoriya sosloviy v Rossii: kurs chitannyy v Moskovskom Universitete v 1886 g.*, 3rd edn., Petrograd, 1918.

—— *Kurs russkoy istorii*, in id., *Sochineniya*, i–v. Moscow, 1957–9.

—— *Peter the Great*, tr. L. Archibald, London, 1958.

—— 'Podushnaya podat' i otmena kholopstva v Rossii', in *Sochineniya*, vii. Moscow, 1959, pp. 318–402.

—— 'Russkiy rubl' XVI—XVIII v. v yego otnoshenii k nyneshnemu', in ibid., pp. 170–236.

—— *Skazaniya inostrantsev o moskovskom gosudarstve*, Petrograd, 1918.

Knabe, B., 'Die Struktur der russischen Posadgemeinden und der Katalog der Beschwerden und Forderungen der Kaufmannschaft, 1762–7', *FOEG* 22 (1975), pp. 1–396.

Knyaz'kov, S., *Iz proshlogo russkoy zemli*, 2 pts., St. Petersburg, 1914-Petrograd, 1917.

Kobeko, D., *Tsesarevich Pavel Petrovich, 1754-1796: istoricheskoye issledovaniye*, St. Petersburg, 1882.

Kochetkov, A. N., 'K voprosu ob istorii, tekstologii i bibliografii "Nauki pobezhdat'" A. V. Suvorova', in Sukhomlin, *Suvorovskiy sbornik*, pp. 157-82.

Kohl, J. G., *Reisen in Südrussland* (pt. 2 of *Reisen im Inneren von Russland und Polen*), 2nd edn., Dresden and Leipzig, 1847.

Kolokol: gazeta A. I. Gertsena i N. P. Ogareva, 1857-1867: faksimil'noye izdaniye, fasc. 4 (1861), Moscow, 1962.

Kolokol'tsov, D. G., 'Leyb-gvardii Preobrazhenskiy polk v vospominaniyakh yego starogo ofitsera s 1831-go po 1846 god', *RS* 38 (1883), pp. 273-310, 593-622, 40 (1883), pp. 329-54, 69 (1891), pp. 635-74.

[Komarovsky, Ye. F.], 'Iz zapisok general-ad'yutanta grafa Ye. F. Komarovskogo', *RA* 1867, 2, 5, 6, 10; 1887, 7.

König, F. *et al.* (eds.), *Beiträge zur Militärsoziologie* (*Kölner Zeitschrift für Soziologie und Sozialpsychologie*, Sonderheft 12), Cologne and Opladen, 1968.

Kopanev, A. I., 'Naseleniye russkogo gosudarstva v XVI v.', *IZ* 64 (1959), pp. 233-54.

Korb, J. G., *Dnevnik poyezdki v moskovskoye gosudarstvo . . . 1698 g.*, tr. V. Zhenev and M. I. Semevsky, St. Petersburg, 1866.

—— *Tagebuch der Reise nach Russland*, ed. G. Korb, tr. E. Leingärtner, Graz, 1968.

Korf, M. [A.], 'Materialy i cherty k biografii imperatora Nikolaya I-go i k istorii yego tsarstvovaniya' [1857], *SIRIO* xcviii (1896), 1-100.

Korolyuk, V. D. and Miller, I. S., *Vosstaniye 1863 g. i russko-pol'skiye revolyutsionnye svyazi*, Moscow, 1960.

Kotoshikhin, G., *O Rossii v tsarstvovaniye Alekseya Mikhailovicha*, 4th edn., St. Petersburg, 1906, repr. The Hague and Paris, 1969.

Koz'min, B. P., 'N. G. Chernyshevsky v redaktsii "Voyennogo sbornika": iz vospominaniy D. A. Milyutina', *LN* 25-6 (1936), pp. 234-7.

Kretchmer, V. A., 'Vospominaniya', *IV* 31 (1888), 3, pp. 631-53, 4, pp. 125-41, 361-80.

Kudryavtsev, A., 'O distsiplinarnom ustave 1875 g.', *VS* 167 (1886), 1-2, pp. 90-121.

Kukiel, M., 'Military Aspects of the Polish Insurrection of 1863-4', *Antemurale* 7-8 (Rome, 1963), pp. 363-96.

Kulomzin, A. N. (ed.), *Finansovye dokumenty tsarstvovaniya imperatora Aleksandra I*, *SIRIO* xliv (1885).

Kurakin, B. I., 'Gistoriya o tsare Petre Alekseyeviche i blizhnikh k nemu lyudyakh, 1682-1694' [1723-7], in *Arkhiv knyazya F. A. Kurakina*, ed. M. I. Semevsky, 6 vols., St. Petersburg, 1890-6, i (1890), 39-78.

Kurochkin, I., 'Odinochnoye zaklyucheniye v voyennoy tyur'me', *VS* 236 (1897), 7, pp. 111-30, 8, pp. 271-89, 237 (1897), 9, pp. 115-26, 10, pp. 341-57.

Kursakov, V., *Spravochnaya knizhka dlya vol'noopredelyayushchikhsya, postupayush-chikh v sukhoputnye voyska . . .*, St. Petersburg, 1898.

Lakhtin, M., 'Pomoshch' ranenym voinam v XVII v.', *RA* 1904, 10, pp. 262-9.

—— 'Voznagrazhdeniye vracham v moskovskoy Rusi', *RA* 1904, 12, pp. 609-14.

Langeron, Count A., 'Russkaya armiya v god smerti Yekateriny II: sostav i ustroystvo russkoy armii', tr. V. N. M., contrib. N. K. Shil'der, *RS* 83 (1895), 3, pp. 147-66, 4, pp. 145-77, 5, pp. 185-202.

Lappo-Danilevsky, A., *Organizatsiya pryamogo oblozheniya v moskovskom gosudarstve so vremen Smuty do epokhi preobrazovaniy*, St. Petersburg, 1890, repr. The Hague and Paris, 1969.

Lavrov, N. F., 'Diktator 14-go dekabrya', in Oksman and Shchegolev (eds.), *Bunt*, pp. 129–222.

Lebedev, A. (ed.), *Russkaya armiya v nachale tsarstvovaniya imperatritsy Yekateriny II: materialy dlya russkoy voyennoy istorii*, Moscow, 1898.

Lebedev, P. S., 'Preobrazovateli russkoy armii v tsarstvovaniye imperatora Pavla Petrovicha, 1796–1801', *RS* 18 (1877), pp. 227–60, 577–608.

Lebedev, V. I. (comp.), *Reformy Petra I: sbornik dokumentov*, Moscow, 1937.

LeDonne, J. P., 'The Administration of Military Justice under Nicholas I', *CMRS* 13 (1972), pp. 180–91.

—— 'Appointments to the Russian Senate, 1762–1796', *CMRS* 16 (1975), pp. 27–56.

—— 'Catherine's Governors and Governors-General', *CMRS* 20 (1979), pp. 15–42.

—— 'Civilians under Military Justice During the Reign of Nicholas I', *CASS* 7 (1973), pp. 171–87.

—— 'The Evolution of the Governor's Office, 1727–1764', *CASS* 12 (1978), pp. 86–115.

—— 'Outlines of Russian Military Administration, 1762–1796', pt. I: 'Troop Strength and Deployment', *JGOE* 31 (1983), pp. 321–47.

—— *Ruling Russia: Politics and Administration in the Age of Absolutism, 1762–1796*, Princeton, 1984.

—— 'The Territorial Reform of the Russian Empire, 1775–1796', *CMRS* 23 (1982), pp. 147–85.

Leitsch, W., 'The Russian Nobility in the Eighteenth Century', *East European Quarterly* 11 (Boulder, Colo., 1977), pp. 317–40.

Leont'yev, A. K., *Obrazovaniye prikaznoy sistemy upravleniya v russkom gosudarstve: iz istorii sozdaniya tsentralizirovannogo gosudarstvennogo apparata v kontse XV pervoy polovine XVI v.*, Moscow, 1961.

Leont'yev, G. A., *Sluzhiliye lyudi vostochnoy Sibiri vo vtoroy polovine XVII—pervoy chasti XVIII vv.: po materialam Irkutskogo i Nerchinskogo uyezdov: avtoreferat dissertatsii*, Moscow, 1972.

Leslie, R. F., *Reform and Insurrection in Russian Poland, 1856–1865*, London, 1963.

Ley, F., *Le Maréchal de Münnich et la Russie du XVIIIᵉ siècle*, Paris, 1959.

Leyev, F., 'Doreformennaya armiya: po zapiskam grafa P. D. Kiseleva', *Vestnik vsemirnoy istorii* 2 (1901), 11, pp. 96–125.

Leykina-Svirskaya, V. R., 'Andrey Potebnya', *RSR* iii (1963), 83–115; also in Miller, I. S. and Smirnov, A. F. (eds.), D'yakov, V. A.(comp.), *Za nashu i vashu svobodu! Gerio 1863 g.: sbornik*, Moscow, 1964, pp. 121–64.

—— 'Petrashevets N. A. Mombelli', *Byloye* 26 (1941), pp. 61–70.

—— and Shidlovskaya, V. S., 'Pol'skaya voyennaya revolyutsionnaya organizatsiya v Petrograde, 1858–1864 gg.', in D'yakov, V. A., Korolyuk, V. D. and Miller, I. S. (eds.), *Russko-pol'skiye revolyutsionnye svyazi 60-kh gg. XIX v. i vosstaniye 1863 g.*, Moscow, 1962, pp. 7–48.

Likhachev, N. P., *Razryadnye d'yaki XVI v.: opyt istoricheskogo issledovaniya*, St. Petersburg, 1888.

Lincoln, W. B., 'The Ministers of Nicholas I: a Brief Inquiry into Their Backgrounds and Service Careers', *RR* 34 (1975), pp. 308–23.

—— *Nicholas I: Emperor and Autocrat of All the Russias*, London, 1978.

—— 'A Re-examination of Some Historical Stereotypes: an Analysis of the Career Patterns and Backgrounds of the Decembrists', *JGOE* 24 (1976), pp. 357–68.

—— *In the Vanguard of Reform: Russia's Enlightened Bureaucrats, 1825–1861*, DeKalb, Ill., 1982.

Lobachevsky, V., 'Bugskoye kazachestvo i voyennye poseleniya: letopisnye nabroski', *KS* 19 (1887), pp. 591–626.

Longworth, P., *The Art of Victory: the Life and Achievements of Generalissimo Suvorov, 1729–1800*, London, 1965.

—— 'The Pretender Phenomenon in Eighteenth-Century Russia', *Past and Present* 66 (Oxford, 1975), pp. 61–83.

—— 'Transformations in Cossackdom, 1650–1850', in Király and Rothenberg (eds.), *War*, pp. 393–407.

Lopukhin, I. V., *Zapiski*, London, 1860, repr. Newtonville, Mass., 1976.

Lorer (Lohrer), N. I., *Zapiski dekabrista*, ed. M. N. Pokrovsky, annotated by M. V. Nechkina, Moscow, 1931.

Lotman, Yu. M., 'Dekabrist v povsednevnoy zhizni: bytovoye povedeniye kak istoriko—psikhologicheskaya kategoriya', in Bazanov, V. G. and Vatsuro, V. E. (eds.), *Literaturnoye naslediye dekabristov*, Leningrad, 1975, pp. 25–74.

Löwenstern, V. I., *Mémoires du général-major russe baron de Löwenstern, 1776–1858*, ed. M.-H. Weil, 2 vols., Paris, 1903.

Luciani, G., *La Société des Slaves Unis, 1823–1825: panslavisme et solidarité slave au xixe siècle*, Bordeaux, 1963.

Luckett, R., 'Pre-revolutionary Army Life in Russian Literature', in West, G. and Wheatcroft, A. (eds.), *War, Economy and the Military Mind*, London and Toyota, NJ, 1976, pp. 19–31.

Luig, L., *Zur Geschichte des russischen Innenministeriums unter Nikolaus I*, Wiesbaden, 1968.

Luppov, S. P., *Istoriya stroitel'stva Peterburga v pervoy chetverti XVIII v.*, Moscow and Leningrad, 1957.

Lur'ye, L. Ya., *Evolyutsiya chislennosti, soslovnogo, professional'nogo i vozrastnogo sostava deyateley russkogo osvoboditel'nogo dvizheniya na dvoryanskom i razno-chinskom etapakh . . . Avtoreferat dissertatsii*, Leningrad, 1981.

Lyall, R., *Travels in Russia, the Krimea, the Caucasus and Georgia*, 2 vols., London, 1825, repr. New York, 1970.

Lykoshin, A. S., 'Voyennye poseleniya', in Dzhivilegov, A. K. *et al.* (eds.), *Velikaya reforma: russkoye obshchestvo i krest'yanskiy vopros . . .* , 6 vols., Moscow, 1911, ii. 86–106.

Madariaga, I. de, *Russia in the Age of Catherine the Great*, London, 1981.

—— 'Spain and the Decembrists', *European Studies Review* 3 (1973), pp. 141–56.

Makeyev, N., 'N. G. Chernyshevsky—redaktor "Voyennogo sbornika"', *VI* 1949, 4, pp. 65–82.

Maksheyev, A., *Voyenno-statisticheskoye obozreniye Rossiyskoy imperii*, St. Petersburg, 1867.

Maksheyev, F. [A.], *Voyennaya administratsiya: posobiye dlya slushateley starshego kursa Nikolayevskoy Akademii General'nogo shtaba*, fasc. 3: *Voyennoye khozyaystvo ili ustroystvo tyla*, St. Petersburg, 1895.

—— *Voyenno-administrativnoye ustroystvo tyla armii,* fasc. 1, St. Petersburg, 1893.

Man'kov, A. G., 'Krepostnoye pravo i dvoryanstvo v proyekte Ulozheniya 1720–5 gg.', in Pavlenko *et al.* (eds.), *Dvoryanstvo,* pp. 159–80.

—— *Razvitiye krepostnogo prava v Rossii vo vtoroy polovine XVII v.,* Moscow and Leningrad, 1962.

Manstein, C. H. von, *Contemporary Memoirs of Russia from the Year 1727 to 1744,* London, 1770, 2nd edn. 1868, repr. London, 1968.

[——] *Zapiski Manshteyna o Rossii 1727–1744,* ed. M. I. Semevsky, contrib. A. F. Bychkov, suppl. to *RS* 12–14 (1875).

Margeret, [J.], *L'Estat de l'empire de Russie et grand duché de Moscovie . . . ,* Paris, 1607.

Markevich, A. I., *Istoriya mestnichestva v moskovskom gosudarstve v XV—XVII v.,* Odessa, 1888.

Markov, M. A., 'Vospominaniya starogo invalida o sluzhbe leyb-gvardii v Pavlovskom polku, 1828–1835', *RS* 68 (1890), pp. 81–135.

Marmont, A. F. L. V., *Voyage de M. le maréchal, duc de Raguse . . . dans la Russie méridionale . . . ,* 2nd edn., 4 vols., Paris, 1837.

[Martos, A. N.], 'Zapiski inzhenernogo ofitsera Martosa o turetskoy voyne v tsarstvo-vanii Aleksandra Pavlovicha', *RS* 77 (1893), 2, pp. 305–68, 449–68, 496–542.

Maslovsky, D. F., *Iz istorii voyennogo iskusstva v Rossii v pervoy polovine XVIII v.: stroyevaya i polevaya sluzhba russkikh voysk vremen imperatora Petra Velikogo i imperatritsy Yelizavety: istoricheskoye issledovaniye,* Moscow, 1883.

—— *Materialy k istorii voyennogo iskusstva v Rossii,* fasc. 1: [1708–1760], *Chteniya* 146 (1888), pp. i–xxxii, 1–24, 153 (1890), pp. i–xvi, 1–294, 159 (1891), pp. i–xiv, 1–148.

—— *Materialy [Zapiski] po* [sic] *istorii voyennogo iskusstva v Rossii,* fasc. 2: *Tsarstvo-vaniye Yekateriny II, 1762–1764 gg.,* 2 pts., St. Petersburg, 1894.

—— *Opis' del sekretnogo povyt'ya Moskovskogo otdeleniya Obshchego arkhiva Glavnogo shtaba: 47-aya opis',* Moscow, 1890.

—— 'Pomestnye voyska russkoy armii v XVII stoletii', *VS* 195 (1890), 9, pp. 5–36.

Masson, C.-F.-P., *Mémoires secrets sur la Russie, et particulièrement sur la fin du règne de Catherine II et le commencement de celui de Paul Ier, formant un tableau des mœurs de St.-Pétersbourg à la fin du xviiie siècle,* 4 vols., Paris, 1804.

Mayevsky, S. I., 'Moy vek . . . 1779–1848', *RS* 8 (1873), 8, pp. 125–67, 9, pp. 253–305, 10, pp. 427–64, 11, pp. 754–81.

Mazour, A. G., *The First Russian Revolution, 1825: the Decembrist Movement: its Origins, Development and Significance,* Stanford, 1937, repr. 1965.

McConnell, A., 'Alexander I's Hundred Days: the Politics of a Paternalist Reformer', *SR* 28 (1969), pp. 373–93.

—— *Tsar Alexander I: Paternalistic Reformer,* New York, 1970.

McNeal, R. H., 'The Reform of Cossack Military Service in the Reign of Alexander II', in Király and Rothenberg (eds.), *War,* pp. 409–21.

Medvedev, S., *Sozertsaniye kratkoye let 7190, 91 i 92, v nikh zhe chto sodeyasya vo grazhdanstve,* ed. A. Prozorovsky, Moscow, 1894.

Meehan-Waters, B., *Autocracy and Aristocracy: the Russian Service Elite of 1730,* New Brunswick, NJ, 1982.

—— 'The Muscovite Noble Origins of the Russians in the Generalitet of 1730', *CMRS* 12 (1971), pp. 28–75.

—— 'The Russian Aristocracy and the Reforms of Peter the Great', *CASS* 8 (1974), pp. 274–87.

—— 'Social and Career Characteristics of the Administratiye Elite, 1689–1761', in Pintner and Rowney (eds.), *Russian Officialdom*, pp. 76–105.

Meier-Welcker, H. *et al.* (eds.), *Handbuch der deutschen Militärgeschichte, 1648–1939*, Frankfurt, 1964.

Mel′gunov, S. P., *Dela i lyudi aleksandrovskogo vremeni*, Berlin, 1923.

—— *Religiozno-obshchestvennye dvizheniya XVII—XVIII vv. v Rossii* [1911–12], repr. Moscow, 1922.

Menning, B. W., 'The Emergence of a Military–Administrative Elite in the Don Cossack Land, 1708–1836', in Pintner and Rowney (eds.), *Russian Officialdom*, pp. 130–61.

Meshcheryakov, G. P. (ed.), *A. V. Suvorov . . . dokumenty*, 4 vols., Moscow, 1949–53.

Miller, F. A., *Dmitrii Miliutin and the Reform Era in Russia*, Charlotte, NC, 1968.

Miller, I. S., 'Russko-pol′skiye revolyutsionnye svyazi v period vosstaniya 1863 g.', in Rybakov, B. A. (ed.), *Istoriya, fol′klor, iskusstvo slavyanskikh narodov*, Moscow, 1963, pp. 120–58.

Milyukov, P. N., *Essais sur l'histoire de la civilisation russe*, tr. P. Dramas and D. Soskice, Paris, 1901.

—— *Gosudarstvennoye khozyaystvo Rossii v pervoy chetverti XVIII st. i reforma Petra Velikogo*, 2nd edn., St. Petersburg, 1905, repr. (microfilm) Ann Arbor, 1964.

Milyutin, D. A., *Vospominaniya*, i. bks. 1–3, Tomsk, 1919, repr. with introduction by B. Lincoln, Newtonville, Mass., 1979.

[——] 'Voyennye reformy Aleksandra II', *VEv* 1882, 1, pp. 5–35.

[Minayev, I. M.], 'Vospominaniya Ivana Men′shago, 1806–1849', *RS* 10 (1874), pp. 46–59.

Mironov, B. N., 'Dvizheniye khlebnykh tsen v Rossii v 1801–1914 gg.', *VI* 1975, 2, pp. 45–57.

—— 'Dvizheniye tsen rzhi v Rossii v XVIII v.', *Yezhegodnik po agrarnoy istorii Vostochnoy Yevropy za 1965*, Moscow, 1970, pp. 156–63.

—— 'O dostovernosti vedomostey o khlebnykh tsenakh XVIII v.', *Vspomogatel′nye istoricheskiye distsipliny*, fasc. 2 (Leningrad, 1969), pp. 249–62.

—— 'O metodike obrabotki istochnikov po istorii tsen: k issledovaniyu problemy obrazovaniya russkogo natsional′nogo rynka', *Yezhegodnik po agrarnoy istorii Vostochnoy Yevropy za 1968*, Leningrad, 1972, pp. 154–65.

—— ' "Revolyutsiya tsen" v Rossii v XVIII v.', *VI* 1971, 11, pp. 49–61.

Modzalevsky, B. L. (ed.), *Arkhiv Rayevskikh*, 4 vols., St. Petersburg, 1908–12.

[Mombelli, N. A.], 'Izvlecheniya iz dnevnika', in Desnitsky, V., (ed.), *Delo petra-shevtsev*, 3 vols., Moscow and Leningrad, 1937–51, i. 240–308.

Monas, S., *The Third Section: Police and Society under Nicholas I*, Cambridge, Mass., 1961.

[Mordvinov] *Arkhiv grafov Mordvinovykh*, 11 vols., St. Petersburg, 1901–3.

Mordvinov, N. V., 'Iz zapisok voyenno-sudebnogo deyatelya', *IV* 111 (1908), pp. 855–94, 112 (1908), pp. 117–37, 531–49.

[Mosolov, S. I.], 'Zapiski otstavnogo general-mayora Sergeya Ivanovicha Mosolova: istoriya moyey zhizni', *RA* 1905, 1, pp. 124–73.

[Müller, J.-B.], *Nouveaux mémoires sur l'état present de la Grande Russie ou Moscovie, où l'on traite du gouvernement . . . des troupes . . . de ses finances . . . depuis l'année*

1714 jusqu'en 1720: par un allemand résident en cette cour, 2 vols., Amsterdam, 1725.

Müller-Dietz, H. E., *Der russische Militärarzt im 18. Jahrhundert*, Berlin, 1970.

Murav'yev, A. M., *Zapiski*, tr. S. Ya. Shtraykh, Petrograd, 1922.

Murav'yev, A. N., 'Avtobiograficheskiye zapiski', ed. Yu. I. Gerasimovaya, in Azadovsky, *Dekabristy*, pp. 137-230.

Murav'yev[-Karsky], N. N., 'Zapiski', *RA* 1885-9, 1891, 1893-5 *passim*.

Muromtsev, M. M., 'Vospominaniya . . .', *RA* 1890, 1, pp. 59-81.

Myshlayevsky, A. Z., 'Ofitserskiy vopros v XVII v.', *VS* 247 (1899), 5, pp. 32-57, 6, pp. 285-309.

—— *Petr Velikiy: voyennye zakony i instruktsii, izdannye do 1715 g.* (Sbornik voyenno-istoricheskikh materialov, fasc. 9), St. Petersburg, 1894.

N., K. L., 'Vospominaniya o dunayskoy kampanii, 1853-1854 gg.', *VS* 89 (1873), 1, pp. 169-91, 2, pp. 367-418.

[Nashchokin, V. A.], 'Zapiski Vasiliya Aleksandrovicha Nashchokina, generala vremen yelizavitinskikh', *RA* 1883, 2, pp. 243-352.

Nasonov, A. N., Cherepnin, L. V. and Zimin, A. A. (eds.), *Ocherki istorii SSSR: period feodalizma: konets XV—nachalo XVII v.*, Moscow, 1955.

[Nazarov, P. N.], 'Zapiski soldata Pamfilova Nazarova, v inochestve Mitrofana, 1792-1839 gg.', contrib. V. I. Lestvitsyn, *RS* 22 (1878), 8, pp. 529-56.

Nechkina, M. V., *Dvizheniye dekabristov*, 2 vols., Moscow, 1955.

—— *Obshchestvo soyedinennykh slavyan*, Moscow and Leningrad, 1927.

—— (ed.), *Revolyutsionnaya situatsiya v Rossii v seredine XIX v.: kollektivnaya mono-grafiya*, Moscow, 1978.

—— 'Svyashchennyy artel'', in Alekseyev and Meylakh (eds.), *Dekabristy*, pp. 155-88.

—— 'Soyuz spaseniya', *IZ* 23 (1947), pp. 137-84.

Neizvestnyy (pseud.), 'Za mnogo let: vospominaniya neizvestnogo, 1844-1884', *RS* 81 (1894), 2, pp. 172-90, 82 (1894), 7, pp. 109-34, 83 (1894), 9, pp. 44-62, 84 (1894), 10, pp. 67-80, 85 (1895), 2, pp. 121-53, 5, pp. 111-31, 86 (1895), 7, pp. 145-65.

Nepluyev, I. I., *Zapiski, 1693-1773*, St. Petersburg, 1893, repr. Newtonville, Mass., 1974.

Neupokoyev, V. I., 'K voprosu o formirovanii revolyutsionnykh nastroyeniy v russkoy armii nakanune i v gody revolyutsionnoy situatsii (1859-1861 gg.): po materialam Dinaburgskogo protsessa', *RSR* i (1960), 213-23.

Neuville, F. de la, *Relation curieuse et nouvelle de Moscovie . . .* , The Hague, 1699.

Nikitenko, A. V., *The Diary of a Russian Censor*, abridged, ed. and tr. H. S. Jacobson, Amherst, Mass., 1975.

Nikitin, A. V., 'Oboronitel'nye sooruzheniya zasechnoy cherty XVI—XVII vv.', in Voronin, N. N. (ed.), *Materialy i issledovaniya po arkheologii SSSR* xliv (1955), 116-213.

Nikitin, N. I., 'Voyennosluzhiliye lyudi i osvoyeniye Sibiri v XVII v.', *IS* 1980, 2, pp. 114-33.

Nordmann, C. J., *Grandeur et liberté de la Suède, 1660-1792* (Travaux du Centre de recherches sur la civilisation de l'Europe moderne, fasc. 9), Paris, 1971.

Novitsky, V. I., *Vybornoye i bol'shoye dvoryanstvo XVI—XVII vv.*, Kiev, 1915.

Novosel´sky, A. A., 'Pobegi krest´yan i kholopov i ikh sysk v moskovskom gosudarstve vo vtoroy polovine XVII v.', *Trudy Rossiyskoy assotsiatsii nauchno-issledovatel´skikh institutov*, Moscow, 1926, pt. I, pp. 327–56.

——'Pravyashchiye gruppy v sluzhilom gorode XVII v.', *Uchenye zapiski Instituta istorii RANION* (Moscow, 1928), v. 315–35.

—— 'Raspad zemlevladeniya sluzhilogo "goroda" v XVII v. po desyatnam', in Ustyugov *et al.* (eds.), *Russkoye gosudarstvo*, pp. 231–54.

[——] 'Rospis´ krest´yanskikh dvorov, nakhodivshikhsya vo vladenii vysshego dukhovenstva, monastyrey i dumnykh lyudey po perepisnym knigam 1678 g.', *IA* (1st series, 1936–54) 4 (1949).

—— *Votchinnik i yego khozyaystvo v XVII v.*, Moscow and Leningrad, 1929.

—— and Ustyugov, N. V. (eds.), *Ocherki istorii SSSR: period feodalizma: XVII v.*, Moscow, 1955.

[Obreskov] 'Ob umen´shenii sroka sluzhby nizhnim chinam: proyekt taynogo sovetnika Obreskova, 1808 g., naydennyy v kabinete imperatora Aleksandra Pavlovicha po yego konchine', contrib. M. I. Bogdanovich, *RS* 9 (1874), pp. 245–51.

Obruchev, N. [N.], 'Iznanka Krymskoy voyny', *VS* 1 (1858), pp. 545–86, 2 (1858), pp. 429–76, 4 (1858), pp. 239–306.

Obruchev, V. A., 'Iz perezhitogo', *VEv* 95 (1907), 3, pp. 122–55, 96 (1907), 6, pp. 65–95, 98 (1908), 5, pp. 504–42.

[Odintsov, A. A.], 'Posmertnye zapiski generala ot infanterii Alekseya Alekseyevicha Odintsova', *RS* 64 (1889), pp. 289–322, 65 (1890), pp. 21–34.

Odintsova, M. K., 'Soldaty—dekabristy', *Sibirskiye ogni* 6 (1928), pp. 217–21.

Oksman, Yu. G. *et al.* (comps.), *Dekabristy: otryvki iz istochnikov*, Moscow and Leningrad, 1926.

—— and Shchegolev, P. E. (eds.), *Bunt dekabristov: yubileynyy sbornik, 1825–1925*, Leningrad, 1926.

Olearius, A., *The Travels of Olearius in Seventeenth-Century Russia*, tr. and ed. S. H. Baron, Stanford, 1967.

Ol´shevsky, M. Ya., 'Pervyy kadetskiy korpus v 1826–1833 gg.: vospominaniya', *RS* 49 (1886), pp. 63–95.

Opochinin, F. K. (contrib.), 'Zapiski grafa Grigoriya Petrovicha Chernysheva, 1672–1745', *RS* 5 (1872), pp. 791–802.

Orlov, M. F., *Kapitulyatsiya Parizha: politicheskiye sochineniya i pis´ma*, ed. S. Ya. Borovoy and M. I. Gillel´son, Moscow, 1963.

Orlovsky, D. T., *The Limits of Reform: the Ministry of Internal Affairs in Imperial Russia, 1802–1881*, Cambridge, Mass. and London, 1981.

Ostrogorsky, G., 'Das Projekt einer Rangtabelle aus der Zeit des Caren Fedor Alekseevič', *Jahrbuch für Kultur und Geschichte der Slaven* 9 (Breslau, 1933), pp. 86–138.

P., P., 'Vospominaniya kavaleriyskogo ofitsera: epizody iz turetskoy voyny 1828 g.', *Sovremennik* 46 (1854), pp. 89–127.

[Panayev, N. I.], 'Rasskaz . . . podpolkovnika Panayeva . . .', in Semevsky, *Bunt*, pp. 65–131.

Panteleyev, L. F., *Vospominaniya*, Moscow, 1958.

Pavlenko, N. I. *et al.* (eds.), *Dvoryanstvo i krepostnoy stroy Rossii XVI—XVIII vv.: sbornik statey posvyashchennyy pamyati A. A. Novosel´skogo*, Moscow, 1975.

Pavlenko, V. N., 'Vedomosti XVIII v. o khlebnykh tsenakh kak istoricheskiy istochnik', in Ustyugov, N. V. *et al.* (eds.), *Voprosy sotsial'no–ekonomicheskoy istorii i istochnikovedeniya perioda feodalizma v Rossii: sbornik statey k 70–letiyu A. A. Novosel'-skogo*, Moscow, 1961, pp. 301–6.

Pavlov-Silvansky, N. P., *Gosudarevy sluzhiliye lyudi: proiskhozhdeniye russkogo dvoryanstva*, 2nd edn., St. Petersburg, 1909.

Pecherin, Ya. I., *Istoricheskiy ocherk rospisey gosudarstvennykh dokhodov i raskhodov s 1808 po 1843 g. vklyuchitel'no*, St. Petersburg, 1896.

Pelenski, J., 'State and Society in Muscovite Russia and the Mongol–Turkic System in the Sixteenth Century', *FOEG* 27 (1980), pp. 156–67.

'Perepiska velikogo knyazya Pavla Petrovicha s grafom Petrom Paninym v 1778 g.', *RS* 33 (1882), pp. 403–18, 739–64.

Pesni sobrannye P. V. Kireyevskim, 2nd edn., fascs. 6–9, Moscow, 1864–72.

[Peter I], *Zhurnal ili podennaya zapiska . . . Petra Velikogo s 1698 g. dazhe do zaklyucheniya Neyshtatskogo mira*, 3 vols., St. Petersburg, 1770-2.

[——], 'Ukazy i pis'ma imperatora Petra I k moskovskomu komendantu, a potom sibirskomu gubernatoru, kn. M. P. Gagarinu', ed. F. A. Bychkov, *SIRIO* xi (1873), 116–56.

Peterson, C., *Peter the Great's Administrative and Judicial Reforms: Swedish Antecedents and the Process of Reception*, Stockholm, 1979.

'Petr Velikiy i yego armiya', *VS* 85 (1872), 5, pp. 225–52.

Petrov, A. N., *Russkaya voyennaya sila: istoriya razvitiya voyennogo dela ot nachala Rusi do nashego vremeni*, 2nd edn., 2 vols., Moscow, 1892.

—— 'Ustroystvo i upravlenie voyennykh poseleniy v Rossii: istoricheskiy obzor, 1809–1826', in Semevsky, *Materialy*, pp. 85–207.

'Petrovskaya brigada: polki leyb-gvardii Preobrazhenskiy i Semenovskiy, 1683–1883 gg.', *RS* 38 (1883), pp. 239–72.

Petrushevsky, A. F., 'Suvorov vo svoikh pomest'yakh', *VEv* 93 (1882), 3, pp. 550–88.

Pintner, W. McK., 'The Evolution of Civil Officialdom, 1755–1855', in Pintner and Rowney (eds.), *Russian Officialdom*, pp. 190–226.

—— 'Civil Officialdom and the Nobility in the 1850s', in ibid., pp. 227–49.

—— and Rowney, D. K. (eds.), *Russian Officialdom: the Bureaucratization of Russian Society from the Seventeenth to the Twentieth Century*, Chapel Hill, 1980.

Pipes, R. [E.], *Russia under the old Regime*, London, 1974.

—— 'The Russian Military Colonies, 1810–1831', *Journal of Modern History* 22 (1950), pp. 205–19.

[Pirogov, N. I.], *Sevastopol'skiye pis'ma N. I. Pirogova, 1854–1855*, St. Petersburg, 1899.

[Pischevich, A. S.], *Zhizn' A. S. Pishchevicha*, Moscow, 1885.

[Pishchevich (Piščević), S. S.], *Izvestiye o pokhozhdenii Simeona Stefanovicha Pishchevicha, 1731-1785*, ed. N. A. Popov, Moscow, 1884.

Platonov, F. N., ['Vospominaniya'], in Meshchaninov, I. V., 'Iz vospominaniy o P. S. Vannovskom', *IV* 124 (1911), 5, pp. 505–13.

Platonov, S. F., *Ocherki po istorii Smuty v moskovskom gosudarstve XVI—XVII vv.: opyt izucheniya obshchestvennogo stroya i soslovnykh otnosheniy v Smutnoye vremya* [1899], repr. Moscow, 1937.

Plavsić, B., 'Seventeenth-Century Chanceries and their Staffs', in Pintner and Rowney (eds.), *Russian Officialdom*, pp. 19–45.

Pleyer, O., 'Allerunterthänigste Relation von dem jetzigen moskowitischen Regierungswesen, 1710' in Herrmann (ed.), *Russland*, pp. 121 ff.

Plotho, C. von, *Über die Entstehung, die Fortschritte, und die gegenwärtige Verfassung der russischen Armee, doch insbesondere von der Infanterie* . . . , Berlin, 1811.

Podyapol'skaya, E. P., 'K voprosu o formirovanii dvoryanskoy intelligentsii v I-oy chetverti XVIII v.', in Pavlenko *et al.* (eds.), *Dvoryanstvo*, pp. 181–9.

Polievktov, M., *Nikolay I: biografiya i obzor tsarstvovaniya*, Moscow, 1918.

Porokh, I. V., 'Vosstaniye Chernigovskogo polka', in Druzhinin and Syroyechkovsky (eds.), *Ocherki*, pp. 121–85.

Pososhkov, I. T., *Kniga o skudosti i bogatstve i drugiye sochineniya*, ed. B. B. Kafengauz, Moscow, 1951.

Potto, G. M., *Utverzhdeniye russkogo vladychestva na Kavkaze*, iii. pt. 1: *Vremya A. P. Yermolova, 1816-1826 gg.*, Tiflis, 1904.

Potto, V. and Bukovsky, *Istoricheskiy ocherk Nikolayevskogo kavaleriyskogo uchilishcha, byvshey shkoly gvardeyskikh podpraporshchikov i kavaleriyskikh yunkerov, 1823-1898*, St. Petersburg, 1898.

Predtechensky, A. V., *Ocherki obshchestvenno-politicheskoy istorii Rossii v pervoy chetverti XIX v.*, Moscow and Leningrad, 1957.

Presnyakov, A. E., *14-go dekabrya 1825 g.*, Moscow, 1926.

—— *Emperor Nicholas I of Russia: the Apogee of Autocracy, 1825-1855*, ed. and tr. J. C. Zacek . . . , Gulf Breeze, Fla., 1974. [*Samoderzhaviye Nikolaya I*, Petrograd, 1923.]

—— *Moskovskoye tsarstvo: obshchiy ocherk*, Petrograd, 1918. (Ed. and tr. R. F. Price as *The Tsardom of Muscovy*, Gulf Breeze, Fla., 1977.)

'Prevratnosti sud'by . . . : vospominaniya polyaka na russkoy sluzhbe v tsarstvovaniyakh Anny Ioannovny i Yelizavety Petrovny: perevod s neizdannoy rukopisi', annotated by A. A. Chumikov, *RA* 1898, 4, pp. 479–508.

Prokof'yev, E. A., *Bor'ba dekabristov za peredovoye russkoye voyennoye iskusstvo*, Moscow, 1953.

Pushkarev, I., *Istoriya imperatorskoy rossiyskoy gvardii*, St. Petersburg, 1844.

Pushkarev, L. N., 'Soldatskaya pesnya—istochnik po istorii voyennogo byta russkoy regulyarnoy armii XVIII—pervoy poloviny XIX v.', in Shunkov *et al.* (eds.), *Voprosy*, pp. 422–32.

Putilov, B. N. *et al.* (eds.), *Istoricheskiye pesni XVII v.*, Moscow and Leningrad, 1966.

P—v, P., 'Dvukhsotletiye sformirovaniya gvardeyskikh polkov, 1687–1887 gg.', *IV 28* (1887), 4, pp. 240–2.

Pypin, A. N., *Obshchestvennoye dvizheniye v Rossii pri Aleksandre I*, 3rd edn., St. Petersburg, 1900.

Rabinovich, M. D., 'Formirovaniye regulyarnoy russkoy armii nakanune Severnoy voyny', in Shunkov *et al.* (eds.), *Voprosy*, pp. 221–32.

—— 'Ofitserskiye "skazki" i posluzhnye spiski nachala XVIII v.', in Kashtanov, S. M. *et al.* (eds.), *Aktovoye istochnikovedeniye: sbornik statey*, Moscow, 1979, pp. 108–22.

—— *Polki regulyarnoy russkoy armii pri Petre I*, Moscow, 1977.

—— 'Sotsial'noye proiskhozhdeniye i imushchestvennoye polozheniye ofitserov regulyarnoy russkoy armii v kontse Severnoy voyny', in Pavlenko, N. I. *et al.* (eds.), *Rossiya v period reform Petra I*, Moscow, 1973, pp. 133–71.

— 'Sel'skoye khozyaystvo i pereselenie odnodvortsev v 30e—50e gg. XVIII v.', *Tezisy dokladov i soobshcheniy XIV sessii mezhdurespublikanskogo simpoziuma po agrarnoy istorii Vostochnoy Yevropy, Minsk—Grodno, 25-29 sentyabrya 1972 g.*, Moscow, 1972, fasc. I, pp. 141-3.

— 'Strel'tsy v pervoy chetverti XVIII v.', *IZ* 58 (1956), pp. 273-305.

— *Sud'by sluzhilykh lyudey 'starykh sluzhb' i odnodvortsev v period formirovaniya regulyarnoy armii v nachale XVIII st.: avtoreferat dissertatsii*, Moscow, 1953.

[Radchenko, E. S. (comp.)], *Kolokol: izdaniye A. I. Gertsena i N. P. Ogareva, 1857-1867: sistematizirovannaya rospis' statey i zametok*, Moscow, 1957.

Raeff, M., *Comprendre l'ancien régime russe: état et société en Russie impériale*, Paris, 1982 (Eng. edn. *Understanding the Old Regime in Russia*, tr. A. Goldhammer, New York, 1984).

— *The Decembrist Movement*, Englewood Cliffs, NJ, 1966.

— 'The Domestic Policies of Peter III and His Overthrow', *American Historical Review* 75 (1970), pp. 1289-1310.

— *Imperial Russia, 1682-1825: the Coming of Age of Modern Russia*, New York, 1971.

— *Origins of the Russian Intelligentsia: the Eighteenth-Century Nobility*, New York, 1966.

— 'The Russian Autocracy and Its Officials', *Harvard Slavic Studies* 4 (1957), pp. 77-91.

— 'Staatsdienst, Aussenpolitik, Ideologie: die Rolle der Institutionen in der geistigen Entwicklung des russischen Adels im 18. Jahrhundert', *JGOE* 7 (1959), pp. 147-81.

— 'Uniformity, Diversity and the Imperial Administration in the Reign of Catherine II', in Lemberg, H. *et al.* (eds.), *Osteuropa in Geschichte und Gegenwart: Festschrift für Günther Stökl zum 60. Geburtstag*, Cologne and Vienna, 1977, pp. 97-113.

Ragsdale, H. (ed.), *Paul I: a Reassessment of His Life and Reign*, Pittsburgh, 1979.

Rakhmatullin, M. A., 'Generalissimus A. V. Suvorov: yego iskusstvo pobezhdat'', *IS* 1980, 5, pp. 64-90.

— 'Soldaty v krest'yanskom dvizhenii 20-kh gg. XIX v.', in Shunkov *et al.* (eds.), *Voprosy*, pp. 351-8.

Ransel, D. L., *The Politics of Catherinian Russia: the Panin Party*, New Haven and London, 1975.

[Rayevsky, V. F.], 'Vospominaniya', introd. M. K. Azadovsky, *Dekabristy—literatory*, *LN* 60(i) (1956), 47-128.

Raymond, D. de, *Tableau historique, géographique, militaire et moral de l'empire de Russie*, 2 vols., Paris, 1812.

Reimers, H. von, 'Peterburg pri imperatore Pavle Petroviche v 1796-1801 gg.', tr. E. P. V—a, *RS* 39 (1883), pp. 443-74.

Rexhauser, R., 'Adelsbesitz und Heeresverfassung im Moskauer Staat des 17. Jhd.', *JGOE* 21 (1973), pp. 1-17.

Richelieu, A. E., Count, 'Journal de mon voyage en Allemagne, commencé le 2 septembre 1790', in Polovtsov, A. A. (ed.), 'Gertsog Armand-Emmanuil Rishel'ye: dokumenty i bumagi o yego zhizni i deyatel'nosti, 1766-1822', *SIRIO* liv (1886), 111-98.

Rieber, A. J., *The Politics of Autocracy: Letters of Alexander II to Prince A. I. Bariatinskii, 1857-1864* (Etudes sur l'histoire, l'économie et la sociologie des pays slaves, 12), Paris and The Hague, 1966.

Rogov, A. I., *Russko-pol'skiye kul'turnye svyazi v epokhu Vozrozhdeniya: Striykovsky i yego khronika*, Moscow, 1966.

Romanovich-Slavatinsky, V. A., *Dvoryanstvo v Rossii ot nachala XVIII v. do otmeny krepostnogo prava*, 2nd edn., Kiev, 1912.

Rossov, Captain, 'Istoricheskiy ocherk prizreniya otstavnykh voyennykh chinov v proshlom veke i v nachale nyneshnego stoletiya', *VS* 30 (1863), pp. 375–98.

[Rostopchin, F. V.], '1812 g. v zapiskakh F. V. Rostopchina' [1823], tr. I. I. Orens, *RS* 64 (1889), pp. 643–725.

Rozengeym, M. P., *Ocherki istorii voyenno-sudnykh uchrezhdeniy v Rossii do konchiny Petra Velikogo*, St. Petersburg, 1878.

Rozhdestvensky, S. V., *Ocherki po istorii narodnogo prosveshcheniya v Rossii v XVIII—XIX vv.*, St. Petersburg, 1912.

—— 'Rospis' zemel'nykh vladeniy moskovskogo boyarstva 1647-8 gg.', *Drevnosti: trudy Arkheograficheskoy komissii Moskovskogo arkheologicheskogo obshchestva* 3 (1913), pp. 193–238.

—— *Sluzhiloye zemlevladeniye v moskovskom gosudarstve XVI v.*, St. Petersburg, 1897, repr. The Hague and Paris, 1966.

Rubinshteyn, N. L. (ed.), *Voyenno-istoricheskiy sbornik* (Trudy Gosudarstvennogo istoricheskogo muzeya, 20), Moscow, 1948.

—— (ed.), *Voyennye ustavy Petra Velikogo*, introd. and commentary by P. P. Yepifanov, Moscow, 1946.

Ruffmann, K.-H., 'Russischer Adel als Sondertypus der europäischen Adelswelt', *JGOE* 9 (1961), pp. 161–78.

[Rusinov], 'Izvestiye o nachale, uchrezhdenii i sostoyanii regulyarnogo voyska v Rossii . . .' [1796], *Zapiski sobrannye po poveleniyu Pavla I o nachale regulyarnogo voyska . . . i o voyennykh shkolakh* (Sbornik voyenno-istoricheskikh materialov, fasc. 16), St. Petersburg, 1904.

Rüss, H., *Adel und Adelsoppositionen im Moskauer Staat* (Quellen und Studien zur Geschichte des östlichen Europas, ed. M. Hellmann, 7), Wiesbaden, 1975.

Russett, B. M. (ed.), *Peace, War and Numbers*, Beverly Hills, Calif., 1972.

Russia, Ministry of Finance, *Ministerstvo finansov, 1802–1902*, 2 vols., St. Petersburg, 1902.

Ruud, C. A., *Fighting Words: Imperial Censorship and the Russian Press, 1804–1906*, Toronto, 1982.

Rzhevsky, S. M., contrib., 'O russkoy armii vo vtoroy polovine Yekaterininskogo tsarstvovaniya . . .', *RA* 1879, 3, pp. 357–62.

Sablukov, N. A., 'Reminiscences of the Court and Times of the Emperor, Paul I of Russia, up to the Period of his Death: from the Papers of a Deceased Russian General Officer', *Fraser's Magazine* 72 (London, 1865), Aug., pp. 222–41, Sept., pp. 302–27.

—— 'Zapiski', in *Tsareubiystvo 11 marta 1801 g.: zapiski uchastnikov i sovremennikov*, St. Petersburg, 1907, pp. 1–105. (Excerpts in 'Iz zapisok', *RA* 1870, cols. 1869 ff.)

Sakharov, A. N., *Obrazovaniye i razvitiye rossiyskogo gosudarstva*, Moscow, 1969.

Schiemann, T., *Geschichte Russlands unter Kaiser Nikolaus I*, 4 vols., Berlin, 1904–19.

[Schwan, C. F. (?)], *Merkwürdigkeiten der russischen Geschichte unter Peter dem Dritten . . .* , Narva, 1790.

Ségur, L.-Ph., Comte de, *Mémoires, souvenirs et anecdotes . . . Correspondence et pensées du prince de Ligne*, annotated by M. F. Barrière, 2 vols., Paris, 1859.

Semenova, I. V., *Rossiya i osvoboditel'naya bor'ba moldavskogo naroda protiv ottomanskogo iga v kontse XVIII v.*, Kishinev, 1976.

[Semevsky, M. I. (ed.)], *Bunt voyennykh poselyan v 1831 godu: rasskazy i vospominaniya ochevidtsev*, St. Petersburg, 1870.

—— (ed.), *Materialy k noveyshey otechestvennoy istorii: graf Arakcheyev i voyennye poseleniya, 1809-1831*, Moscow, 1871, repr. Newtonville, Mass., 1973.

Semevsky, V. I., *Krest'yane v tsarstvovaniye imperatritsy Yekateriny II*, 2nd edn., 2 vols., St. Petersburg, 1903.

—— 'Mikhail Aleksandrovich Fon-Vizin: biograficheskiy ocherk', in id., Bogucharsky, V. and Shchegolev, P. E. (comps.), *Obshchestvenniya dvizheniya v Rossii v pervuyu polovinu XIX v.*, vol. I, St. Petersburg, 1900, pp. 1-96.

—— 'Volneniye v Semenovskom polku v 1820 g.', *Byloye* 13 (1907), pp. 1-36, 14 (1907), pp. 83-123, 15 (1907), pp. 96-121.

—— *Politicheskiye i obshchestvennye idei dekabristov*, St. Petersburg, 1909.

Seton-Watson, H., 'Russia: Army and Autocracy', in Howard, M. (ed.), *Soldiers and Governments: Nine Studies in Civil-Military Relations*, London, 1957, pp. 101-14.

—— *The Russian Empire, 1801-1917*, Oxford, 1967.

Sh., 'Dvoryanstvo v Rossii: istoricheskiy i obshchestvennyy ocherk', *VEv* 22 (1887), 3, pp. 239-84, 4, pp. 531-71, 5, pp. 186-210, 6, pp. 421-52.

Shakhmatov, M. V., *Kompetentsiya ispolnitel'noy vlasti v moskovskoy Rusi*, pt. I: *Vnutrennyaya okhrana gosudarstva* (Zapiski Nauchno-issledovatel'kogo ob'yedineniya, 4), Prague, 1936.

Shakhovskoy, Ya. P., *Zapiski, 1709-1777*, St. Petersburg, 1872, repr. with introd. by R. E. Jones, Cambridge, 1974.

Shapiro, A. L., *Agrarnaya istoriya severno-zapadnoy Rossii*, Leningrad, 1971.

Shatilov, D., 'Mysli po povodu unichtozheniya telesnykh nakazaniy v voyskakh', *VS* 33 (1863), 10, pp. 363-74.

Shchegolev, P. E., *Istoricheskiye etyudy*, St. Petersburg, 1913, repr. London, 1980.

Shcherbachev, G. D., 'Dvenadtsat' let molodosti: vospominaniya', *RA* 1890, 1, pp. 87-130, 2, pp. 215-84, 1891, 1, pp. 29-76 [with title 'Iz vospominaniy', that is, censored].

Shcherbinin, M. P. (comp.), *Biografiya general-fel'dmarshala knyazya Mikhaila Semenovicha Vorontsova*, St. Petersburg, 1858.

Shchukin, P. I. (ed.), *Bumagi otnosyashchiyesya do Otechestvennoy voyny 1812 g.*, 10 fascs. and index vol. (1912), Moscow, 1897-1908.

—— (ed.), *Sbornik starinnykh bumag, khranyashchikhsya v muzeye P. I. Shchukina*, 10 vols., Moscow, 1896-1902.

—— (ed.), *Shchukinskiy sbornik*, 10 vols., Moscow, 1902-12, i-vi.

Shepelev, L. E., *Otmenennye istoriyey: chiny, zvaniya i tituly v Rossiyskoy imperii*, Leningrad, 1977.

Shil'der, N. K., *Imperator Aleksandr I-iy: yego zhizn' i tsarstvovaniye*, 4 vols., St. Petersburg, 1897-8.

—— *Imperator Pavel I-iy: istoriko-biograficheskiy ocherk*, St. Petersburg, 1901.

Shmidt, S. O., 'Mestnichestvo i absolyutizm: postanovka voprosa', in Druzhinin *et al.* (eds.), *Absolyutizm*, pp. 168-205.

—— *Stanovleniye rossiyskogo samoderzhaviya: issledovaniye sotsial'no-politicheskoy istorii vremeni Ivana Groznogo*, Moscow, 1973.

Shpakovsky, N. I., 'Strel'tsy', *ZhMNP* 319 (1898), 9, pp. 137–51.

Shteyngeyl', V. V., *Nastol'nyy khronologicheskiy ukazatel' postanovleniy otnosyash-chikhsya do ustroystva voyenno-sukhoputnykh sil Rossii, 1550–1890 g.* . . . , St. Petersburg, 1890.

Shtorkh, P. A., 'Materialy dlya istorii gosudarstvennykh denezhnykh znakov v Rossii s 1653 po 1840 g.', *ZhMNP* 137 (1868), pt. 2, pp. 772–847.

[Shtrandman, G. E. von], 'Zapiski . . . , 1742–1803', *RS* 34 (1882), pp. 289–318, 43 (1884), 7, pp. 55–86, 8, pp. 271–88.

Shunkov, V. I. (ed.), *Voprosy voyennoy istorii Rossii: XVIII i pervaya polovina XIX v.*, Moscow, 1969.

Siegelbaum, L. H., 'Peasant Disorders and the Myth of the Tsar: Russian Variations on a Millenarian Theme', *Journal of Religious History* 10 (Sydney, 1978–9), pp. 223–35.

Simpson, M. S., *The Officer in Nineteenth-Century Russian Literature*, Washington, 1981.

Singer, J. D. and Small, M., *The Wages of War, 1816–1965: Statistical Handbook*, New York, London, and Sydney, 1972.

Skaryatin, N., 'Iz vospominaniy molodosti', *RA* 1893, 5, pp. 18–22.

Skrynnikov, R. G., *Rossiya posle oprichniny: ocherk politicheskoy i sotsial'noy istorii*, Leningrad, 1975.

Slovutinsky, S. T., *General Izmaylov i yego dvornya* [and] *Otryvki iz vospominaniy*, Moscow and Leningrad, 1935.

Smel'nitsky, M., 'Proiskhozhdeniye poteshnykh voysk', *VS* 318 (1911), 3, pp. 101–10.

Smirnov, A. F., *Revolyutsionnye svyazi narodov Rossii i Pol'shi: 30-e—60-e gg. XIX v.*, Moscow, 1962.

—— 'Zigmunt Serakovsky [Sierakowski]', in Miller, I. S. and Smirnov, A. F. (eds.), *Za nashu i vashu svobodu! Geroi 1863 g.: sbornik*, Moscow, 1964, pp. 9–67.

Smirnov, I. I., *Ocherki politicheskoy istorii russkogo gosudarstva 30-kh—50-kh gg. XVI v.*, Moscow and Leningrad, 1958.

Snytko, T. G., 'Novye materialy po istorii obshchestvennogo dvizheniya kontsa XVIII v.', *VI* 1952, 9, pp. 111–22.

Sofronenko, K. A. (ed.), *Zakonodatel'nye akty Petra I*, *PRP*, fasc. 8, Moscow, 1961.

Sokolovsky, M. K., 'Imperator Nikolay I v voyenno-sudnykh konfirmatsiyakh', *RS* 124 (1905), 11, pp. 397–420.

—— 'Iz pyli arkhivov: iz voyennykh rasporyazheniy imperatora Pavla I', *Varshavskiy voyennyy zhurnal*, 1904, 4, pp. 286–92.

—— 'Iz russkoy voyenno-ugolovnoy stariny: vysochayshiye konfirmatsii imperatora Pavla I-go po voyenno-sudnym delam', *RS* 123 (1904), 7–9, pp. 353–68.

—— (contrib.), 'Russkaya gvardiya, 1816–1834 gg.: prikazy komandirov', *RA* 1905, 9, pp. 5–68.

Solov'yev, N., 'Kratkiy istoricheskiy ocherk organizatsii russkikh regulyarnykh voysk v pervoy polovine XVIII stoletiya, 1700–1761', *VS* 209 (1893), 1, pp. 91–113, 2, pp. 306–26.

—— 'Kratkiy istoricheskiy ocherk raskhodov na armiyu i denezhnogo dovol'stviya voysk v Rossii v pervoy polovine XVIII stoletiya, 1700–1761', *VS* 214 (1893), 12, pp. 215–57.

—— 'O pensiyakh za voyennuyu sluzhbu v Rossii v XVIII i XIX st.', *VS* 210 (1893), 3, pp. 302–12.

Squire, P. S., *The Third Department: the Establishment and Practices of Political Police in the Russia of Nicholas I*, London and New York, 1968.

Staden, H. von, *The Land and Government of Muscovy: a Sixteenth-Century Account*, tr. and ed. T. Esper, Stanford, 1967.

Stanislavsky, A. L., 'Boyarskiye spiski v deloproizvodstve Razryadnogo prikaza', in Kashtanov, S. M. *et al.* (eds.), *Aktovoye istochnikovedeniye*, Moscow, 1979, pp. 123–52.

Starr, S. F., *Decentralization and Self-Government in Russia, 1830–1870*, Princeton, 1972.

Stashevsky, E. D., 'Byudzhet i armiya', in Dovnar-Zapol'sky, M. V. (ed.), *Russkaya istoriya v ocherkakh i stat'yakh*, iii. Kiev, 1912, pp. 411–17.

—— 'Sluzhiloye sosloviye', in ibid., pp. 1–33.

—— 'Smeta voyennykh sil moskovskogo gosudarstva na 1663 god', pt. 2, *Voyenno-istoricheskiy vestnik* 10 (Kiev, 1910), pp. 55–87.

—— *Zemlevladeniya moskovskogo dvoryanstva v pervoy polovine XVII v.*, Moscow, 1911.

Stcherbatow [Shcherbatov], General, *Le Feld-maréchal prince Paskévitsch: sa vie politique et militaire, d'après des documents inédits*, tr. 'un Russe', 4 vols., St. Petersburg, 1888–93, i.

Stein, F. von, *Geschichte des russischen Heeres vom Ursprunge desselben bis zur Thronbesteigung des Kaisers Nikolai I. Pawlowitsch*, Hanover, 1885, repr. Krefeld, 1975.

Stein, H.-P., 'Der Offizier des russischen Heeres im Zeitabschnitt zwischen Reform und Revolution, 1861–1905', *FOEG* 13 (1967), pp. 346–507.

Stepanov, R. N., 'K voprosu o sluzhilykh i yasachnykh tatarakh', *Sbornik aspirantskikh rabot: pravo, istoriya, filologiya*, Kazan', 1964, pp. 52–70.

Stevens, C. B., 'Belgorod: Notes on Literacy and Language in the Seventeenth–Century Russian Army', *RH* 7 (1980), pp. 113–24.

[Stogov], E. [Ya.], 'Ocherki, rasskazy i vospominaniya', *RS* 22 (1878), pp. 301–16, 616–32, 23 (1878), pp. 99–118, 499–530, 631–704, 24 (1879), pp. 49–80, [52 (1886), 10].

Stökl, G., 'Gab es im Moskauer Staat "Stände"?', *JGOE* 11 (1963), pp. 321–42.

Stolypin, D., 'Ob uprazdnenii voyennykh poseleniy: iz lichnykh vospominaniy', *RA* 1874, 1, pp. 765–72.

Storch, H., *Historisch–statistisches Gemälde des russischen Reiches am Ende des 18. Jhd.*, 8 vols., Riga, 1797–1803, i.

Stork, E. von, *Denkschrift über die Kaiserlich Russische Kriegsmacht, in besonderer Beziehung auf den Krieg gegen die Türken . . .* , Leipzig, 1828.

[Storozhenko, A. Ya.], 'Iz zapisok senatora A. Ya. Storozhenko', *KS* 10 (1884), pp. 447–77.

Storozhev, V. N., 'Desyatni i tysyachnaya kniga XVI v.', *Opisanie dokumentov i bumag, khranyashchikhsya v Moskovskom arkhive Ministerstva yustitsii* 8 (1891), § 3.

'Streletskaya sluzhba v XVII v.: pistsovyy nakaz 7185/1677 g.', *RA* 1895, 1, pp. 17–22.

Strokov, A. A., *Istoriya voyennogo iskusstva*, 3 vols., Moscow, 1955–67, i. *Rabovladel'cheskoye i feodal'noye obshchestvo.*

Strumilin, S. G., 'K voprosu ob ekonomike Petrovskoy epokhi', in Beskrovnyy *et al.* (eds.), *Poltava*, pp. 179–89.

—— 'Oplata truda v Rossii' [1930], in id., *Ocherki ekonomicheskoy istorii Rossii i SSSR*, Moscow, 1966, pp. 23–99.

Studenkin, G. I. (contrib.), 'Ukazy, rasporyazheniya i rezolyutsii imperatora Pavla, 1796–1801 gg.', *RS* 7 (1873), pp. 491–516, 622–34.

Sudebniki XV–XVI vv., ed. B. D. Grekov, Moscow, 1952.

Subtelny, O., 'Russia and the Ukraine: the Difference that Peter I Made', *RR* 39 (1980), pp. 1–17.

Sukhomlin, A. V. (ed.), *Suvorovskiy sbornik*, Moscow, 1951.

Suvorov, A. V., *Nauka pobezhdat'*, Moscow, 1950.

[——] 'Polkovoye uchrezhdeniye', in Meshcheryakov (ed.), *Suvorov*, i (1949), 73–168.

[——] *Suvorovskiy sbornik*, ed. 'Varshavskiy voyennyy zhurnal', Warsaw, 1900.

Svatikov, S. G., *Rossiya i Don, 1549–1917: issledovaniye po istorii gosudarstvennogo i administrativnogo prava i politicheskikh dvizheniy na Donu*, Vienna, 1924.

Syrnev, A. (ed.), *Vseobshchaya voinskaya povinnost' v imperii za pervoye desyatiletiye, 1874–1883 gg.* (Statisticheskiy vremennik Rossiyskoy imperii, seriya III, fasc. 12), St. Petersburg, 1886.

Syroyechkovsky, B. E. (comp.), *Mezhdutsarstviye 1825 g. i vosstaniye dekabristov v perepiske i memuarakh chlenov tsarskoy sem'i*, Moscow and Leningrad, 1926.

Syromyatnikov, B. I., *'Regulyarnoye' gosudarstvo Petra I i yego ideologiya*, Moscow and Leningrad, 1943.

Tański, J., *Tableau statistique, politique et moral du système militaire de la Russie*, Paris, 1833.

Tarlé, Ye. V., *La Campagne de Russie: 1812*, tr. M. Slonim, 16th edn., Paris, 1950.

Taubin, R. A., 'K voprosu o roli N. G. Chernyshevskogo v sozdanii "revolyutsionnoy partii" v kontse 50-kh—nachale 60-kh gg. XIX v.', *IZ* 39 (1952), pp. 59–97.

Thackeray, F. W., *Antecedents of Revolution: Alexander I and the Polish Kingdom, 1815–1825*, New York, 1980.

Tikhomirov, M. N., *Rossiya v XVI v.*, Moscow, 1962.

Tkacheva, N. K., 'Iz istorii odnodvortsev v XVIII v.', *Yezhegodnik po agrarnoy istorii Vostochnoy Yevropy za 1968 g.*, Leningrad, 1972, pp. 133–41.

Toll, C. F., Count von, *Denkwürdigkeiten aus dem Leben des kaiserlichen russischen Generals v. d. Infanterie C. F. Grafen von Toll*, ed. T. von Bernhardi, 2nd edn., 4 vols., Leipzig, 1856-8, i.

Torke, H.-J., 'Adel und Staat vor Peter dem Grossen, 1649–1689', *FOEG* 27 (1980), pp. 282–98.

—— *Die staatsbedingte Gesellschaft im Moskauer Reich: Zar und Zemlja in der altrussischen Herrschaftsverfassung* (Studien zur Geschichte Osteuropas, 17), Leyden, 1974.

Troitsky, S. M., *Finansovaya politika russkogo absolyutizma v XVIII v.*, Moscow, 1966.

—— *Russkiy absolyutizm i dvoryanstvo v XVIII v.: formirovaniye byurokratii*, Moscow, 1974.

Trudy imperatorskogo russkogo voyenno-istoricheskogo obshchestva, 7 vols., St. Petersburg, 1909-12, i–iv (1909).

Truvorov, A. N., 'O vremeni uchrezhdeniya Preobrazhenskogo i Semenovskogo polkov', *IV* 30 (1887), 10, pp. 142–64.

Tuchkov, S. A., *Zapiski . . . , 1766–1808*, ed. K. A. Voyensky, St. Petersburg, 1908.

'Turetskaya voyna pri imperatritse Anne: sovremennaya rukopis'', foreword by
S. Safonov, *RA* 1878, 1, 3, pp. 255-74.

Turgenev (Tourguéneff), N. I., *La Russie et les russes*, 3 vols., Brussels, 1847.

'Uchrezhdeniye Preobrazhenskogo polka', *VS* 254 (1900), 8, pp. 225-47, 255 (1900),
9-10, pp. 25-40, 228-45.

[Ulozheniye] *Sobornoye Ulozheniye 1649 g.: posobiye dlya vysshey shkoly*, ed. M. N.
Tikhomirov and P. P. Yepifanov, Moscow, 1961.

Urlanis, B. Ts., 'Lyudskiye poteri vooruzhennykh sil v yevropeyskikh voynakh', in
id., *Narodonaseleniye: issledovaniya, publitsistika: sbornik statey*, Moscow, 1976,
pp. 150-216.

—— *Rost naseleniya v Yevrope: opyt ischisleniya*, Moscow and Leningrad, 1941.

—— *Voyny i narodonaseleniye Yevropy: lyudskiye poteri vooruzhennykh sil yevropeyskikh stran v voynakh XVII-XX vv.: istoriko–statisticheskoye issledovaniye*, Moscow,
1960.

Ushakov, A. F., 'Kholernyy bunt v Staroy Rusi', *RS* 9 (1874), pp. 145-62.

Uspensky, F. I., 'Znacheniye vizantiyskoy i yugoslavyanskoy pronii', in *Sbornik statey
po slavyanovedeniyu sost. i izd. uchenikami V. I. Lamanskogo po sluchayu 25–letiyu
yego . . . deyatel'nosti*, St. Petersburg, 1883, pp. 1-32.

Ustryalov, N. G., *Istoriya tsarstvovaniya Petra Velikogo*, i-iv, vi, St. Petersburg,
1858-63.

Ustyugov, N. V. *et al.* (eds.), *Russkoye gosudarstvo v XVII v.: novye yavleniya v
sotsial'no–ekonomicheskoy, politicheskoy i kul'turnoy zhizni*, Moscow, 1961.

Vagts, A., *A History of Militarism: Romance and Realities of a Profession*, London,
1938; rev. edn., London, 1959.

[Vasil'yev, Lieutenant], *Dnevnik poruchika Vasil'yeva, 1774-1777*, foreword by
E. Shchepkina (Pamyatniki drevney pis'mennosti, 119), St. Petersburg, 1896.

Vazhinsky, V. M., *Zemlevladeniye i skladyvaniye obshchiny odnodvortsev v XVII v.:
po materialam yuzhnykh uyezdov Rossii*, Voronezh, 1974.

Venediktov, I. I., 'Za shestdesyat let: vospominaniya, 1820-1894', *RS* 127 (1905),
pp. 253-85, 580-605, 128 (1905), pp. 39-79, 332-50.

Venturi, F., *Roots of Revolution: a History of the Populist and Socialist Movements in
Nineteenth–Century Russia*, introd. by [Sir] I. Berlin, London, 1960, New York,
1966.

Vereshchagin, G. A., 'Materialy po istorii buntov v voyennykh poseleniyakh pri
Aleksandre I', *Dela i dni* 3 (Petrograd, 1922), pp. 148-65.

Vernadsky, G. V., *The Tsardom of Moscow, 1547-1682* (A History of Russia, 5),
2 vols., New Haven and London, 1969.

—— *et al.* (eds.), Pushkarev, S. (comp.), *A Source Book for Russian History from
Early Times to 1917*, 3 vols., New Haven, 1972.

Verzhbitsky, V. G., *Revolyutsionnoye dvizheniye v russkoy armii: s 1826 po 1859 gg.*
(Trudy Gosudarstvennogo istoricheskogo muzeya, fasc. 39), Moscow, 1964.

—— 'Sochuvstviye peredovykh ofitserov i soldat russkoy armii vengerskoy revolyutsii
1848-1849 gg.', *IA* 8 (1962), 4, pp. 121-33.

—— and Frumenkov, G. G., 'Rasprostraneniye "Kolokola" i proklamatsiy A. I.
Gertsena i N. P. Ogareva v tsarskoy armii, 1854-1862 gg.', *IA* 2 (1956), 5, pp. 210-15.

Veselovsky, S. B., *Issledovaniya po istorii klassa sluzhilykh zemlevladel'tsev*, Moscow, 1969.

—— *Feodal'noye zemlevladeniye v severo-vostochnoy Rusi*, i. Moscow and Leningrad, 1947.

—— 'Smety voyennykh sil moskovskogo gosudarstva, 1661–1663 g.', *Chteniya*, 1911, 3, ii. 1–60.

Vigel', F. F., *Vospominaniya*, 7 vols. in 3, Moscow, 1864–5.

Vish, N., 'Telesnye nakazaniya v voyskakh i ikh otmena', *VS* 279 (1904), 10, pp. 133–42, 11, pp. 113–24, 280 (1904), 12, pp. 113–48.

Vladimirsky–Budanov, M. F., *Gosudarstvo i narodnoye obrazovaniye v Rossii XVIII-go st.*, i. Yaroslavl', 1896.

Vodarsky, Ya. Ye., 'Chislennost' naseleniya i kolichestvo pomestno-votchinnykh zemel' v XVII v.: po pistsovym i perepisnym knigam', *Yezhegodnik po agrarnoy istorii Vostochnoy Yevropy za 1964 g.*, Kishinev, 1966, pp. 217–30.

—— 'K voprosu o sredney chislennosti krest'yanskoy sem'i i naselennosti dvora v Rossii v XVI–XVII vv.', in Beskrovnyy *et al.* (eds.), *Voprosy istorii*, pp. 117–30.

—— *Naseleniye Rossii v kontse XVII—nachale XVIII v.: chislennost', soslovno-klassovyy sostav, razmeshcheniye*, Moscow, 1977.

—— *Naseleniye Rossii za 400 let, XVI—nachalo XX v.*, Moscow, 1973.

—— 'Pravyashchaya gruppa svetskikh feodalov v Rossii v XVII v.', in Pavlenko *et al.* (eds.), *Dvoryanstvo*, pp. 70 ff.

—— 'Sluzhiloye dvoryanstvo v Rossii v kontse XVII—nachale XVIII v.', in Shunkov *et al.* (eds.), *Voprosy*, pp. 233–7.

Volkonsky, P. D. (contrib.), 'Arkhiv svyatleyshego knyazya P. M. Volkonskogo', *RS* 4 (1871), pp. 646–66.

[Volkonsky, P. M.], 'Rasskazy knyazya P. M. Volkonskogo, zapisannye s yego slov A. V. Viskovatovym v yanvare 1845 g.', *RS* 16 (1876), pp. 176–90.

Volkov, M. Ya., 'Ob otmene mestnichestva v Rossii', *IS* 1977, 2, pp. 53–67.

Vorontsov, S. R., 'Zapiska . . . o russkom voyske, predstavlennaya imperatoru Aleks-andru Pavlovichu v 1802 g.', *AKV* x (1876), 467–92.

Voskresensky, N. A. (ed.), *Zakonodatel'nye akty Petra I: akty o vysshikh gosudarst-vennykh ustanovleniyakh*, i. Moscow, 1945.

Vostokov, A. A., 'O delakh General'nogo dvora', *Opisaniye dokumentov i bumag khranyashchikhsya v Moskovskom arkhive Ministerstva yustitsii*, 5 (Moscow, 1888), pt. 2, pp. 1–42.

Voyensky [de Breze], K. [A.] (ed.), *Akty, dokumenty i materialy dlya istorii 1812 g.*, ii. *Baltiyskaya okraina v 1812 g.*, St. Petersburg, 1911.

—— *Istoricheskiye ocherki i stat'i, otnosyashchiyesya k 1812 g.*, St. Petersburg, [1912].

Vyazemsky, A. I., 'Zapiska voyennaya, pisannaya . . . v noyabre 1774 g.', in Sherem-etev, S. D. (ed.), *Arkhiv knyazya A. I. Vyazemskogo*, St. Petersburg, 1881, pp. 3–20.

Vyazemsky, B. L., *Verkhovnyy taynyy sovet*, St. Petersburg, 1909, repr. The Hague and Paris, 1969.

Vyazemsky, P. A., *Zapisnye knizhki, 1813–1848*, Moscow, 1963.

Walicki, A., *A History of Russian Thought from the Enlightenment to Marxism*, tr. H. Andrews–Rusiecka, Oxford and Stanford, 1979.

Wandycz, P. S., *The Lands of Partitioned Poland, 1795–1918* (History of East Central Europe, 7), Seattle and London, 1974.

Warner, R. H., 'The Kožuchovo Campaign of 1694, or the Conquest of Moscow by Preobraženskoe', *JGOE* 13 (1965), pp. 487–96.

Warnery, C. E. de, *Rémarques sur le militaire des Turcs et des Russes . . . avec diverses observations sur les grandes actions qui se sont passées dans la dernière guerre d'Hongrie*, Breslau, 1771.

Weber, F. C., *Das veränderte Russland, in welchem die jetzige Verfassung . . . vorgestellt werden*, Hanover, 1721.

Whitworth, C., 'Doneseniya i bumagi chrezvychaynogo poslannika angliyskogo pri russkom dvore Charl'za Vitvorta s 1704 po 1708', *SIRIO* xxxix (1884).

—— 'Doneseniya i drugiye bumagi . . . Vitvorta i sekretarya yego Veysbroda s 1708 g. po 1711 g.', *SIRIO* l (1886).

Wieczynski, J. L., 'The Mutiny of the Semenovsky Regiment in 1820', *RR* 29 (1970), pp. 167–80.

Wilson, Sir R. T., *Brief Remarks on the Character and Composition of the Russian Army, and Sketch of the Campaigns in Poland in the Years 1806 and 1807*, London, 1810.

—— *A Sketch of the Military and Political Power of Russia in the Year 1817*, London, 1817 (French tr.: *Tableau de la puissance militaire et politique de la Russie en 1817*, Paris, 1817).

Woehrlin, W. F., *Chernyshevsky: the Man and the Journalist*, Cambridge, Mass., 1971.

Wortman, R. S., *The Development of a Russian Legal Consciousness*, Chicago and London, 1976.

—— 'Power and Responsibility in the Upbringing of the Nineteenth–Century Tsars', Group for the Use of Psychology in History *Newsletter* 4 (Springfield, Ill., 1976), 4, pp. 18–27.

Yakovlev, A. I., *Zasechnaya cherta moskovskogo gosudarstva v XVII v.: ocherk iz istorii oborony yuzhnoy okrainy moskovskogo gosudarstva*, Moscow, 1916.

Yakubov, K. I., 'Rossiya i Shvetsiya v pervoy polovine XVII v.: sbornik materialov . . . , 1616-1651 gg.', *Chteniya*, 1898, 1, pp. 289–494.

Yakushkin, E. I., 'S'yezd chlenov "Soyuza blagodenstviya" v Moskve 1821 g.: otvet N. M. Ogarevu', *RS* 6 (1872), pp. 597–602.

Yakushkin, I. D., *Zapiski, stat'i, pis'ma*, ed. S. Ya. Shtraykh, Moscow, 1951.

Yatsunsky, V. K., 'K voprosu o sobiranii i publikatsii materialov po istorii urozhayev i tsen v Rossii', *Problemy istochnikovedeniya* 4 (1955), pp. 350–7.

Yepifanov, P. P., *Ocherki iz istorii armii i voyennogo dela v Rossii, vtoraya polovina XVII—pervaya polovina XVIII vv.: avtoreferat dissertatsii*, Moscow, 1969.

—— 'Voinskiy ustav Petra Velikogo', in Andreyev, A. I. (ed.), *Petr Velikiy: sbornik statey*, Moscow and Leningrad, 1947, pp. 167–213.

—— 'Voysko i voyennaya organizatsiya', in Artsikhovsky, A. V. (ed.), *Ocherki russkoy kul'tury XVI v.*, i. *Material'naya kul'tura*, Moscow, 1976, pp. 336–79.

Yermolov, A. P., *Zapiski . . . o voyne 1812 g.*, London and Brussels, 1863.

Yeroshkin, N. P., *Istoriya gosudarstvennykh uchrezhdeniy dorevolyutsionnoy Rossii*, 2nd edn., Moscow, 1968.

Yevropeus, I. I., 'Bunt novgorodskikh voyennykh poselyan 1831 g.', *RS* 6 (1872), pp. 547–58.

—— 'Sluzhba v voyennykh poseleniyakh i graf Arakcheyev, 1820–1826 gg.', *RS* 6 (1872), pp. 225–42.

Yevstaf′yev, P. N., *Vosstaniye voyennykh poselyan Novgorodskoy gubernii v 1831 g.*, Moscow, 1934.

[Zagorodnikov, I.], 'Dnevnik russkogo soldata, vzyatogo v plen pri Bomarzunde v 1854 g.', contrib. P. S. Lebedev, *RS* 80 (1893), pp. 185–212.

Zagorodsky, V. P., *Belgorodskaya cherta*, Voronezh, 1969.

Zagoskin, N. P., *Ocherki organizatsii i proiskhozhdeniya sluzhilogo sosloviya v dopetrovskoy Rusi*, Kazan′, 1875.

Zagoskin, S. M., 'Vospominaniya', *IV* 79–80 (1900), pp. 51–72, 403–29, 790–815.

Zatler (Sattler), F. V., *Opisaniye rasporyazheniy, po snabzheniyu Krymskoy armii v voynu 1854–1856 g., prodovol′stvennymi i ognestrel′nymi pripasami i suda nad intendantstvom*, 3 vols., Leipzig, 1877.

Zavalishin, D. I., *Zapiski dekabrista*, 2nd edn., St. Petersburg, [1906].

Zayonchkovsky, P. A., 'D. A. Milyutin: biograficheskiy ocherk', in id., *Dnevnik*, pp. 5–72.

—— *Dnevnik D. A. Milyutina* [1873–80], 3 vols., Moscow, 1847.

—— (ed.), *Istoriya dorevolyutsionnoy Rossii v dnevnikakh i vospominaniyakh: annotirovannyy ukazatel′knig i publikatsiy v zhurnalakh*, i. XV–XVIII v., Moscow, 1976, ii. 1801–1856, 2 pts., Moscow, 1977, iii. 1857–1894, 3 pts., Moscow, 1979–81, iv. pt. 1, 1895–1917, Moscow, 1983.

—— 'Podgotovka voyennoy reformy 1874 g.', *IZ* 27 (1948), pp. 170–201.

—— *Pravitel′stvennyy apparat samoderzhavnoy Rossii v XIX v.*, Moscow, 1978.

—— *Voyennye reformy 1860—1870 gg. v Rossii*, Moscow, 1952.

[Zeydlits (Seydlitz), K. K.], 'Vospominaniya doktora Zeydlitsa o turetskom pokhode 1829 g. v pis′makh k druz̧yam', *RA* 1878, 3, pp. 412–35.

Zhuravsky, D. P., 'Statisticheskoye obozreniye raskhodov na voyennye potrebnosti, 1711 po 1825 gg.', *VS* 10 (1859), 11–12.

Zimin, A. A., *Reformy Ivana Groznogo: ocherki sotsial′no-ekonomicheskoy i politicheskoy istorii Rossii serediny XVI v.*, Moscow, 1960.

—— (comp.), *Tysyachnaya kniga 1550 g. i dvorovaya tetrad′ 50-kh gg. XVI v.*, Moscow and Leningrad, 1950.

Zisserman, A., *Istoriya 8-go pekhotnogo kabardinskogo . . . knyazya Baryatinskogo polka, 1726–1880*, 3 vols., St. Petersburg, 1881.

Zubow, V., *Zar Paul I: Mensch und Schicksal*, Stuttgart, 1963.

INDEX

Occasionally with sub-entries in this index logic is preferred to strict alphabetical order.